President Robert B. Kamm

OKLAHOMA STATE UNIVERSITY

~ Since 1890

BY PHILIP REED RULON

OKLAHOMA STATE UNIVERSITY PRESS • 1975
Stillwater, Oklahoma

THIS INSTITUTION
is a part of a great democracy. Whether it succeed or fail in its great
ambition to bring happiness to human kind, will depend much
upon the unselfishness, the high standards, and the ability of those
who shall lead, and their vision and unselfish devotion may depend
greatly upon what they take from this institution into actual life.

BRADFORD KNAPP, *1927*

Preface

In the pages which follow, Dr. Philip R. Rulon presents the story of Oklahoma A&M College from the time of its beginning in 1890 until the changing of the name of the institution to the Oklahoma State University in 1957. In a detailed and well-documented manner he portrays the struggles of the institution to fulfill its high Land-Grant calling and to achieve recognition as a quality institution.

What about the years since 1957? To what measure have the hopes and the dreams of those who served during the first nearly seven decades of this institution been realized?

The qualities of vigor, resilience, innovation, and ability to "stretch dollars" which characterized Oklahoma A&M continue to characterize the Oklahoma State University. Building on the achievements of those of earlier days, the '60's and the '70's have seen the Oklahoma State University "come of age" and to be recognized regionally, nationally, and internationally as a university in the fullest sense. Today, strengths in the arts and in the humanities, in the social and behavioral sciences, and in the applied areas of business and education, stand side-by-side with traditional Land-Grant institution strengths in the biological and physical sciences and in their applied areas of agriculture, engineering, home economics and veterinary medicine. Growth in graduate enrollments and offerings at both the masters and doctoral levels, together with growth in research, extension and public service, have also been substantial in recent years.

In a period of more than usual unrest on American campuses during the '60's, the Oklahoma State University remained a stable campus where teaching, research, and service to students and off-campus publics continued without interruption. At the same time those qualities of freedom and responsible dissent which are so essential to a creative and productive institution were preserved and enhanced. This blend has led some to appropriately refer to OSU as a "progressive conservative" university.

The growth of an institution can be measured in many ways. One easily quantified way is to look at amounts of annual budgets. In the last year of Dr. Henry G. Bennett's service as President in 1951-52, the annual total budget figure was $14,417,252. In 1957-58, the newly-designated Oklahoma State University's budget had risen to a figure of $18,727,798. In 1965-66, the last year of Dr. Willham's presidency, the total budget figure was $35,294,449. It had taken 76 years of development to achieve that figure. The next eight years, however, led to more than a doubling of the budget, from the 1965-66 figure of $35,294,449 to a 1973-74 OSU budget total of $71,442,599.

In the '60's and the '70's the largest building program in the University's history occurred on each of OSU's three campuses. (In addition to the main campus at Stillwater and the OSU School of Technical Training at Okmulgee, which is mentioned in the pages which follow, a Technical Institute was established as a branch campus of OSU in Oklahoma City in 1961.) Among recently completed facilities on the Stillwater campus are the Seretean Center for the Performing Arts, the Colvin Recreational Center, the Business Administration Building, Engineering North, Life Sciences West, the Mathematical Sciences Building, Agriculture Hall, the 10, 12, and 14 story Residence Halls, the Physical Sciences Building, the Central Foods Building, the International Mall, the Beef Cattle facilities, a Library addition, a Student Union addition, and the Student Union parking garage. Major upgrading and renovation has also been accomplished in such facilities as Lewis Stadium, Morrill Hall, Life Sciences East, Engineering South, and in a number of the older residence halls, to mention but some. Campus parking, lighting, drainage and landscaping have been improved. Increased private giving has augmented state and federal funds in accomplishing the substantial physical plant developments of recent years.

Perhaps the most significant developments in the "coming of age" of the Oklahoma State University have occurred (and continue

x

to occur) in the areas which are central in the University's operations—in the classrooms, in the laboratories and in counseling and advisement programs. One distinguished national educational observer and writer has noted recently that "Oklahoma State University is currently producing as great a variety of educational reforms as can be found anywhere in the United States." Another has spoken of the "purposeful community" and the quality of "hope" at the Oklahoma State University.

People—and what happens to people—continue to be, uppermost in the activities of the University. "Emphasis '72-'73—PEOPLE," as an example, underscored the importance to do all possible to help each person, whatever his or her background, to be "at home" on the OSU campus and to become the best of which he or she is capable.

Student and faculty achievements in competitions in various academic disciplines, as well as in out-of-class competitions in such activities as 4-H, athletics, debate, livestock judging, and ROTC continue to bring national recognition to OSU. In 1969, OSU received a Distinguished Service Award from the *Readers Digest* Foundation and the Institute of International Education for its leadership and service in "international education and cultural relations." (In the past two decades the University has served in some 20 nations throughout the world.) Since 1968, the Oklahoma State University has served as national headquarters for NASA's Space Science Education program, working out of ten locations throughout the nation in fulfilling its responsibilities in the 50 states, Puerto Rico, and the Virgin Islands. In 1969, OSU received one of the National Science Foundation's coveted "Center of Excellence" awards. Recently a decision was made to locate the United States Wrestling Federation's National Wrestling Hall of Fame on the OSU campus, thereby joining Kappa Kappa Psi and Tau Beta Sigma, national band fraternity and sorority, in their OSU-based locations.

Considerable reorganization of the Unversity has occurred in an effort to better meet the demands of growth and of the rapidly changing world of the '60's and the '70's. New programs have been added, and some have been dropped. New relationships among departments and among personnel have been achieved, including the recent development of a University Environmental Institute and a Community Development Institute. New talent is constantly being recruited; and, as needs arise, new positions are created. An example of the latter is the recent appointment of a full-time Director of the Affirmative Action Program at OSU.

Today finds the Oklahoma State University with a total enrollment of more than 22,000 students in residence on its three campuses at Stillwater, Oklahoma City, and Okmulgee, with some 65 different nations represented in the student body. Some 50,000 additionally come to the Stillwater campus annually to participate in conferences and short courses. Another 250,000 are served annually by the University's extension and public service programs. Still other hundreds of thousands are reached each year through the University's national and international efforts.

The Oklahoma State University continues its commitment, as a Land-Grant university, *to promote liberal and practical education* on the campus, throughout the State of Oklahoma, and in those areas of the nation and world where its "know-how" can be put to use. *Competency* and *relevancy* are key words, as it builds on past accomplishments, realistically serves in "the now," and carefully plans for the future. The University's Planning Council has recently re-stated OSU's mission as follows:

"The mission of the Oklahoma State University is to provide an environment in which its constituents can discover, examine critically, preserve, and transmit knowledge, wisdom, and values that will help ensure the survival of present and future generations, with enrichment in the quality of life."

In my inaugural in 1966, these hopes were expressed for this University:

"I hope that the Oklahoma State University will measure up fully to the great Land-Grant mission which is ours—I hope that the Oklahoma State University will experience a great 'academic breakthrough' in the years ahead—I hope that we may have a great sense of community among all who are a part of OSU . . . I hope that freedom may flourish on this campus . . . . ."

In part these hopes have been realized; in part they remain to be realized. Our challenge is to realize them fully.

President Robert B. Kamm

The Oklahoma State University

Introduction

The Civil War bent, but did not break, the grand optimism of the American nation in democracy and education. During the summer of 1862, with the tragic conflict still in progress, the Congress of the United States enacted the Homestead and the Morrill Acts, two pieces of legislation which used the public domain to inaugurate bold social experiments. The importance of these measures in the settlement of the West is evidenced by the effect each of them had on the shaping of Oklahoma and her state university in Stillwater. The Homestead Act brought thousands of people to the borders of neighboring states in 1889 for the first of the several famous rushes for land. There they awaited the signal that would permit them to stake a claim and to become residents of the territory. The adoption of the Morrill Act by the Territorial Legislature the following year insured that the doors of higher educational institutions would not be closed to the masses. One could study the various "pursuits and professions in life" close to home and at little personal expense. To some, the ownership of property and the opportunity for their children to earn a college degree meant that the limits of democracy would expand with the passage of time. Yet, change in the United States is an evolutionary, not a revolutionary, process. It is often the second and third generation that achieves success instead of the first. This book is an examination of the region and the educational movement that established Oklahoma State University, the last of the major land-grant colleges to have its history in print. Both those who founded the institution and the state discovered that the incorporation of new ideas into the social fabric is a challenge that sometimes drives men to their breaking point.

The Sooner State, for all of the attention that it received at its birth, did not live up to the high promise that some held for it. Carpetbag government delayed entrance into the Union; the lack of federal planning before the land rushes retarded the development of viable political institutions; drought prevented the prairie grasslands from blooming in the spring; the discovery of oil led to the formation of lawless boom towns; racial and religious prejudice led to terror in the night; repeated international wars drained the farms and cities of their youth; and depression caused a substantial migration to the sunnier climate of California. Nevertheless, a belief in the future and in the faith of one's father kept the people from despair. The seeds planted in 1889 did bear fruit, but most of the pioneers did not live to see the harvest, for it is only within the last quarter-century that Oklahoma has acquired institutional cohesion. The latest census reveals that the state is growing again and that increased industrialization is bringing the region into the mainstream of American society.

The vocational-scientific movement in higher education spawned by the Morrill Act was slow to reach its full potential, too. In all public, private, and religious colleges, seventy in number, accepted the provisions of the land-grant idea: that is, the teaching, researching, and popularizing of functional educational practice and thought. The organic legislation provided direction but the vague procedures for implementation caused political division within the individual states that left a bitter heritage. The sale of land or land-script sometimes resulted in speculation and graft. Few men or women were prepared to teach subjects dealing with the industries of life. Local legislators often refused to appropriate supplemental revenues, because they believed land-grant colleges to be national, not state, organizations. And finally, classical and denominational institutions resented the encroachment of an upstart upon a domain over which they had exercised exclusive control for many centuries. Personnel associated with higher education, however, also believed in the realization of the impossible dream, and dedication to a mission of social service slowly brought respectability to the People's College. By the end of World War I, these institutions had demonstrated the wisdom of federal aid to higher education.

The development of Oklahoma State University parallels that of the land-grant movement and the state after which it was named.

The institution had to endure the enmity of its classical counterparts and upon more than one occasion it reflected the turbulence that occurred as the diverse elements who entered the territory struggled for economic and political dominance. Then, too, coming of age during a transitional period in American life, the organization mirrored the conflict between agriculture and industry, city and country, science and religion, and traditional and industrial education. The university, therefore, could not depend upon the past for precedent. It had to find its own way and forge its own response to change on the local and national scene. Because Oklahoma State was a product of, as well as contributed to, the surrounding environment, her growth must be viewed within the perspective of the land-grant movement and the history of the state. To do less would be an injustice, for institutional and human biography both must be placed within the context of the times in order to be called history. This study focuses upon the collegiate administration; the men and women held responsible for interpreting and implementing legislation and policies, solving crises, and shaping the institution for the future. That the path to the heights was beset with difficulty is revealed in the fact that it took sixty-seven years to attain stability and university status.

Oklahoma State University's history divides itself into three chronological periods, each of which corresponds to a different form of regential control. For seventeen years after its founding in 1890, the institution had a separate governing board. It employed no less than five presidents in an attempt to find a mission and to establish an identity for the small college located in Stillwater. This phase brought several important firsts and generated much excitement, but little progress could be achieved because of financial problems, ineptness, and even outright corruption. As such, the organization performed largely a teaching mission for it did not have the personnel or the equipment to extend its influence far beyond the perimeters of the campus. From 1908 to 1944, the second period, the Oklahoma Board of Agriculture guided the affairs of the college. Growth, both in quality and quantity, occurred during these thirty-six years, with programs, especially those related to extension, encompassing the entire state. In addition, nine presidents directed the work of the faculty and supervised the training of students who served the nation in times of war and peace, depression and prosperity, and reunion and reform.

In 1944, the constitution of the State of Oklahoma was amended to create a separate Board of Regents for all of the state's agricultural and mechanical colleges. These men, in turn, secured the services of two outstanding executives, individuals who strengthened the institution internally and who extended the land-grant idea overseas under the auspices of the Point Four Program. The third stage ended in 1957 when the organization received authorization to change its name from the Oklahoma Agricultural and Mechanical College to Oklahoma State University. Today, under the leadership of Robert B. Kamm, whose Preface precedes these comments, the institution is beginning a new life as a part of the marrow of the nation's state university system. That story, however, must be written by one who has more detachment than the present narrator.

For those who may wonder, the writer is entitled to call Oklahoma State University his *alma mater,* for he resided upon the campus from 1964 to 1967. The book, however, is not an official history nor were any institutional funds expended in the forming of the manuscript. On the other hand, the writing and research could not have been accomplished without the cooperation of many people associated with the institution. The project began as a doctoral dissertation under Theodore Agnew. Other members of the committee included: Homer Knight, Daniel Selakovich, and LeRoy Fischer. It was the latter individual, incidentally, who suggested the topic when he noted in a conversation that over three-quarters of a century had passed without Oklahoma State's participation in the land-grant movement being told. President-emeritus Oliver S. Willham and President Robert B. Kamm were kind enough to spend many hours with the author and without their help it would have been impossible to undertake the project. In the five years in which this study was under active investigation, neither person failed to respond to a question, to open a file drawer, or to render a requested favor. Early documentary and photograph collections were gathered by Angie Debo, Robert Cunningham, and Berlin Chapman. Their preliminary work not only facilitated the completion of this manuscript, but it also created a deeper interest in the history of the university itself. The editorial comment of Glenn Shirley, LeRoy Fischer, and John Hamilton is deeply fused into many of the pages which follow. The original, at times, is difficult to separate from the blend. Moreover, Murl Rogers, Secretary of the Former Student's Association, E. Moses Frye, University Legal Counsel, and Robert Erwin, former Director of University Development, have extended more courtesies than can properly be acknowledged here. Several friends and colleagues have read portions of the manuscript. In particular, the thoughtful advice of Joe Hubbell, James Morrison, William Lyon, and O. A. Hilton, is appreciated. Any inaccuracies of fact and judgment which may remain, however, should not be charged against them.

Archivists and librarians are surely the unsung heroes of the historical profession. It is in this area that my heaviest debts have been accumulated. For expert assistance in Oklahoma, I am grateful to the following people: Edmond Low, Roscoe Rouse, Guy Logsdon, Heather Lloyd, John Stratton, Marguerite Howland, Richard King, and Tony Moffeit, of the Oklahoma State Library; Louise Cook, of the Oklahoma Historical Society; Joe Hurt and M. C. Collum, of the Oklahoma State Board of Education; Chancellor Elijah Dunlap, Vice-Chancellor Dan Hobbs, and Tom Sexton, of the Oklahoma State Regents for Higher Education; President James Ballinger, President Billy Ray Gowdy, Clara Behnke, Secretary, and Carl Junghanns, of the Oklahoma Board of Agriculture; Forrest McIntire, Secretary and Administrative Assistant, and Thelma Woodson, of the Board of Regents for Oklahoma State University and Agricultural and Mechanical Colleges; Mrs. Charles Penfold, of the Stillwater Public Library and the Payne County Historical Society; and Mrs. Edna Spaulding, Clerk, City of Stillwater.

Outside of Oklahoma, the following persons or institutions deserve recognition and thanks: Ralph Huitt, Executive Director, and Garven F. Hudgins, Office of Research and Information, of the National Association of State Universities and Land-Grant Colleges; Richard Maxwell, Assistant Director, Social and Economics Records Division, of the National Archives and Records Service; Philip D. Lagerquist, Research Archivist, of the Harry S. Truman Presidential Library; Ann Turner, Reference Librarian, Norwich University; Gene Decker, Newspaper Archivist, of the Kansas State Historical Society; and Ted Fitch, Reference Librarian, of Northern Arizona University. Individuals associated with the American Antiquarian Society, the University of Maryland, the Denver Public Library, and the Jerome Frampton Library of the Frostburg State College in Maryland graciously provided genealogical information. Maryanna Thomas typed the manuscript in less time than anyone had the right to expect. My wife and sons deserve a special commendation for their many sacrifices. This book is dedicated to them.

Philip Reed Rulon

Flagstaff, Arizona

Contents

Illustrations following pages 140, 204 and 268

I   A Lamp For the Prairie

Old Central, now the oldest higher education building in Oklahoma, is a constant reminder that the history of the state is directly tied to the development of its institutions. It is the petroleum industry, the railroad corporation, the township enterprise, the agricultural organization, the church, and the educational system—not the wild-catter, the wagoner, the real estate speculator, the homestead farmer, the self-ordained evangelist, or the itinerant school master—that should be lauded for modernizing the region. Moreover, initial progress within the state is more closely connected to economic and social leadership than that provided by the political parties. In the territorial period, officials, especially those appointed instead of elected to office, sometimes violated the trust placed in them by the people. On the other hand, confirmation by majority vote did not necessarily guarantee good government. Oklahoma had more than its share of agrarian demagogues, men so embittered with the hardships of their age that they could not offer a viable direction for the future. State institutions of higher learning, therefore, with their

emphasis upon transmitting the cultural heritage, deleting obsoles-
cent ideas, and augmenting the body of knowledge that is held by
society at any given point in time, deserve far more study than they
have received in the past. The educated elite, through the classroom
and the laboratory, enabled some Oklahomans to bypass many of the
difficulties experienced by their counterparts on earlier frontiers.
It is understandable then that both the farmer and the laborer
looked to the land-grant college for assistance. The institution was to
represent a world that had been left behind.[1]

The township of Stillwater, located near the junction of the
Arkansas and Cimarron Rivers, organized the Agricultural and Mechanical College of Oklahoma Territory in the unstable social
evironment created from opening the last of the Louisiana Purchase
to colonization.[2] It is somewhat prophetic that the founding bill
received passage on Christmas Eve in 1890, for the institution in
subsequent years would form a relationship with the region which
is now identified as the Bible Belt. The pioneers, however, who
settled the north central section of the territory in Payne County
probably did not have the leisure to ponder the future.[3] They had
arrived in the most unusual manner of any western migration and
most were preoccupied with the immediacy of present day events.
On April 22, 1889, as the result of a proclamation issued by President Benjamin Harrison, tens of thousands of prospective citizens
gathered near Arkansas City, Kansas, to await the sound that would
blazon the opening of a virgin agricultural land for permanent
occupation.[4] That day at high noon a blue uniformed cavalry officer
rode to a point where "he could be seen for miles each way, with one
hand raised a bugle to his lips and gave the signal, while with the
other hand he waved a flag."[5] A human avalanche, both there and
elsewhere, then descended upon the territory and competition for
the new lands began.

The Oklahoma land-rushes, a local manifestation of social
Darwinism, consisted of people who belonged to nearly every walk
of life, including businessmen, ranchers, farmers, lawyers, teachers,
and physicians. Undoubtedly, the forces which motivated this im-
mense migration must have varied with each man and woman. But,
in general, the placement of nomadic Indian tribes on reservations,
the westward advance of the transcontinental railroad, the ever-in-
creasing population pressures of the East, and the enactment of the
Homestead Act hastened the occupation of the second tier of states
beyond the Mississippi River. As pioneers filled the land, the United
States Superintendent of the Census reported that a person could no
longer draw any frontier line between civilization and the wilder-
ness. It was a simple statement, yet one that symbolically marked the
close of an important phase of American development. And the
territory of Oklahoma became caught squarely in the middle of the
growing urban-rural conflict.[6]

When the people who were fortunate enough to locate un-
claimed land lighted, they found conditions as bad as, or worse than,
those they had recently forsaken. One early resident of Stillwater

exclaimed: "Times were hard, the entire community being made of poor people who had made the 'run' . . . from other states. Few had any worthwhile property."[7] While this statement is not totally accurate, the primitive conditions that prevailed partially explains the faith that the masses have placed in the educational system. An early Oklahoma writer holds in this regard that one of the most pressing anxieties of the plainsmen was the fear that "on the new frontier their children might grow up in ignorance."[8] In a nearby midwestern state a young professor of history stated the situation in a less negative manner when he spoke in 1896 at the dedication of a high school in his boyhood home town. He urged the people in Portage, Wisconsin to make their school a community center, a social and intellectual force with which to preserve the democratic heritage of the frontier experience.[9]

The American people have often been accused of anti-intellectualism.[10] Yet, whether or not this belief is true, it is quite clear that the first generation of the frontier followed the lead of their forefathers in developing educational institutions as quickly as possible in order to transplant the "best of Eastern culture to their Western communities."[11] In Stillwater, for instance, one of the first projects initiated by the community as a whole was to work toward the establishment of an agricultural and mechanical college. It was sought to educate the unlettered and to bring federal and state revenues into an economically depressed region. The struggle proved long and painful, and the battles which ensued left deep scars that affected the history of the institution to be founded there for many years to come.

While the educational age of the residents of Oklahoma Territory may have been low, Stillwater included a sizable number of educated people. Edward Clark, John Clark, Frank Hutto, and Charles McGraw, to name but a few, had each at one time or another been public school teachers. Frank Wikoff, a banker, Robert Lowry, an attorney, and William Knipe, a businessman from nearby Perkins, had actually attended land-grant institutions in the states where they resided before moving to Oklahoma. In addition, the settlement contained a large proportion of the territory's oversupply of lawyers, and some of these men had been trained in college before they embarked on their legal careers. John Clark, Sterling King, Robert Lowry, Van Martin, Alexander Neill, Thomas Richardson, Jerome Workman, and Frank Wikoff fit into such a classification.[12] Finally, the township could count at least ten clergymen in its midst. Several of them, including Simon Myers and William Davis, possessed enough schooling to qualify for local educational work.[13] It was these individuals, who, for the most part, constituted the elite of the community and they were among the first to suggest the possibility of building a college in the middle of a prairie dog town.[14]

With the organization of Oklahoma into a territory during the summer of 1890, the six original counties in the central portion of the state developed an increased interest in state politics, with each

3

speculating on its chances for securing one of the public service institutions.[15] The city of Stillwater entered into the contest with unbounded enthusiasm. In July, a mass meeting convened at Swope Hall on the corner of Ninth and Main Streets in order to "advise the one who was to represent Payne County in the coming first Territorial Assembly . . . in getting some territorial plum."[16] There is some indication that the people considered the possibility of obtaining the site for the state capital but the prison most likely would not have been turned down. There was rampant lawlessness and it appeared as if many guards would have to be employed. The meeting, though a decision was not made to commit the delegation to any one particular institution, did stimulate the *sub rosa* section of the town council, named the "Sanhedrin" by George Uhl, to pursue the matter further.[17] A concerted effort followed.

The townspeople caucused in the local post office after the results of the first territorial elections were announced. Permanent community leadership had not developed at this point, yet it seemed evident that Frank Duck, Robert Lowry, Charles McGraw, J. B. Murphy, William Swiler, and Frank Wikoff would play a leading role in shaping future strategy. At the second conference, those men who had attended or who were acquainted with the function of agricultural and mechanical colleges, suggested that the county seriously consider pursuing a Morrill institution. Later, George Gardenhire, James Matthews, Lowry, and Wikoff met at the latter's office on East Ninth Street to formulate arguments to initiate legislation.[18] Meanwhile, other forces were moving toward the same end.

The First Legislative Assembly of Oklahoma Territory met on August 27, 1890 at the McKennon Opera House in Guthrie, the city which had been designated as the temporary capital. This body was composed of a Council of thirteen members and a House of Representatives which contained twice that figure. The election of these men had been called for by George W. Steele, who had been appointed governor by President Harrison.[19] At some point before he drafted his initial message to the Legislature, Steele re-established contact with an Indiana boyhood friend in Washington, D.C. James Clinton Neal, then of the Florida Experiment Station, brought to the governor's attention the recent passage of the Hatch Act, a measure which he thought would be of the utmost importance in converting Oklahoma into a modern agricultural state. In later life, Neal recalled:

"Still few knew what a bonanza it was, and in my correspondence with the first governor, in 1890, his ideas were so very hazy as to its value and importance that I gave him line upon line, letter after letter, even to the extent of an outline of the law, embracing the results of some years of experience of one of the oldest, and best conducted, and stable colleges in the United States."[20]

Obviously moved by these remarks as well as by the extensive drought on the Great Plains, Steele incorporated in his message to the Legislature on the evening of August 28, 1890, a plea for the establishment of an agricultural experiment station in Oklahoma.[21]

4

Three weeks later he brought the newly passed Land-Grant College Act of 1890 to the attention of the legislators. "I have the honor to transmit herewith certified copy of an act approved August 30, 1890, providing," he said, "for the more complete endowment and support of the colleges for the benefit of agriculture and the mechanic arts . . . . and I recommend early legislation with a view of having the advantage of the liberal donation provided in said act."[22] Steele further suggested that the legislators petition Congress for permission to use the initial grant to construct a college building, as the so-called Granger Amendment of the Second Morrill Act limited expenditures to paying instructional salaries and purchasing classroom and laboratory teaching aids.[23] The executive believed that the request might be granted, because of the recent organization of the territory, the crippled condition of the predominantly agricultural economy, and the fact that homestead farms would not be subject to taxation for at least four more years.

The Legislature wasted little time in acting upon the information provided by the governor. The day after the message had been distributed, House Resolution 14, which accepted the provisions of the bill in question, was given to the Committee on the Location of the Capital and other Public Institutions for deliberation. Subsequently, the Assembly forwarded a letter to Washington which requested that any federal funds due the state under the Morrill and Hatch Acts be earmarked for the erection of an instructional building. Councilor Gardenhire assisted in this effort, probably having much to do with the speed in which the business was conducted. This information, no doubt, attracted the attention of his constituents and must have intensified interest in securing an agricultural and mechanical college for the Stillwater community.[24]

While the Oklahoma Assembly immediately accepted responsibility for implementing the Morrill Act, it did not designate where such an institution should be located. Steele, in this regard, advocated that the counties bid against each other for the sites where the land-grant college, and the other service agencies that would be needed in the state, should be placed. He said: "I would earnestly impress upon you the importance of so legislating as to invite competition for locating them, according to the benefits the people of the several counties may place upon them . . . ."[25] Gardenhire, a Populist, had been selected as president of the Council because it had been evenly divided between the two major political parties. In view of his unique position, he attempted to explore the possibility of a mutually advantageous deal. Gardenhire met with interested parties in a smoke-filled upstairs hotel room. He promised to support the Democrat's bid for the territorial capital, if, in return, they would vote to place the land-grant institution in Payne County.[26] With this concession in his pocket, the lawmaker returned to Stillwater for grassroot consultations.

Gardenhire, however, found that the residents' aspirations had increased since his last visit. Overestimating the councilor's political strength, the voters held yet another town meeting, deciding now to seek the site for the capital itself. The legislator left immediately to resume his post in Guthrie, determined to pursue his latest instructions. But soon after his departure, Hays Hamilton, a citizen who had attended the strategy session, reflected that the assemblage had asked for more than it could realistically hope to keep, for the township did not have a railroad at this point. At dawn, so legend has it, he headed toward the business district and persuaded several influential men in the community to reconsider the decision that had been made the night before. Hamilton won his point. He then relayed a message to Gardenhire which stated that the "voice of the people clamored for the College."[27] From that moment, the community, according to an early member of the faculty, sought the college with the "unfaltering patience which inspired Knights of old in questing for the Holy Grail."[28]

The Land-Grant Act of 1862 received passage only after a spirited sectional debate,[29] and almost every state that founded an agricultural and mechanical college became embroiled in a long political struggle. Sometimes the controversy centered upon the location of the institution. In other instances it involved discussion of how the most money could be obtained from the land or land script provided by the organic bill. Payne County discovered that the implementation of their objective would be much more difficult than they had envisioned, too. Frustration first developed in Stillwater when Councilor Gardenhire found that his projected "combine" had failed to form. Instead, Governor Steele, who held a firm rein on the state's political machinery, introduced his own brand of horse trading.

In order to spearhead a simultaneous attack in both chambers of the Assembly, four separate bills were introduced to locate the Oklahoma Agricultural and Mechanical College in Payne County. Gardenhire sponsored Council Bill 14; Ira Terrill submitted House Bills 30 and 31; and James Matthews added a fourth, House Bill 32. Each of these measures became the object of an intense debate. A particularly heated argument occurred on September 24 but the session finally ended with the passage of Terrill's first bill. One week later, J. L. Brown, the Chairman of the Committee on the Location of the Capital and Other Public Institutions, brought the document to the floor of the Council where it also gained the required majority. Now, since the bill had passed both chambers of the Assembly it appeared as if Payne County would get the institution she desired.[30]

An unforeseen event, however, came to the surface on October 14, which temporarily dashed the hopes of the county for the institution. Governor Steele returned House Bill 30 on that day without his signature. The executive, in a personal letter addressed to Representative Arthur Daniels, noted, with some embarrassment, that the Legislature had adopted his earlier recommendation in regard to the land-grant college. Then he explained that he had been informed by William Stone, the Assistant Commissioner of the Oklahoma Land Office, that the bill was unconstitutional. Since

Oklahoma still had territorial status, it did not qualify for federal funds under either the Morrill or the Hatch Act. While Steele hoped that the United States Congress or the Secretary of the Interior would ultimately give assistance, he stated that he would not sign the bill until officials in Washington clarified the matter. In point of fact, however, the measure was not contrary to the provisions of the two bills, and in view of James Neal's many letters to Steele in connection with such organizations, it leads one to suspect that the chief executive simply wanted to delay action for purely private reasons.[31]

Undismayed by what amounted to a veto of the bill, Councilor Gardenhire decided to continue moving in the same direction. He feared that a loss of momentum would be detrimental to the wishes of the good citizens of Stillwater. In less than two weeks he drafted another measure and introduced it as Council Bill 52. Its wording was much like the previous attempts, but a sub-committee succeeded in pigeonholing the document, permanently. Representative Darius Farnsworth of Kingfisher proposed a companion piece in the House in order to continue the dual approach. It, too, became the object of delaying tactics, thereby clearing the way for James Matthews to initiate House Bill 82 entitled "An Act to locate and establish an agricultural college in Payne county, Oklahoma Territory" on November 20. Terrill, using a North Dakota law passed in 1887 as a pattern, sponsored a governance measure. Councilor Leander Pittman, on the next to last day of the session, tendered still another bill which dealt with bonding procedures to be used by future members of the Board of Regents. The latter two proposals passed as written. House Bill 82, however, was less fortunate.[32]

Matthew's bill moved to the Committee on Public Lands and Buildings, where it lay in a dormant condition for nearly one month. This long delay presumably related to the governor's earlier disapproval. D. W. Talbot brought it to the floor of the lower legislative body on December 17 and strongly urged adoption. Late that evening, the document passed by a 14 to 2 vote. Two days afterwards, Gardenhire directed the proposal through the upper house by an equally lopsided margin. Steele, now apparently convinced of the "legality" of the legislation, added his name on Christmas Eve, the last working day of the first session.[33]

In spite of the wide margin of victory, the bill did not escape criticism from some members of the Legislature. Councilor Brown of Oklahoma County, for example, decided to explain his negative ballot, and probably spoke what was in the minds of several of his colleagues when he commented: "This legislature has been charged with bribery and corruption, and rumors in this regard have pointed to no delegation as it has to that of Payne county. Under the circumstances," he continued, "to see the best institution in the Territory, go to that county is the reason why one should hestitate and I therefore vote 'No.' "[34] These words cast a shadow over the college, thwarting its support in Guthrie for some years to come. In addition, the law itself evoked criticism from an expert, James Neal.

7

He pointed out the the bill establishing the institution was a queer medley of "bad English, uncertain phrase and indirectness that makes it one of the curiosities of legislation." On the other hand, Neal offered credit where it seemed due. He added that the "members of the stormy first session of the territorial legislature builded much wiser than they knew when they asked for the agricultural college, and 'through thick and thin' worked, schemed, intrigued, and nobody knows what else . . . to get it."[35]

Several amendments were tacked onto the founding bill during the final week of the session. In general, each pertained to the procedures to be employed in financing and locating the institution. First, since no site had yet been designated, the Assembly authorized Governor Steele to appoint three commissioners to ascertain the best possible location, thereby initiating competition at the local level. The communities of Cimarron City, Clayton, Forest City, Ingalls, Payne Center, Perkins, Windom, and Stillwater, however were considered the most logical choices as each had a post-office and most of the other minimum services required to sustain a small educational plant. Second, the county or municipality receiving the site designation had to donate no less than eighty acres of land for the use of the college and experiment station. Third, the town closest to the institution was to be responsible for issuing bonds in the amount of ten thousand dollars which had to be delivered to the territorial secretary of state for sale "at not less than their par value, the proceeds thereof to be placed to the credit of such institution, such bonds to run twenty years after the date of their issuance and draw five per cent interest. . . . . "[36] A fourth provision stipulated that the local money had to be used for the construction of a college building. And last, if the community did not provide bonds in a reasonable length of time, the college could be located elsewhere in Oklahoma.[37] The passage of these measures constituted an important victory for Stillwater, yet the city fathers would soon discover that it often takes many battles to win a war.

On May 31, 1891, Governor Steele, who had waited for six months while the interested communities prepared for an inspection, named the necessary commissioners. The three nominees, W. Merton, G. W. Campbell, and J. M. Stovall, appeared to be more than qualified to carry out their assigned duties, since each had been reared on a farm, had been associated in one way or another with education before moving to Oklahoma, had belonged to the First Territorial Legislature, and perhaps more important to the chief executive, had served in the Civil War. Steele, like the man who had appointed him to his office, trusted ex-military men to carry out governmental duties efficiently and with integrity.[38]

The preparations for the commissioner's visit to Stillwater were largely, but not exclusively, made by the "Sanhedrin." This body initially became involved with the college project when members assisted with the Payne County bond election of February 3, 1891. It was believed that this experience would be helpful in garnering support for placing the land-grant institution and experiment station in the county seat. Unfortunately, the bonds failed by a margin of 776 to 375, probably because the electorate had recently voted favorably on a railroad subsidy. Moreover, the proposition did not carry because the election had been held without adequate campaigning, the haste being necessary so that the county could attempt to qualify for federal money during the current fiscal year. Stillwater, then, if it persisted in its desire for a college, would have to bear alone the responsibility for securing the required land and bonding measures. Other interested localities, of course, possessed the same opportunity.[39]

The failure of the county bond program meant that Stillwater would have to incorporate before the community could vote on a bond issue. On March 23, accordingly, the town council presented the necessary petition to the Payne County Board of Commissioners. It requested permission for the people to hold an election to designate three temporary city officers to supervise the incorporation process. On April 7, the electorate selected J. E. Sater, T. J. Lester, and John Caldwell for these positions. They, in turn, divided the township into the required districts and called for a second ballot to be cast on April 20 so that the newly created offices could be filled on a permanent basis. On that date, Charles Knoblock, W. F. Ramsey, and Lester were confirmed as trustees, with J. B. Murphy, J. H. Swope, O. M. Eyler, and T. J. Hueston placed in lesser positions.

Now incorporated into a municipality, the city fathers set May 4 as the day for voting on the bond issue previously rejected by the county. The *Oklahoma Hawk* and *Stillwater Gazette* newspapers were chosen to publicize the event and the *Wichita Eagle* was commissioned to provide the blank bonds if the proposed measure passed. This time the voters acted favorably. Councilor Gardenhire personally took the engravings to Robert Martin, the Secretary of Oklahoma Territory.[40] No effort, however, was made to sell them, because, as an early resident wrote, buyers of bonds were extremely scarce. He remembered that this period preceded the panic of 1893, which "had been incubating over Kansas and the great West for two years already, and [Jacob] Coxey's army was even then dreaming of visiting the capitol steps in Washington."[41]

With the date nearing for the committee appointed by Steele to visit Stillwater, the local residents directed their attention to finding a tract of land suitable as a site for the college. A committee consisting of John Clark, George Gardenhire, James Matthews, and Frank Wikoff hoped to obtain a 200 acre section which lay to the north and west of the city. This property was owned by four farmers, Alfred Newton Jarrell, Charles A. Vreeland, Oscar Morse, and Frank Duck.[42] Of the four pieces of land, the latter's seemed the most valuable because it joined the proposed college site with the boundaries of the city. The team initially inspected this location as two of the men had offered to donate some part of their claim. A. E. Jarrell, in his declining years, reported his father as saying to Duck: "If you will give your northwest forty, I will give my north-

9

east forty . . . and we will locate the Oklahoma A. and M. College and the Experiment Station, so none of the politicians can ever move it, and we will have a school capable of giving our children all the education they are capable of holding."[43]

For the most part, the land in question had not been claimed long enough for final homestead proof to have been made. Yet the site had to be acquired by giving such proof, after which the property could then be deeded to the town officers. Consequently, Duck converted his entry to cash on June 13; Jarrell and Vreeland followed suit on November 3; and Morse completed similar arrangements two days later. It is believed that Duck and Vreeland gave their forty acres without charge. Jarrell, however, received enough money to pay his filing fee and Morse, who offered twice what the others did, received compensation at the rate of fifteen dollars per acre. These charitable acts are evidence that some people, as opposed to the more commercially minded members of the territorial Legislature, who never once in the published debates discussed the potential advantages of a land-grant institution, foresaw the benefits that could accure to the state and community from having a center of higher learning in their midst.[44]

While these negotiations appeared to be forthright and honest, one should not be surprised to learn that real estate speculators entered the scene, hoping to make a profit from the attempt to found the college in Stillwater. The peculiar manner in which Oklahoma became opened for settlement provided the opportunity for claim-jumping and other unethical practices. Though the facts of this particular case are not complete, it has subsequently been alleged that some members of the "Sanhedrin" returned to Duck's house, telling him that in order to consumate the proposed donation of land to the city that he also had to sell his south eighty acres. No original documents of this second conference have been uncovered, but several memoirs suggest that the young farmer was offered a substantial amount of money for the additional acreage. Whatever the figure tendered, the property did change hands, with Duck maintaining that he received only $800 in payment. Moreover, the city did not gain title to the land. It was purchased by a Guthrie real estate syndicate headed by Joseph W. McNeal, who then hired Frank Wikoff to subdivide the property and sell it to individuals looking for homesites. Later, Wikoff denied participation in the deal, and he said that it was transacted without his knowledge, assistance, or desire to benefit by it.[45]

On the evening of June 24, 1891, the governor's commissioners, Campbell, Merton, and Stovall, arrived in Stillwater to discuss the location of the college. They were accompanied by several unnamed national legislators. Councilor Gardenhire took the room next to the delegation at the City Hotel, fearing, perhaps, leaving anything to chance. The next morning, the visitors ascertained, they thought, the legality of the last bond election and proceeded to inspect the 200 acre site offered by the community. Having finished their work in Stillwater, they then rode to Perkins, a small town to the south. Here the inspectors were so impressed with the rich loam soil and the high blue-stem grass of the region that they were tempted to option this location without further hesitation. But Charles Donart, Hays Hamilton, Frank Hutto, and Robert Lowry, however, arrived from Stillwater before the committee could place its recommendations on paper. These men "rescued" the investigators from an enthusiastic street celebration in their honor and returned the commissioners to their overnight accommodations in the county seat. The people of Stillwater, not to be outdone by their leaders, treated the inspectors to champagne and a wild turkey and prairie chicken dinner. Captain William Knipe, from Perkins, who became suspicious of the sudden departure of the commissioners, walked in on the late evening banquet. One glance at the red-eyed delegation indicated to him that the contest for the college site had been lost.[46] He told his companion Warren Chandler that "We are sunk. These Stillwater fellows are just a damned shrewd bunch of horsetraders."[47] Two weeks later Knipe's worst fears materialized. The official report to Governor Steele stated that the commissioners had "selected a body of land containing 200 acres, that contained the various qualities of soil as we thought would be most suitable . . . and asked the citizens of the town of Stillwater . . . to make a formal tender of deed . . . ."[48] The title to the property was transferred to the Board of Regents on November 25, 1891.[49]

At this point in Stillwater's development, the townspeople seemed to think that the decision to move to Oklahoma Territory had been a wise one. The city had been designated as the county seat and a courthouse was under construction in hopes of making the designation permanent. Then, too, the governing board of the college had decided to begin classwork in the local Congregational Church, for, as in the case of the courthouse, it was believed that if formal instruction was underway, it would make it more difficult for the legislators to move the institution elsewhere. Furthermore, the town council had passed a six mill levy in order to pay the interest on the educational bonds once they had been sold. And finally, ten clergymen were available in the immediate vicinity to tend to the spiritual needs of the community. Charles Becker, the editor of the *Gazette*, expressed the thoughts of many of his readers when he encouraged others to come to Stillwater. He proudly exclaimed in an editorial that the community was now a civilized place to live.[50]

Beneath the surface, however, the city's institutions were not as secure as some believed. The most immediate problem in regard to the college concerned the fact that the bonds had not been sold. They had been delivered by Councilor Gardenhire to Robert Martin, who now was acting governor; but, no real effort had been made to find a buyer. College and community officials, therefore, joined together to locate prospective investors. On March 3, 1892, the Stillwater Board of Trustees invited Robert J. Barker, the president of the Oklahoma Agricultural and Mechanical College, to meet with them. This conference was the first indication that a potential buyer had become interested enough in the bonds to investigate the financial condition of the city.[51] Charles McGraw told the assembled leaders that he was in the process of gathering records associated with the bond election. In addition, he said that he had prepared a transcript of the last property "valuation of all the real estate within the boundaries of the city."[52] These documents were being assembled for an individual named Vandergraff, who had previously indicated to Governor Martin that his company might take the certificates.

This news, no doubt, aroused much interest and hopeful speculation. Yet, it failed fast, because the trustees soon received a message which stated that the bond election had been illegal. Vandergraff's firm had found a federal statute which stated that "no political nor municipal corporation, county, or other subdivision in any of the Territories of the United States shall ever become indebted in any manner or for any purpose to any amount in the aggregate . . . exceeding four percentum on value of taxable property . . . ."[53] Charles Donart, the assessor, confirmed the accuracy of the statement. He told the board that the city had only $110,000 worth of taxable property, which was $140,000 short of the figure needed to tender a $10,000 bond issue.[54] And to add to the growing gloom, Donart stated that the latest census figures revealed that the town had insufficient population to incorporate.

Undaunted, the city fathers moved to comply with the provisions of the federal legislation which had been called to their attention. First, the members commissioned Hays Hamilton to review the census count. He approached his task with determination, producing enough names to make the incorporation procedures legal. Thirty-seven years later, however, a friend disclosed that Hamilton had accomplished his job by including the names chiseled on tombstones in the local cemetery. Second, Charles McGraw, who replaced Charles Knoblock as chairman of the town's trustees, appointed Van Martin as a special city assessor. His valuation survey revealed that Stillwater had experienced a near miraculous growth in taxable property, up to $263,000. This figure was more than adequate to call for a vote on new bonds. With the new statistics in hand, Knoblock moved that the board schedule another election for July 26 to authorize a second issue, including interest. The question passed by a margin of 167 to 6. In August, the bonds were delivered to officials in Guthrie and renewed efforts were made to sell them.[55]

On September 23, the *Gazette* stated that the college bonds had been sold and that construction on the first permanent building would begin in the near future. Both statements were premature, although the town council did have a plan of action in mind. [The editor probably knew the true situation, but he may have wanted to stimulate interest in enrollment as the first full length academic year was about to begin.] Eli Reed, Treasurer of Payne County, had been engaged for several months in an effort to sell $50,000 worth of county bonds to the St. Joseph Loan and Trust Company

12

through its agent George Theiss. Reed, a strong community booster, promised to negotiate a package deal, combining the county and college bonds into one portfolio. When this news became public, however, some people feared that the move might jeopardize the county issue. But before a court injunction could be obtained, and at a time when it had been announced that the St. Joseph firm had sent a representative to Stillwater, the treasurer disappeared, mysteriously. Rumor had it that he had been kidnapped. This explanation seemed somewhat plausible, because many infamous outlaw bands periodically ventured from No Man's Land into Oklahoma Territory. Fortunately, however, for the county interests, Reed returned just at the moment that Theiss agreed to purchase both sets of bonds. He looked none the worse for his "frightful" ordeal. On November 2, 1892, the president and clerk of the town council were authorized to sign the documents that pertained to the college. Other details, supposedly, were of a routine nature.[56]

The Missouri business firm agreed to take the college building bonds. It did not, however, offer a specific amount of money while its agent was in Stillwater, because most people assumed that the securities would be sold for less than par value in view of the depressed economy. Later, Theiss stipulated that he would pay seventy-eight cents on the dollar if the company was awarded a bonus of $381. This move made it possible to recall the first set of bonds from Guthrie, destroy them, and forward a request to the Legislature to approve the latest transaction. Led by a member of the college faculty, a group of local citizens rode to Orlando to meet their emissary. He told the excited delegation that the last obstacle blocking the construction of a college building had been removed.[57]

Even though the Legislature approved of the sale of bonds to the St. Joseph Loan and Trust Company, the officials of the city were soon to be disappointed again. The Missouri buyer decided to withdraw his offer at the last minute, probably because he had found out about the irregularities associated with the last city valuation and population count. This announcement created the possibility that the Legislature would move the college to a more richly endowed community, such as Guthrie or Oklahoma City. McGraw, however, devised an alternative plan. He contacted the land syndicate owned by Joseph McNeal, the man who had purchased Frank Duck's south eighty acres. McNeal and his wife paid $7,825 for the bonds, which, as it turned out, proved to be slightly more than the previous offer.[58] W. A. Swiler, W. E. Hodges, Frank Wikoff, and Hays Hamilton met McGraw's stage and demanded to see the proof that the bonds had been sold. Later, the businessman recalled: "When I offered the deposit slip they lighted a match, read the slip and rushed to town. . . ."[59] Band instruments were produced in the middle of the night so that the good news could be blown to the community in an appropriate fashion.

At last, there remained only one more requirement to be fulfilled. Since the bonds had been sold for $2,175 below par value, this sum needed to be raised as quickly as possible so that a $10,000

13

voucher could be mailed to Guthrie. To meet this obligation fifty-five local citizens, including a few members of the college faculty, purchased city warrants in the amount of thirty-three dollars each. Buyers could not be found for an amount about equivalent to eleven shares and this deficit was secured by a loan from the Farmers and Merchants Bank in Stillwater. Alexander Campbell accepted an unsecured personal note and provided the funds without delay. The loan received redemption through the sale of saloon licenses, and the warrants were retired as revenue became available. But, the biennial interest payments posed a more serious problem, as special warrants had to be issued and funds had to be borrowed from the Road and Bridge account. This money, when added to the six mill levy already in effect, provided for complete restitution.[60] Frank Wikoff commented upon the seriousness of the affair in a letter to a close friend. He said that these events seemed like "life and death to us. We practically fought, bled and died for the college . . . ."[61]

The bond sale was not completed without considerable comment. *The Oklahoma Hawk,* an organ of the Democratic Party, contained a column in April, 1893, which criticized the Republicans who had handled the negotations. The writer began by stating that we "have this week made it our business to interview the knowing ones and found out what we could about the transaction and below give the whole affair."[62] The reporter then listed the expenses incurred by the town council in securing the sale of the bonds, especially as the transaction pertained to the St. Joseph Loan and Trust Company. It was alleged that a total of $530 had been paid to F. C. Hunt, C. Knoblock, C. McGraw, J. J. Shaffer, and to the Missouri firm itself. Furthermore, the columnist charged that a competitive bid submitted by M. L. Turner had not even been considered, and that expenses had been abnormally high, with politics playing an important part in determining who got the bonds and how much money had been paid for them.[63]

Notwithstanding the fact that there may have been some truth in the allegations, the residents of Stillwater were elated that the long struggle to sell the bonds had come to an end. Even the partisan *Gazette* did not take time to rebut the editorial in the *Hawk.* Instead, the editor suggested that his readers channel their energy into securing additional support for the construction of a college building. Shortly afterward, the Legislature approved a $15,000 revenue measure.[64] It permitted the Board of Regents to let the contract for the first permanent building on the campus to H. Ryan of Fort Smith, Arkansas, on June 20, 1893. Old Central, as this landmark would be called in the future, came to symbolize the difficulty of bringing vocational and scientific education to the state of Oklahoma. Freeman Miller, an eye-witness to many of the events described to this point in the institution's development, movingly expressed such a sentiment in an anniversary address delivered in 1929. He stated that he hoped the building would "stand for decades to come as a reminder of the days when men dared

14

much and accomplished more—when out of poverty they beheld great visions and adventured forth with brave hearts to achieve victories they coveted . . . . To them," Miller added, "should be the homage of good men and women forever."[65]

In retrospect, the founding of the Oklahoma A. and M. College at the state level evidences no deep commitment to either land-grant or democratic educational ideas. The institution was viewed simply as a means whereby federal funds could be brought to an undeveloped region.[66] Much of the delay in obtaining the legislation that chartered the organization must be attributed to the uninspired leadership of Governor George Steele. His policy of encouraging competition may be construed as a local manifestation of national *laissez faire* economic principles, but more important, whether the policy was sound or not, it created jealousies that extended far beyond the territorial period, leaving college administrators with the haunting fear that the institution might be moved at any time.[67] Not only were the counties who did not receive the organization disappointed, but their elected officials lobbied in subsequent legislative sessions until they secured an educational institution for their own locality. This situation resulted in the construction of colleges that have remained inadequately financed and staffed.[68] Gaston Litton, an Oklahoma historian, has correctly conjectured in this regard that the state's educational history would read much differently if the normal school, the state university, and the land-grant college had been incorporated into a single institution of excellence.[69] Guthrie actually proposed such an arrangement. Its political leadership offered to locate a multi-purpose institution of higher education in Oklahoma City if that community would vote to retain the capital where it was on a permanent basis. Litton, however, did not rule out the development of regional community colleges or a state college system to serve as feeders for the combined university.

At the local level, the businessmen were also interested in obtaining the much coveted federal funds; yet, there is little doubt that some of these individuals possessed an understanding of how a land-grant college could aid in the more complete development of the community's human resources. In addition, the donation of land by four farmers suggest that this class, too, appreciated the potential of higher education. The nation was in the process of shifting from an agrarian to an urban economic base and training in the "industries of life" was needed to aid in the transition. The economic and social elite, especially those men who had attended Morrill institutions, provided direction. This group formed committees and organizations to implement the goals of their neighbors. These agencies, then, secured the funds and balloting strength required to locate the Agricultural and Mechanical College of Oklahoma Territory in Stillwater. And whether the city initially sought the institution out of greed or an enlightened cultural attitude, the four year struggle produced the determination necessary to create and sustain an educational lamp for the prairie. The pioneers of

Payne County were rich in faith and they believed in the American dream. How could the future bring anything except progress?

II THE ITINERANT YEARS

While the townspeople waged the economic and political battle to locate and retain the Oklahoma A. and M. College in Stillwater, the first board of regents, the first president, and the first faculty labored to implement the diffuse law that established the institution. This task proved much more difficult than initially anticipated because most of the regents were inexperienced in the field of higher education,[1] possessed inadequate funds and physical facilities with which to promote teaching, extension, and research,[2] and had to shape academic policy for students who were not prepared for collegiate work.[3] These conditions prevailed throughout most of the territorial period and therefore must be classified as rather routine problems. More noteworthy, however, are the efforts of the administration and faculty to formulate institutional objectives. It was thought that a college needed to have goals, to stand for certain principles, and to have a program which could be supported by the general public.[4] The adoption of a mission, however, was a decision that could not be made overnight, for the Legislature, the governing board, the college presidents, the students, and the members of the community often held divergent educational views. Thus, these individuals and organizations came into conflict during the period from 1891 to 1894. This stage of development may best be labeled the "itinerant years," for the institution had no permanent buildings of its own and classes had to be conducted in local churches, the offices of businessmen, the county courthouse, and the homes of the instructional staff.

Most of the statute entitled "An act to locate and establish an agricultural college in Payne County, Oklahoma Territory" concerned the composition, the method of appointment, and the duties and responsibilities of the Board of Regents, the agency charged with overseeing the corporation. This body was endowed with dictatorial powers, but if a more stable political environment had prevailed, it is possible that a cooperative spirit between the Board and other members of the college could have been effected. During the "itinerant years," however, no one had been appointed to review the decisions of the regents, and they decided to reserve most of the administrative powers for themselves, instituting policy without seeking the advice and consent of concerned educational specialists.[5]

According to law, the Board was to be composed of five persons, with the governor serving as a sixth in an *ex officio* capacity. The founding legislation charged the state's chief executive officer with the function of submitting names to the Legislature when vacancies existed. Two regents were to be appointed for two years and three for four years, thereby insuring a degree of continuity. If a resignation took place when the Legislature was not in session, the governor could fill the void and his nominee would serve until the Assembly convened again. The most notable exception to this design related to the fact that if an Oklahoma Board of Agriculture was created, it could have the privilege of forwarding two names to the governor that he was obliged to appoint. Coordination between the trustees and the college came from having the secretary of the Board serve as the president of the land-grant institution.

The Trustees were granted supervisory authority in almost every area that related to the life of the college organism. The Board possessed the power to appoint and release personnel from the president down to student experiment station employees, direct the expenditure of federal and territorial funds, audit vouchers, approve reports submitted to Guthrie and Washington, determine the sum of all salaries, and share with the faculty the privilege of conferring degrees on students who passed the required examinations and who were known to possess a good moral character. Finally, the law limited the number of times that the trustees could meet as well as the amount of compensation that a member of the Board could claim. More than passing notice should be taken of the latter provision, because it was the only limiting amendment in the organic act that critics could use to check the Board when disputes arose.[6]

While these duties should not have been too difficult for a mature and established institution of higher education, they were

18

onerous at a time when the college only nominally existed in the hearts and minds of the people directly associated with it. In addition to the above, the Board assumed direction of the Oklahoma Experiment Station. But the members, generally speaking, did not believe this organization had much scientific value; they thought of it primarily as a subsidiary of the college, a place where a profit could be made to increase the instructional budget.[7] And, as with the educational plant, the founding law was vague in regard to the station,[8] clearing the way for politicians to use the farm to employ friends and relatives who were in need of employment. The latter situation caused the station no end of petty troubles on a day-to-day basis, and it marked the agency as a spot where serious trouble would erupt in the near future.[9]

Governor George Steele forwarded his nominations for the first Board of Regents the same day that he signed the law creating the college. Five names were submitted to the Legislature, with four of them being members of the lawmaking body. Robert Barker, Logan County, forty-two, a farmer and member of the Republican Party; the Reverend J. P. Lane, Cleveland County, thirty-eight, a clergyman and member of the Republican Party; Arthur Daniels, Canadian County, a Populist, who served as Speaker of the House of Representatives; and John Wimberly, Kingfisher County, twenty-four, a farmer and member of the Democratic Party, were the solons suggested for service. Amos Ewing, Kingfisher County, twenty-eight, an employee of the Choctaw, Oklahoma and Gulf Railroad Company and a lifelong Republican, became the final candidate. With the exception of Daniels, all were approved. Governor A. J. Seay, successor to Steele, later forwarded the name of M. T. Little to fill the fifth position.[10]

The first formal meeting of the Board took place in the Old Heriott Building in June, 1891 at Guthrie.[11] It is highly likely, however, that some of these individuals had been in touch with each other before this conference, because Barker, Ewing, and Lane, the men who belonged to the Grand Old Party, were the only individuals present. The most important item on the agenda pertained to the selection of a college president and a secretary for the Board. Three years later, Robert Barker, then testifying before a special legislative investigating committee, revealed what had taken place. He stated: "The Board of Regents of the A. and M. College was organized . . . by electing Robert J. Barker, President and Secretary; A. Ewing, Treasurer."[12] The secrecy of the meeting and the lack of detail suggests that political party alignments played an important role in the selection process.

With the Board now operational, the remainder of the year was devoted to making plans for instruction to begin. At the second meeting, which was held in August, the regents reported that James Neal had agreed to become the director of the experiment station. Leaving his family in Indiana, he moved to Stillwater and began formulating an agricultural and horticultural program designed to meet the immediate needs of Oklahoma farmers. The Board met

19

again in November, making some historic decisions. First, it was decided to use the facilities of the local Congregational church so that classes could be formed the following month.[13] This move was made possible by the city fathers who agreed to rent the building, purchase the equipment needed to convert the structure into classrooms, and provide money for janitorial and utility fees. Federal funds could not be used for such purposes and the state had not yet appropriated revenues for higher education, at least in regard to Oklahoma A. and M.[14] Second, the Board announced that Alexander Covington Magruder, a graduate of the Mississippi landgrant college, had consented to teach courses in agriculture for the incoming class of students. Third, John Wimberley, a member of the Board, accepted election as superintendent of building, and he was authorized to submit plans for the construction of an inexpensive residence for the station director and college farmer as well as some temporary laboratories, barns, and sheds. All of these buildings were to be modest in scope, as it was anticipated that only $3,000 would be available for building during the current fiscal year.[15] Last, Captain L. J. Darnell and Edward Clark were offered, and they accepted, appointments as military commandant and principal of the preparatory school.[16]

Publication of the news that classes would begin in December, 1891, caused much excitement in Stillwater and the immediate vicinity. The residents of the community, since most of the urgent business had now been attended to, decided to express their appreciation by holding a banquet for the Board. Professor Neal, the first member of the faculty, served as master of ceremonies. He introduced President Barker, who, as the main speaker, summarized the recent steps that had been taken by the trustees. Other regents and politicians offered a variety of toasts and best wishes, including T. G. Lowe, John Lane, George Gardenhire, J. R. Keaton, A. A. Ewing, John Wimberley, T. S. Jones, A. N. Daniels, and John Clark. The occasion was a festive one. The postmaster, caught up in the spirit of good will, invited the visitors to spend the night at his house instead of having them take quarters at the Wagon Yard.[17] With the exception of letting contracts for the temporary buildings, the hiring of A. V. McDowell as manager of the farm, and the employment of George Latimer Holter as station chemist the remainder of the academic year was routine. The trustees met in June to review the year's work. No public statements were issued, yet it was assumed that the college had gotten off to a good beginning under their watchful eye.[18]

Considering its relative obscurity, the Oklahoma A. and M. College, during the territorial period, probably had more than its share of capable presidents. Henry Elijah Alvord and George Espy Morrow, each had a national reputation in the field of agricultural education. Edmond Dandridge Murdaugh added much color to the campus and the state as a result of his oratorical ability. Moreover, he brought with him an expert knowledge in the teaching of industrial arts that he had acquired in Maryland. The administration of Angelo Cyrus Scott evidenced the initiation of some aspects of a state university in Stillwater. His tenure as president still remains a landmark in the history of the institution. Robert Barker, however, the first president, has remained something a mystery, for he was a quiet and colorless diplomatist.[19]

President Barker moved to Oklahoma during the first land rush. Born on April 23, 1848, near Hinton, Virginia, he received his common school training at the Cheshire Academy in Ohio. His collegiate work was taken at the Hale Normal College in West Virginia, where he graduated in 1869, having pursued a special course in civil engineering. Barker then taught the primary grades in Jumping Branch, West Virginia, and Sulpher Springs and Kokomo, Indiana. In 1880, he decided to abandon the teaching profession in order to enter the furniture business in Pomeroy, Kansas and Jefferiesville, Missouri. Never one to miss an opportunity, the move to Oklahoma Territory was taken because it seemed to be a good chance to acquire inexpensive land for raising shorthorn cattle. This educational and business background endowed Robert Barker with more ability than some of his neighbors in Crescent City, so it was logical for them to nominate him to serve in the first Legislature.[20]

Representative Barker, according to his contemporaries, had many favorable personal characteristics. Coming from the antebellum South, he evidenced much of the poise and bearing that sometimes is associated with men of the planter class. Harry Thompson, who worked closely with Barker for nearly three years, described him as a "congenial, companionable, intelligent citizen . . . a warm friend to those he liked."[21] He had his critics, too. Some of the college faculty resented the manner in which he obtained the presidency and his close relationship with the Republican Party. Yet, Thompson maintained that not even his bitterest rival could accuse him of even the slightest trickery.[22] Horticulturalist Frank Waugh agreed. "He was strictly honest," he said, "and though in his political relations, surrounded by malfeasance and peculation, he never misappropriated so much as a postage stamp nor stooped to the faintest dishonesty."[23] Subsequent investigations of the college by territorial legislators corroborate the accuracy of these evaluations.

While it is true that the first president possessed a college degree and had served a ten year apprenticeship in the public school system before moving to Oklahoma, he came to Stillwater with some educational disadvantages. He was not a scientist by nature, nor had he a clear idea as to the intent and purpose of the Morrill Act.[24] Barker, as late as 1892, corresponded with John Noble, the Secretary of the Interior, in an attempt to seek further information about the federal bill which established land-grant colleges. He wrote: "We understand . . . the Agricultural and Mechanical College of Oklahoma Territory is entitled to 90,000 acres of public land as a permanent endowment. How to proceed to have it set apart is what we do not understand."[25] Having been a member of the Legislature when the whole question of federal aid had been discussed in Guthrie, the executive should have known that the institution was ineligible for such support at this time. And, even if he missed those discussions, it is surprising that he would wait for almost an entire year before contacting Washington. But, on the other hand, Barker was never one to rush into action and sometimes conflicts were avoided because of his slowness to respond to a crisis situation.

The very title that Barker assumed upon taking office indicated some hostility toward the new sciences, especially those of an empirical nature being pioneered on the campuses of land-grant institutions. The initial catalog, which he wrote himself, listed his position as "President and Professor of Moral and Mental Science."[26] Whereas such terms were once used by college executives to guard the religious orthodoxy from theological heresies, it is much more likely that this designation was employed in the late nineteenth century to "discover the distinction between science and philosophy and to detect the fallacy of identifying science with a metaphysic of positivism or naturalism."[27] Barker himself hinted that this view was in the back of his mind early in his administration when he said that upon becoming president he realized that

the destinies of these students were entrusted to my care. I recognized that whatever is retained is not necessarily the idea in its entirety, but the effect of the idea upon the mind and *ad infinitum*. Dark and evil sentiments produce like effects, rendering turbid and vicious the mind impressed by them, while good impressions like sparkling water tends to purify all with which they come into contact.[28]

Holter, Magruder, Neal, and Waugh, who were all graduates of older and better established state universities, probably did not like this point of view, for it is one that reflects a belief in revealed truth and *in loco parentis*. With the exception of Neal, these men had graduated from land-grant colleges which were breaking with the traditions of the past.

President Barker had one other liability which adversely affected his administrative tenure. When he moved to the territory, he initiated a homestead settlement on a 160 acre tract in April, 1889, making entry the next month at the Kingfisher land office. This filing meant that if he wanted to keep possession of his claim, the residency requirements of the 1862 land bill would have to be fulfilled. Barker, therefore, had to leave his family in Crescent City in order to qualify for a clear title to his property. Consequently, he commuted to Stillwater and arranged for only temporary quarters while in town. He took almost every possible opportunity to return home for visits with his wife and children. His close attachment to his family is understandable, yet when problems on the campus developed, no executive office was present. This left the faculty to cope with routine as well as extraordinary business matters, a situation which most resented. Ill-feelings evolved, leading to an internal struggle between the two elements as early as the beginning of the first full-length academic year.[29]

22

With Barker preoccupied with his property in Crescent City, regential duties, classes in mental and moral science, and the attempt to sell the college bonds, it is improbable that he had, or took, the time to develop goals for the institution entrusted to his leadership. Instead, he seems to have continued to operate under those principles that had guided him when he taught common school, thereby relegating Oklahoma A. and M. to the status of a simple agricultural academy. It is true that on one occasion he told a group of legislators that "in this institution we consider that we have but a reflection of the Agricultural and Mechanical College of Kansas."[30] But this statement must be considered a gross exaggeration, for that organization by this time had achieved a level of sophistication that did not exist in Stillwater. Furthermore, there is no evidence that the administrator attended the meetings of the Association of American Agricultural Colleges and Experiment Stations or requested information from nationally prominent state universities. This lack of direction led to many problems. In particular, the Legislature was not educated as to the nature of the responsibilities that had been assumed when it founded the institution. The subsequent lack of money and moral support irritated the faculty and retarded development.[31]

Tensions mounted to the boiling point in the summer and fall of 1892. Barker, having spent several weeks in Crescent City, returned to greet the incoming students and then went back to his home for what appears to be a three month period. By late October, the faculty began to discuss issues in their weekly meetings which suggest an academic mutiny afoot. On the 24th, with James Neal chairing the session, George Holter moved that a committee be appointed to create a disciplinary code for the students. This motion not only pointed to a serious behavior problem, but it also disclosed that standing committees had not been organized. Magruder, at the same meeting, recommended that several of the faculty talk with the Board of Regents about a proposed division of the preparatory class. This action, of course, constituted a break in the chain of command. Magruder's motion was tabled and subsequently withdrawn. It evidences, however, a growing dissatisfaction with Barker. Also, another colleague asked that a common set of parliamentary rules be adopted. Perhaps this motion, too, commented adversely upon the manner in which the affairs of the institution were being conducted.[32]

The "Minutes of the Faculty" for the months of November and December reveal that the gulf between the instructors and the administration was growing wider. In November, Professor Magruder moved that "everything affecting students or Faculty shall be discussed, voted upon and carried, ordered published by the Faculty prior to any announcement to that effect by the president or any member of the Faculty."[33] Later, Clark, the head of the preparatory department, introduced another item which implied that the organization badly needed its executive in residence. He requested that a committee be appointed to "confer immediately with the

City Council in regard to wood to supply the present need of this college."[34] Moreover, the twin insurgents of the institution—Holter and Magruder—were nominated to request of Barker that he chair the delegation. Student conduct came under discussion as well. Several cases of theft and drunkenness had been reported. Punishments were meted out, but Barker, who had responded to the plea to return, promptly declared the new disciplinary code invalid. He did, however, acquiese on the matter of appointing standing committees. Nevertheless, the antagonism between him and the faculty became worse and a principal-teacher, not president-professor, relationship continued.[35]

The quality of instruction increased during the third academic year. In addition, Barker took more of an interest in the institution, especially in the crucial area of legislative relations. Here his experience as a territorial politician worked to the benefit of the college. But the burst of energy arrived too late. The Secretary of Agriculture had already expressed disappointment in the progress of the Oklahoma organization and he suggested a change in leadership. Barker, not being in a position to defend himself, resigned. The faculty conveyed silent approval by voting no commendations, nor did a single newspaper, including the student publication, lament the passing of the first chief executive. The ex-president left the campus sometime during the summer of 1894 and returned to tend his farm and a furniture store which his family had purchased. An administrator on a business trip in 1937 to Kansas City, Missouri, where Barker then was living, reported him to be in good health, further adding that he was a "doctor." The college planned to bring the ninety-one year old gentleman to Stillwater for a Founder's Day celebration, but advanced age prevented travel. Little else is known about his declining years.[36]

Robert Barker's difficulties with his faculty did not all stem from personal ineptness or a lack of interest. The younger instructors had come to the campus from other institutions that were just beginning to burst into greatness, and each was anxious to mold the Oklahoma institution into the image of his *alma mater*. The president realized that the organization he headed was not yet in a position to implement many of the bold educational ideas being discussed elsewhere. Thus, he often became the "heavy" who had to check the enthusiasm of his staff. An early student, however, realized that an indelible mark had been left. She said that other executives may have had greater gift or ability, but that Barker had made a good beginning with the meager resources which had been placed at his proposal. Yet, even this hindsight praise does not make it possible to credit the first president with forming the initial organizational mission. That honor belongs to the faculty.[37]

In the last decade of the nineteenth century there were many exciting developments connected with land-grant colleges. Probably nothing, however, supersedes the contributions to Morrill institutions made by the experiment stations attached to them by the Hatch Act of 1887.[38] These organizations were charged by legislation to aid "in acquiring and diffusing among the people of the United States useful and practical information on subjects connected with agriculture, and to promote scientific investigations and experiments . . . ."[39] The fusion of "experiment" or "research" stations to academic institutions had an important effect on higher education. They multiplied the number of trained resident scientists on college campuses, improved the general character of instruction as men who spent part of their time researching made abler teachers, brought stations and instructional centers into a closer contact with the public, and "lifted research from local and immedate tasks to great fundamental problems—that is, from applied to pure science."[40] In addition, the stations influenced teaching methodologies, course titles, and subject matter content.

While it may have been the intention of the framers of the Hatch Act to use experiment station personnel purely for investigative functions, it was not long until prominent members of the government, such as Edwin Willets, the Assistant Secretary of Agriculture, were urging scientists to be more conscious of disseminating the results of their laboratory experiments to a wider audience than the classroom. Land-grant college presidents generally concurred in this view, too. Louis L. McInnis, Texas A. and M., and George Atherton, Pennsylvania State, in particular, were vocal on this point: The former man is on record as saying:

In my opinion, the practical relation between the agricultural experiment stations and the colleges is that the stations are to occupy a coordinate position with the college departments having instruction for their purpose. Their purpose is investigation, but the final use of investigation is instruction; not necessarily the instruction of youth, but the instruction of all studies and teachable minds.[41]

There was no debate at Oklahoma A. and M. as to whether station investigators should teach in the classroom. Both a shortage of funds and faculty made it a necessity. In fact, the staff at times had to teach at the expense of research. But, in the long run, the faculty, by working double shifts, found it possible to serve two masters and made the college an important data distribution center.[42]

James Clinton Neal, the oldest and most experienced member of the station staff, dedicated his life to the study of science at an early age. A student of his recalled that his position at the institution would have been difficult for most men to fill, because, in addition to administrative duties and participation in joint research projects, he taught geometrical drawing, physical geography, physiology and hygiene, botany, entomology, meteorology, biology, and geography.[43] To these duties he added others. He wrote to his sister in 1894 that "I have been [Acting] President for the last three weeks . . . . I have two classes each day now, and . . . am writing two bulletins, reports and a correspondence that is quite large, often 50 letters per week."[44] Also, time was found to serve as a physician when such services were required. This sense of duty commanded the complete respect of his colleagues, and they accorded him the distinction of getting the college established.[45] A faculty resolution read: "He, more than any other, laid the foundations of our institution."[46]

Neal, like many of those men who had made the run into Oklahoma Territory, was a veteran of the Civil War, serving two enlistments. He first saw action with the 138th Regiment, Indiana Infantry, where his name became associated with William Mershon, the youth who won fame as the drummer boy at the battle of Shiloh. His next enlistment began in March, 1865, but Neal by this time had already decided that he did not like military life.[47] He wrote that "war is stern, savage, awful in the huge cannon, the long lines of earthwork, the hordes of glistening and gleaming bayonets . . . . War is cruel, gloomy, when patients come in from the front, mangled, bruised, torn, lame and crippled for life."[48] This letter concluded by saying nature, by contrast, was beautiful. While the war loosed in some men a lust for the adventurous life, it worked just the opposite in Neal. He vowed, therefore, to devote whatever years he had ahead of him to humanity. Upon discharge from the service, the ex-soldier enrolled at the University of Michigan. There he received two degrees, the latter a medical-pharmaceutical-scientific course which entitled him to be addressed as doctor. The Smithsonian Institute and the Florida A. and M. College employed Neal before he moved to Stillwater in 1891.[49]

For his day, Professor Neal held a conservative view of what the purposes and function of an experiment station should be. He believed that the Oklahoma station should provide farmers with information about practical things—soil, temperatures, rainfall, and crop varieties—instead of concentrating on abstract investigations.[50] Since the territory had only recently been organized, this type of activity seems appropriate; yet, to be in line with national practices, he probably should have stressed theoretical as well as applied experiments.[51] Conversely, however, the director appears progressive in the sense that he steered the state's farmers away from the production of cotton, a staple which had caused the Deep South severe economic problems. Finally, Neal urged his staff to perform largely a teaching function, but here he was not an absolutist either. His annual report for the year 1894 included a remark to the effect that the ideal situation was one where research and instruction were combined to the mutual advantage of both.[52]

Neal, in getting the experiment station underway, had two persistent sources of irritation. First, the Board of Regents, the college president, and the Legislature were lax in providing funds and moral support. One trustee, a grain dealer in Guthrie, who is thought to be somewhat typical, once stated that he could hire a good stenographer for his office at seventy-five dollars per month and he could not see why a member of the faculty should ask for more.[53] Second, the founding law made it difficult to determine whether the director of the station or the farm superintendent had the most authority. Frank Northup, a reporter for the *Gazette*, believed that the former often hindered Neal and his subordinates

26

from conducting scientific investigations. To illustrate, the farm manager told Northup: "I show these young squirts where to get off. When it comes to farming I know my stuff."[54] This man, the journalist further declared, certainly was related to those practical rural philosophers who felt themselves experts because they had worn out several homesteads before coming to Oklahoma.

After several years of fighting institutional financial problems, trying to get along with political appointees on the college farm, and seeing his family live in quarters where his daughters had to place an umbrella in their room to prevent snow from blanketing their beds, Neal sought the presidency.[55] He believed that the higher salary and the additional prestige might alleviate some of his personal problems. Failing health, a lack of spectacular achievement at the station, and the prevailing political climate, however, made this objective beyond his reach. In 1895, he was relieved of his administrative duties, retaining, though, a position on the faculty. His replacement, Colonel Henry Glazier, did not have a professional background. Instead, as a member of the faculty and the Board of Regents, he pushed "model" or "practical" farming. *Home, Field, and Forum*, an agricultural journal, protested the personnel change by publishing editorials which ridiculed the man. One column stated that the students knew more about horticulture than Glazier, for they knew Johnson grass from Toesits and would not advocate "hanging horseshoes onto fruit trees in order so that they might have an abundant supply of iron."[56] Another issue charged that the director pruned trees and vines in August, a time when sap still ran. The writed concluded: "This is, indeed, experimenting with a vengeancy, and we must insist is a very impractical kind of 'practical'."[57] Yet, the appointment stood.

In spite of his conservative outlook, James Neal represented something of a transitional scientific figure at Stillwater. His training at Ann Arbor had been completed before Darwinian concepts had penetrated the methodology of the biological and social sciences. Being of the old taxonomical school, Neal felt that science was merely another name for the great lessons of the Infinite[58] and he spent much of his time in the search for all-encompassing natural laws.[59] Consequently, the director did not attempt to structure data into forms that would explain cause and effect relationships. But, on the other hand, he did nothing to prevent his younger colleagues from doing empirical research while he became a competent administrator, coordinating and facilitating the work of the station. Neal, then, made it possible for an agricultural triumvirate composed of George Holter, Alexander Magruder, and Frank Waugh to give direction to the future.

Holter, the leader among these three men, was credited by his contemporaries as being the best trained man on the staff. After graduating from the Pennsylvania State College and studying in two German universities, he came to Oklahoma A. and M. to teach chemistry, a subject regarded as the first real science of the new age.[60] "Uncle George" impressed the early Aggies because he had a large personal library and he could read books published in the German language. Also, he attempted to instill an appreciation for scholarship in his students. One young man explained: "He gave us vision and inspiration and did all that a great teacher can do—he led us to the fountain of science where it was up to us to drink."[61] Besides being a capable instructor, Professor Holter realized that his pupils needed someone to assist them in developing self-discipline and to explain the advantages of a college degree. In a stern, friendly, but uncompromising way, the Pennsylvanian assumed this task, as well as carrying on valuable research. His abrupt demeanor, however, did not appeal to college presidents and business minded regents. They tended to tolerate him as his work and students were highly regarded by the Department of Agriculture but he was never considered for the presidency when it became vacant. He later, in fact, lost his position because of his frankness.[62]

Alexander Magruder, the second member of this trio, was the son of a prominent English professor, who taught for many years at the Mississippi Agricultural College.[63] Handsome, well-tailored, a military veteran, and a man who turned many a lady's eye as he rode his horse "Damit" along Stillwater streets, Magruder had a good conception of the land-grant mission. He, buttressed with a degree from the college which employed his father, post-graduate work in Germany, and practical experience at the West Virginia Experiment Station, set out to accomplish two goals. First, the instructor tried to create a respect for scientific agriculture and academic excellence by presenting a gold medal to those students who excelled in scholarship. Magruder knew that no one would be graduating for several years and he hoped that the award would provide some much needed incentive. Second, he established an experimental plot, a piece of land which now ranks next to the University of Illinois's Morrow Plot for continuous agricultural research.[64] Here he grew experimental crops and made important soil tests. Moreover, Magruder joined Holter in scouring the United States and Europe by mail to search for procedures to increase research productivity at the college.[65]

The students loved Magruder for his devotion to teaching and for his uncondescending attitude toward them. He initiated the lecture system on the campus in order to transmit information about his soil experiments. Realizing that many individuals in his classes did not know how to take notes, he often stopped at midpoint in his daily discourse to show "how to condense in order to retain the full thought and at the same time advance at a fair rate of speed."[66] Magruder wrote friends for assistance with his teaching problems when his own initiative failed. On one occasion he asked his former minister in Mississippi, the Right Reverend Hugh Miller Thompson, to refer him to "two or three striking places in the life of Christ which seem specifically designed to impress upon us the 'dignity of labor'."[67] The response, presumably, was passed on to the students, as they never were enthusiastic about working on the farm.

28

The Board dismissed Magruder during the summer of 1895, without any advance notice. Upon returning from a short summer vacation, he was informed that his services would not be needed for the coming academic year. Governor William Renfrow promptly offered him the position of Territorial Superintendent of Instruction, but the professor declined to accept, choosing instead to attend Tulane University, where he received a medical degree in 1900. In part this decision had been made earlier, for Magruder's wife of less than a week died of a sudden illness. In October, 1894, Bessie Duncan and her sister took their mother to Orlando, Oklahoma, where she was to catch a train for Norman. It was a sad occasion as the older lady was to enter a sanitarium at the end of her journey. On the return trip, Bessie got drenched in a chilling rain and contracted quick consumption. She and Magruder were married in a home that they had already built and furnished. Her premature death made medical research an important priority for the rest of his life. The twenty-six year old instructor, however, did not depart the campus without leaving a permanent imprint for he fathered the excellence which has always been associated with the college of agriculture. Then, too, his memory is still perpetuated by the plot site that bears his name.[68]

Frank Waugh, the last member of the triumvirate, joined the faculty in February, 1893. He had just completed the requirements for his Master of Science degree at Manhattan, Kansas. A short, homely, but extremely likable, chap of twenty-three, Waugh was the most popular member of the faculty outside the classroom. He was in constant demand to chaperone parties and to discuss personal problems. His contribution to the college and to the nation, however, came in the area of horticultural research. He, along with Liberty Hyde Bailey of Cornell University, led the American movement aimed at de-emphasizing the curricular concepts of a French scientist named Antoine Poiteau. Professor Waugh believed that science classes should be taught as technical and liberal arts courses instead of being limited to a vocational classification.[69]

Poiteau, a horticulturist himself, constructed a model for teaching his specialty as a vocational subject that became widely adopted by many people in the United States. Waugh believed it permissible to employ this instrument if one were teaching in a technical school but he felt that courses at the college level ought to be a "disciplinary study in a scheme of liberal education."[70] Horticulture, then, should encourage a student to observe, to reason accurately, to present thoughts cogently, and to cultivate the aesthetic tastes—these items to instruct in the development of a whole man.[71] To illustrate this premise, Waugh wrote a paper entitled "Ideals of Horticultural Instruction." In it, he maintained that there were three elements to the discipline of horticulture, "each laid in a different field of knowledge: (1) a science, a branch of botanical science; (2) a philosophy, based on the science and typified in the evolution course; (3) an art, illustrated in landscape gardening." Moreover, he stated in this same manuscript that a college course embodying such principles could teach a vocation as well as provide a liberal education. The paper concluded by comparing the advantages of this approach to the one espoused by the Poiteau, pointing out that those who follow the lead of the latter individual

cultivate the practical side of the subject, in preference to the liberal aspect; their idea is an institute of horticultural technology. The followers of Professor Bailey bring into the foreground the requirements of a liberal education; and while they teach technology, treat it as of secondary importance. Horticulture is a required study in agricultural colleges generally. For students who do not follow that occupation in after years, the technology is of comparatively little value; while the student who pursues a course shaped according to the second ideal develops in a manner to increase his satisfaction in life, whatever his surroundings may prove to be.[72]

In the end, Bailey and Waugh's position prevailed, much to the consternation of many freshmen who had enrolled in general education science courses.

Waugh's instructional concepts and his interest in scientific horticultural research irritated several members of the Board of Regents. A journalist reported that he was "fired to make a place for an auctioneer-farmer near Orlando who was prominent in politics . . . ."[73] After leaving Stillwater, he studied in France and Germany, and went on to write more than thirty books and a hundred articles while a member of the faculty of the Massachusetts Agricultural College. The demotion of Neal, the replacement of Magruder and Waugh, and the eventual release of Holter established an unfortunate trend at Oklahoma A. and M. It illustrates that the governing board wanted to institutionalize a mission from the top in spite of the fact that it often meant destroying viable programs. Even the students recognized that the institution had been "badly crippled by the appointment of ne'er-do-wells . . . ."[74] There is little need, however, to mourn the passing of the first faculty, for these men established a dedication to service and scholarship that would not die. While a mission was not spelled out in detail, a good precedent had been set, one that would serve as a guide to others in the future.

The earliest instruction was not collegiate, since no qualified students could be found for the freshman class. President Barker, therefore, invited advanced common school pupils to transfer to the college's preparatory department. During the "itinerant years," two men, Edward Clark and Harry Thompson, secured and taught those individuals who elected to enroll in the sub-collegiate organization. Clark, the first principal, moved to Stillwater to teach in a subscription school. A graduate of an unidentified normal, he conducted classes in the Swope Building, the Congregational Church, and the Methodist Church.[75] In 1891, Clark got into difficulty with the parents of one of his male students over a disciplinary procedure that he had employed. Simon Myers, a Presbyterian clergyman who had been sent to the territory the year before by the Board of Home Missions, chaired a committee which exonerated him. Nevertheless, Clark decided to resign and he accepted Barker's offer to teach at the college. His first class consisted of almost fifty students.[76]

A dynamic lecturer, Clark became a popular instructor. As an environmentalist he believed that the things which a person learns in his youth will set the pattern for future conduct. The teacher, though educated as a mathematician, used the discipline of history to form a code by which students could live. His speech, "Honor and Integrity," found him emphasizing the value of choosing prominent historical figures as personal models. Clark believed that history

with its various unfoldings of the human character and its record of greatness and failings of men and nations, furnishes an abundant source wherein the true seeker may find mental food essential to the development of a noble mankind or a pure womenhood. Bible history furnishes the reflective mind many characters imbued with many virtues. This history of the Old World is made to read with fascinating charms by virtue of the nobleness of its numerous martyrs to faith, government, and justice. Yet I am too patriotic to believe that it is strictly necessary for an American youth to go without the limits of our own beautiful domain to seek an ideal worthy of his admiration. The pages of our history, with which every youth should be familiar, are resplendent with renowned and illustrious characters which, for their nobility of purpose in the establismment of liberty and the nurturing of free institutions of learning have received the plaudits of the civilized world.[77]

Trained historians might quibble with Clark's utilitarian use of their discipline. The Aggies, however, enjoyed such statements, even requesting that they be published in the campus newspaper so that the ideas could be circulated throughout the state.

In 1892, Professor Clark accepted an appointment to teach mathematics at the college level. He remained in Stillwater for six more years. A student verse reported that he died of "lymphatics" at an early age. Harry Thompson, the son of a Princeton educated clergyman, replaced him and arrived on the campus during the summer of 1893. Born on August 27, 1865, at Farmouth, Kentucky, Thompson received his elementary education from his father. He attended the Catawba County common schools, and then took a normal training course at the Southern Normal School [Western Kentucky State College]. Thompson taught public school in Irving, Kentucky, and Little River, Texas, before assuming a high school principalship.[78]

Thompson proved to be a skillful headmaster. He was a tough, unsympathetic recitation grader; however, he hated to see his students get into serious trouble. His position, according to one of the earliest male students, required a "heman" in order to "tame all the wild animals and get them started in the right direction."[79] Tall, lanky, and affable, Thompson pointed many of his charges toward the serious pursuit of knowledge. In addition, he protected the promising ones until they could mature. Tom Hartman recalled: "I am grateful to Thompson for helping me out of a heap-o-trouble one night in Old Central when a free for all fight occurred in the Sigma Literary Society . . . .Thompson cleared me before the faculty. He had them believing I was a hero—struck down in the line of duty, as it were."[80]

Neither Edward Clark nor Harry Thompson were as academically gifted as their colleagues at the experiment station. Both men were graduates of teacher training institutions, organizations which were finding it difficult to compete with the more comprehensive state universities of the country. But Thompson and Clark did, however, measurably contribute to the development of the Oklahoma A. and M. College. Each individual believed in the positive value of a higher education for the masses. Thus they attempted to apply enough academic luster so that their students could enter the collegiate program. These men, as such, were as close to the land-grant idea as any of their fellow instructors. More than one prominent chemist, home economist, and government bureaucrat owed his or her start in life to these two patient and exacting teachers. They shared their love of learning with students whom no one else wanted.

Three diverse and distinct forces shaped the fledgling college from 1891 to 1894. First, the Board of Regents, who may best be visualized as merely an extension of the Legislature, played a somewhat negative role in the development of the early institution. The trustees, with the possible exception of Robert J. Barker, were men of the business class who compared the supervision of a college to the operation of a marketplace. The Board supervised the building of a physical plant, appointed personnel to tend the store, and expended funds for the purchase of station equipment, but for being so close to the institution, they had a remarkable lack of vision. There were no dreams of creating a Cornell, a Michigan State, or a University of California. Instead, these individuals were rather ordinary men—truly products of their own Gilded Age.

The college administration, headed by Barker and Neal, became the second force which shaped the institution during the founding period. The former, who had an adequate knowledge of the nation's common school system, seems to have wanted to develop a high school program. And, as with the other regents, he could not see the value of extension service or laboratory research. His close attachment to his family, as well as his desire to become a landowner, robbed him of much of the vitality required to develop excellence. The latter man, perhaps, would have been a better choice to head the college. He was a graduate of a leading state university, had grown up with the land-grant movement, and knew many nationally prominent educational leaders. Moreover, he had a personal disposition which inspired confidence and trust. If he had a fault, it was that he spent too much time in detail. This trait contributed to a gradual loss of health and this hindered him in carrying out institutional objectives.

In conclusion, the faculty, more than any other element, colored the institution during the "itinerant years." Because of modern academic training, these men steered the organization toward service, whether it be in the form of teaching, extension, or research. They conducted classes for students who were ill-prepared for college work and they produced experiment station bulletins with only

32

crude scientific equipment at their disposal. Also, it was a rare occasion when one of them would turn down an opportunity to speak at an agricultural or horticultural meeting, in spite of the fact that they often had to dig into their own pockets for travel. Furthermore, the faculty continued to push for higher standards and a more comprehensive program. Clark, Holter, Magruder, Thompson, and Waugh, then, were a combination of practical and progressive men in touch with their times, but with hopes for something different in the future. To them belongs the credit for planting the land-grant seed into the rich, red, Oklahoma soil.

III DEMOCRACY'S SCHOOL

Oklahoma Territory became opened for settlement in 1889 with little attention devoted to local and state government; hence, the only officials who possessed any real authority were a handful of deputy marshals whose jurisdiction was limited to breaches of federal law. When Governor George Steele arrived on May 23, 1890 at the Santa Fe Railroad depot in Guthrie, he was greeted by thousands of citizens, because, as one observer said, the executive represented "government of the people, for the people and by the people by agents of their own choosing in local affairs under the forms of democratic rule to a land thus far a stranger to such blessings."[1] The thirteen months without elected government had several important social consequences. Not the least concerned the fact that, unlike some of the states created under the auspices of the Northwest Ordinance, "there were no provisions for public schools."[2] When one remembers the high regard that Americans have had for education, this situation seems most unusual. However, it should be remembered that the absence of educational action and thought

34

on the Dixie frontier had caused the second and third generation to be less learned then the first. Oklahomans, with strong ties both above and below the Mason-Dixon line, faced a dilemma, for there were two altogether different precedents that could be followed. In Stillwater, the elite motivated the homestead farmers to look north instead of south. The community created schools based upon public subscriptions until the Legislature could authorize the development of a state system.[3]

Though the claim has never been proven, it is often alleged that Stillwater established the first public school in the state. Initial classwork was held in churches, the courthouse, and in vacant rooms above downtown stores. Public spirited citizens, such as W. A. Swiler, donated lumber for the construction of benches and tables, because without property taxes there were no community funds to support common schools.[4] The Reverend Simon Myers, president of the local school board, reported on the state of the elementary school in 1890. He wrote that the

room used is very small for the number of pupils; the seats are not fastened to the floor and placed too close to pass between them. Not being fastened to the floor the seats frequently work and shove from their place. The room is cold. There is no room for recitation seats. Thus depriving the Teacher from having his class separate from the School during recitations. During windy days the noise and dust . . . are very annoying. The room being so near to the business part of town is also of much annoyance.[5]

The educational process suffered because of disciplinary problems, too. A certain Miss Dunn, whose first name is unknown, complained that it was nearly impossible to manage the boys and girls who had been placed under her care.[6] Furthermore, absenteeism constituted an economic as well as an instructional disruption. Even as late as 1898, a college bulletin announced that conditions were so bad that "it is not possible to maintain good schools for more than a few months each year in some parts of the Territory."[7]

In view of these conditions, the city of Stillwater welcomed Robert Barker's disclosure that the Oklahoma A. and M. College would develop a preparatory school on its campus. This institution filled a deep void. It served as a feeder for the freshman class and it offered advanced elementary and high school training at little direct cost to the community. From 1891 to 1904, this arrangement proved popular, but in the latter year, the townspeople decided to build an independent high school. The college, then, designed a pre-collegiate short course in agriculture and domestic economy, leaving the citizenry with the responsibility for providing regular high school instruction. The presence of the preparatory department meant much to the state of Oklahoma. It guaranteed a better than average education to those who did not have a high school in their locality and it offered instruction to individuals who did not have the time nor the money to obtain a traditional degree. In addition, the preparatory institution provided leadership for the burgeoning high school movement.[8]

Many nineteenth century state universities established subcollegiate departments on or near their campuses. One of the curiosities of the post-Civil War period is that no effective link had yet been devised to weld the college and the common school together. Land-grant institutions, who were committed to the concept of a higher education for everyone, often established preparatory institutions to serve as a bridge between the "public elementary school and the public university.[9] The organization in Stillwater fell partially into this category. It offered training in arithmetic, grammar, geography, and history, these being the subjects which required mastery if one wanted to pass the examinations necessary for admittance into the college program. Moreover, the institution accepted pupils who simply wished to take a short course in farming and prepared young men and women for the tests needed to obtain a territorial teaching certificate. And last, many mature students elected to attend classes, so that they would not be embarrassed because of their age.[10]

For the most part, the preparatory department had a conscious democratic character. The college founding law specified that all citizens of the territory, whether male or female, between the ages of twelve and thirty, "shall be admitted to instruction therein, if they apply as students . . . ."[11] Two years later modifications were made in the original act but even the second bill was not stringent in regard to admissions. It stated that all residents from fourteen to thirty, "who shall pass a satisfactory examination in reading, arithmetic, geography, English grammar, and United States History, and who are known to possess a good moral character, may be admitted to all the privileges of the institution.[12] Moreover, the costs of attending were geared so that the masses could afford it. The college newspaper published a study in 1895 which revealed that student expenses at Yale ranged from $900 to $1,000 per year, with the Lawrence Scientific School of Harvard running only slightly lower. By contrast, men and women at A. and M. paid much less. An early bulletin suggested that pupils should plan on spending $100 for board and room, $10 for clothing, the same for textbooks, and approximately $30 for incidentals per academic year. Most, if not all, of these sums could be earned in residence by working on the station farm at a rate which fluctuated between eight and ten cents per hour. No tuition, either in- or out-of-state, was assessed.[13]

While not specified by state law, one important exception to a truly open admissions policy existed in practice. Emma Dent, one of the first students, later recalled that a young Negro girl was denied permission to enroll solely on account of race.[14] This incident illustrates that public school segregation during the territorial period was subject to county option. In Payne, if more than five black children resided in a township, separate accomodations were to be provided. Such regulations had an important effect, contributing to two unique developments in Oklahoma. First, many Negroes voluntarily retreated to rural enclaves, hoping thereby to eliminate the "tormenting and humilating subordination in bi-racial communities."[15] Second, the state's black citizens, who in 1890 had the lowest rate of illiteracy in the South, fell well below the national average maintained in the four decades preceding 1930. One college president said that he did not personally believe in segregation, but he felt it wise not to antagonize a citizenry which had such a large white southern element.[16]

But, for its age, the Stillwater sub-collegiate department was democratic. This attribute is notably evident in a public address given at the college by the Reverend R. B. Foster, the pastor of the local Congregational Church. Echoing sentiments similar to those expressed by Jonathan Baldwin Turner in his "Plan for an Industrial University" and Edward Bellamy in his *Looking Backward*,[17] the minister stated that in the "past society had been divided into privileged classes and the masses. The classes were expected to be educated; the masses, to inherit a life of toil and to be content with the minimum of intellectuality."[18] Morrill institutions, the speaker continued, were designed to break down these barriers. He advised the working men in his audience to take up the challenge of democracy, putting "religion in your hearts, education in your heads, and money in your pockets, and take your rightful place—the world cannot keep you from it."[19] Foster, then, thought that education would bring back the social mobility which existed on the American frontier.

When the preparatory department opened its doors in December, 1891, the first classes were held in the local houses of worship. Other higher educational institutions in Oklahoma, such as the Edmond Normal School, had a similar experience. In Stillwater, the earliest students met in the Congregational Church, transferring later to the First Presbyterian and the Methodist Episcopal Church, South, While it was not intentional, this wedding of church and state left a lasting imprint on Oklahoma A. and M. The public came to expect that the institution would instill the Judeo-Christian tradition in its students. Then, too, the agrarian myth, which had religious roots, became popularized, in part, through the close association with Protestant churches. Perpetuated through the curriculum, as well as by the church and the family, the state's populace formed a relationship with the geographic region known as the Bible Belt. This situation later made it difficult to industrialize and to secularize education at a time when the nation as a whole was de-emphasizing agriculture and religion.[20]

The territorial church structures utilized by the earliest students do not compare with the modern architectual wonders of today. Frank Northup, a printer who came to Stillwater in 1893, described one building. He said that it was uncomfortable in the winter because it was only heated by woodburning stove. In the "summer the winds sifted fine dust over students, seats, and books with indiscriminate regularity."[21] Both professors and students complained. George Holter remembered that the practice of separating rooms by partitions on rollers was less than satisfactory.

Frequently, he recalled, the ability to "hold a recitation became merely a question of ears, lungs, capacity, and endurance."[22] A memoir by A. E. Jarrell concurred. He wrote that there

were four or five movable wooden partitions, about eight feet high and twelve feet long, mounted on rollers. The partitions set apart the instructor's desk and the corner seats, thus making a small room with a blackboard or two. Persons in the improvised recitation room were not visible from the main room. The small room was lighted by windows and some light came over the partitions.[23]

Surrounded by uninspiring facilities, the Aggies often expended excess energy by defacing the walls and seats. James Hastings, a farmer, claimed that a different church had to be employed each year, for "one term was about all any one church could stand the wild birds among them."[24] Yet, instruction did begin and a new land-grant college beckoned the masses to gather at its gates.

Almost fifty students enrolled in the preparatory department on the first day of class. Many of them were not quite sure of what to expect. Neither they, nor most of their parents, had attended a high school. On the other hand, it may be stated with certainty that the group believed that the presence of a college in their community afforded a unique opportunity. The parents of Alfred Jarrell, who were unlettered, urged him to enroll as they thought teachers in the preparatory department would be better than those employed in the subscription school. James Homer Adams felt that the fact instructors were called professors instead of teachers was incentive enough to attend. Tom Hartman registered, so he said, because he hated to get up before the sun to do farm chores. Penniless, in ragged clothing, and with little conception of the nature of higher education, Tom was able to convince Holter that he had the wherewithal to profit from instruction. "Uncle George" took Hartman to a local restaurant, secured him a job as a dishwasher, and persuaded Barker to admit him to classes. Green as the prairie grass from whence they came, these young men, and others like them, were eager to quench their thirst for knowledge. First, however, they needed a thorough orientation.[25]

If a reminiscence of James Adams is representative, the pupils who appeared at the Congregational Church on December 14, 1891, were confused and a little frightened. James, leaving his brother Arthur at home because of an illness, walked to the church and took a seat in the back of the classroom. President Barker welcomed the incoming students and then offered a short devotion. He was followed by Professor Neal, a man who seemed friendly but who spoke of things that were difficult to understand. He began by talking about the purpose of the preparatory department, the course of instruction, and the need of students to sign a mysterious document called the "Matriculation Pledge." When Neal finished, he asked each boy and girl to step forward one by one in order to sign his name at the bottom of the vow concerning future conduct.

Adams, whose name was first on the list, was called to approach the desk in the front of the room. It took a great deal of courage for the thirteen year old boy to take the pen offered by the speaker. His hesitation prompted Neal to ask if he understood what was required of him. Silently, James nodded his head from side to side in a negative gesture. This act evoked another, and more lengthy lecture. Now, James decided to sign the document which had been placed before him, in spite of the fact that its meaning still was not very clear. He would make the attempt to understand it later. To those in charge, this academic ignorance indicated that the faculty would have to develop some type of communication with the students. The instrument selected for this important task was a system of rewards and punishments based on military discipline.[26]

In part, the Morrill Act of 1862 received approval because northern Congressmen believed that the emphasis on military education in the Confederacy had significantly increased the capacity of that section to prolong the Civil War. President Dabney, Tennessee University, confirmed the validity of this hypothesis in 1898. Speaking before the Association of American Agricultural Colleges and Experiment Stations, he reported that almost all of the one thousand graduates of the Virginia Military Institute had served in a leadership capacity for Lee's Army. Military instruction in land-grant colleges, then, was patterned after southern collegiate practices. When peace returned, however, Morrill institutions, especially those of the West, maintained a military department for purposes other than the training of soldiers.[27]

The Kansas Agricultural College, one of the oldest land-grant institutions in the midwest, devised a twofold post-Civil War military program. First, military science was thought to have merit as a means by which to "impart manliness, alertness, respect for authority and consideration of others." Second, the faculty, in a day when the harmful effects of German academic practices were being widely publicized, believed time devoted to physical culture would promote "health, bodybuilding, and correction of unnatural positions."[28] To these two concepts, the Oklahoma A. and M. College added one more.[29] It thought that military instruction and drill could be used to combat the "indolence and indispositions always found to exist in a warm climate."[30]

Captain Darnell and Professor Magruder devised the military course employed on the Stillwater campus. The former man, who had had a distinguished career in the Union Army, took the drillmaster position with some reluctance. But Barker hit upon his local sympathies by asserting that the city might lose the educational plant if every letter of state and national law in regard to such institutions were not fully complied with. Magruder, perhaps for the same reason, agreed to write and to deliver twenty-four lectures on the organization and combat practices of foreign armies. The combination of drill and instruction in military science, it was hoped, would provide the bases for a system of discipline in the sub-collegiate school. The earliest efforts in this direction, however, were more often humorous than instructive.[31]

One reason that Commandant Darnell did not want to participate in the training program is that Barker, through a misunderstanding of the Morrill Act, felt that females as well as males should
participate in drill. Premonitions of disaster materialized on the
first day of practice. The drillmaster appeared at the designated
spot wearing his "Civil War uniform with army belt, cap, and huge
square-toed shoes. . . ."[32] He then began to explain the various
military commands, beginning with the proper position for attention. "Eyes front, heads up, chins in, shoulders back, chests out,
stomachs in, toes out," and as the old soldier warmed to his task,
"the second finger of your hand on the seam of your pants."[33] The
last comment was followed with a moment of silence, a snort, and a
giggle. Darnell, regaining his composure, turned his company loose,
shouting to a nearby faculty member: "This is the hell of an
army."[34]

Future drills assumed a more orderly and dignified atmosphere.
The boys liked the drill sessions and took much pride in learning
military bearing. Yet, they were a peculiar looking group, with
long and short coats, high and low heeled boots, hats of all varieties, and weapons that resembled broomsticks. But when the handsome West Point gray and black uniforms became the order of the
day, the cadets evidenced an eagerness to display their talents before visitors and townspeople. On one festive occasion, the corps
drummer became so engrossed in his work that he beat the head
out of his drum. This enthusiasm suggests that communication had
been established between the faculty and the students.[35]

The female drill experience was not unlike that of the males.
Professor Holter has preserved a picturesque account of how an
April practice looked to a new member of the faculty. He wrote:

The first sight of this cadet corps a couple of days later burned a hole in my
memory, and the hole is there yet. You have possibly seen a cartoon of an
Irish Brigade, but if you have, it certainly does not give you much light on the
subject for a sight of this cadet corps beggars description. Picture if you can,
a lot of girls in long dresses, in short dresses, in old dreses, in new dresses, and
you have an idea, possibly, of the general appearance of the uniforms . . . .
Now take this battalion . . . of girls, form them into a company, and drill them
in an average Oklahoma wind, and if the sight does not leave an indelible impression in your memory, you are certainly puncture proof to all ordinary
sights.[36]

In 1894, the wives of Henry Alvord, Freeman Miller, James Neal,
and Frank Waugh, at the request of the faculty, designed a uniform
for the females. The ladies sketched a sailor dress pattern, with a
loose blouse waist, a plain full skirt, and a seaman's cap. The girls,
however, were excused from military exercises before the dress code
became mandatory. Nevertheless, the common attire and the willingness to perform as a team, facilitated the forming of a relatively
casteless student body. Bonds were devised which remained long
after graduation.[37]

The faculty employed military procedures to punish students
who broke the institution's rules, whether the infractions were of an
academic or an extracurricular nature. The "Matriculation Pledge,"

which had to be signed during the first week of school, placed the students firmly under the control of their mentors. It read:

Being now about to enter as a student of the Agricultural College of Oklahoma I do hereby acknowledge my obligation and bind myself to obey all its laws and regulations and I pledge myself on honor that so long as I am a student of the College during term or while I remain at the College during vacation I will not have in my possession any deadly weapons except such arms as are furnished by the Military department without the consent of the President or Faculty. And I do further pledge myself on honor that I will not join or form any connection with, either directly or indirectly, any secret club, society, fraternity, or other organization, composed in whole or in part of students of the College, or attend the meetings or wear the badge of any such secret organization. And I do further pledge myself, on honor that I will not treat with disrespect by shouting or otherwise any applicant for admission to the College. And I will not engage in 'hazing' or any other maltreatment of a student lately admitted to the institution.[38]

The demerit system, which did not reach full bloom until the second academic year, fostered the development of student responsibility in a number of ways. For example, tardiness carried two demerits, an unexcused absence from chapel three, and a willful violation of any college rule twenty-five. When the latter figure had been reached, a letter of warning was mailed to the student's parents; the accumulation of forty points in one term meant automatic dismissal.[39] These rules were enforced. The "Minutes of the First Faculty" for the 1895-1896 academic year note that nearly fifty pupils were expelled.

George Holter, who in later years found time to reflect upon the stringent demerit system, has provided an evaluation of the disciplinary procedures utilized by the preparatory department. He said: "We had peculiar ideas in those days and as I look back upon some of our disciplinary measures I think a great many were crude . . . but, they had one point of merit; they worked to perfection and with little friction."[40] In point of fact, they did. The faculty found a method to regulate and standardize conduct; the students knew precisely what was expected of them; and institutional rewards and punishments were meted out with justice and uniformity. Also, the rules bound the young people together. Investigators could seldom find an eye witness who would inform on his classmates if trouble occurred.[41]

There were, of course, aspects of the system that many educators would lament. The rigid rules prohibited individuality and non-conformity. In Septmber, 1896, for instance, two Quaker brothers named Oldham requested that they be excused from military drill because of certain religious convictions they held. The faculty temporarily granted the petition, but a week later they and their sister left school, which suggests that the rules were not amended on a permanent basis.[42] The next year, a male student, who had only recently been admitted to the freshman class, asked if he could be excused from attending chapel. Two reasons were given in support of the request. First, the boy said that he believed the founders of the American nation had intended that religious freedom be granted to all. Second, he pointed out that land-grant institutions

41

should be "free to all citizens of the United States and Oklahoma, without regard to their religious views."[43] This student also left the campus and in this instance the record indicates that his plea was denied.

While such specific instances are to be regretted, a defense may be made for the militaristic policy. Those individuals in positions of authority recognized that preparatory students were exceptionally young and they therefore should be subject to the concept of *in loco parentis*. The teaching staff, however, hoped for something more than just setting a pattern for conduct. They wanted to create a sense of responsibility in each individual so that the learning process could begin. As collegiate classes formed, the administration and faculty relied more and more on upperclassmen to set academic and behavioral standards. Thus military discipline was not envisioned as a permanent part of the institution. It was a transitional stage which a frontier college had to pass through in order to accomplish higher objectives.

Those students who entered the preparatory school were expected to complete their studies in one or two years, depending upon their public school background. Generally speaking, the departmental curriculum was divided into two broad areas. First, the morning classes, which were conducted in the church, emphasized the subjects usually taught in high school. Second, the afternoon sessions were principally devoted to *practicums:* that is, working at the college farm or experiment station to apply the data transmitted in the classroom. When circumstances warranted, the latter periods were also used to give pupils practice in military drill and in advanced reading and writing exercises. The course of study, then, included both applied and theoretical knowledge.

During the first year of operation, the cadets received instruction in English grammar, composition, arithmetic, history, and geography in the morning, with the afternoons reserved for military tactics, lectures in agriculture, and drill in reading and writing. Advanced students were permitted to take algebra, civics, geography, and physics. Horticulture was substituted for agriculture in the afternoons. The *practicum* for each program took about two hours per day; but, when this obligation had been satisfied, the Aggies could continue working to earn funds which could be applied toward their fees. Girls worked side-by-side with the boys on the farm. They learned how to plant and harvest crops as well as take care of livestock. In addition, the students learned to respect the importance of self-help.[44]

The teaching methods utilized by the faculty consisted of both time-honored and more modern techniques. The instructors adopted textbooks for their classes but the lack of a bookstore made published materials difficult to obtain. Newcomers were urged to bring their old schoolbooks with them and the city was scoured at periodic intervals to find suitable works. One early inventory of the library revealed that the institution had borrowed almost two hundred and fifty books from the United States Department of Agriculture to fill some of the void. Also, visual aids received attention. Professor Magruder ordered animal model reproductions from the Richard Krey Company in New York City. Later, Thompson secured globes, maps, and charts for the individual classrooms. Together, these items provided the students with a varied educational diet.[45]

Some, but certainly not complete, information is available concerning course content. In arithmetic, Joseph Ray's *New Practical Arithmetic* (Cincinnati: Van Antwerp, Bragg, and Company, 1887) was used. Fractions, their laws and operations through decimals, elementary banking, square and cube roots in their relation to mensuration, and the metric system of weights were taught. History classes studied Edward Eggleston's *History of the United States* (New York: Appleton and Company, 1888). The explorations of the Norsemen, the Spanish, the English, the French, and the Dutch were reviewed in connection with the "germ theory," an idea being popularized by Herbert Baxter Adams of Johns Hopkins University. The class concluded with an examination of American political history from the sixteenth to the nineteenth century. Physiology students memorized the contents of Joel Dorman Steele's *Hygiene Physiology* (New York: Barnes and Company, 1889). This book touched upon the structure of the human body with a special emphasis on health habits, including a lengthy unit dealing with the harmfulness of alcohol and tobacco on the nervous system. English classes were geared toward rhetoric, not literature. W. H. Maxwell's *Advanced Course in English Grammar* (Chicago: American Book Company, 1891) served as the principal text. Finally, physical geography, a course which seemed particularly pertinent for Oklahomans, included an analysis of local climatic and geographical patterns as well as laying a foundation for further study in physics and geology. E. A. Houston's *New Physical Geography* (Philadelphia: Eldredge and Brothers, 1891) provided systematic guidance.[46]

The school curriculum remained essentially the same from 1891 to 1902. In the latter year, President Scott appointed G. D. Hancock to head the preparatory department. He, a recent graduate of William Jewell College, reorganized the course of study. At the same time, the age for admission increased from fourteen to sixteen and entrance requirements were strengthened. Furthermore, the mission of the organization changed. Now called the school of agriculture and domestic economy, this agency became the only part of the college to offer practical instruction in agriculture. Classes were conducted from October to March 15th. Those persons who wanted to do regular collegiate work were permitted to remain after the short course had ended.[47]

The merits of the preparatory school in relation to the general land-grant mission are not easy to assess. Approximately one thousand pupils attended the college in the first decade of its existence, but few of the sub-collegiate students went on to earn four year degrees. For example, some sixty-four young men and women

43

matriculated in the preparatory department during the initial academic year, yet only six stayed long enough to fulfill college graduation requirements.[48] This high rate of attrition seems not just peculiar to Stillwater. Professor H. W. McArdle, North Dakota Agricultural College, observed that the "large number of students enrolled in the preparatory course as compared with the number in college shows the need of such a department. It is a lamentable fact that so few continue their work beyond the preparatory classes."[49] Other sub-collegiate schools reported similar experiences.[50]

One very real and important aspiration of the preparatory students was to have their own instructional building. Also, the faculty and the residents of the community wanted to see a permanent campus established. These three groups, no doubt, were excited when the editor of the local *Gazette* reported in August of 1893 that work "is being pushed for our Oklahoma Territorial Agricultural College building. The campus, heretofore sod, has been broken and seeded to cowpeas preparatory to making the lawn."[51] The article should have added that James Neal had already sketched a landscaping design and that college students had volunteered to assist with the construction process in order to bring the project to a completion. Gloom, however, still existed in many quarters, because those who were well informed knew that serious political problems were surfacing. Some were severe enough to endanger the very existence of the college.[52]

The most serious obstacle blocking further construction concerned the fact that William Renfrow, a Democrat, had been appointed territorial governor by President Grover Cleveland. With the exception of Robert Barker, Renfrow replaced the entire Board of Regents, selecting J. C. Caldwell, Frank Caruthers, John Clark, Henry Glazier, and J. W. Howard to serve in the place of the former trustees. The incumbents contested this move and refused to turn over the balance of unexpended federal funds to the new trustees. Simultaneously, other problems developed. The federal government elected at this time to open the Cherokee Strip for homestead filings. Many students and faculty deserted, temporarily, their posts to stake a claim. Next, the actual location of the first college building site became the object of a bitter dispute between the institution's administration and the local citizenry. And last, as has been previously noted, the organization's building bonds had not been sold.[53]

Of these various problems, the manipulation of the Board of Regents caused the most serious repercussions. Charles Becker, the editor of the *Gazette*, tried to keep his readers informed of statewide developments by reprinting materials from other territorial newspapers. Three excerpts appeared on August 18, 1893. They each surveyed the political reaction following the reorganization of the regents. The first, which came from the *Edmond Sun*, suggested that the changes in the Board had been made because Governor Renfrow owned a bank in Norman and wanted trustees in office who would permit him to use the funds of the college as capital

44

for it.[54] A Democratic newspaper, as might be expected, defended the standard bearer of its party. *The Guthrie News* maintained that Renfrow had attempted to force the former Board into action, but these individuals left town rather than to risk a confrontation on their own "dunghill." The writer continued by adding that a conference between the two factions would have been a meeting of "honesty and rascality. Of courage and cowardice. These men have robbed the territorial treasury and they felt that they were thieves and criminals, and so feeling did not dare await the coming of Oklahoma's executive."[55] One by one, the individual actions of the former regents received equally colorful analysis.

A *Guthrie Capital* reprint presented yet another point of view, citing the substance of an interview with Amos Ewing, the treasurer of the old Board. This article stated that the current trouble had been precipitated by M. L. Turner, the Guthrie man who had purchased an option on the college bonds for $2,500 but discovered that he could not sell them for a profit. Ewing thought this transaction should be nullified and that the "earnest" money should be used to rent an instructional building in Stillwater until the entire situation could be disentangled.[56]

Editor Becker, knowing the propensity of Oklahoma newspaper editors for exaggerating, provided a reasoned explanation for the vitriolic reprints. He concluded:

The *Gazette* is not disposed to uphold the regents or anyone else in rascality. No one can say we are doing it now . . . . The facts are that the governor concluded to appoint democratic successors for them and then someone, probably some democratic editor at Guthrie, anxious to gain a little notoriety, started a rumor going that their work had been crooked, and without stopping to investigate or wait for the proper parties to make charges before a proper officer that gaseous members of the democratic party over the territory swelled up, and proceeded to gloat over the crime alleged to have been committed by republicans.[57]

The writer completed his commentary by saying that if Renfrow had evidence of wrongdoing, he should take the matter to court rather than letting territorial newspapers try the case.

The controversy continued. Two months later an anonymous letter received publication in the *Gazette*. It asserted, "That the governor of a commonwealth would use his influence to defeat the best interests of his wards is a charge too unreasonable to claim even passing notice."[58] The writer then explained that Renfrow was simply holding up the sale of the college bonds until Caruthers could be sworn into office as treasurer of the Board of Regents. Ewing responded without delay. He told the editor of the *Gazette* that the governor had promised to release the bond money by the time construction started on the college building, but he had not. Moreover, he, as had the writer for the *Edmond Sun,* thought Renfrow to be "dragging-his-feet in order to use the money for his bank at Norman."[59] In addition, Ewing sent a note to the college faculty, asking them—as well as the townspeople— to petition the chief executive for assistance with the building program.[60] Meanwhile, events occurred which led to settlement of the controversy.

In December, 1893, the federal government forwarded a check from the Morrill fund in the amount of $19,000 for deposit with the territorial treasurer. Trustee Ewing instituted legal proceedings to obtain the money, claiming that the real issue was who constituted the lawful Board of Regents. A Guthrie court, however, refused to accept jurisdiction. In March, and before a new petition could be filed for a hearing, Governor Renfrow decided to try for an out-of-court settlement because a Republican newspaper editor had charged him with misappropriating some $21,000 in connection with land sales in the Cherokee Strip. The chief executive, then, in order to give full attention to this development, commissioned C. A. Galbraith, the Oklahoma Attorney General, to drop the unfiled charges against Ewing pertaining to his refusal to release institutional funds entrusted to his care while he was on the Board. Subsequently, Ewing and Renfrow made enough money available to complete the construction of Old Central. On June 14, 1894, President Barker, as one of his last official duties, presided at the dedication of the building.[61]

The importance of Old Central in relation to the townspeople has already been discussed; in short, it signified that the Oklahoma A. and M. College would remain in Stillwater. The building, however, meant as much or more to the faculty and students. Erected on the forty acre tract nearest to the city limits, its tall, distinctive spires pointed towards the sky as if to say that a higher education could bring young Oklahomans to the pinnacle of success in their chosen fields. Professors Neal and Magruder were so proud of the red brick structure that they invited K. Allen, the publisher of the *Sentinel*, to take a "ramble" with them through the building. Later, he reported to his readers that it was the finest building in the territory. The middle story had six lecture rooms, with a large hallway which ran the entire length of the floor. The basement added space for storage and laboratory experiments. The top level contained an office for the president and director of the experiment station, two small recitation rooms, and an auditorium that would seat four hundred people. The latter was most important, for now the students had a place to assemble for extracurricular activities, such as meetings of the local literary societies.[62]

In the last three-quarters of a century, many articles, books, and poems have been written about Old Central. Some students have returned from long distances to see where they carved their names. The alumni have rallied time and time again to save the structure when they feared its continued existence was in danger. Educators and politicians have used its facilities to make important speeches. Yet, one of its finest tributes came from the pen of a young English major, Vingie Roe. Just after the turn of the century, she composed a short poem entitled "On the Steps." Miss Roe captured the real spirit of Old Central in her concluding lines.

Tall, black, and shadowy, the College stands.
And sitting here upon the steps which make

A dim, white bulk amid the darker gloom,
A dream, born of twilight, fills my heart—
A dream of all the faces which have passed
In at these portals, and come forth again
In armor strong, invincible, to meet
The world.[63]

"Democracy's School," the first instructional department of the Oklahoma A. and M. College is an excellent example of the versatility of the American land-grant college movement. Students and their parents became acquainted with the work of the agricultural experiment station, the intellectual ability of the masses to engage in the political processes increased, and the children of the frontier generation acquired some aspects of a liberal education. Then, too, in a day when farm families were thought to be socially isolated from their city cousins, the sub-collegiate school served as an important link in bringing rural people into the mainstream of American life. Heightened human resources meant that the government formed by the founding fathers could survive in an age of trial. Phenomena of this type illustrate, as one historian has written, "that although democracy is supposed to begin at the bottom and grow upward, it can often begin at the top and pull the bottom to it."[64] Herein is the basis for the democratic characterization of the sub-collegiate school.[65]

IV THE CRISIS OF 1894

By April, 1894, the Board of Regents appointed by Governor William Renfrow had gained firm control of the administration of the Oklahoma Agricultural and Mechanical College. Led by the incoming president, John Clark, the trustees met in Stillwater at the end of the month to discuss certain changes in personnel. The first notable substitution involved replacing A. V. McDowell with B. J. Conley of Kingfisher County as superintendent of the station farm. Since the former man had generated considerable friction between the faculty and staff, most individuals in the community and associated with the college believed that the removal would benefit the institution. Therefore, they did not protest the action. T. M. Upshaw, on the same day that Conley signed his contract, agreed to assume secretarial duties for the college. Some people felt that this position had been created specifically for him. This appointment, too, created little adverse reaction because a clerk had been needed for a long time. The reorganization touched a popular member of the faculty in May. W. W. Hutto, whose brother Frank belonged to the hierarchy of the Grand Old Party, was released from his position as an instructor of English.[1] The Republican *Gazette* protested the firing, stating that Hutto had gained the "love and esteem of the students and the respect and confidence of the patrons of the college."[2] Nevertheless, the Board selected a capable man to succeed him.

Freeman Miller, the replacement, was a native of Indiana. He received his undergraduate and Master's degree from DePauw University. Miller moved to Texas to open a law practice but he had suitable academic training in history and literature for teaching. In fact, he had graduated as valedictorian of his class. But even with these credentials, the *Gazette* still charged that his appointment resulted from "right political thinking" rather than from a strong subject matter proficiency. The Democrat *Sentinel* disagreed. A member of the college faculty offered a different analysis. He believed that Miller had received the nomination because he had been making deep inroads into the law practice of John Clark. Regardless, however, of the divided local feelings about the appointment, the instructor performed well and became the first resident member of the instructional staff to publish widely, eventually receiving from many state newspapers the title of "poet laureate of Oklahoma."[3]

It is important to note that these activities took place while the institution did not have a full time executive officer on the campus. The trustees seized this moment to grasp control of the organization. President Barker, sensing that the Board wanted to remove him, had earlier retired to Crescent City and he now served the college only in a lame duck capacity. His successor remained throughout the summer in Washington, D. C. trying to wind up his duties as a deputy assistant to the United States Secretary of Agriculture. When he finally did arrive in Stillwater, it immediately became apparent to him that he could not avoid involvement in the state's political struggle. Conflict, then, developed between him and the Board of Regents.

When Norman J. Colman became the first Secretary of Agriculture in 1889,[4] he felt that his department should create a closer working relationship with the Morrill colleges. The third secretary, J. S. Morton, believed much the same way, and it was at his request that Henry Elijah Alvord received consideration for the administrative vacancy in Stillwater. Since this suggestion came from a figure in high national office, and because Major Alvord, as he liked to be called, had had a distinguished career in agriculture and engineering, the Board of Regents felt they had no choice but to confirm him as the second president of the Oklahoma A. and M. College. Had the trustees known more about the views of their newly appointed executive officer, they might not have employed him, for he had previously resigned the presidency of the Maryland Agricultural College because of a clash with his superiors.[5]

By the time he arrived on the campus in September, 1894, Henry Alvord, an eighth generation descendent of the prominent

Alexander Alvord of Windsor, Connecticut and Northampton, Massachusetts,[6] had virtually assumed direction of the land-grant college movement in the United States. He had, as Liberty Hyde Bailey once said, "rare ability as an executive."[7] Major Alvord rose to prominence because he was one of the first men in the country to recognize that agriculture and engineering had to organize in order to build a viable system of vocational and scientific higher education. As such, he helped to found the Society for the Promotion of Agricultural Science in Rochester, New York, serving twice as its president. When George Loring, the Commissioner of Agriculture, called for this group to meet in Washington in 1882 to lobby for additional educational legislation, Alvord attended. He returned for similar conferences in 1883, 1885, and 1887. Under his leadership, the Society for the Promotion of Agricultural Science played an instrumental role in getting the Hatch Act passed and in forming the Association of American Agricultural Colleges and Experiment Stations.

The Association of American Agricultural Colleges and Experiment Stations quickly developed into an important organization. Henry Alvord became the first chairman of the executive committee and he remained in that capacity for eight years before resigning to accept the presidency in 1894. During his tenure, the agency succeeded in securing abundant financial aid for land-grant colleges, in funding and implementing the Hatch Act and the Second Morrill Act, and in developing a clearing-house for the dissemination of scientific information at home and abroad. Collectively, these accomplishments brought Morrill colleges to the end of their pioneering period: that is, it gave state universities the vitality and coordination necessary to combat the stranglehold of classical and denominational colleges on the nation's system of higher education. In addition to this organization, Henry Alvord served as an executive officer for the New York State Agricultural Society, the New York Dairy Association, the American Jersey Cattle Club, the National Cattle Growers Association, and the American Association for the Advancement of Science. Also, he maintained an active membership in the Royal Agricultural Society, the British Dairy Farmers Association, the American Statistical Association, the National Geographic Society, and the French Order of *Merite Agricole*.[8] His political and scientific contacts brought "respectability to the presidential office of Morrill institutions at a point in time, when many administrators were held in low esteem, both in grange and legislative halls."[9]

Henry Alvord, before coming to Oklahoma as a college president, visited Indian Territory on two occasions, once as an army officer and once as a special emmissary for President U. S. Grant. As a boy of sixteen in 1860, he enrolled at Norwich University, where Justin Smith Morrill served as a trustee. This institution, one of several founded by Captain Alden Partridge, was the first civilian college to offer instruction in both agriculture and engineering. Its proximity to Greenfield, Massachusetts, Alvord's home, made Norwich a more convenient place to attend than West Point. A popular student, Henry became editor of the *Reveille* and *University Quarterly* newspapers. In 1862, he enlisted in the "College Cavaliers" in response to the governor of Rhode Island's plea for an all-student volunteer Civil War regiment. The youth, elected First Sergeant, completed a ninety day tour of duty with the Seventh Cavalry and then returned to Northfield, Vermont to receive his Bachelor of Science degree. AC. E. and an honorary LL. D. were obtained in 1870 and 1890, respectively. Subsequently, Alvord enlisted in the Second Massachusetts Cavalry and served three years under Philip H. Sheridan. Later, he enjoyed speaking and writing about his role in defending the city of Washington from the ill-planned and poorly executed attack of General Jubal Early. His boyhood letters also reveal that he was present at Appomattox when Robert E. Lee surrendered to U. S. Grant.[10]

In spite of the fact that he thought of himself as more of an engineer than a soldier, Alvord, according to his service record, accepted a regular army commission at the end of the war. Before leaving for the West, he served with Oliver Otis Howard in the Freedmen's Bureau. He then assumed duty posts at Fort Riley, Kansas and Forts Arbuckle, Cobb, and Gibson in Oklahoma. Besides his work as an adjutant and road and bridge construction supervisor, Alvord learned to speak the Comanche dialect and was instrumental in preventing George Custer from further slaughter of the Kiowa tribe.[11] Instead of killing the Indian, Alvord, a humanitarian officer, believed in establishing reservations where natives could be taught to "read and write, plow the fields, and live in cabins."[12] The interest in Indian education continued, for he became nominally affiliated with Richard Henry Pratt in founding the Carlisle Indian Barracks in Pennsylvania.[13]

In September, 1869, Major Alvord began his lifelong association with the American land-grant college movement. In this year he became the first army officer detailed from West Point to a Morrill campus to offer instruction in military tactics. But before he could become deeply involved with his assignment at the Massachusetts Agricultural College, Alvord, along with Professor Edward Parrish, returned to Indian Territory as a Special Indian Agent. President Grant commissioned the young soldier to meet with Satanta, the incarcerated Kiowa chieftain, and to bring representatives of the Apache, Arapaho, Caddo, Comanche, Delaware, Keechie, Towoccaroe, Cheyenne, and Wichita tribes to Washington for a conference. Upon completion of this mission, he returned to Massachusetts to study agriculture under the noted Charles A. Goessman, a highly competent German who had received his degree in analytic and organic chemistry from Göttingen. Alvord then resigned his commission to take a position on the faculty of the Massachusetts Agricultural College as well as a part time appointment at the nearby Williston Seminary. Simultaneously, he inaugurated scientific dairy experiments at his home in Fairfax, Virginia. From there he helped to develop cooperative creameries in the East, to direct the chautauqua "School of Farming," and began to publish. Seven chapters were contributed to J. P. Sheldon's *Dairy Farming*, a book marketed by Cassell and Company in London. His article, "The American Cattle Trade," brought a medal from the Royal Agricultural Society of Great Britain.[14]

The publicity gained as a member of the faculty of the Massachusetts Agricultural College brought other opportunities. In 1881, Professor Alvord accepted the directorship of the Houghton Farm in Cornwall, New York, an experiment Station patterned after Rothamshed in England. The plan of investigation there included studies in soil physics, plant physiology and pathology, animal breeding, and nutrition. When Congress passed the Hatch Act, Charles Kendall Adams of Cornell offered Alvord the chance to head the experiment station at Ithaca. He refused in order to become president of the Maryland Agricultural College. He popularized the "People's College" concept while at College Park and conducted research on tomatoes, potatoes, fodder, strawberries, and on the composition and digestibility of the corn plant. Friction, however, developed between him and the Board of Regents because of the heavy emphasis placed on agriculture. His tenure terminated in 1893, Alvord went to Washington to serve as a special assistant to the Secretary of Agriculture. It was during this period that the executive learned of the presidential vacancy at the Oklahoma A. and M. College.[15]

In addition to his experience as a farmer, teacher, and soldier, Henry Alvord brought with him to Stillwater an aura of greatness. Moreover, he had a genial personality and a strong desire to push the Oklahoma A. and M. College into the vanguard of the land-grant movement. Harry Thompson, the gadfly of the faculty, who boarded with his senior colleague, said that he "knew him quite well and liked him."[16] James Neal, a man whose judgment may be trusted, wrote to an Oklahoma legislator in 1895 that there were "few men his equal as a College President, and none in the United States his superior."[17] Unfortunately, these views were not shared by the Board of Regents. The members resented federal interference in local matters and decided among themselves that the destiny of the college should be determined from within the state itself. Thus, the new president was in trouble from the moment that he stepped on the campus.

The fourth academic year of the college started on September 12, 1894. The term began with eight faculty and approximately 120 students. Only a senior class remained to be formed for the organization to offer a full-fledged undergraduate program. The faculty, this year, were more tired than usual, for they had had to bear the responsibility for transferring equipment from the Methodist Church to Old Central during the summer months. In addition, some of them had helped to landscape eight of the forty acre site on which the first building had been erected. The campus, with the roads that had been constructed earlier, now began to reflect the image of a real institution of higher education. Though there is not documentary evidence to confirm it, it is likely that the instructional staff had furnished the president's office in advance of his arrival. Two men, James Neal and Alexander Magruder, must have known Alvord by reputation, as they had attended meetings of the Association of American Agricultural Colleges and Experiment Stations. The faculty, no doubt, was pleased to obtain a person of Henry Alvord's stature. Consequently, there must have been an effort to make him feel welcome.[18]

Arriving after the semester's work was underway, the new executive threw himself into the many tasks which confronted him. Presidential duties are always cumbersome but the recent reorganization made things even more difficult. The most pressing obligation at present concerned the preparation of the institution's annual report. Barker should have completed the document by the end of the fiscal year. But when he resigned from the Board of Regents in 1893, cool relations developed between him and the other trustees. He decided, therefore, to return to the solitude of Crescent City on a permanent basis. Barker had, however, gathered most of the necessary data and locked it in his desk drawer in Old Central for the use of his successor. The compilation of the report proved tedious and time consuming, yet it afforded Alvord an opportunity to assess the current state of A and M. and to make recommendations for change to the Board of Regents. The completed analysis revealed the ability of the second president to locate weak spots.

Fluctuating enrollments is the first item which captured the attention of the report writer. He stated that

students do not seem to appreciate the necessity for persistent application in their work, their needs and opportunities now offered to them. And parents are too prone to permit, or even encourage, absences for every insufficient reason. The full strength of the College and its teaching force is exerted to . . . impress the importance upon the minds of the students themselves, as well as upon parents, of punctual and regular attendance . . . .[19]

Second, Alvord commented on the present status of the military department. Morale seemed low and he believed that a request should be submitted to the War Department for a regular army officer to be detailed to Stillwater from West Point. Third, the Board's attention was directed to several problems related to instruction. While some improvements had been made in adjusting teaching loads, the new executive felt that additional professors and teaching assistants should be employed so as to free more faculty for research and extension work. Moreover, instructional and staff salaries needed immediate consideration, for they were not equitably divided. Fourth, departments needed to be reorganized to permit more emphasis on the needs of Oklahoma. Next, the writer pointed out that a female should be hired "to give proper advice as to study, health, and conduct to girls and young women who are for the first time removed from home influences, and at a critical age."[20]

The concluding and longest section of the report dealt with the necessity for more departments and buildings. Legislators were reminded that they had in essence contracted with the federal government to support the development of a comprehensive college when they accepted the provisions of the Second Morrill Act. Domestic economy and mechanical arts were the departments which required relief without delay. The former should go on the drawing board before the latter, since almost one-half of the student body consisted of females. In regard to buildings, construction should begin on at least two during the current academic year. The first should be designed to contain plant houses, propagating pits, a boiler room, and work rooms for attendants. Also, provisions should be made for faculty offices. A second building was to house the departments of chemistry and physics, with space reserved for zoology and comparative anatomy lectures. Old Central, in this regard, had already proved inadequate because odors, fumes, and gases could not be controlled and they reached every part of the building.[21]

Not just content to make recommendations, President Alvord moved to augment his report. He started by realigning the existing departments and by reducing the number of administrative duties that the faculty had been forced to assume as a result of the prolonged absences of the former administrator. The professors, however, were formed into standing committees as usual. Magruder and Alvord were placed in charge of the military department; Clark, Miller, and Waugh were directed to study questions pertaining to room and board for students; and Miller agreed to develop a plan for strengthening the library. Moreover, entrance requirements for both the preparatory school and the college were upgraded. Finally, it was decided to make the wearing of military uniforms mandatory for students.[22]

By far the biggest project undertaken at this time concerned the codification of the rules relating to student conduct. Clark and Magruder assumed responsibility for this matter. Other instructors standardized daily forms, created new report procedures, and initiated guidelines for regulating the literary societies on campus. Collectively, the faculty met to coordinate the amount of work required for classes. In this same area, it was recommended that the students give more public performances, including a declamation, essay, or oration during the last quarter of the sophomore year, an oration at the conclusion of each subsequent undergraduate year, and an address at graduation exercises. The same group scrutinized the thorny subject of *practicums*. Here is was agreed that two hours of labor on the farm should be counted as the equivalent of one hour of classroom work and that grades for such activities should be reported separate from regular course offerings.[23]

With Old Central operational, the faculty and departments reorganized, the rules governing student conduct and literary societies revised, and provisions made to free more faculty for research, it was now possible for President Alvord to focus on public relations and to tend to the matter of student enrollment. Besides stepping up his speechmaking,[24] he composed promotional brochures. One that is thought to be representative began with a brief statement on the mission of Oklahoma A. and M. The writer stated that the object of the institution was to provide a liberal education and to offer training in "chemistry, physics, mathematics, botany, geology, and entomology in connection with agriculture."[25] Other pages described scientific equipment housed at the college and discussed possibilities for student employment. Next, the institution was compared to the West Point Academy, because it was believed that the cadet image would be more glamorous than an agricultural one. Last, local communities throughout the state were invited to request members of the faculty to participate in meetings of the various horticultural and agricultural society meetings. Also, Alvord urged parents, boys, girls, school teachers, farmers, lawyers, doctors, merchants, mechanics, and politicians to visit the campus so that they could promote the college and its work.[26]

It is not known how the Board of Regents reacted to the reorganization but subsequent events suggest that some hostility had been generated, for a direct confrontation soon occurred. The initial dispute concerned a policy matter instead of a clash over a specific decision or incident. Sometime in September or October, 1894, the trustees issued a directive which stated that President Alvord and Professor Neal had to swear to the accuracy of all vouchers that passed over their desks for payment. This meant that each such document had to be notarized. Both men resented such treatment, because it questioned their personal integrity. Henry Alvord, less cautious than James Neal, stated flatly that he could not comply with the condition. As chairman of the executive committee of the Association of American Agricultural Colleges and Experiment Stations, he knew that other collegiate administrators were not required to give testimony of this type. Thus, he decided to appeal the Board's ruling to a higher authority.[27]

Instead of arguing with the trustees, President Alvord wrote to the Secretary of Agriculture in order to obtain an official policy statement from Washington. Alfred True responded, posting his letter to Oklahoma on November 9. He stated that, in general, the governing board should have a voice in determining priorities but then it should be up to the executive officer to decide how funds should be spent in order to carry a particular project to its natural conclusion. Expenses were to be incurred only with the consent of the president of the college and he was to be responsible for issuing vouchers at regularly scheduled intervals. On the other hand, the trustees were charged with auditing the institution's accounts. The only items which required sworn affidavits were those "in which proper vouchers could not be obtained and notarial fees are not a necessary or proper charge against station funds received from the United States except in such cases."[28] Major Alvord had won his point and he probably did not lose a minute in conveying the contents of the letter to his superiors.

The incoming administrator, before a compromise could be reached, received a call to Washington. The next annual meeting of the association of land-grant colleges was scheduled to convene at the end of November, and, as a member of the steering committee, the president had little choice but to be present. During the course of the convention, the chairman of the executive committee performed his duties in an efficient manner. In reflecting, however, upon the magnitude of the problems that existed in Stillwater, he decided to resign his position in the organization. He then asked the delegates to replace him. The membership respected his wish but decided to recognize his past service by electing him as the next president of the association. The educator accepted the new post as it was honorary in nature and had few duties attached.[29]

While in Washington, Alvord attended to several college business matters. This suggests that the executive had no intention of leaving Oklahoma in the near future. In particular, he attempted to locate materials that would strengthen the institution's library. The administrator learned from a friend that a complete set of *Harper's Magazine* would be sold. He inspected the periodical collection and forwarded a note to Freeman Miller in regard to condition and price before boarding a train for the return trip to Stillwater. The leather-bound volumes were purchased and they made their way to the same destination only weeks later. This transaction provides some evidence at least that Henry Alvord had not been job hunting and that he had not forgotten that his primary allegiance still belonged to the organization that paid his salary. Nevertheless, his appearance on the campus proved to be a signal for more trouble.[30]

Since it was the custom of the Secretary of Agriculture to attend the meetings of the agricultural colleges and experiment stations, it is likely that Henry Alvord conferred with him about the ugly situation developing in regard to the land-grant college in Stillwater. When Alvord returned to the institution, at any rate, there no longer was a willingness to compromise. The president met with the Board of Regents and requested that they cease certain questionable practices which he had outlined in a long written report. Moreover, he demanded that the trustees turn the daily operation of the college over to him. The regents still resented the attempt to curtail their powers, and they refused to adopt the suggestions that had been made. Major Alvord responded by verbally tendering his resignation. He was a man who felt that he had a high calling in life and he did not intend to waste his time dealing with petty people.[31]

The offer to resign, from all appearances, was presented in haste, without premeditation. Later, the subject of the controversy provided the members of the Board with an opportunity to review their stand. The trustees refused to do so, however. And, after the next meeting, which was held in Stillwater, the editor of the *Gazette* announced what had taken place. He said that the regents had accepted the resignation of Alvord "and then proceeded to elect a successor, a man of whom they knew nothing and cared less."[32] The same newspaper published the official letter of resignation. In it, the ex-president explained that the Board had allocated large salaries to positions at the college and station for which the duties performed did not justify the expenditure. "The result," he added, "is nothing less than a diversion of public funds from the objects for which they are specifically provided."[33] Both the letter and a copy of the latest report of the president were mailed to the Secretary of the Interior and the Secretary of Agriculture in Washington."[34]

A public letter of appreciation, which was printed in the *Messenger*, the *Oklahoma State Sentinel*, and the *Eagle-Gazette*, followed shortly thereafter. Alvord addressed these notes to the "good people of Oklahoma" and appealed for public-spirited citizens to insist through their legislators that the "college not be used for selfish, personal, or political ends, but that it . . . be conducted solely for the public good."[35] Several immediate reforms were suggested. First, the college needed a treasurer who lived near the institution. Second, more honest and capable men should be appointed to the Board of Regents. Last, the second president of the Oklahoma A. and M. College, thoughtfully, but somewhat strangely, commended John Clark, the regent from Stillwater. He said that he had done a good job and deserved reappointment if and when a new Board was formed.[36]

Most of the local newspapers commented on Alvord's resignation; however, it was the *Messenger* that set the tone for future action. An editorialist declared that Henry Alvord would not resign and send a "stinging" report to Washington if he could not substantiate his charges. Therefore, the writer called for an investigation by the Territorial Legislature.[37] The next day James Neal wrote Representative Robert Lowry that real trouble was afoot. He stated that Alvord had already left for Washington to become, he thought, Assistant Secretary of Agriculture. Also, Neal said that he had been apprised of two plans that concerned the relocation of the college and experiment station. The first centered upon moving both institutions to another locality in Oklahoma. The second involved transferring just the station to an area that had better soil. Naturally, the director opposed each idea. Initially, he spoke against the latter proposal, claiming that the two institutions complemented each other and should not be separated. In regard to the relocation of both, he warned Lowry that as

soon as a College gets on wheels, its value is gone, and it then is a football for successive Legislators to use as a plaything, and possibly a means of getting 'rakeoffs' . . . . No matter what the arguments as to suitability of location, poor soil, out of wayness and that Payne County got it by 'finesse and trading'. The facts are that Payne County has worked for all she was worth, and sacrificed both time and money to hold it, and here it should stay. Some of these days a Railroad will make this place as accessible as Guthrie or Oklahoma City, and all the other objections can be overcome.[38]

Others joined in the fight. Hays Hamilton wrote to Lowry on January 15, 1895 that most of the people in Stillwater supported the idea of an immediate investigation. He felt it would be a good tactical move for the local legislator to introduce such a motion himself.[39] Neal added more. He said that he had contacted Alvord and asked him to reconsider, providing that a new set of regents were appointed. But, he appended: "I think it doubtful if he would serve except on his own terms."[40] The *Sentinel,* following the lead of the *Oklahoma City Times-Journal,* requested that the Board of Regents not accept the president's resignation until such time as an investigation had been concluded. The suggestion, however, came too late, for Hamilton informed Lowry that Edmond Dandridge Murdaugh had been selected to become the third president of the college.[41]

Meanwhile, other developments were taking place in Guthrie. Representative Angelo C. Scott, a newspaperman, former candidate for governor, hosteler, and member of the Assembly, introduced a motion in the Legislature which asked that Alvord withdraw his resignation. The resolution passed, the solons being unaware of the events that had transpired in Stillwater at the last meeting of the Board.[42] In addition, a joint resolution received consideration. It, in substance, made members of the agricultural committees of the House and Council a special *ad hoc* group to investigate "the affairs of the Territorial agricultural and mechanical college . . . ."[43] The sessions were to be held in Guthrie but members of the sub-committee were authorized, if necessary, to visit the campus as often as needed. The legislators were also instructed to issue process for such witnesses and records as they deemed necessary as well as to look into the

financial management of the institution, including the disposition of government funds belonging thereto; the appointment and dismissal of instructors, employees and officers; the matter covered by the last report of the president of said college, and of the director of the experiment station. . . . [44]

The Legislature appropriated $300 to pay the expenses incurred by the investigating body.

James Neal, who had hoped for the presidency himself, took the lead in organizing local support and formulating plans for further reorganization. Before the *ad hoc* committee could convene its hearing, he contacted Representative Lowry in Guthrie. Neal suggested that the number of trustees be increased from five to nine. He felt that the governor would not replace his own appointees, so the next best thing was to request that more members be added. Concurrently, J. A. Stephenson, of Stillwater, forwarded to Lowry the names of businessmen in the community who had offered to help in any manner possible. C. D. Shaffer promised to "handle" the Populists if their votes were needed in the Legislature. Thus, the townspeople, in spite of political differences, were united in their effort to save the college for their community.[45]

On February 5, 1895, the investigating committee called the public hearing to order in Guthrie. Twenty-one days later its report came off the press. Fifteen witnesses were asked to testify during the three week interval, including the current governor, an ex-governor, a former college president, several members of the Board of Regents—both past and present—, and a number of faculty and staff. S. H. Kelsey, billed as an "expert accountant," agreed to audit the institution's books. As might be expected, the territorial newspapers capitalized on the situation, reporting the entire proceedings in picturesque detail.

The committee used the report Henry Alvord had sent to Washington to guide its investigation. In this document, the ex-president had identified what he considered the most troublesome problems associated with the college and station. His most important criticisms included: (1) the experiment station had been operated as a model farm, and the Board seemed intent on making it operate at a profit; (2) the Legislature had been negligent in providing funds, especially in regard to the construction of new buildings; (3) the superintendent of the farm was a political appointee, ignorant of scientific principles and paid an excessively high salary in relation to that of the faculty; (4) the college secretary was a patronage appointment and incompetent to perform his duties; (5) the trustees had spent federal funds foolishly, paying themselves abnormally high salaries; (6) former treasurers had not kept proper financial accounts; and (7) faculty salaries were unequally divided. Finally, Alvord believed a new Board of Regents should be formed and a larger faculty should be recruited in order to carry out the mission of the college.[46]

A. V. McDowell, the superintendent of the station farm, testified first. He told the committee that he had worked at the institution from April, 1892 to June, 1894, resigning shortly after the "democratic board of regents" got possession of the books and seal. McDowell's job entailed both timekeeping and supervisory work. He received $75.00 per month, a figure as much or more than what some of the faculty earned. The farmer was not charged with wrongdoing but he did admit that he had not had a harmonious relationship with the station scientists. His general attitude is reflected in a statement wherein he said that if the academic personnel used a little "bit more of good common horsesense and a little less science, that our farmers would appreciate the station more than they do."[47]

On the same day, the committee held a lengthy session with James Neal. The experiment station director fielded questions on a wide variety of topics, including the general use of the Hatch and Morrill funds, the recommendations of ex-president Alvord, faculty salaries, the expenditures of the Board of Regents, the status of the college water supply, and the quality of Stillwater soil. His most revealing testimony, however, concerned the manner in which the regents had purchased supplies for the institution. Neal said that Wimberley, Lane, and Little were paid substantial amounts for expenses in their capacity as purchasing agents but that the faculty had done most of the work. Then, too, most of the Hatch funds had been used for instructional salaries, and $5,516.06 had been spent to build a new road at the station. The latter expenditure seriously embarrassed the college as barely enough money remained to pay faculty salaries.[48]

59

Next, Amos Ewing took the stand. His testimony concluded the events of the first day. The legislators questioned the former regent in regard to travel expenses, faculty appointments, money which still might be in his possession that belonged to the institution, and the location of the banks where federal funds were placed on deposit. Most of Ewing's replies were interesting. However, those in connection with the latter proved the most damaging to his reputation. The treasurer acknowledged that institutional funds had been deposited regularly in banks at Guthrie and Kingfisher. The books of these establishments indicated that no interest had been paid on unexpected daily balances. When quizzed as to whether he had personally received interest payments, he said he had not. But, he admitted that after the "peremptory writ of mandamus was sued out, some of the parties with whom I had deposited, as I understand it, agreed to pay counsel when the question arose as to whether or not the governor of this territory of his own motion could remove the board of regents."[49] Ewing "forgot" to mention that Joseph McNeal was president of the Guthrie bank, and that he himself had an interest in the Kingfisher establishment. Nevertheless, no formal charges were filed against him.

Tazewell Upshaw, the man who took the witness stand after Ewing, has been identified by one historian as the chief trouble maker at the A. and M. College.[50] His qualifications for his position as secretary included clerking in a drugstore, serving as deputy registrar of deeds, and sales experience in wholesale drug and fire insurance firms. Initial testimony related to circumstances surrounding Upshaw's appointment to the college staff. The clerk said that he had been hired by the Board of Regents, and, when Dr. Neal presented him with a list of duties, he promptly took the paper to John Clark who scratched off all the items except one. The trustee also wrote on the bottom of the paper: "Prescribed by the board of regents."[51] Upshaw carried this document with him during duty hours. If he was asked to perform a job not on the list he lost no time in producing the paper so as to avoid additional duties.

The other questions that the committee put to Upshaw indicated that the investigating body had done its homework. First, he was asked if he had hired Emma Dent, a student, for four dollars per month to assume his job while he was absent. Second, someone inquired if he had ever used alcoholic beverages to excess and if he had boasted that his job had been awarded for political reasons. Last, a member of the committee asked whether he had been hired to spy on Alvord. Each reply indicated that there was a degree of truth in all these allegations. In regard to the last query, the secretary stated that a good part of his position consisted of keeping the Board informed of Alvord's activities. He reported, for instance, that the president had said that the "first duty of the faculty was to educate the board of regents, and that when they were properly educated they could run things to suit themselves."[52] The legislators finished with Upshaw in one day but the remainder of the hearing often touched upon his conduct.

Frank Caruthers, a graduate of the Texas A. and M. College, took the witness stand after Upshaw. Caruthers, a member of the successful Norman law firm of Ross and Caruthers, refused to answer almost every question directed to him, insisting that he could not recall the specific circumstances surrounding most of the early history of the college. However, in spite of his reluctance to give straightforward information, two questions of themselves caused the spectators to titter. The first requested whether he knew that Tazewell Upshaw was wanted in the state of Texas on a murder charge. Caruthers, of course, gave a negative response. He did say, however, that there had been rumors which suggested involvement in several shady deals. The second question related to the ownership of banks where college funds were deposited. Caruthers explained that the institution had approximately $23,000 on hand at the present time. One-fourth of this amount had been placed in Guthrie at McNeal's bank. The remainder was on deposit at the Norman State Bank. The regents drew upon funds at the former institution to pay monthly bills while Norman money had not been drawn upon, except for emergencies. The lawyer was then asked who owned the latter bank. Caruthers replied that William C. Renfrow, the governor of the Territory of Oklahoma, held most of the stock.[53]

Following Caruthers, two former members of the governing board, J. E. "Shorty" Quien and John Wimberley, appeared before the committee. The questioners bore in heavily on the latter man, especially in regard to his activities as purchasing agent and superintendent of the college building program. Eventually, it was determined that he had received compensation for both positions simultaneously. Moreover, testimony revealed that some of Wimberley's financial transactions in connection with the experiment station were somewhat out of the ordinary. He admitted, for example, that he had engineered the sale of three horses owned by a neighbor to the college. Two of the animals proved incapable of heavy work. One went blind and the other contracted a crippling lung disease. Furthermore, Wimberley's brother had been paid an exhorbitant sum to bring the horses to Stillwater. The regent tried to justify his actions but the committee abruptly dismissed him.[54]

William Campbell was subpoenaed next. He had been a member of the team appointed by Governor Steele to locate a site for the Oklahoma A. and M. College. Campbell said little of interest. Then Robert Barker took the witness chair. The committee pressed immediately for additional information about the activities of the first Board of Regents. His responses made it clear that much of the blame for the failure of his administration was due to the unwise decisions of the trustees. Testimony confirmed that funds had been spent indiscriminately, junkets had been taken which resulted in no positive benefits, and that the faculty had not been consulted in regard to the creation of purchasing priorities. As to the lack of visible accomplishments at the experiment station, the ex-president shouldered the complete blame, refusing to slander or diminish the character of James Neal. In fact, he said: "J. C. Neal, who is also director of the station, is one of the best men I have ever met in my life; honest, upright, sensible and unassuming; he takes great pleasure in his work, nothing passing that is not right, nor any duty ever neglected."[55] It became apparent, as the proceedings moved ahead, that Barker had often disapproved of the Board's actions, but that he was incapable of taking corrective measures, because the trustees were frequently in league with the territorial governors.

The Reverend J. P. Lane, ex-governor A. J. Seay, John Clark, and William Glazier were the last witnesses brought before the investigating committee. The Reverend Mr. Lane admitted receiving double salaries; Seay could not recall whether he had been simply a stockholder or a director of the bank in which college funds had been deposited while he was in office; John Clark provided a character reference for Tazewell Upshaw; and Governor Renfrow pleaded innocent to any wrongdoing, claiming that he had been hoodwinked by the regents in some of their manipulations of personnel. Colonel Glazier, who had replaced Alexander Magruder, acknowledged the general accuracy of the report sent to Washington by Henry Alvord. None of the testimony offered enhanced the reputation of these witnesses. The investigating committee decided that they had heard enough and they ended the hearing.[56]

The *ad hoc* committee reviewed the findings of Captain Kelsey, the man who had been hired to audit the books of the college, before compiling the final report. His investigation, in general, corroborated the information supplied by those individuals called to the witness stand. Kelsey found that the accounting system employed by the regents was not adequate. There were many vouchers missing and some of those that had been made available were so oversimplified that it was almost impossible to ascertain why, how, and by whom money had been spent. Consequently, he could not prove specific instances of graft. Kelsey did hint, however, that the opportunity had been present for wholesale corruption. After all, most of the former trustees were businessmen; they were individuals who should have had a thorough knowledge of proper bookkeeping procedures. On the other hand, the auditor did commend the accounting system inaugurated under Henry Alvord. These records were clear, concise, and free from error.[57]

With this information in hand, the investigators drafted their report for the Legislature. The completed document contained eleven sub-divisions. It implied that many of the problems which had arisen in the last three years were the result of inexperience. Then, too, the founding law, as has been mentioned, had been loosely drawn, with few safeguards written into it. Nevertheless, the committee did identify some outright instances of wrongdoing. Trips taken to Kansas, Ohio, and Texas under the guise of inspecting other land-grant institutions had really been made to visit relatives. The investigators believed that these junkets were gross violations of the public trust placed in the Board of Regents. The college, in order to survive, badly needed the advice and counsel of sister land-grant institutions but none had been forthcoming.[58]

The body of the report condensed the testimony of the various witnesses and then made the following observations. First, it appeared that the site for the Oklahoma A. and M. College had not been well chosen. Besides poor topsoil, the institution suffered from a lack of water. Thirteen wells had been drilled, yet drinking water still remained in short supply. Second, two positions needed to be abolished, that of the farm superintendent and that of the college secretary. Third, officers of the organization were reminded of the necessity for keeping better records. Fourth, administrators were instructed to expand the geographic locale from which students were recruited. Many of these recommendations pointed to the manner in which the city of Stillwater had acquired the college. Henceforth, the institution was to be a state, not a local organization.[59]

While many people were charged with the responsibility for the poor showing of the institution, the concluding section of the report laid most of the blame on the Board of Regents. The writers said that in our

examination into the financial management of this institution we have found little to commend and a great deal to condemn. Where public officers rendered: for every day in the month, including Sundays, and then in addition collected pay in the territory for the same period of time that they have charged the institution for service as an agent in another capacity, it is time such officials in charge of educational institutions should be taught to observe a law which is older than colleges, states, or nations.[60]

These words implied moral laxity but confirmed that the laws of Oklahoma Territory had not been broken. The Legislature, therefore, did not suggest that punitive action be instituted in the courts. The report of Henry Alvord was ignored, too. Predictably, however, one adverse reaction did develop. The investigation intensified the ill feelings between the two major political parties. This resulted in a contest to move the Oklahoma A. and M. College to another community.

With the new Board of Regents continued in office, the leadership of the college anticipated both personal and institutional recriminations. On February 11, 1895, Professor Neal wrote to Robert Lowry and pleaded with him to sponsor a bill to increase the size of the governing board. He feared that if the same people were held over that "no Republican stands a ghost of a chance in the faculty after June, and that all the abuses that are now at work, as to Upshaw, will be continued . . . ."[61] Three days later the *Gazette* reported that a measure had been introduced in the Council to move the college to El Reno.[62] And, to add to the city's problems, Representative Knipe, of Perkins, initiated a plan in the Legislature to extend the Payne County "line nine miles into Lincoln County and to move the county seat to Perkins."[63] The destruction of the Stillwater courthouse by fire seemed to forecast success.

The business, educational, and political elite of Stillwater, how-ever, were determined to keep *both* of their prized possessions. The *Sentinel* warned the opposition that when "you tackle Stillwater and her institutions you will be facing Spartans."[64] Charles McGraw led the fight to preserve the county seat. "If you get the common gobbler started an assertion is soon a positive fact," he said to Lowry, "and continues to get larger. Kill the Knipes Bill in the Committee. We will send the money to do so."[65] It is not known whether Lowry had to resort to the use of bribes, but the problem was resolved in favor of Stillwater. In return, F. C. Hunt penned a letter of appreciation to the legislator. He stated that the city planned a reception for Lowry once the current session came to a close.[66]

Also, Robert Lowry deserves the credit for retaining the land-grant college in Stillwater. When he ran for office in 1894, his pop-ularity was such that he had been mentioned as an odds-on-favor-ite to become the next Speaker of the House of Representatives. The position was thought to be particularly important because many people believed the occupant of this seat would be appointed the next territorial governor. Cassius Barnes, a man who started his political career as a clerk in the Guthrie land office, opposed Lowry for the speakership. Lowry, however, in spite of support from stal-warts, such as Henry Asp, John Dille, and Frank Greer, decided to let Barnes have the job. But he did obtain an important pledge from his opponent. Barnes said: "Now Bob, I want to be speaker . . . . If you do help you may be assured I will appreciate and re-member your friendly aid in a time of need, and shall reciprocate in any way within my power."[67] Cassius Barnes did become Speaker of the House of Representatives and governor of Oklahoma Terri-tory. Lowry called for his "favor" in connection with the relocation crisis and the institution remained in Stillwater without a public political fight. Moreover, the legislative proceedings do not indi-cate that any other serious effort to put the "college on wheels" took place in the immediate future. The organization now could begin to extend its influence through teaching, research, and extension.

The crisis of 1894 and the investigation of 1895 proved to be a turning point in the history of the Oklahoma A. and M. College. Though Henry Alvord was not given the treatment or the tenure he deserved, his work made the institution more closely approxi-mate a real center of higher learning. It also provided officials in Guthrie and Washington with accurate facts in regard to the status of the college. Major Alvord, in less than six months, completed a reorganization that might have taken less experienced men several years. Yet, the problems were by no means resolved on a permanent basis. More than thirty-five years would pass before the Department of Agriculture would issue a clean bill of health for station accounts. Then, too, almost half a century would elapse before Oklahoma politicians decided to let the land-grant college develop without interference in its internal operations. On the other hand, it would have been impossible for anyone to shape A. and M. so that no future changes were needed. Educational organizations are never done; each generation must shape them to meet their own needs.

V   A SINNER AND A SAINT COME TO STILLWATER

The legislative investigation of the Oklahoma A. and M. College proved sensational but it initiated few permanent policy reforms, for most of the institution's urgent problems had been resolved before the committee started its work. The revision of the Christmas Eve founding law occurred long before the public hearing, the bookkeeping system prepared by the second presidential administration received the approval of Captain S. H. Kelsey, and the controversial secretary of the college resigned his position to accept employment in an Oklahoma judicial office. Meanwhile, Henry Alvord took leave of the campus to be in Fairfax, Virginia before New Years' in order to spend the holiday with his wife. A subsequent announcement in a local newspaper stated that the ex-president had taken a professorship at the Vermont Agricultural College. The next year, the Secretary of Agriculture appointed him as the first Chief of the Dairy Division of the Bureau of Animal Husbandry. In Washington, Alvord won international recognition because of his writing on the cattle industry and his conduct of American agricultural exhibits at foreign expositions. His propensity for hard work contributed to an early death. He collapsed at the St. Louis World's Fair on October 1, 1904. The medical examiner who tended the ailing man said that acute exhaustion had contributed to bulbar paralysis.[1]

The Board of Regents remained in a "special" relationship with high territorial officials during the next collegiate administration, with the trustees continuing to use the Oklahoma A. and M. College as a political pawn. The alliance regrouped through the publication of rumors designed to discredit the reputation of Alvord. The Board hired a president whom they hoped would be content to act as a figurehead. But he refused to cooperate. A new, and enlightened, Board of Regents then tendered an offer to another man, a distinguished elder statesmen of the land-grant movement. This individual promulgated an educational program which nearly every one in the state wholeheartedly embraced. His love for agriculture and farming proved contagious; it generated much goodwill throughout all of the counties in Oklahoma.

Edmond Dandridge Murdaugh, the third president of the land-grant college in Stillwater, came to Oklahoma in January, 1895. A strikingly handsome man with steel gray hair, impeccable clothes, and a military type of poise and bearing, Murdaugh easily qualifies as the most colorful individual to preside over the faculty in the pre-statehood period. He, in subsequent years, acquired a reputation as being one of the most able political orators in either Indian or Oklahoma Territory, too. Murdaugh discovered, however, that following a vigorous executive in office is a difficult, if not impossible, task. His lack of interest in agriculture and his inexperience in higher education, when added to the above, predestined a short tenure. With the exception of one brief interlude, he remained active in Oklahoma educational circles for the rest of his life. Murdaugh played a significant role in shaping the character of the regional state colleges. Some feel that he should be identified as the father of this system.[2]

Edmond, the son of the Reverend E. C. Murdaugh, a Morengo County, Alabama Anglican clergyman, descended from an illustrious Old Dominion family. The father, not long after Edmond's birth, returned to his native state in order to become Bishop of the Diocese of Virginia. While there, Edmond may have attended the University of Virginia but registration records do not provide documentation to this effect. He did, however, enroll in the preparatory school of William and Mary College in 1867 and entered the collegiate program the year following. A degree was not earned, yet the educator later claimed it had. Murdaugh also asserted in later life that he had been awarded a Doctor of Pedagogy diploma from the Maryland State Board of Education. Contemporary evidence for the latter certificate is also missing.[3] But regardless of Mudaugh's academic background, his aristocratic ancestry always made him stand apart from his contemporaries. A close friend at the Central State

67

College called him a disciplinarian of the old school, one who believed that "the educational process worked best under strict tutelage . . . . A southerner to the manor born, he never betrayed his Virginia antecedents.[4]

It has often been suggested that Murdaugh received his appointment to head the Oklahoma A. and M. College because he was the personal choice of Henry Alvord. This assertion, however, is probably not valid, for it is doubtful that the second president had any influence left with the Board of Regents. More likely is the possibility that the new executive obtained his position because of his eighteen years at the helm of a vocational school located in Eaton, Maryland, a city on the eastern shore of the Chesapeake Bay. Many regarded this institution as the leading one of its kind in the state. Furthermore, the principal had become well known for his lectures on pedagogical and psychological topics. He was in the vanguard of the movement to professionalize public school administration and teaching.[5]

Murdaugh, a Cleveland Democrat who was appointed by a Board of Regents of the same political persuasion, gained immediate acceptance in the community and at the college. The editor of the *Gazette* wrote that the institution needed sympathy in the loss of Major Alvord but that a real gentleman had been chosen to take his place. He believed that Murdaugh had many talents, including natural oratory which was shown by the "master manner in which he handles subjects which daily arise."[6] The students concurred. One young male observer let it be known that faculty meetings were so orderly that they usually lasted for only a short time. He concluded: "It is talked on the streets that President Murdaugh is the right man in the right place. He is always polite, gentlemanly, and easy on all occasions."[7] The coeds especially seemed to take to the handsome administrator, for on the appropriate day many brightly decorated Maybaskets were deposited at the door of the president's residence.

Initially, Murdaugh's colleagues accepted the mid-year replacement. The "Minutes of the First Faculty" suggested that routine business was quickly dispensed with on February 4, the initial staff meeting of the new administration. The same held true for the next two months. A minor crisis arose in March when thirteen students had to be expelled for misconduct; however, no faculty splits evolved over the matter. The single innovation through this period, and it also was not controversial, related to the establishment of a press bureau headed by Freeman Miller. President Murdaugh probably created this agency to counteract the adverse publicity received by the institution during the recent legislative investigation.[8]

Faculty relationships began to deteriorate toward the end of the 1894-1895 academic year. A local newspaperman got wind of the strife first, stating that there was something peculiar about the dozen or so men employed at the college that the average person found difficult to comprehend. He said: "Their duties are not cumbersome, and, to the outside world, it appears, that as soon as a man has been duly elected and installed in that institution his head starts to swell, and . . . he . . .seeks to breed discord in the premises and in consequence has the entire institution in a turmoil."[9] Though the writer did not identify to whom he was referring, he probably had in mind a growing rift between James Neal and Edmond Murdaugh. The conflict proved severe enough so that by summer the entire faculty lined up behind one or the other person. The cause for the disagreement can only be conjectured. It seems possible, however, that the operation of the experiment station lay at the root of the matter. The former president had been critical of its work. Then, too, Murdaugh had not been trained in agriculture. These two factors may have been responsible for driving a wedge between the two men. But regardless of the nature of the dispute, the regents again decided to intervene. They chose this particular time to institute yet another reorganization.

Captain Kelsey, the person chosen to replace John Clark in March, led the latest purge. His business background dictated a simple solution to the jealousy that existed among the faculty. He proposed to fire the higher paid senior professors and restaff the institution with less expensive personnel. Following Kelsey's suggestions, the trustees took the following actions during the summer of 1895: First, the Board informed President Murdaugh that he would not be rehired for the coming academic year. Second, James Neal received notification that he had been relieved of his duties as director of the experiment station, although he could elect to remain as a professor of natural science at $500 less than his present salary. Third, both Frank Waugh and Alexander Magruder were fired outright. Last, the college farmer was told that the institution no longer required his services. Of the original faculty, only George Holter now remained on the payroll.[10]

The Board of Regents carefully timed the public announcements of these changes, selecting a date when it was known that most of the students and members of the faculty would not be on the campus. Professor Thompson heard the news of his release from Freeman Miller by mail in late June. Expressing what must have been in the mind of many people, Thompson said: "Heavens and Dante! What an avalanche has swept down upon the faculty. Are our feet on the rock or are we on sinking sand? The mill of the gods grind slow, but they grind to powder."[11] Even vacationing students became alarmed. One wrote to Miller that rumors concerning the faculty were circulating over the entire territory.[12]

Oklahoma newspapers, of course, responded in print. Local editors, particularly, regretted the release of Magruder and Waugh, because they feared many of the experiments in progress at the station would be lost. Statewide comment, however, centered primarily on the release of the popular Edmond Murdaugh. The *Guthrie Leader* began the political analysis. The writer of several articles published in June and July charged that an unholy alliance had turned out the administrator. He believed that Governor Renfrow had wanted to keep Murdaugh but that Captain Kelsey, backed by Tazewell Upshaw and James Neal, had conspired to obtain the votes needed for dismissal. Kelsey attempted to refute these allegations in order to maintain the integrity of the trustees. He gave his side of the affair in the *Gazette*.[13]

S. H. Kelsey hinted that either President Murdaugh or a close friend of his had composed the stories published in the *Leader*. Next, he said that the regents were required by law to oversee the Oklahoma A. and M. College and that they therefore had to assume the responsibility for making personnel decisions. The accountant maintained that politics had absolutely nothing to do with the aforementioned changes. He added that Governor Renfrow had been present when the faculty dismissals were voted upon, and, if the same man had been at the meeting where Murdaugh was fired, he would have approved of this action, too. The president, the regent explained, had lost his position because of immoral conduct.[14]

The seriousness of the charge demanded proof. It was common knowledge in the community that some of Murdaugh's personal habits were not within the realm of conduct that people in Oklahoma expected of their educators. Two months before he had been dismissed, he had been invited by John Clark to accompany some of the "boys" on a camping trip. The group took a generous supply of alcohol along to their overnight site on Stillwater Creek. The liquor was responsible, according to an early resident, for the trouble that ensued. Frank Wikoff related that the "Doctor" and some of the other members of the party had too much to drink. Then, during the festive hours of the night, someone took a pair of shears to Murdaugh's hair, leaving abundant evidence that a barber had not done the trimming. Early the next morning, the president "had his hair smoothly clipped."[15] The *Sentinel* reported this incident just before the end of the academic year.[16]

Now, Kelsey indicated other such incidents had occurred. He said that reputable sources had informed the Board that Murdaugh had been under the influence of alcohol in a neighboring city. In fact, the regent said that his behavior was so poor that a local Sunday School instructor had used the president as an example of intemperance in one of his classes. It was also alleged that Murdaugh drank to excess in his hotel room and that he was in the habit of sending out for liquor. And, even if this hearsay testimony was inaccurate, the Board felt vindicated in their action, because the present executive had appeared on the streets of Stillwater, in the saloons, and at his hotel room on the evening of his discharge in "a maudlin condition from the effects of liquor."[17]

It is difficult to ascertain if the charges levied against Edmond Murdaugh were true, for no formal investigation was made nor do many documents pertaining to his administration currently exist. But there are circumstances that suggest the accusations may have been exaggerated in order to justify a change in leadership. Captain Kelsey, a Union Army veteran, and a Republican, replaced John Clark, a Democrat, as president of the Board about two months after Murdaugh had been sworn into office. It was not at all un-usual in the late nineteenth century for such vicissitudes to signal sweeping changes. When Populists and Democrats succeeded in capturing control of the neighboring state of Kansas in 1896, they canceled all of the faculty's contracts at the Manhattan A. and M. College. Professors were then brought in who were of the right political persuasion. The turmoil in Oklahoma bears a marked resemblance to the Kansas maelstrom.[18]

Edmond Murdaugh did not leave the state after being re-lieved of his presidential duties. He, at the suggestion of Harry Thompson, made application for and obtained the senior position at the Central State College, an institution which in this period had the largest student enrollment in the state. In subsequent years, the educator organized the Northwestern Normal School at Alva, served as superintendent of the Woodward public school system, and pre-sided over the Claremore Military Academy. Between the time he held the latter two positions, Murdaugh returned to the state of Maryland to start a new teacher's college, the Frostburg Normal School. Oklahoma, however, still held a strong attraction for him. He accepted the presidency of the Southwestern State College and ended his academic career as a professor of psychology at Central State. If Murdaugh had possessed an immoral character, as Captain Kelsey claimed, it is unlikely that so many prestigious positions could have been secured. On the other hand, there may have been some truth to the allegations because he changed positions with amazing rapidity.[19]

There may have been one more mark against Murdaugh which adversely affected his tenure in Stillwater. At the time he came to Oklahoma Territory the administrator was widely known for his interest in vocational education, especially as it pertained to engi-neering. The men who served on the Board of Regents were dirt farmers as well as businessmen. Undoubtedly, they believed that the program of the Oklahoma A. and M. College should primarily, if not exclusively, emphasize agriculture to serve the homestead element of the state. This point of view, in part, was shared by other leaders of the land-grant movement. The fact that engineering was not mentioned in the organizational name of the Association of American Agricultural Colleges and Experiment Stations is sig-nificant. Then, too, the federal agency in charge of Morrill colleges was the Department of Agriculture. Except for a few isolated insti-tutions, such as the Massachusetts Institute of Technology, engi-neering would have to wait until the end of World War I for modern academic development.

Murdaugh did not publicly contest the decision of the trustees to release him, nor did he attempt to defend his administration. Thinking the matter settled, the regents at the end of the fiscal year commissioned Captain Kelsey to obtain a new executive. He decided to extend an offer to George Espy Morrow of the Univer-sity of Illinois. While details of this transaction are not available, one letter to Morrow has been preserved. It suggests that the educator had not sought the position and that an annual salary rate of $2,000 had been decided upon. "Hearty support" and "administrative assistance" was offered if Morrow would agree to direct the Oklahoma A. and M. College in the future.[20]

Born on a farm in Warren County, Ohio, on October 19, 1840, George Morrow first acquired an interest in pioneer farming methods through his frequent attendance of fair exhibits in the western portion of the state. Morrow's early education, as that of his nine brothers and sisters, came from his father who taught him how to read. Afterwards, he was permitted to sample the large collection of books in the family library. George, at fifteen, entered the Mainesville Academy, graduating in 1856. He planned to enroll at Miami University in Oxford but instead enlisted in the Union Army. When the war ended, Morrow attended the University of Michigan and obtained his law degree in 1865. He elected, however, not to open a law practice, because he had already decided to become an agricultural journalist.[21]

Morrow, along with Liberty Hyde Bailey and Eugene Hilgard, was one of the American academicians who popularized the study of agriculture. He had much to do with establishing the subject as a science. But whereas the other two men entered the academic field early in their lives, the former acquired his knowledge as a publisher of farm newspapers. He first became associated with the *Western Rural*. When this paper moved to Chicago, Morrow went along as a cub reporter, subsequently becoming one of the nation's leading authorities on agriculture. Later, he and an older brother bought the *Western Farmer*. The mid-1870 depression, however, caused a fatal decline in circulation. The eventual failure of the newspaper motivated Morrow to accept a teaching position at the Iowa Agricultural College.[22]

The announcement of Professor Morrow's appointment at Ames in 1876 was greeted with much enthusiasm. The *Progressive Farmer* carried an item which stated that the agriculturalist had been chosen unanimously and that no one had ever "embarked in a difficult enterprise with so universal a confidence on the part of the public that he could achieve success."[23] Morrow, however, did not stay in Iowa long enough to fulfill these high expectations. In less than a year he decided to accept a position with the Illinois Industrial University. There his literary fluency, broad knowledge of agriculture, and engaging personality "all conspired to make him a most entertaining . . . lecturer before farmers."[24] His work at the university itself received favorable attention, too. In his initial address, Morrow evidenced that he had a clear idea of the nature and intent of the Morrill Act. Both agriculture and engineering should be stressed, he said. Moreover, he believed that these new institutions of higher education should serve the public so that the people could receive the benefits of scientific research.[25]

At Urbana, George Morrow acquired an international reputation. His writing and research brought him a full professorship and promotion to several administrative posts. Still, he did not accomplish all that he wanted to, for students seemed more interested in industrial than agricultural education. When enrollment in his classes decreased to the point of alarm, he stumped the state to search for pupils. Increasingly, travel took up so much time that the institution had to employ a teaching assistant for instruction in agriculture. In the end, the tide toward urbanization and industrialization could not be turned back. His most lasting influence pertained to the creation of the Morrow Plot, a soil experiment in the improvement of corn production which preceded the Hatch Act by ten years. When the offer to head the Oklahoma A. and M. College arrived, Morrow accepted without delay. He felt that in Stillwater he could develop a truly outstanding program in agriculture.[26]

George Morrow brought with him to the campus many things that the college desperately needed at this point in its development. The president was more outgoing than Barker or Alvord and he thought of himself as a common man. He spoke and acted as if he were a part of the people, not someone above them. In addition to his many years of experience in journalism and the academic world, Morrow had traveled abroad, to Denmark, Holland, and England. Therefore, even though he had a practical bent, the new man did not qualify as a provincial. Last, but not least, the educator's wife and children accompanied him to Stillwater. He was the first executive to bring his family. On the whole, Morrow's tenure at A. and M. proved important. He implemented the reorganization started a year before and put the institution on solid ground. Advanced age and obsolete agricultural ideas were his only real handicaps.[27]

By the time he got to Stillwater, the fourth president had developed a distinct philosophy of agricultural education. His ideas paralleled those of Jonathan Baldwin Turner and John Milton Gregory,[28] yet there were enough differences in his approach so that one can credit him with a degree of originality. In order to assess his intellectual make-up, one should first examine the presidential address that he delivered to the Association of American Agricultural Colleges and Experiment Stations. It was presented the year before Morrow left Illinois for Oklahoma. Alfred True, in the *Experiment Station Record,* called this speech the beginning of a deeper national interest in the teaching of agriculture.[29] The document, in short, made a majestic plea for the preservation of rural life.

Morrow began with the premise that agriculture constituted the basic industry of the world. Then he said that the rapidity of rural change was threatening the primacy of agriculture as there had been a migration from the country to the city as well as from the older lands in the east to the newer lands in the west. He thought this development a mistake. Land-grant colleges should take up the challenge of making agriculture more popular and profitable, thereby slowing down the urbanization process. Academicians, in this regard, needed to create better methods of instruction by systematizing what needed to be taught in order to recruit more able students. Experiment stations, too, should do their part by finding new uses for old crops and by increasing the number of commodities that could be grown in a particular geographic area.[30]

This theme received expansion as soon as the new president arrived on the campus. Morrow noted for a Stillwater audience that Morrill institutions were founded for undertaking only limited tasks; they were not general education in the ordinary sense. Next, he pointed out that land-grant colleges were designed not merely for the benefit of individuals but for the welfare of all mankind. Finally, the president explained that institutions of higher education could be divided into three categories: the general, the professional, and the industrial. A. and M. colleges, according to this scheme, belonged under the latter classification, as they were primarily concerned with the earth as a producer of food. Thus the

Industrial institution has as its paramount purpose to give its students the largest use of their brains and bodies in the actual industries; to enable them to use every power whose possibilities nature has bequeathed to them; to join the trained mind and the trained hand together for the conquering of the world, for the subjugation of the hostile forces of nature. This special purpose, which may be called the 'manu-mental,' may well be termed the highest.[31]

Morrow concluded his presentation by warning his listeners against discarding general and professional colleges. They should be retained along with industrial universities to form an educational trinity.

Morrow, as had his predecessor, took charge of the Oklahoma Experiment Station. This situation makes it necessary to understand how the executive thought the station and college should fit together. Departing somewhat from the position held by Neal, Morrow thought that the station could make the land-grant college unique for it provided the information and skills which ought to be taught to students in the classroom.[32] In a paper entitled "The Relation of Teaching to Experiment Work," the scientist explained how the process generally should work. He said that a college and station should work side-by-side as two helps to one end.

Let the teacher carefully study the experiments now in progress as well as those grown venerable with age and make much use of them as object lessons. Let there be the freest consultation between the teacher and experimenter, and so far as it is practicable without injury to assigned work, let each help and work in the other's field.[33]

The agriculturist, then, felt that both college and station should promote empirical science, not just be a technical institute or a model farm. Research is what set Morrill colleges apart from classical institutions.

As in the case of Alvord and Murdaugh, the professors and students accepted their new leader without hesitation. In September, 1895, the campus newspaper reported: "If ever a college was blest with a good man as president, ours is. We don't know whether to scorn or pity the Illinois institution from which our president

74

came."[34] Harry Thompson, who served as administrative assistant to the president, called Morrow's lectures "epics of science," and added that when he spoke "he showed his superiority over the heads of other institutions."[35] Others agreed, especially the broader community of the state. This support aided the executive in instituting an ambitious expansion program, the first in the organization's history.

President Morrow spent most of his initial year in Stillwater publicizing the institution he headed throughout Oklahoma. He took a "swing around the circle" to counteract the distasteful coverage given the reorganization of 1894 and the release of Edmond Murdaugh. He also found time to interview young people who might qualify as potential students. In addition, Morrow delivered speeches aimed at building rapport with territorial farmers, a prerequisite to developing adult extension courses. The extent of the speechmaking becomes apparent when one traces the president's first month in office. He spoke in Oklahoma City, lectured at the college on the subject of "Some Privileges of College Students," and talked at public school teacher's meetings in El Reno, Oklahoma City, Perry, and Pond Creek. Moreover, he attended agricultural and horticultural gatherings in Guthrie and Oklahoma City.[36]

The administrator stayed in Stillwater during the month of October but he did devote some time to discussing the importance of close contact with the public. In a newspaper interview, Morrow said: "It is the desire of the college authorities to make the college a helpful influence to the community as a whole. Citizens will always be welcome as visitors to all public exercises."[37] Harry Thompson scheduled more trips for November and December. Taking his wife along, the president visited with farmers in Guthrie, Oklahoma City, and El Reno. In the next three years, he seldom turned down an invitation to meet the public. The entire family made many sacrifices to help Morrow champion the "Holy Earth," a phrase made popular by Liberty Hyde Bailey.[38]

The first harvest of these seeds appeared in 1898 and 1899. Morrow, drawing upon comments given to him personally, as well as responding to newspaper criticism concerning the dull and technical nature of Oklahoma agricultural experiment station bulletins,[39] encouraged the faculty to assist him in making direct contact with the public because "in a country with so many important and unsettled problems, such meetings should be of great value."[40] And indeed they were. Informal talks and papers led to the establishment of extension courses and extension courses evolved into semi-permanent instructional centers located throughout the state. Shawnee, Hennessey, Perkins, and Perry hold the distinction of being the first. Many more, however, were added later. If the people would not come to the college then the college would go to the people.[41]

In order to expand the services of the Oklahoma A. and M. College even more, President Morrow decided that the size of the faculty had to be enlarged. Here the executive was more fortunate than his predecessors. He had two presidents of the Board of Regents who had complete confidence in him because they knew of his work at other land-grant institutions. These men dedicated themselves toward improving the college that Morrow now headed. Robert Lowry, the lawyer, became acquainted with the president while he was teaching at the Iowa Agricultural College. When Lowry left Stillwater to fight in the Spanish-American War he was succeeded by Frank Wikoff. The latter man, then a banker, had gotten to know the educator at the University of Illinois. Both of these individuals respected the administrator. They worked with him to locate bright young scholars who believed in teaching, extension, and research.[42]

Most of the new professors were recruited from other land-grant college campuses. Many of them found working conditions so pleasant that they remained through the so-called "Golden Age" of Angelo Cyrus Scott. The most noteworthy individuals who came to Stillwater from 1895 to 1899 were: (1) E. E. Bogue, botany and entomology, a graduate of the Ohio State University; (2) J. W. Fields, chemistry and physics, a graduate of the Pennsylvania State College; (3) J. F. Bone, agriculture, a graduate of the Ohio State University; (4) L. L. Lewis, veterinary medicine, a graduate of the Iowa Agricultural College; (5) R. E. Chandler, mechanical engineering, a graduate of the Stevens Institute of Technology and Cornell University. Robert Tucker, foreign language, a graduate of the College of William and Mary, joined the instructional staff at the recommendation of Alfred True shortly after Morrow retired. Last, but not least, A. C. Scott replaced Freeman Miller, whose outspokenness and personal habits irritated many people. These professors assumed much of the responsibility for the day-to-day operation of the college. Under Morrow, the point arrived where the faculty delegated power to the president, not the opposite. The process became so smooth that in June, 1898, the *Gazette* reported that the entire teaching corps had been re-elected for the following year.[43]

The most troublesome problem faced by the Morrow administration concerned the matter of increasing the amount of financial aid granted by the state. Governor Cassius Barnes reported to the Secretary of the Interior that in 1895 the Stillwater institution had received from the federal government almost $20,000, of which $14,701 belonged to the experiment station. Besides these funds, the college obtained a small amount of cash from the sale of crops grown on the station farm. The Legislature provided assistance from time to time, but it was so sporadic that advance planning became almost an impossibility. Collectively, the institution's funds were hardly sufficient to support an organization that housed two hundred students. Therefore, the administration initiated an intensive effort to raise more money.[44]

The Board of Regents located one new source of revenue. The exact amount, however, also fluctuated so much that the institution was not able to budget it ahead of time. In 1893, the United States

Congress empowered the executive branch of the government to reserve certain public lands in the Oklahoma Panhandle for such purposes as the local Legislature might designate. Consequently, sections thirteen and thirty-three were leased, with the proceeds earmarked for improvement of the general welfare. The federal lawmakers, in order to begin generating revenue as quickly as possible, created an *ad hoc* committee consisting of the governor, the secretary of the territory, and the superintendent of instruction to supervise the leasing process until the Legislature itself could assume responsibility for the task. This committee decided to permit several agencies to share in the benefits, including institutions of higher education.[45]

In 1897, the Oklahoma A. and M. College received $7,500 as its share of the leased land revenues. The amount dropped, however, to $5,000 in 1898, finally bottoming out in 1899 at $900. The third year decrease produced a sharp reaction from both Morrow and Wikoff. In the institution's annual report, they reviewed the situation in depth. They began: "The opinion that this institution is well provided with funds rests on a false assumption . . . ."[46] Then the writers reprimanded the Legislature for neglecting the organization in time of need. The section on finances asked whether Guthrie representatives were keeping the bargain they had struck with the federal government at the time the provisions of the Morrill and Hatch Acts were accepted. The report made it clear that the two men thought they had not.

Just when it seemed as if some significant strides forward might be made, a major economic reversal occurred. The issue of school segregation, which had been receiving increased attention as a result of Negro migration from the South, came to the political surface. Large numbers of blacks began applying for admittance to Oklahoma institutions of higher education. In 1895, an Aggie newspaper reporter wrote that the question had recently been raised in Edmond, and that Stillwater could expect the "disturbing" problem to come up in the very near future. It did. The Legislature dragged its feet but two years later it passed a bill which provided for segregated instruction.[47]

The solution in regard to higher education involved the creation of a new university in Oklahoma. The Second Morrill Act, it will be remembered, permitted states and territories to construct "separate but equal" colleges for Negroes. As a result the Legislature established at Langston the Colored Agricultural and Normal University of the Territory of Oklahoma. The founding law required that Oklahoma A. and M. donate $15,000 of its funds on hand to Langston, and thereafter it was to share all federal monies on a percentage basis. The move had some clever aspects. The lawmakers found a method of appeasing Negroes, of preserving the supremacy of white institutions, and of adding another state university without spending any more money. On the other hand, the division of the Washington endowment did much injustice to both land-grant institutions. The Oklahoma A. and M. College recovered from the blow but Langston remained underfinanced and unaccredited until the Korean War.[48]

Community and college reaction in Stillwater varied. The *Gazette* piously announced: "Won't it be a benefit to the farmers of the Territory to have two experiment stations, one at Stillwater and one at Langston, twenty miles from each other?"[49] The students were more realistic and sincere in their analyses. One asked whether it was feasible to combine agricultural, mechanical, professional, and normal training under the same roof? He added, however, that he wished the institution good luck just the same.[50] Another said: "Abstractly considered, colored young people have a right to attend the school for whites, but, in view of existing feeling or prejudice, it seems better to provide separate schools."[51] Tens of thousands of teen-aged Negroes, therefore, were left to endure the pitfalls of a sub-standard education. Moreover, the state of Oklahoma failed to develop the talents of people who had come to the border states hoping to share more fully in the nation's democratic heritage.

The inadequate financial aid given to the Oklahoma A. and M. College in the past, and the loss of federal funds to Langston, relegated the organization to a low place in land-grant statistical ratings, both those prepared by the federal government and those compiled by other schools. There were sixty-four Morrill institutions in 1898, of which fourteen were for the exclusive use of Negroes. Stillwater, according to figures published by the Department of Agriculture, ranked in the lowest ten percentile in number of students, in value of permanent funds and equipment, in general revenues, and in equipment additions for the previous year. These measurements were borne out by charts and graphs developed by the Pennsylvania State College. Their study placed Oklahoma forty-eighth in assessed valuation of property, the same in annual appropriations, fortieth in fixed state appropriations, and twenty-eighth in equipment owned. If these statistics were accurate, A. and M. was so poorly endowed that it ranked below many of the southern all-Negro colleges.[52]

Both James Neal and Major Alvord had asked the Legislature for more funds. But little help had been forthcoming. George Morrow and the Board of Regents made similar requests in 1896 and 1897, again to no avail. In September of the latter year Morrow decided to state specifically what was needed. He hoped that his itemized list would impress upon the Legislature the urgency of the problem. Increased enrollment and services, the president said, necessitated the construction of (1) quarters for the department of domestic economy; (2) a building and equipment for the department of mechanical engineering; (3) instructional and research laboratories; (5) a library study room; (6) a dairy building with laboratory and experiment rooms; (7) recreational facilities; (8) a museum; (9) a print shop; and (10) additional book space. Seven months later the Board took what action it could with the funds that were available and approved plans for the construction of an engineering building. Furthermore, the collegiate curriculum was broadened so as to include courses in bookkeeping, foreign language, music, stenography, and typewriting.[53]

The trustees let the contract for the engineering building in May, 1898. The structure was to be a two story affair 80' x 32' with an annex for a boiler and engine room. The blueprint called for a lower floor that could be used for iron and woodworking shops and an upper chamber divided into lecture and apparatus rooms. The next year the regents committed themselves to a new chemical laboratory and to expansion of the library. These improvements started the institution moving again and made it possible to increase student enrollment. Moreover, the building program squelched rumors that the organization would be moved. Thus the politics of patience and moderation proved more successful than thunder from Washington.[54]

Not only did Morrow get the college moving again physically, but he also presided over the institution when the first senior class was formed. In 1896, both townspeople and professors observed a noticeable change in the men and women who had arrived in Oklahoma only a few short years before in covered wagons. George Holter remembered that standards of excellence then were even higher than those of today based upon percentage of failure for a given term. The *Populist* newspaper published an item at the beginning of the academic year which stated that most of the Aggies were serious about their studies and that they retired to their rooms by seven o'clock in the evening. But prepared or not, six young men became candidates for degrees at the end of the Spring term.[55]

The graduation exercises of June 9, 1896, were commemorative, devotional, elaborate, and sentimental. Even the fact that just one-half dozen cadets qualified for a degree after five years of operation could not dampen the enthusiasm of the large crowd that assembled in Old Central to see Arthur Wesley Adams, James Homer Adams, Frank Ellsworth Duck, Alfred Edwin Jarrell, Ervin Gibson Lewis, and Oscar Matison Morris receive the Bachelor of Science they had earned. To prove their competence, the students had maintained high standards; they all passed both written and oral examinations, and had composed a senior thesis. Their projects were entitled: (1) "The Esthetics of Motion"; (2) "The Study of Nature"; (3) "Sir Humphrey Davy"; (4) "Abraham Lincoln"; (5) "Man, the Master"; (6) and "Pictures in the Fire." These topics do not indicate a preoccupation with agricultural subjects. Instead, they suggest that the college faculty had devised a well-rounded academic program within the limits and scope of the institution.[56]

It must have seemed to the graduates as if every person in the state of Oklahoma made a speech sometime during the commencement week. To single out one as being more important than the others is extremely difficult. But, because of its breadth, the address of Robert Lowry given at an Old Settlers reunion in Stillwater one week before graduation captured the spirit of the moment, best.

He said that the prairie, where once Mother Nature reigned supreme, had been civilized as a result of the labor of numerous individuals, few of whom were famous. Lowry concluded his talk by providing an answer to those who might inquire as to who had made this land. He said:

> I cannot tell. I only know
> He heard God's voice and came
> In the white caravan across the prairie sea,
> To work for country, God and me.
> The soil he broke, felled the huge oak,
> And from the soil, with horrid toll,
> Dragged forth its gnarled, and twisted foot.
> No granite monument, is chiseled with his name.
> No trumpet blazons forth his fame.
> A city there, a school, a church spire tall.
> The farms, the homes, the villagers, - all -
> These be his monuments and these alone
> He needs no urn of bronze and no memorial stone.[57]

In some respects these words characterized the experience of the first Oklahoma A. and M. graduating class, for the students knew that they too qualified as pioneers. They had survived the drought years in Stillwater churches, endured the embarrassment and humiliation of carpetbag politicians who had used educational funds for their own advantage, and suffered quietly while favorite professors left for more stable academic institutions. Yet, in spite of adversity, the six young men in question finished their degree programs. The graduates moved to other cities and states, but a fondness for their *alma mater* remained with them as long as they lived. Their affection echoes that of Daniel Webster when he defended the interests of Dartmouth College before the Supreme Court in the landmark sanctity of contract case. He whispered: "It is . . . a small college and yet there are those who love it."[58] Then he wiped away a tear which clouded his vision as he remembered the halls in Hanover. Many of the earliest "plowboys and blacksmiths" felt the same toward the institution that had trained them.

It was almost three years to the day after the first graduation that George Espy Morrow left the campus. The struggle for respectability had been a long one, and it had taken a heavy physical toll. President Morrow introduced his successor to the students in June, 1899 and then departed for Paxton, Illinois, where he died less than a year later.[59] Alfred True posthumously hailed him as the man who had fathered excellence in agricultural instruction. Former Colleagues in the American Association of Land-Grant Colleges and Experiment Stations paid tribute as well. In Stillwater, the faculty joined those throughout the nation who mourned the loss of a gentle leader and a revered friend. A resolution stated that we

have heard with profound regret of the death of Professor George E. Morrow. . . . As a scholar the range of his learning was wonderful; as a specialist in his chosen pursuit his services were of conspicuous and enduring value; as a teacher he was suggestive and inspiring; as an administrator he was honorable and faithful; as a man his life was stainless and above reproach; and he was a christian citizen, doing his full duty by the State. Through all the future history of this institution his name will be honorably associated with its early struggles and triumphs.[60]

Most eulogies are overly sentimental and they tend to give the deceased more credit than he deserves. But the faculty tribute to George Morrow may well be called a conservative memorial: an important part of the humanity of the nation had been lost.

The Oklahoma A. and M. College gained in stability from 1895 to 1899, although it took the rude dismissal of another executive to bring about the appointment of an honest and dedicated Board of Regents. Edmond Murdaugh, the sinner, should not have been employed as president, because he was not willing to make personal sacrifices in order to retain his job. He came from a family which had status and believed in living the good life. George Morrow, the saint, should probably not have been employed either. He championed a way of life which was slowly dying and could not be revived. Then, too, he was too old to grow alongside the state of Oklahoma. The institution needed a young man with strength; a man whose eyes were locked upon the future, not the past. And yet, the land-grant college was most fortunate to secure the services of Morrow. His patience and personality resulted in much goodwill and some increased funding at a critical point in time. He richly deserves the title of patron saint.

VI   THE NEW EDUCATION

By the beginning of the twentieth century, the land-grant colleges
of the United States were exhibiting much of the promise that their
intellectual architects had earlier ascribed for them. These institutions insofar as teaching and learning are concerned, had had to
think through many puzzling problems. First, the organizations
were confronted with the fact that they were both state and federal
in nature. This situation involved the acceptance of financial assistance from the federal government without letting agencies, such as
the Department of Agriculture, unduly influence them. It also
meant convincing state and territorial legislatures that they were
regional instructional centers and that local financial support was
necessary for their continued existence. Second, the Morrill colleges,
especially after they had shed their practical image, had to combat
the ruthless criticisms levied at them by their classical and denominational counterparts. Princeton's James McCosh went so far as to
suggest that national endowments should be discontinued and given
to the burgeoning high school movement. President Warren Can-
dler of Emory College, later a Southern Methodist Bishop, spoke to

82

the Georgia Legislature in 1889 in an effort to convince the lawmakers that higher education was a function of the church, not the state. This attitude, of course, reflected a growing concern for the secularization of Academia. Third, land-grant universities, as they incorporated the word "state" into their names, had to decide whether to put their resources into general culture or agriculture. In this regard, utopian idealists, practical vocationalists, sectarian classicists, and military enthusiasts each had a different conception of where such organizations should proceed in the future. With a temporary political settlement affected in the territory, the Oklahoma A. and M. College had to face these same problems, thereby launching a program designed for the next century.[1]

In her 1897 commencement oration, Jessie Thatcher, the first woman graduate of the Stillwater college, evidenced one more major challenge that her *alma mater* would have to cope with in the opening decades of the new era. She began with the statement that if "you and I could have chosen when to exist, I think there could have been no more inspiring time than now." To illustrate the magnitude of change taking place in society, she commented at length upon recent technological innovations in the communication and transportation industries and the growing importance of women in the world. Then she devoted the remainder of her talk to educational institutions. They were, Jessie believed, the "one all-important thing, paramount to everything else . . . ." She explained:

The future race will, perhaps, be one of specialists. This will be necessary, on account of the vast knowledge involved, but, in all probability, the whole volume of human knowledge will be gradually rewritten and condensed . . . . The sciences themselves will be scientifically systematized, and by the aid of that process it will be possible for the future specialist to be better versed in all departments than the specialist of today in his own.[2]

Last, Miss Thatcher pointed out that the greatest contribution of the nineteenth century to American life had been the abolition of slavery. Now, with the liberty outlined in the Declaration of Independence a possible reality, the educational system could spin its magic. These institutions could help all citizens to benefit from the democratic process.[3]

While a student could forecast what the new education should be concerned with generally, it took specialists like Cornell's Liberty Bailey to spell out for college presidents what should be done. His report to J. G. Schurman in 1904 detailed how agricultural instruction should be modified. He said:

In the epoch just closing colleges of agriculture have concerned themselves mostly with technical farming, largely with the increasing of the productiveness of the farm. In the epoch just opening great emphasis is also to be laid on the farm home and family. We are to reach the farmer as well as the farm. Certain great public questions touch the farmer very closely; these must be considered in the College of Agriculture . . . both in its regular academic courses, and in its extension work. Some of these questions are farm labor, rural organizations, good roads, means of communication in the country, sanitation, architecture of farm buildings, cooperation with churches and societies in introducing better ideals of farming and citizenship.[4]

Herein was a rationale for wedding engineering and agriculture with the social sciences so that land-grant colleges could provide a better and fuller life for the masses.

The First Territorial Legislature played an instrumental role in shaping what would be taught to the Oklahoma A. and M. students. The founding act charged the administration with developing a program which would emphasize practical instruction in agriculture and the mechanic arts. The legislators, using the so-called Granger Amendment as a guide, enumerated the subjects that could be offered when the institution opened its doors. The organic act stated that the curriculum must embrace the English language and literature, mathematics, civil engineering, agricultural chemistry, animal and vegetable anatomy and physiology, the veterinary art, entomology, geology, and "such other natural sciences as may be prescribed; political rural, and household economy, horticulture, moral philosophy, history, bookkeeping, and especially the application of science and the mechanic arts to practical agriculture in the field."[5]

It was, of course, impossible for a small faculty to institute such a broad program. Neither time nor money existed in quantities large enough to fulfill all the provisions of the founding law. Nevertheless, the college attempted to be as faithful as it could to the charge that had been given. The catalog clearly stated, for example, that the object of the institution was not to offer a university education; it was to provide training in the industries of life. Moreover, the Aggies were warned that pursuance of the latter did not mean there would be an absence of physical work. One writer declared: "It is not expected that students enter upon a course of study for the purpose of passing a few years in pleasantry, but . . . it is presumed that the attainment of useful knowledge and skill is the dominant motive, which prompts young men and women to enter the institution."[6]

The collegiate department was formed in September, 1892, with a new class added each year until 1896. Graduate work was not developed until after statehood. The nine month academic year usually was divided into three equal quarters in order to accommodate students who had to return home to help on the farm at seed and harvest time. The curriculum, as in the preparatory institution, included textbooks, classroom lectures, laboratory experimentation, and college farm *practicums*. The last item received much emphasis, for the catalog stated that "four years without labor, wholly removed from the sympathy of the laboring world, during the period in life, when tastes are rapidly formed, will almost invariably produce disinclination, if not inability to perform the work and duties of the farm."[7]

Both the faculty and students shared the responsibility for setting academic standards. The instructors used a one hundred point grading scale, with at least one mark being recorded each month. To pass a particular course, the Aggies needed to maintain an overall average of seventy per cent besides achieving at least the fiftieth percentile on final examinations. *Practicum* grades were kept separate. Seniors, in addition to satisfactory marks, had to write a three to five thousand word thesis.[8] The student body participated in that they persuaded the faculty to adopt an honor system in 1895. After the instructor distributed an examination, he did not remain in the room to act as a "watchdog." When the class period was over the examinee would simply write on the bottom of his paper: "I hereby certify on honor that I have neither received nor given assistance on this examination."[9]

In order to graduate a candidate had to complete 314 quarter term credits.The young men and women—if the suggested sequence was followed—took sixteen courses in mathematics, agriculture, English, military science and tactics, and bookkeeping the first year. Eighteen subjects were attempted the sophomore year, including mathematics, agriculture, science and mechanical drawing. The third year contained the same number of hours, with history being the one new addition. The subjects required for the senior year decreased by two, but the classes were more varied. Agriculture, science, English, mathematics, law, and philosophy, military science, psychology, and surveying completed the undergraduate course of study. The faculty called this program "general science" and certified students who completed the four year program for a Bachelor of Science degree.[10]

In addition to the Legislature and the personnel directly associated with the college, other individuals and groups influenced the collegiate curriculum. The land-grant association set up a model course of study, hoping that some standardization would occur across the country. The nation's intellectual elite took part in the Darwinian conflict as well as the less publicized war between the classics and English, modern languages, and history. The National Grange, as well as local and regional agricultural organizations, often expressed deep concern over the status of higher education in the South. And clergymen, such as the Right Reverend Robert Brooks, The Episcopal Bishop of Oklahoma, closely observed collegiate affairs to make sure that scientists did not forget God while they looked for the secrets of the universe.[11]

The students, perhaps, comprised the most outspoken group in the state. Two noteworthy methods of comment in regard to the curriculum evolved. First, the staff of the college newspaper wrote or solicited articles dealing with teaching and learning. Some pertinent examples are "The Department of Chemistry"; "The Mechanical Engineering Department"; "Should Examinations be Abolished"; "Am I Educated?"; "The Department of Agriculture"; "After Graduation"; "The Benefits of a College Education"; "College Influences"; "Specialization in Education"; and "Brain Culture and Agriculture." Second, the students organized discipline clubs in order to discuss pedagogical techniques. The Chemistry Club received the first group charter. Agriculture, biology, and engineering came later. In 1895, the students and faculty formed the College Club. It served as an interdisciplinary educational forum on the teaching process. Papers entitled "Physical Culture," "The Use and Abuse of Textbooks," "How to Teach Science," "The New Education," "Electives," and "Textbooks, Lectures and Laboratory Instruction" were read during the initial nine months of operation.[12]

The Oklahoma A. and M. College may have placed an undue stress on practical agricultural instruction in the beginning, but even its narrow approach seemed to some an improvement over the curriculum of many classical institutions. Mr. Dooley, Peter F. Dunne's satirical bartender, described the status of such organizations in a fictional dialogue between a typical president of a liberal arts college and a young Irishman who was not strong enough to contend for high honors as a middleweight. The former said:

Me dear boy, what special branch iv larning wud ye like to have studied f'r ye by our compitint profissors? We have a chair iv Beauty an' wan iv Puns an' wan iv Pothry on th' Changin' Hues iv th' Settin' Sun, an' wan on Platonic Love, an' wan on How Green Grows th' Grass, an' wan on th' relation iv Ice to th' Greek Idee iv God . . . .[13]

Contrasted to this, the students of land-grant colleges were exposed to both inductive and deductive scientific reasoning processes. One Stillwater student began a discussion of the new education by saying that Louis Pasteur had obtained some of his best ideas from predecessors who were unable to follow the facts to a logical conclusion. He continued:

Interest in science must be beyond a mere curiosity to know a fact, but when you study science for the sake of science as such, when the enjoyment of completeness and accuracy are more desirable than the indolence of ignorance, when the desire for orginality is great enough to stimulate work then the mind has passed the stage of blind intellectual instinct.[14]

President Robert Barker pieced together the initial course of study a week or so before the institution opened its doors for instruction. Since no class schedules were printed, and because the elective system was just then coming into vogue, it is impossible to ascertain which classes were taught first. It is apparent, however, that Barker attempted to include most of the subjects prescribed by the Legislature in the founding law. The only exception to the provisions of the organic act was Latin. Professor Freeman Miller wrote the textbook, *The Latin Inflections: Together with Their Elementary Principles* (Stillwater: Gazette Printing Company, 1896). As in the preparatory school, regular academic classes came in the morning and the afternoons contained drill, *practicum,* and laboratory work.[15]

The analysis and evaluation of the undergraduate curriculum is of such importance that it warrants a separate study. It is necessary here, however, to sample the educational views of the faculty, the different teaching methods, the more important textbooks, and some of the course titles in order to see how the college generally charted its course at the turn of the century. Since academic areas had been departmentalized, the treatment follows the organizational lines established by the first administration. The college contained four major departments in 1893. These were supported by seven smaller sub-divisions. Agriculture, horticulture, chemistry, and physics each had departmental status, while mathematics, philosophy, psychology and ethics, natural science, English, literature, and history formed the lesser instructional units. The faculty approved a course of study based upon this organization in May. Later, Edward Clark and Frank Waugh requested each department chairman to turn into them a report containing course titles, class schedules, textbooks, points to be covered, and a description of teaching methods. This information was included in the 1894 catalog. This makes it possible to review with some degree of accuracy the earliest practices of the various departments.[16]

Alexander Magruder chaired the department of agriculture. He believed that both practical and theoretical instruction was necessary to turn out a well-rounded student. The first course in agriculture came during the sophomore year. It stressed animal husbandry, particularly methods of dairying. The course also touched upon "farm drainage; surface and subsoil drains; hillside ditching; terracing; action of flowing water; irrigation, and the duty of water." In the spring an advanced offering took pupils outside of the classroom to learn the use of the level, leveling rod, and drainage tools. Seniors concentrated on farm economy, natural and artificial manures, treatment of alkali soils, the work of the Department of Agriculture, state experiment stations, and foreign farm practices. The upperclassmen were taken on a tour of the territory to observe "crops, location of dwellings, barn, sheds, pastures, fields, and water supplies."[17]

Horticultural studies were supervised by Professor Frank Waugh. He conducted two terms of classwork and *practicum*. Freshmen received an overview of the subject as well as specific information on large and small fruits, vitaculture, forestry, landscaping, and vegetable gardening from L. H. Bailey's *Talks Afield: About Plants* (Boston: Houghton, Mifflin and Company, 1885). Men and women were formed into separate classes during the junior year. The former were taught how to apply the principles of horticulture to the climate and geography of Oklahoma, while the latter studied such parts of the fruit and vegetable cultures as seemed best to suit their future needs as homemakers. Waugh offered to design special courses for advanced students. All of his pupils were encouraged to plan and execute original work.[18]

George Holter of the chemistry department felt that standards were important and he hoped to make his organization "second to none in the college." The Harris Chemistry Series and C. Remigius Fresenius's *Manual of Qualitative Chemical Analysis* (New York: Wiley and Company, 1897) served as texts. Holter attempted to imbed the "facts" of these books into the minds of his classes by insisting upon the necessity of thought, frequent recitations, and periodic examinations. The same standards prevailed in the laboratory. He admonished his charges with these words: "The work accomplished must be work well done, and an analysis nearly right is an analysis not at all right. When a student is given a sample containing four elements, these four elements must be found, and only these, no more, no less." Both students and instructor appear to have taken the subject seriously. Tot Walker became so engrossed in an experiment in 1899 that she inhaled too much ammonia hydrate and passed out at her table in the laboratory. Later, Professor Holter breathed too much hydrogen sulfide and fainted in front of the entire class. The usual remedy for such accidents was to carry the student or the teacher to the open window. The fresh air brought the victim back to consciousness. Then class continued. "Uncle George" also presided over the department of physics. He used Joel Dorman Steele's *New Popular Physics* (New York: Barnes Publishing Company, 1887) to provide instruction in motion, force, energy, matter, changes in matter, sound, heat, light, electricity, and dynamics.[19]

Instruction in the natural sciences included classes in entomology, botany, geology, zoology, and meteorology—all of which were taught by James Neal. Alpheus Spring Packard's *Entomology for Beginners: For Young Folks, Fruitgrowers, Farmers, and Gardeners* (New York: Holt Publishing Company, 1888) was used to acquire general concepts. The students then directed their attention to local problems, for Neal believed that "no science is of more value to the farmer than practical entomology, since in most cases his success depends upon the extent to which his crops suffer from insect ravages." The accompanying *practicum* consisted of collecting samples and devising chemical formulas to eradicate insects. Geology classes used J. LeConte's *Compend of Geology* (New York: Appleton Publishing Company, 1884). Lectures and recitations were the usual method of covering the material but field trips were scheduled in order to observe rock formations in the state. The instructor devised his course to "make observers rather than mere book scientists." Botany, however, was Neal's favorite course. Here he paid less attention to application and more to theory. The Aggies were expected to master C. E. Bessey's *Elements of Botany* (New York: Holt Publishing Company, 1884) and then move on to the series published by Asa Gray. Germination and decay, physiology, and the structure of plants received emphasis.[20]

Philosophy and psychology were given only passing attention. The inclusion of these courses under one departmental heading should remind one that psychology was once more a philosophical discourse than a behavorial science. Robert Barker handled such instruction for the "itinerant college." He believed these subjects should be taught inductively,

no theory or doctrine being urged for acceptance which is not based upon a philosophical induction. The student is taught to subject every statement of fact or principle to the test of his own experience. A full and free discussion of opposing views is encouraged. Recent research in physiological psychology receives special attention.[21]

Professor Clark taught the four year sequence in mathematics. Trained as a classicist, he thought that the purpose of such instruction was to "secure full possession of the leading principles and methods, to exhibit practical applications, and to lead the student to form accurate and precise methods of thinking." The books written by Joseph Ray were used to study inequalities, indeterminate equations, series, and logarithms. Clark employed E. Wentworth's *New Plane and Solid Geometry* (Boston: Ginn Publishing Company, 1888) for the study of geometry. Here some attempt was made to understand the application and utility of the mathematical sciences. Trigonometry and surveying were introduced in the senior year.[22]

Professor W. W. Hutto supervised the teaching of the English language, English literature, history, and constitutional law for the college. He used several textbooks for English, including T. W. Harvey's *Elementary Grammar and Composition* (Cincinnati: Van Antwerp Publishing Company, 1880), Adams Sherman Hill's *Principles of Rhetoric and Their Application* (New York: Harper Publishing Company, 1885), William Swinton's *New World Analysis* (New York: Ivison Publishing Company, 1888), and V. Waddy's *Elements of Composition and Rhetoric* (Cincinnati: Van Antwerp Publishing Company, 1890). Freshman concentrated upon the construction of sentences and the history of their native tongue. The junior year brought work in the area of explanation, argument, laws of mind and languages, and literary criticism. The classics were introduced during the senior year in a capstone course. English *practicum* consisted of public orations, usually held in conjunction with chapel exercises or graduation ceremonies.[23]

History students used W. Swinton's *Condensed History of the United States* (New York: Ivison Publishing Company, 1878). Research, however, served as the heart of the course. Students selected individual topics for investigation and then proceeded to the library where they developed hypotheses from the facts they sorted out from dusty documents. Hutto regarded constitutional law as the practical aspect of history. His course on this subject provided an acquaintanceship with both federal and state laws, especially as they pertained to the governance of Oklahoma.[24]

The author of the catalog for 1896-1897 summed up faculty attitudes toward pedagogical techniques. He explained:

Varying in detail with the nature of the subject, there is a combination of the use of text and reference books, lectures, laboratory work, library research, with oral and written reviews. It is the attempt, while avoiding educational 'fads,' to make use of the best methods of teaching, a leading feature of which is an insistence on the subject's seeing, handling, working with things and subjects rather than simply reading or being lectured to about them. Greater importance is attached to securing right methods of study, training for the best use of such methods in the future, and acquiring the knowledge of where and how to find information than to the accumulation of a mass of facts[25]

It is difficult, if not impossible, to assess what constitutes good teaching, and to guage the effect of instruction upon students. Nevertheless, it should be pointed out that a number of the early graduates did go on to distinguished careers. Businessmen, bankers, lawyers, politicians, and school teachers were abundant. Several became university professors and one even went on to a college presidency. Others pursued graduate work at other institutions. Andrew Caudell, an Indian, enrolled at the Massachusetts Agricultural College; Oscar Morris studied at Cornell, later joining the faculty; Frank Griener stood at the head of his class at Pennsylvania State; Lewis Miller entered the Yale School of Forestry; Cora Miltimore took a special library course at the University of Kansas; and George Stiles received his Doctor of Philosophy degree from Johns Hopkins. He afterwards assisted Harvey K. Wiley in rewriting the nation's laws governing the packaging, manufacture, and sale of food and drugs.[26] Wiley was so impressed with Stiles— and several others who worked under him—that he told Angelo Scott in 1905 that "you either have an exceedingly strong department of chemistry here or exceedingly bright men as students."[27] While such data is not conclusive evidence of quality, it does suggest that some Oklahoma A. and M. College students could compete with graduates of other institutions on an even keel.

Engineering did not receive departmental status in Stillwater until 1908. This discipline should have merited more attention earlier as it constitutes one of the nation's most impressive educational success stories. The West Point Academy pioneered the subject in the United States because men like Henry Knox and Alexander Hamilton realized that warfare was changing. They felt that if the country wanted to be secure, it would have to train artillery and fortification officers the equal of those being turned out at Woolrich in England and Ecole Militaire in France. President Jefferson signed the bill making the garrison at West Point a national academy. He also appointed Jonathan Williams to be the first superintendent. One of this man's students, Alden Partridge, left the institution in 1817 to develop Norwich University in Vermont. From 1819 to 1900 his school graduated around 550 engineers. These men literally changed the face of America by constructing innumerable bridges, canals, mines, railroads, and telegraph and telephone lines. The Van Rensselaer Institute, the Sheffield and Lawrence Scientific Schools, and the Massachusetts Institute of Technology aided in developing the subject as an academic discipline. The land-grant colleges, after the passage of the Morrill Act, popularized engineering as a field of study for the masses.[28]

George Morrow hired R. E. Chandler to head an engineering sub-division the year before he retired as president. In September, 1898, twelve male students reported for class in the newly constructed mechanical arts shop that the college valued at $10,000. While the catalog stated that the course was purely mechanical in nature, it, in reality, also contained the basic elements of electrical. As elsewhere, the program proved both popular and profitable. One hundred twenty two people graduated by 1912, holding degrees in the architectual, civil, electrical, and mechanical fields. These men secured positions in almost every state in the Union as well as Hawaii, Japan, the Philippine Islands, Mexico, and Russia. President Morrow's successor stated in 1903 that the demand for engineering graduates could not be filled, implying that program should be extended further.[29]

The engineering course initially took a back seat to agriculture, and it was not until 1927 that the number of engineers in a graduating class exceeded the number of graduates in agriculture. New faculty, such as Walter E. Rowe, took a major step forward when they directed the program toward rural technological problems. This pleased many students, for they were reluctant to study farming but they wanted to get into something that was not wholly unrelated to it. Enrollments reflected the growing interest in the discipline. The majors in the division increased over twelvefold from 1898 to 1914. The regents enlarged physical facilities to keep pace. The Board authorized the construction of an engineering hall in 1902, expanded it in 1906, and built a completely new building in 1912.[30]

Professor Chandler defined engineering as "the art of directing the great sources of power in nature for the use and convenience of man . . . . at a minimum outlay of materials and energy."[31] Majors pursued many of the same courses as other students did in the mornings. In the afternoons, however, they took *practicums* in blacksmith, electrical, lathe machine, and woodworking shops. Sometimes, as in 1900, the Aggies repaired discarded equipment—a road grader in this instance—and then used the machinery to gain practical experience, such as beautifying the campus. The faculty required theses for graduation. The earliest remaining titles suggest that a broad range of topics received exploration in the classrooms and laboratories. R. Morton House discovered that high standards had to be complied with, as he came very close to not getting his degree in 1903 because of an incomplete in geometry.[32]

With the local and national demand for engineers exceeding the supply, the college found itself confronted with several pressing problems in 1904. First, legislative appropriations, as usual, were slow in coming. President Scott estimated that only $23,000 had been provided for engineering studies during the last six year period. The lack of funds became so acute that the faculty voted to eliminate the two year sub-collegiate course in mechanical arts. Second, informed people in Stillwater discovered that the University of Oklahoma had petitioned the Legislature for permission to offer engineering at Norman. Scott immediately wrote to Governor Tom Ferguson in Guthrie protesting this move as an "unnecessary and inadvisable duplication." He could not, however, block this development. Yet, in spite of these problems, the college scraped together enough money to improve its offerings, and graduates often left the campus with a higher salary than that paid to the faculty.[33]

Largely because of the stimulus caused by growth in engineering, the Oklahoma A. and M. College joined many of its sister state universities in developing a curriculum which included electives. While the administration did not have the staff nor the funds to offer degrees that did not have a common core, it still became possible to come up with major and minor programs. Both students and faculty welcomed the adoption of this innovation. The former could now tailor their course of study to meet individual interests; the latter were able to teach more classes in their respective specialties.

The first steps toward instituting electives were taken during the administration of Henry Alvord. He thought that students should be permitted to substitute one class for another, providing they could get the consent of the individual instructors involved as well as the faculty as a whole. The first record of such activity is found in the "Minutes of the First Faculty" for September 25, 1894. On this date, the faculty permitted Arthur Adams to choose something in place of agriculture.[34] Within two years the practice became commonplace. In 1896, a newspaper reporter predicted: "It is about certain now that in future years elective courses will be provided for the students of the Junior and Senior classes."[35] Apparently he had inside information, for five days later the faculty issued a directive which stated that juniors henceforth could choose their own course of study. During the first term, the student could either take analytical chemistry, general history, chemistry, or botany; the second term electives included descriptive chemistry, general history, chemistry, or botany; the third term choices were horticulture, veterinary science, mechanics, botany, comparative anatomy, or zoology.[36]

Because of certain abuses, the instructors decided to create a standardized policy to govern the elective system. President George Morrow, George Holter, and Freeman Miller were formed into a committee in May, 1896, to investigate the situation and to make recommendations to the faculty. Their report suggested that a student could not: (1) take an elective unless he had all the necessary prerequisites; (2) enroll in an elective unless his classroom and *practicum* registration totaled more than twelve hours per week; (3) choose an elective until he agreed to carry the subject to its logical conclusion; and (4) select his own schedule if the entire faculty did not approve. Finally, the committee stated that the system could only operate so long as it did not place an unnecessary burden upon the instructional staff. The report was adopted, unanimously.[37]

In 1897, the faculty broadened the elective system so that it encompassed the senior year, too. This meant that if a student decided to major in chemistry at the end of his sophomore year, he had to stay with that subject until graduation. Exceptions to this rule could only come from the faculty as a whole. More controls were added the next year. Students were no longer permitted to choose commercial work, music, typewriting, or shorthand as a major.[38] And finally, the campus newspaper reported in 1900 that the course of study is so arranged that only "the work of the freshman year is the same for all."[39] The age of specialization had arrived.

The students and staff found many ways to broaden the curriculum prescribed by the First Territorial Legislature. Student organizations, and expanded library, guest lecturers, chapel services, and a variety of visual teaching aids enriched the instructional program. Of these, the improvement of the library was probably the most important step forward. Under the watchful eye of Freeman Miller, it became a viable part of the institution even though located in a cubbyhole in Old Central. In 1894, the book shelves contained about 1600 volumes as well as copies of most of the major Oklahoma newspapers. Jessie Thatcher became Miller's assistant in 1897. She helped to catalog 2,500 new acquisitions that had to be filed in the stacks.[40] At the close of the territorial period, a writer estimated that there were 43,000 items housed in the library, including 13,000 bound volumes. He also stated that the

books are kept in fire-proof stack rooms, and the general reading room of the college is immediately adjoining. In this room are kept all of the chief current magazines, representative metropolitan newspapers, and the leading and many of the local newspapers of Oklahoma, dictionaries, encyclopedias, and other books of ready reference, historical, literary, and scientific.[41]

The library then, as later, received excellent value for the dollars invested by the state.

Chapel services played an important role in molding the character of the institution during the "itinerant years." But with the construction of Old Central in 1894, this activity assumed a more secular nature, causing a gradual decline in prestige. Cadets frequently used the early morning worship hour for mischievous pranks. One time a president found a human skeleton sitting in his chair. A cow greeted the sleepy-eyed students as they entered for prayer on another occasion. Perhaps the most unforgettable incident related to the placing of some chemicals in the ventilation system. These materials combined with the warm air in a shaft and produced such an offensive odor that services had to be canceled. Members of the faculty also contributed some humorous moments. James Hastings recalled that one "purely political appointee aspired to shine all the time. He thought that he should be permitted to lead convocation and did, but he did not know the Lord's Prayer. So one of the good sort would sit behind him and coach him quietly when he came to a halt."[42]

Chapel began to take on the atmosphere of a high school assembly during the administration of George Morrow. Professor Scott, for example, often used this time for short lectures on English grammar. In addition, visitors were permitted to use this period. This custom dates back to the Alvord tenure. He instituted the first regularly scheduled lecture series on the campus. Speakers included the Reverend R. B. Foster, Bishop Robert Brooke, Mary E. Lease, Alfred True, Champ Clark, and Robert McIntyre. The topics covered ranged from Populism to fun on the farm. Being isolated from the main stream of American educational thought and practice, the lecture series informed as well as entertained.[43]

Music played an integral part in the life of the frontier college. Since it was not initially included in the curriculum, the students had to assume responsibility for this activity themselves. The Sigma Literary Society, particularly, sought members who possessed musical talent. This organization purchased an organ and sheet music on their own. The Webster Debating Club followed suit by buying several horns. These and other instruments were used to play such popular melodies as "After the Ball is Over"; "Sweet Bunch of Daisies"; and "Pride of the Ball." The literary societies created an interest in music and had much to do with getting the subject added to the regular course of study.[44]

The college as well as the preparatory school employed visual aids and laboratory equipment in their classes. In addition to the usual books, charts, and maps, the institution used some of its federal subsidy to obtain grain and animal papiermache and plaster of paris models. One simulation of a horse cost $920. Fifteen microscopes valued at $1,100 were received in the same shipment, adding substantially to the six which the institution already owned.[45] Holdings in this area became so extensive that Major Alvord wrote to Washington that "this college has now in use an equipment greater in variety and cost than all the other educational institutions of Oklahoma combined, higher in grade than the district school."[46]

The library, the series of lectures presented by local and national personalities, the informational chapel services, the music programs, and the instructional aids all enhanced the curriculum, making campus life more interesting and more bearable. The disproportionately high number of college professors and public school teachers turned out by the Oklahoma A. and M. College suggests that the faculty gave creditable and stimulating performances in the classroom and that many students therefore wanted to imitate them. The old was not forgotten, but it was the departure from the classical curriculum that brought the masses to Stillwater. The mystique of science and the hope for good jobs guaranteed increased enrollments each year. To the Aggies, the twentieth century promised to be a demanding and exciting age. There were hungry people in the world to be fed and modern cities to be built. Four years in the classroom and the laboratory seemed a small price to pay in order to share the challenge of the future. The new education did not lack for disciples.

VII THE PLOWBOYS AND BLACKSMITHS

The American university student in the past has not been the object of scholarly historical research.[1] This situation seems strange in view of the fact that so many of the nation's leaders, including political figures, even as far back as the colonial period have been college graduates. There are many reasons which account for the low esteem of students held by collegiate personnel and the general public, but the principal one probably is related to the concept of *in loco parentis,* a term that implies intellectual immaturity, the need for paternalistic supervision, and the belief that higher education should teach something more than just vocational skills or training in the professions. Largely because of this concept, then, the student has not been granted *Lernfreiheit* or been permitted a meaningful voice in the governance of our universities.[2] One contemporary writer believed that the lack of freedom to learn hurt the intellectual development of higher education in the United States. He explained: "The college in America could not become a marketplace of ideas so long as it regarded its students as both gullible and perverse."[3] But with few exceptions, the early classical and denominational colleges did not identify their students with the term scholar.

Land-grant institutions were a significant force in attacking the merits of *in loco parentis*. Since these organizations came into being to train young men and women to be investigators, patterned themselves after German rather than English university models, and often lacked schools of theology and law, their faculties were less concerned with moral training than were their classical cousins. In the case of the Oklahoma A. and M. College, the first students, particularly those of the preparatory department, received instruction in Christian ethics and what then was considered to be proper public conduct. But when scientific men gained control of the institution, the curricular stress in this area diminished. Gradually, the Aggies were permitted more intellectual freedom and given a voice in shaping the objectives of the college.

The campus life of the individuals who enrolled at A. and M. reflected the frontier environment from which they had so recently emerged. The students were poor in terms of dollars and cents and material possessions, often employed violence to settle personal disputes, fervently sought any type of entertainment, feared the twin pestilences of smallpox and typhoid, and possessed a high degree of courage and self-reliance. Yet, while the barbarism of the Oklahoma plains was almost always evident in the territorial period, the Aggies were able to overcome cultural limitations. Many acquired the skills and the intelligence needed to lead. The educational system to which they were exposed had deficiencies, but it did help them to advance more quickly than through trial and error. The new education was of great importance insofar as the future was concerned; however, the transmission of culture proved beneficial to the present.

Most of the early students were recruited from Payne County and were less than fifteen years of age on the average.[4] As many of their parents, such as those of Alfred Edwin Jarrell, were barely making ends meet, the young men and women had to earn the money for their own personal and educational expenses. The cadets, besides working on the experiment station farm, accepted employment as dishwashers, maintenance men, clerks in the local stores, and almost anything else that could be obtained.[5] One somewhat typical student, a Swedish boy named Lewis Miller, assisted his widowed mother to run a hand laundry, served as a janitor at the college, and hired out as a handyman for a local church over a six year period in order to secure the funds needed to complete his degree program. When he graduated, Miller stated in his senior oration: "And now, we go out to face the stern realities of life."[6] This comment amused a local citizen who believed the lad had faced hardships as severe as he would ever encounter. Later, Lewis attended the Yale School of Forestry and eventually became a section chief under Gifford Pinchot in Washington.[7] The Aggies did not seen to mind the difficulties that had to be endured. Frank Rector, a contemporary of Lewis Miller who also became a government bureaucrat, wrote that "to those of us who were privileged to get our first taste of higher education in the new institutions in the raw territories there was implanted a restlessness and zeal for the acquiring of knowledge that has persisted throughout our lives."[8]

One method of saving money utilized by the students involved the forming of boarding clubs. The college itself barely had enough space for classes and equipment, much less excess funds with which to provide dormitories and cafeterias. Students, consequently, had to locate their own accommodations. A few lived at home, some rented rooms from local residents, and one ingenious and hardy soul even occupied the bell tower of Old Central. Private clubs helped to alleviate such extreme conditions and offered food and lodging at well below the going rate. The College Boarding Club, which was simply a large plain structure owned by a local businessman, contained twenty-two rooms. The Aggies rented the building, employed a cook to prepare meals, and paid classmates to serve as waiters. In this manner as much as one dollar per week could be shaved from previous expenditures. The administration of the college maintained no control over such organizations.[9]

Procedures for disciplinary measures varied from president to president. The faculty, however, took a strong intermediate role as the institution was much too young and too poorly endowed to afford the luxury of a nonteaching dean to regulate behavior on the campus. The military system of discipline used for preparatory students under Robert Barker applied to collegians, too. Henry Alvord lessened the severity of the rules during his administration but demerits continued to be used for minor infractions. The faculty handled more serious breaches on an individual basis, with the president held responsible for the execution of correctional measures. According to the "Minutes of the First Faculty," offenses ranging from drunkenness, "improper behavior" between the sexes, chicken stealing, eating peanuts in class, insubordination, pranks turned sour, and other such items.

With many students living close to the subsistence level, it was not unusual for the Aggies to leave the campus for a part of the academic year. In addition to homesickness, scholastic failures, and discouragement, disciplinary measures increased the drop-out rate.[10] One contrite young man, who had been expelled for accumulating fifty demerits in one term, realized that he had not made the most of the opportunity given him. He wrote to Freeman Miller: "Well, Prof, I'll treat you professors right and you do me the same. Trust me with a loose rein, but if I try to bust the sinch. Sock the rall to me rights." Then, perhaps to evidence that a change of heart had occurred, he added: "I should like to talk with you on some certain subject that is on some ancient religion and the Bible. I don't want to become a peddler of the Gospel, but I want to study languages and don't know the meaning of some whole chapters. They seem like a myth."[11] The college readmitted this student. He became the manager of the John Slack Boarding Club.

The austere surroundings often led students to devise pranks to break the monotony of campus life. Some of the attempts to add spice to the humdrum existence brought trouble. One recorded incident relates to the wedding of Professor George Holter. The chemist and Mable Hodges were married on November, 1894, at St. Andrews Episcopal Church. The bride seemed particularly vulnerable in that she was the daughter of W. J. Hodges, the recognized social leader of Stillwater. About a week after the ceremony, several male students wheeled an old cannon to the front of the teacher's home, loaded it to the muzzle, and then discharged the vintage weapon. The concussion was so great that it not only aroused the young couple from sleep, but it also shattered every window in the house. In class the next morning, the bridegroom demanded that the guilty culprits dig into their pockets in order to produce enough cash to repair the broken window panes.[12]

The frontier students lived close to death. Both disease and human violence took tragic tolls. One male returned to the campus from his Christmas vacation in 1900 infected with smallpox. He recovered, but classes from January 23 to February 6 had to be discontinued so as to prevent the infection of his classmates. Another student's bout with typhoid ended more sadly. Ross V. Taylor, one of the most popular men on the campus, came down with the dreaded fever while he was visiting his parents in Ohio. He shared his last wish with his parents just before he died. He requested that he be "brought back to his fellow students, and for them all to meet him at the end of the journey."[13] College cadets met the incoming train and provided their friend with an escort to the local cemetery.

Not all of the early student deaths can be attributed to natural causes. Just a short time before the cannon escapade, Max Stubblefield, who lived at the James Bruce residence in the College Addition, was shot above the right eye. His roommate had purchased a rusty pistol which accidentally projected a bullet in the direction of Stubblefield. The missile lodged in the brain, where a local physician said it would have to remain. The boy's parents took him back with them to Lincoln County. After a long recuperative period it seemed as if he might recover. Max clerked at a Chandler store and subsequently returned to classes at the Central State Normal School. One month later, however, death knocked again, and this time would not be denied. President Edmond Murdaugh personally accompanied the lifeless body back home.[14]

The relationship between the college students and their youthful city counterparts led to violence, too. The list of items which provoked trouble included a shortage of girls, poorly lighted streets, band concerts on the intersection of Ninth and Main, a lack of spending money, and the absence of recreational facilities for teenaged youths. Numerous battles took place between the two factions before an incident occurred which served to cool inflamed tempers.

The local boys found a champion in the presence of a large muscular Negro lad. This individual, not being able to distinguish between college students and those of Stillwater, would ask males if they were a "boomerah." If someone answered in the affirmative, he immediately was told to defend himself. Ill-feelings mounted until one cadet was pushed through the window of a Main Street butcher shop. Thereafter, a more sensible atmosphere prevailed. On the other hand, friction between town and gown never completely subsided.[15]

Collegiate life produced a spirit of *camaraderie*. Classes on the first day of each new academic year brought joy as well as sorrow because some former friends were found and others were not. Furthermore, those in attendance often sought to lessen the ideological differences which separated them. A college essayist, for instance, believed churches should discard their narrow sectarianism and unite in a new religious organization that might be titled: "The United Brethren Church."[16] Romantic bonds between males and females also formed. Norris "Gib" Gilbert evidenced that such relationships existed when he penned the following lines in the *Autograph Book* of Willa Adams. He wrote:

> May the names of those who love you
> Whose hearts are true and kind,
> When you are in life's twilight
> Rest gently on your mind.[17]

And they did. Miss Adams returned to the campus almost fifty years later and she compiled the history of the literary society to which she had belonged. This task brought back many reminiscences of her undergraduate years.

Although it is impossible to pinpoint a specific date, the college campus eventually became a world unto itself. A community came into being which may be called the collegiate way. Pep rallies, modes of dress, dating customs, and many other things became institutionalized and prescribed certain forms of behavior. New students, in order to gain acceptance into this youthful society, had to conform or else they were forced to remain apart from the center of student activity. This style of living which resulted often set the standard for one's future conduct. In addition, the collegiate way influenced intellectual development. For example, the bull sessions held in rooms and in local recreational establishments often supplied the means to adjust the social ideas dispensed in the classroom to an actual life situation. The importance of these aspects of collegiate life should not be underestimated. It is entirely possible that peer group associations stimulated more behavioral change than anything else at the institution.

Edward Everett Dale, the frontier historian, believes that the origins of literary societies have been lost in the "mists of antiquity." In the prairie West, however, he thinks that the development of such organizations stemmed from the Friday afternoon exercises of rural schools.[18] Parents, on this day of the week, frequently visited classes, a situation which produced a good deal of restlessness on the part of the students. "During this period the children eagerly anticipated two entire days of freedom . . . . and the teacher with nerves worn to a frazzle by the week's hard work was nearly certain to be jumpy, over-critical, and acutely sensitive."[19] Classes, therefore, were often suspended and a "literary" held instead. These meetings not only solved the Friday afternoon problem but they also created an informal adult education program.

Many of the students who enrolled at the Oklahoma A. and M. College had attended common schools in the West. In addition, some of the faculty, such as Robert Barker, Harry Thompson, and Edward Clark, had taught in public schools. Both students and faculty, therefore, probably were instrumental in bringing the literary society to the college campus. In January, 1892, less than a month after the beginning of classes, the faculty granted a charter to the Star-Crescent Literary Society. The precise details are not available, but the organization seems to have had a twofold purpose. First, and perhaps most important, it provided entertainment for both students and residents of the community. The society became so popular that nearly every member of the preparatory school joined. The group selected "Ad Astra per Aspera" as a motto.[20] Second, the Star-Crescent provided a forum by which students could discuss the burning social issues of the day. What is thought to be the first program involved a debate among Earl Myers, Phede Shearer, Julian Murphy, and Lille Emmons. The topic for this meeting has not been preserved; however, a subsequent one held in April centered upon the movement to grant women the right to vote. In June, the boys of the first class held a surprise box supper social for the girls. The students made an attempt to reorganize the next year. But for some reason the effort met with little success.[21]

The literary societies which were founded after the demise of the Star-Crescent Club should not be associated with Greek letter fraternities and sororities. The students believed such organizations were undemocratic and should be banned from the campuses of land-grant colleges. Instead, the societies filled gaps in the curriculum, stimulated intellectual growth, promoted social contact between the sexes, and provided practice in debate and oratory. The latter skills were among the most important learned at college, because before television and radio they provided much entertainment. Then too, political leadership depended, in part, upon one's ability to communicate with the masses. Consider, for example, the eminence of the Fourth of July speech in rural communities. It was the local State of the Union address and an event not to be missed if one could possibly help it. Consequently, membership in a literary society was considered prestigious and a sign that a particular student had leadership potential.[22]

On October 16, 1893, the male collegiate students met at the Methodist Episcopal Church to discuss the formation of a new literary society. "Gib" Lewis and Alfred Jarrell presided. After much discussion, it was decided to petition the faculty for permission to charter a club to be called the Webster Debating Society. Presumably, the name referred to the oratorical talents of Daniel Webster, who had preceded William Jennings Bryan as being the most prominent speaker of his time. Fourteen males, upon gaining preliminary approval from the appropriate faculty committee, met again the following week to draft a constitution and elect officers. The personable Frank Waugh received the majority of presidential votes. This instance is the only record of direct faculty participation in any of the activities of the literary societies. As long as the students followed the procedures outlined in their constitution, they were usually free to conduct business without interference.[23]

The constitution of the Webster Society, as students usually referred to it, stated that the purpose of the club was to strengthen the membership in debating, general literature, and social development. To this end, the weekly gatherings were to consist of a calling of the roll, a reading of the previous minutes, the initiation of new members, a business session, a debate, the report of the debate critic, and the formulation of plans for the next meeting. Professor Holter had insisted on such systematic procedures, for he did not trust the students to be entirely on their own without supervision. He regarded the constitution the same as a college regulation and it therefore had to be adhered to without deviation.[24]

Faculty restrictions lessened with the passage of time but the society remained essentially a debating club. The weekly resolutions covered a wide variety of topics, with popular ones being frequently repeated. Most of the subjects fell into five major categories, namely: (1) educational; (2) historical; (3) political; (4) philosophical; and (5) social. The close correlation to current coursework is obvious, suggesting perhaps that the students were not always permitted a free and full discussion of controversial subjects in class. A listing of some representative titles follows:

Educational

1. November 18, 1893: Resolved that a student should choose his profession before entering college. Negative decision.
2. February 10, 1894: Resolved that the study of mathematics is of more use than the study of English. Affirmative decision.
3. January 12, 1895: Resolved that the studies of the classes of the college should be set back one year. Affirmative decision.
4. September 28, 1895: Resolved that training is more the object of education than information. Affirmative decision.

Historical

1. November 25, 1893: Resolved that Washington deserves more credit for defending his country than does Columbus for discovering it. Affirmative decision.
2. January 6, 1894: Resolved that Arnold should not have been deprived of his command at the time he was. Affirmative decision.

3. January 19, 1895: Resolved that the character of Napoleon should be admired. No decision recorded.
4. February 29, 1896: Resolved that the warrior has done more for civilization than the statesman. Affirmative decision.
5. April 7, 1896: Resolved that the feudal system was favorable to civilization. Affirmative decision.

Philosophical

1. October 28, 1893: Resolved that there is more pleasure in pursuit than in possession. No decision recorded.
2. January 20, 1894: Resolved that curiosity will lead a man further than necessity will drive him. Negative decision.
3. February 24, 1894: Resolved that country life is better than town life. Affirmative decision.
4. November 2, 1895: Resolved that there is more happiness in the savage than in the civilized state. Affirmative decision.

Political

1. January 13, 1894: Resolved that Oklahoma now should be admitted as a state. Affirmative decision.
2. January 27, 1894: Resolved that the Queen of Hawaii should be returned to her throne. Negative decision.
3. March 10, 1894: Resolved that the Chinese laborer should be excluded from the United States. Affirmative decision.
4. November 3, 1894: Resolved that the Government should own and control the railroads of the United States. Affirmative decision.
5. February 15, 1896: Resolved that the national banking system of the United States should be abolished. Affirmative decision.

Social

1. May 26, 1894: Resolved that poverty causes more crime than ignorance. Affirmative decision.
2. October 13, 1894: Resolved that capital punishment is justifiable. Affirmative decision.
3. January 5, 1895: Resolved that Indians have received worse treatment by the whites than the Negro. Affirmative decision.
4. November 4 1895: Resolved that the lawyers have proved a curse on the country, and are not necessary under our present state of civilization. Affirmative decision.[25]

Student critics judged the debates and rendered a verdict. The decisions listed at the end of each topic above should not be taken as representative of the thinking of the entire student body, however. Willa Adams, who occasionally served as a critic, has written: "I see by the [Sigma] minutes that I was appointed a judge a few times, and I am wondering just upon what I based my decision, whether on the strength of the arguments, or on my personal preference or feeling toward debaters."[26] V. Williams, one of Willa's classmates, added in a newspaper article entitled "An Unloved Friend" that the critics were accused of having personal biases and sometimes were unpopular as the result of their decisions. The essayist reminded his readers that every person could benefit from criticism, whether it came from professor, literary critic, family, or classmate. In conclusion, Williams said that while the debate itself was important as far as judging was concerned, incorrect speech, rude manners, imperfections in morals, uncultivated tastes, and general ignorance were other items that needed to be considered in rendering a verdict.[27]

The Sigma Literary Society became the third group to receive a charter from the faculty. Maggie Hutto and Elsie Parker, perhaps feeling left out because the Websters excluded females from membership, approached President Barker in October, 1893, in regard to the possibility of establishing another organization. The executive did not appear sympathetic to the idea, but Professor Waugh, who was also in the room, assisted the girls by posing leading questions and prompting the type of responses that led to the presentation of a convincing case. Grudgingly, Barker gave his qualified approval.[28]

The Sigmas held their first formal meeting on October 20, 1893. They selected as their motto the phrase previously used by the Star-Crescent Society. Then nine male and female students assumed the task of writing a constitution. Holter, the chairman of the faculty committee on literary societies, announced three days later that the document had been completed. Some objections, however, must have been voiced because it was three weeks before the instructional staff as a whole accepted the instrument. This delay probably involved redrafting the constitution so that it coincided more closely with that of the Websters. When completed, the document stated that the objectives of the association included oratory, general literature, and the promotion of fellowship.[29]

In spite of constitutional similarities, the two organizations were markedly different. First, the Sigma membership consisted of both men and women, thereby providing more opportunities for dating, an activity that had been popular at frontier literary society meetings. Second, the programs of the co-educational group emphasized music. In fact, Miss Katie Neal composed an official song entitled "The Sigma Waltz." Third, the last group to be chartered had much more variety than its other campus counterpart. A typical program included: (1) opening music, usually a vocal solo; (2) a calling of the roll; (3) a declamation; (4) a dramatic reading; (5) more music; (6) a debate; (7) practice in extemporaneous speaking; (8) drill in parliamentary procedure; (9) a reading of the minutes of the previous meeting; (10) the report of the critic; (11) general criticisms from the audience; and (12) assignments of future responsibilities.[30]

With the two groups competing for new members and community approval, it was inevitable, perhaps, that rivalry should develop. The first recorded instance of hostility occurred in 1893, when a joint debate ended in a Sigma victory. The men walked away complaining that they had not understood the ground rules. James Adams rationalized: "The Webster speakers had prepared for long arguments, and, when, the chairman limited them to ten minutes each, they were not prepared to concentrate their remarks and consequently lost the debate."[31] To evidence their resentment, the all-male society passed a motion which instructed their secretary "to inform the Sigmas that they did not desire another joint meeting."[32]

Petty bickering turned into serious trouble in 1896. The societies—contrary to regulations—voted at the beginning of the academic year to purchase organizational badges to be worn on member's clothing. By November competition had grown more pronounced with open malice becoming evident. The specific event which produced conflict was a special Thanksgiving program scheduled to be held in the Methodist Church. Each of the organizations had applied for faculty permission to hold a holiday session, but the Sigmas received approval, because this group had canceled a previous meeting so that the teaching staff could hold its annual reception. On the designated evening, someone wired the contacts of the buzzer system together. The bell began to ring just as Norris Gilbert rose to introduce the topic for debate. The Sigmas blamed the Websters for the interruption.[33]

The hostilities continued. At the request of the faculty, the students scheduled a joint program for Friday evening, December 4. But before the meeting could begin, a fist fight developed among several young men, with some receiving severe bruises and cuts.[34] A *Gazette* news item revealed that the controversy had reached the public, for the paper reported: "There is quite an ill-feeling between the two college literary societies, that has caused quite a disturbance for the past few weeks, we hope that this will be overcome, and that the societies will work in harmony with each other."[35] A reconciliation, however, did not come about. Toward the end of the academic year, the Sigmas stole some refreshments of the Websters; in turn, the latter group "spiked" a bushel of Sigma apples with quinine and cayenne peppers. The year came to a close with tempers at a boiling point, a situation which prompted Professor Holter's committee to conduct a lengthy investigation.[36]

The faculty interrogated the membership of the two literary societies and suspended nine male students for a three week period. The refusal of the Aggies to inform on each other irritated Holter's committee to the point where it ordered both societies disbanded. The membership, at least in the case of the Sigmas, met once more to divide among themselves the funds that remained in the treasury. The last meeting must have been a sad occasion, because five decades later one girl remembered almost every detail of what had taken place on the evening in question.[37] Unable to meet on campus, the literary clubs, though not under the same names, went underground. The collegiate administration discovered one that met in an upstairs room of the Payne County Bank. Another investigation ensued, with the faculty subsequently publishing an open letter which explained the relationship of the students to the college. In part, the communication read: "It is the sense of the Faculty that the students of this institution are under the control of the

104

Faculty from the time they enter College until their connection therewith is severed by withdrawal, suspension, expulsion, or graduation."[38]

But in spite of the stern tone of the announcement, the college did permit new societies to be formed in the future. The Omega Society formed next and it had a continuous existence until 1905. The College Legislature Club, the Alpha Society, the Young Ladies' Society, the Philomathian Society, and the Social Club followed. Nevertheless, the demise of the Webster Debating Club and the Sigma Literary Society marked the end of the heyday of such organizations at Oklahoma A. and M. In place of them, the students formed discipline clubs, a further sign of specialization. The bias toward sororities and fraternities gradually decreased, too. The Aggies, then, created local chapters of national organizations in rapid succession.[39]

In general, the literary societies helped in many ways to color and shape campus life. One specific contribution which continues to the present day is the development of a college newspaper. Because of a lack of money and the absence of a printing press, the earliest editions were handwritten. Later, club dues, subscription fees, faculty contributions, and advertising revenues were combined to produce a published paper. *The Oklahoma A. and M. College Mirror,* the predecessor of the *College Paper,* the *Orange and Black,* the *Progressive Agriculturalist,* the *Aggievator,* the *New Education,* and the *O'Collegian,* came out in 1895. The literary societies compiled notes and sent them anonymously to the editors of local newspapers before the advent of published papers. People, such as Charles Becker, received items signed: "No Man"; "Mirza"; "Vanquished"; "The Populist"; "G. A. S."; and "Pagoda." The owner of the *Gazette,* after receiving several barbed and biting columns, decided that future submissions would have to be signed with a name of a person currently enrolled. The students, therefore, decided to find another method of reporting campus events.[40]

The unpublished papers were designed to be read at the meetings of the literary societies. "The Riverside Review," edited by Willa Adams and an unnamed colleague, is an example of such a newspaper. The one remaining issue is numbered volume ten, number five, suggesting that it was a part of a regular series. The ten pages of news items were carefully inscribed on ruled tablet paper. Content of the make-shift weekly contained stories of both students and faculty. The issue in question carried the details of a coming engagement, the results of a particularly difficult chemistry examination, a condensation of a chapel address by Robert Barker, and several humorous happenings of the previous week. One of these items noted that Lieutenant Gilbert had given an improper military command in drill, resulting in his company marching over the top of him.[41]

In 1895, the year that the literary societies reached their zenith on the campus, the membership of the Sigmas and Websters formulated plans to publish their heretofore manuscript newspaper. Under the leadership of Jessie Thatcher, the news items for the first printed edition were gathered during the month of April.[42] Charles Becker of the *Gazette* instructed on lay-out and predicted that "the first issue of the 'Oklahoma A. and M. Mirror' will come out about May 13."[43] The *Mirror* arrived on schedule. The students distributed it just before commencement exercises. The paper contained general news stories, educational information, local gossip, notes of community affairs, and business advertisements. Of special interest to this study is the fact that many of the earlier issues of the *Mirror* carried historical reminiscenses. Thus, many gaps in the development of the college were filled.[44]

One factor which motivated the literary societies to publish their own paper was the national student newspaper exchange, a phenomenon which paralleled the rise of inexpensive urban dailies. High school, college, and university students, all eager to extoll the merits of their own institution, printed newspapers and magazines which dealt with the activities of their *alma mater*. Extra issues were mailed to any educational organization willing to reciprocate The Aggies at one point exchanged with over one hundred institutions scattered throughout the country, including organizations located in Arkansas, California, Massachusetts, Michigan, Nebraska, New York, and Pennsylvania. While it is not known how other members of the national exchange accepted the *Mirror,* the reviews in Oklahoma newspapers were quite complimentary.[45]

Among other things, the campus newspaper was designed to promote the mission of A. and M. and to popularize the new education within the state. An early editor said that though our

first purpose is to advance the best interest of our own institution, both at home and abroad, we want the teachers in the common and high schools to feel that in our columns they may find assistance and encouragement. To this end we cordially invite teachers and all others interested in educational matters to contribute their best thoughts, and aid us in making our paper more and more useful.[46]

Besides reprinting popular lectures, original compositions, and news of the land-grant movement, the editors published biographies of prominent scientists and literary figures. Portraits of Louis Agassiz, William Cullen Bryant, Charles Darwin, Robert Fulton, Asa Gray, Karl Wilhelm von Humboldt, Thomas H. Huxley, Nathaniel Hawthorne, Washington Irving, James Russell Lowell, Charles Lyell, Isaac Newton, Edgar Allan Poe, and John Greenleaf Whittier were carried in 1895-1896. The selection of these particular names is most interesting, for it reflects a change in emphasis at the college. Shortly afterwards, the institution modified its single degree program from science to science and literature. These articles, therefore, forecast the creation of a modern arts and science college.[47]

The first venture into the newspaper business ended in failure. In June, 1896, the editor sensed that the future looked bleak. He said we

have done the best we could with the means at our command. If we have done even a little to direct attention toward the institution, to educate people to proper understanding of what the institution is and of what our work is, to bring students to our institution and to increase its influence and power, we are satisfied.[48]

The paper, however, did not receive new life until September, 1897. It evidenced, then, considerable reorganization. First, the head of the department of English agreed to supervise the editing and lay-out work. Second, the faculty formed a committee under the direction of E. E. Bogue to assist with financial problems. More advertising was secured, but in the end, the professors usually had to apportion a deficit among themselves by donating in accordance with the amount of pay that they received from the state.[49]

The following year Angelo Scott found a solution to many of the problems which surrounded the publication of a student newspaper. He felt that high printing costs could be reduced if A. and M. had its own printing press.[50] Such machinery, too, could be used to publish experiment station bulletins, for costs had risen sharply due to "the unreasonably high prices charged for work done under the contract for printing made by the Territorial Legislature in 1897."[51] This move not only proved financially expedient, but it also provided the campus with hardware for a new vocational program. The existence of the press greatly aided the effort to improve the quality of their newspapers and it created an interest in professional journalism as well.

Collegiate athletics, either intramural or extramural, received little attention during the founding years. With no campus, a meager budget, a scarcity of nearby institutions with which to compete, and the absence of a railroad for rapid transportation, this omission is understandable. James Adams described the extent of athletic activities in these words:

The athletic sports, outside of an occasional game of football, and some talk about baseball, were all concentrated and merged into one day—Washington's birthday. The sports consisted of a game of football, a foot race, sack race, three-legged race, potato race, pie-eating race, running jump, high jump, and a tug-of-war.[52]

Student interest gradually increased and by 1895 the men were quite vocal in support of an organized program. The *Mirror* said: "The continued talk about athletic sports in our college is becoming tiresome in the extreme."[53] While farm work at the college provided physical exercise and eliminated the need for an intramural program, the demand for extramural sports grew more intense.

Those who promoted intercollegiate athletic teams offered several arguments to support their position. Some believed the day was past when students should be associated with "glasses or . . . a scholarly hump on his back."[54] Instead, they pointed out, as did the author of an article entitled "The Value of Athletics," that the ancient Greeks thought "a strong and symmetrical body was necessary to perfect the development of the mind."[55] Another rationalized that there "seems to exist an intimate relation between vigorous athletics and the receptive powers of the mind; and that institution which leads in excellence of its games turns out the best prepared men mentally and physically."[56]

The Aggies found a somewhat unlikely champion in President Scott, a man who looked much like the public conception of a scholar. He, with the approval of the Board of Regents, constructed an athletic field which local people said was the finest such facility in the territory. Furthermore, Scott paved the way for A. and M. to join the Oklahoma Intercollegiate Athletic Conference and the Oklahoma Intercollegiate Oratorical Association, two agencies which scheduled simultaneous contests. Stillwater students fared well in both organizations, probably not deserving the "plowboy and blacksmith" nickname attached to them by their "tea-sipping" University of Oklahoma cousins.[57]

The initial athletic teams, like the literary societies, academic organizations, and boarding clubs, were self-supporting. The faculty, however, did appoint a standing committee to regulate sports. On February 2, 1904, this group set forth institutional policy in regard to student participation in intercollegiate athletics. The statement said that contests had to be cleared in advance, players who lived off-campus had to register with administrative officials when they traveled with the team to an away game, satisfactory grades had to be made in seventy-five per cent of the previous semester's work, missed classes had to be arranged for with the appropriate instructor, ineligible athletes had to be suspended from the team, and no one sport was to have a monopoly on engagements held in other communities. Last, the socials and dinners given by the student body to finance the various teams had to be approved in advance by a majority vote of the faculty.[58]

Football aroused the most enthusiasm on the campus.[59] Again, it was Scott who paved the way for the Aggies to form a team and to compete on an intercollegiate basis. His views on the subject were expressed to F. L. Shallabargar, a Guthrie stationed newspaper reporter for the *Kansas City Journal*. The executive wrote that the institution he headed favored the game without reserve, except that contestants had to preserve their standing in class. Scott then added that the occasional "accidents on the field are to be deplored, certainly; but even the elements of risk and danger I do not regard as an unmixed evil. Besides giving health and strength, the game develops self-reliance and courage."[60] Angelo Scott, a man who weighed less than a hundred pounds, and who always was in delicate health due to chronic insomnia and a childhood accident, became an avid fan. It was not unusual for him to faint on the grandstand floor during a particularly exciting contest.[61]

The college colors, orange and black, and the Tiger nickname were chosen by students in one of George Holter's classes. The selection of the Princeton standards most likely was a tribute to Harry E. Thompson, for his father had been a graduate of that institution. This association suggests, too, that land-grant colleges yearned at times for identification with established educational organizations. The Tigers of Oklahoma A. and M. wore their colors proudly in their first intercollegiate football contest, beating Kingfisher College by a score of 22 to 0. Both townspeople and students developed an intense interest in the sport. Special trains were chartered to away games after the railroad came to Stillwater in 1900. Besides having a formidable team during the early years, the Aggies won a reputation for gentlemanly play.

The first meeting of the University of Oklahoma and the Oklahoma A. and M. College football teams occurred in 1904 at Island Park in South Guthrie. The gridiron rivalry between these two institutions has generated much enjoyment for fans and provided many exciting stories for newspaper writers and sportscasters. The most famous touchdown, however, in almost three-quarters of a century of competition, came during the initial contest. On the fourth play of the game, O. P. Callahan, of Stillwater, punted from his own goal line. The ball went up in the air rather than downfield. The wind caught the pigskin and it finally landed behind the A. and M. goal line in Cottonwood Creek. A Norman and Stillwater player both started to wade into the water, when the former remembered that he could not swim. He ducked his opponent's head while a fellow player retrieved the ball after a ten yard swim and made a touchdown. This score remains the strangest of the series. Stillwater lost the game to Norman, setting a pattern which extended far into the future. It was not until World War I that the Aggies finally bested their bitterest adversary.[62]

The athletic teams of the late territorial era consistently were of high quality. One of the most memorable moments in the athletic history of A. and M. occurred on May 23, 1900. The literary and track teams combined to score a double victory to bring the prized Douglas Cup to Stillwater on a permanent basis. Alice Jenkins placed first in the Oklahoma Intercollegiate Oratorical Association contest with a speech entitled "Ideals." The thinclads defeated the Edmond Normal School, the Kingfisher College, and the University of Oklahoma for the track championship. Since the victory was the second in a row for Stillwater, A. and M. was entitled to keep the trophy donated by a Guthrie jeweler. The University of Oklahoma disputed the claim to permanent possession, because one event had to be canceled on account of darkness. Yet, the title stood.[63]

The increased emphasis on athletics, particularly football, generated campus controversy in 1901. Miss Lila Nelson in November forwarded an article called "One View of Football" to the editor of the *College Paper*. In her essay she maintained that the game should be banned as it endangered life and limb, was too violent to be healthful, and cultivated a rough and unsympathetic spirit among the students.[64] Such a statement, of course, could not go unheeded for long. R. H. Kerr submitted a counter-position in the form of a discourse entitled "A Defense of Football." Kerr admitted that serious injuries had occurred in the past but he believed that Americans by nature were a people who enjoyed competitive sports. In fact, the article concluded, it was competition that had made America great. Because of it, the flag of the United States currently flew halfway around the world, and the nation had never suffered a military defeat. Kerr ended his essay by stating that Chancellor Otto Von Bismarck had said that two-thirds of the German university students "die young as a direct result of their college course."[65] This statement implied that football was not as destructive physically as scholarship.

In conclusion, it is important to note that the earliest athletic programs were self-supporting. Both federal and state funds were preserved for the institution's primary mission. As better equipment became available to protect the health of the combatants, the opposition to football and other contact sports crumbled. The teams, in the end, had much to do with developing school spirit. Many chants and cheers reflect student and alumni interest. One favorite, the first school song, came from the pen of Angelo Scott. Set to rousing music, it proclaimed:

> Oh, we are the students of the O. A. M. C.
>   Ki Yi! Ki Ye!
> The wearers of the black and orange, we
>   Rip Zip! Hooray!
> We haven't any great excess of cash,
>   Yell O. A. M. C.
> And that's why we don't do anything rash,
>   O. K. L. A.
> Chorus.
> Ki Yi! Ki Ye! Rip Zip! Hooray!
>   Hooray! Hooray!
> Yell O. A. M. C.! O. K. L. A.!
>   O. K. L. A.![66]

The collegiate students of the Oklahoma A. and M. College measurably contributed to the institutionalization process. They, as some of their state leaders, envisioned the territorial college as a stepping stone to the construction of a mature university. While student organizations were unquestionably geared toward self-fulfillment, they also tried to enhance the image of their *alma mater*. The public performances of the literary societies evidenced to the community that culture as well as vocational skills had been acquired through the course of study. Moreover, the *Mirror* and the *College Paper* kept interested people abreast of educational developments. The athletic teams turned the eyes of more and more laymen to the institution and facilitated the expansion of the organization. Thus it may be concluded that the Aggies themselves had much to do with making the Oklahoma land-grant experience a successful one.

VIII ANGELO CYRUS SCOTT

Shortly before the Christmas vacation of 1898, Angelo Cyrus Scott, a founder and leading citizen of Oklahoma City, delivered a public lecture at the Oklahoma Agricultural and Mechanical College. Anticipating the resignation of a colleague in the near future, the faculty had extended this invitation in order personally to assess the talents of a man whom some people have regarded a "wonder of the frontier" and *the* cultural leader of the territory.[1] In addition, President George Morrow penned a note to Chancellor Francis Huntington Snow of the University of Kansas to check on the academic credentials of the speaker from Oklahoma City. The reply described the candidate in glowing terms. In part, it read:

Mr. Scott is one of the most highly respected and talented graduates of the University of Kansas. He has remarkable abilities and attainments of a literary character. He was at one time invited to become a member of the faculty at this University, but at the time, much to our disappointment, had other plans that could not be lightly set aside. I am thoroughly familiar with him . . . . I should consider your institution exceedingly fortunate to secure his services.[2]

111

On the basis of this favorable recommendation, an outstanding record of past accomplishments in the state of Kansas and in Oklahoma Territory, as well as the inspiring lecture delivered in the auditorium of Old Central, Scott was elected chairman of the department of English. He was appointed over a hundred or so other aspirants who had applied for the position from all parts of the nation.

While at Stillwater from 1898 to 1907, Scott gained a reputation as an exceptional teacher and lecturer, which on one occasion prompted the alumni magazine of his *alma mater* to ascribe him with near divine qualities, calling him a man who spoke with "tongues of men and angels." When Morrow retired during the summer of 1899, Scott became the unanimous choice of the Board of Regents for the college presidency. The executive used his varied talents to carry on the spirit of his predecessor's administration, and, as the fifth president of the Oklahoma A. and M. College, he developed an institution of considerable excellence sometimes referred to as the "Princeton of the Prairie."[3]

The selection of a man with the new president's background for an administrative position in a land-grant institution is, at this time, of especial significance, for unlike many of his counterparts, Dr. Scott was not an agriculturalist. Instead, he thought that state universities, which many of the older Morrill colleges had become, should play an important role in preparing citizens to participate in the nation's democratic political system and in shaping the environment for the welfare of the general public. Scott, therefore, qualifies as one of those unsung land-grant educators of the late nineteenth century whose pen and tongue paved the way for popular acceptance of the reforms of the Progressive Era.[4]

In the 1890's, the agricultural experiment stations attached to land-grant colleges and universities were responsible, as has been mentioned, for initiating the most far-reaching educational innovations of the day. As the empirically trained investigators brought data from their laboratories to the classrooms, they had to devise new courses and teaching methods to convey the results of their research to students. Preparatory schools, extension courses, short term winter institutes, and station bulletins carried reforms to the public. Visionary college presidents, however, also aided in the process of modernizing institutions of higher education. Following the lead of his predecessors, Angelo Scott moved the college one more major step. He dreamed of constructing a multi-purpose state university.[5]

In spite of some of his later statements, it is debatable whether Justin Morrill knew specifically what he wanted to accomplish when he introduced the Land-Grant Act of 1862. If he did, there certainly were many of his early devotees who possessed different ideas on the subject. But by the decade before the turn of the century, a general consensus was aborning in the minds of educators as to what the proper goals of a state agricultural and mechanical college should be.[6] Even the father of the movement began to reflect this unanimity, for in a speech given to the students of the

Massachusetts Agricultural College in 1887, the twenty-fifth anniversary of the legislation in question, he said that the objective of his bill was to open the doors of such colleges to the masses by being close at hand and to offer the people a liberal education. "It would be a mistake to suppose that it was intended that every student should become either a farmer or mechanic," he continued, "when the design comprehended not only instruction for those who hold the plow or follow a trade, but such instruction as any person might need - and without the exclusion of those who might adhere to the classics."[7]

President Scott concurred. He adopted the same view, however, for altogether a different reason. He had found it difficult to persuade students to enroll in agricultural courses. Farmer's sons and daughters did not want to attend college to learn how to plow. Neither did their parents desire them to. Farming, they thought, particularly in these depression years, was hard, unglamorous, and often unprofitable; thus the elder generation preferred their offspring to pursue loftier goals.[8]

In 1907, the president consented to being interviewed by Miss Blanche Little, a young lady who later became a close friend of the Scott family. The results of this conversation were published in the *School Journal,* a popular educational magazine of the day. Fully aware that his administration would come to an end when Oklahoma Territory became a state, the educator spoke frankly. He said that many people thought of the Stillwater institution as a place where they "farmed some and carried on high school work."[9] Such an image made it difficult for him to implement the late nineteenth century concept of what a Morrill college should be. Consequently, the executive declared that he would like to see the name of the institution changed to Oklahoma State College, thus broadening its appeal and its acceptance by the public.

The revamped organization should have a curriculum which would emphasize both the liberal arts and sciences, as well as develop a probing mind. Speaking at the dedication of a Carnegie Library in Oklahoma, President Scott recalled for his audience Thomas Carlyle's famous statement that a university was a collection of books. Then he explained why this definition was somewhat dated. He said "We have moved away from the day of Carlyle. With the coming of Science into the Kingdom of learning, the preeminence of books is challenged by the microscope, the spectroscope, the theodolite, and the chemical reagent, and the university which does not number these and a hundred other handmaids of Science . . . is poor indeed."[10] Also, an institution had to guard against training students to be mere technicians of science. "I believe." Dr. Scott said in another speech, "the narrowly trained mind is apt to remain narrow, while the broadly trained mind, if used right, is certain to grow and expand . . . ."[11] The former skills could best be learned in the laboratory, but the latter was to be derived from a study of literature, history, philosophy, science, and law.

The educational views of the fifth president were mirrored in the many academic changes he pioneered at Stillwater. As early as 1900, Scott, in his first biennial report to the Board of Regents, declared that a Bachelor of Science degree could now be obtained in six areas, including (1) general science and literature; (2) agriculture, also embracing studies concentrating in horticulture and veterinary science; (3) mechanical and electrical engineering; (4) chemistry; (5) botany; and (6) biology. Furthermore, students could elect to enroll in other courses, such as foreign language and typewriting; however, a degree would not be granted for such pursuits.[12] This curricula, which was far removed from the single prescribed agricultural course outlined by the Legislature in 1890, Scott explained in a speech entitled "The Place of the College of Agriculture and Mechanical Arts in the School System of the State," made A. and M. a "college in the highest sense of the word - a part of that new educational movement which professes that 'higher education may and should render a broader service to humanity' than was formerly possible bringing the trained mind and hand, and modern science, to the help of human industry . . . ."[13]

A short time later, the president and the faculty cooperated in raising entrance requirements and reducing the "practical" agricultural course to the sub-collegiate level. The latter step was viewed as a move to give elementary farming information to boys who would return to the family homestead, thereby clearing the way for teaching to become more scientific. In the area of entrance examinations, the subjects in which tests were administered remained the same, but a student reporter stated that the faculty became so zealous in preparing these tests that the questions were submitted to the whole body for consultation and review. In 1903, for the first time in the college's history, some students—perhaps as many as fifty—were not permitted to enroll because of academic deficiencies.[14] In addition, the senior colleague of the faculty stated that a "discriminative tuition fee of five dollars a term or fifteen dollars a year, upon students entering from other states . . . ." was applied.[15]

There were, of course, some dangers attached to these innovations. With increasing enrollments coming at last, the institution had to depend more and more upon the Legislature for appropriations. The day was passing when federal subsidies were enough to finance the institution. If a decrease in enrollment had occurred, the organization might have suffered a serious economic reversal. But just the opposite happened, for by the end of the Scott administration in 1908, the student body had passed the thousand mark, as compared to about two hundred when the executive took office. The educator expanded the geographical area from which students were recruited, too. The year before these changes took place, the regents were informed that young men and women from Illinois, Indian Territory, Indiana, Iowa, Kansas, Missouri, New Mexico, North Carolina, Oklahoma Territory, Pennsylvania, and one foreign country attended the A. and M. College.[16]

Not content just to initiate new programs, President Scott determined to meet the public to explain and defend the increasing services of the institution. He stumped the territory, making hundreds of speeches to Chautauqua gatherings, farmer's organizations, womens' clubs, religious meetings, and various kinds of local and state governmental functions. Each success, large or small, inspired him to devote more of his energy toward championing the cause of the new education. He pointed out in a newspaper article in 1903 that he was disposed to "work day and night for the upbuilding of the institution and for the welfare of the students . . . ."[17] Regardless of these efforts, however, this aspect of his administration met with only partial success, for increased state appropriations to meet the needs of a growing student body and a more diversified curriculum were still difficult to obtain.

As might be expected, the educational views of Angelo Scott were accepted more readily by the students of the college than by the public. Nevertheless, the president diligently did the necessary spadework required to bring about popular support on the campus. Reared in a rural community, and being a devout Calvinist of the Presbyterian variety, a type of background which many of the later progressives shared,[18] the administrator fervently sought to create a college and community environment where cultural and intellectual activity could thrive. After Scott's death, his wife stated that it was in this effort her husband had been most successful.[19]

While he was president, the executive manifested an interest in both the mental and physical needs of his students. Each academic year was opened with an expression of personal concern for those individuals left in his care. A typical speech came at the beginning of the 1902-1903 term. The students were warned of the twin perils associated with leaving home and entering the collegiate way. "The first," he explained, "is the peril to achievement . . . the second to character." Expanding on the former, the speaker suggested that five evenings per week be spent studying, for upon "no other plan of procedure can you hope to accomplish what you are here to do." Referring to the latter peril, Scott encouraged the selection of the right kind of friends. "Above all, don't get the idea," he further admonished, "that it is an unmanly thing to lead a straight, clean and decent life. It is the manliest thing in the world, and the best."[20]

A simultaneous effort was initiated to create what the president thought would be a more suitable environment in the surrounding community. Scott supported the establishment of a town band, directed several operettas, participated in the meetings of the local school board, provided leadership for a variety of religious organizations, and loaned faculty members to the community in times of crises, such as when L. L. Lewis cooperated with the county health department to curtail a small pox epidemic. These activities led Scott to believe that he had a vested interest in Stillwater and that he could denounce things that he did not like. In 1903, for example, armed with a Temperance speech over ninety pages long, he spoke at length to a group of townspeople on the "evils" of liquor and gambling. These conditions, he explained, were particularly prevalent in this frontier community, thereby presenting temptations to his students. Finally, the diminutive man accused city officials of being in league with the unlawful elements. To buttress his point, he urged them to sue him for slander if he had pointed his finger unjustly. No known court contest ensued.[21]

Scott's numerous speeches were often spiced with personal examples to illustrate that a college education was worth whatever a poor farm boy or girl might have to sacrifice for it. On one occasion, he explained some of the difficulties he and William Allen White had in working their way through the University of Kansas. Scott concluded his presentation by telling how he had stretched his own meager food budget as a student. He said:

I had the pleasure of cooking my own food and washing my own dishes through a large part of my college course . . . and I tell you it is perfectly amazing how well and cheaply one can live on oatmeal and soupbones. Why, the evolution of a soupbone is something wonderful - first the soup, and then the cold meat, and then the stew, and back to the soup again. I tell you, there's food for reflection in a soupbone.[22]

Knowing that many of the Aggies were attending the institution on borrowed money, the president tried to help them find jobs so that they could pay back their benefactors and save enough money to launch their careers, which often meant that they had to leave Oklahoma. The Legislature, in 1905, was requested to permit the A. and M. college to share the teacher training function of the Edmond Normal School so that students could obtain teaching certificates. A measure granting such a request received approval in the Senate, but a student newspaper article reported the bill failed, for "the Normal School combination jumped sideways in the House, tore its hair, waved its arms, and killed the bill by a narrow margin."[23] Scott was successful, however, in securing a large number of the "scientific aid" scholarships established by the Department of Agriculture for graduate study in Washington, D. C., thereby eliminating the necessity for students to work before earning advanced degrees. Many of the individuals who received grants later achieved national attention for their work in testing the purity of manufactured foods and drugs.[24]

A number of incidents could be cited to indicate the closeness of Angelo Scott to his students. He helped them to get a printing press for their campus newspaper, championed the cause of intercollegiate athletic and debating teams, asked the Aggies not to address him as professor, retained confidences in spite of intense pressure from parents, and generally treated the "plowboys and blacksmiths" with genuine respect. He said at the time he left office that kindness wins more with students than severity, so he made the former his guiding star. His relationship with Vingie E. Roe serves as an example of his deep concern in this area.[25]

One day while reading the *Perkins Journal*, the president came across a poem entitled "The Flight of the Wolves." Scott, believing the writer had promise, wrote to his friend Congressman Victor Murdock, editor of the *Wichita Eagle*. He asked him to give the poem wider circulation by including it in a forthcoming edition of his newspaper. In addition, he sent a note to the young authoress, inviting her to come to the campus to study under him personally. Miss Roe came, but the combination of her genius and shyness did not blend well with the less mature student body. She soon left. Before her exit, however, the young girl spent many hours with her mentor, discussing with him the future literary career she envisioned for herself. Many of these conversations later evolved as plots for the thirty-one novels and numerous screenplays that she wrote. One of these, *The Great Trace* (1948) which is generally conceded to be Vingie Roe's best, she dedicated to the president.[26] The debt was also acknowledged in a letter to an Oklahoma historian. "Dear man. He believed," she said, "in the light, which was, in all truth, to be the one great flame of my life."[27]

Robert Henry Tucker, on the fiftieth anniversary of the Oklahoma A. and M. College, gave a detailed account of the institution's appearance in 1899, the year Angelo Scott took office. Tucker wrote that the campus contained two hundred acres, possessed one medium-sized building, several smaller less pretentious ones, and had a faculty of fourteen or fifteen to teach the two hundred students enrolled. When President Scott resigned in 1908, by contrast, the campus contained one thousand acres, while funds were received from the Second Morrill Act, the Hatch Act, the Adams Act, a territorial tax levy, and the Cherokee Strip leased land fund. Moreover, the educational organization received a 250,000 acre land-grant from the federal government. Physical facilities increased, too. A new agricultural building, a dairy structure, and an engineering hall had been added. Tucker, a former "vice-president" of A. and M., attributed these gains to the "fine leadership of President A. C. Scott, assisted by an energetic faculty . . . ."[28] This generalization is correct; however, it does not shed light upon the vital question that needs to be answered at this point: "What was the most important quality of Scott's leadership?"

Many midwestern agrarians in the late nineteenth century were suspicious of corporate business organizations and practices, probably because of the failure of the Alliance and Grange,[29] but Dr. Scott, a lawyer and businessman himself, belonged to a rural movement that from 1890 to 1920 took an important step in the process of forming an accommodation between the farmer and big business.[30] One immediate by-product, as far as the administration of the college is concerned, was for the executive to implement techniques of modern leadership, such as financial and personnel efficiency, long-range planning, and the recruitment of talent who could bring fresh ideas into the organization. In addition, Scott believed a spirit of cooperation should be developed among the administration, the Board of Regents, the faculty, the students, and the public at large. In short, the president was an organization man, and herein lies the secret of his term of office.[31]

At the time Professor Scott became associated with the college, his father and two brothers held important state and national posts, a situation which gave him a firm economic, political, and social base from which to operate. John Scott, the father, who by this time had reached an advanced age, sat in the Oklahoma House of Representatives, having run on a platform of promoting education in the territory. Because of his previous legislative experience in Kansas, he was highly esteemed in the eyes of his colleagues. Only an untimely death prevented him from rendering yeoman service to his educator son. William, a brother, also resided in the territory and published the influential *Oklahoma City Times* newspaper, which he and Angelo had started on May 9, 1899. Moreover, William was at one time a member of the Legislature himself. Both of these men were in a position to assist Angelo, and he quite often asked them to do so.[32]

Charles, the third son of John Scott, occupied an office which enabled him to render valuable service to his educator brother. As a regent for the University of Kansas, he was able to secure invitations for "Angie" to speak at Lawrence on noteworthy occasions. As a United States Representative from Kansas, he had been appointed to chair the committee on agriculture by the untidy, but colorful, "Uncle Joe" Cannon. Charles aided his brother directly when circumstances warranted. Other times, he introduced him to prominent Congressmen who helped him to make substantial gains for the institution he headed. Charles and Angelo were the closest of the three brothers. They kept in touch with each other by mail when they first left home, and after their careers started to rise, the summers were spent together at the Sprague Ranch or at the Scottage, both located in Estes Park, Colorado.[33]

Moreover, the presidential administration of our subject was enhanced by his own educational and occupational achievements. He received, as a youth, tutoring from his father and a retired Williams College mathematics professor. Deciding to attend the University of Kansas where John Scott served as a regent, Angelo graduated in 1873 as class valedictorian. Two years later the same institution conferred a Master of Arts degree on him. His LL.B and LL. M. came from the Columbia School of Law in 1884. Professional experience before his elevation to the A. and M. presidency included teaching in a common school and working as a legal clerk in Iola, Kansas. Scott then moved to Washington, where he became executive secretary to an ex-Kansas governor who served as state school land commissioner. Coming to Oklahoma in the Run of 1889, he opened a law office, helped to found the city that is now the state capital, published the first newspaper in Oklahoma City, became a United States Commissioner, sat in the Legislature, and chaired the Oklahoma World Columbian Exposition Committee. In 1892, the young man barely missed being appointed the second governor of the territory.[34]

The background of President Scott, along with his family connections, would have been enough to permit him to make significant progress at Stillwater. A conscientious Board of Regents and an extremely capable director of the Oklahoma Experiment Station contributed as well. The chairman of the Board, Frank Wikoff, who

118

had attended a land-grant college himself before obtaining a law degree from the University of Cincinnati, brought much practical knowledge about fiscal policy and Oklahoma politics to his office. John Fields, whom the president nominated to head the station, was a graduate of the Pennsylvania State College. There he had achieved considerable fame as the co-discoverer of tuberculosis in cattle, assisting Leonard Pierson.[35] Fields, Scott, and Wikoff labored as a team, and in the executive's own words became a "sort of sub-board of regents," taking over between regularly scheduled meetings.[36]

This trio set as a major goal the expansion and strengthening of the faculty. President Scott used his contacts in the academic world to secure the names of young scholars, and the Board of Regents found the funds needed to employ them. Scott's friendship, for example, with David Starr Jordan, with whom he vacationed in Colorado, resulted in the acquisition of Dr. Walter Shaw, a graduate of Stanford University. Edwin Mean Wilcox became the first holder of the doctorate from Harvard University to join the faculty. Other men migrated from the University of Chicago, John Hopkins University, the University of Maryland, and the University of Wisconsin. These men, combined with the professors previously recruited by George Morrow, composed a body of scholars who rivaled any other Morrill college in the vicinity. A new era had clearly dawned at Stillwater.[37]

Until the advent of the Scott administration, the largest source of income at the disposal of the college was the annual $25,000 provided by the federal government under the auspices of the Second Morrill Act. The so-called Granger Amendment, a provision of the bill in question, limited the expenditure of these funds to the payment of faculty salaries and the purchase of teaching apparatus. Consequently, the majority of the buildings on the campus were in a poor state of repair, students were stuffed into overcrowded classrooms, and office and laboratory space remained almost non-existent. An illustrative complaint came from the caustic pen of George Holter, who published the following remarks in the student newspaper:

I am supposed to have a recitation at 8 o'clock, four days each week. In order to do this, I must have heat. This morning my lecture room had the delightful temperature of 59 degrees. It is absolutely impossible for me to give chunks of wisdom at this temperature. I am religiously opposed to playing a game of 'freezeout' with students.[38]

Fully aware of such conditions, the collegiate administration began pressuring Payne County legislators for increased financial support. Senator Freeman Miller and Representative James Matthews, in addition to William Scott, answered the call, obtaining a three-tenths mill levy in 1901 and a four-tenth mill levy in 1902. These funds were earmarked for an expansive building program. Miller, the following year, got the Guthrie solons to provide an additional $54,000 but the governor vetoed the measure. He took the matter to court and succeeded in gaining a partial restoration of funds. It proved, however, a Pyrrhic victory. The leading territorial Democrats resented the manner in which the court decision was obtained; thus it became difficult, if not impossible, to secure more local legislative assistance at this time.[39]

The first noteworthy public criticism of the Scott administration came in the form of a scathing newspaper editorial published on January 16, 1903, in the *Stillwater Democrat*. The writer charged: (1) no members of the Democratic Party were on the Board of Regents; (2) members of the faculty who belonged to the Democratic Party were replaced as quickly as possible; (3) the president had campaigned for Republicans who were running for local and territorial offices; (4) members of the faculty were permitted to do the same; and (5) staff employees of the college and station had been released for "improper" voting behavior. The article concluded: "It is time that this prostitution of a great institution, this debasement of the greatest educational establishment of the territory should forever cease."[40] The following day, the *Gazette* contained an editorial which showed the absurdity of these charges. Later, President Scott denied the allegations, too, stating that he only knew the politics of one man on his staff and he was a Socialist. Nevertheless, the damage had been done. Oklahoma A. and M. returned, as in the founding years, into the rough-and-tumble of territorial politics.[41]

In 1905, the president concluded that without a powerful catalyst Oklahoma was no longer a fruitful place in which to seek funds for his building program. Although displeased with some federal officials, especially the United States Division of Forestry for what Scott considered undue meddling in state affairs, he and John Fields decided to seek the aid of the national Congress in Washington. These two made a trip to the capital under the guise of attending the annual meeting of the Association of American Agricultural Colleges and Experiment Stations. Contacting Scott's brother, the lobbyists identified three objectives. First, they wanted to get a law modified which Congressman Dennis Flynn had introduced sometime earlier in order to prevent the construction of new public buildings in Oklahoma until the territory became a state. Second, the duo hoped to obtain a larger portion of the Cherokee Strip leased land revenues. And finally, the visitors tried to get a section of school land which lay adjacent to the college campus ceded to the institution. It was a tall order, but one which Scott believed could be accomplished. Enlisting the support of Speaker Cannon and Senator Albert J. Beveridge for his cause, the president systematically visited each congressional committee that might be concerned with the bills he wanted approved. After five weeks of intensive groundwork, the measures were passed during the "unanimous consent" hour. Happily, the educator boarded a Baltimore and Ohio train for the return to Stillwater.[42]

Meanwhile, John Fields, who had earlier attended the land-grant college association meeting in Washington with his senior colleague, traveled to Guthrie in order to request that the Legislature appropriate money for the erection of a new building at the college and to improve certain designated facilities at the station. Succeeding in getting such bills introduced, he then turned his attention to soliciting the support of the Oklahoma Territorial Board of Agriculture for them. Since Fields had presented the general scheme of organization for this agency and Scott had courted the group from its creation, it was a relatively easy task to get a resolution approved which supported the requests.[43] The final draft read:

Resolved that the earnest efforts for the development and dissemination of accurate information concerning all lines of agriculture, on the part of the Oklahoma Agricultural and Mechanical College and Experiment Station are of the greatest importance to the future of Agriculture in Oklahoma, and that the needs of this institution as incorporated in the bills now before the Legislature (1) approximately $30,000.00 for the securing, improving, stocking, and equipping of the section of land recently granted by the Congress to the College, (2) appropriating $100,000.00 for the erection of an Agricultural building, additional shops, and a gynasium, and (3) amending the law for the free distribution of . . . vaccine [should be passed] . . . . With more than three-fifths of the people of Oklahoma engaged in Agricultural pursuits; expenditures for higher education along these lines in the Territory should, in some measure, bear a similar proportion to the total expenditure for higher education.[44]

This endorsement, however, had no immediate effect. In later years a plea from this agency would have received the prompt attention of the lawmakers. But, in 1905, the Board was not well organized and it lacked political power. Therefore, Fields and Scott had to devise other steps to win the votes necessary to pass their measures.

The two men now decided to hold an open house at the college, inviting members of the Legislature and friends of the institution personally to inspect the needs of the physical plant. On Friday, February 17, a chartered train brought four hundred people, including a large number of legislators, to Stillwater from the capital. The guests were treated to a colorful reception at the depot, served a luncheon prepared by the young ladies of the domestic economy department, and then seated for a round of speechmaking. Scott spoke last. He began: "I don't like lobbying. But when the mountain comes to Mahomet, it seems to me it is entirely fit and proper to place the claims of the Agricultural and Mechanical College before the Legislature . . . ."[45] An impassioned address followed. If a stanza of a student poem published in the campus newspaper is accurate, the president left nothing to chance, for he had coached the student body in advance when to applaud. The verse in question reads:

> And when he raid gymnasium
> My! How the boys did yell!
> You know he tole em to do that,
> (But den you musn't tell."[46]

Two months later the annual appropriations increased by $5,000, while twice that figure became available to pay the claims of those who had leases on the school land section. Approximately $92,000 was designated for the construction of an agricultural building.

John Fields dispatched an urgent letter to Professor Bailey of Cornell asking for the loan of a "set of plans and specifications of any building which your institution may have erected for similar purposes . . . ."[47] It seemed, on the surface, as if complete victory had been won.[48]

In reality, however, the passage of these bills further unified the Democratic opposition. The party had been forced to support Scott's program, because to oppose agricultural bills would have hurt the organization at the polls. But on the other hand, L. W. Baxter, the state auditor, and J. C. Strang, the state attorney general, refused to honor a voucher for the expenses of the Washington expedition, claiming that the expenditure of funds for advancing or advertising the interests of an educational institution was illegal.[49]

About the same time, an Oklahoma construction firm, Sherman and Kruger, contested the legality of the contract issued by the Board of Regents to O. A. Campbell and S. A. Layton to build Morrill Hall, the name to be given to the new agricultural structure. Kruger, who acted as spokesman for his firm, complained to Governor Tom Ferguson that his agency had the low estimate on the brick and iron contracts, but that other companies tried to bribe him so that he would not bid. In addition, he stated that the Campbell-Layton firm had been permitted to submit a second bid because a Stillwater banker, who also served on the Board, had informed the opposition that a small premium would be paid on the Oklahoma City warrants. Both the governor and the regents conducted investigations. These revealed that the protestor was correct; his bid had been nearly $5,000 lower than the one submitted initially by the Campbell-Layton Company. Consequently, Ferguson called for a meeting of all parties concerned on November 15, 1905.[50]

Kruger appeared at the hearing bearing nearly one hundred affadavits from merchants, bankers, businessmen, and reputable citizens who swore to his skill and good name. The Board seemed inclined to make the matter right, but the *Advance Democrat* concluded that "Dennis Flynn, the chief attorney for the Frisco Railroad and the Poobah of republican politics in Oklahoma, demanded that the contract be given to Campbell for party reasons; and the Board cringed and cowered before his orders like a set of whimpering puppies at a bear hunt."[51] The original contract stood. Rumors circulated, however, to the effect that $20,000 of the $78,000 amount was "velvet" and had been secretly returned to the trustees. The incident was not reported to President Theodore Roosevelt as some had threatened; however, the *Oklahoman* newspaper correctly asserted that there "is a packing house scent about the transaction that will not down, and some men in high places have fallen from the pedestal of popular esteem as a result of the affair."[52]

In spite of the personal embarrassment these charges must have caused the president, Scott remained an effective executive for the institution. He again returned to Washington in 1906 to make sure that, when statehood replaced territorial status, the Stillwater college would get the endowment to which it was entitled under the Land-Grant Act of 1862. But the educator discovered upon arriving at the nation's capital that President David Boyd and Henry Asp of the University of Oklahoma were there too. These men had found an antiquated statute dating back to 1850 "which provided land-grants to newly-formed states in lieu of swamp lands and for public improvements."[53] Scott now had to make a momentus decision. Should he join them, or should he go it alone?

The question proved to be a difficult one to resolve. Under the provisions of the Morrill Act of 1862, the Stillwater institution could certainly expect to receive no less than 210,000 acres of land. The alternative was to gamble, along with Asp and Boyd, and seek 40,000 acres more. After consulting with Senators Joseph Foraker and Chester Long, Scott elected to join forces with his fellow Sooners, for the Congressmen pointed out that the Morrill endowment would almost certainly have to be shared with the Negro institution at Langston. Subsequently, legislation granted 500,000 acres of land to the colleges in Norman and Stillwater. The leased lands were preserved as well. Scott regarded these measures as an "important step in the history of the college."[54] But upon returning to Oklahoma, the lobbyist sensed the winds of change. Little public attention was accorded his latest triumph for the institution. Instead, the populace seemed preoccupied with prospects for statehood; and with such a long awaited and exciting event in sight, sweeping changes in higher education were introduced and executed with little or no criticism. Every major college president in the state lost his position as well as a majority of the faculty.

The first significant change adopted by the Legislature was to reorganize the personnel and structure of the Oklahoma A. and M. College Board of Regents. On June 6, 1907, the Board of Agriculture assumed jurisdiction of all the agricultural colleges in the state. Governor Charles Haskell five months later appointed J. P. Conners, J. Roetzel, R. F. Wilson, D. N. Robb, G. T. Bryan, E. White, D. Diehl, R. S. Burns, J. C. Elliott, R. W. Lindsay, and S. D. Dennis to replace the existing governing body. The new members met on November 21 at the Royal Hotel in Guthrie, deciding to make a quick on-the-spot inspection of the institution in Stillwater. While the Board did not unduly interfere with the daily operation of the college on this visit, it did initiate some major financial changes. Unexpended funds, with the exception of a few thousand dollars, were removed from Frank Wikoff's bank. The monies that remained were henceforth to draw three per cent interest.

The reorganization of the Board of Regents also heralded a change in the collegiate administration. Not wanting to face the humiliation of being fired, Angelo Scott in late fall submitted his resignation. He asked, however, that it not take effect until June 30, 1908. The regents accepted the document as written. On January 22, 1908, the college committee of the Board of Agriculture interviewed three candidates for Scott's position. James H. Connell, the Dallas,

Texas editor of the *Farm and Ranch Magazine,* was elected president at an annual salary of $4,500, effective July 1. Scott graciously congratulated his successor and advised him that when the Legislature convened, the new man should be in attendance to safeguard the interests of the college, while the other individual remained in Stillwater to tend to routine academic affairs.[55] This suggestion was sound but it did not appreciably help the institution. William "Alfalfa Bill" Murray, who chaired the Constitutional Convention, had the matter of agricultural education well in hand. In the future, elementary schools, high schools, and most institutions of higher learning would all give instruction in practical agriculture. On the other hand, the concept of building a multi-purpose university at Stillwater received a major setback. This idea did not become effectively resurrected until Henry Bennett came to the helm of the organization in 1928.[56]

During the months of May and June, 1908, the outgoing administrator made several farewell speeches, each of which revived memories of his tenure as president. A curtain of gloom descended upon the campus in spite of the fact that graduation ceremonies, usually a happy event, would soon be held. The speaking engagements began with a talk at the annual Junior-Senior Banquet. Next came an address to the local chapters of the YMCA and YWCA. A special chapel symposium on the subject of "honor" followed. On the Monday before diplomas were distributed, the students gathered *en masse* outside of Morrill Hall, where the Board of Regents were holding a meeting. "We want President Scott," they shouted. The slender man left the business session and introduced his successor to the group. He ended his remarks by pointing to Connell, saying: "The King is dead, long live the King."[57] The next evening several husky athletes carried Scott on their shoulders to an athletic banquet. Prolonged applause, however, made speaking a useless endeavor.[58]

At commencement, Angelo Cyrus Scott delivered his last public message as president of Oklahoma A. and M. College. City newspaper reporters noted a peculiar silence and moist eyes on the part of many in the audience. Scott introduced James Connell who spoke on the value of intelligent labor and the need for universal education. The outgoing administrator then turned his attention to the assembled students. He ended his remarks by saying that the

choicest memory I take with me in leaving the A. and M. college is that of the friendship and the affectionate loyalty of its students . . . . Though this particular student body will pass beyond the walls of the institution, there is a certain symbolism about a college which one does not forget, and I am sure I shall never see your orange and black without also claiming it as mine, or hear your multitudinous yell without feeling moved to join in it.[59]

As Scott prepared to leave his office three weeks later, he typed a memorandum for posterity. He began this document by stating that he had been president for nine years, and that he had written ten to fifteen thousand letters concerning college business which he hoped had some good result on the state as well as the young men and women who had passed through the portals of the institution during his administration. He completed his thoughts with these words: "And so, with undiminished love for the college and best wishes for its prosperity and usefulness for all the years to come, I subscribe myself for the last time."[60]

Not long after the writer's departure, the *Gazette* predicted that most of the faculty, either voluntarily or involuntarily, would follow. They did, leaving on both scores. Nevertheless, the service educational philosophy and the exceptional administrative ability of the last territorial president of the Oklahoma A. and M. College measurably assisted in developing a state institution sensitive to the needs of the masses several years before the Progressive Movement hit its zenith. The emphasis on the "new education," the use of "causal scientific precepts" for the regulation of the frontier environment, and the implementation of the "gospel of efficiency" to motivate change all contributed to making the territory a better place in which to live. As such, the man and the institution, both of whom were ahead of their times in Oklahoma, deserve recognition for their contributions to society.[61]

Leaving Stillwater, the ex-president continued providing educational leadership for his adopted state. He immediately accepted an invitation to replace Vernon Louis Parrington at the University of Oklahoma, a person who had also felt the ire of the new political administration. But before the next academic year began, Scott accepted a counter offer to become dean of the Oklahoma City University graduate school. Later, he renewed this ties with the Norman institution and devoted the remainder of his ninety-two years to extension lecturing, writing textbooks and historical literature, and generally creating a more sophisticated cultural level in the state. Public recognition came late in life for Scott, yet numerous honors were accorded him in the twilight of his long career. On one of these future occasions, the alumni magazine of the University of Kansas pictured him as he most likely would want to have been remembered. Speaking of the individual who received the first distinguished service citation issued by Scott's *alma mater*, the writer said: "He looks like an actor; he would like to have been a preacher; he has been an editor, a lawyer, and a politician; he is a teacher."[62]

IX   THE PROGRESSIVE PERIOD

Both the educational and political progressivism of the first two decades of this century are difficult to define, for each were multi-faceted reform movements.[1] It is clear, however, that Oklahomans, who celebrated the coming of statehood just at the time when muck-rakers were questioning the viability of American institutions, be-lieved that a new age had arrived for them. An editorialist for the *Peoples Press* in November, 1907, joined the populace in faulting the federal government and the so-called "robber barons" for the lack of progress during the territorial period, saying that now the fairest of the French Territory will "assume the prerogative of self-government, from out of the cesspool of graft, incompetence, mis-rule, and the bondage of railroad masters onto the high plain of self-government, onto the mountain heights of full and complete citizenship."[2] In addition, the seventeen year statehood apprentice-ship created a bitterness toward urbanization and the industrial revolution as well as the federal government. J. P. Conners, of the

126

Board of Agriculture, certainly believed this way. He thought that Oklahoma's "Corn Field Lawyers" were the ones who could bring the region freedom through laws that would preserve the independence of the farmer class. Consequently, the people looked for a champion who could preserve Populism by using the reform techniques advocated by the leaders of the Progressive Movement.[3]

William Henry David Murray became this man. Born on the windswept plains of Texas, he hoped—in addition to political action—to bring the new era to the Sooner State by means of an educational system steeped in Agrarianism. Thus this rural evangelist, both a lawyer and a certified common school teacher, sponsored measures in the Constitutional Convention that (1) inaugurated an extensive farmers' institute program; (2) replaced the Board of Regents of the land-grant college in Stillwater with the Oklahoma Board of Agriculture; and (3) made instruction in agriculture, horticulture, animal husbandry, stock feeding, forestry, domestic science, roadbuilding, and rural economics mandatory in the public schools. Finally, the Democrat, according to his own written testimony, established five two-year agricultural and mechanical colleges in Lawton, Goodwell, Helena, Broken Arrow, and Tishomingo by intimidating a delegate to the Constitutional Convention who had passed a bad check in a poker game. These were institutions, it should be added, that "Alfalfa Bill' promptly named after cronies who had helped him get his platform enacted.[4] Nevertheless, the "Sage of Tishomingo" remained proud of his accomplishments, observing that "whatever errors or wrongs I have ever done, the destruction of Educational Institutions will never be charged against me."[5]

In shaping his reorganization of educational institutions in Oklahoma during the transition from territory to statehood, Murray relied heavily upon the advice of James H. Connell, a man with whom he had taught common school in Texas. Believing the Dallas editor to be the best scientific and practical agriculturalist that he had ever known, "Alfalfa Bill" asked Connell to draft plans for revamping the Board of Agriculture and for creating a statewide farmers' institute program. Murray was so pleased with these efforts that he named the new junior college at Helena after his friend, and upon the recommendation of John Fields, Frank Northup, and Ewers White, he worked to get James Connell appointed as the sixth president of the Oklahoma A. and M. College, a position that he held until 1914. Then Robert L. Williams became the chief executive of the state. This individual urged the release of Connell from his Stillwater post and in 1917 he abolished the school which Murray had named after him.[6]

In January and February, 1908, William Murray introduced President Connell to the Oklahoma populace, predicting that his leadership would do much toward bringing prosperity to the Sooner State. In Stillwater, he said that Connell was eminently qualified to head the land-grant college, and that "with his traveling over the state lecturing to farmers on how to grow crops, how to protect them from insects and how to feed their stock, he will earn for the state twenty times what any other officer or employee will do . . . ."[7] And in truth he did.[8] The institution, during the Connell administration, strengthened its regular academic programs, increased institute and short course offerings, organized numerous boys' and girls' agricultural clubs throughout the state, expanded enrollments and physical facilities, and multiplied the number of popular scientific bulletins published. These activities led to the development of one of the most extensive extension programs in the United States. This brought legislative appropriations in ever larger quantities. But uniform greatness, however, was delayed because of the state's political infighting.[9]

Mass education moved to the forefront of American life early in the twentieth century. The official newspaper of Oklahoma A. and M. College made much of the fact that Dr. Woodrow Wilson was the first professional educator to assume the national presidential office, and that he regularly called upon collegiate personnel for advice and counsel. The writer of one particular column dealing with this subject stated: "When recognition of this sort is coming to men whose claim to honor is based on merit of achievement, we then have reason to feel more security for the future of American democracy."[10] James Connell penned these words not just because he was a staunch Democrat, but because he believed Wilson's election would make it easier for land-grant institutions to extend their system of public service to the byways and hedges of his adopted state. He thought that A. N. Hume put the difference between pre- and post-Civil War higher education quite well in an article entitled "Making American Colleges More Useful by Improving Their Extension Work." The writer said: "The old idea of college and university administration is aristocratic, the new is democratic."[11] Both Connell and Wilson believed this statement to be true.

Before coming to Stillwater, the sixth president had achieved some national recognition. Connell, as a boy, had witnessed the laying of the cornerstone for the Mississippi Agricultural College. He enrolled at State College on October 31, 1884, listing his "nativity" as Macon, Mississippi, the place where his merchant guardian resided. Four years later Connell and his classmate Alexander Magruder received their Bachelor of Science degrees. The former man then joined the faculty of the University of Kentucky. Later, he acquired a regional reputation at Texas A. and M. College for his institute work and dairy experiments. Connell resigned his teaching position to become editor of the *Farm and Ranch Magazine*. This office enabled him to broaden his contacts and meet most of the important academic and governmental people associated with the land-grant college movement.[12]

The publisher's reputation as a lecturer in agriculture and a farm organizer preceded him to the campus. Both his ability to relate to "plain folk" as well as academicians had given him the distinction, according to William Murray, of having spoken on the campus of every Morrill institution in the United States. Moreover, Connell served many professional associations in an executive capacity, including the Association of American Agricultural Colleges and Experiment Stations, the Southern Cotton Growers Association, the American Association of Farmers' Institute Workers, and the Texas State Farmers' Congress. Temporarily appointed secretary of the Oklahoma Board of Agriculture while he waited for President Angelo Scott to complete the remainder of his last term of office, Connell found that he had so many invitations to speak at extension meetings and teachers' gatherings that he scarcely had time to add to the sixty farmers' institutes that existed in the territory before statehood.[13]

Though a good orator, the new executive repeated the same basic speech over and over again. He favored having boards of agriculture serve as regents so that a "practical" mission could be implemented in American land-grant colleges. Furthermore, he frequently cited the *Old Testament,* Martin Luther, and John Milton to illustrate for his audiences that labor—particularly agricultural labor—was a blessing, not a curse, to mankind. Finally, the Texan usually ended his addresses by attacking the cities for their low birth rate and high death rates, then showing that farms by contrast served as the breeding ground for all of the great civilizations and nations of the world. These themes, despite being simplistic, were what many people in Oklahoma wanted to hear.[14] A *Bristow Record* reporter in 1910 reflected general farmer reaction when he wrote after one of Connell's talks that if

Creek County could send a hundred boys each year to the Agricultural School it would mean more to the future of the county and state than the greatest oil field the mind could imagine. It would create more wealth - more lasting wealth - than a gold mine. A hundred boys graduating from A. and M. College in 1914 would mean at least seventy five educated farmers, the kind who wouldn't know a chattel mortgage if he met it in the road, and the kind who are buying automobiles.[15]

Notwithstanding the fact that President Connell headed an institution which now had to serve both of the territories that comprised the state of Oklahoma, he did not get the opportunity to attend to his daily administrative functions until December, 1908. He greeted incoming students on September 10, and then embarked upon an extensive travel itinerary. First, Ewers White, J. P. Conners, and Connell left late in September for a ten day inspection trip of several sister land-grant institutions in order to get firsthand information in regard to a projected expansion program. Ideas on this tour were garnered from personnel associated with Morrill institutions in Iowa, Minnesota, Kansas, and Wisconsin. Second, the president visited other educational organizations located in Illinois and Michigan. And last, in November, he attended national professional meetings in Washington, D. C. Armed with the data collected from these junkets, James Connell set about shaping the college to meet new objectives. He devised a plan which brought more students to Stillwater than to any other educational center in the state, and he implemented an extension system that made it possible for Oklahoma A. and M. to come into direct contact annually with more than 150,000 community residents. In short, the administrator wanted to make his institution the hub of Oklahoma life.[16]

Connell, in most respects, proved capable of dealing with the problems that stood in the way of accomplishing his goals. Although not as scholarly as Angelo Scott, he had a firsthand knowledge of the hardships related to the pioneer environment, recognized that the region had limited financial resources so that priorities had to be established, and correctly surmised that an inadequate communications and transportation system in the state would make his job exceptionally difficult. On the other hand, the educator had been endowed with the health, mentality, and personal stature to equip him for getting his program underway. His friend, Charles Evans, described him, in fact, as a man among men, being over "six feet in height, straight as an arrow, broad in shoulder and lithe of limb, and with large, fearless clear eyes . . . ."[17] Furthermore, he always appeared in public immaculately dressed, presenting such a commanding figure that most colleagues and associates found it easy to trust him and his judgment.

President Connell did have critics, however. Some individuals resented his making B. C. Pittuck, a foster son, dean and business manager of the state agricultural schools, and handpicking former friends, such as John Craig, to direct the affairs of the Oklahoma Experiment Station. Then, too, those members of the faculty who had worked for President Scott often expressed hostility, because a scholar had not been chosen for the vacant presidency. George Holter, who led this element, made absolutely no effort to hide his disgust. Professor H. G. Seldomridge once stated that he presided as toastmaster at a public function where both Connell and Holter were present. The former man gave the keynote address for the banquet, and when he had concluded, Holter, in a voice loud enough to be heard by all, said: "I feel like a man who has just buried his wife, and rides back from the cemetery with his mother-in-law."[18] Seldomridge believed the comment in bad taste, yet he also added that Connell could not have retained his position without political assistance.

Most of the faculty recruited in 1908 were of good quality, with one real gem in the person of Carl Gunderson, a Norwegian who had taken work at Leland Stanford and Columbia University. Other professors, such as W. P. Webber, University of Cincinnati; C. S. Bushnell, University of Chicago; William Lawrence, University of Indiana and Chicago; Hardee Chambliss, Virginia Military Institute, Vanderbilt University, and Johns Hopkins; Arlington P. Little, University of Vermont, and L. B. Rose, who had done work in Germany, also brought a wealth of teaching and research experience to the Stillwater campus. These men were loyal to both the college and the state. They had much to do with an announcement in 1912 which said that annual elections of faculty could now be dispensed with. Less frequent personnel changes enabled Connell to build a team that had both dedication and continuity of purpose. [19]

Initially, the student body enthusiastically supported the policies of the new administration. The executive left few stones unturned in an attempt to increase enrollment and to make life away from home as pleasant as possible. In 1908, the registrar processed nearly 800 fulltime students. This figure more than doubled by the time James Connell left office. A survey of application forms published in the *New Education* in September, 1913, evidences that inquiries for admittance had been received from practically every post office address in Oklahoma and that scattered requests for information were on file from many states. When classes started later in the month it was found that men and women from Arkansas, Texas, Kansas, Illinois, Iowa, South Carolina, and Missouri were in attendance. Even foreign countries, England and Russia, were represented.[20]

College officials tried to improve living conditions and develop an atmosphere where school spirit could increase. A newspaper columnist claimed that the Aggies condoned no artificial social distinctions, were loyal, and that each individual was as "eager to enroll new students in the various departments as to cheer their football squad on to victory."[21] Having mustered such support, the president persuaded the governing board to appropriate nearly $100,000 in order to erect the first collegiate dormitories in the state. The Women's Building, placed to the East of Morrill Hall, was designed to contain a living room, a gymnasium with plunge and shower, classrooms for domestic science courses, a kitchen, a reception hall, and eating facilities for approximately 160 students. When the Boy's Dormitory, located North of the Civil Engineering Building, was finished in 1911 it contained similar accommodations, except that the cadets shared eating facilities with the women. On occasion, an orchestra was hired to perform on the veranda during the meal. Both the dorms and the entertainment proved popular and more than one student wrote home that the institution was a pleasant place.[22]

Student clubs flourished during this period. President Connell recommended that boys and girls bring along a "church letter" when they left home so that they could enter into the religious life of the community. Also, he arranged with the registrar for students to pay YMCA and YWCA dues at the time they paid their regular activity fees. Faculty wives and community leaders supervised the college "Y" programs, which included both social meetings and intensive *Bible* study. Literary societies continued to exist but by this point much of the luster surrounding them had diminished. The Omega Society, established in 1906, developed to where two groups—one for males and one for females— had to be formed. Likewise, the popular Philomathean Society created an "A" and "B" division, both of which combined to sponsor the publication of the *Orange and Black,* the new campus newspaper. Debates still remained the predominant club activity, and each group tried to select an interesting topic for the Saturday evening meeting.[23]

A variety of social and discipline clubs were active from 1908 to 1914, suggesting that pluralism was becoming more and more evident. The Campus Club (Lahoma), supervised by the wives of Connell and Holter, was created to care for the needs of young girls who were away from home for the first time. Two years later ten females organized the Affinity Club. It hosted dances and generally fostered social contact among students. The agricultural, chemical, and engineering clubs continued to be the most stimulating discipline organizations. The Teachers Club formed by Dr. John Bowers, however, proved surprisingly strong. Finally, athletic, pep, and letter societies received charters in order to render support for sports programs.

A new social precedent was set in 1909 when the faculty gave its permission for the Delta Sigma fraternity to incorporate. Being the first of its kind on the campus, the organization began with seventeen male members on March, 1910 amid much fanfare and publicity. Both students and townspeople attended the dedication, bringing gifts that could be used to furnish the building located to the East of the college physical plant. Not only did this agency add another dimension to campus life, but it also promoted ties that encouraged lifelong interest in the university.[24]

As did his predecessor, Connell took an active interest in the economic welfare of his students. His first year in office he arranged for those individuals who could not afford tuition to take a free course in the industrial arts. The next year the Board of Agriculture was persuaded to allot $5,000 for student employment. People were paid to work in the dairy and stock barn, the print shop, the orchard, the garden, and on the construction of new buildings. The president also succeeded in getting Oklahoma railroad authorities to grant free transportation to and from short courses held in Stillwater as well as permitting college men and women to purchase roundtrip tickets from their homes to the school for about one and one-third of the normal fare. Moreover, the state passed legislation which granted a full scholarship to one male and one female from each Supreme Court district in Oklahoma.[25]

This concern brought student body support in times of crises. Two incidents stand out as especially important. First, Connell went directly to Governor Lee Cruce in an attempt to justify an annual college budget of $1,500,000 in 1911. This sum far superseded past allocations. The students, in appreciation for this effort, turned out *en masse* for an evening bonfire rally, cheering their leader for his tenacity.[26] Second, the editor of the *Orange and Black* assembled almost all of the student body in 1913 to protest charges by the Board of Regents that academic standards had deteriorated. The following resolution received unanimous passage.

We wish to state that class work has progressed in the last few years . . . .Our graduates are on equal footing with the graduates of other colleges throughout the Southwest. We further wish to state that no dissension exists in the student body. And still further, we, the students who have enrolled in the College for

132

from one to five years, believe that we fully understand the conditions existing at the present time and those that have existed for the past time mentioned, and feel that we can make the statement that actual records and statistics showing growth and improvement in both equipment and progress of all departments and phases of college work will show that the charges of incompetency and dissension are unfair . . . .[27]

Growing support made James Henry Connell an important educational figure in Oklahoma. In addition, his personal prestige elevated the presidential position of A. and M. to the point where it carried the second highest salary within the state. On the other hand, the increased stature of Connell caused him to play politics in order to launch an ambitious expansion program. Initially friendship with William Murray and close alignment to the Democratic Party worked to the advantage of the institution. But, in the end, it brought the Connell administration to a close. The power structure of the state was in the process of changing. The college profited from the arrangement at first but it later paid a high price for political involvement.

James Connell may be regarded as a builder by almost any criterion. Besides Gardiner and Crutchfield dormitories, he secured the funds with which to erect an engineering building, now called Gunderson Hall, that contained a $40,000 heating plant for the use of the college. Completion of this structure brought the number of permanent buildings on the campus to eight. An auditorium provided more space for large classes. Lesser construction included a cafeteria, a bookstore, several greenhouses, a livestock pavilion, a piggery, and a new barn. The president, in addition to enlarging the Stillwater complex, made numerous trips to the five feeder junior colleges to help the local administration to get these institutions off the ground.[28]

Curricular increases were more impressive. Taking advantage of new legislation, the college developed a teacher training department in 1908. Provisions were made the same year to offer a Master of Science degree with emphasis in agriculture, natural science, engineering, and domestic economy. R. O. Baird received the first of such awards for his advanced work in chemistry and bacteriology. Individuals who elected to do their graduate work study elsewhere, found, as reported by the *New Education* in 1913, that they could successfully compete against students in more prestigious universities. Undergraduates as of 1914 were able to choose classes from seven schools, including veterinary medicine, commerce and marketing, agriculture, engineering, domestic science, science and literature, and education.[29]

While significant progress occurred on the campus of Oklahoma A. and M., the extension activities of the institution soared almost beyond belief. But, before beginning a major push in this direction, President Connell plugged two weak spots. First, he hired E. J. Westbrook, a journalist, to take charge of the publishing and printing plant, because the "college was hardly known outside of the adjoining counties of Payne . . . ."[30] This was a sound move, and, besides regular duties, Westbrook published *The Orange and*

Black, the *Progressive Agriculturalist,* and *The New Education* newspapers. These carried accounts of the projected extension program throughout the state. The latter paper constituted the most successful of these journalistic ventures, for it eventually reached a bi-monthly circulation of over 50,000. Second, Connell attempted to strengthen the experiment station. He began by creating a summer Cotton Institute devoted to breeding, raising, and marketing this product in all its phases. Personally, the president opposed cotton farming in Oklahoma as it was injurious to the soil. But when production rose to almost 1,000,000 bales in 1910 he thought it best to help farmers learn how to raise the crop with the least damage. Next, the money needed to diversify the variety of stock owned by the farm was secured. The Legislature appropriated funds to add to the Shorthorn, Aberdeen, Angus, and Jersey cattle owned by the college in 1909. Additional stock came from prize herds in Iowa and Missouri. Dorset ewes and Shropshire lambs were imported from Scotland under the direction of Jim Craig. He promised to make Stillwater the center of sheep research in the nation.[31]

Simultaneously, a national move to upgrade the quality of rural life got underway. On May 28, 1908, Theodore Roosevelt spoke before a group of distinguished scientists assembled on the campus of the Michigan Agricultural College. He said: "If there is one lesson taught by history it is that the permanent greatness of any State must ultimately depend more on the character of its country population than any thing else."[32] A year later he asked Liberty Hyde Bailey to accept the chairmanship of the Commission on Country Life to explore the whole of rural society in America. This development set in motion an effort to improve the economic, political, and social life of the small independent farmer. The Oklahoma Boys' and Girls' Agricultural Clubs were formed with this thought in mind.

The Board of Agriculture and the Oklahoma A. and M. College, with guidance from John W. Wilkinson and Henrietta Kolshorn, designed what they called a junior agricultural program in 1910. Its stated purpose, according to the college catalog, was to (1) acquaint young people in the state system with industrial education; (2) vitalize studies in the common schools; (3) develop a system of education in elementary schools suited to the children of the common people; (4) lead boys and girls and men and women to study farm problems in their home communities; (5) give the people a sense of the importance of farm life; (6) inculcate class sentiment and a feeling of independence in the minds of farm children; and (7) organize the farm as a social unit for future generations. In conclusion, the framer of these objectives wrote: " In its broader sense it means to educate the hand, the eye and the heart, as well as the mind; to study things as well as books; to become a doer as well as a dreamer."[33]

Wilkinson, in an effort to get the project started, mailed organizational literature to the county school superintendents, the secretary of the Farmers' Institute, and the secretary of the local

134

womens' Institute Auxiliary. These announcements reported that five or more youngsters from nine to eighteen were needed to secure a charter and compete in the corn, cotton, bread, flower, vegetable, and sewing prize contests. Incentive for membership came from many sources. First, the Board of Agriculture offered seventy-five expense paid trips to meetings conducted by the district agricultural schools. Second, the college provided thirty-two full scholarships to subsidize attendance at an annual one week institute at Stillwater. Third, Senator T. P. Gore promised to bring to Washington the individual who raised the best corn with the highest yield. Last, the state fair committee extended an additional $700 cash award to a winner in the same category.[34] Governor Lee Cruce added his support to the junior program by sending a public letter to President Connell, stating that he wanted most heartily to "endorse the movement inaugurated in this state for the purpose of developing among the girls and boys of Oklahoma, a stronger inclination toward agricultural pursuits."[35]

It had been expected that these organizations would grow, but membership mushroomed far beyond even the most optimistic predictions. From 539 the first year, the number multiplied to 30,517 in 1913, with the participation divided among thirty-eight counties and 1,200 clubs. Prizes the latter year totaled more than $5,000. And, even more impressive, the circulation of *The New Education,* which eventually became the chief instrument for communication with local chapters, steadily climbed to the point where 120,000 issues were mailed to subscribers each year. Then, too, agricultural correspondence courses for high school students and teachers in 1913 increased 150 per cent over the previous twelve month period. Even public school literary societies caught the spirit. It was suggested that every fourth Friday evening be devoted to the reading of papers pertaining to farm life.[36]

Concurrent with the establishment of the agricultural youth clubs, the college initiated a series of two and six-day Summer Encampment Schools, called Chautauquas in a Tent, in Adair, Choctaw, Kiowa and Kingfisher counties. These programs were usually conducted in the open but other facilities were employed as they became available. At Pauls Valley, for instance, a county judge felt the idea so important that he adjourned "taking the jury and witnesses and attorneys to some other room so the school could be conducted in the district court room."[37] Lectures for these meetings usually concerned "farm crops and soils, marketing, dairying, and husbandry including poultry, veterinary science, and insects and silos."[38] All activities were offered without charge. Evening movies assured a good crowd. Projectors were placed on the floor of a wagon and focused on a curtain or sheet stretched between two trees. Attendance ranged from 500 to 1,500, leading the Board of Agriculture in 1912 to provide for two sessions instead of one in each of the state's Supreme Court districts.[39]

The Populist faction of the Democratic Party in the territorial period, locally led by Freeman Miller, believed that the railroad industry had retarded progress by robbing "merchants and shippers in ways that are countless and methods that are too numerous to be catalogued."[40] Most A. and M. officials, however, thought just the opposite was true. Professor R. E. Chandler, head of the school of engineering, stated in a speech that without modern transportation it would be impossible to link the state and nation together. James Connell felt much the same way, for early in his administration he solicited the aid of Oklahoma railroads for his extension program. His efforts in this direction met with much success. In 1913 the student newspaper reported that almost "every railroad in the state has shown a willingness and, in fact, an eagerness to assist the A. and M. College in any work that looks toward the upbuilding of the agricultural interests of the State."[41]

Receiving support from the Oklahoma Board of Agriculture and State Corporation Commission, the president created an extension concept that consisted of exhibiting agricultural practices and products through college-manned trains. Under the supervision of T. M. Jeffords, James Wilson, and R. C. Potts, the first train left Stillwater in 1910. The trip lasted twenty-one days and played to 60,000 people. When the initial train returned, it was met by the college cadet corps and band, 500 students, and many townspeople. Jeffords, despite the extreme cold weather, invited the crowd to examine the displays, making sure that news photographers had plenty of opportunities for recording the event on film. On the following Friday evening, he gave two illustrated lectures at the local opera house entitled "The Farming Industry" and "The Fly Pest." The students viewed the same program three days later in the new auditorium. The material was so well received both in Stillwater and on the road that a second train formed, and in February an additional 75,000 onlookers had the chance to profit from this extension concept.[42]

With the assistance of the Santa Fe, Frisco, Katy, and Fort Smith and Western Railroads, the demonstrations continued. In 1911, 20,000 visitors turned out the first week, with attendance increasing each week thereafter. The "College on Wheels" captured the imagination of many Oklahomans. It even appeared as if the good will and publicity that had been generated would make the institution one of the most popular in the region. This project, however, along with the other extension services, consumed so much energy and drained so many resources that the organization lost sight of its research mission. A letter written by Alfred True to James Wilson in May, 1910, forecast serious trouble both with the Department of Agriculture and the state of Oklahoma.

In his correspondence, True pointed out that the station research had almost ceased and that a vigorous policy for improvement had not been implemented. Furthermore, he said that reports on federally funded projects were being returned sporadically. None at all had been submitted in the area of horticulture. It also was alleged that research personnel seemed to be teaching so much that they did not have the time to do research and that college and station salaries seemed excessively high. Two years afterwards A. and M. received a written reprimand for purchasing library books from the Adams and Hatch Act funds. Benjamin Hennessey, of the Board of Agriculture, fired James Wilson as station director, indicating that the fault for the poor performance was his. Alfred True, however, blamed the trustees. He said that until a "liberal and settled policy is adopted toward the station which will recognize its administrative and technical needs its fund cannot be used in a way to give the return which should be expected. . . ."[43]

The situation deepened and widened. Officials in Washington finally became so disgusted that they followed through on an earlier threat to withhold federal funds altogether for nine months, citing as reason the failure of the administration to keep Hatch, Adams, and station sale accounts separate. The *Gazette* said that the move made history, for it was the first time since the Morrill Act of 1862 had been passed that such an action had been taken.[44]

While the station experienced trouble with Washington, the college began to have state problems. In 1909, a Stillwater newspaper carried a front page headline that read "Eleven Canned." J. F. Lawrence, Richard Sauerhering, Cornelius Beatty, Cora Snapp, Rudolph Rosen, L. S. Weatherby, E. E. Bascomb, and George Holter had, the reporter said, received dismissal notices. Moreover, the writer hinted that he possessed inside information in regard to the firing of three other members of the faculty. Holter's leaving was thought to be especially sad, for the columnist believed that "he is, and has been for years, the best loved by students. He has been their friend and mentor, and has always had the courage to stand by them."[45] The Board, adding insult to injury, refused to permit the chemist to resign as it had the others, saying that "Holter has been insubordinate and that he has attempted to promote sentiment against the board of agriculture and the management of the college."[46] All of the departing instructors were docked one month's pay without warning or explanation.

The next year more faculty were dismissed. L. A. Moorhouse, H. P. Miller, and John Craig were charged with being disloyal. In addition, O. M. Morris, W. R. Wright, L. J. Barton, and M. J. Otey resigned. The trustees retracted just a bit in May in reference to Miller, claiming that he had just been dismissed for disloyalty but for reasons of economy. Several local papers lamented the loss of Craig because of his national reputation. The bitterness grew more pronounced when word arrived from San Antonio, Texas, that he had died less than two months after leaving the campus. An obituary in *The Breeder's Gazette* reprinted in a Stillwater newspaper claimed that Craig had done yeoman work at the Iowa Agricultural College and that he was the foremost authority on sheep in the United States. It also noted that he had published the best book in print on stock-judging. Thus it seemed that the man had been treated unfairly by the Board of Regents.[47]

The latest purge caused the staff of the Stillwater *Gazette* to do some calculating in regard to loss of faculty. A news story claimed that the college and station had employed 89 instructors during the past two year period, of which fifty had left, with twenty being fired.[48] *The Peoples Press* appointed itself as defenders of the regents. In a two-column article dealing with charges of ex-Governor Tom Ferguson that corruption existed at the college, a writer employed a mock trial technique to discuss the situation in full. The essayist identified the people who had been released from teaching and administrative positions, giving afterwards the conclusion that each man and woman had been incompetent. The final verdict read:

It is therefore ordered and adjudged that the Democratic Party be and shall remain in control of the state government of Oklahoma and all its institutions forever . . . . The demur is sustained and Tom Ferguson, the G. O. P., *et al,* are forever prohibited from making unwarranted charges against a party that has given Oklahoma the best constitution ever written and such good laws as the Initiative and Referendum, Primary Election Law, Jim Crow Law, Bank Guarantee Law . . ., and last but not least, the Grandfather Amendment.[49]

This latest controversy aroused the students of the college. On April 26, the Aggies asked President Connell for permission to use the chapel to conduct a mass protest against the Board of Regents. Denied the use of campus facilities, they met at the Stillwater courthouse. Noel H. Walton, a junior, called the group to order in a room which overflowed. He asked his classmates to sign the following document: "To the Board of Regents of the A. and M. College, Stillwater, Oklahoma. Gentlemen: We the students of the Oklahoma A. and M. College, believe the usefulness of the college calls for a change in the administrative head of the institution. Respectfully submitted."[50] Venting their anger now at Connell instead of the trustees, all of the students present signed the petition. Walton even urged some individuals to act as runners in order to find other sympathizers in the "pool halls, the theaters, and anywhere you can find a student."[51] In the interim, those in the room sang songs, gave college yells, and generally enjoyed themselves. The seriousness of the matter, however, can be seen in the fact that two hundred students signed the ouster document.

The academic year drew to a close with the regents deciding to come to Stillwater for a meeting. The membership hinted to local newspaper reporters that the students had retracted their petition, but a subsequent letter signed by thirty-two people sent to the letter-to-the-editor column of the *Gazette,* vehemently denied the statement. Further repercussions came when two of these boys were notified by the trustees on June 10th that they had been expelled for "contempt." This action probably was not popular with the student body, for R. N. Allen, one of the individuals in question, had been slated to be the business editor of the *Orange and Black* the following year. Meanwhile, the faculty came to the defense of their senior colleague. They passed a resolution which expressed confidence in Connell and asked the students to remain calm.[52]

Alfred Boyd, dean of the college of engineering, has written that James Connell had been engaged in political battles during the whole of his administration. Whether this situation was of his own making or not, continuous political turmoil existed from 1910 to 1914. The local community, before the war was over, would employ Initiative, the Referendum, and the Recall in an attempt to bring sanity back to the college campus. In 1914 the stage was reached where three separate bodies claimed to be the official regents. On one occasion these groups met simultaneously in Stillwater. They spent most of their time arguing with each other and asking the faculty and students who they thought was the legally constituted authority.[53]

According to governmental provisions adopted by the people and the state Legislature, the members of the Oklahoma Board of Agriculture were to be selected by Farmers' Institute delegates. Democrats, by the summer of 1911, had split into two major factions, and the Republicans attempted to take advantage of the situation by discrediting both groups. Some of this animosity evidenced itself in the annual Institute meeting held in August at Stillwater. Correspondence between some of the interested parties reveal that widespread corruption existed at this time. For example, Charles Scott, of Stigler, Oklahoma, wrote to W. A. Tucker in Custer County that one of the members of the Board of Agriculture was running the Connell State School of Agriculture for his own personal benefit. Scott himself had been dismissed as president. He felt others would be fired if they did not help re-elect the incumbent Board. Scott said: "I heard one member of the Board say that 'It cost from $250.00 to $1,000 to fix the delegates' and the State will have to pay the bill."[54] Moreover, G. N. Kneeland corresponded with Charles Lamb asking that the latter individual vote for the man Scott opposed, because "the Board of Agriculture is the only body in the state that Cruce's crowd can't handle and anyone who wants to keep that bunch from filching the state poor ought to work for the Board of Agriculture *as it now stands*."[55]

The summer meeting of 1911 lived up to advance billing and perhaps even superseded expectations. It ended mainly as a fight among the Democrats, but Ewers White did inject some partisanism in it. The editor of *The Peoples Press,* who viewed the proceedings, stated that two or three fistfights nearly broke out on the campus, and that Campbell Russell, one of the insurgents, had been darting "around through the crowds, raising his head every once in a while like a little dog in high oats . . . ."[56] Also, Russell tried to disrupt the balloting process, and Ewers White, his protagonist, stood so long to be recognized that in the excitment he forgot whom he was to place in nomination. Even William Murray got into the act. But for him the drama closed on a happy note. His candidate O. A. Brewer won the key election by a 43 to 36 vote margin. On the other hand, Russell was not placated. He afterwards sued Brewer for $20,000 claiming that his reputation had been slandered.[57]

Neither was the *Stillwater Gazette* pleased with the re-election of the incumbents. An article printed on September 8 stated that the regents had done a good job in the past, but "as is usually the case where laws are so drawn as to give unlimited power, they abused the power so freely placed in their hands."[58] The writer reiterated, too, the charges previously made by Charles Scott against the Democratic Party. Leaders were alleged to have hired campaigners with state money to continue the Board in office and to have threatened state employees with loss of their jobs if they did not cooperate. Later, the paper charged that corruption had existed at the forming of the state junior agricultural colleges, for politicians located these institutions near property they owned in the various cities.[59]

Comments such as those above brought a reaction from the citizenry of the state. J. K. Armstrong, Secretary-Treasurer of the Peoples Power League, assisted by the state auditor and state examiner, received authorization to investigate the books of the college. *The Peoples Press,* which also opposed the incumbent Board of Regents, decided to give Armstrong direction by posing questions that would lead him to the source of any wrongdoing. The below listed are representative.

1. To what fund were the salary and expenses of O. A. Brewer charged when visiting the Grant county farmers' institute last fall which he attended solely for the purpose of sewing up the election of satisfactory delegates?
2. We ask that your report show the cost of the legislative lobby maintained at the Lee-Huckins hotel last winter, and from what fund same paid.
3. To what fund were the salary and expenses charged of one Hardy Dial, who posing as a cotton lecturer, spent time taking care of his boys?[60]

J. B. Phillips of Altus employed the Initiative in an attempt to bring about some system of coordination among Oklahoma institutions of higher education. He introduced a bill in the Legislature through public petition which would have restructered and relocated almost every college in the state. Phillips recommended that the University of Oklahoma be moved to Stillwater and combined with the land-grant organization. The discontinued college in Norman would then be used to house a school for the blind. In addition, the reformer wanted to transfer Central State to Durant so that "young ladies and girls in their teens may not be tempted by the road houses of Oklahoma City and the evil men who dwell therein."[61] This act would enable an insane asylum to be built in Edmond. Legislator Oliver H. Akin believed Phillips's bill a joke, but he did offer a counter proposal to eliminate thirteen state colleges. As precedent for combining the Norman with the Stillwater institution, Akin pointed out that Missouri, Minnesota, Illinois, Nebraska, Florida, Tennessee, West Virginia, Wisconsin, Ohio, and Kentucky had one state university. The Legislature did not adopt either proposal.[62]

The 1912-1913 academic year brought more controversy. In September, James Connell found himself in court. Ruth Gray, the

Central Building (Old Central)

Library Building (Williams Hall)

R. J. BARKER, first
president Oklahoma
A. and M. College,
1891-1894.

HENRY E. ALVORD,
President, 1894-1895.

EDMUND D. MURDAUGH,
President, January
18 to June 30, 1895.

GEORGE E. MORROW,
President, 1895-
1899.

ANGELO C. SCOTT,
President, 1899-
1908.

JAMES HENRY CONNELL,
President, 1908-1914.

LOWRY L. LEWIS,
President, 1914-
1915.

JAMES W. CANTWELL,
President, 1915-
1921.

JAMES B. ESKRIDGE,
President, 1921-
1923.

GEORGE WILSON,
President, June 4
to July 28, 1923.

RICHARD GAINES TYLER,
Acting President,
August 1 to September
23, 1923.

BRADFORD KNAPP,
President, 1923-
1928.

CLARENCE H. McELROY, Acting President, May 1 to June 30, 1928.

First faculty Oklahoma A. and M. College, 1892. George L. Holter, Chemistry, at left; Alexander C. Magruder, Agriculture; Willis W. Hutto, English Literature; and Frank A. Waugh, Horticulture.

President, faculty, and college secretary, 1895. Frank A. Waugh, Horticulture, at left; Freeman E. Miller, English and Literature; H. E. Thompson, Principal Preparatory Department; Miss Ella Hunter, Instructor Preparatory Department; Dr. J. C. Neal, Director Experiment Station and Professor of Natural Sciences; T. M. Upshaw, Secretary; A. C. Magruder, Agriculture; Edmund D. Murdaugh, President; E. F. Clark, Mathematics; George L. Holter, Chemistry and Physics.

Class '96

First graduates Oklahoma A. and M. College, June 10, 1896. Standing (l. to r.), Homer Adams, Arthur W. Adams, Erwin G. Lewis, and Oscar M. Morris. Seated (l. to r.), A. Edward Jarrel and Frank E. Duck.

Miss Jessie Thatcher, first woman graduate, Class of 1897.

Experiment Station director's
dwelling and part of the College Farm. At right, Dr. J. C.
Neal, 1893.

Budding, grafting and pruning short course, 1904.

An agronomy field trip, about 1916.

Filling the campus silo. Below, a Case tractor on campus in 1915 with boy's dormitory (now Crutchfield Hall) in background and Experiment Station director's dwelling and greenhouse to the left.

College Barn, 1908.

Feed lots at the College Farm in 1900. Road at left is now Athletic Avenue.

Stock judging at A. and M. College in 1898.

Feeders Day, Animal Husbandry Department, 1930.

Prize-winning beef cattle at the College Barn in 1900.

daughter of J. T. Gray, brought suit against him. Because of a shortage of funds, Connell and J. L. Hasselle had earlier decided to charge students a $5 admission filing fee. Miss Gray believed the assessment illegal. Judge A. H. Huston ruled for the plaintiff. The administration appealed the case, however, for these funds were considered necessary for the continued operation of the college. The Supreme Court sustained the lower court decision. Not only did Connell now have to face a serious financial deficit but he also discovered that more than one group claimed to be the legal Board of Agriculture.[63]

In November, 1912, the state's electorate voted in favor of a measure which provided for the Recall of the Board of Agriculture. Campbell Russell, of the Peoples Power League, spearheaded this action with Initiative Bill 23. It had been written as a result of the investigation conducted by J. K. Armstrong. The Farmers' Institute convened on January 15, 1913, to hold another election. Confusion developed, however, because the state question left some doubt as to how delegates to the convention should be chosen. Consequently, two different slates were nominated. The one faction met in Stillwater, as usual. It selected a ticket headed by J. H. Persinger. G. T. Bryan, of the old Board, recognized the claims of Democrat Persinger and turned the books and official seal of the organization over to him. The second faction only held district meetings. This group put forth a slate with Ewers White at the helm. With the exception of George Vincent and George H. Hinds, who were unopposed, all of the other seats became contested. White, then, hired Freeman Miller to represent his delegation in a *quo warrento* proceedings.

The 1912-1913 academic year closed without a decision from the courts. Becoming alarmed, the Stillwater Chamber of Commerce requested that the Persinger Board meet with them so that the two groups could discuss the fate of the college. The Board did meet on the campus; however, it refused to talk with the city fathers and it also reneged on a promise not to re-elect James Connell as president. Moreover, the membership decided at this time to dismiss approximately five percent of the faculty, including W. E. Schreiber, the athletic director, and James Wilson, the man who headed the Oklahoma Experiment Station. One trustee did explain why no action had been taken in regard to Connell. He said that an attempt to recall the Board of Agriculture for the second time seemed imminent. It was. On July 31, a member of the Legislature from Shawnee pushed through a bill to hold another state election. Shortly thereafter, a constitutional amendment received passage in the form of State Question 60. In August, accordingly, the membership of the Board was reduced from eleven to five. Also, the governor received the power to nominate candidates instead of the Farmers' Institute. In September, Lee Cruce appointed J. F. Darby, G. A. Ramsey, G. T. Bryan, I. C. Renfro, and Frank Gault to office. Now, three different groups claimed to be the lawful board.

This situation brought the courts into the picture again.

District Judge G. W. Clark unseated the Darby-Ramsey Board in January, 1914. He granted, however, a supersedas order staying the effect of his judgment until the Supreme Court had time to review the case. He cited as reason for his verdict that the constitutional amendment voted in August had been improperly voted upon. This left the Persinger-Eliott faction in charge of the college, for Freeman Miller had failed to appear in court to defend the claim of Ewers White. The Supreme Court reversed Clark's decision six months later, leaving the Darby-Ramsey group as the duly constituted Board of Agriculture. Republican White could have challenged the ruling but he decided not to push his petition any further.[64]

Meanwhile, President Connell attempted to operate the college as best he could in view of the existing circumstances. In a move to counteract the unfavorable publicity, he earlier persuaded Stillwater businessmen to co-sponsor the production of four films dealing with the institution's programs. These movies were then shown in Oklahoma and adjoining states and probably had something to do with preventing a drop in enrollment.[65] In addition, the executive drafted a lengthy letter which he ordered mailed to the student's parents. The body of the document denied corruption existed within the college. The concluding section carried a message for parents who might be concerned about the quality of education. "Friends of the institution and parents of students," he wrote "should bear in mind that this is a fight between boards; that classroom conditions of the Agricultural and Mechanical college are not affected; that there is absolutely no reason why any parent or guardian of students should feel disturbed."[66]

The new regents initiated swift action. They terminated the services of James Connell and B. C. Pittuck without giving them the option of resigning. J. F. Darby, on behalf of the Board of Agriculture, requested L. L. Lewis to supervise the affairs of the college until a qualified man could be found to replace Connell. In addition, he and some of his colleagues went to Washington in order to discuss the resumption of federal payments under the Hatch Act. Both local and national officials seemed anxious to reach a settlement and an agreement was made without delay. When the Oklahoma delegation returned to the state, they interviewed several men for the vacant presidency in Stillwater. Those who received consideration were: A. St. Clair MacKenzie, dean of the graduate college at the University of Kentucky; E. A. Burnett, dean of engineering at the University of Nebraska; and William Carlyle, director of the Idaho Experiment Station. None of these men, however, were extended an offer. The Department of Agriculture apparently laid down some rather stringent guidelines and the Board of Regents believed it best to study the situation further before making a decision.[67]

In spite of the problems of the last year, it could be seen at the departure of James Henry Connell that the Oklahoma A. and M. College had matured under his administration. The number of permanent buildings increased and he left a faculty of about eighty-five to instruct some 2,500 students who were enrolled in thirty-one departments. It is not possible to estimate how many people in the state benefited from the extension program, but the total, if available, would probably stagger the imagination. The Alumni Association, then headed by Loyal F. Payne, reported in 1914 that the college had graduated some 431 men and women, most of them during the past seven years. Connell had been able to keep the institution moving ahead. The president, however, did more than simply increase enrollment and programs; he made the people of Oklahoma care about their land-grant college in Stillwater. Enough so, that they demanded the appointment of honest men to oversee it.[68]

Frank Gault, the president of the Board of Agriculture, devoted the entire 1914-1915 annual report of his agency to the Oklahoma A. and M. College. He surveyed most of the institution's service programs, particularly stressing the economic, intellectual, and social benefits that residents of the state could expect to derive from the organization. In the Preface, Gault summarized the general attitude of the Board in regard to the mission of the college. He wrote: "Agricultural education of the right kind is the very foundation of this commonwealth, and should receive the intelligent support and encouragement of every citizen. All other lines of business are dependent upon agriculture."[69] Faces and policies changed, but the belief in the agrarian myth persisted.

X   THE WAR YEARS

The first two governors of the state of Oklahoma came from the region formerly known as Indian Territory. Haskell and Cruce, both Democrats, proved that the people of Little Dixie were capable of exerting a strong influence on the political scene. These men were astute politicians "brought up in the hard school of Indian tribal politics" and "knew infinitely more of statecraft and political matters than their neighbors to the west."[1] The election of 1914, however, seemed to some individuals as one that might bring a change in direction. Democrat Robert L. Williams of Durant, called "Corporation Bob," experienced a vigorous challenge from J. B. A. Robertson and Al Jennings, the former outlaw. The Republican Party nominated John Fields, who now published a successful agricultural newspaper in Oklahoma City. Some discontented farmers, since Fields was a former director of the Oklahoma Experiment Station, thought he might be more sympathetic to rural problems than his major opposition. Williams won the Democratic primary but his chances for victory in November appeared bleak,

144

because most of the Bull Moose Republicans had returned to the fold of the Grand Old Party.[2]

Robert Williams and John Fields were opposed by two splinter groups. The Progressive Party, which had lost much of its strength since the last national election, chose John Hickman as it standard-bearer. A prominent spokesman for this organization stated that Theodore Roosevelt, Albert Beveridge, Victor Murdock, Henry Allen, and Hiram Johnson would be imported to revive interest in the organization, yet little was accomplished, even with outside money and speaking talent. The Socialist Party put forth the name of Fred Holt. Most of his support came from the element which in a few years would constitute the so-called "Green Corn Rebellion." This group opposed the entry of the United States into World War I, suggesting instead that the country pay more attention to domestic problems, especially those of the tenant farmer. Williams defeated Fields 100,597 to 95,904. Holt received 52,703 votes, enough to turn the tide either way. For the third consecutive time, however, Oklahoma remained in the hands of a politician from Indian Territory.[3]

Governor Williams, an Alabamian, was born in 1868. He had resided in Durant for eighteen years prior to his election as head of state. In 1907, he obtained a position on the Oklahoma Supreme Court and acquired a reputation for hard work, honesty, and energetic support of measures that he personally favored. One person who evaluated his tenure as governor added that Williams seemed a person "of good intentions and a tenacious champion of clean government."[4] Yet, in order for the southern wing of the state Democratic Party to remain in office, it was necessary for the chief executive to support the rural spoils system controlled by the Board of Agriculture, an agency that during this period of its history closely resembled the urban political machines of Boston, Cincinnati, Kansas City, and New York City. The correspondence of the Board from 1915 to 1937, when Frank Gault, John Whitehurst, and Harry Cordell were in power, suggests that many administrative, staff, and faculty appointments at the Oklahoma A. and M. College were made to reward party faithful. The relationship between the office of the governor and president of the Board of Agriculture became clear to the citizens of the state in the 1920's. The Legislature then brought impeachment charges against Whitehurst and Cordell as well as Governors Jack Walton and Henry Johnston.[5]

Frank Gault moved from Sullivan County, Missouri, to Geary, Oklahoma, to farm, ranch, and breed cattle.[6] He had not held a paid public office prior to his election as head of the Board of Agriculture in 1914. In campaign advertisements, he explained that he now sought such a position because the governor had appointed him as a member of the Board and he had found bad conditions "existing at the A. and M. College and in the Department in general."[7] The trustees, under Gault, possessed a sincere interest in the college and received firm support from farmers throughout the state. The existence of a patronage system often meant old-fashioned horsetrading rather than outright corruption. With the Washington difficulties taken care of through the direct assistance of Woodrow Wilson, the regents decided to call a meeting of the college department heads to discuss what should be done about the vacant presidency in Stillwater.[8]

The abrupt departure of James Connell and other high ranking executives seriously crippled the Oklahoma A. and M. College because the campus in late summer and early fall was almost devoid of administrators. The situation became further complicated by the fact that the institution had been reorganized in 1913, changing from divisions to schools, a move which indicated a need for more, not less, supervisory personnel. During the summer the Board of Agriculture interviewed three prospective presidential candidates; however, none of these men appeared to possess the special skills needed at Stillwater. The regents continued to hunt for a chief executive until November but then decided to make an acting appointment from within the college itself in order to secure more time for an extensive search. The documents remaining from this period are not clear on the point, but it seems as if the trustees wanted to find a man who was not an agriculturalist. President Connell had emphasized this aspect of the institution's program to the neglect of others. Therefore, in seeking a temporary president, the Board looked to the second strongest division in the college, the school of science and literature. The first dean, William Walter Johnston, even though he had an influential brother and prestigious academic credentials, had just resigned. Laymon Lowery Lewis, who also served as dean of veterinary medicine, took his place.[9]

Even before his official appointment, there was an informal consensus among the members of the Board that Lewis should take care of routine business in the absence of a president. It was the dean who had found out from Connell what should be done before he left and had assumed responsibility for hiring new men, scheduling vacations, purchasing supplies, buying insurance, and advertising for students. Moreover, he personally wrote the memorandum requested by the federal government so that the college could obtain demonstration funds from the Smith-Lever Act.[10] The student newspaper supported Lewis for the presidential position. A columnist said that he never had an enemy and was not interested in politics and this had enabled him to weather "every storm that ever involved the institution . . . ."[11] While he was on an emergency leave to visit his ailing father, the Board decided formally to appoint Lewis as acting president. Later, it added $125 per month to his salary as compensation for the additional duties.[12]

President Lewis, the son of S. J. and Jaleh Lewis, a family of Irish and German extraction, was born on September 3, 1869, at Newport, Tennessee. He accompanied his parents when he was ten years old to western Texas, and, after graduating from a local high school, he enrolled at the Texas A. and M. College in 1887. From there, he moved to Ames, Iowa, where he earned a degree in vet-

146

erinary medicine. George Morrow hired Lewis in 1896 and found an office for him in the basement of Old Central. Five years later he married Georgina M. Holt who had come to Stillwater from Topeka, Kansas to teach in the business department. The couple had two children, Samuel and Ruth. Professor Lewis, from 1896 to 1921, held so many positions at the Oklahoma A. and M. College that it took sixteen lines in the catalog to list them. He was genuinely loved by his colleagues and students. In addition, he made noteworthy contributions to science during the course of his academic career. When he died, a spokesman for the institution reported that practically every nation in the world had requested his pamphlets on veterinary medicine.[13]

In spite of recent problems, the community believed that A. and M. seemed destined for greater heights in the immediate future. The *Gazette* in July, 1914, published a comprehensive article on student and program growth in the last twenty-three years and looked for gains to continue. The editor acknowledged, however, that evolution was a slow process, but the coming year, with Lewis as president, appeared very bright.[14] The campus yearbook took a similar view. One writer, as he reflected upon the events of this period, wrote: "A new spirit . . . seemed to be borne this year, terminating in a good upward creative impulse, all striving for a higher A. and M."[15] Disaster, unfortunately, struck in the midst of this enthusiasm. Two Stillwater citizens noticed a fire at the college on the morning of August 7. They called the fire department, but since rain had not fallen for over two months, Morrill Hall, the pride of the campus, burned to the ground, except for two small rooms. Lewis personally led the firefighters, yet little could be done without water.

The blaze began on the third story roof of the building and ate its way down to the ground, one floor at a time. The offices of the president, financial secretary, and registrar were gutted and student and experiment station records destroyed. Only a broken water pipe saved the two remaining rooms.[16] One young reporter had the presence of mind to record his impressions as he watched the flames engulf the structure. He wrote that the

pictures formed by the heat waves, shudderingly turned their faces to the wall. The stairways charred, and fell. The floors crashed down, bending and twisting large steel girders. The uncanny light flickered through those long dim halls, where so many happy throngs had been. In the classroom deserted chairs, desks, seats, calmly awaited their inevitable fate. To the bewailings of the people gathered about the slowly burning building were added the inaudible voices of the many who had come and gone through the years . . . .Then the day came and Morrill Hall was a mass of smoking ashes, twisted steel, and bare, smoke-grimed walls.[17]

President Lewis, a perennial optimist, predicted that the Board would authorize repairs without delay. Despair, however, continued to linger in the eyes of those who watched the catastrophe.

Fire visited the campus again on October 16, the day of the Harvest Carnival. The faint din of hammers could still be heard in the distance, but by noon, most of the booths for the festival had been constructed. Suddenly, someone shouted an alarm loud enough so that it could be identified above the noise. The coeds, sensing that it was their dormitory on fire, rushed into the Women's Building and began throwing their personal possessions out the windows. Coats, hats, pillows, pennants, banners, pictures, and blouses floated to the ground. The boys, in pairs, rescued pianos, chairs, and beds for the flames had started in the attic and provided a few minutes in which to save college equipment. In the end forty young women found themselves without a place to live. The second fire assumed an unusual grotesqueness in that many of the students were attired in costume. A German peasant, a French chef, and a football player scurried in and out of the building, while a clown in red and white tights rescued a young Indian girl trapped by the flames. No lives were lost. President Lewis estimated the damage at $10,000, an amount which the regents appropriated without delay.[18]

"Doctor Lew," as nearly everyone who knew the president called him, served as the executive of the college for less than twelve months. Though much of his energy had to be expended upon restoring that which had been lost by fire, his tenure, in retrospect, is quite significant. He changed the name of the domestic science program to home economics and helped the normal school to become a school of education. Moreover, the administrator assisted the faculty in making the transition from a quarter to a semester system so that time would be left for a substantial summer school session. It was also Lewis who persuaded the Board of Agriculture to standardize instructional salaries. The following scale received adoption.

Position	Salary Range
Deans	Open
Professor	$1,800 to $2,500
Associate Professor	$1,500 to $2,000
Assistant Professor	$1,200 to $1,700
Assistant	$ 900 to $1,400
Instructor	$ 675 to $1,000
Graduate Assistant	$ 360 to $ 600

While these amounts were not really competitive with other land-grant institutions, nothing could have increased faculty morale more.[19]

The trustees adhered to the established guidelines in the immediate future when employing faculty, yet they continued to use extension and staff positions for the repayment of political debts. George Wilson, for example, who had little experience and no degree, was added to the payroll of the extension department at an annual salary of $2,000, a good sum for even a full professor. President Gault personally recommended this appointment. On the other hand, the Board hired an excellent man to direct the experiment station. William Carlyle, the new appointee, had experience in judging livestock and had held important positions at universities located in Wisconsin, Colorado, and Idaho. Furthermore, he had spent several years in the employ of the federal government, specializing in French, Belgium, and Russian breeding practices. Carlyle, in turn, secured the services of William L. Blizzard for the college, an individual who had studied under the prominent R. J. Kinzer and worked for Arthur Capper in Kansas. Blizzard brought national attention to the Oklahoma A. and M. College. He also trained a young Randlett, Oklahoma boy for the presidency of the institution.[20]

Lewis wrung some noteworthy concessions from the regents concerning the experiment station when he hired William Carlyle. First, station funds would henceforth be allocated separately from college funds, with the state contributing at least half as much money as that gotten from the federal government. Second, no appointments were to be made at the station without the prior consent of the president of the college and the dean of agriculture. Third, the station director was to be instructed that no new programs could be launched without the approval of the college executive officer. But after gaining consent, the director would be free to carry out his projects without interference. Fourth, the Board agreed to implement the provisions of the Smith-Lever Act of 1914 in Oklahoma. This bill provided for the employment of county extension agents who would demonstrate good farming practices in the various communities. William Bentley, a former associate of Seaman Knapp, the individual who conceived the idea, became the father of the system in the Sooner State. Together, Bentley and Carlyle brought the extension and station programs back into the mainstream of modern agricultural practice and thought.[21]

Besides being a capable administrator, President Lewis became an invaluable public relations man for the college. He spoke well and "with modesty" on the subject of "The College and the Governor" at a banquet in Stillwater in late October. Lee Cruce seemed flattered by Lewis' talk, but he warned that the institution should not expect too much from the Legislature by way of appropriations. The governor, as it turned out, was more interested in urging the townspeople to vote in the coming elections to "drive every gambler and bootlegger out of the country."[22] Later, Lewis arranged for the Oklahoma Press Association to hold its annual meeting on the college campus and he provided a dinner in which all of the food had been grown in the state of Oklahoma, a move that secured the institution much favorable publicity. Finally, the local chamber of commerce appreciated the president's foresight in supporting programs to train young men and women for business careers. As a result, the Oklahoma A. and M. College established the first school of commerce and marketing in the nation.[23]

Toward the end of the year, the chamber of commerce forwarded a letter of appreciation to the Board of Agriculture on behalf of the acting executive. The writer reported that the contents had the unanimous consent of the business and professional segment of the community. In it, the group stated that they knew

Lewis was not an aspirant for the presidency on a permanent basis, yet the townspeople wanted the trustees to know that they were indebted to them for the harmony that prevailed at the college. Respect for the veterinarian's work also developed on the campus. Earlier, the students named the athletic field for him and in 1914 it was decided to dedicate the first yearbook to the popular professor. The inscription thanked Lewis for always being a "patient and reasonable listener to the student's grievances, and a general, warm-hearted friend to all."[24] The faculty honored their colleague by establishing a research club that bore his name. However, even if Lewis had decided to seek the presidency, it would not have been possible for him to get it, as the Board had already found a man to fill the vacancy.[25]

On June 15, 1915, Frank Gault sent a telegram to James Cantwell, the superintendent of schools in Fort Worth, Texas. He informed the candidate that he had been "unanimously elected President of the A. and M. College, at Stillwater, Oklahoma, on roll call vote . . . ."[26] Documents in the files of the Board reveal that the recipient of the telegram had been born on March 6, 1868, in Douglass, Texas, the son of John and Mary Cantwell. James earned a B. A. and M. A. from Baylor University and a second undergraduate degree from Yale. His educational experience included teaching in country schools and serving as the principal of the Southwestern Academy at Magnolia, Arkansas. In addition, he had accepted appointment as superintendent of school systems at Texarkana, Arkansas and Corsicana, Texas. In the latter state, he received recognition from his colleagues in 1907 when they elected him president of the Texas State Teachers Association. Cantwell married Ada Westmoreland of Dawson, Texas, on May 24, 1895. He belonged to the Democratic Party, the Methodist Church, and the Masonic Lodge.[27]

James Cantwell accepted the offer extended by the Board of Agriculture, promising in return to dedicate his "best self to the educational interests of Oklahoma."[28] Many Texans regretted the administrator's decision to leave the state and he had repeated offers to return. But Cantwell, fortunately for A. and M., did move to Stillwater where he became loved almost as much as the gentle "Doctor Lew." He arrived in June and set up an office in the Engineering Building, as Morrill Hall still had not been repaired. The new executive worked at the college and in the land-grant association to promote agriculture. His most immediate objective, however, was to strengthen other programs.[29] Not long after he assumed his duties as president, he told the students that the "main effort now will be a correction of the notion people have concerning education in agricultural and mechanical college and industrial trade schools. We have got to show them that we teach cultural subjects here, and teach them as well as they are taught in other schools."[30]

The first major task confronting Cantwell was to review the personnel roster, a list which by this time had reached almost one hundred and fifty people.[31] Several full professors were hired with-

150

out delay, including Dr. Charles Chambers of George Peabody College; Dr. L. Charles Raiford of the University of Chicago; and F. M. Rolf of Clemson College. Furthermore, a familiar face returned. Freeman Miller, now a prominent attorney and frequent contributor to state and national literary journals, regained a position on the English faculty. He taught for one year before leaving the institution for good.[32]

Both the administrative staff and the faculty grew in quantity and in quality during the Cantwell administration. The president personally persuaded Dr. Harry Granger Knight to leave the University of Wyoming in order to become the fourth dean of agriculture, succeeding W. A. Linklater, O. O. Churchill and William Carlyle. Alfred True regarded Knight as "one of the best . . . in this work to be found in the country."[33] He, as a young man, had wondered far from his home in Benington, Kansas to attend college. By 1904 Knight had been awarded a B. A. and M. A. from the University of Washington and he received his Ph. D. from the University of Illinois for graduate work done there and at the University of Chicago. Dr. Herbert Patterson, who possessed a Ph. D. from Yale University, came to Stillwater to succeed John Bowers, the first dean of the school of education. Patterson, with the assistance of S. L. Reed, formerly of Gustavus Adolphus, created a modern department. Patterson had an interest in educational research but his publications did not earn him a national reputation.[34]

Ruth Michaels, an attractive young lady who caught the eye of many people as she moved around the campus in her long dresses, has the distinction of being the first dean of home economics. She taught courses in food science, being assisted in instruction by Nora Talbot, a specialist in textiles and clothing. Two of Oklahoma's all-time "greats" joined the instructional staff at the time Miss Michaels assumed her administrative position. Professor Carl "Hog" Thompson, who had gotten his master's degree at Stillwater, returned to the college after being awarded a Ph. D. in animal husbandry from Ames, Iowa. In addition to being a capable classroom performer, he was an entertaining 4-H and Rotary speaker. On more than one occasion he bested his friend and imitator Will Rogers in humorous after dinner quips. Some people believed that the latter man patterned his humorous monologues after Thompson. The most famous member of the faculty at this time, however, was Dr. Hilton Ira Jones, a former Charles Warren scholar at Harvard University, now known across the nation as the Wizard.[35]

Professor Jones received his nickname from the Redpath Lyceum Bureau, an agency that booked speakers for the summer Chautauqua circuit. He developed chemistry on the campus to the point where almost a thousand students enrolled in that subject each year. Moreover, local church leaders had difficulty in securing quarters large enough for him to hold his Sunday School classes. Jones used his own books in his college courses and is sometimes credited with writing the first text in organic chemistry in the nation. Though Cantwell was able to secure substantial raises for his faculty, it was not in his power to keep a man of Jones' stature on the payroll. H. P. Harrison, the director of the Redpath Bureau, dogged the instructor during his entire six year stay in Stillwater in order to lure him away from the institution. Eventually, he got his way, but not until he made the chemist a regional supervisor and built him a new laboratory in Chicago, Illinois.[36] Men, such as Thompson and Jones, inspired students and some even dared to dream of bigger and better things for the institution. A female writer for the student newspaper in 1917 shared some of her innermost thoughts with her readers. She said that she foresaw a beautifully landscaped campus, complete with a union and sunken gardens. Her article closed by saying: "Such an institution as pictured herein—Oklahoma State University—is to be within the future; is to be desired."[37]

President Cantwell attempted to translate the young coed's dreams into reality. He wrote to the Board of Agriculture that the college had a great advantage over older educational organizations because it was unhampered by centuries of tradition and was "free to search for truth and to teach the truth, and it relies on science as a basis for progress."[38] Also, he followed the lead of his predecessor in that he wanted to convince the public that Oklahoma A. and M. was much more than a preparatory school or an agricultural college. Besides Oklahomans, he courted national and foreign visitors. One group, headed by Sebastian Lomanitz, an agriculturalist from the Mexican province of Santa Cruz, believed that the president had helped the institution to take giant strides forward. Lomanitz declared: "We have visited Cornell and Pennsylvania Agricultural colleges as well as a number of others in the East, and when we take into consideration the age and wealth of these states as compared with Oklahoma, I would say that you here are far in advance of them."[39] This compliment, of course, was a qualified one, yet the delegation correctly observed that the service to the state continued to be an integral part of the institution.

Students were not forgotten in the effort to improve the Oklahoma A. and M. College. Early in his administration, the president spoke to the Aggies about the dangers of drifting, the necessity of being happy, eating well, and studying hard. In another speech he suggested that those on the campus divide their day into three parts, devoting one-third to sleep, one-third to recreation, and one-third to school. The townspeople, because of the lack of dormitory space, were urged to care for their youthful boarders as if they were their own children. Landlords should, he added, be sure that the students had access to a bathtub because cleanliness and godliness went together. Businessmen were asked to support the institution, and they did in many ways. One of the least significant, but most popular, was the practice of making reduced train tickets available for the annual football contest in Oklahoma City with the University of Oklahoma.[40]

In December, 1915, President Cantwell made many friends when he announced the appointment of a committee consisting of

152

Dean Lewis, Professor Miller, and M. J. Otey to make plans for a quarter-centennial celebration.[41] These men invited former students, legislators, presidents, and faculty to attend the event planned for January 7, 1916. History, as one person remarked, was permitted "to run rampant throughout the program."[42] In addition to seventeen different toasts at the banquet, Robert Lowry spoke on "Stillwater and A. and M."; A. W. Adams on "Early Student Life at A. and M."; L. G. Pittman on "The First Legislature"; Angelo Scott on "Reminiscences of a Former President"; and Freeman Miller on "The Friends Who Have Passed Away." Two hundred adults gathered to hear the speeches.[43]

The twenty-fifth year also marked another important event. In February, 1916, the college executive conferred with the Board of Agriculture about the necessity of maintaining high academic standards. Mindful of these remarks, the trustees ordered Cantwell to tour other land-grant colleges in order to gather information which could be used to prepare Oklahoma A. and M. for its first North Central accreditation visit. Little is known of this inspection, except that the institution did pass. It could now take its place with other educational organizations in the Mississippi Valley region. Shortly thereafter, ninety-one students received degrees at graduation exercises. This class was the second largest in the history of the college. Thus, in many respects, the quarter-centennial year marked an important turning point.[44]

Frank Gault, in his customary folksy fashion, indicated at the end of Cantwell's first year that he was pleased with his work. When asked by a friend what he thought of the president and how he would characterize him, Gault said: "Well, the best way I can describe him is this - if the state militia boys were sent to shoot all of the college professors in Oklahoma, they never would shoot at Cantwell."[45] It is not known how the Yale man reacted to this description, but he must have been pleased when he was re-elected to his office without a dissenting vote.[46] Yet, there were problems. The most serious involved a squabble among Gault, Attorney General S. P. Freeling, State Treasurer W. L. Alexander, and State Examiner Fred Perkinson. The dispute related to the question of which agency in the state should receive and expend the federal education funds forwarded from Washington. Governor Williams resolved the dilemma but not to the satisfaction of Gault. He commented on the situation to Cantwell by letter, saying: "Oklahoma seems to have and oversupply of statesmen without statesmanship, lawyers without legal ability, legislators without experience, and hell is to pay at the college with no pitch but to bear the wounds caused by incompetent advice from the state examiner and inspector's office."[47]

In the summer, the president finally found the time to compare his organization with the other institutions that he had visited. After sifting facts and comparing data, the administrator identified several items that required his immediate attention. First, it was painfully clear that the college obtained much less support from the

153

state than any university he had inspected on his trip. A. and M., for example, only got $81,000 per year in direct aid whereas the Iowa Agricultural College received a healthy $940,000. Moreover, as has been stated, the manner in which funds became available caused numerous headaches. Second, the school of engineering on the campus remained, for the most part, instruction in shop and almost no provisions had ever been made for research. Likewise, support for home economics lagged. Third, teaching loads throughout the college needed to be lowered in order to permit faculty to publish and to supervise candidates seeking graduate degrees. And last, the school of education could not lose its normal identification without more equipment and personnel. While money does not insure excellence, quality in academic circles cannot be obtained without it. The day when education could be equated with an instructor and student engaged in dialogue on a log was over. Science required many supple minds and much expensive hardware.[48]

Governor Williams met with the Board of Agriculture in January, 1917, to discuss the matter of legislative appropriations. He agreed to issue a deficiency certificate to pay overdue bills and promised to provide at least a million dollars [including federal funds] in the next biennium for the institution. Then, somewhat unexpectedly, the college received assistance from Washington. Congress passed the Smith-Hughes Act in February. Later, President Woodrow Wilson formed a committee called the National Research Council to explore the establishment of engineering research stations on the campuses of agricultural and mechanical colleges. Cantwell related these developments to the faculty with much enthusiasm. In addition, he asked their cooperation in getting underway programs that were ready for implementation.[49]

Meanwhile, there were other events in progress which would deeply touch the Oklahoma A. and M. College. In April, Woodrow Wilson requested that Congress declare war on the nation of Germany for it had announced its intention to resume unrestricted submarine warfare.[50] The call to make the world safe for democracy meant not only that young men would be drafted into the armed forces, but also that civilians would have to mobilize and redirect domestic resources. The provisions of the Lever Act passed in August, 1917 had the most immediate consequences for the college. This bill requested the regulation of agricultural products "to prevent . . . scarcity, monopolization, hoarding, injurious speculation, manipulations . . . to establish and maintain governmental control of . . . necessaries during the war."[51] D. F. Houston, United States Secretary of Agriculture, was largely responsible for the exact composition of the measure. He, however, had consulted with the leadership of land-grant colleges before putting the final draft together. In addition, Houston charged these men with much of the responsibility for implementation. He said: "I shall not offend you by attempting to impress upon you the need of continued effort to increase production and to promote conservation and economy. There must be no breakdown on the farm - no failures of goods,

154

foodstuffs, and clothing."[52] The rapid response of agricultural and mechanical colleges proved their basic soundness and versatility.

Both the state and college loyally supported the war. There were antidraft riots in three or four counties, but the poor and unorganized tenant farmers were incapable of serious and sustained support. The Oklahoma Council of Defense, even before the urging of the National Creel Committee, searched schools for unpatriotic books and teachers. A. and M. fared better than many of the smaller state colleges, thanks largely to the cool head of James Cantwell who refused to lose his composure in the heat generated by the crisis. In Stillwater, Edward Gallagher, the athletic director, captained the home guard, while newspapers pushed the sale of bonds and threatened so-called Socialists, who ate meat as often as they could get it, with retribution. The students joined in support of the war. Many of them encouraged their classmates to sign the pledges supplied by the Payne County Council of Defense and joined hands with other young people across the country in raising money.[53]

The Board of Agriculture promised its complete cooperation to Cantwell so that the Lever Act could be implemented in Oklahoma. Frank Gault renounced middle men and speculators who, in his opinion, were getting rich and stated that Sooners stand "ready, willing and anxious to divide with those having a common interest in her vast agricultural resources."[54] Cantwell worked to increase agricultural production. But he also thought of the war as an opportunity to sell higher education to the public. He told the regents that the

nation must train its inhabitants in civic and patriotic duties and the nation has no other agencies for this work than its public schools and colleges. If national happiness, prosperity and security depend upon efficient production, distribution, thrift, cooperative endeavor, loyalty and such characteristics, they must be made a part of the education of a broader and more useful curriculum of studies that must find their way into our educational institutions rendering the highest service to the state.[55]

Moreover, the president called upon his counterpart at the University of Oklahoma and persuaded him that the two institutions must both work together, something the two organizations had never done before.[56]

The initial wartime contribution of the college came in the general area of agriculture, especially animal husbandry. Professors "Hog" Thompson and W. L. Blizzard assisted Oklahomans in improving breeding practices and brought much credit to themselves because of their excellent stock-judging ability. In 1917, Oklahoma A. and M. won eleven major prizes at the Chicago International Livestock Exposition. The next year Cantwell reported to the Stillwater Chamber of Commerce that the institution led the nation in number of awards earned at fairs and livestock shows. He stated: "Two hundred and thirty-eight money prizes were taken, of a total cash value of $3,894.50; also, five silver medals, one bronze medal, two silver trophies; and numerous blue ribbons."[57] These achievements continued after the war as well. In 1923, Blizzard announced that 226 ribbons had been won in competition that year, including 102 prizes. Two years later Thompson supervised an exhibit at the Royal American Stock Show and returned with 54 ribbons. Then, too, the national food crisis spurred the further development of research activity at the Oklahoma Experiment Station, particularly in the production of animal vaccines. Carlyle and Cantwell, however, did not see eye to eye on administrative policy, so the Board relieved the former man and charged the president with supervision of both college and station. Emma Chandler of the home economics department did her part by conducting the state household food survey and Professor C. E. Sanborn created a correspondence course in bee-keeping in order to help alleviate the acute sugar shortage in the state.[58]

Until World War I, military training at the college had never really been taken seriously, except for a brief period before and during the Spanish-American fiasco. President Lewis initiated the practice of full scale maneuvers in 1914, but the cadets seemed to think of this more as an opportunity to have a good time than to train. Drill usually concluded with the losers treating the victors to free beer at Pecks, a tavern located near the campus. The girls participated by preparing meals for the men in the field and sewing flags. With announcement of the war, however, things began to change. First Lieutenant Arthur J. Davis arrived from West Point in September 1916. He reorganized the military program and put it into step with practices suggested by the Department of War. One month later, the Board of Regents applied for the junior provisions of the Reserve Officers Training Corps. Several trips were made to Washington, and by the beginning of 1917, the college stood ready to train leaders for the combat and technical services of the army.[59]

In April, Davis, who had just been promoted to captain, held an assembly for all of the collegiate males. He asked the cadets either to volunteer for the regular army, the navy, or the national guard within a week or to enroll in the ROTC program underway at the college. About one hundred men enlisted, including Henry L. Thomson, B. A. Ahrens, A. H. Nelson, and G. J. Moore of the faculty. These men were permitted to stay until graduation. Clarence Ousley, former editor of the Fort Worth *Record-Herald* and now director of the extension service of the Texas A. and M. College, and the Reverend Edward Henry Eckel, secretary of the Southwest District of the Episcopal Church, spoke at commencement as well as at special services for these men who were entering the army. The volunteers were sent to Fort Logan H. Roots in Arkansas, where eighteen eventually received commissions. Concurrently, Walter Stimmons of the college notified Senator Thomas Gore of Oklahoma that 400 males were eligible for military training on the campus.[60]

In 1918, President Cantwell informed the Board of Agriculture that 600 men had enlisted in the armed forces. Both the college and Department of War, however, were beginning to have second thoughts about conscripting students, because it was felt that undergraduates should stay in school until they received degrees. Consequently, the institution, as a result of a meeting of university presidents at Fort Sheridan in Illinois, decided to participate in the Students' Army Training Corps, a program designed to prepare men for the technical services as opposed to the combat arms divisions. To be eligible for the ninety day program, students had to possess a high school diploma and be over eighteen years of age. The president and military commandant of the college were empowered to recommend which individuals should be commissioned. The regents permitted the SATC program to commandeer all male dormitories on the campus and they remodeled the Livestock Pavilion to provide additional living quarters. Every able-bodied man was required to undergo training.[61]

The Students' Army Training Corps operation began in September, 1918, with 343 men enrolled. Captain Michael McDonald, a retired army officer who replaced Davis, swore the men in during the month of October. The war ended, however, before the first class graduated. Many people on the campus were not disturbed to see the program terminated, because the SATC students did not seem particularly interested in scholarship. Nevertheless, the college did elect to continue ROTC as it was revised by the National Defense Act of 1920. Both President Wilson and the Association of American Land-Grant Colleges played a role in modifying the earlier legislation on which it was based. The second act divided collegiate military training into two segments. The first two years were designed to fulfill the basic provisions of the Morrill Act and then those students showing initiative and powers of command were selected for "enrollment in the advanced course during the last two years of college."[62] The new program was academically more sound than the first. It would, however, take another catastrophe before military would be comparable to collegiate instruction.[63]

The war stimulated rather than retarded growth at Stillwater. Since Oklahoma A. and M. was a developing institution, the organization did not experience a decrease in enrollment as did some other land-grant colleges. In fact, it even forged ahead. President Cantwell, for example, secured almost $65,000 worth of surplus aviation equipment at the urging of his pilot son Robert to initiate instruction in gas combustion engines and in flight "training, radio work, aerial photography, and air gunnery and bombing."[64] Robert joined the faculty and taught classes until he became more interested in the air freight business. Moreover, the president persuaded the Board to allocate funds for the acquisition of additional machinery under the Caldwell Act, a law which enabled the college to purchase equipment at 15% of the original price. These materials enabled the school of engineering to broaden its base and undertake research and instruction in fields other than agriculture.[65]

After the war, the college agreed to assist with the retraining of disabled combat veterans. The federal Congress passed a law on July 11, 1919, designed to provide vocational instruction for 100,000 men, of which Stillwater initially assumed direct responsibility for about 200. These individuals proved to be excellent students and they received pay from $80 to $147 per month depending upon their family status. Henry C. Dunlavy, the coordinator for the Fourteenth Federal District, served as liaison between Stillwater and Washington. The vocational students and their families became staunch supporters of the Oklahoma A. and M. College.[66] They formed study groups to examine their own unique problems and encouraged the development of student maturity in general. Furthermore, during the dark days of 1921, the students voluntarily "organized to go out to the country school houses and spread the gospel of education."[67]

The post-World War I era brought changes in the political machinery of the state, too. In November, 1918, the electorate placed James Brooks Ayres Robertson in the governor's office. He was forty-eight years old, a native of Iowa, and lived in Chandler, Oklahoma, where he shared a law firm with Brigadier General Roy Hoffman. Robertson won his office without difficulty, defeating Horace McKeever of the Republican Party 104,132 to 82,865. The Socialist vote deteriorated to the point where Patrick Nagle only received 7,438 ballots. Thus the party did not play an important role in determining the outcome of the election. Though the Democrats who controlled the House and Senate were badly split, most people at the college hoped for an increase in appropriations, because the governor as a young man had been a public school teacher, and often rode miles out of his way to see the spires of Old Central on the horizon. Then, too, the economic picture looked bright as compared to the past, for the state of Oklahoma now was producing more oil than anyone else in the nation, including California and Texas. This situation, however, did not insure prolonged prosperity. The price of cotton, corn, wheat, and oil tumbled fifty per cent in a matter of months. This situation had many consequences, of which not the least was increased tensions among the races.[68]

Also, the November elections brought about a change in the leadership of the Board of Agriculture. James Cantwell, who believed that this event would mark the end of his administration, warmly thanked the outgoing executive, saying that the

history of our troubles during these four years will probably never be written but the President of the College would like to have reported the one fact that the Board has supported the President of the College fully through the entire time and it is to this support that success is due. I believe that no matter what policies the new administration may have in mind for the A. and M. College that it is in infinitely better condition to hand over to our successors, for all of which I again express my deep gratification and good wishes to our President, Mr. Gault.[69]

John Whitehurst, a member of the Board whose campaign had been engineered by his brother George, replaced Frank Gault. The new head had been born in Monticello, Florida in 1869, and spent his boyhood years on a large plantation in Texas. He came to Kansas to enter the mercantile business before moving to Oklahoma in 1910. Robert Williams appointed him to the Board six years later.

Whitehurst acquired a reputation as a builder in that he secured over one million dollars for the construction of eleven major structures on the campus. He retained Cantwell as president, and, much to his surprise, doubled his salary. Moreover, he awarded him a four year contract, a first in the twenty-five year existence of the college.[70]

Whitehurst wanted to use his position in order to win the gubernatorial office. Initially, he moved quickly to get construction started on the Science Hall and Armory-Gymnasium, both of which had been authorized by the Legislature in 1918. The Board then persuaded the solons to appropriate an additional $400,000 to begin work on structures to house home economics, the central administration, and a library. Whitehurst and Cantwell, in order to get this money, invited seventy-five members of the Legislature to visit the campus. Governor Robertson pared down the figure; however, the budget still permitted the expenditure of $1,600,000 over the next two years.[71] President Cantwell exhibited visible excitement at a banquet held in April at Stillwater. He told the assembled friends of the organization that "as sure as the world goes around we are to have the greatest college in the southwest."[72] The community responded with equal enthusiasm and the leadership placed the educational institution within the city limits and promised to make improvements in streets and sewers.[73]

The college, however, still found itself in extreme financial difficulty through 1919 and 1920. The Legislature had been generous but it had not produced adequate revenues for maintenance, nor had it provided for substantial salary increases for the faculty. Many buildings on the campus were in desperate need of repair. Chester H. Lowry and Mrs. Harry Bahntage, two members of the Former Students' Association, circulated a petition on behalf of Old Central, yet nothing was done to modernize other structures. The Board of Regents initiated a salary study at the request of President Cantwell. Some help became available in recruiting but veteran instructors slipped further and further behind. In fact, many of them had to do extra work because the war had drained specialists from college campuses.[74] On the other hand, definite improvements had been made, and, at the end of the 1919-1920 academic year, the senior colleague of the faculty stated that the demoralizing effect of World War I had been overcome and that the "school year just closed has been one of the most prosperous and successful in the history of the institution . . . . "[75] Shortly thereafter, Baylor University awarded William Howard Taft and James William Cantwell honorary Doctor of Laws degrees for their service to the nation in time of crisis.[76]

The next year provided some time to prepare for the coming decade. From September to December, the president of the college developed a master plan to present to the Board of Regents. The report began by reminding the trustees that the institution had been accredited by North Central and that vigilance was needed to preserve this position. It stated, too, that quantity had not come at the expense of quality. "Education," Cantwell said, "has become more and more a work of the laboratory, of the shop, of the stock barns of the farm, gardens, orchards, etc. and still a better knowledge of English, history, government, science and commerce have been achieved."[77] The document concluded with a plea for additional planning, especially in regard to finances. Some method was needed so that the institution did not have to live from hand-to-mouth each year. Stop-gap building programs were no longer feasible and teaching, research, and extension funds must be separated. In short, President Cantwell called for the conversion to a multi-purpose university.

The Eighth Legislature convened about a month after the report was submitted to the Board of Agriculture. Because of divided leadership, the body adjourned without making any appropriations for the institution in Stillwater. Cantwell, discouraged at this development, resigned at the March meeting of the regents. J. N. Roach requested that the executive reconsider his actions in view of the fact that Governor Robertson had already called a special legislative session; however, the executive refused to change his mind. Whitehurst withheld the news from the public until the special session finished its business, for he did not want the people to become disheartened. The *Gazette* made the announcement public. Sometime later, in an annual Founders' Day address, Cantwell hinted that the problems he had to face were far more serious than anyone had ever imagined. Yet, he had succeeded in making progress as the result of persistence and hard work. The action of the Legislature seems to have been poor repayment for loyal service.[78]

Lewis's successor left Stillwater in June, 1921. He returned to Texas where he negotiated a tuition increase for the disabled veterans on the Oklahoma A. and M. campus. President Cantwell had invested much of his salary in real estate, so there was no need to seek immediate employment. He even reserved time for a vacation in Colorado and a course in educational administration at Columbia University in New York City. The next September, he became director of the Texas Juvenile Training School at Gatesville. Later, he moved to Wichita Falls as superintendent of schools. The presidency of the Texas Technological College was offered but Cantwell elected to stay in Wichita Falls until his death in April, 1931.[79]

The popular esteem that should have been Cantwell's in Oklahoma came to him in Texas. One measure of the affection accorded him is evidenced by the fact that seven ministers officiated at his funeral in the First Methodist Church of Wichita Falls. In addition, the Booker T. Washington school, the Rotary Club, and the Masonic Lodge held simultaneous memorial services in other parts of the city. All schools in the district suspended classes for two full days. Mrs. W. W. Silk, a member of the committee that authorized the observance, summed up the feelings of many of her fellow citizens when she said that "the board is fatherless now. Cantwell was our leader. The entire eight years that he was here saw not one instance of dissatisfaction, of disagreement."[80] The acceptance of this man's resignation may have been the most serious mistake made by the Board of Agriculture under John Whitehurst's tenure. The coming decade was to be filled with economic, social, and political disillusionment as well as racial and religious hatred. More than ever, the Oklahoma A. and M. College needed the firm, but gentle, hand of James William Cantwell, a devoted public servant.

XI   SCHOLARS AND KLANSMEN

Oklahomans found it difficult to return to peacetime. The Committee on Public Information and the American Protective League, along with the Oklahoma Council for Defense, had aroused emotions that were difficult to still.[1] One commentator called the post-war period an age of insecurity, with state and nation reeling from challenges by alien forces, a somewhat strange experience for a country which had been isolated for so many years. "Bolsheviks, foreigners, the Pope, the crime and corruption of the big cities, the apparent breakdown of the traditional morality," he explained, "all seemed to be destroying the America with which native-born Protestants were familiar."[2] Moreover, anti-Negro and anti-Semitic agitation returned, leading to a resurgence of vigilante justice in both the rural and urban sections of the state. The Ku Klux Klan rode in rowdy oil boom towns[3] and in Tulsa on one occasion the Knights of Liberty took "a party of IWW members from the police, bore them to the edge of town, whipped and tarred and feathered them and ordered them to leave the community."[4] In brief, the state of Oklahoma was ripe for a demogogue. However, a prolonged quarrel between the Legislature and the gubernatorial office prevented any one individual from gaining political supremacy.

Xenophobia and racial hatred were not the only reasons for social discontentment. The rapid decrease in oil and farm prices affected the situation as well. The Honorable Henry Wallace, the United States Secretary of Agriculture, thought that falling prices had fomented a depression in all of rural America. He wrote to President R. A. Pearson of the Association of Land-Grant Colleges that

most of us can remember times when prices of the principal farm products were lower than they are now as measured in dollars and cents, but I think our history does not record a time when prices of farm products were so low as compared with the cost of production or so low as compared with the cost of other things the farmers have to buy.[5]

A spokesman for the American Farm Bureau agreed, yet he believed the situation could be reversed if transportation could be improved so that surpluses could be marketed overseas. Growing trade restrictions on the international scene, however, prevented the implementation of this suggestion and the economic decline continued. Thus the Board of Agriculture had to seek a new president for the Oklahoma Agriculture and Mechanical College within an atmosphere of both social and economic unrest. Their selection, in order to be successful, would have to be a patriot as well as a person who could assist in bringing prosperity back to the farming class.[6]

The trustees did not look beyond the confines of the state for a man to replace James Cantwell. Two weeks after the regents received a formal resignation, they interviewed James Burnett Eskridge, who currently presided over the Southwestern State Normal School at Weatherford, Oklahoma. He accepted the position without hesitation and became the first president of A. and M. to possess an earned doctorate. The incoming administrator had been born in 1866 at Nashville, Tennessee, the son of John Harper and Catherine Castleman Eskridge. He received an M. A. at Burritt College at Spencer and a Ph. D. in psychology and philosophy in 1897 from Cumberland University in Lebanon. During this period, Eskridge instructed at the East Side Academy in Nashville and headed the Shelbyville Training School and the Collegiate Institute in Springfield. He taught between 1897 and 1912 at the Latin and Mathematics Boys' Training School in Montgomery, Alabama, the Texas Christian University in Fort Worth, and the University of Texas in Austin. Meanwhile, he added to his academic credentials by finishing requirements for a second M. A. and Ph. D. in classical languages at the University of Chicago. With four graduate degrees in hand, Eskridge moved to the Oklahoma Women's College at Chickasha. In 1915, he accepted the presidency of Southwestern. Eskridge and his wife had four children, two girls and two boys. One of the latter became a physician and member of the Oklahoma Medical College faculty. Both he and his father were listed in *Who's Who in America*.[7]

A scholarly-appearing individual with pince-nez glasses, President Eskridge was a man of wide interests and many talents. He had learned as a boy how to plow a straight furrow and to navigate a raft down the Cumberland River. Therefore, he knew something about farm people and rural life. The townspeople in Weatherford supported his administration and defended him against critics who suggested that he obtained the Stillwater position because of political influence. The Oklahoma Board of Education had confidence in Eskridge, too. He held the Weatherford presidency longer than any other man before him, changed the normal school into a four year college, and operated the institution without a deficit. The governing board thought so much of him that they voted the executive a four week vacation with pay when he left, a sign that he was much esteemed. The faculty, with one or two notable exceptions, respected their senior colleague. His degrees and a book entitled *The Influence of Cicero upon Augustine in the Development of Oratorical Theory for the Training of the Ecclesiastical Orator* (Menasha, Wisconsin: George Banta Publishing Company, 1912) suggested that he was a classical scholar of the first rank.[8]

Excluding his background and experience, the Oklahoma Board of Agriculture hired James Eskridge for two reasons. First, he knew the political situation in the state and in the past he had placed friends of prominent Democrats, such as Henry Johnston, at Weatherford as long as they were reasonably well-qualified. Second, there was no doubt in the minds of the members of the Board as to the loyalty of the individual they had just employed. At Southwestern, for instance, he had assented to the firing of C. H. Simpson, a professor of agriculture who opposed America's entry into World War I. Simpson did not support the conflict as he thought it was a plot to kill off males so that white girls would have to marry Negroes.[9] Then, too, the president encouraged his faculty to sign loyalty oaths and he took a strong stand against foreigners, especially Bolsheviks and Reds. Like many people in Oklahoma, he believed that the home, the church, and the school were the cornerstones of American society and that they should be protected at all costs. Some of these institutions, he once said, were diminishing in importance because of the increasing "contempt for good government, and for law and order, while radicalism of all kinds is growing rampant, and anarchy lifts its lurid hand to engulf society in wreck and ruin."[10] Indeed, the Board had found its patriot and the members felt that they could handle agricultural problems without assistance.

The students of Oklahoma A. and M. were the only group in Stillwater to oppose the appointment of President Eskridge. Much of their disenchantment was not personal but simply pertained to the fact that they liked Cantwell and did not understand why he had resigned. Otis Wile, a young journalist, called the new administrator "pompous" and wrote that he probably would be incapable of coping with the state's more astute politicians. Another individual was a bit more charitable in that he thought Cantwell's replacement had a sincere interest in academic excellence but that he just did not know how to handle people. The student body as a whole disapproved of a ban on cars, a return to the quarter system, and a move to make each person sign an oath at the beginning of the academic year in regard to future conduct. By Christmas, however, most of the Aggies had warmed up to Eskridge and had accepted the idea that Cantwell was gone for good. Later, after the president had shed some of his aloofness, the students realized that he had their welfare at heart and they placed their complete trust in him.[11]

President Eskridge found many problems facing him when he arrived on June 6, 1921. His most immediate concern centered upon the need to replace two deans, Ruth Michaels of home economics and R. H. Bringhurst of engineering, and three members of the faculty who had been unexpectedly released. The local *Gazette* did not help recruiting in that it published a story which spoke of political meddling and the annual guillotining of faculty. Yet, the vacancies were filled by August. The appointments, however, of Ed Brewer and J. F. Campbell to staff and administrative positions suggests that there may have been a grain of truth in the analysis provided by the newspaper. A second concern arose when Eskridge discovered that the college owed the city of Stillwater $4,500 in unpaid utility bills.[12] Whitehurst and Robertson attempted to obtain passage of a one-half mill levy for schools and roads to provide additional funds. The measure, however, was defeated by such a large majority that the former man lost a great deal of prestige. In fact, the *Tulsa World* felt that irreparable damage had been done to the political career of the head of the Board of Agriculture and his followers. One editorial observed that it

requires no political philosopher to understand that the political ambitions of . . . President Whitehurst went glimmering with the decision, for they had valiantly supported 'our chief' and went stubbornly to the pen for the last round of a battle that ordinarily informed men fully understand was lost when they started it.[13]

As early as September, 1921, it became clear to Eskridge that the Stillwater presidency would be more demanding than his Weatherford office. The initial press of business was so great that he decided to delay his formal inauguration until the month of November, combining it then with the Harvest Carnival and the thirtieth anniversary of the college. This delay left time to establish a department of publicity and to create a correspondence division on the campus. For the first position, Eskridge selected R. Charles Evans. He was charged with maintaining continuing contact with high school seniors throughout the state. Professor R. J. Campbell, formerly of Southwestern, received the appointment as director of the correspondence school, a job which paid $3,000 per year. Campbell supervised the preparation of courses that carried from two to four hours credit each and set up a pay scale for those faculty who wished to instruct in the new venture. Also, the president authorized the development of three four week short courses in agriculture for people over sixteen years of age who did not want to enroll in a degree program.[14] Toward the middle of the month, he delivered a series of outdoor lectures in psychology and pedagogy at George Peabody College and George Washington University. In Washington, Eskridge visited about college matters with officials in the Department of Agriculture and with Warren G. Harding, a man he thought was "very unassuming; democratic, congenial, [and] friendly."[15]

The inauguration of James Eskridge was held on November 1, 1921. Clarence McElroy, the chairman of the festivities, mailed three thousand invitations for the event. Ex-president Edmund Murdaugh added a dash of color to the occasion by serving as toastmaster of a banquet held on Halloween. The students provided the entertainment at dinner, putting on a burlesque of past and present faculty. Professor Jones of the chemistry department served as grand marshal for the inaugural parade and endeared himself to many people, particularly the American Legion, by suggesting that the federal vocational students take the lead position. The following morning several thousand townspeople jammed the lawn adjacent to the auditorium to hear the speechmaking. Inside, the faculty and visiting dignitaries were seated so that they could see the school colors which hung from the balcony. The college seal, set in the middle of an autumn scene, decorated center stage.[16] President John Whitehurst, one of the first to address the assemblage, drew prolonged applause when he announced that the ailing "Doctor Lew" had been made dean of the college and that he was to be allowed to "go anywhere at anytime, and to pursue the work of his office in his own way."[17]

Next, President Eskridge arose to deliver his remarks. He was a skillful orator, but on this day, he decided to pursue a practical course. He spoke plainly and with a sense of urgency in his voice. Eskridge told the audience that the

state of Oklahoma is marvelously wealthy in oils, minerals, and other resources, but, long after these things shall have been exhausted and the story of them become as a tale that is told, her people will be maintaining themselves from her agricultural resources, and enriching their coffers from the product of her soils. Her horses, swine, sheep and cattle, together with her farms by the thousand . . . will be her treasures, and for the enlargement and increase of these material possessions and for the maintaining of liberty and the purity of her homes, she will look to her sons and daughters who come to institutions like this.

Here is to be had training in those things that make for the building of the home and for the uplift of society. Experts of all kinds - in agriculture and cognate industries in the various branches of engineering, in home economics, in education, in science, literature and art, in commerce and business administration, in veterinary medicine, and in many other subjects - are to be found in the various departments of the college. They cannot fail in the end, of great achievement if they receive that support from the state to which those who look to this institution for instruction and guidance are entitled.

The impression abroad seems to be that the A. and M. college rolls in luxury, and revels in the fat of the land. The truth is, it is hard pressed on every side, even for the plain necessities of a meager existence, with no margin whatever for expansion. There are about 25 per cent more students in attendance now than there were this time last year, and it is conservatively estimated that next year will find a still greater increase over this year. It is a standing reproach to this great commonwealth that young men and women of slender means and towering ambitions cannot find adequate dormitory facilities when they enter for instruction.

There are, in this very presence, young men and women fighting a desperate battle against poverty, some eating hard bread and black sorghum, taking long chances with their constitutions, who, by every token of decency and fairplay, should have extended to them a kindly and sympathetic hand of helpfulness. I wonder where our large-hearted, large-brained men and women of easy finances and most fortunate circumstances are! In the name and for the sake of such heroic young men and women as these are known to be, there ought to be a foundation established of at least $100,000 judiciously invested, the income of which could be lent to these young people annually.

This school proposes to be a leader and not a follower in this program of reform . . . . Had we our way all these things [books, tuition, room, and board] would be furnished to our students free.

It is high time, it seems to me, in these days of laxness and growing contempt for law and order and the recognized rights of well-ordered society, that institutions, secular as well as religious, should take their bearings, sound their waters and ascertain whether it is in the direction of danger or of safety they are sailing. Every system of education, whether it be cultural or scientific, professional or vocational, should be firmly established on the rock of eternal justice and higher morality and dedicated forever to the services of mankind in its humblest as well as in its most exalted conditions.[18]

At the end of the day, the speaker left Stillwater for New Orleans to attend the annual meeting of the Association of Land-Grant Colleges. There was no time to rest with important work to be done.[19]

President Eskridge seemed to think that he would have a long tenure at the Oklahoma A. and M. College. He began, therefore, as had almost all of his predecessors, by reorganizing the institution, beginning with the administrative staff. Here he sought the advice and counsel of Earle Albright whom he appointed as his administrative assistant. The selection of L. L. Lewis as dean of the faculty and his untimely death in September, 1922, provided the opportunity to elevate Clarence Hamilton McElroy to head the school of science and literature and veterinary medicine. A Creek Indian, he had graduated from A. and M. in 1906, returning to the institution three years later, as he said, to act as a "chambermaid for a bunch of hogs on the hill" in addition to teaching physiology and bacteriology for $35 per month. Red-haired, poker-faced, and keen-witted, McElroy completed his doctorate in veterinary medicine at a college in St. Joseph, Missouri. Not one to be shaken by a crisis, he provided able leadership for many years. In 1927, Professor A. A. Arnold, head of the department of foreign languages, became vice-dean, enabling McElroy to devote more time to the college as a whole.[20]

With the changes in veterinary medicine and science and literature completed, President Eskridge turned his attention to home economics. The women's division had earned the right to share more of the institution's resources, for the girls had shown remarkable maturity during the recent war. They undertook military training, sold bonds, created a loan fund for students, established a Red

Cross chapter on campus, performed nursing duties, edited the student publications, and wrote letters to former classmates on the front. One of their most spectacular accomplishments was to design a service flag which contained one thousand stars, with the name of a serviceman embroidered on each. The women on the faculty evidenced that they had talent, too. Ruth Michaels and Edith Smith published numerous extension bulletins on dietetics, nutrition, and home economics. Annie Smith, who had attended Virginia College, Syracuse University, Pratt Institute, New York City University, the Chicago School of Fine Arts, and the Cincinnati Art Academy, became the first female department head on campus outside of home economics, directing instruction in art classes. And Ora Ardell Black left an indelible imprint in the minds of her colleagues when she died as a result of Spanish Influenza which she contacted while nursing ailing students back to health. Her death seemed particularly tragic in that she had struggled twelve years to obtain her undergraduate degree in English.[21]

Eskridge appreciated loyalty and thought it ought to be rewarded. He appointed Ella Nora Miller as dean of home economics and urged her to develop a viable program. She lost no time in obtaining the funds with which to remodel the Home Builder's Cottage and created a *practicum* for majors. Also, Dean Miller followed the lead of Cornell University and the University of Wisconsin in having the college adopt orphans who would live in the cottage, while teams of girls watched and cared for the baby in six week shifts. In September, 1921, a group from Stillwater drove to the Oklahoma Children's Home in the state capital and brought back the first of a line of young kings, whom the girls named Baby David. Omicron Nu, the honor society in home economics, provided the money needed to care for the child by selling buttons which read "Baby David Fund." Males majoring in agriculture provided fresh milk and processed dairy products. L. L. Lewis personally inspected the conditions under which these provisions were secured.[22] The coeds, apparently, were good "mothers," for in December, 1921, "A great sturdy, rosy-cheeked, and laughing boy was delivered to a family for adoption."[23]

Baby David became the center of attention on the campus as well as receiving some state and national publicity. Arthur Brisbane, a reporter for the *New York Evening World*, wrote a lengthy story on the baby which was syndicated by the chain owned by William Randolph Hearst. Because of this publicity, RKO Pathe News shot a film clip for newsreels which the college estimated reached some 50,000,000 people. This national coverage insured that the child care experiment would be retained. Baby David II, however, arrived in Stillwater on February 2, 1922, under unfortunate conditions. He had been given morphine at the orphanage to stop his crying and by the time of his arrival in Stillwater he was an addict. Miss Marie Baird, with the assistance of a local physician and several girls, supervised his care during convalescence. He left the campus completely recovered.[24]

168

The third, and last, Baby David was referred to the college by the foster mother of the first. He entered Morningside Orphanage in Tulsa because his real mother, a cripple, had two older children in a fatherless domicile and she could not afford to feed the latest arrival. The child, even after three months at A. and M., still evidenced the prior neglect as the malnourished boy only weighed seven pounds. But again, the expert care provided by the senior girls enabled the baby to regain his health. Later, Miss Baird attempted to adopt a girl so as to break the male line. One of suitable age, however, could not be found. The program ended in 1923 as a result of unrest on the campus. Nevertheless, the publicity obtained through the program did much to secure the funds and staff needed to create a modern school of home economics.[25]

The establishment of a service-oriented school of education is perhaps the most important development during the early post-war period. Both state and national public schools needed attention. In January, 1921, Henry Noble MacCracken published an article entitled "Religio Magistri" in the *Atlantic Monthly* magazine. In it, he assessed the impact of World War I on the educational system. Teachers, he said, had fared worse than any other class in the conflict. Normal school enrollments significantly decreased, partly due to budgetary problems and partly due to censorship and loyalty oath controversies. The situation deteriorated to the point where some elementary classes had over sixty pupils in one room. This led districts, such as Poughkeepsie, New York, to vote strict enforcement of teacher's contracts in order to keep the student-teacher ratio from getting even higher. College faculty felt the crunch, too. In North Dakota, the Non-Partisan League invited instructors to join trade unions and in another place students picketed an administration building with signs that read "FEED THE PROFS."[26]

Unquestionably, the Oklahoma public school situation was worse than the national average. The Legislature finally recognized the gravity of the problem and in 1921 appointed a state committee consisting of R. H. Wilson, J. A. Duff, Charles L. Brooks, George Southard, Cyrus S. Avery, and J. S. Vaughn to make a "thorough investigation of the public schools of Oklahoma, including the rural schools, the city schools, and the high schools and colleges."[27] The commission's report confirmed the worst fears of educators. It discovered that the state had 673,106 school-aged children, of which only 355,999 attended classes regularly and nearly 80,000 did not attend at all. In order to instruct the pupils who did enroll, the state provided a meager $26,298,611 to equip classrooms and to pay 13,170 grade and 2,540 high school teachers. Finally, the commission concluded that Oklahoma had far too many one, two, and three room schools. The consolidation movement had only begun to make an impact in this area. Eskridge, with his pedagogical academic background and his teaching and administrative experience in normal schools, was the logical man to upgrade public education in the Sooner State.[28]

Fortunately for the college, the Stillwater institution had capable education faculty. Professor John H. Bowers organized the summer school and during the war he began to offer formal courses for individuals already teaching in the public system. By 1922 this aspect of the college's program had developed to the point where Eskridge believed that it should have its own commencement. It was Dean Patterson, however, who shaped the academic year teacher training curriculum. Moreover, he persuaded Cantwell to provide a separate facility, the Old Chemistry Building. This structure, then, was remodeled, turning the third flood into lecture room, laboratories, and administrative offices; the second into large lecture halls for introductory classes; and the first into experimental rooms for psychological research. Students could select coursework which led to the Master of Science, the Bachelor of Science, a State Life High School Certificate, a Special Education Certificate, and Grammar Grade and Two Year Certificates. Intelligence tests were used to screen prospective candidates and contracts were negotiated with public schools for the training of student teachers. Patterson made a special effort to enroll females so as to give them an alternative to home economics.[29]

Though Dean Patterson published two textbooks, one in spelling and one in tests and measurements, his educational ideals are best expressed in the articles prepared for inclusion in professional journals. In an essay submitted to the *Educational Review* in 1922 entitled "Can College Teaching Be Improved?" he called attention to the undue emphasis of legislators upon buildings, of poor academic preparation for teaching, of low scholarship, and of the lack of instructional evaluation in higher education. Later, in an address called "An Experiment in Supervising College Teaching" given at the Sixth Annual Meeting of the Southern Association of Teaching Training Institutions in Nashville, he presented a statistical model for measuring teaching effectiveness. Three articles in *School and Society*, "An Experiment in Automatic Spelling," "Teaching Ethics Through Manual Training," and "A New Approach to the 'Formal Discipline' Controversy," touched upon problems related to public school instruction. Patterson also wrote an essay for the same journal which dealt with the rights of teachers in regard to annual contracts. His enthusiasm and leadership brought the school of education to the point where it had more majors than any other college on campus.[30]

President Eskridge, while his subordinates were reorganizing the individual schools, stayed busy. He spoke as often as he could in and out of the state specializing in commencement and baccalaureate addresses. Moreover, he examined in detail the financial status and the bookkeeping systems of the college. Additional government surplus items found their way to the campus because equipment could be purchased cheaper than from regular supply outlets. Then, too, college and station scientists were ordered to charge physicians who sent laboratory samples to the institution for analysis and then sold the results for their own personal gain. Student fees, in spite of his inaugural address, were re-examined and faculty were warned about ordering supplies, especially alcohol, without prior administrative approval. A claim presented by Simon Duck, W. H. Adams, and Frank Hutto against the college over land formerly owned by Frank Duck received prolonged attention. In addition, Eskridge approved the creation of the first dry cleaning course in the nation. And last, the executive requested that the Board of Agriculture name the men's dormitory after W. W. Crutchfield, a local YMCA secretary who died in 1921. This act proved exceedingly popular with students and local Protestant ministers.[31]

In May, 1922, the trustees voted unanimously to return Eskridge to the presidency. The second year in office was approached with much optimism for both appropriations and enrollments looked encouraging. Businessmen, led by Dale Lytten, formed a committee to advance the interests of the college with the Legislature. Furthermore, the Board joined with their executive officer in planning the launching of a campaign to solicit five million dollars from private citizens to construct a central office building, a dairy barn and milk processing plant, two new dormitories, a livestock judging pavilion, a student and veterinary hospital, and to install a modern water system at the college. A local newspaper editor announced with much pleasure that almost all of the faculty had been returned to their posts and that students were pouring into the city from over most of the United States to look for work before classes began in September. In fact, the registrar predicted that freshmen would reach the one thousand mark for the coming year. Unfortunately, however, an ill omen surfaced amidst this activity. One week after Armistice Day fire hit the campus again, destroying the horse barn. Three students and three former graduates who lived there lost everything, and 4,500 bushels of corn, oats, and wheat were engulfed by the flames. In the recent past, fire had been a disaster signal and in this instance, though perhaps contemporaries did not make the connection, it foretold that the time for state elections neared again.[32]

The election of 1922 was the most colorful and spectacular ever held in Oklahoma. The Robertson-Whitehurst faction of the Democratic Party lost power, yet the conservative wing did put forth the name of Judge Thomas Owen for the August primary. He, in turn, experienced a vigorous challenge from R. H. Wilson, former regent of the Oklahoma A. and M. College and state Superintendent of Education. Wilson, just before the balloting, obtained a public endorsement from the Ku Klux Klan. Additional controversy surrounded his candidacy when he announced a plan whereby all children in the state would have to attend public schools, even those enrolled in parochial systems. Both Owen and Wilson had to contend with a third Democrat for the nomination. John Calloway "Jack" Walton, who currently served as the mayor of Oklahoma City, decided to seek the gubernatorial office. He had solid support from disgruntled Democrats and from Roman Catholics. In addition, the Farmer-Labor Reconstruction League—an agency affiliated with the North Dakota Nonpartisan League—used its organization to help Walton. This combination enabled him to defeat Wilson by 35,000 votes and Owen by 50,000.[33]

Republican John Fields opposed Walton in November and James Wilson, who also had been director of the Oklahoma Experiment Station, ran against John Whitehurst for the presidency of the Board of Agriculture. As the campaign drew to a close, Walton and Whitehurst joined forces in an attempt to defeat the opposition. The former man adopted most of the platform of the Farmer-Labor Reconstruction League and employed a jazz band to follow him as he toured the state. Whitehurst contributed his share to the partnership, for he was an excellent orator and many farmers and businessmen in Oklahoma were indebted to him for past political favors. Yet, the outcome remained in doubt, because Walton wanted to abolish capital punishment, called bankers crooks, and stood for free school textbooks and for state ownership of cement plants, warehouses, elevators, and utilities. Some members of the State Democratic Central Committee, such as Judge A. A. McDonald, refused to support the party's nominee and implied that Walton was a Socialist. Then, too, the candidate irritated the Klan by stating that its membership represented a lawless element, which, if not curtailed, would take Oklahoma back to the vigilante period. In the end, however, hard campaigning and good organization brought victory as well as the grandest inaugural celebration that the state had ever seen. An old-fashioned fiddler's contest replaced jazz bands and overalls and dresses substituted for boiled shirts and fancy gowns. Carloads of cattle, hogs, sheep, and chickens were barbequed over giant trenches while 8,000 gallon pots brewed coffee. Nearly 100,000 people attended the festivities.[34]

Friends of the college sought to take advantage of the situation. Stillwater businessmen raised several hundred dollars so that the Aggie band could play at the inauguration. John Whitehurst introduced Walton at the quarterly meeting of the Farmers' Union in order to bring the newly elected executive closer to rural leaders. Meanwhile, President Eskridge invited key members of the Legislature to a banquet at the college where they were lavishly entertained as well as made aware of the financial needs of the institution. In March, he submitted a budget which called for one million dollars over the next biennium for construction of new buildings, salaries, maintenance, and summer school. Beyond that, Senator Harry Jones of Stillwater requested half as much again for scholarships, dormitories, and replacement of the feed that had burned. The Legislature pared down some of these requests. But it still sent a generous bill to Walton for his signature.[35] He indicated, however, that the attempts to win his goodwill had failed, for he vetoed several of the larger appropriations measures and warned that university budgets "if not checked, sooner or later would involve the commonwealth in bankruptcy."[36]

Not content with holding spending at a minimum, Governor Walton decided to make some personnel changes in higher education. He threatened to fire the president of the University of Oklahoma and actually replaced five of the six regents of that institution. Next, the executive committee of the Farmer-Labor Reconstruction League demanded repayment for their support in the last election and asked Walton to appoint George Wilson in place of James Eskridge. Wilson had held several minor teaching and administrative positions at A. and M. from 1910 to 1918 before he resigned to run for state Superintendent of Education. Walton resisted granting the requested favor; however, he did make Wilson the director of vocational education in Oklahoma. The latter man had a dubious reputation in the state. He did not possess a college degree, having only a teaching certificate earned at the normal school in Edmond. Walton surmised, correctly, that the appointment of such a man could cause serious political trouble.[37]

Rumors of George Wilson's elevation to the presidency of A. and M. became more and more pronounced toward the end of the second semester of the 1922-1923 academic year. Some members of the Former Students Association anticipated what was coming and became incensed. George Young, a Chicago engineer who had graduated in 1915, expressed the opinion of many alumni in a letter he wrote to the editor of the *Orange and Black*. Young said: "Instead of getting Oklahoma State College entirely out of politics, the Oklahoma State student body, faculty and alumni must carry their institution far deeper into politics than she has ever been if their *alma mater* is to come into its own."[38] The *Gazette*, usually well informed on college matters, cautioned against extremist reaction. Perhaps, however, the paper should have taken a stronger stand, for on May 18 John Whitehurst found himself in deep trouble at a meeting of the Board of Agriculture. H. M. Stillwell, Pete Coyne, and J. E. Royce, all Farmer-Labor Reconstruction League men appointed to the Board by Walton, insisted upon talking about the renewal of Eskridge's contract instead of discussing graduation plans. Whitehurst attempted to head off the discussion, but the next day, over his wishes, the Board elected George Wilson president of the Oklahoma A. and M. College.[39] Believing that he had been double-crossed by the governor, President Whitehurst called Eskridge to state that the new man would assume office on June 1 and predicted that the election would be "a tragedy to the college and university life of Oklahoma."[40]

The Reconstruction League championed Wilson's appointment for it believed his election would foster hope in the minds of farmers in the nation that someone was interested in their problems. On the other hand, it is also clear that the organization did not expect any serious protest. Yet, opposition did develop, even before the regents met. The students drafted letters to their parents and told them that the North Central Association might withdraw accreditation if a man without a degree was appointed president. Moreover, petitions were mailed directly to Walton and Wilson.[41] On May 23, 2,500 people jammed the auditorium at the college to discuss the situation further. Senator Jones, Major J. B. Pate, military commandant, and Ray Etheridge, a student, led the debate. Both college and townspeople urged immediate action. J. A. Tolson, professor of ancient languages, received applause when he stated that "I am a man first, a teacher second. I feel the time has come when faculty members should shed their reluctance, forget any fear of losing their jobs, and take a stand for the right. Every man worthy of the name of teacher should lift his voice." J. M. Mellett, a local teamster, offered to take interested people to Oklahoma City without charge to see the governor. Frank Hayne encouraged the residents of Stillwater to get involved, too. He said:

There's lots of yellow in Stillwater. Folks say a demonstration will hurt business. That's a small matter. A principle is at stake. When dirty politicians put their hands on the schools, it is time for men to come forward and stand on their rights as citizens.[42]

The League had greatly understimated the pulse of the community.

The unrest continued after the mass meeting. About 2,000 students organized a downtown march, shouting chants such as "Down with George Wilson"; "To Hell with George Wilson"; and "We want Educators, Not Agitators." Many carried homemade signs, with the most popular reading "Keep Our School Out of Politics"; "Present Attendance at A. and M. Is Largest in History—Keep It Growing"; and "President Eskridge Has Made Good—We Want Him Returned." Edgar Bass, at the downtown rally, urged a mass demonstration in Oklahoma City and Senator Jones promised the introduction of legislation to change the method of selecting regents. Later, 1,000 people gathered on the steps of the state capitol and one-tenth of that number crowded in the office of Governor Walton. The executive appeared visibly nervous at the confrontation. As the protestors spoke, he paced his office with a letter in one hand and a corncob pipe in the other. Walton rejected the request to reinstate Eskridge and grew impatient with the persistence of his critics. Finally, he told the assemblage that the college belonged to the state, not Stillwater, and that if the people of the community did not behave themselves, he would tell them when to get up in the morning and when to go to bed.[43] Senator Jones did not like being threatened by martial law and he spoke for many of his constituents when he said: "The governor is a big man today. When the legislature meets again, we will have 154 other men here, each of whom will be a man as big as he is."[44]

During the month of May President Eskridge took little action on his own behalf, because the change seemed inevitable. Much of the time he spent with his sister and ailing mother in Tulsa, so he could avoid both state and national reporters who wanted to get his views on the situation. He did return to the campus for a convocation, however, and warned faculty and students against violence, saying that "the children of men must walk together, in harmony, peace and brotherly love: for only in this way can they accomplish the highest and in this way, only, can our republic

174

abide."[45] Afterwards, he discovered from Whitehurst that the Farmer-Labor Reconstruction League men on the Board had made a mistake by making Wilson's term of office begin on June 1 instead of July 1. This situation meant that both individuals held valid contracts because Eskridge's term of office did not end until the close of the fiscal year. The law firm of Lillard and Edwards was hired to seek an injunction which would prevent Wilson from assuming the presidency. Its brief stated that Coyne, Stillwell, and Royce wanted the latter individual installed without delay so that they could destroy the financial records of M. J. Otey, treasurer. The petition further alleged that there was a shortage in the books of $100,000.[46]

This charge brought quick action from Governor Walton. He secured a decision from his attorney-general to the effect that the Board could name anyone president at anytime, yet Eskridge had to be paid a salary until the end of the fiscal year. The incumbent, then, decided that he would not leave the campus until forced to do so and he returned to preside over the graduation ceremonies. Walton delayed a confrontation until most of the students had left for the summer. It was not until June 6 that he sent four national guard officers, Joe Campbell, Abe Hershowitz, Charles Daley, and A. H. Ferguson, along with several enlisted men, to accompany Attorney-General B. H. Markham in an attempt to oust Eskridge by force. Wilson appeared in Stillwater shortly after the arrival of these men, being escorted by Judge Brown Moore and Abraham Lincoln Bowline. In advance of the Oklahoma City party, some unidentified persons turned loose the black sheep owned by the college farm and painted the word "agitator" in several conspicuous places. Others placed the Oklahoma and United States flags at half mast and ran a red bed sheet up above them. Meanwhile, James Eskridge, with sleeves rolled over his elbows and a large bandana tied around his head to prevent perspiration from running into his eyes, hurriedly emptied his desk drawers. There were signs of deep remorse in his eyes, for B. H. Markham had been a student of his at the Texas Christian University.[47]

The governor's delegation requested the keys to the buildings from E. E. Brewer and Earle Albright, but both men said that the group would have to deal with Eskridge personally. George Wilson asked Markham to get the keys from Eskridge. The latter man made a telephone call to John Whitehurst and then turned them over. The ex-president, however, refused to talk with his successor and he told his former student you can "tell your swashbuckling governor that I keenly resent this show of military force, and that I consider it an outrage upon me, upon the citizens of Stillwater and upon the state of Oklahoma."[48] Leaving the city by train, James Eskridge paused for a moment at the station to say goodbye to a recent Aggie graduate, Oliver S. Willham. Neither man knew at the time that the younger of the two would become president of the college himself, and that his administration would mark the end of undue political meddling into the internal working of the organization.[49]

Many newspapers in the state and region published stories on the strange changing of the guard in Stillwater. Floyd Miller, a former student of Wilson's at Alva, Oklahoma, was one of the few editors to defend the new executive. In the *Skiatook News*, he called the silver-haired man a person of high courage and said that he should be given a fair trial. On the other hand, H. G. Spaulding of the *Shawnee Morning News* reported that none of the members of the Oklahoma State Press Association had a good word for Wilson. Also, he personally accused the college head of having spent most of his youth walking the streets of small towns talking about Socialism.[50] The *Wichita Daily Eagle,* a newspaper that became close to the college during the administration of Angelo Scott, did a series of articles on the educational and political situation in Oklahoma. The editor called Governor Walton to find out more about his views and to question him concerning the appointment of Wilson. In regard to the latter, the politician stated that the Board of Agriculture had made the change at the request of the farm community.[51] Next, the editor telephoned Wilson himself. The latter man said that he was not going to turn the institution into a soviet camp; that he did not intend to restrict teaching to "bugs"; that he was not going to shoot a hole through every American Legion button in the state; and that he was not going to "fly the red flag from the fence corners, despite the anger of the thoroughbred bulls and the Oklahoma City patriots."[52]

President George Wilson had the shortest tenure of any chief executive in the history of the Oklahoma A. and M. College. When he assumed office, he was about fifty-two years of age and had two children, one eight and one thirteen. Had circumstances been different, and if he had had a university degree, it might have been possible for Wilson to win the presidency on his own, for he was an able man. He desperately wanted to institute an educational program which would help the agricultural element within the state. Now, however, he, and many of his followers, were embittered because of their inability to improve themselves economically and because of the public persecution that haunted those who pursued a collectivist philosophy. But by this point in time the distance between Wilson and the mainstream of life in Oklahoma was so great that it prohibited dialogue and prevented any chances for success. Wilson's appointment was in danger from the moment that he took his oath of office.[53]

The Walton men on the Board of Agriculture introduced the incoming president to the faculty in early June. Numerous newspapermen were in the audience of the auditorium to hear the executive's address but the speaker refrained from making any radical statements. He closed his remarks by stating that he needed the cooperation of the staff in order to make the Oklahoma A. and M. College a greater educational facility than it had been. "This institution," he said, "is bigger than the president, bigger than the faculty, because it is the institution of the people, and it is the people we must serve if we are to hold our places in their hearts."[54] The entire Board of Regents met on the campus after the presentation. John Whitehurst presided, as usual, and informed the trustees that there was widespread dissatisfaction among the faculty and that many were planning on leaving Oklahoma in protest. John E. Guberlet, one of the men who resigned, had five years of service as a parasitologist at the station and as an assistant professor of zoology. He wrote that his "status as a college teacher and research worker, as well as that of the teaching profession in general, would be lowered by continuing in the new administration."[55] Others expressed similar sentiments.

The exact number of resignations is not known. The Board, however, did decide to make additional personnel changes, especially in the supervisory machinery of the college. When the latest reorganization had been completed only fifty-five members of the faculty and staff were scheduled for service in the coming academic year. And, in order to prevent problems with insubordination in the future, Pete Coyne suggested at the July meeting of the trustees that all individuals associated with the college should in the future hold their appointments at the pleasure of the Board "rather than to be employed on the contract basis."[56] The loss of seasoned faculty was a severe blow but the administrative juggling almost brought the institution to a standstill because only Clarence McElroy and M. A. Beeson were able to retain their positions. In quick fashion, Edward Boyd replaced R. G. Tyler in engineering; E. S. McCabe took the place of Herbert Patterson in education; J. T. Herner succeeded H. F. Holzclaw in commerce and marketing; Blanche Freeman became dean of women in lieu of Mary Brogden; and home economics remained vacant. The reorganization far surpassed anything in the history of the college up to this point.[57]

In addition, the Board of Agriculture came to the realization that they would have to declare other positions in the state vacant if they wanted to retain their political power in Oklahoma. H. M. Stillwell, amidst much parliamentary maneuvering, moved that forty-nine other offices should be declared open and that they should be filled by individuals who were 100% for Oklahoma. John Whitehurst took strong exception, yet he lost and a new salary list received adoption. The victory, however, by the Farmer-Labor Reconstruction League men did not stand, as Governor Walton decided that too much unfavorable publicity had been generated against his administration. He disavowed any special relationship with Coyne and Stillwell and appointed Mrs. Frank King, a Democratic committee woman, and Harry Blake, president of the Oklahoma Shorthorn Breeders Association, to serve on the Board in their stead. They, along with A. T. Whitworth and J. E. Royce of the old group, voted unanimously to oust Wilson and to retain most of the people previously fired. Only one overt act of retribution occurred. President Whitehurst called Washington to seek approval for the release of M. A. Beeson who had been friendly to George Wilson.[58]

Wilson left the campus without causing a disturbance of any kind. He was officially relieved as of July 31, 1923, having served just fifty-eight days in office. His successor, Richard Gaines Tyler, formerly dean of engineering, learned of his advancement through the newspapers while stationed at Fort Sill, where he was attending a reserve officer summer camp. The appointment, he learned later, was only temporary. He had already accepted a teaching position at the Massachusetts Institute of Technology, his *alma mater,* beginning October 1. Wilson invited Tyler to share his executive quarters in order to assure a smooth transition. The engineer, however, refused the offer and rented a room in the Scott Hotel in Oklahoma City until the presidential office had been vacated. Since Earle Albright had refused to serve as administrative assistant to Wilson, and had not been reinstated to his position, Tyler selected Raymond Etheridge, late student body president, to assist him in planning for the coming academic year.[59]

In a four installment memoir published twenty years after his acting presidency, Richard Tyler recounted some of the problems that he faced during his tenure as chief executive of the college. His brief rebuilding assignment was made particularly difficult because Governor Walton demanded that certain faculty and staff be retained on the payroll. Then, too, Walton set the entire state in a turmoil by declaring martial law in certain sections of Oklahoma because of increased Ku Klux Klan activity. Milton R. "Slick" Gallion, who had been appointed superintendent of buildings by Wilson, directly involved Tyler in this action. He stated to a Tulsa newspaper reporter that the president was a member of the Klan and that he had permitted the organization to use college facilities for meetings. It is true that some students and faculty belonged to the white-robed group, yet there is no evidence that Tyler had any sympathy for the Klan. He retaliated by firing Gallion despite the fact that Walton had told him that the superintendent was to be retained in his position. The Board of Agriculture upheld Tyler and charged that Gallion had been hired by Walton "to throw the skids under the college authorities."[60]

Together, John Whitehurst and Tyler did a remarkable job of putting the crippled college back on its feet. In fact, enrollment in September actually increased by one-tenth. The duo expressed appreciation to the American Legion and the alumni for their help in securing the release of George Wilson. Two men, H. L. Kent, president of the New Mexico Agricultural College, and Henry J. Waters, editor of the *Kansas City Star* newspaper, were interviewed for the vacant presidential office, but both individuals refused to accept the position. Moreover, Tyler and Whitehurst examined the books of the college and found a shortage so great that the faculty and federal vocational students could not be paid their full summer stipends. State officials, then, were brought into the investigation and proceedings were set into motion which lasted until 1933.[61]

The M. J. Otey case is one of the strangest in the history of the college. The treasurer graduated from Oklahoma A. and M. in 1902 and six years later he was invited to assume financial responsibility for the various college accounts as the Board believed that Angelo Scott was not a good businessman. During the Cantwell administration, three men were appointed to audit the books of the institution; however, they did not report any wrongdoing. Otey informed Frank Gault by letter in November, 1917, that the books were being checked again because of a $1,286.56 overdraft in the Morrill fund. The treasurer, allegedly, made up this money himself because he said that he did not want the college to be embarrassed.[62] President Eskridge, who had established an excellent bookkeeping system at Weatherford, requested that Otey provide him with a complete financial accounting when he assumed office. The treasurer, however, refused to comply. Although he did not follow through on the matter Eskridge did write Whitehurst that "I do not know the real condition of the financial affairs of the College, that I have never known them, and that so long as the present policy is pursued, that I fear I shall never know them."[63] He recommended a new set of procedures, all of which were promptly rejected.

The current investigation of the books surfaced because of Otey's support of George Wilson. When students claimed that North Central would deny accreditation to the college if a man without a degree was appointed president, the treasurer irritated many people opposed to Wilson by writing to Kendrick C. Babcock, the Chairman of the Commission on Institutions of Higher Education. Babcock stated that the allegations of the students were not true, especially if Wilson agreed to appoint a vice-president who had an academic background. Wilson, however, surprised Otey by suspending him until such time as the accounts had been examined.[64] Later, Whitehurst requested that G. P. Balfour, an agent in the state auditor's office, John Barry, assistant attorney-general, and J. W. Reece, county attorney, review the books in an attempt to confirm a discrepancy of $134,687.93. The Board president said that he did not know where the money was or who had taken it if it was gone. He thought, however, the guilty party might be the "old bunch of reds, who filled my office with gunmen last spring."[65] Whitehurst never clarified this statement for the public record, yet it is believed that he was referring to the members of the Board who belonged to the Farmer-Labor Reconstruction League.

In January, 1924, the regents filed suit in Oklahoma County against the New Amsterdam Casualty Company, the firm who held Otey's bond. In addition, a Payne County court arraigned Otey on an alleged embezzlement charge the same month. On the counsel of his attorney, Chester H. Lowry, the treasurer pleaded not guilty, smugly stating that "I won't run an inch. I'll stay right here in

Stillwater and meet the issue."[66] The trial concluded in May, 1924. John Barry related that the account ledgers were in such terrible shape that they were almost indecipherable. He further maintained that Otey had withdrawn college funds and deposited them in his own personal bank account. Lowry tried to refute the charge. He said that Otey, who currently had a son enrolled in Stillwater, should be commended instead of reprimanded for he had used some $10,000 of his own funds to aid the college in time of need. The jury could not decide the truth of the matter. The judge dismissed the jurors after twenty-eight hours of being deadlocked. A second trial in February, 1925, resulted in conviction. The next month the defendant was fined $500.00 and sentenced to eight years in the penitentiary. Otey, then, dismissed his second lawyer and hired Freeman Miller to file an appeal. He won a new trial for his client and succeeded in getting the decision reversed in January, 1928. The Board of Agriculture remained unconvinced of the treasurer's innocence and it was not until 1933 that funds were appropriated to clear the deficit from the books.[67]

Meanwhile, prominent political leaders found themselves in difficulty. Governor Walton, who had resisted calling the Legislature into session for fear of being impeached, finally did so. His worst fears were confirmed on October 23, 1923, when twenty-two charges were filed against him. The Ku Klux Klan dominated this session of the Legislature and its membership led the fight against Walton. The list of offenses included misappropriation of public funds, graft, malfeasance, interference with a grand jury investigation, suspension of *habeas corpus,* the unwarranted imposition of martial law, impeding the freedom of the press, abuse of pardon and parole powers, violation of the oath of office, and general incompetence. On November 19, eleven impeachment counts were sustained. The governor remained active in state politics for some time, but he never acquired a significant following again. M. E. Trapp succeeded Walton.[68]

Immediately afterwards, Representative W. E. Disney filed nine impeachment charges against John Whitehurst. He accused him of nepotism, of padding the payroll, and of illegal financial procedures. The trial lasted thirteen days, with a vote coming on April 11, 1924. Vice Chief Justice N. E. McNeil announced that none of the allegations had been sustained. Whitehurst thanked those who had acquitted him and he privately resolved to dedicate himself to the betterment of the Oklahoma A. and M. College. It was a promise that he tried to keep. Less than a year later, George Wilson killed himself. Walter Benson and J. K. Wright, the men who investigated the death, maintained that the shooting had been an accident. Wilson was found in his home by his wife and daughter. With Walton and Wilson both out of office, the state and college were ready for a new start.[69]

180

XII   "INSTITUTIONS HAVE SOULS"

The Board of Agriculture secured a new president without much public debate or delay. Bradford Knapp, the man chosen to succeed Richard Tyler, attained immediate acceptance because he possessed exceptional leadership qualities and belonged to one of the most distinguished families in American agriculture. Seaman A. Knapp, his father, descended from an English line which had crossed the ocean with Sir Richard Saltonstall in 1630. He began his rise to prominence as an educator when he replaced George Espy Morrow as Professor of Practical and Experimental Agriculture at the Iowa State College in 1879. Knapp served the land-grant institution at Ames in many positions, including president, before leaving to promote modern farming methods in the South for the United States Department of Agriculture. He achieved international recognition for his Farmers' Cooperative Demonstration Work program, a plan devised to exhibit procedures developed by state experiment stations. In 1914, Congress institutionalized this idea by passing the Smith-Lever Act. Bradford Knapp and Walter Merritt Riggs added important amendments. The nation commemorated the contributions of the father of demonstration work in many ways, but perhaps the dedication of the memorial connecting arch between the Administration and South Building of the Department of Agriculture in Washington in his name and the establishment of the Seaman A. Knapp School of Country Life at the George Peabody College in Nashville, Tennessee are the highpoints.[1]

Two of the four children raised by Seaman and Maria Hotchkiss Knapp entered the field of agricultural education. Herman, the oldest, graduated from the Iowa Agricultural College and remained at the institution in an executive capacity for almost half a century. Bradford, a middle child, who was born on December 24, 1870, at Vinton, Iowa, replaced his father as chief of extension work in the South. Also, he accepted appointment as dean of agriculture at the University of Arkansas and president of the Oklahoma A. and M. College, the Alabama Polytechnic Institute, and the Texas Technological College. He married Stella White, the daughter of L. A. White of Enid, Oklahoma, forming a union that produced five children, of which two made agriculture a career. Marian studied dietetics in Stillwater and interned at George Washington University Hospital before accepting a teaching position in the public schools at Sapulpa. Bradford, Jr., received his undergraduate degree from the same institution that his sister attended and then earned a Master of Science at Ames. Subsequently, he entered government service, being employed first at Kingsville, Texas, the place where his father had earlier started his career. Seaman Knapp started a family tradition that continued for several generations.[2]

In Iowa, Bradford, and his younger brother Arthur, were expected as boys "to shoulder their share of the household chores as the father had been taught to do back on the old farmstead near Lake Champlain."[3] Seaman, who had been crippled by an unfortunate accident, had to depend on his sons for assistance and by age eleven Bradford could operate and repair heavy equipment, including steam engines. This mechanical bent remained, resulting in a lifelong love affair with the automobile. Knapp enjoyed tinkering with the machines, kept detailed records of gasoline mileage and the time needed to drive certain distances, and he constantly attempted to best the "records" he had established. Sometimes the penchant for speed led to accidents. One of these involved several of his own students. President Knapp enrolled at sixteen in an agricultural course at Ames but he earned his baccalaurate degree in chemistry from Vanderbilt University in 1892.[4]

If the automobile was a first love, athletics proved to be a close second. At Vanderbilt, Bradford played tackle on this institution's first intercollegiate football team. He had to switch to coaching, however, when he suffered a torn shoulder ligament in the second game of the season. Still, his black jersey with a gold "V" sewed on the front became the pride of his life and he often wore the sweater, even while a college president. The injury did not prevent him from acting as captain of the track team, nor from playing polo,

182

tennis, and golf. And on one occasion, he performed as a football referee for two teams now competing in the Big Eight Conference.[5] Thirty-five years after his days as an active player, a student reporter wrote that mention of the gridiron never failed to make the "grayish glints of his silvery eyes sparkle and dance as if he were on the field . . . ."[6] The penchant for athletics did not diminish in later life and at Stillwater Knapp brought some of the finest coaching talent in the country to the campus.

The twelfth president of the Oklahoma A. and M. College did not look like an athlete. Professor D. C. Mooring, who introduced Knapp as a guest speaker during the Lewis administration, referred to him as a good example of Darwin's theory, a humerous reference to the hairless condition of the guest's head. Instead, he gave the appearance of a scholar and he often behaved with the indicisiveness of an intellectual, especially as a young man. When he left Vanderbilt, he managed a cane and cotton plantation in Louisiana but left in order to study law at the University of Michigan. The course was completed in 1896. Knapp then gained valuable executive experience by serving as an assistant to his brother at Ames, by establishing law practices in Belmont and Clarion, Iowa, and by acting as county attorney for two years. From 1909 to 1919, he worked for the federal government and lectured on agricultural subjects in Europe and in the United States. This assignment provided the opportunity to develop his speaking capabilities and to establish broad contacts in the field of agriculture.[7]

The Washington years brought maturity and recognition. The speaking talents, for instance, often produced invitations to address conventions, such as the Association of American Agricultural Colleges and Experiment Stations, where he spoke on topics entitled "The Place Which Demonstrations Should Have in Extension Work"; "The Written Project System as Affecting the Work of the County Agents"; "The General Scheme for Carrying on Extension Work with Women"; and "Special Responsibilities of the Land-Grant Colleges to Agriculture." In addition, Knapp published dozens of articles on industrial and agricultural subjects and wrote two books entitled *How the Whole Country Demonstrated* (Washington: Government Printing Office, 1915), and *Safe Farming* (Washington: Government Printing Office, 1916). The University of Maryland awarded the executive an honorary Doctor of Agriculture degree for his service to the nation in his chosen field. Besides speaking and writing, Knapp belonged to many organizations. He sat on several national agricultural advisory boards, served on the executive committee of the National Council of Boy Scouts in America, and participated in the activities of the Royal Economic Society of England, the American Economic Association, the National Economic League, the Masonic Lodge, the Rotary Club, and several collegiate honor associations. A deeply religious man, the bureaucrat became attached to William Jennings Bryan and this friendship may have resulted in a political conversion, from Republican to Democrat.[8]

In 1920, Knapp left the government to become the dean of agriculture at the University of Arkansas. Three years later, during the summer, he drove his family to Enid to visit relatives, thereby presenting John Whitehurst with an opportunity to talk with him about the upcoming presidential vacancy at Oklahoma A. and M. Dean Knapp, who had spoken at the college many times in the past and had assisted William Bentley with the extension program, consented to an interview in Oklahoma City with the trustees on September 7, 1923. The regents, in view of the need to replace Tyler before he left for Cambridge, offered the presidency to the candidate at $8,000 per annum. Knapp hesitated, telling Whitehurst that he had heard the executive had no power of his own and that one could not hire even a janitor without the advance permission of the Board.[9] The promise of a free hand brought acceptance. He wired the secretary of the college from Fayetteville on September 3, 1923, that "I will be with you before long, ready to unite with you in faithful service to the people of Oklahoma."[10]

Bradford Knapp arrived in Stillwater ten days later. It was only then that he realized the enormity of the task that he had undertaken. The college had inadequate physical facilities, less than a full complement of faculty, little money with which to instruct the 4,634 students attending classes, the 725 people enrolled in correspondence courses, and the 400,000 individuals associated with state agricultural clubs and the county agricultural and home demonstration programs. Then, too, the organization had had four different executives in less than four months, a situation which posed many practical bookkeeping problems. Later, Knapp hinted that he wished he had not taken the position;[11] however, in a speech entitled "What Is an Institution" delivered in 1936, he left the impression that the tenure in Stillwater had a marked influence on him. He said: "Institutions are not made only of mortar, stone, and cement, but have souls—composite souls made up of something of each one of its students, faculty members, and general workers. And while each one that came here left a part of himself, he took away with him part of the soul of the institution, unconsciously."[12] It is most certain, nevertheless, that Bradford Knapp gave more than he received. He belonged to that rare breed who hold service to mankind as the highest form of life.

In the early part of his administration President Knapp benefited from the crisis precipitated by the appointment of George Wilson, for the upheaval had been serious enough to break the apathy of the public. Governor Trapp cooperated with Knapp in an attempt to bring sanity back to the campus. He visited the college as often as he could and did his part to untangle the knotty financial situation. In fact, so much money became available that in June, 1924, $6,000 was returned to the state's general fund. With his political fortunes on the wane, John Whitehurst turned educational statesman: he gave Knapp a free hand and toured other land-grant plants to get ideas for a comprehensive building program. Stillwater, too, did its part. The chamber of commerce appointed a blue ribbon committee consisting of Paul Reed, W. H. Wilcox, C. H. McElroy, H. H. Allen, Ruth Strode, and Jake Katz to aid in securing larger legislative appropriations. The Former Students Association, thoroughly aroused by the events of the previous summer, gave increased attention to the organization of alumni clubs in the various Oklahoma counties. And finally, the news media gave almost unqualified support to the college as it struggled to regain that which had been lost.[13]

Knapp did everything that he could to cement a harmonious relationship between the college and the state. He, and when appropriate, his wife, joined dozens of organizations. These ranged from the Farmers' Union to the Old Settlers Association. Also, the executive secured the support of the powerful American Legion again. It took much time, however, to maintain contact with so many groups and it is fortunate that the president had the stamina of a draft horse.[14] At one point during his first year in office, he discovered that his secretary had booked him for eleven appearances [each in a different city] in a fourteen day period. He then told some students that to make "a bum speech seems the only way for me to keep from being hooked."[15] Besides meeting the people in their home environment, the administrator got them to come to the college in large numbers. One member of his staff in 1927 calculated that almost 100,000 automobiles visited the campus in a one year period.[16]

The Board of Agriculture, the faculty, and the students were not forgotten in the move to restore confidence. Knapp, unlike Eskridge, attended every meeting of the Board and attempted to conduct the affairs of the college in a business manner. Three bids were on the table before him when approval was asked for a maintenance item. Every faculty, staff, and extension appointment had the prior consent of the appropriate department head or dean and letters of recommendation and transcripts bulged in a briefcase by his feet where one could get them in the event of a question. Moreover, Knapp spaced pleas for leaves of absence, special raises, and promotions among items that did not cost money so that it would appear he was not asking for too much at one time. Whitehurst gave Knapp a $2,000 raise and requested Trapp to place all the district colleges under him. The governor, however, vetoed a bill which contained the latter proposal.[17]

Bradford Knapp devoted as much time as he could to increasing faculty morale during his first three years in office. The politically appointed deans were replaced with men of national reputations. The executive explained to the Board that good administrators were needed because the "ability, personality, training and experience of these men will become the measure of the progress of the institution."[18] Also, leadership offices were combined when possible in order to save money to provide higher faculty raises. These requests were couched in terms that were difficult to refuse. Knapp "begged" an additional $300 for Earle Albright who had been rehired to prepare the budget and act as as administrative assistant to the chief executive. Other increases rewarded those who were performing exceptionally well or had earned recent degrees. The faculty, too, appreciated receiving the back pay that they had lost under Wilson. Even clerical personnel were given periodic increases and paid overtime, something which had not been done before.[19]

The faculty grew in size and quality during this period. Between 1923 and 1926, the number of professors increased by 45%, from 117 to 170. Of these people there was a 133% increase in earned degrees. The personnel roster of the latter year listed twenty doctorates, sixty masters, and eleven professional degrees. The new faculty published in greater quantity than the old. *The O'Collegian* reported in 1928 that nineteen instructors used textbooks that they had written themselves. Even more impressive is the fact that some of these books did not pertain to agriculture. The humanities and social sciences, at last, were coming into their own. And, strangely enough, the music department had a man named John W. Brigham who gained more than a little national attention as a result of three comic operettas that he had composed.[20]

Knapp and the students got along well with each other from the beginning. In September, 1923, the "Prexy," as the Aggies called him, received spontaneous applause as future plans for the institution were outlined. Teaching, extension, and research was stressed, especially in connection with the needs of Oklahoma. Moreover, the value of a "cultural" education received emphasis. The students were informed as well that the Board had not asked questions concerning the personal politics of the president. In appreciation, the speaker informed the Aggies that no political meetings could be held on campus so that he could never be accused of partisanship. For those in the audience who wondered if Knapp would root for the University of Arkansas when it invaded Lewis Field on November 29, the president made it clear that the Cowboys were his team. Last, the administrator invited the students to get to know him. He said: "I want you to feel perfect freedom in approaching me. If I do not recognize you the second time I meet you, remind me of your name. I want to be friendly with you."[21]

The Aggies were encouraged to become goodwill ambassadors for Oklahoma A. and M. and in turn President Knapp did all he could to develop school spirit. Students going home for vacations were reminded that people would judge the institution by their public behavior. Those who stayed were invited to take holiday meals at the executive's house. The college sent questionnaires to the business community in order to find jobs for men and women who needed to work in order to stay in school. Achievement by present and past students received recognition. Knapp established an honor roll and personally provided the funds to purchase a loving cup for the individual who had the best grade point average each year. In addition, the Board was encouraged to award honorary doctorates to former students who had achieved success. In June, 1927, Dr. William L. Burlison of the 1905 graduating class

186

received a Doctor of Agriculture degree in recognition for his entry into *Who's Who in America*. Also, Dr. William A. Tarr, class of 1904, had a Doctor of Engineering degree bestowed upon him at the same time. Both men held full professorships at the University of Illinois.[22]

Generally speaking, the president succeeded in maintaining a good relationship with students but problems did develop from time to time. The automobile particularly caused difficulty. The Board of Regents banned them from campus in an attempt to reduce immorality and to increase academic efficiency. Knapp, however, found that enforcement was almost impossible. On one occasion, the *Oklahoma City Times* accused him of neglect in this area and he retorted publicly that in a ten day period he had expelled three and placed twenty-four on probation. Moreover, behavior at athletic contests sometimes caused embarrassment. One year a local fan at Lewis Field threw an empty soft drink bottle which injured a University of Tulsa coed. The president, therefore, had to issue an apology, much to his chagrin.[23] Next to the automobile ban, the thing which rankled students the most was Knapp's acceptance of a position on a local board of censors. The city appointed him at the time it passed an ordinance which called for "prohibiting any and all immoral, indecent, lude and lascivious shows, whether moving picture shows, carnival or tent show, theater or any other form of entertainment."[24] Time healed most of the wounds suffered by one side or another. In the end, the collegian believed Knapp when he said that "autocratic rule at . . . college has never produced the best results. Best results can only be obtained by good leadership and from understanding of right and wrong."[25]

The college administration attempted to upgrade all departments on the campus but initially the team focused on agriculture and engineering. In the former field, Knapp provided personal leadership by performing as a researcher and writer himself. He spoke and wrote extensively on the value of diversified farming so as to discourage the practice of growing single crops in the South. Publications were sporadic, yet one lengthy series of articles was composed for the widely read *Oklahoma Farmer-Stockman*. Then, too, the president expanded summer institutes, reorganized the demonstration train idea, and took great care in the selection of county extension agents.[26] The Board was told that they could no longer appoint such people on the basis of politics. "As private citizens," he explained, "we expect them to vote as they please and to worship according to the dictates of their own conscience."[27] A department of botany and plant pathology was authorized and placed under the direction of F. M. Rolfs, a graduate of the Iowa Agricultural College and Cornell University. He was instructed to collect all types of plant growth in Oklahoma for study and display.[28] Blizzard and Thompson were singled out for special roles. They brought agriculture back to the position it once held on the campus. In 1925, B. H. Heide, executive secretary of the Chicago

International Stock Show, wrote to Knapp that never "in the colorful history of the International has one state collected in one year so many fine honors and trophies as did Oklahoma this year."[29]

President Knapp failed in his bid to develop a modern college of engineering, because the Board did not have any real interest in the subject. Some progress, however, did materialize. Edward P. Boyd, the replacement for Richard Tyler, worked with his superior to improve engineering extension. Then, too, O. B. Badger was commissioned to conduct short term institutes throughout the state. Professor DeWitt Hunt received a charge to solicit funds from the railroad and refining industries so that the institution could train students specifically for employment in these areas. The organization also attempted to move into petroleum geology and engineering, but the University of Oklahoma opposed duplication of its school, as it was feared that existing resources would be spread too thin.[30] Nevertheless, Knapp requested the regents in December, 1925, to create an engineering experiment station. Forty-eight land-grant colleges had such a center already in existence. He said:

If the school of engineering at this institution is to take the place which it ought to be, it must do a number of things. First, it must be interested in the particular problems that relate to the work of this institution, and second, it must of necessity encourage a spirit of research, and particularly is this true, in the fields of automobile engineering, chemical engineering, mechanical and electrical engineering, as well as in agricultural engineering. Unless this spirit of research is developed, the school will become a back number, and I claim it cannot be developed except by a man who has experience in research work.[31]

The Board, then, permitted the executive to fire Boyd and begin search for a more qualified dean. It authorized a generous salary, yet it proved difficult to get a top man to move to a substandard operation.

Two departments in the school of science and literature indirectly profited from the inability of the president to reorganize engineering. First, Knapp concentrated upon English. Under Angelo Scott and Freeman Miller, this organization had achieved a degree of excellence. In recent years, however, it had suffered at the expense of what was thought to be more useful subjects. Now, the president hired J. Frank Dobie, a professor at the University of Texas, to head the department. A specialist on the folklore of the Southwest, Dobie had an adjunct appointment at Austin, where he was just beginning the career which would win him national acclaim. The new department head published during his stay in Stillwater, writing several articles and signing a contract for a manuscript entitled "Trail Drivers of the Southwest." The students liked him immensely and they often followed him as he smoked his large pipe while loping across the campus to class. In the end, administrative duties took too much of his time for research and he returned to Texas.[32]

The department of history received strengthening, too. This subject had been severely neglected both before and after the terri-

188

torial period. In 1926, Professor J. H. Caldwell, a mathematician, became the first head of the department. In a memoir, he discussed the development of the discipline at the institution. Caldwell pointed out that James Connell created the first chair of history, but the initial courses were conducted by a home economics instructor. This person was succeeded by W. H. Morehouse. He had earned degrees at Beloit College and the University of California before moving to Stillwater to serve as dean of the college of commerce and marketing. Next, G. W. Dunlavy of fine arts occupied the history post. He was assisted by Albert S. Hiatt and A. H. Burris. From 1924 to 1926, Dean McElroy handled instruction. He and Knapp were interested in the history of Oklahoma A. and M. College and together they gathered some pertinent documents, including photographs of all the institution's presidents. These were hung in the office of the president.[33]

On May 5, 1926, the Board of Regents confirmed the appointment of Thomas Reynolds as chairman of the department of history. Reynolds completed his first graduate degree in history under the prominent Herbert Boulton at Berkeley and then took his Ph. D. at George Peabody in Nashville, where he stayed on as a member of the faculty. Although he had spent his boyhood climbing the foothills of the Cumberland Mountains, he developed a problem with his health, so he came to Oklahoma. A vigorous jogging program aided his recovery and he found the energy to provide direction for the fledgling organization placed under his care.[34]

Reynolds, in many ways, is typical of the faculty employed from 1923 to 1927. He capitalized on the president's interest in Oklahoma history by having him speak to classes. Also, he instructed J. L. Coffey to gather materials related to the famous runs, towns, and Indian chiefs. Later, the department head hired Berlin Basil Chapman who had studied under Frederick Jackson Turner at Harvard University to expand upon Coffey's beginnings. Chapman had a long career at Oklahoma A. and M. and did much valuable work. Professor Reynolds published books and articles dealing with Latin America and took an active interest in the development of the library and graduate studies. His popularity and effectiveness is demonstrated in the fact that enrollment in history doubled in less than six months. He knew the direction that his department should take; however, heavy teaching loads sapped much of the strength of the faculty.[35]

As the college pushed forward, President Knapp sought means to publicize new programs. But it was difficult to reach the public in conventional ways during the 1920's because of the intense competition to reach those people who were bored with the assembly line or the monotony of farming. The institution continued to pepper state newspapers with information, yet it was not enough.

Following the lead of the University of Illinois and the Iowa Agricultural College, the organization decided to get into the radio business. This development was logical, for engineering and physics departments of land-grant institutions had done much to perfect film projection equipment and had done much of the experimentation on radio transmitters and receivers. Knapp, something of a showman himself, felt that mass media could be of use in extending the perimeters of the college and he linked the agency to radio station KFRU. It was located in Bristow, Oklahoma and advertised itself as the "Voice of Oklahoma."[36]

At first, the station simply broadcast athletic contests and carried short announcements called "Aggiegrams." When KFRU increased its power from 500 to 5,000 watts, however, the chamber of commerce in Stillwater decided to sell "subscriptions" in the community so that the college could build its own remote control facilities in order to expand its offerings. An item in the local newspaper stated that Bristow had one of the five largest stations in the country and that programming would reach at least 150,000 sets in Oklahoma.[37] The writer preceded requests for donations by reporting that the broadcasting center would provide "constructive educational advertising for Stillwater, the Oklahoma Agricultural and Mechanical College and the state of Oklahoma."[38] Professor J. C. Kositzky installed the necessary equipment in the auditorium so that programs could be relayed to Bristow. On April 8, 1925, the college initiated its first broadcast, one which reached people located as far away as North Dakota, Illinois, and Iowa. Subsequent programs included music, lectures, and interviews. Later, the Bristow station changed hands, with the call letters switched to KVOO. The college then established regular air times as well as continuing to transmit extension and institute information.[39]

Better academic programs and increased coverage by the media stimulated enrollment. In 1925, President Knapp stated that the college had become a national university, suggesting that its fame had spread over all the earth. The statement, of course, was an exaggeration, but statistics released from Washington did prove that the organization had grown "more than any other institution of its nature and rank in the entire United States."[40] The report revealed a 37% increase in students during the Knapp administration. In 1926, 246 degrees were awarded, a number which constituted a new record. The Legislature responded to the growth in a positive manner and the same year the budget reached the one million mark. Nevertheless, problems continued. The college had trouble with its drinking water, lacked a modern cafeteria, and many of the early buildings sagged with the weight of the years. Some stacks in the library worked loose from their braces and 5,000 books tumbled to the floor. Fortunately, no serious injuries occurred. Old Central continued to deteriorate at an alarming rate and finally the state condemned it, although the building still had to be used. Moreover, inadequate fire fighting equipment and a lack of water cost the college dearly. The largest barn on the campus burned just before the 1924-25 academic year, causing over $50,000 worth of damage. Knapp, with bandana over his head and his sleeves rolled up, worked alongside the fire department, but the flames did not subside until nothing remained.[41]

Not long after the fire, President Knapp decided to seek support for a major building program. It seemed as if the time for such a move was ripe in that John Whitehurst had let it be known to friends that he would not run for office again. Then, too, the courts declared that M. E. Trapp was ineligible to file for the governor's office, even though he had only finished the unexpired term of Jack Walton. Knapp and Whitehurst, therefore, plotted feverishly to raise money before the next political campaign. In February, 1925, the two presidents invited a delegation from Oklahoma City to inspect the crowded classrooms and the dilapidated condition of the older buildings. The visit was successful, in spite of rumors to the contrary, and the Legislature authorized the construction of an administration complex and two dormitories, one for males and one for females.[42]

All three buildings were badly needed. Since 1914, for instance, the college had been without adequate offices for the executive staff. The new structure, however, marked a sharp departure from the past because the Legislature permitted the expenditure of $250,000 instead of the customary $100,000. When completed, the new building was the third largest in Oklahoma, being surpassed only by the state capitol and Central High School in Tulsa. The floor space measured 55,000 square feet.[43] In September, 1925, Bradford Knapp suggested that the Board name the edifice after someone who had loyally served the institution. He waited until Whitehurst left the room during a meeting and said:

In the belief that a recommendation which honors someone in the State of Oklahoma would be acceptable to the people, and since the building is as much or more agricultural than it is administrative, I want to recommend to the Board that the building be designated 'Whitehurst Hall,' in honor of the Honorable John A. Whitehurst, President of the Board of Agriculture. During his administration, this institution has grown enormously, - 1511 to 4064 . . . . He has been a firm rock of safety in time of trouble and has stood loyally by the best interest of the institution in every way during his administration.[44]

The two dormitories commemorated people associated with the college. On July 2, 1925, Knapp requested the Board's permission to name the dormitory for men after Carter G. Hanner, a former student who lost his life in 1918 on the Champagne front in France. His widow still lived in town and the local American Legion had named its hall after him.[45] The other dormitory was named after Jessie Thatcher Bost, the first female to graduate from the college. She seemed deeply touched by the move and wrote Knapp to thank him for his thoughtfulness. In part, her letter said that " I have just learned of the very great honor that has been bestowed upon me, at your suggestion. I wish to thank you, President Knapp, for this unique way of expressing to the world the honor to the pioneer; and I am so glad I was a pioneer at A. and M."[46]

The administrative staff and faculty approached the elections of 1926 with much trepidation. Henry Johnston, a lawyer born in Evansville, Indiana on December 20, 1870 and a longtime political power in the Democratic party since he moved to Perry in 1903, opted to run for the office that M. E. Trapp would vacate. Johnston had served as temporary chairman of the Constitutional Convention in 1906. He also held the position of Grand Master of the Masonic Lodge in Oklahoma. Supported by the Anti-Saloon League and the Ku Klux Klan, some people called him "Sinless Harry," the meatless, smokeless, cussless wonder. His campaign began with several sharp statements. Johnston urged religious toleration, supported the idea of taking educational institutions out of politics, wanted better treatment of widows and orphans, and he promised to keep a close eye on the treasury of the state. Whether he loved his mother and liked apple pie is not known.[47]

William J. Holloway shared the Democratic ticket with Henry Johnston. The candidate for Lieutenant-governor had been born in Arkansas, educated at Ouachita College in Arkadelphia, and moved to Durant at twenty-two years of age, where he acquired an interest in politics. Quiet, unassuming, and businesslike, he, perhaps, would have been a better selection for the governor's office. Both men won without undue difficulty. When Governor Johnston took office, he surprised many people in the state by appointing a certain Mrs. O. O. Hammonds of Okmulgee as his private secretary. She attempted to prevent office seekers from getting to her boss, earning for herself the title of "Mrs. Colonel House" or "Rasputin." Many members of the Democratic Party considered this a hostile and unfriendly act.[48] President Knapp knew the chief executive only slightly, but he must have been pleased to see the *Gazette* quote the governor as saying that a better man "could not be found in the United States for president of the Oklahoma Agricultural and Mechanical College in Stillwater."[49]

The Honorable Harry Cordell replaced John Whitehurst as president of the Oklahoma Board of Agriculture. An anti-Murray Democrat, Cordell had been born in 1871 at Pleasant Hill, Missouri. Small, blue-eyed, affable, and possessing a good sense of humor, he had attended Wentworth Military Academy at Lexington before staking a claim in Kiowa-Comanche county in 1901. Eleven years later, he entered the Oklahoma Senate and established himself as a proponent of quality education. He and Whitehurst met together on December 20, 1926, in Oklahoma City to assure a smooth administrative transition. No severe problems seemed to exist, except that the college budget had been overspent and it was necessary to secure a deficiency certificate from the governor. Many people breathed a sigh of relief. The election was over and no blood had been spilled.[50]

Having secured all that he could from Oklahoma City, Knapp now thought it was time for the college to secure money from other sources. He told the Board that I

192

believe the time has come when those who believe in the institution, who have benefited from it, and those who look forward to a larger and better influence from the work of the institution would be willing to help it do some things which the legislature of the state may not feel like doing and which most institutions do not ask the legislature to provide for.[51]

Specifically, the speaker suggested that the organization attempt to obtain $500,000 to launch the largest building program in the history of the institution. His plan included: (1) the construction of a student union which would house the alumni association, student organizations, the post office, and recreational facilities; (2) the building of a football stadium and a gymnasium for intramural basketball; and (3) the razing of Old Central and the erection of a campanile tower in its place. The latter would serve as a memorial to the Aggies who had died during World War I. The regents endorsed the plan but it did not receive implementation for several years. Regardless of the delay, however, a new concept had been born at the Oklahoma A. and M. College. The institution no longer was to depend solely upon the Legislature for appropriations and the idea of a master plan to prepare for the future had been born.[52]

The president requested and received an additional $100,000 for operations from the Legislature in 1927. He decided, however, to continue to seek other sources. Consistent with his democratic educational philosophy James Eskridge had reduced student fees to a minimum. This action stimulated enrollment [the college, for example, expected 5,000 students for the 1926-1927 academic year], yet the state was not able to keep pace with the growth. Knapp pointed out to the Board that other similar institutions received far more revenue from fees than did Stillwater. Whereas A. and M. only obtained $8,000 per year, the land-grant colleges in Iowa, Kansas, Pennsylvania, and Washington got $390,000, $250,000, $600,000, and $190,000, respectively. Therefore, it seemed that Oklahoma should begin charging again for library services, registration, and use of laboratory equipment.[53]

The physical condition of Old Central at any given point in time is a good bellwether to the status of the college. A significant crisis occurred in 1927 in regard to both the building and the institution. State engineers condemned the structure in 1925 and by 1926 the landmark housed just the alumni and student publication offices. On February 1, a loose piece of ceiling plaster fell upon the head of Raymond Bivert, a graduate student. The chunk of mortar barely missed Paul Miller and C. E. Trout. Bivert received medical treatment and was confined to his quarters for a few days. Meanwhile, Knapp closed the building and fenced it in so that students or young children in the neighborhood would not be injured. As months passed, stones near the casements slipped out of place and some people threw rocks which damaged the window panes themselves. The structure took on an air of abject loneliness and it seemed to many as if the fortunes of the college were on the wane.[54]

Trouble came from many quarters, including the students. Young people on college campuses during the 1920's became caught up in a movement which questioned many of the traditional values of the educational system. The Aggies fell somewhat behind in not celebrating "Hell Week" or participating in "panty raids," but they did become quite concerned about censorship, especially as it applied to the student newspaper. President Knapp in 1924 authorized the publication of a daily called the *O'Collegian*. Secure in his position at that time he gave the editor a good deal of freedom, admonishing him only to tell the truth, to uphold moral standards, and to not print stories which ridiculed or hurt others unless a principle was a stake. Across the nation both sanctioned and underground papers were becoming more popular. However, when the pages of these publications began denigrating certain time-honored customs confrontations occurred. In 1927, student editors in Texas and California were fired and Chancellor Charles M. Snelling of Georgia summarily dismissed five young people for circulating an underground newspaper named the *Iconoclast*. The Oklahoma A. and M. College campus reflected what was happening elsewhere.[55]

In the fall of 1926, President Knapp invited the editor of the *O'Collegian* into his office for several discussions. The executive had been receiving criticism from people off the campus because of the paper's editorial philosophy. Knapp, at this point, maintained that the newspaper should be under the supervision of the committee on publications and that the general policy should be "to uphold the highest standards of Christian moral standards, and no halfbaked thing."[56] In January, the controversy became personal and serious. A student named Pader wrote an editorial entitled "Youth's Revolt Against the Moral Code." The essay summarized a report delivered by Dr. Edith Swift, a physician and authority on social hygiene who had recently spoken at the National Student Conference at Milwaukee, Wisconsin. The editorial stated that one need not apologize for pre-marital sexual relations, for new developments in transportation and communication had combined "to make sex freedom absolutely accessible to our young people without the stigma of consequences which restrained young people of another day."[57] Knapp strenuously objected to the subject matter of the editorial, for Oklahomans still considered sex a subject that one did not discuss in public.

The editor resigned his position under fire and left the campus in order to enroll at the University of Missouri. The student body felt that the paper had been unfairly censored and directed several pointed barbs at Bradford Knapp. One writer, Stella A. Coward, voiced popular sentiments in a poem carried by the *O'Collegian* entitled "Censorship." She wrote:

> Stop their shows and watch their play,
> Guard your precious Sabbath Day,
> Drag them off to Sunday School,
> Preach to them the Golden Rule,
> Watch their papers and their books,
> Then be shocked if they are crooks,

If they lack backbone and guts,
If they live and move in ruts,
After they've been left to stew,
With nothing big or great to do.
Keep the lid good and tight,
And try to hold your children in,
Guard them well from needed light—
And think you're keeping them from sin.[58]

The Aggies did not forgive Knapp for several months. As it became time for his presidential appointment to be renewed, the *O'Collegian* pleaded for a fourth term. A writer reported in May that he thought "Knapp and his administrative aids have accomplished more during his three years here than any head of the college heretofore."[59] But, later in the month, as a result of a poor attendance at a special convocation, the executive requested a mandate from the student body. He asked: "I want you to let me know before the end of this term whether you believe in the college as it is now operated or whether you do not, and I shall judge your actions by what is said and what is done."[60]

During the same month, the Board of Agriculture began to challenge the judgment of the president. The regents reappointed the executive but rumors persisted that the financial status of the college was in peril. The trustees, rather high-handedly, gave some credence to the whispers by refusing to appoint H. A. Andrews as chief clerk and E. E. Brewer as purchasing agent.[61] This move stunned Knapp; it was the first time that such a thing had happened to him. He returned to Stillwater and spent most of the next month composing a 5,000 word treatise which he delivered to the Board on June 1. In it, he stated that there were no irregularities at the college and that he had been the first administrator to submit an annual budget in advance. Also, he deeply resented the attempt to impugn his character. "I have nothing in the world," he said, "except my own good name and reputation. I have never benefited out of a job I have held in the world except for my living . . . .My family for generations past have borne the proud name of having served the public well."[62] Moreover, Knapp questioned the advisability of making a politician an officer of the college, for the Board wanted to put an ex-state Senator in the position sought by Andrews. Last, the president suggested that if the Board got its way in this matter, it would make the college again a dumping ground for politicians out of work. His exact words are worth repeating. He said that no matter how sincere the Board might

be in dictating an appointment at the A. and M. College, the moment such action is taken, you have destroyed the efficiency of your machine, and have unsettled the minds of every man and woman at the college, because they will believe that the President is no longer in authority, and that they must seek political pull in order to hold their positions, or in order to obtain one. When that happens, you do not need a President. You have supplanted him entirely. Men and women at the college will no longer obey him as your direct representative, but will go over his head to you, bringing about conditions that were the absolute downfall of this institution in 1923.[63]

Harry Cordell denied that the Board was disenchanted with Knapp, yet many people suspected that the college would experience a change in administration in the near future.[64]

From July to December, 1927, political events in Oklahoma turned the state inside out. The Board of Agriculture confirmed the appointment of Andrews and Brewer; however, they hired Clyde F. Lytton of Stillwater to become business manager and gave him authority over Knapp's men. Then, too, the Oklahoma Board of Education relieved President J. P. Battenberg of Northwestern State Teachers College and forced the resignation of President J. W. Turner of Southwestern State Teachers College. In Oklahoma City, members of the state Legislature attempted to meet in special session to bring impeachment charges against Henry Johnston. The governor thwarted this action by placing three companies of the 179th Infantry on guard at the State Capitol. Later, he got Judge Tom J. Chambers to issue a restraining order against the rambunctious solons.[65]

The Legislature, however, would not be denied. The House wanted to attempt to remove the governor in 1928, but the Senate did not concur at this time because the membership feared that the method of convening was unconstitutional. On January 18, 1929, shortly following the last national election in which Johnston had supported Governor Al Smith of New York for the presidency, the Oklahoma City solons filed formal impeachment charges. The Senate found Johnston guilty of general incompetence by a vote of 35 to 9 on March 20, 1929. William J. Holloway replaced Johnston as chief executive. Impeachment proceedings were also initiated against Harry Cordell. He survived, as did Whitehurst before him, probably because he had many friends in the Legislature. Bradford Knapp, no stranger to politics himself, sensed the outcome of the power struggle. In February, 1928, he completed arrangements to purchase the Snowden Farm for the college, a transaction that he had had in mind for sometime. Then, toward the end of the month, he announced to the Board of Agriculture that the Alabama Polytechnic Institute at Auburn had him under consideration for the presidency of that institution. In March, he made his resignation public and stated he had requested to be relieved of his duties as of June 30, 1928. The decision to accept or reject the Alabama offer was a difficult one. Knapp decided favorably on two counts. First, he feared that his family name might be tarnished in the current political squabble. Second, he had developed a heart condition and it was hoped that a less strenuous job would prolong his life.[66]

The resignation of Bradford Knapp rocked the entire state. President W. B. Bizzell, of the University of Oklahoma, asked Knapp to stay and stated that the administrator had "no superior as a college executive."[67] The editors of the *Stillwater Gazette,* the *O'Collegian,* and Carl Magee of the *Oklahoma News,* who wrote a column called "Turning On the Light," urged that the president reconsider his decision and asked that the Former Students Association take a firmer interest in the destiny of the college. On the A. and M. campus, Theta Nu Epsilon, a secret political fraternity, became active.[68] But it was not possible to get the resignation withdrawn. In April, President Knapp bade the Board goodbye. He did not enter into the public controversy which developed and he canceled almost all of his scheduled speeches so that reporters could not have easy access to him. Moreover, he stated that many newspapers had printed exaggerated accounts of the relationship between him and the trustees. He said that he had

appreciated the many acts of courtesy and cooperation on the part of the Board. I am not responsible for any of the editorial material which has gone out in this affair. I will say frankly I have tried to conduct myself that I might win friends, because I felt friends were necessary to the institution, but I have never favored these friends, and have not appointed personal friends to positions at the college. I know that the board has not been responsible for many things that have been charged against it. I want you to know that I understand fully, and my sole desire is to leave this Board with the utmost of respect for each individual member of it, I have earnestly endeavored to so conduct myself that I would leave this state with the finest feeling in the world.[69]

The regents offered the presidency of the institution to W. B. Bizzell of Norman. When he turned them down, they asked Clarence McElroy to oversee the college on a temporary basis until a successor could be found.[70]

In May, 1928, the college and community gathered to honor Bradford Knapp. He was given a reception in the annex of the cafeteria and presented with a Westminister clock. It was inscribed with the words "From the Faculty of the Oklahoma Agricultural and Mechanical College, 1928." Graduation day came at the end of the month. Knapp and his wife Stella composed a touching farewell for publication in the *O'Collegian* and then joined with Harry M. Rogers, president of the Exchange National Bank of Tulsa, in handing out degrees. The largest graduating class in the history of the institution received diplomas. Other than saying that unfair charges had been levied against him, the educator refrained from offering any explanations for his leaving.[71]

The end of the Knapp administration caused many heads to roll. Two deans, C. T. Dowell and Blanche Freeman, found themselves suddenly unemployed. Adrian Daane, L. A. Mitchell, R .B. Thompson, A. S. Hiatt, and C. E. Trout of the faculty and staff were given dismissal notices as well. The latter, it was said, had lost his job because he failed to muzzle the student newspaper which had scored Harry Cordell on several occasions. President Knapp directed the Alabama Polytechnic Institute from 1928 to 1932 and then returned to the Southwest as president of the Texas Technological College. He stayed there until his death on June 11, 1938.[72] The latter institution drained from him whatever strength his body still possessed. He, in the midst of an agricultural depression, had to combat economy-minded regents whose budget slashes worked hardships on the organization. The historian of Texas Tech stated his case very simply. She wrote: "He wore himself out in the effort to perform his duty."[73] Bradford Knapp, however, according to his own characterization of institutions, did not die, for he left a part of his soul wherever he went.

XIII COMING OF AGE IN AGGIELAND

Unlike the "lost generation," the young men and women of Oklahoma A. and M. College did not suffer from the extreme disillusionment so prevalent on many campuses in the two decades preceding the Great Depression.[1] Most of them, for instance, would not have understood F. Scott Fitzgerald when he wrote to his daughter that even though "I loved Princeton I often felt that it was bywater, that its snobby institutions were easy to beat and to despise and unless I was a natural steeplechaser or a society groom I'd have to find my own private and emotional life."[2] Moreover, the Aggies did not have the time nor the money to indulge themselves in the excesses described by B. H. Lehman in *Wild Marriage,* a best selling novel which depicted collegiate life at Harvard University in the Post-World War I era. It is true that Oklahoma students consumed alcohol and smoked cigarettes, but they did not question the church, the capitalistic system, the instructional process, the institution of marriage, or the intervention of the American government in the affairs of other nations. As a matter of fact, Lehman's book, and several others just like it, was suppressed at some midwestern and southwestern colleges.[3]

Whereas many larger institutions from the turn of the century to the conclusion of the war in 1918 continued in traditional hell-raising,[4] the land-grant organizations "gave the less well-to-do an opportunity for college training, undermining the established elite."[5] Yet, the Oklahomans, for the most part, still qualified as "plowboys and blacksmiths." One should not, however, classify the entire student population under one heading, for Elam Dunster, the main character of *Wild Marriage,* reminds the reader on the last page of the book that each Cambridge man was different and that on the campus there were "twenty-four or five hundred separate histories."[6] But while the overall image remained the same, there were many differences. The Stillwater student body increased in numbers; more individuals enrolled in graduate courses; the schools of education, science and literature, and engineering challenged the supremacy of agriculture; political activism heightened; nationally-ranked athletic teams took the field; and, more important, the men and women initiated dozens of new organizations. Both those of a social and intellectual nature flourished.

The campus, at this point, did not have a student union, but Theta Pond, which received its name because of its proximity to the Kappa Alpha Theta sorority house, provided a popular gathering place in the evenings. It was a quiet corner where a person might take a solitary stroll or find a spot to walk arm-in-arm with a current "flame," who most likely was a home economics or an elementary education major. The pond dated back to 1893. At first, it was used to water horses. Later, however, a windmill propelled water to the top floor of the chemistry building, where it then became piped to other buildings. The pond fell into disuse after 1910, except for the annual freshman-sophomore tug-o-war. Bryan Thompson, the landscape superintendent, used Works Progress Administration and National Youth Act labor to clean and deepen the channel as well as to add spillways under quaint rustic bridges. Limestone and four colors of water lillies, which were blended into the surrounding flora, made it once again a favorite trysting place and a convenient location where neighborhood children could fish for blue-gill or bass and feed ducks.[7]

The most striking change in the student body concerned the new freedom gained by the coeds. The institution, at the beginning of the Lewis administration, carefully regulated contact between the sexes. The girls could not attend dances without written permission from home and faculty chaperones saw to it that no couples left the ballroom without reporting their destination. During the war, however, the women assumed added responsibilities, because many of the men on campus were connected with the military and had little or no time for extra-curricular activities. This situation permitted both academic and social maturation. One sign of increased professionalization occurred in February, 1923. The college then secured a charter for a local chapter of the American Association of University Women. Appearances changed, too. An observant male reporter for the *O'Collegian* described his female classmates as healthy, vivacious, and attractive enough to make men compete for their affections. But, he added, the girls were different than the flapper. They did not smoke in public, controlled their tongues, and were interested in home and family. Occasionally, though, a coed experienced serious problems. In 1921, one young lady died from drinking carbolic acid because she feared prosecution on a bad check charge.[8]

When minor sports—tennis, golf, swimming, and gymnastics—came to the campus, the girls developed an active interest in athletics. They formed a Women's Athletic Association in order to participate in an organized intramural league, including soccer ball and a modified hockey game. Such talent, of course, could not long be ignored by the academic world, and it became possible in the 1920's for women to obtain a Bachelor of Science degree in physical education. The coeds assisted the rise of major sports by sponsoring social activities designed to make money. A carnival in 1920, for instance, netted over $600, a tidy sum for that day. Finally, sororities competed against each other in major sports. On one occasion, the Pi Beta Phi and Kappa Alpha Theta teams played a close basketball contest which ended in an 8 to 7 score.[9] The football coach, who had agreed to referee, declined, however, to accept other invitations of this type. He explained: "I was threatened by bodily harm, social ostracism and other dire consequences and those tears were too much for me."[10]

While the status of women increased during and after the war, the men still dominated college life. Chester Gould and Oliver Willham were not typical, but they illustrate that the male population did have talent. In 1917, Frank Martin, from Sallisaw, went to Pawnee with a friend for the weekend. While there, Martin could not help but boast to the townspeople about the recent victory of the football team over the University of Oklahoma. It was the first time that the Stillwater eleven had beaten the Norman opponent. Gould, a high school student, borrowed the program of the game. When it was returned later to Frank, Chester had drawn some sketches of the players. These cartoons were carried back to the college and published in the next edition of the student newspaper.[11]

In 1918 and 1919, Ray Skinner and Maud Cass, because of the lack of male students, invited the Pawnee youth to Stillwater to assist with the preparation of the college yearbook on weekends. Gould composed most of the drawings which introduced the various subdivisions of the annual. In addition, he continued to prepare caricatures for the *Orange and Black,* devoting most of his attention to athletics. He also took time to portray other activities, including the 1919 tug-o-war across Theta Pond. The artist did a series on the attempt of the sophomores to capture the colors of the freshman class as well. They had been suspended in a cottonwood tree near the Old Central building. Some of these contests must have taken much advance preparation, because a panel in 1920 exhibited boys armed with bags of soot and a mechanical device which emitted tear gas spray. This particular endeavor lasted several hours. The men did their best to impress the female audience, who hugged the sidelines, with their athletic prowess.[12]

Gould enrolled as a freshman in the school of commerce in 1920, his father having secured employment in the college print shop. Chester, a small boy, with glasses and short-cropped hair parted to the right side, became, without a doubt, the most popular male on the campus. There almost always was a crowd gathered around him as he poked good-natured fun at professors and classes. In particular, he seemed fascinated with Hilton Jones and the subject a chemistry. To most people Gould must have appeared a frivolous student, yet he had a more serious side. He drew a cartoon entitled "Exam Jinx" which an editor published in the 1920 issue of *The Judge* magazine and the following summer he earned money for his education by working as a reporter and artist for the *Oklahoma City Times*.[13]

The Oklahoma environment shaped the future direction of Chester Gould's talent. During his sophomore year, the student exemplified the earnestness of his fellow Aggies by working long hours in the *Redskin* office to perfect his sketches, but he continued to select popular topics which would appeal to his classmates. On the whole, however, Gould was more influenced by conditions within the state than on the campus. First, he matured in a city where Gordon "Pawnee Bill" Lillie, a former partner of William Cody's wild west show, established a permanent home. This man represented a bygone era when law and order was thought to have come from rugged individualism.[14] Second, the lawlessness of the oil towns, the resurgence of the Ku Klux Klan, and renewed racial tensions established the need for an ordered society in the collegian's mind. Frank Martin remembered that Gould often thought about the subject of injustice. He wrote that his friend had a desire "to lead a crusade against some wrong preying on society. At that time his plans were very vague, but his heart was set on bringing a picture of actual conditions to the people and being a leader in moulding sentiment against such activities."[15]

In 1922, Gould, after many self-centered parting statements in the *Redskin*, left Stillwater to enroll at Northwestern University, where he could get more specialized training. His departure left an enormous void; many years afterwards his colleagues would remember his antics with fond affection and respect. Gould developed a cartoon strip entitled "Radio Cat" in 1924 but it failed to attract wide attention. The next few years were spent along the water fronts, in police stations, and at the Northwestern crime bureau. It was not until 1930 that he created the character that would make his name a household word, Dick Tracy. Martin felt that the "immortal detective" was present in his thoughts many years before the idea of leading a crusade returned. "In reality, Dick Tracy," he

202

said, "was created in his mind even before he had left high school; yet the exact person, form and position he would take was not worked out until later years."[16]

Oliver Willham enrolled at Oklahoma A. and M. College the same year as Chester Gould, A tall, handsome, genial lad, he had been born on June 26, 1901, at Clearwater, Kansas, where his father farmed and raised cattle. The family, in 1907, decided to move to Randlett, Oklahoma, when the Big Pasture was opened for settlement. Oliver, and his sister Time, completed high school in this community and then elected to attend the land-grant institution in Stillwater. Father Willham, a church elder, would not consent to this move, however, until he had personally surveyed the institution. After a visit to the old homestead in August to tend to some business, he stopped at the community that housed the college. There he met Professor Carl Thompson in a local grocery store. Both the man and the institution passed inspection. In fact, Thompson agreed to rent his two spare rooms to Oliver and Time.[17] The two students left home, with a stern, but loving, admonition from their mother, one that they would remember many years later. She said: "I will help you all I can but remember you are to stay up there for a whole year. I want no coming home for holidays or anything else."[18]

The freshman class of 1920 numbered 425; thus academic competition was becoming increasingly difficult. Willham proved more than capable. He elected an agricultural major but enjoyed chemistry under H. I. Jones, physical education from Ed Gallagher, and military instruction from Captain Michael McDonald. The student posed some peculiar problems for the latter individual. He gained seventy-five pounds his first year on the campus and it was next to impossible to keep him in a cadet uniform. Harry Orr and C. H. McElroy taught Willham the value of scholarship; however, it was W. L. Blizzard who became the boy's model. This man did not have a reputation as a good classroom instructor. He knew farm animals, however, as well as, or better than, any person in the country. Oliver enjoyed his association with him and made the stock-judging team which provided him with many adventures. In Chicago, he had all of his clothes stolen, except for those on his person. And in El Reno, he once stayed at the Old Southern Hotel, while the Ku Klux Klan paraded through the street holding burning crosses that illuminated most of the city.[19]

Willham's popularity on the campus developed more slowly than Goulds. But after completing his two years of introductory courses, the junior found more time for social activities. He often attended church-sponsored activities, although he was not one to wear religion on his sleeve. There seemed to be an air of wholesomeness, a spirit of sincerity, and a dedication to service that easily set him apart from his classmates. By the time graduation day arrived, it was apparent that Willham had an unusually bright career ahead of him in the academic world. He had excelled in his classes and belonged to many organizations, including Block and

Bridle, Alpha Zeta, the Oklahoma Academy of Science, and Phi Kappa Phi, the highest honor society on campus. Leaving Stillwater, Willham obtained employment at the Panhandle A. and M. College. There he learned much about the political machinery of the state and met his wife, a home economics instructor named Susan Hurt, formerly of Ash Grove, Missouri. Summers were devoted to graduate study in animal husbandry at the Iowa Agricultural College. Both the M. S. and Ph. D. were in hand by 1934. He then returned to Stillwater for additional experience. And though the future had great things in store for him, Oliver Willham never forgot what he owed to his *alma mater* or to the people of Oklahoma. He was a democrat by birth, by training, and later by choice.[20]

With students, such as Gould and Willham, leaving to take post-graduate study at other institutions, and with the increased need of Oklahoma society for more advanced technology, it became apparent to the administration that the Oklahoma A. and M. College needed to develop graduate programs of its own. As early as 1910, R. O. Baird, a teaching assistant, petitioned the faculty for permission to pursue a master's degree. The Board of Agriculture, toward the end of the year, empowered President James Connell to prepare a statement for the college catalog. He appointed a committee consisting of C. E. Sanborn, J. H. Bowers, C. K. Francis, Carl Gunderson, and N. O. Booth to help him.[21] The first announcement of a graduate program appeared in 1911. It stated that the

degree Master of Science will be granted upon completion of twenty-eight hours' work carried for one year or fourteen hours' work carried for two years and the presentation of a satisfactory thesis. Graduate students can be registered only upon approval of the heads of the departments concerned, the faculty, and the president of the college. Those who desire to register as graduate students are advised to communicate with the president or with the head of the department in which they desire to do work.[22]

Baird received the first post-Bachelors degree in 1912. It was awarded two years after his initial request, in the field of chemistry.[23]

During the first decade after formal authorization, graduate study languished at Oklahoma A. and M. Most of the faculty realized the importance of advanced study, for they had received their training from institutions which offered higher degrees. Time and money for such programs, however, were difficult to obtain.[24] About two dozen students made application for admission to the graduate division in 1916 but World War I interrupted this growth. Nevertheless, the interest did justify the appointment of C. E. Sanborn to head a permanent committee to protect standards and to let students know precisely what was expected of them.[25] Sanborn, in spite of adverse circumstances, possessed the credentials for keeping the program moving. He received a B. A. and M. S. from the University of Kansas and began his academic career at Texas A. and M., where he taught and did research in the field of entomology. Immediately before coming to Stillwater, he directed the

Dairy Building (right). In later years served as headquarters for student publications.

The last word in the manufacture of butter and cheese, including a power driven churn, 1916.

Shops and Boiler House

Electrical Laboratory

Machine Shop

Setting Up A Traction Engine

An engineering class in 1909 with two traction engines.

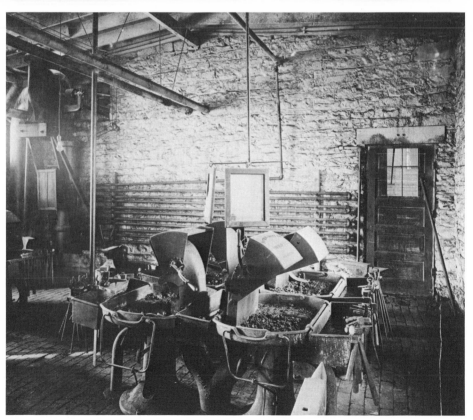

Blacksmith Shop

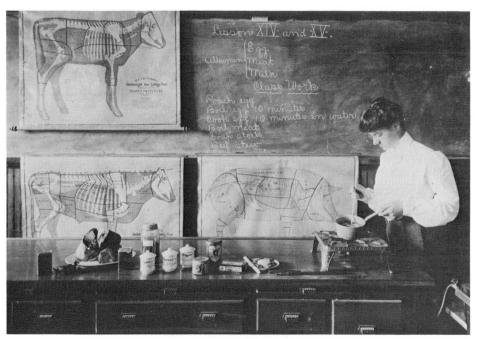

Illustrative Lesson in Cookery

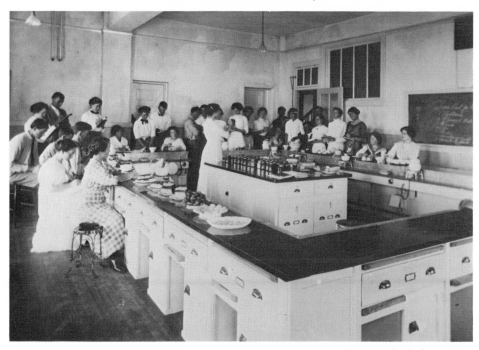

After the girls in the Department of Domestic Economy had finished their baking, the boys were invited to help dispose of the products.

A Sewing Class

Botanical Laboratory with Class

Zoological Laboratory with Class

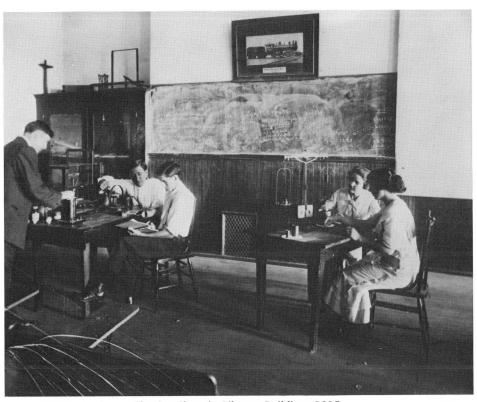

Physics Class in Library Building, 1915.

Campus entertainment. The Sigma Serenaders, 1897. Standing (l. to r.), T. J. Hartman, Cora Miltimore, N. T. Gilbert, Willa Adams, George Bowers, and Minnie Dysart. Seated, Earl Myers and Jessie Thatcher.

First boy's dormitory, 1899.

Early OAMC Band. At right, a representative of the military.

Football team, 1904.

First girl's basketball team, 1904.

OAMC track team, 1903.

Girl's hockey team.

Entire student body and faculty photographed on the steps of Morrill Hall in 1907.

The OAMC skyline at the turn of the century. . .

from the South Gate. . .

from the southeast, 1905. . .

from the southwest, 1906.

New buildings were added. . .

Morrill Hall, the "Showcase of Oklahoma" before the fire of 1914. The ornaments along the edge of the roof were not replaced during reconstruction.

Women's Building (Gardiner Hall) in 1910 with residents on the steps and balconies.

Gundersen Hall

The Auditorium

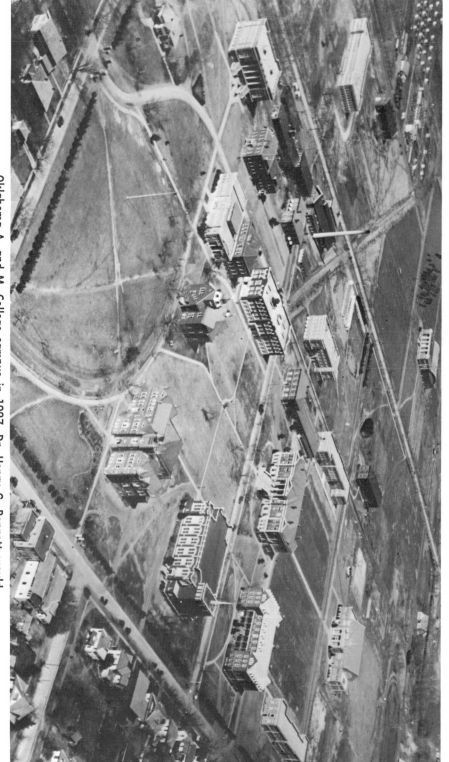

Oklahoma A. and M. College campus in 1927. Dr. Henry G. Bennett would become president the next year to begin the "Twenty-Five Year Plan."

insect breeding laboratory at the University of Illinois. Sanborn moved to Oklahoma in 1909 and served as head of the entomology department for twenty-five years prior to being relieved at his own request in 1934. He became one of the founders of the Oklahoma Academy of Science as well, and gained distinction for his work with "anaplasmosis, an important disease affecting cattle, and with flies as carriers of disease."[26]

The beginning of legitimate graduate work stems from the death of the respected L. L. Lewis. In 1924, the faculty, and many of those students interested in pursuing advanced degrees, commemorated the death of the former president by gathering on Thursday afternoons under the name of the Lewis Research Club. Bradford Knapp attended these sessions and encouraged every department in the institution to discuss ongoing research and to think about the development of graduate programs. He also envisioned the formation of a graduate division. Furthermore, he requested the regents to support post-graduate work through teaching and research assistantships.

This move, however, had overtones of being an economy measure. Clarence McElroy and Tom Reynolds, representing agricultural and social sciences, respectively, were selected to guide the monthly activities of the Lewis Research Club. They invited their colleagues to read papers on different subjects and promoted the creation of a powerful campus lobby on behalf of graduate study. The students, particularly, benefited from this organization as they gained a broad research perspective, averting the narrow specialization becoming so common at other institutions."[27]

In 1926, Professor Sanborn revamped the graduate program. The following year over one hundred students filed a plan of study, with fifteen actually receiving degrees at commencement. Bradford Knapp's successor decided that enrollment had reached the point where a school and a dean should be provided. He hired Daniel Cobb McIntosh, a sparkling-eyed Irishman, for the task of setting up a separate division. McIntosh, if for no other reason, appears to have been a good choice because he possessed more earned degrees than any other person on campus. He held a B. S. in agricultural education, a B. A. in chemistry, and M. A. in educational administration, a Ph. G. in pharmacy, and a Ph. D. in psychology and administration. The new dean also had considerable experience. He began teaching in the Greene County, Indiana public schools in 1900, served overseas in World War I, and accepted a position at Texas A. and M. prior to his move to Stillwater. Dean McIntosh, between 1929 and when he retired in 1953, personally awarded 3,500 of the 4,300 graduate degrees earned by the Aggies. He also pioneered doctoral study on the campus.[28]

In addition to institutional poverty, the graduate program at Stillwater suffered because of the high wages paid by industry. Students, therefore, left the institution as soon as possible to find employment. Dean M. A. Beeson conducted a survey in 1922 and reported that the average annual wage of recent graduates approached $3,000, a figure higher than the salary of many faculty. L. H. "Lew" Wentz, a wealthy Ponca City oil magnate, donated $50,000 [and added more later] to the college to inaugurate a permanent loan fund in 1926, yet there still was not enough money available to encourage students to spend an additional year or two in residence. Jake Katz, a local businessman, instituted another scholarship fund, and, on occasion, the college organized a special drive for needy students. Large scale financial aid, however, did not materialize until the Great Depression. Student assistance at one point reached such a critical stage that the administration suggested young men bring livestock with them when they enrolled, so that they could use the profits to pay expenses. Professor A. C. Baer directed this operation and Wendell Emmons is the first known student to take advantage of it. He maintained two dairy cows which netted him over one dollar per day.[29]

The college developed a "self-help" program for students during the early stages of the Depression. Schiller Scroggs, the director, supervised the employment of about two hundred students who engaged in cabinet making, farming, making brooms, needlecraft, ceramics, and in a duplicating service. Scroggs, in order not to antagonize the community, hired a disinterested outside authority to see what businesses could be started on the campus without competing against townspeople. The institution then secured $150,000 to be used as capital. Both men and women were eligible to work for a maximum of four hours per day, provided that they enrolled in at least twelve hours of classes and maintained an above average grade point. The program was designed to break even; however, if a profit was made, college officials added it to the Wentz fund.[30]

The first students to receive employment were assigned to the college farm, the one near Perkins. Some twenty young men there became involved in the cultivation of wheat, cotton, and oats. Almost as many men accepted assignments in the shops, where they constructed desks, chairs, and other furniture. DeWitt Hunt, the director of the program, was a skilled public relations man as well as an able craftsman. When conferences were held on the campus, he asked his students to make emblems to commemorate the visit. He also saw to it that each new governor of the state received a handsome desk and matching chair as a gift from the college. The ceramics plant employed about the same number of people as the farm and the shops. Headed by M. G. French and L. F. Sheerar, the boys, aided by equipment donated by William Bellis, made flower pots and interior and exterior decorating tile. H. C. Floyd, formerly of Berea College, directed needlecraft, but it never assummed the importance of some of the other projects.[31]

The broom factory proved to be the most successful college self-help program. Under the direction of J. R. Arnold, the institution rented the back portion of the Robert A. Peery Building on Lewis Street. This operation employed one hundred students in two shifts, which were supervised by A. W. Wahler and R. L. Owens.

The brooms could be identified by a diamond shaped trademark and the words "Oklahoma A. and M. College Self-Help Industries." In addition, Arnold selected an advertising slogan that read "Our Project: Boys and Girls of Sterling Worth." Five full time salesmen took the product throughout the state. Since nine-tenths of the world's broom corn was grown within a 300 radius of Wichita, Kansas, the broom industry had no difficulty in obtaining supplies. The factory had a weekly payroll of $600. Schiller Scroggs estimated that 2,000 acres of broom corn were needed to supply production needs.[32]

Not all of the students, of course, were impoverished, and many had time to participate in the numerous organizations that characterize this phase of the institution's history. In January, 1915, the presidents of the various clubs met in order to form a student constitution. The Aggies solicited data from thirty other colleges and universities over a three month period before drafting their own document. It was presented to the student body for ratification on April 6. The finished product provided for the four customary officers as well as a twelve man senate. In May, the students elected their first representatives, with Joe Robinson defeating Grady Thompson for the presidency by a 282 to 66 margin. Jerry Johnson obtained sufficient support at the polls to nail down the combined offices of secretary and treasurer and Fern Lowry, representing the coed element, easily won the vice-presidential post.[33] The senate had many functions, according to the constitution, including the development of student government

to bring about a closer relationship with the faculty, the student body, and the Board of Agriculture; to recommend, maintain, and regulate the customs and traditions of the College, and take such steps as may be advisable and necessary to support and carry into effect any policy to uphold the name of our college . . . .[34]

Revised in April, 1925, the constitution assumed the important task of chartering and regulating student publications and organizations.[35]

Good communications is probably the major reason that student organizations were so successful during this period. In 1924, the Board of Agriculture approved a format for a bi-weekly newspaper entitled the *O'Collegian*. It became responsible for providing the information and publicity that nourished interest in club activities. Students paid one dollar per year to cover printing costs. The initial issue came out on September 4. The paper had paid staff positions, and, in order to keep it from becoming strictly a local affair, arrangements were made with Walker Stone, who headed the Associated Press Bureau, for his Oklahoma City man to telephone 2,000 words nightly from the state capital. President Knapp, though he later regretted the support he gave, assisted the students in making the *O'Collegian* a daily the second quarter of the 1924-1925 academic year.[36] The stated policy of the paper was to publish "the news which is of vital interest to a large number of the student body. No discrimination shall be made in favor of any group or organization, but this paper shall strive to serve as an accurate and timely record of news of the campus."[37] By 1930, the *O'Collegian's* circulation grew so large that a new press had to be installed. It could print from seven to thirteen columns and turn out 3,500 pages in an hour. The expansion, however, caused some problems. J. R. Brown, tax ferret, attempted to include the paper on the tax rolls. Raymond Bivert took issue with him, and succeeded in getting George Tabor to reverse Brown's decision.[38]

The students published other items, too. In a less serious vein, the *Aggievator* and the *Earthquake* appeared sporadically. The home economics department sponsored a magazine entitled *The Oklahoma Home*. Besides one at the Iowa Agricultural College, it was the only such publication in the country. However, most of the students' enthusiasm was reserved for the *Redskin*, the annual yearbook. It came out first under the Connell Administration in 1910 and followed the general format of most other collegiate annuals. The book had sections on the faculty, the campus, classes, cadet life, the discipline clubs, and social highlights. In Chester Gould's day there were many jokes and an occasional "hell" or "damn." But, for the most part, the Aggies exhibited tastes that would not offend adult readers. The earliest issues of the magazine are pleasurable to thumb through simply to view the ingenuity with which students photographed buildings, such as Old Central. While traditional in orientation, the *Redskin* evidenced quality even though the editor claimed only a modest objective.[39] He wrote: "Here will be found no lofty climaxes, and extraordinary displays of literary knowledge; but only simple expressions of what we have thought, felt, and seen during our college days."[40]

Unlike the *O'Collegian*, the *Redskin* had to charge directly for its sales, although it did receive advertising revenues from local businessmen. In 1921, Claude L. Walsh came up with a novel idea which helped to keep the yearbook in the black. He asked his California motion picture executive father to come to Stillwater to arrange a weekly film series, with the proceeds going to the annual. The program became operational in September in time so that the first films could be scheduled in the evenings after football games. College authorities screened the movies in advance in order that everyone could be assured the "production to be shown are those which any student or citizen of Stillwater would be glad to see."[41] With admission pegged at thirty cents per person, most of the Aggies could afford to see productions such as "The Raven," "Humoresque," "Town Nigger," and David Wark Griffith's "The Fall of Babylon," an epic which had a cast of over 125,000. The *Redskin* and the film program were both well received by the students and townspeople.[42]

The most influential, but not necessarily the largest, organization on the campus in the pre-Depression years was the Young Mens' and Young Womens' Christian Association. In reality, these were two separate institutions, but, since they had a joint governing board, they may be treated here as one. President Scott had assisted

208

the "Y" to get a good start. It declined in popularity under his successor, because of inadequate financial support.. The students tried to persuade the Board of Agriculture to subsidize it to the extent of hiring a full time director. It initially refused on the basis that state funds could not be used for religious purposes. Later, the regents relented, finding, apparently, some method of justifying the expenditure. The "Y," before institutional funds became available, planned campus social activities and often joined with sister chapters across the country in sponsoring special events. In 1918, for instance, the Stillwater membership united with 200,000 other students in a Christ and World Democracy Crusade. Three years afterwards, with increased funding, the organization hired a director and expanded its activities. The first man thought to have held this position is Frank Morse of Reno, Nevada. The second supervisor, however, is the individual who again made the "Y" a viable institution.[43]

Stanhope Reid Pier arrived in Stillwater on August 27, 1925. He was a native of Greeley, Colorado, had attended high school in Lynchburg, Virginia, and received his undergraduate training at the University of Nebraska. From there, he moved to nearby Omaha, where he became director of the local YMCA, a position he resigned in order to serve in the United States Navy during World War I. Pier travelled after the war for eighteen months with the Student Volunteer Movement, "an organization known for its promotion of missionary education and recruiting and securing of students for foreign missionary work."[44] He also accepted a ten week overseas assignment on behalf of European student relief. These contributions brought him recognition, and, just before his move to Stillwater, he became the National Secretary of the Student Volunteer Movement, headquartered in New York City. "Stany," as the students called him, assumed the Oklahoma position at thirty-four years of age. He provided much social and spiritual leadership at Oklahoma A. and M. before his departure in 1928.

In some respects, Pier served as a substitute dean of students. The director organized mixers at the beginning of each quarter, conducted campus forums, booked guest speakers, found vacant rooms for visitors, and created an odd job bureau for those who needed money. In addition, the "Y" retained an active interest in national and international affairs. The Aggies, for example, joined with other American university students in debating the merits of United States membership in the Permanent Court of Military Justice. Most of the A. and M. membership agreed with the 100,943 individuals who voted in favor of this move as opposed to the 27,825 who did not. The most useful service provided by the organization was the publication of a so-called Freshman *Bible,* a 147 page booklet which spelled out college rules and regulations, presented tips to freshmen, outlined the campus social and athletic calendar, and listed honor societies and students yells and songs. The businessmen in the community picked up the tab for printing.[45]

The organization decreased in popularity after Stanhope Pier left the campus. DeWitt Hunt, the chairman of the advisory board, recommended George Bullock for the directorship. He seemed to possess the necessary qualifications as he had a degree from the University of Texas and had done graduate work at Yale. Students, however, as in the case of the literary societies, were beginning to have other interests. Only mixers continued to be popular. One young man in 1929 established a record for drinking punch. He consumed sixty-nine cups in a single evening, a mark which still stands to the present day.[46] In 1928, President Knapp's successor built upon the Christian tradition established on the campus by the "Y" and proclaimed that henceforth five days each school year would be set aside for devotions and meditation. He noted: "It is fitting and proper that this week be set aside in Stillwater and on the campus as Religious Emphasis Week during which time all people may be given the opportunity to consider the fundamental realities of morality, religion, and deity."[47] The two branches of the "Y" and Religious Emphasis Week, along with the church study centers, provided a Christian environment for those that wished it. And, perhaps, for some who did not desire it.

The YMCA and YWCA served a useful purpose, because they were organizations that looked after the welfare of the entire student body. The newer clubs, those which were chartered in the decade or so before the stock market crash, were elitist: the sororities and fraternities catered to the social and economic upper class; and the local branches of honor societies depended upon superior scholarship for admittance. There were, however, a few exceptions. The campus did contain a Cosmopolitan Club, an agency that served foreign students in residence at Stillwater. Its membership regularly included undergraduates from South America, the Philippine Islands, Russia, China, Czechoslovakia, Spain, and India. Moreover, students interested in activities as diverse as dairying or ACACIA, a student fraternal lodge, elected officers and conducted business in line with the specialized interests. The campus also contained a secret society, Theta Nu Epsilon. It attempted to influence campus and state elections and last, some individuals debated chartering a local chapter of Alpha Pi Sigma, an organization incorporated by Wilson D. Bush, a Kleagle in the national Ku Klux Klan.[48]

As has been mentioned, the first fraternity established on the campus, Delta Sigma, came in 1909. With the barrier broken, others followed: The male students founded Delta Sigma Alpha in 1916; Lambda Chi Alpha in 1917; and Kappa Alpha and Kappa Sigma in 1920. The females, not to be outdone, attempted to secure a Kappa Alpha Theta chapter. They began working toward this end as early as 1910. The faculty did not encourage them in this pursuit, so the coeds held secret meetings under the name of the "After Tea Girls." Persistence finally prevailed. In September, 1919, national officers initiated the group, making it unnecessary for the girls to fear further faculty raids, some of which had sent them scurrying into town where they requested that local bankers hide their records in vaults. Ten years later, the *Redskin* listed eight sororities, and fifteen fraternities as well as a Panhellenic Council.[49]

Honor societies replaced the discipline clubs. Alpha Zeta, the first on the campus, represented agriculture. Installation ceremonies were conducted on September 30, 1916, by John MacArthur of the Kansas Agricultural College. He currently served as national secretary. The following roster indicates those groups established on the campus by the end of the Knapp administration. It should be noted that four were founded by Oklahoma A. and M. College. The students did not think it inconsistent to include religious organizations alongside honor societies, for they held scholarship and religious faith both in equally high esteem.[50]

Name	Oklahoma A. and M. Chapter Date	Founding Institution and Date of First Chapter
Alpha Zeta (agriculture)	1916	Ohio State University (1897)
Omicron Nu (home economics)	1920	Michigan State University (1912)
Chi Delta Phi (English)	1925	University of Tennessee (1919)
Kappa Delta Pi (education)	1921	University of Illinois (1910)
Sigma Tau (engineering)	1923	University of Nebraska (1904)
Chi Sigma (chemistry)	1920	Oklahoma A. and M. College (1920)
Alpha Sigma (radio electronics)	1925	University of Oklahoma (1922)
Pi Delta Kappa (forensics)	1925	Ripon College (1913)
Kappa Tau Pi (men's religious society)	1920	University of Oklahoma (1918)
Pi Zeta Kappa (international women's society)	1920	University of Oklahoma (1909)
Pi Epsilon Alpha (Methodist Church society for women)	1926	Oklahoma A. and M. College (1926)
Kappa Kappa Psi (band)	1919	Oklahoma A. and M. College (1919)
Kappa Phi (Methodist Episcopal Church society)	1921	University of Kansas (1916)
Farraguerra (women's military society)	1927	Oklahoma A. and M. College (1927)
Scabbard and Blade (men's military society)	1920	University of Wisconsin (1905)

Phi Kappa Phi (all academic honor society) 1920	University of Maine (1897)
International Relations Club (peace society)	Carnegie Endowment for International Peace (no date listed) [51]

Two of the above listed groups, Kappa Kappa Psi and Phi Kappa Phi, deserve additional discussion. In connection with the former, the college was fortunate in 1915 to hire Bohumil Makovsky to head its music department. "Boh," as he was known throughout the state, brought A. and M. great fame for his role in establishing the first national collegiate band society. Until he reached seventeen, Makovsky lived in a Bohemian town named Frantisky. There he and his mother eked out a living on a small fourteen acre farm, his father having died before he was born. In the United States he became a cigar maker's apprentice in the daytime, while he gained experience as a musician in the evenings. In Czechoslovakia he had learned to play several instruments from an uncle who instructed in the royal band of Russia. Farm chores, however, left little time for practice, except for what he could get as he walked to school each day. It did not take "Boh" long to realize that he did not want to make a career of making cigars. He quit to tour the country for eight years with a traveling band. Then he settled down in Oklahoma City where he taught at the Old Music and Art Institute and directed bands in Yukon, Dent, Shawnee, and Woodward.[51]

In 1916, President Cantwell hired Makovsky to teach in Stillwater. Rumor had it that he attempted to quit when informed that he was to be chairman, yet he stayed until his retirement. He liked to teach woodwinds and prided himself in instilling a love of music rather than developing techniques. Besides regular classes, "Boh" conducted a ninety piece concert band, an all-school band, and seventy-five piece military band. One writer estimated that in one way or another the teacher involved about eight hundred people per year in his music program. In addition to organizing Kappa Kappa Phi and drawing the attention of the great John Philip Sousa to the college, Bohumil Makovsky focused the eyes of the Southwest on A. and M. through his concert tours and marching bands. Music remained his work and his life until he died.[52]

Phi Delta Kappa, sometimes called the most prestigious honor society in the nation, did not permit the founding of a chapter in Stillwater because the organization represented scholarship in the liberal arts to the mutual exclusion of the sciences. Therefore, L. L. Lewis and Harry Orr, who had joined Phi Kappa Phi at the Kansas Agricultural College, requested that a branch of this honor society be installed at A. and M. On April 22, 1920, E. H. Wells, a professor of economics at Nebraska Wesleyan, joined Lewis and Orr in organizing a chapter. He recounted for his audience the fact that this organization had been conceived by a group of academicians in Washington, D. C. in 1895. They established the first chapter at the University of Maine the following year. Moreover, he reminded his audience that Phi Kappa Phi represented "unity and democracy of education, and its general object is to unite college graduates of high rank without regard to department, course of study, or sex, for the advancement of highest scholarship."[53] The establishment of clubs and societies, even those of the caliber of Phi Kappa Phi, did not mean, however, that all were viable organizations. The student and local newspaper often contained editorials on apathy.[54]

Although disinterest sometimes hampered the honor societies, it did not transfer to athletics. In 1915, the Aggies were electrified to hear that Ed Gallagher would return to the campus as director of athletics. Gallagher, a legendary track star in the Southwest, graduated from Oklahoma A. and M. in 1909. He served as track coach for four years under W. E. Schreiber before leaving to head the sports program at Baker University, the oldest institution of higher education in Kansas. His decision to return to his *alma mater* marked the entrance of the institution into big time athletics. The students, too, contributed to this new image by shedding the Princeton Tiger, choosing instead to identify their teams with their own region. They selected "cowboy" as their nickname and created a mascot patterned after Frank "Pistol Pete" Eaton, a veteran of the Old West who resided in nearby Perkins.[55]

The year before Gallagher returned, President Lewis brought the Oklahoma A. and M. College into the Southwestern Intercollegiate Association. This organization, of which the institution was a charter member, incorporated on December 8, 1914, at Houston, Texas. Its membership included the University of Texas, Texas A. and M., Rice Institute, Baylor, Southwestern University of Arkansas, the University of Oklahoma, and Oklahoma A. and M. In 1920, college officials decided to seek admission into the Missouri Valley Conference. Ed Gallagher filed the formal request at a meeting in Oklahoma City. The committee turned down this petition by a five to four vote but President Knapp succeeded in reversing this decision on December 9, 1924. The victory, however, was short-lived, because in 1927 the University of Nebraska, the University of Oklahoma, the University of Kansas, and the Kansas A. and M. College secretly decided to create a new athletic association, joining with the University of Missouri to form the Big Six Conference. This move, which left Stillwater to face weak competition, infuriated Knapp and it undoubtedly had something to do with his resignation from the presidency.[56]

But in spite of this setback, the students and community supported the institution's athletic program without reservation. Football, in keeping with the spirit of the age, commanded the most attention. Pep rallies were held throughout the week, and on the night before the game, the Aggies built huge bonfires which illuminated the darkness so that hundreds of people could participate in the cheering and singing. Many of the football contests were filmed and exhibited throughout the Southwest in order to recruit players and to increase enrollment. In 1919, the college made arrangements to give the Aggies instant coverage of away games. Maintenance personnel stretched a long wire across the stage of the auditorium which could be marked to indicate the loss or gain made on each play. Then a student would listen to a telephone report and place a device on the wire to indicate what happened on each down. Knapp replaced this crude form of communication five years later with a $1400 electronic machine which would signal everything from a punt to a fumble. Also, the instrument could be used as a scoreboard for home games.[57]

The football mentor, next to the college presidency, seems to have had the least tenure of anyone on the campus. E. E. Parry, the first paid coach, took the position at an annual salary of $1,000, half of which was to be paid from gate receipts and half from the Student Athletic Association. When he complained that the students were behind in their payments to him, the Board fired him. It also demanded the resignation of Boyd Hill, the athletic director. Paul J. Davis, Parry's successor, laster longer. Davis had graduated from Dickinson College in 1907 and come to Stillwater in 1909. He had a season record of 7-2-1, the high point being a 134 to 0 drubbing of Phillips University. This score set a national record. But, after looking over the prospects for the future, Davis decided to seek greener pastures one year later. The players hated to see him leave, and, as a token of their affection, they awarded him a large loving cup which they had purchased with their own money.[58]

The employment of John George "Pinky" Griffith indicated that the day of big time collegiate football had arrived. Under him, the team played its first Missouri Valley opponent, though it was not in the conference yet. In Griffith's two year tenure, he compiled a 8-9-1 record. It was an excellent performance in view of the fact that the schedule had been greatly strengthened. In order to accomplish this feat, however, the popular red-haired man had to draw upon all of his fourteen years of coaching experience at the University of Idaho and the University of Iowa. Griffith brought the forward pass to Stillwater and captured the admiration of Aggie fans all over the state.[59] A yearbook writer recalled: "He was discussed on the side lines, at the bookstore, at the Rooter's meetings, in the study room and then 'Prexy' began to talk about him in chapel and finally the whole state began to talk about him for he was a new coach in charge with a new style of football . . . ."[60] Unfortunately for the Cowboys, the New Mexico A. and M. College lured him away from the campus.[61]

E. A. Pritchard, Griffith's replacement, compiled a winning record in 1917 and 1918. His two year mark of 8-7-0 does not really reflect the regard students had for him, because he succeeded in defeating the University of Oklahoma by a score of 9 to 0. It was the first time that Stillwater had ever beaten its Norman rival. Reed Coldiron, the quarterback, engineered the win, with splendid assistance from Guy "Looky" Lookabaugh, who made bone-crushing plunges into the Sooner line. College officials in order to increase attendance for this contest, scheduled the game on neutral ground in Oklahoma City. Five thousand fans paid to watch their favorite team. Pritchard won twice as many games as he lost in 1918 but decided to move anyhow. Next, James E. Pixlee tried his hand. Coming from Missouri Wesleyan College, he failed to produce a winning season in two attempts, so Gallagher replaced him in 1920.[62]

John Frederick "Maulie" Maulbetsch, an All-American halfback at the University of Michigan in 1914, remained at Oklahoma A. and M. College from 1921 to 1928. He brought the team into the Missouri Valley Conference, and won the title in 1926 with a squad captained by Harold "Red" Weissinger. The coach endeared himself to Cowboy fans by tieing or beating the Oklahoma Sooners four times. This feat brought Maulbetsch national recognition. He became one of the first athletes to endorse products packaged by the wizards of Madison Avenue. His specialty was adhesive tape. Maulbetsch, his last year at Stillwater, was voted one of the top ten coaches in the country. In addition, the University of Michigan selected him as one of their ten greatest alumni.[63] The Aggies honored him, too. They dedicated an issue of the *Redskin* to him, stating that he was their

loyal friend, inspiring coach, and exponent of true sportsmanship, who by his fine personality, devotion to the welfare of the students, and unselfish service to the Oklahoma A. and M. College, has gained the admiration and gratitude of countless friends.[64]

Not everyone connected with Oklahoma A. and M. agreed with the students' assessment. Gallagher had trouble with Maulbetsch over money, and Knapp became disturbed with him over the conduct of people who attended away games. In June, 1927, L. A. Clinkenbeard of the Board of Agriculture suggested that he be fired but the other members voted the motion down. Nevertheless, Maulbetsch resigned at the end of the year to make room for the son of Bishop Ernest Waldorf, a player who had been an All-American tackle at the University of Syracuse. Lynn Waldorf, with one possible exception, turned out to be the greatest football coach in the history of the institution. He, in six seasons, compiled a 34-10-6 record, including four state championships and two Missouri Valley Conference titles. Moreover, he accomplished a near Herculean task in fielding teams that never lost a game to the University of Tulsa or the University of Oklahoma, both of whom were usually national powers on the gridiron. When Waldorf left in 1934, he was replaced by his genial assistant, A. A. Exendine, who had been an outstanding player at Carlile.[65]

Basketball, as compared to football, did not fare well on the Aggie campus during its early years. In fact, the college dropped the sport in 1914 because the facilities were so poor that the game always lost money. The increased attention being devoted to the activity at other institutions caused the students, out of pride more than anything else, to request that intercollegiate competition be reinstated, in spite of the fact that the gynasium was only one-half regulation size. Until the completion of the new facility in 1920, the teams, which usually were headed by the football coaches, scheduled mediocre opposition and played almost all of their games away from home. The 1916-1917 season proved to be one of the few bright spots. Led by Reed Coldiron, the Tigers won the state championship and beat the Chilocco Indian School on its home court, a feat which no other team had been able to do for ten years.[66]

In 1920, the college basketball team played for the first time on a new regulation sized court. But because the institution was preoccupied with returning to peacetime activities, the coach did not have time to arrange a complete schedule of games in advance. James Pixlee fielded three separate teams during the season, as players lost interest when they did not know on a Monday who would be played the following weekend. Conditions did not significantly improve the next year, with the boys only winning two contests. Both victories came at the expense of a weak Oklahoma Baptist five. John Maulbetsch developed basketball into a major sport at Stillwater. In 1922 his team defeated several strong opponents, including the Kansas A. and M. College, the University of Oklahoma, and the Southern Methodist University. Moreover, the freshman team did well and prospects for the future brightened.[67]

From 1923 to 1925, the team, now competing in the Southwest Conference, improved steadily, placing fourth, third, and first, respectively. Clifford T. "Red" Dean, led the team in scoring and was voted All-Conference center. George Conner of Sapulpa, a guard, received league honors the following year. The Cowboys that season were favored to win the championship but had to wait until the final game to do so. Clyde Hall, in a contest with the University of Arkansas, made the winning basket just seconds before the final gun sounded. Later, Maulbetsch developed teams that could almost compete on an even keel with members of the Missouri Valley. His players won their first conference game against the University of Washington by a score of 29 to 26. Otherwise, there was little to cheer about from 1925 to 1927. Then, in 1929, when prospects looked good, two of the best players decided not to return to school, and, a third player, now the only veteran on the squad, received a letter stating that he was ineligible for further competition. George Rody, a man who had played basketball under Forrest "Phog" Allen at the University of Kansas, followed Maulbetsch. He coached throughout the 1931 season with success.[68]

In 1934, the Oklahoma A. and M. College found a man who could bring excellence in basketball. Sometime during the winter, the president and business manager, along with Vernon Snell, a leading sports writer in the state, met with Henry Iba in an Oklahoma City hotel room. Iba, the basketball coach at the University of Colorado, had been employed at Classen High School for two years and at Northwest Missouri State College for four years. He already had a national reputation, for he was one of the originators of center-post play, a strategy which had spread until most of the leading teams in the country were using it. Iba decided to leave

216

Boulder and come to Stillwater to coach basketball and baseball. In addition, he became athletic director when Ed Gallagher's health failed. With the completion of Gallagher Hall in 1938, then called Iba's folly, the "Iron Duke" developed the Cowboys into a national basketball power. More than once, though, he had to sign personal notes for athletic equipment as money always was in short supply.[69]

Neither track or baseball achieved prominence before World War II. In 1914, President Lewis brought Claude Allen, the world champion pole-vaulter, to coach track. He resigned shortly afterward, leaving Gallagher to handle the thinclad teams until 1927. Pete Fannema had an undefeated mile season and Floyd Beanblossom set a new hop-step-jump record at the Pennsylvania Relay. Otherwise, the sport received little recognition. Roy W. "Wash" Kenny replaced Gallagher. Kenny recruited in the high schools, extended the training season, and obtained a new cinder track in 1929, yet nothing seemed to help. Baseball fared worse. In 1931 it was temporarily deleted from the schedule. The students, however, did not appear to mind, for they discovered a new sport, one that would bring national and world attention to their college.[70]

Edward Gallagher, as wrestling coach, sent teams to the mats which from 1915 to 1938 won 130 dual meets, losing only five times and three of these losses came in the same season. At one point, the Cowboys placed first in seventy-four consecutive meets, a record that probably will never be equalled again. In addition, Gallagher wrote the standard textbooks for the sport and served as president of the American Association of Wrestling Coaches. Then, too, he was the first man to send athletes to the Olympic Games from Stillwater. His proteges, known as Gallagher's Men, assumed important coaching jobs upon graduation in colleges and universities all over the nation. Few men ever dominated a sport in the manner that Edward Gallagher did wrestling.[71]

One of six children, the wrestling coach was born on September 5, 1887, at Perth, Kansas, the son of Alfred and Susan Gallagher. He enrolled as a preparatory student at Stillwater in 1904. The next year he gained admittance as a regular student. Edward worked his way through school, as the family did not have much money. He served as a janitor and later purchased a chemical formula for dry cleaning clothing, a move that ended his financial worries. Gallagher majored in engineering; however, time was always found to compete in organized athletics. Taking after his grandfather, who had been a wrestler, and his father who sprinted, Edward played football and excelled in track. A popular student, he married Stella Taylor, a home economics coed.[72]

Initially, the Cowboys won their matches simply by superior strength. Extensive analyses of diet and new training methods made wrestling more scientific. Moreover, Gallagher applied his engineering skills to the study of anatomy. Often his students found him tucked away in a corner of a biology laboratory where he could be observed "stringing rubber bands over human skeletons to learn how

217

to apply the principles of leverages to wrestling."[73] Next, he mastered Jinto and proceeded to devise holds which would enable the Aggies to best their competition in spite of weight differences. Gallagher recruited men who had a particular type of build, too. He sought boys who were tall and slim and who possessed a slow heart beat and large blood vessels. His indomitable will and revolutionary training methods made the Oklahoma A. and M. College virtually unbeatable. Almost singlehandedly, Edward Clark Gallagher made wrestling, a minor sport elsewhere, a major one in the Southwest.[74]

Wrestling excellence had a tremendous impact on the state of Oklahoma. Before World War II, the image of the state of Oklahoma had deteriorated in the eyes of many people in the nation. John Steinbeck, the novelist, published a book entitled *The Grapes of Wrath* which portrayed Sooners as ignorant and backward. Had the state been more alert, its leadership might have capitalized on the fame of Will Rogers; however, it did not. Therefore, Gallagher's teams brought the college and community favorable publicity at a time when it needed it most. Nevertheless, the recognition did not end the migration westward. Thus, at a time when Oklahoma needed more revenue, it lost much of its labor force, and the Great Depression settled in until the nation mobilized for yet another war. The college and the state, as at no other time in their history, needed one of its own to emerge as a progressive leader.[75]

XIV "A Dreamer of No Little Dreams"

On June 1, 1928, the Board of Agriculture met in Oklahoma City to elect a president for the Oklahoma A. and M. College. The membership approached their task with confidence, for the regents had appointed no less than eight men to this position in the last twenty-five years. The trustees had had an individual in mind for some time, but the public outcry against the acceptance of the resignation of Bradford Knapp has been so great that the Board decided to go through the motions of an extended search. Henry Johnston, who knew that a second attempt would be made to impeach him in the near future, promised not to interfere in the selection process. Moreover, the governor stated that he personally favored bringing in an experienced executive from outside the state. On this day, therefore, eighteen names were under consideration. Several members of the Former Students Association were in attendance, too. W. A. Melton, president of the organization, presented four other names to the Board for consideration. His list included: George I. Christie, director of the experiment station and dean of the college

219

of agriculture at Purdue University; Andrew M. Soule, president of the Georgia State College of Agriculture; Julian A. Burress, president of the Virginia Polytechnic Institute; and Harry L. Dent, president of the New Mexico State College. It was clear to everyone in the conference room that this meeting was a special one because a stenographer had been hired to record every word.[1]

Harry Cordell and W. A. Melton dominated the conversation. The former man, from the original list of eighteen names, recommended that Henry Garland Bennett, the president of the Southeastern State College in Durant, Oklahoma, be confirmed as Knapp's successor. The latter man did not oppose the nomination, but he did not support it either. The two men eventually reached the point where they could only glare at each other across the table. This break in the action prompted Ferne King to move, and George Van Noy to second, a motion to employ Bennett. She said: "Ever since I have been a member of this Board, I have wanted to see the A. and M. College in the hands of a man capable of putting it where it belongs, or where it ought to be. It has never been there yet, and I think that Dr. Bennett can put it there, and will make a success of that college."[2] Her statement placed Melton in something of a quandary. He believed that Cordell's candidate was a capable individual but he felt that his appointment would involve the land-grant institution again in the politics of the state. Melton knew Bennett had been a college classmate of William J. Holloway, the lieutenant-governor of Oklahoma, and that Dial Currin, president of the First National Bank, had driven the candidate to the capital city the day before. Both men resided in Durant and both men were prominent in the Democratic Party. Moreover, Melton had been informed that Bennett was waiting in a nearby room, ready to be introduced at the proper time. In other words, the decision had already been made. The only question now concerned whether or not to lodge a formal protest.[3]

The Alumni Association had investigated Henry Bennett prior to requesting that some of the membership be permitted to attend the meeting in Oklahoma City. The people interviewed believed Bennett an able, if not an outstanding man. Melton reported: "In our investigation we have found little or nothing of criticism of Doctor Bennett which is justified. We found many men in various walks of life, in the portion of the state around Durant, who spoke in the highest terms of Bennett's ability, integrity, and honesty of purpose."[4] If the investigation had been more thorough, there would have been less hesitation about the nomination. Bennett had been born in Nevada County [near New Hope], Arkansas in a log cabin on December 14, 1886, five years to the day before the A. and M. college opened its doors. Of medium height, the raspy voiced executive possessed an abundance of personal charisma, a trait shared by many of the state and national political leaders of the coming decade. By 1928 Bennett had adopted the Sooner State as his own and in the future he would reject many offers to leave it on a permanent basis. In return for the many kindnesses extended by his fellow citizens to him and his family, the educator vowed to employ his leadership talents for the betterment of Oklahoma. He was, as Senator Robert Kerr once said, "a dreamer of no little dreams . . . ."[5]

Henry, the son of Thomas Jefferson and Mary Elizabeth [Bright] Bennett, had been a devout Christian since youth. He and his sisters lived on the family farm before moving to Texas with their parents. The Bennetts remained in Texas until it was time for their children to begin formal schooling. They then returned to Arkansas, to Arkadelphia. Henry enrolled in the primary department of Ouachita College when he was eight years old, staying until 1907 when he received his Bachelor of Arts degree. The boy proved to be an apt pupil at the Baptist institution and made excellent marks in his studies, most of which were classical in nature. He served as president of the Philomathian Literary Society, vice-president of the student athletic association, and business manager of *The Bear,* the campus newspaper.[6]

Henry worked his way through school with his hands. He earned his tuition by collecting laundry, driving a grocery wagon, and delivering mail. Thomas Bennett preached in nearby towns and his wife Mary took in boarders to support the family. On occasion, Henry's income was used for family as well as school needs. He obtained a teaching certificate and taught at a business college in Texarkana following graduation but quit after a few months to sell textbooks. On one trip, Bennett visited Boswell, Oklahoma, a community which needed a teacher. He gained the position through the assistance of friends and soon became principal of the school and superintendent of Choctaw County. His popularity was such that several colleagues nominated him for the presidency of the Oklahoma Teachers Association. From 1909 to 1919, the young man matured as an educator and took a better paying position at Hugo. He learned to respect the residents of southern Oklahoma. In turn, they never forgot Henry Bennett's affection and gentleness. He was a man who truly possessed the common touch.[7]

Bennett, during the years that he spent as superintendent of schools in Hugo, met Vera Pearl Connell, the daughter of J. V. Connell, a businessman, lawyer, and federal judge. Miss Connell envisioned an educational career, too. She attended a Presbyterian Indian mission school and the University of Chicago. The couple enjoyed the company of each other; however, when a proposal did not immediately materialize, Vera accepted a teaching position in Alva, the home of a small normal school. In this case "absence did make the heart grow fonder" and the two repeated their marriage vows on January 27, 1913, at Judge Connell's home in Durant. The bride wore a wedding dress made by Madame LaRogue of Louisville, Kentucky. Vera and Henry's two daughters, Liberty and Mary, and the wives of their three sons, Philip, Henry, Jr., and Tom, all wore the same gown at their weddings. The lifestyle of the Bennett family coincided with an analysis of Oklahomans drawn by J. Frank Dobie. He said that the thing which set Sooners apart from other people was their simplicity—in diet, religion, and loyalties. Of these attributes, religion meant the most to the Bennetts. Henry and Vera died at the same time. The family *Bible* was the top item in the handbag which lay between them.[8]

Henry Bennett accepted the presidency of the Southeastern State Teachers College at Durant in 1917. He was in an excellent position to know the strengths and weaknesses of the institution for he had enrolled in a summer institute there before buildings had been erected on the campus. The educator remained in Durant for more than a decade. Enrollment increased from 300 to 1,500 during this period and funds were obtained for an outstanding physical plant. In particular, Southeastern specialized in training rural school teachers. The president wrote textbooks for the public schools and he brought in nationally prominent educational lecturers. Some people believed that the institution ranked among the best of its kind in the country. Besides his presidential duties, Bennett held executive positions in the Baptist Church, the Lions, and the Rotary. However, he seldom accepted personal praise for his accomplishments.[9] He explained in 1934 in a speech at Durant that my

success personally, so far as there might be adjudged to have been any, was largely due to the capable and unselfish staff who worked with me in the achievement of our commonly accepted aims, to the loyalty and unfailing co-operation of the business and professional people of this City, and to the good-will, hearty support, and united effort of the people of the district.[10]

President Bennett continued his own education while employed in Durant. He completed his intermediate degree at the University of Oklahoma in 1924. Two years later Columbia University awarded the Ph. D. His dissertation was written in a remarkably short period of time and entitled "The Coordination of the State Institutions of Higher Education in Oklahoma." More practical than theoretical, the study argued for the creation of a unified system of higher education in the Sooner State. The period spent in New York City brought acquaintance with Thomas H. Briggs and George D. Strayer, two professors who almost singlehandedly developed educational administration as an academic field. Both of these men believed that schools could be used to overcome evil [politicians] and usher in the Golden Age [rule by the masses]. Henry Bennett agreed with this point of view and he did much to popularize Brigg's and Strayer's ideas in Oklahoma.[11]

In 1918, Henry Bennett, along with others, such as M. A. Nash, T. T. Montgomery, and J. P. Battenberg, founded a secret fraternity to bring schoolmen together. Southeastern Oklahoma educators composed the nucleus of the group at first. The organization, though purely social on the surface, originated at a point in time when education was evolving into a profession and when educators recognized the need for active involvement in politics in order to make changes. Perhaps, then, it was more than coincidence that the early members of the society gradually gained control of many of the state's public school and college administrative positions. On the other hand, the organization primarily provided a much needed social release. Teachers in the first two or three decades of this century were often judged by the same standards as those applied to clergymen. The group chose as its name The Ancient and Beneficient Order of the Red Red Rose. It is believed that the title stemmed from the practice of putting a rose in the lapel of initiates. The wives of the membership, not to be outdone by their husbands, created an auxiliary, the Blue Blue Violets.[12] The goals of the Red Red Rose included:

1. To furnish a meeting place where friendship may be encouraged, isolation eliminated, false dignity laid aside where teachers may meet and eat with increasing pride.
2. To foster fraternal cooperation and the development of all agencies which shall be for the advancement and profit of the teachers.
3. To work for the professionalization of teaching and the improvement of public schools and to relentlessly war against all forces opposed to these ends.[13]

More humorous objectives are listed in the WILL OF THE GRAND OLD MAN.

There were few formal trappings during the early years of the organization. The agenda usually consisted of a dinner and certain other activities designed to breakdown the stone-faced facade sometimes associated with public servants. The humor grew less coarse and the titles of members more impressive as the society expanded in size and influence. Some of the more colorful positions were: The Exalted Grand High Mokus of the Universe; the Exalted Grand High Provider; The Exalted Grand High Eulicidator; The Exalted Grand High Inner Wicket; The Exalter Grand High Organizer. The Red Red Rose offered the rural school teacher much of value. Poorly educated and paid, it gave him an opportunity to meet college presidents, university faculty, and governors of the state. The organization also provided some fond memories never to be forgotten. One member stated: "The entertainment and grand association afforded by the conclave has made a valuable and sizeable contribution to the teaching profession." He added: "Yes, as I look back over the past quarter of a century it seems to be that through this 'Noble Order' I had my heartiest laughs, listened to the cleverest wit, ate the most delicious food and had close fellowship with the cream of mankind. For what else can one ask?"[14]

How much of this information W. A. Melton had in the back of his mind as he sat at the conference table in Oklahoma City is not known. In the end, however, he did not oppose Bennett's election at an annual salary of $10,000. In fact, he greeted him at the door when he stepped into the room and asked him to give his first speech as president to the chamber of commerce in Tulsa. After introductions were made and congratulations extended, Bennett met with Acting President Clarence McElroy and Bradford Knapp. The latter man had returned to aid his predecessor with personnel appointments for the coming year. The Oklahoma Board of Education reluctantly released the president of Southeastern from his post. The Rotary and Lions Clubs wrote glowing recommendations of Bennett and forwarded them to their organizational counterparts in Stillwater. More than one person in the Southeastern community broke down in tears.[15] Fellow churchmen, however, probably felt the worst at his departure. The local congregation of the Baptist Church took up a collection to purchase and engrave a gold watch. It was presented with the following statement:

To know Henry Bennett well is to love him . . . . He has the charm of personality that draws most men to him as a magnet. He has the power of leadership that makes other men gladly follow him. He is a democrat and meets with equal ease the low and the high - he treats all men as his equal. He is a clearing house for the troubles and worries of others and is capable of soothing the sick, cheering the discouraged, and lending a helping hand to the man who feels down and out.[16]

This estimate may be too laudatory, but friends and foes alike agreed that Henry Bennett was an unusually talented man.

Though the Board of Agriculture promised a free hand in guiding the affairs of the Oklahoma A. and M. College, the members believed they were free to make personnel changes before the incoming administration took office. Seven members of the faculty and staff therefore received dismissal notices five days after the Oklahoma City meeting. Included in this group were Adrian Daane, H. Clay Potts, R. B. Thompson, A. S. Hiatt, E. C. Campbell, C. E. Trout, and L. A. Mitchell. Shortly afterward Harry Cordell promised the editor of the *O'Collegian* that no further interference would take place. Yet, within a few days, the Board voted to dismiss forty more of its employees, some of whom are thought to have held service positions in Stillwater. Bennett did not object to the release of staff, but he did protest the firing of faculty and several had their names listed on the payroll roster again.[17] Later, he requested that the trustees adopt a written document which he had prepared in response to the dismissals. It was based upon the 1915 tenure statement of the American Association of University Professors. In part, it read:

Be it resolved, that the following statement be stated in writing and be in the possession of both the college and the teacher.

Termination of a temporary short term appointment shall always be possible at the expiration of the term by the mere act of giving timely notice of the desire to terminate. The decision to terminate shall always be taken however in conference with the department concerned. The question of appointments for the ensuing academic year shall be taken up as early as possible.

A permanent or long time appointment shall not be terminated except for cause, and then only after a proper hearing. Exceptions to this rule may be necessary in exceptional cases of gross immorality or treason when the facts are admitted. In such cases summary dismissals shall ensue. In cases where other offences are charged, and in all cases where the facts are in dispute, the accused teacher shall always have the opportunity to face his accuser and to be heard in his own judgment upon the case.[18]

The unanimous adoption of this resolution ended the annual election of faculty. In one stroke the biggest single evil associated with the college since the institution opened its doors in 1891 had been eliminated.

President Bennett began his administration in late June, 1928. He had many advantages that his predecessors did not have. The campus contained 36 buildings and 4,000 students, counting regular and short course enrollments. The September freshman class numbered almost 2,000. This figure included Henry Bennett, Jr., who at fourteen, was the youngest student at the institution. In addition, the president enjoyed the confidence of the chief executive of the state, for William J. Holloway replaced the impeached Henry Johnston in 1929. The former individual praised Bennett on several occasions, and, in turn, the educator wrote speeches for the chief executive and helped him to shape educational policies. Moreover, the two men developed an appropriation formula for higher education in Oklahoma. One, incidentally, which increased the annual budget of A. and M. by more than one-third. Finally, Bennett followed a man in office who had just completely reorganized the entire academic program and had brought the institution into harmoney with modern educational practices and thought. After a quick trip to Washington to untangle some problems relating to the experiment station, Bennett attempted to build upon the foundation laid for him. His immediate objectives included revamping the administrative structure, devising a plan to expand physical facilities, providing additional security for the faculty, and aiding the Alumni Association to overhaul its antiquated organizational structure. This program prepared the institution to move ahead at a rapid pace; only the extent of the Great Depression prevented immediate strides forward.[19]

Henry Bennett believed in the consolidation of power. In short, he was a dictator, though usually a benevolent one. When he became president of A. and M. it had six schools: agriculture, engineering, home economics, science and literature, education, and commerce. To these six, he added one more— a school of graduate study. Agriculture and engineering dominated both at home and abroad. The school of engineering enrolled more students than agriculture; however, the latter brought more state and national recognition to the campus. The livestock teams, for instance, won national and international championships in 1930. But while the general academic program was in good shape, the institution needed to develop a leadership team which could work together for the attainment of common goals. The appointment of new deans and the centralization of power, then, became the president's first major endeavor.[20]

In the past, most of the political pressure had been directed at deans and department heads, a situation which prevented executive continuity. Many of the earlier appointments had not been loyal to the chief executive of the institution and this fact contributed to the rapid turnover in the presidential office. Bennett, in order to counteract this situation, filled vacancies with church friends and with former associates from Durant. Quite often these individuals were people who did not possess the earned doctorate. For those who performed well, the president rewarded them with high salaries and with leaves of absences so that they could complete work on a terminal degree. In this manner a completely loyal staff was obtained. On the other hand, elevation to an administrative position did not necessarily guarantee personal intimacy. Many a dean in the coming years would sit in his chair and stare out of his window toward Bennett's office in Whitehurst Hall and wonder what the "good Doctor" wanted them to do in a particular situation. Moreover, the president often put his staff in competition with each other to keep them alert. If he had an important speech to make, or a major decision, he often asked three or four different men to provide an outline or to weigh arguments for or against a certain proposition. The deans, therefore, struggled against one another for position and power.[21]

The closest advisors to the president were those people who controlled access to him and those who were charged with the financial responsibility for the institution. On Bennett's first visit to the campus he asked Earle Albright and Veta Ware to serve as his administrative assistant and personal secretary, respectively. Both were faithful and closed-mouthed. Sam Stone, president of the Commercial National Bank of Durant, and Clinton R. Strong served as principal financial advisors. W. A. Melton and Haskell Pruett assisted in money matters at various intervals. J. L. Sanderson, a friend of Harry Cordell, remained with Bennett throughout all of his administration. Of these individuals, the president probably relied most heavily upon Clint Strong. When he died, Bennett personally wrote a moving eulogy for him and entitled it "I Had a Friend."[22]

Many of the other early non-academic administrative appointments came from fellow church members or friends from southeastern Oklahoma, too. Julia Stout, who had taught with Vera Connell, replaced Blanche Freeman as dean of women. R. J. Schull, from Hugo, accepted appointment as college physician. D. A. Hamilton and Philip Wilber were both on the faculty when Bennett arrived, but the executive singled them out for special work on remodeling present physical facilities and building new structures. The most difficult position to fill on a permanent basis was that of the librarian. Icko Iben, a graduate of the University in Halle, succeeded Elsie Hand. He was a specialist in the sciences and had almost a decade of experience at the University of Illinois before joining the staff at Stillwater. He was followed by Edmon Low, a native of Oklahoma. Low came to A. and M. from Bowling Green State College. He remained in Stillwater until retirement and brought the institution substantial recognition for his planning and service programs.[23]

Carl Petty Blackwell was probably the most careful appointment that President Bennett made to head a college. He received his Bachelor of Science degree from Oklahoma A. and M. in 1911 and his Master of Science from the University of Wisconsin four

226

years later. Blackwell worked on his doctorate at Cornell but never could find the time to complete the dissertation. E. W. Allen of Washington recommended his election as dean of the school of agriculture and director of the experiment station. His selection for these positions had much to do with the release of $80,000 due the station from the national Congress. The dean came to Oklahoma with his parents from Lampases County, Texas, in 1895. He taught at Wisconsin, Cornell, the University of Texas, and Clemson and worked for the National Fertilizer Association before returning to Stillwater in an executive capacity. Blackwell served as an important link between the college and the national government before his death in 1937. He was an administrator who earned the respect of the majority of students and faculty.[24]

Philip Donnell was selected to oversee the school of engineering. He, as Blackwell, had considerable experience before he assumed an executive post at A. and M. Of New England stock, he had been born in Minneapolis on December 16, 1889. His family possessed the wanderlust and the boy received his pre-collegiate education in schools located in Minnesota, Maine, New Hampshire, Wisconsin, and Iowa. Donnell earned his undergraduate degree in three instead of four years at Clark University and an advanced degree at Harvard. Prior to his work at Cambridge, he was employed by the United States Coast Guard and Geodetic Survey in the Philippine Islands and after receiving his degree he transferred to Alaska with the same organization. He also became associated with the Bell Telephone Company and taught at the Georgia Institute of Technology and the University of Mexico before taking a position in the Bennett administration. In Stillwater, Donnell developed a reputation as a world traveler and a public relations man. He attended the World Power Conference in 1930; headed several New Deal agencies; and fought with the United States Army during World War II. Donnell and Henry Bennett were alike in many respects, for they both possessed a high degree of enthusiasm. The former became the first man in the history of the institution to hold the title of vice president.[25]

President Bennett would like to have replaced Clarence McElroy as dean of the school of science and literature in 1928, but McElroy had too strong a following in the state. Bennett did, however, bring a replacement with him from Durant. Schiller Scroggs, the son of J. W. Scroggs, an Oklahoma writer, and minister, was appointed director of administrative research until the science and literature deanship became available. Scroggs proved capable, yet many disliked and feared him.[26] A writer for the *Redskin* said that he "provokes some to think, some to tears, some to hatred, some to reconsider, some to action, some to respect - but whatever, he is a provocative man."[27] Scroggs traveled extensively before settling in Stillwater. He began his undergraduate work at Kingfisher College but left school before he graduated to enlist in the United States Army. The soldier served with the American Expeditionary Forces in Siberia and spent five years in the Orient before becoming a civilian again. In 1921, Scroggs resumed work on a degree at Southeastern and graduated while Henry Bennett was president. Between the dates that he returned to school and received his degree the military veteran taught public school in Oklahoma and Missouri.

Henry Bennett appointed Scroggs as a professor of secondary education at Durant and head of the James Russell Demonstration School after he graduated. He brought him to Stillwater in 1928 and awarded him leave of absence so that he could complete work on a master's degree at Columbia and a doctor's degree from Yale. Prior to his deanship in 1935 Scroggs provided the statistical data for modernizing the financial structure of the college. Moreover, he wrote the administration's statements on tenure, leaves of absence, and sabbaticals. Some of these documents were drafted into article form and published with Bennett in professional journals, such as the *Journal of Higher Education*. In 1937, Dean Scroggs suggested that the name of the school he headed be changed from science and literature to arts and science. Then he divided it into four administrative units: biological sciences; physical sciences; humanities; and social science. An active man, Scroggs founded the Summer Conference of Academic Deans and published several volumes of poetry. He possessed exceptional organizational ability, yet he lacked the temperament to achieve widespread recognition on the campus. Some people called him the president's hatchet man, a title which was not altogether undeserved.[28]

Herbert Patterson retained his title of dean of the school of education. Bennett, however, had a man in mind to replace him at the appropriate time. Napoleon Conger assumed the leadership of this school when Patterson was appointed to a newly-created office called chair of adminstration. Dean Conger was born in 1882 in Smithville, Tennessee and earned degrees at Cumberland University and the Ohio University in Athens. He taught at Southeastern in Durant and co-authored several grade school textbooks with Henry Bennett. Professor Conger obtained his Ph. D. from Teachers College, Columbia University, where he studied under Thomas Alexander, E. S. Evenden, W. C. Bagley, and J. H. Newton. His dissertation was entitled "Professional Adjustment Service Rendered by Teacher Training Institutions." Conger played a larger role at the Oklahoma A. and M. College than his title would suggest.[29]

Henry Bennett recruited Raymond Thomas to replace J. W. Scott as dean of the school of commerce. Thomas came to Stillwater with a Ph. M. and Ph. D. in economics from the University of Wisconsin and teaching experience at a small college located in Springfield Missouri. He proved to be one of the few deans who did not always agree with his senior colleague.[30] Under Thomas, the college he headed adopted "Looking Ahead with the School of Commerce" as a theme. Moreover, the adiminstrator was one of the only men on campus who did more than just talk about good teaching. He is on record as saying. "There should be brought about, it is suggested, a cross-fertilization of teaching and research effort between and among our rather rigidly defined departments, bringing a mixture of ideas and a cross-breed offspring superior to the traditional pure stock."[31] Thomas even practiced what he preached and on occasion he joined with O. A. Hilton, another Wisconsin graduate, to teach interdisciplinary courses in history and economics. Goals for the school of commerce included growth, practical business experience for students, increased professionalization, the recruitment of superior faculty, and continual scrutiny of the business curriculum to keep it current. Thomas, as did some of the other deans, held several important political positions during the New Deal period.[32]

It was fortunate for the college, perhaps, that Conger and Scroggs were unable to assume deanships immediately. From 1928 to 1931 President Bennett used these two men to draft annual reports which set the tone of the institution's development for the next twenty-five years. The first of these documents informed taxpayers of how their money was spent in Stillwater and outlined future needs, in particular. The report called for increased expenditures for salaries, maintenance, and additional buildings. The writers likened higher education in Oklahoma to a boy who was outgrowing his clothes faster than his parents could afford to replace them. But, while focusing on the present and pointing to the future, it was felt that the past should not be forgotten. Bennett, especially, thought that some buildings, such as Old Central, should be preserved for oncoming generations.[33]

The second report contained almost twice as many pages as the first. It covered much the same ground and then went on to deal with teaching loads, the curriculum, and something called the freshman drop-out problem. It was the third report, however, that had the most impact upon the institution in the future. In a section entitled "A Look Ahead," which drew heavily upon the talents of Philip Wilber and D. A. Hamilton, the document detailed the needs of the college for the next quarter of a century. The building program was so extensive that President Bennett thought that some people might charge that the state had neglected A. and M. in the past. Therefore, he reminded his readers that Oklahoma was still young as a state and that it would be illogical to believe it could have institutions of higher education that matched those of older regions. The designation "Twenty-Five Year Plan" itself was audacious, for completion of it would coincide with Bennett's retirement date.[34]

Henry Garland Bennett was a keen student of educational history. He had studied the beginnings of western universities in Italy, France, and England and had had a chance to visit many of them personally in 1931 when he went on a world tour for the Rotary Clubs located in the Twelfth District. In addition, he knew the traditions of American education and inspected college campuses whenever the occasion arose.[35] Bennett's belief in the formal educational process, whether primary, secondary, or higher, bordered upon the utopian. In an undated speech in Durant he stated that

"I shall be cautious of generalization and not say that the school system is responsible for our social freedom; I shall insist only that the two go together."[36] He said on another occasion that

I should like to see one generation of American youth reared and educated from cradle to maturity with the benefit of all that we know about medicine, health and hygiene, formal education, and psychology. I should like to see one generation of America's children grow up free from disease, social or biological, or mental malnutrition or maladjustment, in happy and healthy learning situations. Truly, I believe that here lies the pathway to Utopia.[37]

Land-grant institutions fit at the top of the educational revolutionary ladder. They retained the old, but popularized the new, always emphasizing service. However, whether time-honored or modern, a college needed leadership. "Great institutions do not result from haphazard development; they are the fruition of years of planned growth under the guidance of wise policy," the president further explained.[38]

Initially, good planning related to the development of a modern physical plant, one that would rate second to none in the United States. However, before one could plan for the future, pride had to be developed in the past. In 1928, for example, President Bennett requested permission from the Board of Agriculture to christen an unnamed girls' dormitory in honor of a pioneer in home economics. He said: "I wish to recommend that it hereafter be called Maude Gardiner Hall, in honor of Miss Maude Gardiner who began the work in Home Economics at this institution in the Fall of 1900."[39] Bennett also saved Old Central from destruction and secured $40,000 to restore it. The interior was almost completely refinished: repairs included new floors, plaster, and paint. The exterior received a face lift as well. Bricks were cleaned, cracks patched, and the roof redone. This renovation added space at a crucial point in the institution's history. The basement floor housed physics, and later geology, while the top floor provided offices for the alumni association, the graduate dean, and student organizations. The second floor continued to be used for classes. If it is true that the state of Old Central at any given point is a barometer to the general health of the college, then the future in 1939 seemed bright indeed.[40]

Both Old Central and Gardiner Hall forecast a distinctive architectual style for the Oklahoma A. and M. College. The president, early in his administration, requested the development of a master plan for construction and campus beautification. The funds granted by the Board were used to employ the services of the Mc-Crary, Culley, and Carhart Company of Denver, Colorado, a firm which had served as a consultant for some thirty other colleges in the Southwest. Their study suggested a location for all buildings, roads, game courts, service units, and experimental plots. Neither Wilber or Hamilton, however, were satisfied with the work of the Denver firm. These two men spent nearly two years in modifying the design so that it would meet the requirements of A. and M. The finished product, the "Twenty-Five Year Plan," envisioned an eventual student population of 8,000. The center of the campus was to be a magnificent library which would be surrounded by some fifty other buildings placed in an aesthetically pleasing setting. Geographically, the campus was to develop from the west, to the southwest, to the northwest. The master plan called for a uniform architecture, one never named, but which layman might refer to as Williamsburg Georgian. The exterior surface proved so striking that one variety of brick was named after the college.[41]

Two obstacles stood in the path of immediate implementation of the "Twenty-Five Year Plan." First, within a year and a half after Bennett assumed the presidency, the stock market crash of 1929 triggered the Great Depression. Payne County, prior to this date, had been the fifth wealthiest in the state. Its oil fields, property, and livestock had a valuation of approximately $75,000,000.[42] By 1930, however, drastic relief measures had to be employed. The Stillwater Council of Churches opened an office on West Seventh Avenue in the last quarter of the year. "It was an outgrowth of a feeling on the part of the church people that charity is an expression of the Christian spirit and should be done to the credit of the church."[43] The assistance was provided without charge, except those that received it were required to attend Sunday School classes. Public officials told the people to exhibit courage and faith, yet a quick recovery did not come. Sheriff M. J. Bradley found that he had to use "unusual finesse and technique" to keep the cells of the county jail empty. Students donated clothing and other items that they did not need. Raymond Thomas dispatched some of his majors to take industrial surveys in hopes of attracting new businesses to the community. In 1931, Will Rogers returned to Oklahoma to stage charity shows; he alone raised almost $100,000 to aid those hardest hit.[44]

Oklahoma educational institutions suffered because of the Depression. Teachers salaries dropped; extension services were curtailed; subjects were cut from the curriculum; and budgets were pared in some areas by as much as 80%. In Stillwater, thirty-five members of the faculty and athletic staff were released at the end of the 1930-1931 fiscal year. Those who remained received two cuts in pay of 20% each, while the operations budget dropped about one-third. The crisis was compounded when college officials permitted students to defer fees and to purchase books and food on credit. Consequently, money was not available to pay even those expenditures which had been authorized by the Board of Agriculture. Then, too, the lenient credit policy led to a 10% increase in enrollment, a situation which complicated matters even further. On March 2, 1933, the chief executive of the state ordered 475 banks in Oklahoma closed. This move provided an opportunity for people to think and to renew their faith in the future. The next Christmas holiday brought improvement and many parents contemplated purchase of gifts for their children once again. President Bennett, however, realized that if the college expected to move ahead it would have to secure funds from the federal government.[45]

The second problem which retarded implementation of the "Twenty-Five Year Plan" related to the meager maintenance allowance that left existing buildings in a poor state of repair. Added to this, the architects who designed the older structures were not aware that the region posed peculiar foundation problems. Cracks had appeared in many basement walls which permitted moisture to seep in at regular intervals. Moreover, many of the buildings were not designed for the special needs of a land-grant institution. Whitehurst Hall burst into flames on July 15, 1931, when hay samples ignited. The next year a spark from an electric refrigerator in the Animal Husbandry Building ignited a leak in the gas line. Four years later a fuel pipe in a subterranean passage underneath executive offices in Whitehurst exploded. The floor below Henry Bennett's desk was lifted from two to five inches. The latter two calamities resulted in damage estimated at $100,000. Two students, Virginia Alexander and Leah Schedler, were seriously injured. Fortunately, the crisis occurred just before lunch; otherwise, the disaster might have been the worst in Oklahoma's history.[46]

Though it would be several years before the college could inaugurate a major building program, the new administration began speculating on how to finance physical expansion almost immediately. In March, 1930 Cordell and Bennett convinced the Thirteenth Legislature to approve the concept of building bonds for higher education. The college received permission to finance as much as 70% of new buildings and to retire debts through self-liquidating bonds. In order to launch the "Twenty-Five Year Plan," the Legislature specifically gave approval for the expenditure of $450,000 for the erection of two girls' dormitories. Bennett, anxious to get his program underway, arranged for J. W. Baker to seek an injunction against Frank Carter, the state auditor, in order to test the constitutionality of the act. The firm of Wilcox and Swank handled argument for the college while J. Berry King represented the opposition. The Supreme Court ruled in favor of the bond measure by a five to three vote. The president then designated that building be started on a site south and west of Whitehurst Hall.[47]

In spite of legislative approval and a favorable ruling by the Supreme Court, bids were not let for almost three years. Meanwhile, Wilber and Hamilton visited Texas in order to observe structures similar to those that they had in mind for the Stillwater campus. Moreover, advice was solicited from people associated with the college before the final plans were drawn. Both buildings upon completion were acknowledged as the finest of their type in the state. Federal, not state, funds were secured for the 30% down payment and the student self-help industries built the beds, tables, dressers, and dining hall furnishings. DeWitt Hunt and Henry Adams supervised labor on the latter. Furthermore, the Charles M. Dunning Construction Company of Oklahoma City hired about 200 workers for a seven month period on the complex located on the corner of College Avenue and Monroe Streets. The project provided jobs for Oklahomans and the college got buildings at depression costs. The program provided a good bargain in more ways than one.[48]

With the beginnings of a new administrative team and the "Twenty-Five Year Plan" underway, President Bennett turned his attention to the faculty. His initial thrust was aimed at improving tenure and sabbaticals, the recruitment of faculty with graduate capabilities, and higher salaries. In part, he was pushed into action because Professor A. S. Hiatt, one of the men fired in 1928, had appealed to the American Association of University Professors for redress. The organization investigated Hiatt's release and stated in its bulletin that there is a

widespread opinion at Stillwater, within and without the faculty, that political and personal influence with board members may determine appointment and tenure of professors. Such suspicions will break down the morale of any faculty and great care should be taken to avoid any apparent justification of them.[49]

The release of 35 instructors and coaches in 1931 brought another probe. Little was done, however, because the complaining party, J. P. Isaac, was not a member of the organization. Bennett, who was a soft touch if the faculty could get to him personally, let Isaac begin a trip to Europe on what he thought was a sabbatical leave. It was only after he was at sea that he received a wire stating that he had been dismissed. In an attempt to bolster morale, for those who remained, the president inaugurated a club to pay recognition to the men and women who had served the college over a long period of time. The first members of the Decade Club were Clarence McElroy, E. E. Brewer, C. E. Sanborn, E. J. Westbrook, and Monte Brattin.[50]

In 1937, Bennett reviewed his tenure policy and found that he had been as successful as one could expect during a depression. He reported in 1928 that the college had 188 full time faculty, of whom only 71% had served five years or less. Eight years later, by contrast, the institution employed 260 full time instructors and 66% of them had over five years of service. He concluded: "I think the generalization is rather safe that professor tenure at Oklahoma A. and M. College is now as stable as it is in any institution of higher learning in the United States."[51] Also, the executive took a position on academic freedom, an issue which none of the other presidents had ever broached. Bennett accepted the principle that an instructor had freedom to teach and write in his specialty without recrimination; however, he cautioned that a teacher should not tear down in a student's mind what he could not replace. It was pointed out that "those who pay the bill shall have the right to say what they shall buy. If professors want complete academic freedom let them also assume complete responsibility for their own salaries."[52] Definite improvements were made, yet when state elections rolled around, the faculty often had to chip in for campaign expenses. In Stillwater, the practice did not become a public issue [except that

Professor Isaac may have been released for not contributing]; at Norman, the situation became so bad that the American Association of University Professors investigated the matter at length.[53]

Comment generated by the situation on the campus of the University of Oklahoma motivated Henry Bennett to attack faculty problems at home. First, he recommended to the Board of Agriculture that it employ no more instructors who did not have at least one year of training beyond the bachelor's degree. Second, he requested that promotion policy "take into consideration not only demonstrated fitness and experience but also graduate qualifications with the end in view of appointing to full professors only those holding doctor degrees."[54] Third, he suggested that the regents adopt a pay scale for the Oklahoma A. and M. College which would be equal to that paid to faculty at the University of Oklahoma. Revenues, however, prohibited the implementation of the latter item, yet the Board did try to achieve parity as quickly as possible. On the other hand, faculty salaries never became a major concern of the Bennett administration. President Bennett believed that people would teach for less money than elsewhere if the institution had high stated purpose and if a superior physical plant was provided.[55] One anecdote is sufficient to illustrate. A visitor, who was being escorted around the campus, once stopped to admire the landscaping around Theta Pond. He asked Bennett how he could justify such elaborate beautification while so many of the faculty were underpaid. President Bennett ignored the question and stated very softly, "But isn't it pretty?"[56]

Though authoritarian, and a devout Christian, Henry Bennett seems to have been less concerned with the development of college rules to legislate student morals than any of his predecessors. He permitted automobiles on the campus, did not oppose the building of taverns near the college when Congress repealed Prohibition, and the editor of the O'Collegian received a free hand. The president believed that the newspaper was to popularize new ideas, not retard their growth. The chief end of college according to Bennett's educational paradigm, was to help a student formulate a personal philosophy of life and a style of living. Therefore, at the beginning of each academic year he pointed out the importance of faith in the American way, the need to practice economy, the necessity of being positive, and the dangers of overspecialization.[57] Most of the Aggies came to believe in the pledge that Bennett made in his first speech to the student body. He said: "I pledge, here and now, life-long loyalty to the ideals of scholarship, character, and service of the founders of this institution to the end that I may loyally serve the College, the state and nation."[58]

Undergraduate enrollment during the Depression increased until 1938 when the total student population numbered about 7,000. In that year the college had some 5,000 regular students and about half that number again taking correspondence and short courses. The mushrooming figures caused many problems in connection with financial aid. Neither the self-help industries nor con-

234

struction jobs on the new buildings solved the need for monetary assistance. Henry Bellmon, the son of George D. Bellmon, was somewhat representative of the students throughout this period. One of thirteen children, he enrolled at Oklahoma A. and M. in 1938 after graduating from Billings High School. He earned his Bachelor of Science degree in agronomy in seven instead of eight semesters and maintained a grade point which was among the highest on campus. He worked his way through college and took jobs that included employment on a poultry farm, waiting on tables, and washing dishes and windows. In addition, Henry picked pears and cotton, served as a laboratory assistant, and wrote for the *O'Collegian*. He also was one of the students who made furniture for the new girls' dormitory. Though he did not have enough money to have his picture taken for the *Redskin*, Oklahomans did become familiar with his image for he was elected the first Republican governor of the state and later became a member of the United States Senate. After graduation, Henry aided others in his family to attend college.[59]

The lack of an adequate operations budget placed unusual liabilities on the students of the Great Depression era. The bond program for new buildings necessitated that undergraduates live in the dormitories, a fact which irriated them as well as the townspeople. Also, numerous fees had to be assessed. The annual catalog of 1939-1940 listed twenty-five separate charges. Occasionally, the students, who were living in a period which was protesting convention, organized to impose certain institutional rules. They chafed at the extensive fee system; rigged elections; balked at eating cafeteria food; and questioned regulations in general.[60] In 1931, the student senate threatened a walkout if the administration did not extend the hours for weekend dances. Gerald "Cowboy" Curtain, a steller athelete, declared that instead "of a democracy on this campus we have a dictatorial aristocracy! It's a deplorable state when students don't have a few rights . . . . How can we expect them [students] to show an interest in construction measures when they are led around like a bunch of sheep?"[61] Ralph Winters and Earl McCafferty joined with Curtain in discussing the situation with the president in his office. The incident closed without ill-feeling, hostility, or violence.

The modern Alumni Association of the Oklahoma A. and M. College may also be dated from the beginning of the Bennett administration. The organization changed its name to the Former Students Association in 1928. W. A. Melton, Orville Savage, L. A. Santee, and Robert Short appeared before the Board of Agriculture in November of that year to ask that the trustees pay one-half of the salary of a permanent secretary. Such an arrangement had existed in the past but now the Board promised to continue the practice on a permanent basis. The association, in return, stipulated that it would act as a service organization for the educational plant. It also became a powerful lobby on behalf of the college within the state. Executives of the institution met with members of the Legislature and with governors-elect to increase appropriations as well as to secure promises of political non-interference with the educational process. In visiting with future governors the association repeatedly requested that one alumni sit on the Board of Agriculture at all times. This man, or woman, could then serve as liaison between the two agencies. The dedication of this group had much to do with the increased stability of the college in the coming years.[62]

The Former Students Association continued to operate a placement bureau, but it moved into other areas as well. In 1928 the agency cooperated with the college in planning an annual Founder's Day on December 14th. Former students and friends of A. and M. then gathered to commemorate the past and to hear Henry Bennett give a birthday speech, a presentation that always centered upon plans for the future. The idea for this event originated with Harry Thompson, a member of the territorial faculty. Often those who assembled on the campus found Bennett's projections hard to believe. Many, for instance, were skeptical when the president predicted in 1931 that he would establish an international agricultural institute in Stillwater to help underdeveloped countries of the world increase food production. Yet, before Bennett left office, such a program existed and to a degree that was more extensive than even the president himself dreamed of.[63]

The Former Students Association designed a new magazine in 1929 to inform alumni of the status of the institution. Called the *Oklahoma A. and M. College Magazine,* the first issue appeared in September. George McElroy served as editor and business manager; Louis Blackburn as associate editor; and Earl C. Fisher assumed the responsibility for soliciting advertisements. Five thousand copies were printed for distribution. President Bennett composed the lead article for the first edition. In it, he said:

It is my opinion that a vigorous, effective Alumni and Former Student's Association is one of the most valuable assets of any educational institution, and I assure you and your association of my fullest support in all of the mutually important problems which will change our joint effects in the future.[64]

The alumni, in response, pledged support of the current administration and promised to cooperate with the president in the future. The Depression posed many problems for the magazine and the organization encumbered heavy debts. Bennett, however, always found enough money to keep it in circulation. A marriage contract between the two had been arranged and it was a vow that neither wanted to break.[65]

Two long term goals were selected by the Former Students Association and both of them were to benefit the college. First, the organization attempted to improve the athletic facilities on the campus, especially the football stadium. Second, the leadership spearheaded an effort within the state to provide A. and M. with a separate board of regents, one such as it had had during the territorial period. Insofar as the former objective is concerned, the association began the movement to build a new football stadium as early as 1922. In that year friends of the college collected money to assist the University of Oklahoma complete a similar project, hoping that institution would reciprocate at a later date. Ed Gallagher and Bradford Knapp tried to move the program ahead. This effort, however, came to a standstill when the latter individual left for Auburn. The Former Students Association revived the project in 1929. The organization asked L. W. Burton to appoint a committee to build a field house which would seat 15,000 people and a stadium to hold twice that number. Clarence McElroy championed the effort on the campus, stating that A. and M. would never assume its rightful place in educational circles until athletic programs in Stillwater were comparable to those at Norman.[66]

Under Bennett, the association created a definite plan of action. Two committees were formed: W. A. Melton, a tireless worker, headed the first; the second group was largely honorary in nature and included the names of people such as Will Rogers. These men divided the state of Oklahoma into areas that concided with Supreme Court districts and subsequently established local chapters. John B. Nichlos, a multi-millionaire from Chickasha, agreed to supervise the overall drive. He hired Frederick Vining Fisher and Harry Edwards Clay of the General Organization Company headquartered in Chicago to collect cash donations and pledges. Fisher, in order to expedite things, believed that the stadium should be dedicated to the men and women who had lost their lives in World War I. He coined a slogan which read: "For Oklahoma and Her Soldiers, Living and Dead, Her Sons and Daughters Long Years Ahead." The Depression slowed progress and prevented the Former Students Association from achieving its goal for many years. But with patience and ingenuity both projects were completed before the bombing of Pearl Harbor.[67]

During the same general period of time, the organization initiated an effort to change the composition of the Board of Regents. The plan was quite similar to what Henry Alvord and James Neal had suggested in 1894 and 1895. Walter Jessee, of Supply, worked out the details for the initial proposal. He sought the creation of a separate governing board with seven members, one of whom would retire each year. In 1928 the alumni distributed a petition which requested a vote by the people on a constitutional amendment to make the change. Both Governor Holloway and Harry Cordell favored the establishment of a separate board.[68] Orville Savage explained the necessity for the move in an article entitled "What About This Separate Board of Regents?" He felt that the institution should have its own governing body so that the A. and M. college could provide leadership for the state "unhampered by politicians, and whose members may serve full terms without being discharged at the will of a governor or some political boss."[69]

Dave Logan, Okmulgee County, co-authored a bill in the Legislature to create a nine member board. The bill passed both houses and received a plurality from the people in November but it did not receive a majority of all ballots cast in the election. Some individuals failed to vote one way or the other. In 1933, and again in 1935, similar bills were drafted. In the two elections held in the thirties, the association attempted to obtain the endorsement of important groups, such as the Grange, the Oklahoma Education Association, and the political parties. The Democrats even incorporated the idea into its state platform. Of the organizations approached, only the American Legion responded negatively. In 1936, the electorate gave the question a 13,000 majority; however, the silent vote killed the measure again. Early Cass, who had replaced Savage as president of the Former Students Association, led a court fight to force J. William Cordell of the election board to certify passage anyway. The Supreme Court ruled on the petition, supporting Cordell. In 1937, the alumni decided not to push the matter any further until they could find a governor who would change the ground rules.[70]

From 1928 to 1931, Henry Bennett reorganized the administrative structure of the Oklahoma A. and M. College and took the steps necessary to strengthen the institution so that implementation of the "Twenty-Five Year Plan" could begin. In only a short period of time he became recognized as a bold and resourceful leader. Randle Perdue, a sometime employee of the college, expressed the opinion of many people when he wrote that Bennett "has done so much for A. and M. . . . that's it's difficult to enumerate even the more important accomplishments."[71] If, however, Perdue had been able to project more clearly, he would have been even more laudatory, because the man he was referring to was destined to become a legend in his own time. Heads of state at home and abroad would pause at Henry Garland Bennett's death to pay homage to a visionary educator and to an institution that was to add a significant new dimension to the land-grant movement.

XV   THE NEW DEAL COMES TO OKLAHOMA

With a friendly governor in office for three years, Henry Bennett easily won re-election to the presidency of the Oklahoma Agricultural and Mechanical College. This tenure provided the time and opportunity to mold the institution he headed so that the "Twenty-Five Year Plan" could be implemented. It was not possible, though, for the executive to launch many of the programs that he had in mind because the Great Depression continued to inflict a terrible toll on the people and institutions of the state. Much energy had to be spent in talking about retrenchment and to spreading an optimistic gospel. The Depression had little personal impact upon the president. He was unconcerned about his own wealth and regarded money simply as an object to provide for his family, to do his work, and to help friends in distress. Bennett's dress and mannerisms suggest that he had not removed himself from the roots that produced him. He spoke with a slow drawl, selected plain clothes, retained a fundamentalistic faith, and sometimes, in an unguarded moment of humor, he exhibited a bias toward members of certain minority groups. Ouachita College granted a Doctor of Laws degree during this period, a sign that contemporaries continued to regard him as one of the clan. The honor, however, had been earned, for substantial gains had been made in the first quarter-century of Henry Bennett's professional life.[1]

A unique opportunity presented itself in 1931. Earlier, President Bennett had accepted the Governorship of the Rotarians Club's Twelfth District. One of the duties connected with this position was to attend the R. I. convention held in Vienna, Austria in 1931. In connection with this trip abroad, Dr. Bennett toured other countries in Europe. When Bennett addressed the incoming students after his return, it was apparent that the executive had lost much of his provincialness. He realized, for example, that the current financial crisis was more than just a periodic economic reversal: it represented a watershed in the history of western man. "Humanity," he said, " is near the breaking point. Collapse of western civilization is in the balance. The economic, political and social principles for which the western nations for five centuries or more have stood are now on trial."[2] The speaker had known poverty but not to the extent that it existed in Europe and Asia. The trip awakened latent educational missionary desires as strong as the religious calls that sometimes motivate men of the cloth to make the trek overseas. Before world problems could be broached, however, there were difficulties in Oklahoma and in the nation that had to be resolved.

On the local scene, the most serious obstacle that had to be dealt with concerned the return of William "Alfalfa Bill" Murray to the political life of the state. He had left the country some years before in order to develop an American agricultural settlement in Bolivia. He decided to run for governor now in an attempt to rebuild the Democratic Party from the stormy impeachments of Jack Walton and Henry Johnston. The politician had not changed much since the Constitutional Convention of 1907, except in personal appearance. His hair had turned grayer, his walk slower, and his eyes duller, yet his sagging frame still possessed a remarkable voice. In fact, there was none like it in the Southwest. Murray, according to his *Memoirs*, went to the bank at Tishomingo and borrowed four dollars to add to the twelve in his pocket. He gave his wife one of these, arranged credit for her at the market, and then began to walk the length and breath of the state in order to speak with the people.[3]

The candidate faced substantial opposition. He was opposed in the summer Democratic primary by E. B. Howard, W. M. Darnell, Frank Buttram, and M. E. Trapp. Republican aspirants included Lew Wentz, Roy Hughes, J. E. Harreld, Earl Flesher, George Nicholson, A. C. Alexander, James Harris, Irving Page, and Ira Hill. Murray and Buttram emerged as the winners in the primary. "Alfalfa Bill' then trounced his opponent in a runoff election held in August. Ira Hill defeated James Harris on the other side of the political fence. It is possible that Murray conducted the best campaign of his life in 1940. He continued to stump the state, as in the primary, but he also relied heavily upon the *Blue Valley Farmer,* a newspaper for which he had purchased the mailing rights. In the end, Hill lost by almost 100,000 votes. Henry Bennett, who had ridiculed Murray in letters to his friends at Columbia University, suspected that a great ordeal was in the making. He met with Murray before he took his oath of office in hopes of preserving the college's budget, but to no avail.[4] The governor-elect had run on a platform which called for stringent economies and he had already decided that the educational system of the state was to "bear the brunt of retrenchment."[5]

Uriah Murray, now close to the century mark, read the oath of office to his son William at high noon on January 12, 1931. The changing of the guard did not have much in the way of ceremonial trappings so as to keep the inauguration in line with the somber mood of the state. The text for the traditional address came from the book of Exodus, chapter seventeen. It suggested that the next four years would be a battle between good and evil. Murray explained: "I am Moses. The Senate is Hur and the House is Aaron. Enemy forces in the state are Amalek."[6] Subsequent events indicated that the personal reference to Moses meant more than the fact that Murray considered himself to be on the side of the Right. He intended to be a strong and independent leader, one who would implement his retrenchment program by employing the executive order instead of working through the Legislature.[7] The extent of the changes envisioned by Murray in regard to the educational system were set forth in his address to the Thirteenth Oklahoma Legislature. Among the more important items mentioned were: (1) no teachers should hold more than one job; (2) pensions and emeritus positions not specifically sanctioned by law were to be eliminated; (3) all operations budgets were to be reduced by a full 30%; (4) administrative salaries were to be cut; (5) the pay of faculty was to be frozen for a two year period; (6) athletic and academic programs which gave students expensive tastes were to be discontinued; (7) institutions were instructed to discontinue their relationship with North Central; and (8) higher educational organizations were told that the state needed to develop some method of coordinating their programs. Some of Murray's ideas had merit, but he sometimes seems to have proposed them for the wrong reasons.[8]

These announcements, coming all at once, took many educators by surprise and originated dozens of rumors within Oklahoma educational circles. State newspapers published United Press releases to the effect that Bennett and Bizzell would both be removed from their presidential positions in Stillwater and Norman. Frank Hall, who worked for a syndicated news service, reported, too, that Murray favored vocational over classical instruction and that he would transfer Bennett to the University of Oklahoma in order to give that institution a more practical bent. In the spring additional stories forecast the release of large numbers of faculty from the land-grant college. Randle Perdue and James E. Miller were fired late in the 1930-31 academic year and Harry Cordell predicted that others, including Sam Stone, comptroller, would go the same route. Some faculty were released, because of a $100,000 budget slash, but the changes were not nearly as severe as some observers had anticipated. The reason for not implementing the more radical measures became public in September, 1931. William Murray had decided to run for president of the United States. His mind, then, was on other matters.[9]

Governor Murray made his first major national speech in Chicago. He told a large crowd that "what the country needed was a man who was intelligent enough not to be deceived, brave enough not to be intimidated, and honest enough not to be bought."[10] In Oklahoma, Henry Bennett sometimes substituted for the presidential aspirant on the speaker's platform. Moreover, he did not discourage the Aggies from beginning the first "Murray for President Club" on a college campus. Led by Sam Hoover, Manly Humphrey, and Miss Tommie Moore this organization spearheaded the establishment of similar organizations at other colleges in the state. T. H. Reynolds of the history department served as advisor to the League of Young Democrats who initiated the movement. Some members of the instructional staff were requested to contribute directly to the campaign chest; others were invited to write public school textbooks and to assign a portion of the royalties to the William H. Murray Educational Foundation. The textbook commission agreed to adopt these books in advance of publication, a decision which provided much incentive. Presumably, the foundation's revenues were used to provide scholarships for the poor; however, some people believed that substantial sums were transferred to support the bid for the presidential nomination. Much to his later dismay, Bennett joined several of the faculty in this endeavor. This act, and the frequent introductions of Murray in Oklahoma, such as in Stillwater on Armistice Day, were gestures that the politician would not forget.[11]

In the end, Murray did not pose a serious threat to the nomination of Franklin D. Roosevelt. He mistook the interest of the press in the color that he provided for voting strength. The defeat brought a commitment to help his own in Oklahoma. President Bennett's "friendship" prevented some budget cuts,[12] but more important, it produced enough cooperation for the two men to work out a plan for coordinating higher education in the Sooner State. In July, 1929, the Legislature at the request of William Holloway passed a law which authorized the creation of a coordinating board. The bill proposed that the Oklahoma Superintendent of Public Instruction, the presidents of five colleges, and two members appointed by the governor form a committee to unify higher education. The commission failed to function effectively but it deserves mention because it facilitated the development of the Oklahoma College Association. During one of its meetings, the Right Reverend Francis Kelley, Bishop of Oklahoma City and Tulsa, gave a speech entitled "The Greater University." William Murray borrowed some of Kelley's suggestions and incorporated them into a bill which he asked the Legislature to pass in 1933. The governor attempted to explain his latest educational program in a public statement called the *Oklahoma Greater University, Coordinating All Colleges, Private and Public, Under One Harmonious System.* Murray, while the lawmakers and people pondered the merits of this measure, issued an executive order to begin implementation.[13]

The executive order proposed "the elimination of certain duplicated departments and courses of study in state institutions."[14] The committee appointed to initiate the reorganization consisted of O. S. Henshaw, Charles Briles, and John A. Murray. The latter man was a cousin of the governor's who taught at the Oklahoma A. and M. College. This group met for the first time on March 20, 1933. The plan that evolved is too lengthy to be detailed here. In general, however, it called for housing all engineering, home economics, agriculture, and business studies in Stillwater. The more traditional professional programs, then, would be centered at the University of Oklahoma. Instruction in pedagogy, by the same token, would be exclusively the domain of the regional normal schools and state colleges. The Legislature passed the Coordination Act in April, 1933. This bill created a fifteen member board which would be appointed by the governor. It would have the authority to reorganize higher education within the state. Clint Strong and Henry Bennett did not agree with everything that Murray proposed but they urged the Board of Agriculture to support the general idea in hopes that the elimination of academic duplication would promote excellence in the agricultural and engineering sciences.[15]

Simultaneously, Governor Murray attempted to develop what he called the Greater University, a concept which bears a resemblance to the super boards and multi-campus universities of a later era. The members of the Coordinating Board were instructed to elect a chancellor who would apportion the funds provided by the Legislature for higher education. The Board itself would be kept operational by assessing each institution fifty cents for each one of its students. Individual colleges would retain the privilege of granting degrees but students in any institution were to be given the option of taking a test in order to qualify for a diploma from the Greater University. The examination, Murray hoped, would spur competition among the colleges to see who could obtain the most "honor" degrees. Charles Briles, John D. Finlayson, M. A. Nash, and Bennett worked with Murray in an effort to implement the Greater University idea. The latter man brought in outside consultants, such as Edward Elliot, president of Purdue University, and persuaded the Carnegie Foundation to award several grants for feasibility studies.[16]

The Coordinating Board and the Greater University failed to get off the ground because the attorney general ruled that it was unconstitutional to pay a chancellor and a research support staff from state funds. Many educators in the state breathed a long sigh of relief at this development, for it prevented the statewide shuffling of academic departments and colleges. The Coordinating Board itself remained alive for a time because President Bennett donated the services of some of his staff, such as Schiller Scroggs, for statistical research. Both Bennett and Murray talked with the latter's successor in an effort to get him to further the idea of coordination. This man commissioned the Brookings Institute to make a study of higher education in the state. L. J. Calvin, who assembled these data, concluded that nothing positive could be done until Oklahoma devised some objectives for higher education and until adequate funds were provided by the Legislature. *In toto,* the report suggested that higher education in the Sooner State was still in the Jacksonian Era. Then, too, the completed document pointed out, as had the American Association of University Professors, that the mischievious system of political patronage was demoralizing to both the public and their elected representatives. So many problems were identified that the corrdination idea was shelved for several years.[17]

William Murray completed his term of office in January, 1935, and left Oklahoma City. The state treasury had a $17,000,000 deficit at the time of his departure, for he had gotten *ad valorum* taxes reduced but substitutes had not been passed to fill the void. Murray tried for the gubernatorial nomination again in 1938, however, his day in Oklahoma politics had passed. The death of his beloved wife Alice in August proved to be a blow from which he never fully recovered. He returned to the capital when his son was elected governor. His last years were spent in writing diatribe, such as *The Negro's Place in the Call of Race.* The election of Murray convinced Henry Bennett that he and the Oklahoma A. and M. College would have to become more active in politics in order to prevent such a man from holding the governorship again. In addition, it prompted Bennett himself to consider running for the office from 1933 to 1941. It is impossible to determine whether he ever really wanted the position. But speculation in regard to his nomination caused prospective candidates to consult with him at frequent intervals.[18]

The scarcity of state funds convinced Henry Bennett that money from outside of Oklahoma must be obtained to stimulate the economy and to increase physical facilities at the A. and M. college. The financial bungling of the Murray administration reinforced this view even more. In January, 1930, President Bennett accompanied T. W. Kelly and W. B. Murphy to Washington to seek additional dollars for the construction of a new post office in Stillwater. Herbert Hoover, toward the end of his term of office, prepared the way for such requests by instituting a policy of using federal funds to erect public buildings which would provide jobs for the unemployed. The city of Stillwater was scheduled to receive approximately $100,000 for this project but the committee felt that this figure was too low. Bennett joined with Murphy and Kelly because he wanted a post office designed which would contain offices

244

for members of his faculty who were associated with the federal government. No immediate action resulted. Later, when the national presidency changed hands, Murray hindered the acquisition of funds because he opposed bringing the New Deal to Oklahoma. In 1933, however, the A. and M. college did obtain $450,000 in order to start construction on two dormitories for women. To prevent Governor Murray from interfering in this matter, the Board of Agriculture wisely decided to name the buildings after the state chief executive. The institution received $135,000 as an outright gift and contracted to pay back the other $315,000 through future rental fees. Murray Hall was built first and an annex named North Murray came afterwards.[19]

The college experienced much trouble in getting the loan and in getting the project underway. Harry Hopkins refused to approve the initial request because he believed the per unit cost too high. Many conferences were held before the deal was adjudicated to the satisfaction of everyone concerned.[20] Moreover, the state contained a number of fiscal conservatives who opposed the concept of deficit spending. Philip Wilber, who had been instrumental in drawing up the "Twenty-Five Year Plan," worked with Henry Bennett in selling the idea of bonding. Sometimes, though, he had his own moments of doubt about the financial arrangements. Bennett dismissed whatever concerns Wilber had by stating on one occasion that "what if it doesn't pay out on schedule? Who will take it away?"[21] Murray Hall was dedicated in 1935 and the bonds were retired eight years ahead of schedule. Ex-Governor Murray appeared for the dedication. Written documents or eye witnesses can not be found to confirm it, but a rumor persists to this day that Murray secured a ladder the night before the ceremonies and climbed upon it to see if his name was *permanently* engraved above the entrance. Other than this alleged incident of skepticism, the project was successful and it turned out to be a significant breakthrough.

Meanwhile, the state's political situation brightened, too, Ernest Whitworth Marland defeated Tom Anglin in the Democratic primary and W. B. Pine from Okmulgee in the general election for governor. Marland's term of office proved to be a significant turning point in the political history of the state. His victory over Murray's man, Anglin, sounded the death knell for the old-style agrarian element of the Democratic Party. There were other departures as well. Marland became the first man from outside the Little Dixie area to serve a full term as chief executive of the state. The new governor received his early education in private schools and he earned a law degree at the University of Michigan. He accumulated a huge personal fortune which some people estimated as high as $100,000,000 as a result of striking oil on the 101 Ranch. Most of this money, however, was lost in the stock market crash of 1929. But instead of attempting to recoup his financial losses, Marland chose to enter politics. He won election to the House of Representatives in 1932 and became chief executive in 1935, campaigning on the slogan "Let's Bring the New Deal to Oklahoma."[22]

Stillwater became interested in and associated with New Deal programs before Marland took office as governor. On August 7, 1933, the city fathers formed a special council under the National Recovery Act to bring the Blue Eagle to the Sooner State. Moreover, farmers of the community moved quickly to apply for payments under the Agricultural Adjustment Act. Faculty, such as Dover Trent, explained the more technical provisions of Roosevelt's legislation to businessmen. He later requested a leave of absence to serve as director of the Arkansas River Valley project. Initially, the town leadership received an introduction to New Deal through the good offices of General Hugh Johnson, who was the son of a former Alva postmaster.Bennett and Albright made many trips to Washington on behalf of the college. When Marland became governor he expanded their contacts by introducing them to bureaucrats that he had met while serving in the House of Representatives.[23]

More noteworthy, as far as A. and M. is concerned, Bennett and Marland seemed to be in virtual agreement about the role that the institution could play in helping the state to recover from the throes of the Great Depression. In the governor's inaugural address he estimated that approximately 150,000 heads of families were unemployed and that another 35,000 males were too old or too sick to work. These men, and their dependents, suggested that nearly 800,000 people in Oklahoma were in need of relief. Marland believed that the technical expertise of A. and M. could be useful in bringing prosperity back to Oklahoma, particularly by fostering industrialization. In exchange for the assistance he hoped to get, the governor promised not to meddle in the internal affairs of the land-grant institution.[24] His position, however, did not mean that professors and students should not be active in politics. "I have been encouraging students for years to get into politics—the science of government . . . . Don't let less educated men run things," Marland said at a commencement in Stillwater.[25] This point of view permitted Henry Bennett and his staff to leave their ivory towers and to become involved in government at the state and national level without fear of retribution.

The college desperately needed to secure more support from the state in order to assume added responsibilities. Fortunately, Bennett's new longevity record provided the prestige necessary for improving the financial situation. He surpassed Angelo Scott in length of service as president at the beginning of the 1935-1936 academic year. His impact on the college itself is reflected in the fact that he had signed 56.75% of the 5,445 bachelor's degrees and 87.65% of the 753 master's degrees awarded by the institution. He spoke now with a commanding voice in Oklahoma. It was opportune that he did, for by the summer of 1935 the financial condition of the college had reached a point of crises. First, more faculty had to be employed in order to take care of a student population which had doubled in size during the last decade. Second, the institution owed over $10,000 for utilities to the city of Stillwater. Third, substantial amounts were required to pay for advertisements in the

Tulsa World and the *Oklahoma Farmer-Stockman*. Fourth, student accounts were in the red as it continued to be difficult to collect fees on time. And fifth, physical facilities had degenerated to where they were well below the level of meeting instructional needs.[26]

The Oklahoma Senate's Committee on Education reported favorably in 1935 on bills to provide money for the construction of additional buildings at the University of Oklahoma and the A. and M. college. The Legislature followed the recommendations given to it and appropriated $44,000,000 for higher education. Marland, however, because of a lack of revenue, had to eliminate the provisions for capital outlay and he decreased the amount allocated for faculty salaries. The final budget for A. and M. was less than that provided in 1926. Funds were, however, made available to pay back bills and to put student accounts on the black side of the financial ledger. President Bennett directed his administrative staff to prepare statistical data which would assist the Board of Agriculture to determine where a reduction in the payroll could be made. Sustained pressure for more funds did help. In 1937, the college received $1,500,000 more than it had during the last biennium. The appropriation, in fact, was so favorable that Representative Ben Huey complained that the Legislature had discriminated against the University of Oklahoma.[27]

Governor Marland fulfilled his promise to call upon A. and M. to assist with certain of the state's economic problems. In 1936, he requested the loan of several faculty to sit on the State Planning Board. During the same year, as a result of consultations with the federal Agricultural Adjustment Administration, President Bennett accepted an appointment to chair Oklahoma's State Soil Conservation Committee. The college took on even more responsibilities in 1937. Marland asked Bennett to develop an agricultural rehabilitation program for first term inmates at the prison in Stringtown. The Legislature set aside 8,000 acres for the project. Plans were made with the assistance of Philip Donnell, J. B. Perky, E. E. Scholl, Lippert S. Ellis, Henry Murphy, and Horace Harper to provide vocational training for approximately 1,000 men. In addition, Raymond Thomas, Carl Blackwell, J. T. Sanders, and Philip Wilber were drafted to serve on other state committees. Quite clearly, the college had entered a new age of service.[28]

From 1935 to 1939, Henry Bennett had a progressive Board of Agriculture to work with. Ernest Marland nominated capable men to assist Harry Cordell, including C. H. Mullendore, Z. H. Lawter, L. E. Waldrep, and Orville Savage. The latter individual was the first graduate of the college to serve on the Board since Tom Hartman. On January 10, 1937 the college lost a friend when Cordell died of a stroke. He was fifty-five years old and in the middle of his third term as president. Cordell, an anti-Murray Democrat, probably cost A. and M. some appropriations because of his open hostility toward "Alfalfa Bill," but he kept his vow to Bennett not to place any more politicians on the faculty. Officials memorialized Cordell's long years of service to Oklahoma by having the corpse lay in state in the rotunda of the State Capitol before burial in Frederick. John Coffey, thirty-nine, replaced the deceased man. He had been born in Texas in 1898 and held two degrees from the Oklahoma A. and M. College.[29] Tom Reynolds, an individual always attune to the political situation in the state, believed that Coffey would prove to be an excellent administrator. He said: "He is a dynamo, ambitious and hard working. I find him very co-operative and a fine fellow . . . ."[30]

One month after Coffey became president of the Board of Agriculture Governor Marland asked him to head the highway commission instead. To replace him, the chief executive selected a "dark horse," but one thoroughly acceptable to Henry Bennett. Joe Scott, in fact, was a member of the so-called "Durant Gang." He moved from Texas to Antlers, Oklahoma when he was eight and earned a Master of Science degree at Stillwater before becoming business manager of the Southeastern State College in Durant. When Bennett left that community, L. A. Crable employed Scott as Assistant Superintendent of Education. Both Scott and Bennett were hewn from the same oak. Each man had a flair for public relations and each was generous, perhaps to a fault. Their personal ambitions eventually came between them and caused a permanent split. Neither of them, however, would permit differences of opinion to bring harm to the college. And, more significant, the duo knew Oklahoma politics as well as anyone in the state.[31]

Together, Marland, Scott, and Bennett began to search for federal funds and they obtained them in almost unbelievable quantities. The technique they perfected during the Great Depression was to be successfully employed time and time again in the future. The initial stage of the operation called for administrators and faculty to secure appointive positions at the state, regional, or national level. These men [or women] would then alert Bennett to programs for which A. and M. could qualify. The grantsmanship of of the 1930's primarily involved the elevation of college deans to federal posts. Raymond Thomas, in addition to being a member of the Oklahoma Tax Commission, became a consulting economist for the Tennessee Valley Authority. Next, Dover Trent welcomed an invitation from Chester Davis to serve in Washington as assistant director of the Commodities Division of the Agricultural Adjustment Administration. Later, he responded to a call from Rexford Tugwell to become a regional director of the Resettlement Administration. Philip Donnell, who in many respects served as the coordinator of New Deal programs on the campus, moved to Oklahoma City where he became state engineer for the Works Progress Administration. Carl Blackwell held many prestigious positions, including the regional directorship of the Texas and Oklahoma Division of the Federal Land Utilization program. He also took Trent's place in the Rural Resettlement Administration. Seventy members of the faculty occupied New Deal posts, too.[32] The extent of these numbers prompted President Bennett to state that "it is doubtful if any college in the country with no larger personnel than A. and M. has contributed as many men to the various recovery measures as A. and M."[33]

While the aforementioned were getting established in their positions, the college continued its press for state funds. Instructional space reached a critical point during the 1936-1937 academic year. In September, the faculty found that it was impossible to locate enough classrooms. Professor Lippert Ellis, for example, discovered that he had an overflow enrollment for his agricultural economics course. The room scheduled for his use held 150 students but he had 180. Investigation revealed that the only vacant room on the campus at the hour he taught was a 10 x 15 office suitable for only fifteen people. The original room was retained but students had to take turns sitting on the floor. Some of the buildings that were used should not have been. In the spring the state and local fire marshals jointly condemned the English and History Building and the Music and Arts Building. President Bennett, in a superb piece of showmanship, requested permission from the Board of Agriculture to install six tents on a grassy quadrangle behind Murray Hall. This spot had been used by coeds for intramural softball games. Photographs were taken when the canvass was in place so that the crowded conditions could be exploited in state newspapers. Many of the stories were accompanied by humorous verses and songs. The Legislature, which just happened to be in session at the time these events unfolded, had little choice but to provide the funds for new buildings.[34]

State funds were used to remodel old buildings as well as to construct new ones. Thatcher and Hanner Halls were refurbished at a cost of $600,000. Two new classroom buildings, one for engineering and one for science, were placed under a construction contract calling for an expenditure of $500,000. In addition, the college erected a "4-H" convention hall to be used by the state's agricultural clubs for their annual meeting. The structure was named after Edward Gallagher and used as a basketball stadium. When told it was the largest in the Southwest, critics called it "Iba's Folly." Simultaneously, federal funds became available. The government approved requests for a student union and a library but Oklahoma could not afford the 30% to float the bond issues. The Works Progress Administration, however, did provide the wherewithal to modernize the Old Biology Building, Lewis Stadium, and the power plant. Smaller projects included: tennis and handball courts, a honey house, manure pits, curbs, gutters, sidewalks, sewers, and new facing for buildings. Indeed, one of the most familiar sights that greeted visitors and students were the initials "WPA" brushed into the cement that dotted the campus.[35]

The combined state and federal funds ran well into the millions. Yet, it was just a beginning. Carl Blackwell secured Rural Resettlement funds to turn 20,000 acres of land seven miles west of Stillwater into a scientific and recreational area. The development eventually contained a 3,000 acre lake, a beach lodge, and rental cabins. The government also authorized the construction of two additional dormitories which together had a capacity to house 950 students. The first, a residence hall for males, was named after the late Harry Cordell; the second, a women's dormitory, was named for Frances Willard, the temperance worker. Bonds for these two buildings totaled more than one million dollars. Investors sold them several times at a profit, a sign that financial experts felt that the affairs of the college were being conducted on a sound basis.[36]

Two new major programs, both innovative, were added to the college just before World War II. The first was establishment in conjunction with the city of Stillwater and the federal government. The local community donated land on the southeastern part of the campus to the Board of Agriculture to build a school of fireman-ship. It was the only such collegiate department in the nation. The building, constructed in the now familiar Georgian style, was 77' x 82' with a five story tower. Colonel Clarence Goldsmith of the National Board of Fire Underwriters gave the dedicatory address. The Association of Land-Grant Colleges and State Universities took particular note of the idea. Lewis Webster Jones in 1948 called it a good illustration of the versatility of the land-grant movement. The other program, a school of restaurant and hotel management, imitated courses of study at Cornell and Michigan State University. Daisy Purdy headed the school and constructed a curriculum which emphasized business laws and management problems. Graduates of both programs were much in demand both at home and abroad.[37]

The Oklahoma A. and M. College brought the Civilian Con-servation Corps and the National Youth Administration to Still-water, too. In 1933 Dover Trent announced that an agreement had been signed with CCC officials to board two hundred males. These men were to be employed on soil erosion projects in Payne County as well as on the beautification of the campus. The college leased land to the government and then secured money from Washington to construct barracks, eating and bathing facilities, and work rooms. Philip Wilber joined with Captain John R. O. Bradley of the United States Army and J. W. Carpenter of the CCC erosion division to complete details. President Bennett, as an incentive to get the program, arranged for one hour of academic instruction to be given the visitors each day, for most of the CCC employees were high school graduates. County agricultural extension agents filled manpower quotas by nominating two people each from their dis-tricts. The program ended in 1936, but the institution received long term benefits in that it was awarded title to the various buildings that had been erected.[38]

Ford Mercer, who left the faculty on a leave of absence in September, 1935, served as the outside contact for National Youth Administration subsidies. One year after Mercer's departure, Bennett sought government money to provide for the education of Oklahoma youth whose parents had been adversely effected by the drought of 1936. In November, he held a conference in Stillwater with Carl Hesley, New York, Richard Brown, Washington, Garth

250

Arkridge, New Orleans, and Houston Wright, Oklahoma City, in regard to NYA funds. Brown agreed to make Stillwater the headquarters for a twelve state area which would bring two hundred more people to the campus for vocational training. These students were to receive instruction in agriculture, welding, automobile mechanics, plumbing, shop, carpentering, drafting, and general education. Also, plans were finalized to lease a dormitory to the government until it could construct a $150,000 industrial arts building. In addition, the college was authorized from $25,000 to $50,000, annually, for student labor. This money was divided equally between men and women, with each person receiving an average of $15.00 per month.[39]

Besides aid from the government, the students sometimes received assistance from industry. The most unique and successful experiment conducted on the campus during the New Deal was a contest which resulted in the perfection of the first parking meter. Carl Magee, editor-in-chief of the *Oklahoma News* newspaper, and a man who had won a national reputation for his exposure of the Teapot Dome Scandal, funded a project which he hoped would do something to alleviate parking congestion in downtown Oklahoma City. A public spirited citizen, Magee had developed an interest in this problem because of his service on the traffic committee of the chamber of commerce. Under the direction of Professor H. G. Theusen, he offered $500 for a design and operation model for a coin device which would eliminate free all-day parking. Competition for both categories ended May 6, 1933. Victor L. Rupe, Vivian Sicks, Wayne Robinson, Marshall Maxwell, Clarence Glasgow, and S. K. Lynn divided the $160 offered for design. Sicks, Lynn, and Rupe, along with Gordon Buckle and J. J. Mosshamer, shared the $240 for an operational model. Magee provided $100 for construction materials so that the students would not have to spend money from their own pockets.[40]

The contest furthered Magee's idea. It did not, however, result in a completely functional design. Professor Theusen then invited a former student, Gerald A. Hale, who now taught in the department of mechanical engineering, to collaborate with him on the project. Together, the two men perfected the first practical meter. They called it the Black Maria, a term used by the local townspeople to refer to the police wagon. Intermittent research continued in order to solve various minor problems related to making deposited coins visible and improving the timing device. Hale left the faculty to go into the commercial manufacture of parking meters. Theusen stayed on at the college until retirement. In 1964, he received the Frank and Lillian Galbreadth Industrial Engineering Award, the nation's highest honor in his field.[41]

The participation of the Oklahoma A. and M. College in New Deal programs began to decrease in 1938. Earlier, the Board of Agriculture drafted a special resolution to thank Franklin D. Roosevelt and Harold L. Ickes for their assistance and cooperation. It was more than appropriate to issue this commendation for Philip Donnell calculated that five-eights of all PWA funds awarded Oklahoma had gone to the land-grant college in Stillwater. Future prospects, however, for the institution appeared less than bright, for the state was scheduled to elect a new governor in 1938. Many newspaper editorialists believed that Henry Bennett would run himself this time, but he did not. Fifteen men sought the Democratic Party nomination. None of them appeared to be sympathetic toward education. The five frontrunners included Jack Walton, William Murray, Ira M. Finley, W. S. Key, and Leon C. Phillips. The latter man labeled Marland a "spender" and promised to wage war on the New Deal. On the basis of this platform, Phillips won the right to run against Ross Rizley, a weak Republican candidate. He defeated Rizley by a 355,740 to 148,861 margin. The large plurality convinced him that he had a mandate to hold state spending to an absolute minimum.[42]

Leon Phillips' term of office as governor was a difficult one, partly because of the times, and partly because of his own personality. He had been born in Missouri in 1890 and moved to Oklahoma Territory with his family when he was only two. As a boy he attended public schools and later studied for the ministry at Epworth University. He changed his mind, however, and transferred to the University of Oklahoma where he received a law degree in 1913. Phillips' astute legal ability, plus the inherited piety of his Pennsylvania Dutch mother and shrewdness of his Scotch-Irish father, brought him respect and recognition. He served in World War I with distinction and afterwards won three elections to the Oklahoma Legislature.[43] When he addressed the latter body for the first time as chief executive Phillips stated that he wanted to create a "progressive program of education to the end that Oklahoma may have an educational system equal in all respects to the best in the country."[44] Yet, it soon became apparent that he would not recommend the appropriation of enough money to turn his statement into a reality. The executive established a debt limit for the state and when schools and colleges violated the ceiling, he held up their money, including the funds needed to pay the salary of teachers and faculty. Additional funds, under his adminstration, were out of the question.[45]

Perhaps the most difficult educational problem which faced the new governor was the intense struggle for power between the state university and the state land-grant college. Because Phillips was a graduate of the University of Oklahoma, he often seemed to go out of his way to give credit to A. and M. The executive frequently stressed the importance of vocational education and he graciously accepted a desk which the Aggies had made for him. His educational philosophy called for appropriations based upon current needs, not past inequities. Nevertheless, some newspaper reporters in the state felt that Phillips protected the element who wanted to choke A. and M. in its attempt to move from a college to a university. Critics believed, too, that the governor reflected a bias toward the land-grant college when he decreed that the faculty at Norman would have to take a smaller pay cut than the one at Stillwater. But more important, like Murray, Phillips did not get along with the administration in Washington. His prolonged attempt to halt construction of the Red River Dam, a $54,000,000 project, brought much unfavorable publicity and probably decreased the flow of federal funds to Oklahoma.[46]

Phillips revived the Coordinating Board created by the Legislature in 1933 in order to save money and end institutional squabbling. He appointed John Kane, Francis C. Kelley, Henry Bennett, W. B. Bizzell, Eugene Briggs, G. W. Hilderbrandt, Robert S. Kerr, A. Linscheid, T. T. Montgomery, M. A. Nash, C. I. Pontius, John W. Raley, John Rogers, V. G. Smoot, and A. G. Williamson to the Board. The first project undertaken by this body was to prepare a lengthy study of higher education in Oklahoma. In 1941, the Legislature approved a bill which authorized the people to vote on a constitutional amendment so that the state could create a unified system. The voters approved the measure on March 11. Article XIII-A contained the following provisions: (1) all institutions which received funds from the state were henceforth to be a part of the Oklahoma State System of Higher Education; (2) a nine member team was to administer the System; and (3) the principal duties of the Board would be to recommend budgets, grant degrees, regulate fees, prescribe standards, and allocate the funds provided by the Legislature. Private and demoninational institutions, if they desired, could come under the System. The members of the Board appointed by Governor Phillips met for the first time in the Blue Room of the State Capitol Building on June 16, 1941.[47]

Whether or not the Great Depression marked a turning point in the history of the nation is debatable. It is clear, however, that the American states became more closely tied to the national government, and, in turn, the country became more aware of world economic and military interdependence. Stillwater took early note of Germany's aggressive tendencies and it regrouped its "Washington Division" to bring defense programs to the Oklahoma A. and M. College campus. This time President Bennett served as the instrument of mobilization. He revealed thoughts that had been with him for a long time when he said: "We are world citizens now. We have an inescapable responsibility to do our part, to bring about world peace, a world fellowship. The minds and hearts of men are the same all over the globe. We must renew our faith and philosophy in the future."[48] Then the contacts made as a result of the New Deal were consulted again.

Philip S. Donnell and Professor V. W. Young went to the nation's capital in August, 1939 to sign agreements with the Civil Aeronautics Authority to teach flying at the college. The program which followed operated independently of the military except that graduates were eligible for commissions in the United States Army. Students, especially those majoring in engineering, were encouraged to apply if they had completed one year of college work and could pass the required physical examination. Participants received $40 per month and free room and board; the college got $300 per year for each student. Twice as many applied for the first class as could be accepted. About forty began receiving instruction in September, 1939. The Board of Agriculture provided free insurance for the volunteers.[49]

Philip Donnell left the campus on a leave of absence in September, 1940. He was placed in charge of the 180th Infantry, 45th Division, of the Oklahoma National Guard. Donnell expected to return to A. and M. in twelve months but more than five years passed before he could resume his normal administrative duties. George Whiteside replaced him as dean of engineering as well as taking over the federal aviation program. Dean Whiteside obtained more money for the college and also secured $300,000 for modernizing Searcy Field, the Stillwater airport. The latter agency eventually received about $2,500,000 from the federal government and the United States Navy. Bennett, the head of one of the first colleges in the nation to offer flight training, became an aviation enthusiast. In particular, he felt that farmers could employ airplanes to feed cattle in bad weather and to spray pesticides on crops. After World War II he helped the Oklahoma Flying Farmers Association to acquire a charter from William Enyart, the president of the National Aeronautics Association. The former group, then, formed the National Flying Farmers, an organization which recognized Henry Bennett as its founder.[50]

In 1940, the war in Europe began to affect Oklahomans. Three months before Franklin D. Roosevelt drew the first name for the peacetime draft, an editorialist for the *O'Collegian* predicted that students would be among the first to be called to service. He wrote:

WAR . . . every able bodied man at Oklahoma A. and M. is threatened by it. WAR . . . every student at Oklahoma A. and M. has been taught the uselessness and ruinous results of it. WAR . . . every man has heard his mother read from the *Bible* those words of God's commandment, 'Thou shalt not kill.' WAR . . .the teeth of it are hungry for human bodies. Your body and mine brother Aggie.[51]

President Bennett, the father of boys of draft age himself, understood the fears of the students. On many occasions he tried to instill in them a belief worth personal sacrifice. He entitled one particularly moving address "The American Way Shall Survive." In it, the speaker stated that Adolph Hitler was a threat to democracy because he represented government by personal authority instead of law. The closing words came from the depths of Bennett's soul.[52] To those who had doubts about the necessity of the draft, he said:

Dark and ominous as the clouds of disaster are that are spreading over the world today, I bespeak on your part, young ladies and young gentlemen, an unshaken faith in the future. In the very unsettled condition of affairs lies the possibility of their reorganization in the dynamic nature of society and of men lies the necessity for the continual struggle to perpetuate a chosen way of life as well as the desirability of time modifications in it; in the long view of history lies evidence of the trend of human progress toward the enhancement of the lives of all; and in the essential unity of our nation for an invincible

254

military and naval prepardness we find grounds for our faith that the American way of life shall not pass away. Let us, rather, pray for a resurgence of that ardent idealism of an earlier day which led men to do great things because they believed in themselves and in their destiny.[53]

The possibility that America would be drawn directly into the war reawakened post-World War I passions in Oklahoma. The fact that students were not eager to be drafted caused many in the state to suspect that college professors had been teaching the wrong things in their classes. The criticism which followed was aimed at instructors whose liberal leanings were interpreted as socialistic. Hitler and Germany received scant attention. Milt Phillips, state adjutant of the American Legion, began holding loyalty hearings. His findings prompted men in the Legislature to action. Representative Tommy Jelks, Grady County, urged colleagues to investigate patriotism on college campuses, especially the University of Oklahoma where two professors had been charged by the Civil Liberty League with being Communists. E. R. "Pete" Weaver, of Stillwater, agreed. He said: "There are not two sides to the question of communism against democracy. There is but one side, and that is the United States, and the preservation of this form of government."[54] Senator H. M. Curhutt favored spending as much as a quarter of a million dollars to ferret out radicals. The Former Students Association of A. and M. held loyalty dinners throughout the state in hopes of countering adverse publicity.[55]

Henry Bennett, whose personal loyalty was never questioned, attempted to use the interest in patriotism to increase the budget of the college. He maintained that higher education should be strong in order to contribute to the national defense. The Board of Agriculture elected him for the fourteenth time in 1941, raising his salary to $12,000, the highest in the state. Legislators were invited to the campus to inspect the institution. In turn, they voted to award A. and M. $300,000 more than that provided over the last two year period. Governor Phillips negated the increase. He had become disenchanted with Henry Bennett because he would not announce his candidacy for the gubernatorial nomination. The educator's reluctance to make his position known left Robert S. Kerr as the frontrunner and Phillips did not like the National Democratic Committeeman.[56]

From October, 1941, to May, 1942 the quarrel between the governor and the president of the land-grant college reached the point where it almost ended Bennett's career. Much of the problem centered upon the wrangling over state funds for higher education. Phillips attacked Bennett because he had not turned down the last raise given him by the Board of Agriculture. His hatred extended to other colleges as well, for he threatened to move Central State to another location as a result of the city of Edmond's refusal to supply free drinking water. In November, 1941, President Bennett went to Washington for a long conference with federal officials. The precise reason for the visit is unknown, but it is likely that the discussion which took place related to the possibility of obtaining

255

more money for defense programs. If Bennett had doubts as to whether he should continue as president of Oklahoma A. and M., these now were dispelled. The free world needed food and young men had to be trained for leadership in the military. Kerr and Bennett consulted with each other about the gubernatorial election in Oklahoma. In July, 1942, Kerr won the Democratic primary and in the November election the office he sought became his for the next four years. He was the first native of the state to occupy the governor's chair.[57]

Robert Kerr and Henry Bennett had much in common. Both had been born in a log cabin, had been reared in the Southwest and lived in Little Dixie, had attended the University of Oklahoma, and had been pillars in the Baptist Church. Then, too, William J. Holloway had given each of them their initial push upwards. He had worked for Bennett's appointment to head the land-grant college and had chosen Kerr to replace J. W. Clark as a special justice of the Oklahoma Supreme Court. It is also possible that the two men found some consolation in the fact that Phillips had turned against each of them. Kerr and Bennett remained close for the rest of their lives. They seldom failed to consult with each other on important matters. When, for example, Kerr accepted an invitation to deliver the keynote speech at the National Democratic Convention in 1944 at Chicago, Bennett helped him draft the message.[58]

Henry Bennett discovered after the election that he needed a friend in public office more than at any other point in his life. Scandal, except for two minor incidents, had never touched his long public career. F. C. Carter in 1932 accused Bennett of spending $99.33 from state funds to send Christmas cards. The matter was dropped when the Board of Agriculture pointed out that presidents had used college funds to defray holiday greetings for the past twenty-one years. The same man alleged that money had been misspent in installing a radio and a heater in the car driven by the president.[59] In 1937, Representative J. E. Taylor suggested that Bennett had supported a bill in the Legislature to build farm ponds and that some of this money would be "used as a slush fund to help nominate Bennett for governor."[60] The measure was defeated by one vote, so the issue was dropped. The next year threats were made against Bennett's life. He turned over two blackmail letters to the Federal Bureau of Investigation but that agency did not make any public announcement about the contents. An attack in December, 1942, however, diminished the president's reputation in some quarters of the state. Large amounts of money were spent and a battery of lawyers had to be employed to end a prolonged court struggle. The fact that the case was settled on a technicality caused Bennett's enemies to continue a whispering campaign against him. This element viewed him as a behind-the-scenes political boss who used influence to terminate the matter. Since grand jury records are sealed, it is impossible to review the actual testimony and evidence offered in the case. The crisis came close to the point where automatic re-election to the presidency of the Oklahoma A.

and M. College was placed in doubt. Bennett's splendid war and post-war record erased the incident from the memory of most people and his popularity reached an all-time high during the Korean War.[61]

Governor Phillips refused to support Robert Kerr to succeed him. Instead, after the Democrat primary, he endorsed W. J. Otjen, a Republican. Just before Phillips left office he appointed Dixie Gilmer of Tulsa a special prosecutor to get to the bottom of alleged school textbooks corruption in the state. Gilmer stated that certain "corporations and distributors of school books, together with various of their agents and employers have . . . entered into a conspiracy to control the price of . . . books."[62] He was given $7,500 to bring prosecution under Oklahoma's anti-trust laws. President Bennett, who had written public school textbooks and assigned some of the royalties to the William H. Murray Educational Foundation, testified before a Tulsa grand jury in 1943. The line of questioning indicated quite clearly that Phillips had had Bennett in mind when he authorized the special investigation. Specifically, Gilmer, a candidate for governor himself in 1946, queried the president about the frequency of book revisions and asked him if he had taken an active part in the campaign of Robert Kerr. Bennett stated that the decision as to whether textbooks should be changed was in the hands of the publisher and that he had not unlawfully participated in Kerr's election. The grand jury, however, indicted the president on three counts of perjury on November 17, 1943.[63]

In February, 1944, District Judge Oras A. Shaw handed down a decision which brought the case to an end. He supported Bennett's contention that revisions were decided by the publisher not the author. Gilmer, of course, was interested in this point because whenever textbooks were modified the state had to purchase new copies for the public schools.[64] Neither did Judge Shaw believe that the educator was guilty of illegal political influence. "In fact," Shaw wrote,

I think that from the standpoint of our general welfare, every citizen owes to himself and to his country to earnestly engage in politics in the sense that he should be acquainted with the political needs of our state, and the nation, and to do what he can to put into effect his ideas in regard thereto, and if all our people do it, we will have a better brand of democracy than we have at this time.[65]

On the other hand, several former public school officials, including one who later became an executive of the Oklahoma A. and M. College, were severely reprimanded but not punished. Shaw stated that in his opinion his court did not have legal jurisdiction.[66] Robert Kerr protected Bennett from undue criticism while the case was on the docket. It was an act which set the cement of the two men's friendship.

Shortly before the governor's office changed hands, the calendar on President Bennett's desk reminded him that he and the college had another birthday to celebrate. On December 14, 1941, it would be fifty years since Robert Barker and James Neal had gathered with students in the Congregational Church to begin instruction. Bennett requested and received permission from the Board of Agriculture to hold a three day conference on the 13th, 14th, and 15th to commemorate the event. He also appointed a blue ribbon committee to aid in the planning. Several prominent men and women were invited to participate in the festivities. Henry G. Knight, Department of Agriculture, was to speak on "Future Markets for Farm Products"; David Cushman Doyle, author and lecturer, on "The Future of Public Works and Services"; Aurelia H. Reinhardt, president of Mills College, on "The Educational Process Fundamental to Democracy"; Edward Howard Griggs, author and lecturer, on "The College and Leadership"; and Clarence A. Dykstra, president of the University of Wisconsin, on "The Next Fifty Years." President Bennett, for his own presentation, decided to discuss "Oklahoma A. and M. College Faces the Future." Yet, before he could compose the words that he wanted to share with those who would gather for the occasion, the nation was stunned by the surprise attack on Pearl Harbor.[67]

Henry Bennett boarded a plane for Washington almost immediately after the radio broadcast the news. He returned to the campus four days later to confer with state officials and members of his staff. The president did, thoughtfully, stop long enough to make a major address to the students where he urged them to continue their studies until it was time to don a military uniform.[68] Bennett resisted a temptation to speak directly on the war at the 50th anniversary celebration. Instead, he simply restated the principles that he had espoused since he became an educator. The body of his talk stressed that education was needed to extend knowledge and that the future would be better. It was, however, a single sentence at the beginning which stood out. "I believe," he said, "in the unlimited perfectability of man (physically, mentally, morally, and in other fields not yet approached)."[69] In the ten years of his life that remained these words would become a guiding principle. The phrase would touch men in Oklahoma, in the United States, and in the deserts and jungles of foreign lands.

XVI   Cooperation and Brotherhood

From 1941 to 1951, Henry Garland Bennett achieved true greatness. The second global war of the century stabilized the political situation in Oklahoma and permitted the dean of American land-grant college presidents to become an educational missionary and spokesman for international peace. Robert Kerr served as a catalyst in the journey outward and upward but stimulation also came from Bennett's belief that governmental programs could touch the people in a positive way. In particular, the preparation of a document entitled *A Report on Public Works Planning* produced for the Oklahoma Planning and Resources Board convinced him of the importance of federal aid.[1] Governor Kerr, in return for assistance to the state, helped the college to make certain organizational changes in the governing board. These had been sought by the Former Students Association since the administration of George Wilson. With new leadership, the Oklahoma A. and M. College embarked upon a mission of service unparalleled in its history.

The governors who followed Robert Kerr were sympathetic to

259

the needs of higher education, too. Kerr's successor, Roy Turner, became the second native son to serve as governor of Oklahoma. Though a millionaire independent producer of oil, he had an interest in agriculture and education. Turner had been elected to the Oklahoma City Board of Education and his ranch near Sulphur was regarded by some as one of the best of its kind in the nation. Henry Bennett and Roy Turner were not close but the two men developed a viable business relationship through Forrest McIntire, the governor's administrative assistant. In addition, the two executives found a common bond in their mutual admiration of President Harry S. Truman. Johnston Murray, the son of "Alfalfa Bill," assumed the governor's post in 1950. He resembled his father in that he was a financial conservative. His ideas on race and education, however, were much more liberal than the family patriarch. Bennett himself ceased to be a candidate for elected political office. Yet he did continue to exert an influence on the state political scene. One of his more successful attempts at lobbying involved bringing the wives of the lawmakers to the campus for an annual Hospitality Day.[2]

The Board of Agriculture continued to elect Henry Bennett to the college presidency without hesitation until 1944. The coolness of Joe Scott caused some, but not insurmountable, problems because the educator seemed more interested in what was happening in Washington than in Oklahoma City. Many national political leaders visited the campus in the upcoming decade and a number of them left a generous tip in the form of support for expanding an old program or beginning a new one. The entire Bennett family followed the lead of the head of the household in fighting for peace. Henry, Jr., a graduate of the Johns Hopkins Medical College, served in New Guinea and suffered a near mortal wound from a Japanese Eagle Bomb. Philip, who now had a law degree from Harvard University, obtained a commission in the Adjutant General's Corps. Tom was stationed in the Pacific Theater. Liberty and Mary, both in their twenties, performed as volunteers on the Stillwater home front. Vera Bennett held the family together. She shielded her husband from minor domestic cares as he searched for new challenges and she instilled a desire in her children fully to develop their many talents. The American Mothers' Committee of the Golden Rule Foundation elected her the state mother of the year in 1943.[3]

The college administrative staff remained fairly constant throughout Bennett's last decade in office. The changes which did occur came as a result of the war or retirement because of advanced age. Edward R. Stapley replaced George Whiteside as acting dean of the school of engineering when the latter entered active military service. Nora Talbot, who had joined the faculty in 1915, and, who had become head of home economics in 1927, requested to be placed on the emeritus list in 1950. Lela O'Toole of the United States Office of Education succeeded her. The new dean had grown up in Thomas, Oklahoma and had earned two degrees in Stillwater before beginning work on a Ph. D. at Ohio State. O. K. Campbell became dean of men in 1948, taking over for Clarence McElroy. The latter man also retired in 1950 after having spent fifty years on the Oklahoma A. and M. College campus. His long tenure was both a testament to his academic ability and to his great personal popularity.[4]

When lists of leading college presidents were published in the 1940's, Henry Bennett usually placed in the top ten. He became the first president to win fame for his work at the college itself. The faculty took pride in the recognition granted their senior colleague but there were many who hoped to see the reign of the "Durant Gang" ended. The fact that the institution did not have a vice-president until after World War II indicated, however, that Bennett did not intend to relinquish his hold on the organization. Salary and retirement pensions, along with fringe benefits, continued to be among the lowest in the nation. In fact, pay actually decreased in 1944. Some of the instructors who accepted commissions, such as Raymond Bivert, O. A. Hilton, A. Richard Williams, and J. Rex Cunningham, must have found that even military remuneration was better than that provided for teaching. Instructors who remained on the faculty, of course, gave their all, especially to war related programs.[5]

On December 29, 1941, President Franklin D. Roosevelt sent telegrams to all of the colleges and universities in the country. No one consulted with the teaching staff in regard as to how the faculty could aid in the war effort. However, committees were formed to study procedures for becoming more efficient and effective. These groups produced documents relating to instruction, publish or perish, the military brain-drain, student advisement, general education, and the improvement of course content. On the other hand, the faculty did take some steps which eventually would make decentralization easier. The local chapter of the American Association of University Professors became stronger and it investigated many aspects of working conditions. The institution also formed a Board of Faculty Representatives. This group initially resembled a company union but it did establish a precedent for increased participation in the decision-making process. The war years, in retrospect, caused academicians to question the wisdom of investing too much power in one man in much the same way as the public contemplated the awesome strength of the national executive branch.[6]

Both faculty and students responded to the mobilization call. To those who felt somewhat uncomfortable about the new role, President Bennett reminded them that "the university is not an isolated institution but an integral part of the social order—and that its greatest contribution to society—is not in the creation of change as a direct objective but rather in its peculiar capacity to understand change and interpret it."[7] During the war, 113 members of the faculty and staff enlisted in the armed forces. Almost all of those who stayed had some connection with the national defense. For example, H. Clay Potts supervised the collection of scrap metal; Professor H. G. Theusen produced time-study reports to stimulate factory production; and other people collected statistics for the Office of Price Administration and conducted investigations into locating new sources of rubber. Oklahoma A. and M. as a whole cooperated with the community in bringing film personalities to Stillwater to sell war bonds. And finally, Henry Bennett spoke to farmers throughout the state, stressing the importance of agriculture in fighting the war and in reconstructing the war torn world once hostilities had ceased.[8].

The character of the student body changed considerably from 1941 to 1951. The draft took many young men but there always seemed to be others to take their place. Fred C. Whitledge, 26, an education major, and the Harrison brothers, Bill and Jack of Supply, were the first Aggies to enlist. They signed their papers on Monday morning following the bombing of Pearl Harbor. Nearly one hundred of their classmates joined them before the month was over. The number of graduates increased from 949 in 1942 to 1,591 in 1948. The latter figure was deemed large enough for the administration to justify a mid-year graduation to be held in January. The number of foreign students climbed higher as well. In 1948, the registrar announced that the institution now enrolled men and women from twenty-eight different foreign countries. If the 16,222 men and 7,250 women who had graduated up to the time of Dr. Bennett's death had taken the time to examine the signature on their diplomas, they would have found that Henry Bennett had signed 21,056 or 88.69% of all degrees and 3,712 or 97.50% of all graduate degrees granted by their *alma mater*. The president brought many things to the campus, including students.[9]

The college conducted twelve programs for the military during World War II. Most of them were administered by the school of engineering. Some 40,000 men and women, as summarized below, received educational service certificates.

VEND Vocational Education for National Defense	3,655
ESMWT Engineering, Science, Management War Training	1,268
STARS Specialized Training and Reassignment School	5,751
CAAWTS Civil Aeronautics Administration, War Training Service	193
CAACPT Civil Aeronautics Administration, Civilian Pilot Training	300
AAFCTP Army Air Force College Training Program	3,980
ASTP Army Specialized Training Program	1,450
AAFTED Army Air Forces Training Detachment	2,585
ASTRP Army Specialized Reserve Program	454
WAVES Naval Training School	10,783
EERM Naval Radar Training School	6,702
SOL School of Oriental Languages	402
	37,523

In addition, the military assumed command of the school of fire-manship and sponsored a national laboratory for testing diseased plants. Funds were provided to employ twenty-four pathologists, one for each two of the forty-eight states. Toward the end of the war, A. E. Darlow left the campus to develop military study centers in Europe designed to assist soldiers in making the transition back to civilian life. The first of these was located in Shrivenham, England. It offered mini-courses in agriculture, commerce, education, engineering, the fine arts, journalism, science, and the liberal arts. Last, but not least, the national government provided funds for agricultural research.[10]

The army, including an air force component, the navy, and the women's auxiliary of each, created military programs on the A. and M. campus. Precise dates and training requirements are difficult to determine because of the restrictions placed on troop movements. George Whiteside, an Annapolis graduate, completed arrangements to bring the first naval operations to the campus. He implemented plans made by a local chamber of commerce delegation which consisted of Roy Hoke, H. G. Bennett, Philip Wilber, Elmer Donart, Claude Bradshaw, Hal McNutt, Ralph Archer, C. R. Bellatti, and L. E. McConkey. These men spent over $6,000 in order to work out the details with Washington. Commander H. W. Olds supervised the navy personnel who came to learn how to operate a secret scanning device for use in detecting aircraft. The men assigned to the radar division lived in the barracks built by the National Youth Administration. Later, the navy spent huge sums of money to enlarge Searcy Field so that pilot training could be offered.[11]

In November, 1942, the collegiate administration emptied Thatcher and Hanner Halls to make room for the air force segment of the United States Army. Regular students were ordered to find rooms or apartments in the city of Stillwater. The faculty who instructed these men were sent to Fort Logan, Colorado for a special orientation course. The initial experiment proved so successful that Major General Jacob E. Fickel sent more soldiers to Stillwater for pre-flight school. The expansion of Searcy Field made it possible to offer actual pilot training. Additional barracks to hold the latter men were brought from Wilburton and Broken Arrow, Oklahoma. When the army ended its programs in 1944, Colonel Howard M. Yost moved the men to Camp Howze, Texas. So many military personnel were stationed in Payne County that some people in Oklahoma believed that the college might be closed to civilians.[12]

Oklahoma A. and M. continued to prepare reserve officers under the National Defense Act of 1920. As has been mentioned before, the college established an infantry unit on the campus first. Just before World War II, in 1937 to be exact, the administration received permission to prepare engineering students for commissions. Signal corps and aviation training were added during the conflict with the Axis. This brought the total number of options to four. The two new programs were open to all students who were pursuing degrees in transportation, aircraft maintenance, engineering, statistical control, meteorology, supply, communications, or armament. The government provided free uniforms and textbooks besides paying students at the rate of $20 per month.[13]

The most popular program on the campus, and the one that received the most publicity, was the Women Appointed for Volunteer Emergency Service, sometimes called the WAVES. Oklahoma A. and M. was one of the first educational institutions in the nation to offer training in this area and it eventually became the largest. The WAVES lived in Willard, North Murray, and the south wing of Cordell Hall. Seven sorority and fraternity houses had to be leased to the government as well, for as many as 1,200 young ladies were stationed on the campus at the same time. Most of them were schooled in clerical duties so that more males could be freed for combat. Lieutenant Helen Sweat commanded. Her group was a diverse one and included an olympic swimming champion, a John Powers model, a golf professional, a Latin American botanist, a New York nightclub hostess, a stage ingenue, a torch singer, and a concert pianist. In all, the WAVE program contained girls from every state in the union.

Local, state, and national newspapers published articles on the "sailorettes." The O'Collegian printed dozens of pictures and one editor even requested the girls to think of themselves as "alumni" of A. and M. once the war had ended. The first WAVE arrived on the campus in August, 1941, and the last one left in January, 1945. Male soldiers expended many jokes about them but the women put in long hours of training. A typical day started at six in the morning and ended with lights out at ten in the evening. Eight hours were spent in the classroom Monday through Friday. The girls never lacked for attention. The Bluejackets of the radar school usually provided a welcoming dance. School children in the vicinity got their names and mailed greeting cards to them on holidays, such as Valentine's Day. The WAVES, in their white blouses and blue skirts, provided much femininity to a campus that heretofore had been largely masculine.[14]

On April 12, 1945, the day Franklin Delano Roosevelt died, Senator Elmer Thomas announced that the facilities vacated by the army would be utilized by the navy to develop a school of oriental languages. Captain John H. Morrill, a war hero who published his experiences in a best-selling novel entitled South to Corregidor, assummed charge of the operation. James A. McAlpine served as the academic director of the school. Bennett selected him for this task because he had been reared in central Japan by missionary parents. Oklahoma A. and M. was scheduled to offer instruction in the Japanese language while the University of Colorado, in a companion venture, would teach Russian and Chinese. The navy expected to send about 150 instructors to conduct training for some 750 to 1,000 college graduates who ranked in the upper 10% of their class.

264

The oriental language program was the first to come to Stillwater which had the possibility of leaving long term academic benefits. The other projects, rumors suggest, had been careless about personnel records, class attendance, and high instructional standards did not always prevail. On the other hand, the experience of simply spending time on a college campus inspired some, such as Robert B. Kamm, a naval radar student from the Little Switzerland section of Iowa, to consider graduate work so that he might return to A. and M. after the war to join the faculty. The school of oriental languages, however, was one of real rigor. It was to consist of fourteen months of intensive work directed by second and third generation Japanese-Americans skilled in language instruction. The initial class was housed in Cordell and Thatcher Halls, with provisions made for married men to occupy quonset huts on Sixth Street. The program ended in the summer of 1946; the surrender of the Japanese seemed to negate the value of the project.[15]

In 1946, President Bennett prepared statistics for the Board of Regents which summarized A. and M.'s role in World War II. He estimated that 6,067 former Aggies had fought from Pearl Harbor to Berlin, from Iceland to Hiroshima. Of these, 4,464 served in the army, 1,162 in the navy, 287 in the marines, 48 in the coast guard, 18 in Red Cross service, 66 in the women's auxiliary corps, and 19 had been nurses or dieticians. Four thousand five hundred ten held commissions while 2,411 had earned decorations. These ranged from the Purple Heart to the Distinguished Flying Cross. Patrick Hurley, George P. Hays, and Joseph Clark won international fame for top eschelon military leadership. Indeed, it may not have been an exaggeration for Bennett to claim that American free public education had won the war. On another occasion, he added that A. and M. had trained twice as many soldiers as all of the other Oklahoma schools combined and that the institution had more service personnel on its campus than any other college in the nation. The record was one in which he understandably took great personal pride. Yet, there was no time to comtemplate the past. The college now had to help the state of Oklahoma to industrialize.[16]

In the attempt to change the direction of Oklahoma's development, from agriculture to industry, it was obvious to President Bennett and Governor Kerr that the institution had to divorce itself from the Board of Agriculture. In 1943, therefore, much pressure was applied to the Legislature to sanction another public vote on the matter. The Legislature responded favorably, setting July 11, 1944 as the date for the people to express their opinion on State Question 310. Robert Kerr used his influence to see that the measure needed only a simple majority to pass.[17] The Former Students Association held several meetings prior to the vote. President Bennett conferred personally with the organization in May, 1944 and offered to "underwrite the cost of printing, mailing, and secretarial help."[18] The alumni, under the leadership of A. O. Martin, purchased numerous newspaper advertisements and posted 125,000 pieces of literature. The bill passed by a margin of 9,147. Kerr appointed the first eight members of the new Board of Regents for the Oklahoma A. and M. Colleges. Joe Scott, as president of the State Board of Agriculture, served on this body in an *ex officio* capacity.[19]

The membership elected B. D. Eddie, the general manager of the Superior Feed Mills, as chairman. Others on the executive committee included R. T. Stuart, vice-chairman, and C. R. Bellatti, secretary. The latter man had exhibited a deep interest in the college for many years in his position as publisher of the *Stillwater News-Press*. Kerr retained Andrew Potter in order to insure some continuity between the old and the new board. Edward T. Davis, Fred G. Drummond, and Joe C. Scott held degrees from A. and M. P. F. Harrill and M. L. Dudley completed the list. Because of his background, President Bennett probably thought that Colonel Stuart would be the organization's key man. Stuart's grandfather had moved from Scotland to Texas while it was still a republic. His great grandmother had southern roots, too. She was the sister of T. J. "Stonewall' Jackson. Stuart started his own life insurance company in 1916. He began selling policies in 1905 for the Equitable Life Insurance Company in Texas and had set a national record by recording $2,000,000 in sales in less than three months. Stuart and Bennett shared many of the same qualities, including a belief that A. and M. was the "most glorious, profound and magnificent institution in America, taking a backseat for no other land-grant college in existence anywhere."[20]

President Bennett anticipated in advance the passage of State Question 310 and he spent many months in preparing suggestions for the Board of Regents. Moreover, he wrote a book published privately in 1945, entitled *This is Colonel Stuart: A Gentleman from Texas*. The membership of the Board held their first meeting on August 7, 1944 in the Blue Room of the State Capitol so that Governor Kerr could attend. M. A. Nash, co-founder of the Red Red Rose, represented the Oklahoma State Regents for Higher Education. These men conferred with the presidents of all the A. and M. colleges in the state, for the Board had been charged with shaping policy for more than just one institution. Consequently, the executives of Cameron State Agricultural College, Conners State Agricultural College, Eastern Oklahoma Agricultural and Mechanical College, Murray State College, Northeastern Oklahoma Agricultural and Mechanical College, and Panhandle A. and M. College had been invited to be present. C. L. Harrison, of Langston University, took part as well. He expressed an interest in having his institution join this group so that he could "follow in the footsteps of Booker T. Washington" in making Langston the Tuskeegee of Oklahoma. Besides this, Langston still had not been accepted for membership in the North Central Accreditation Association. In 1945, the Legislature granted his wish and made provisions to bring the Negro institution under the umbrella of the Board of Regents.[21]

The meetings held throughout the remainder of 1944 touched upon a variety of topics, including further organizational arrangements, the need to compile legislative statutes and court decisions dealing with higher education, designation of an appropriate seal, and the importance of talks to determine the relationship of the Board to the Oklahoma State Regents for Higher Education. Robert Kerr and Attorney General Randell S. Cobb continued personally to offer advice. Tom Sexton frequently attended as a substitute for M. A. Nash. Though the "Minutes" are not altogether clear, it seems as if the Board wanted to create a land-grant college system in Oklahoma, with the other seven colleges under the direction of A. and M. This idea actually was proposed several years later. Henry Bennett usually brought several members of his staff with him, such as C. R. Strong, J. L. Sanderson, and Philip Wilber. In many respects these men served as financial and architectual consultants to all of the schools placed under the jurisdiction of the Board.[22] Schedules were always tight but occasionally a minute could be found to discuss the future. On September 2, 1944, President Bennett suggested that the membership not limit their goals for the Oklahoma A. and M. College. He said:

It is needless to say that the creation of the Board of Regents is the realization of a dream of some twenty-eight years or more of all friends of agriculture and friends of agricultural schools. It is a personal satisfaction to the present Governor. It is up to the Board, whoever the members may be from time to time, not to be content with how the schools have been run . . . . There is no reason why Oklahoma cannot produce schools equal to Ames, Purdue and others.[23]

From 1945 to 1951, the Board of Regents laid the groundwork for the conversion to a state university. The trustees provided additional administrative support, expanded graduate education, sharpened the emphasis on service, and pushed the "Twenty-Five Year Plan" to virtual completion. In the area of administrative support, the college created its first vice-presidential position in 1947. Philip Donnell, who ended his military career in 1946 as Chief of Training within Civilian Agencies, was made vice-president in charge of building and construction. Three years later Randall T. Klemme became vice-president for agricultural and industrial development. Vice-dean of agriculture Oliver Willham assumed a position equal to those of Donnell and Klemme. The selection of the latter two vice-presidents ended much suspense, for many people wondered if a man would be trained to succeed Bennett when he retired.[24]

The expansion of graduate programs proved more expensive and more complex than simply creating new administrative positions. The presence of the Oklahoma State Board of Regents for Higher Education meant that other people besides institutional trustees would have a voice in ruling on additional graduate degrees. Money, of course, had to be considered in this regard but there also with the thorny matter of academic duplication. B. D. Eddie often consulted with M. A. Nash when problems occurred, and, at other times, presidents of the University of Oklahoma and the Oklahoma A. and M. college threshed out matters personally.

In 1947, for instance, Henry Bennett and George Cross, who had replaced Bizzell, met and agreed that Norman would henceforth emphasize geology while Stillwater would stress engineering. Other times, quick solutions were not possible. Each conflict had to be handled one-by-one until such time as general guidelines could be formulated.[25]

As early as 1944, President Bennett began to implement plans to bolster graduate education. He asked the Board in December for permission to appoint five percent of the faculty to honor professorships. These individuals were to be given special pay and released time. During the same year the executive discussed the possibility of establishing a research foundation on the campus. It became operational in 1946, with O. M. Smith as its head. Marvin T. Edmison took his place eleven years later, in 1955. The latter man held degrees from Oklahoma A. and M. and currently held a position at the University of Arkansas similiar to the one offered him at Stillwater. The foundation at first attempted to seek grants for agriculture and engineering but with the passage of time the humanities and social sciences profited from the arrangement as well.[26]

The Board of Agriculture approved a Doctor of Education degree in July, 1938. It was a professional degree established at Harvard University in 1920 to train men and women for administrative positions in education. The degree lacked the prestige of a Ph. D., yet completion of it entailed considerable rigor. In order to graduate, according to the catalog, a prospective candidate had to complete six semesters of work beyond the bachelors, pass a proficiency test, demonstrate a reading knowledge of two foreign languages, write a dissertation, and show evidence of being able to use research tools. The second graduate dean added a new twist to it. He worked out a plan for other departments to offer the degree in conjunction with the school of education. This arrangement, no doubt, had saving money as a purpose. In the end, however, it anticipated by some fifteen years the development of a Doctor of Arts degree; that is, the training of one who is more a popularizer rather than a producer of original research. Expanding university enrollments made good teaching more of a necessity than in the past. The Ed. D., then, turned out to be an enlightened step forward.[27]

In 1946, four years after the first student received a Doctor of Education degree at Oklahoma A. and M., the Board of Regents approved a request to develop a course of study leading to the Doctor of Philosophy. This degree centered upon the ability independently to plan and execute original research instead of teaching and administration. The program initially was limited to animal husbandry and chemistry. The Federal Works Agency tendered a grant the next year to fund doctoral study in veterinary medicine. Oklahoma, prior to this time, had depended upon other states to train men and women who wanted to pursue a Doctor of Veterinary Medicine degree under an arrangement with the Regional Council for Education. Twenty-six students received their D.V.M. in 1951, shortly after the school of veterinary medicine became accredited.

HENRY GARLAND BENNETT, President, 1928-1951.

Veterans' Village housing project in 1946 with more than 1,200 units and a peak population of 4,500 people.

Ground breaking ceremonies delighted Dr. Bennett because they signified another part of the campus development plan sliding into place. Left to right are regents Fred Drummond, R. T. Stuart, P. E. Harrill, and Dr. Bennett.

Dr. Bennett smiles proudly at replica of new men's residence hall that would bear his name while civic club representatives, R. T. Stuart of board of regents, and Senator Robert S. Kerr look on. He was even more delighted with the opportunity of meeting students (left) and particularly those whose fathers or mothers had attended Oklahoma A. and M.

Aerial view of Oklahoma

niversity campus, 1975.

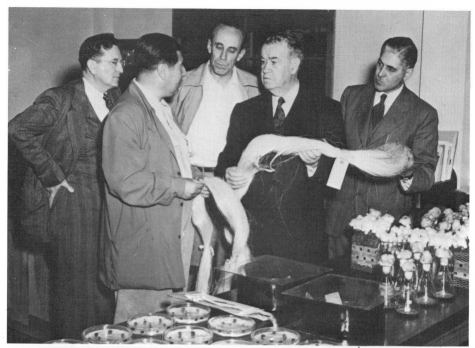

In November, 1950, Dr. Bennett became administrator of the Technical Cooperation Administration, popularly called the Point Four program. Here TCA officials and Bennett inspect Abaca (Manila hemp) fiber at one of the Inter-American Institutes of Agricultural Sciences at Rurrialba, Costa Rica.

Dr. Bennett inspecting a shovel used by an Iraq farmer.

Bennett Memorial Chapel was completed on the Oklahoma A. and M. College campus in 1954 following Dr. Bennett's death in a plane crash near Tehran, Iran, in a blinding snowstorm the night of December 22, 1951.

Expansion of campus facilities was a major concern of Dr. Oliver S. Willham, President, 1952-1966. Many forward-looking changes took place during his 14-year tenure, among them the changing of the institution's name from Oklahoma A. and M. College to Oklahoma State University.

The New Library (above) and Student Union (below), two major projects in the "Twenty-Five Year Plan" were completed in the early 1950's.

The engineering sciences requested the State Regents for Higher Education for permission to add the Ph. D. in agricultural, civil, chemical, electrical, and mechanical engineering in 1952. The Board granted the petition on July 23. Other departments applied for the same privilege as they felt they were ready to handle advanced instruction.[28]

The growth of graduate education necessitated the identification of faculty who had the temperament and professional credentials to guide doctoral students. Professor McIntosh, in the 1930's, consulted with the committee on higher degrees in regard to standards and implementation schedules. Thirteen years later President Bennett authorized a Graduate Council to replace the committee on higher degrees. This group formalized rules for membership to the graduate faculty. The Council decreed that instructors who sought appointment should have a terminal degree in their field of specialization, be a member of the faculty for at least eighteen months, and have an established reputation as a producer of original research. Potential members were nominated by the appropriate department head and then screened by the membership of the Council. In the future, subcommittees met to discuss fellowships and assistantships for students. The research foundation provided released time and money for those who did not qualify to eliminate deficiencies.[29]

The development of the Oklahoma Institute of Technology was the most ambitious project initiated on the campus during the last five years of the Bennett administration. In 1946, the United States Army, as a result of an international reparations agreement, brought the Klockner-Humboldt-Deutz Laboratory from Oberrusel, Germany to Alexandria, Virginia for storage at the Camden Quartermaster Depot. The federal government valued the equipment at $2,500,000. The Department of Commerce selected a retired physicist from the National Bureau of Standards named H. C. Dickinson to head a committee to find a permanent location for the laboratory. Approximately 110 universities and foundations submitted grant proposals. Henry Bennett and Philip Donnell composed one for the Oklahoma A. and M. College. The writers justified their request by stating that a central geographic location would protect the hardware from enemy attack and that the laboratory would help the Sooner State to convert from an agricultural to an industrial economic base. Moreover, it would provide a testing site for engineering just as the experiment station had for the school of agriculture. The argument made sense to Dickinson's committee and the college received an affirmative response to their petition.

Before the equipment arrived, President Bennett asked the Board of Regents to change the title of the division of engineering to the Oklahoma Institute of Technology. He also suggested that the Klockner-Humboldt-Deutz Laboratory be named the Oklahoma Power and Propulsion Laboratory and that it be made a sub-division of OIT. The trustees approved both of these requests and voted the expenditure of $10,000 to construct temporary quarters for the

110,000 pounds of steel until it could be put in working order. The college hired W. S. Burns of England to oversee the operation. He, in turn, scoured the country to find academicians who had the background to assemble the equipment. Burns envisioned the need for a staff of twelve specialists and fifty technicians. Philip Donnell and Burns had become friends in England during World War II. Together they hoped to make Oklahoma the center of deisel fuel research in the United States.[30]

When the seventy-two crates containing the Klockner-Humboldt-Deutz Laboratory were unpacked in Stillwater it became apparent that a good bargain had not been struck. The Russian Army, unknown to the American government, had removed many of the lighter pieces of equipment and taken them back with them to the U.S.S.R. What remained had only a value of $200,000. Dean Donnell convinced Bennett to continue with the project for he felt that industrialization was the key to stopping population losses in the Sooner State. The Board of Regents tried to secure the funds needed to manufacture the missing parts but failed because state appropriations in the late forties fell lower than at any time since the middle of the Great Depression. In the absence of state money the college signed contracts with the navy for defense research. These commitments, however, could not be fulfilled. Bennett's successor had to terminate the project in 1955. The demise of the Power and Propulsion Laboratory became the largest catastrophe of the Bennett administration. Besides deep disappointment, some faculty and staff suffered severe personal losses. Several professors had resigned good jobs at leading universities, such as the University of Illinois, and now found themselves unemployed. At least one man, too, incurred a substantial debt because of double moving expenses.[31]

While the college had only limited success in launching the Oklahoma Institute of Technology, the institution did achieve national recognition for the educational opportunities provided disabled veterans and those who wished to study under the provisions of the "G. I. Bill of Rights" of 1944. President Bennett told the faculty shortly after Italy surrendered to the Allies that it was time to start thinking about post-World War II educational programs. In September, 1943, he reported that Oklahoma A. and M. had almost 7,000 students and predicted that the faculty should anticipate an enrollment of 20,000 in the next decade. Bennett appointed a college committee to make recommendations in regard to future academic programs. Philip Donnell was made a vice-president to order to build the facilities needed to meet this challenge. Here his military background and his long years of experience as an engineer worked to the advantage of the college. Donnell provided the leadership for constructing the largest on-campus veterans program in the country.[32]

On December 1, 1944, Henry Bennett commissioned Vance Posey to open an office to assist students who wanted to secure educational payments under Public Laws 16 and 346. Posey did not have to wait for business because he found the institution already had some 500 veterans, many of whom were married. Housing reached the critical stage in a short period of time. Donnell moved those students with dependents into quarters vacated by military personnel. There never seemed to be enough space, however. Bennett, then, made application to the Reconstruction Finance Corporation to secure funds with which to float bonds for more married student housing. By the summer of 1947 the college had a veteran complex valued at $4,000,000. In addition to the facilities that already existed the institution purchased or built 178 trailers, 410 apartments, and 693 hutments. Much of this equipment had been obtained from military or defense installations in Kansas, Texas, Louisiana, and Oklahoma. The college, however, still had 700 more requests than it could fill.[33]

Veteran enrollments continued to soar. Ethel Prosser and Val Connell, the managers of veterans village, counted a student population of 5,000 in 1949. The first occupants were Leonard West and his wife. Mildred Lucille Bronker, born February 3, 1946, became the first of hundreds of babies to arrive. The village contained its own laundry facility, post office, grocery store, fire station, recreation center, nursery, and maintenance shop. The main streets of the complex were named after the war theaters in which the engineers who built them had served. The roads in the west section were named after islands in the Pacific; the ones in the east section had French names. The smaller streets were christened after towns and counties in Oklahoma. The presence of so many mature students necessitated a drastic change in the regulations that governed undergraduate conduct. The college, therefore, permitted them to form their own government. The veterans met on the evening of March 25, 1946 at the Prairie Playhouse and elected John Kelly of El Reno mayor and Clifford Byrd of Sallisaw vice-mayor. These men supervised the affairs of a city that was larger than many of the towns in Oklahoma.[34]

Henry Bennett took great pride in the development of veterans village and he spoke about the community on the radio as often as he could. Federal and state officials recognized the human interest of the public in the settlement and they often selected the Mooney Recreation Hall, a building named after an immigrant janitor who had helped young wives with plumbing, lighting, and heating problems, as a place to make important speeches and policy announcements. The village incorporated as a municipality and residents obtained the right to vote in state and federal elections. Professor Foster Dowell, Guy Donnell, and John D. Hall, of political science, felt the project important enough that they created a course entitled Problems of Municipal Administration [Political Science 373] so that students could be provided with an opportunity to see social ideas tested in a social situation. The community started its own newspaper, and called it appropriately, *The Village Times*. The paper helped newcomers to get acquainted, highlighted the achievements of the veterans in the classroom and on the sports field,

271

carried low cost food recipes, and reported the names of new born babies. Different people probably liked different features of the *Times*. There must not, however, have been many who did not enjoy hearing about practical jokes that Anita Roberts [the dispensary nurse] and Clyde West [a maintenance man] played on each other. Their antics provided chuckles for young marrieds who needed to retain their sense of humor in order to tolerate the academic, social, and financial stresses of the unusual environment they lived in.[35]

In December, 1943, the same month that Vance Posey set up an office in Stillwater to assist veterans under the "G. I. Bill of Rights," the Board of Agriculture discussed the possibility of doing something for disabled veterans. The Board had sponsored such a program after World War I and now they heard that the Glennan General Hospital in Okmulgee, Oklahoma would be closed and the facility put up for bid. It raised the question of whether or not it might be obtained for a second campus. Okmulgee, the Old Creek Nation's capitol, was located south of Tulsa and fifty miles west of Muskogee. It lay in the center of the industrial belt of the state. One year later, Roy R. Tomkins explored the provisions of Public Law 16. This bill stated that handicapped veterans could be paid as much as $95 per month for on-the-job or classroom vocational training. Philip Donnell and Henry Bennett went to Washington to request the federal government for permission to convert the Glennan Hospital into a facility for technical training. In June, 1948, the Board of Regents submitted a bid of $1,300,000 to be discounted at 100% for future services rendered. The government accepted the offer and the Board of Regents for the Oklahoma A. and M. Colleges assumed control of the buildings and grounds the following January.

The Okmulgee Tech campus opened under the direction of L. K. Covelle, a man personally chosen by President Bennett. The institution emphasized terminal technical education but it also possessed a separate division that operated as a community college. Enrollment quickly climbed from 500 to 1,500. One of the most unusual characteristics of the organization is that it operated without state funds. A student tuition charge of $250 [mostly paid through the federal subsidies received by veterans] supported the various divisions: agriculture, food trades, intensive trades, industrial trades, and related subjects. The only exception proved to be state aid to buy a line-o-type machine and to guarantee bonds for the construction of dormitories. Less than 10% of the students who enrolled had any college training and over 50% had never finished high school. The length of training varied but few programs extended beyond three sixteen week terms. Graduates found jobs which paid from $50 to $75 per week. One survey revealed that 60% of the students who attended from 1948 to 1951 were veterans, of which 2% had a physical handicap. President Bennett had as much or more pride in this program as he did for the veterans village project in Stillwater. Unfortunately, however, he severely neglected the amount of pay provided for the 74 instructors who manned the classrooms. In 1955, state legislators from the Okmulgee region tried to separate the institution from A. and M. for this and other reasons. They failed in their effort, yet the movement did force some changes for the better.[36]

The presence of so many veterans on the main campus brought the Oklahoma A. and M. College to the pinnacle of national sports competition in football, basketball, and wrestling. The institution in 1944 began what one writer has called the "golden decade." The Cowboys in the next ten years won 678 games or dual meets, lost 124, and tied 20. Jim Lookabaugh replaced Ted Cox as coach of the football squad in 1938. The gridiron program improved gradually, reaching a peak in 1944 and 1945. In 1944, the Cotton Bowl officials asked A. and M. to meet Texas Christian University. The Aggies blanked their opponent by a score of 34 to 0. The next year the team accepted an invitation to play in the Sugar Bowl. This time Oklahoma A. and M. met St. Mary's of California. The opposition lost by 20 points, 13 to 33. These two teams produced the first All-American football player in the history of the college, Bob Fenimore. The Cowboys played in the Delta Bowl in 1948. The loss, however, of Coach Lookabaugh affected future football fortunes adversely. He was replaced by J. B. Whitworth, who had been an assistant of Wally Butts at the University of Georgia.

Concurrently, Henry Iba's basketball teams won high national honors. In 1944, the year of the Cotton Bowl, the Aggies were invited to play in the National Invitational Tournament at Madison Square Garden in New York City. The team had a fine record during the 1943-1944 season but prior to that date it had only been conquered four times on its home floor, Gallagher Hall. The University of Southern California broke a 47 game winning streak during the 1940-1941 season. Other losses were sustained at the hands of teams from Creighton University and the University of Kansas. In New York, led by All-American Bob Kurland, the players made their way to the finals where they beat New York University 49 to 44 before a crowd of 18,000 people. The next year, "Iba's Men" defeated the University of North Carolina in the same tournament by a margin of 43 to 40. In the same month, the wrestling team, which had dominated in this sport since the coaching days of Edward Gallagher, won the national wrestling title. In 1945, then, within a period of ninety days, the Cowboys won national championships in football, basketball, and wrestling. Moreover, the victory over North Carolina was the first time that a college team had won the N.I.T. two years in a row.[37]

The increased academic, athletic, and vocational programs, pushed the physical facilities of the Oklahoma A. and M. College once more beyond reasonable limits. In the 1940's, Bennett pleaded with the Legislature for building funds. He encountered intense opposition, for all state agencies were critically in need of funds. The lawmakers did respond to the crisis in 1945 but the Oklahoma State Regents for Higher Education decreed that the lion's share of the increase would go to the state colleges. It was a reasonable decision in terms of the overall needs of the educational system. Bennett, however, could not help but be disappointed. A. and M. had done a commendable job during the war and in providing programs for veterans, yet the college only received $850,000 in capital outlay. The president, instead of admitting defeat, requested the Board of Regents to approve additional building bonds. He now had the enrollment to justify the largest building program in the history of the college and he did not want to see his "Twenty-Five Year Plan" scrapped. In the coming months, the trustees and Bennett's executive staff worked out a scheme to construct or remodel some fifty-one buildings or service facilities at a cost of from $20 to $25,000,000, of which $15,000,000 would be bonded indebtedness. The Board of Regents persuaded the Houston, Texas firm of Moroney, Beissner and Company to buy the bonds in one large package.[38]

The building projects started in the 1940s and ending in 1953 touched almost all parts of the college's anatomy. The recent success of the athletic program, coupled with an announcement by George Cross of the University of Oklahoma that he would support A. and M.'s bid for admittance to the Big Seven Conference, necessitated doubling the seating space of Lewis Stadium. Moreover, the utility and heating system of the institution needed an immediate overhaul. Together, the cost of these two items totaled almost $5,000,000. The administration decided to use the $850,000 from the state for a new classroom building. Two dormitories were included in a package which approached $6,000,000. The school of home economics, long overdue for a modern plant, requested $2,500,000. Almost $9,000,000 was reserved for a student union and a central library.[39] One major item had to be excluded from the design, a center for the humanities. Bennett regretted the omission. Sometime afterward, he told a friend: "At the heart of this college, I dream of a center for those studies and disciplines which inform and illuminate all that we strive to do."[40] It simply was impossible however, to include this facility.

The ground breaking ceremonies for the Home Economics Building took place on February 15, 1949. This building was to replace a structure which had been in use since 1919 when there were only 154 students. Currently, the school, by comparison, had a faculty of 75 and over 4,000 enrolled. The Classroom Building was not completed until after Bennett had left office. It contained 45 instructional rooms and a large auditorium. Approximately 2,000 individuals could be accommodated at one time. Interior colors of light coral, beige, blue, and green provided a pleasant atmosphere for learning. The two dormitories were dedicated to members of the administration. The facility for women was named for Julia E. Stout, who had forty years of educational service to Oklahoma to her credit. The men's dormitory was designed to house 1,100 males and had many special features, such as 200 oversized beds. A concession, no doubt, to Henry Iba's quest for more basketball players

274

the size of Bob Kurland. Colonel Stuart and Senator Bob Kerr were on hand for the dedication ceremonies. They led the movement to name it after the college's president.[41] The inscription of the printed program read:

Dedicated to Dr. Henry Garland Bennett, president of the Oklahoma A. and M. College, whose outstanding record as an educator in war and peace; whose youth development and opportunity programs; whose state public service and citizenship have pioneered the pattern of the vital values by which we live. For his attainments and notable successes as a college leader, on the state, national and international scene; for the reality he has given to the realm of college training and the broad facilities he has provided in the various educational provinces of the College . . . we pay him special tribute on this occasion.[42]

The message must have sparked a glint in the eye of the aging executive. It was the first time that the trustees had named a building in honor of a president.

The next two buildings, the Student Union and the Library, stand as the crowning achievement of Henry Bennett. Sites for both of these structures, especially the latter, had been zealously guarded for several decades. The Student Union was opened for use on September, 1950. It stood six stories high and contained some 200 rooms, including bowling alleys, a restaurant, several lounges, a snack bar, study rooms, conference rooms, a cafeteria, space for alumni, regents, and auxiliary enterprise offices, a motel with 81 units, and rental space for a variety of businesses. President Bennett hired C. A. Tibbetts of Tulsa, Oklahoma to manage it. Convention facilities were among the best in the state and they were designed to keep Oklahomans in constant contact with their land-grant college. David Lilienthal, former head of the Atomic Energy Commission, made the first reservation in the motel. He inaugurated a special lecture series to commemorate the event. Other speakers included Pearl Buck and Frank Lloyd Wright.[43]

Ground for the Library was not broken until the summer of 1950. Certain members of the local community had caused a two year delay by protesting the closing of Washington Street, a major traffic artery that ran through the campus south to north. Governor Turner signed a measure to give the Board of Regents the right to close the street but District Judge Henry W. Hoel ruled the action unconstitutional. The Oklahoma Supreme Court, however, unanimously reversed the decision. As Henry Bennett watched Colonel Stuart, Mac Q. Williamson, Edmon Low, Dial Currin, and Alfred E. Jarrell, the lone survivor of the first graduating class, turn the first spade of earth, he formed an image of the completed structure in his mind. He had been over the plans so many times with Philip Wilber that he knew them by heart. The building would be large enough to shelve 1,000,000 volumes when finished and all sidewalks on the campus would stop at the entrance just as all roads led to Rome. Underneath the electric carillon in the 182 foot tower would be an impressive Georgian front highlighted by Italian marble and kasota stone from Minnesota. Inside, the building would contain books, documents, manuscripts, a music library, browsing rooms, a map room, and study carrels for graduate students and members of the faculty. Edmon Low developed an open stack system patterned after procedures in use at Princeton and Harvard. The structure, when finished, would be the fifth largest in the nation.[44]

If the Library had been finished in 1950, one could have observed the sharp difference between it and Old Central. That building was once again showing the signs of advanced age. In June, during the middle of a psychology class taught by Professor S. L. Reed, the ceiling in room 101 cracked and fell. Students took refuge under their desks to protect themselves against falling plaster and the water which sprayed the premises as a result of a broken sprinkler pipe. Fortunately, no one sustained a serious injury. Repairs were made without delay but the accident signaled trouble; the Korean Conflict broke out in the same month. The local chamber of commerce regrouped their "Washington Division." C. R. Bellatti, Randall Klemme, and Henry Bennett, through the assistance of Robert Kerr, met with Anna Rosenberg, an Assistant Secretary of Defense, to discuss what role the college could play in the current international crisis. In the coming months, the institution substantially increased training for reserve officers, secured more women's military auxiliary programs, worked out details for participation in "Operation Bootstrap," and inaugurated something called the Central Technical Training School to prepare civil defense instructors. Also, the college made special preparations to assist veterans with educational training under Public Law 550, the Korean G. I. Bill.[45]

In addition to these services, the national government requested one more favor from the college. It wanted to secure the president of the institution on a full time basis. The Truman administration, several times in the past, had called on Henry Bennett for assistance. Clinton Anderson, Secretary of Agriculture, selected him in October 1945 to attend the United National Food and Agriculture Conference in Quebec, Canada. The meeting dealt with the distribution of American food in Europe. In February, 1948, Bennett talked personally with Truman, although the subject of the conversation is not known. Later that same year, however, several Oklahomans, including Roy Turner, played an instrumental role in the famous election campaign of 1948.[46] The next year Richard C. O'Brien, Chief of the Overseas Branch of the Department of Army, asked Bennett to serve as an advisor to the Office of the Military Government for Germany. The purpose of the trip, according to O'Brien, was to teach the "sociology and practices of agricultural education, extension and research of the land-grant colleges of the United States."[47] The trip was not taken, however, because the executive could not find the time to be absent from the campus.

The United States Civilian Agricultural Department of the Army and Cultural Relations renewed the invitation that summer. This time the Board of Regents suggested that Bennett take the trip, but they did not order him to go. He left in July, visiting with officials in Washington before he went abroad. The tour increased Bennett's conviction that the free people of the world had to unite in order to maintain peace so that the energies of the people could be released for the production of food. Simultaneously, Senator Elmer Thomas requested President Truman to appoint Bennett to the National Science Board. In addition, the Farm Credit Association elected the educator Director of the Central Bank for Cooperatives. In March, 1950, His Imperial Majesty Haille Selassie of Ethiopia asked the federal government to send an advisor to Ethiopia to develop an institution of higher education in his country along the lines of the American land-grant college. Bennett, therefore, spent a month in Ethiopia. Robert Kerr arranged for him to see Truman on his return. Truman thanked Kerr and requested that Bennett forward a written report of his trip to Washington. He did not disclose why he wanted the document.[48]

In 1949, in his inaugural address, Harry Truman indicated that he would retain the New Deal philosophy, even though he had discontinued to associate with many of Roosevelt's advisors. Most critics have agreed that the fourth point of his acceptance speech was the most interesting. He said that the nation should use the expertise of business, private capital, labor, and agriculture "to embark on a bold new program for making the benefits of our scientific advances and industrial progress available for the improvement and growth of under-developed countries."[49] This move, Truman thought, would be instrumental in turning the poor of the world against Communism. Empty stomachs, one man said, pointed more individuals toward acceptance of Communism than ideology. In September, 1950 Truman signed an executive order instructing the Secretary of State to create the Technical Cooperative Administration, subsequently known as the Point Four Program. The idea for this agency had been suggested by Benjamin Hardy, a talented journalist. The State Department selected Capus M. Waynick, the Ambassador to Nicaragua, to serve as acting head until a permanent director could be found.[50]

In November, 1950, Henry Bennett left Stillwater to attend the annual meeting of the Association of American Land-Grant Colleges and Universities. The decision to take part in the conference in Washington was somewhat unusual in that he had always remained somewhat aloof from this group. The Associated Press speculated in advance of Bennett's departure that he would be placed in charge of the Point Four Program, with rank as Assistant Secretary of State. On the second day of the convention, the educator conferred with Truman. That afternoon he called Earle Albright in Stillwater to state that he had been offered the position. A public statement for consumption at home read simply: "I would be glad and shall consider it an honor to serve the President for a limited time, subject to the approval of the A. and M. board of regents."[51] Time, too, was alloted before the return to discuss details of his appointment with Nelson Rockefeller, who then served as chairman of the Advisory Board for International Development. On

November 17, 1950, the Board of Regents granted Henry Bennett a leave of absence and passed a resolution commending President Truman for the honor he had bestowed on the Oklahoma A. and M. College. Moreover, they made Oliver S. Willham a vice-president and placed him in charge during Bennett's absence. The line of command then passed to Philip Donnell and Randell Klemme.[52]

The next month Henry Bennett, though still president of the Oklahoma A. and M. College, left for the nation's capital. He served as head of the Technical Cooperative Administration for only one year but his period of service left a lasting imprint on many men and many nations. Some felt that he seemed out of his element for he did not wear the Homburg of a diplomat nor the grey flannel of the organization man. Then, too, he had grown slightly round in the mid-section and still wore high lace shoes. Bennett amazed members of Congress, especially J. William Fulbright, by not asking for an increase in his budget. Point Four had to be kept small so that a new bureaucracy did not form. Moreover, Bennett espoused simple objectives. He told an appropriations committee that the United States could not make the world over but maybe it could double the food production of places where they did not have enough to eat. He also made it clear that the men and women of the nations to be served should do the work.[53] Bennett knew, as Truman once said, how the simple ideas of cooperation and brotherhood can make people "work miracles by sharing knowledge to help themselves and each other."[54]

Henry Bennett spent much of his year in national office in visiting underdeveloped nations. He toured Panama, Costa Rica, Ecuador, Peru, Bolivia, Chile, Argentina, Paraguay, Brazil, Venezuela, and Haiti with A. Cyril Crilley and Ben Hardy shortly after taking residence in Washington. Later, he returned to Ethiopia to sign an agreement with Haille Selassie for the improvement of primary, secondary, and higher education in that country. He planned a trip to the Middle East in the fall of 1951. Meanwhile, he testified before Congressional committees, met with the Board of Regents, and made speeches throughout the United States.[55] In May, 1951, he addressed the graduating class of the Oklahoma A. and M. College. His remarks, which he entitled "The Great Basic Hope for Peace," stated that Latin America, Africa, the Middle East, and the Far East looked to the United States for assistance. "We must," he said, "'upon the rubble and the wreckage of the old imperialism erect a new world system—a world system inclusive of all, a world imperialism of morality and justice based upon economic efficiency and security."[56] In another message, "The Human Side of Point Four," which was given before the American Association of Land-Grant Colleges and Universities, Bennett stated that Communism could best be contained by sharing technical information with underdeveloped nations instead of wasting resources on warfare. One of the "soundest ways we can help in the long run is to assist other countries develop institutions like our Land-Grant Colleges, experiment stations, and credit and marketing system."[57] He added, however, that agricultural and mechanical colleges could not be transplanted intact. The people had to mold institutions suited to the needs of their own country.

On November 30, 1951, Henry Bennett, his wife Vera, A. C. Crilley, Benjamin Hardy, and James T. Mitchell left New York City for a tour which included Rome, Athens, Cairo, Amman, Beirut, Baghdad, and Teheran. The trip encountered numerous delays. On December 22, the state department delegation, plus a crew of fourteen, left Baghdad in the middle of a blinding snow storm for Teheran. The Bennetts planned to spend the Christmas holidays there with Ambassador Loy Henderson. The snow and the lateness of the hour prevented the crew from sighting the Miradad Airport. The plane finally sighted the field but could not land. It circled the landing strip for what must have seemed an eternity and then crashed into the side of a mountain only five miles away. The wreckage tumbled down the long, rocky incline, and rolled to a stop in the middle of a narrow ravine at the bottom. The rescue squad found no survivors the next morning. Henry Bennett had died five days after his sixty-fifth birthday.[58]

Neither Oliver Willham nor the state of Oklahoma was prepared for the shocking news or the national and international publicity that followed it. Memorial services were conducted in an interfaith chapel in Teheran, in Gallagher Hall at the A. and M. College, and in Durant, Oklahoma. The family selected the latter site as the final resting place. Testimonial dinners were held for months to come in Washington and throughout the Sooner State. Letters, telegrams, and telephone calls flooded Stillwater. Harry Truman and Dean Acheson sent messages on behalf of the national administration. Almost every major newspaper in Chicago, New York, and Washington carried editorials lamenting the loss. Eric Severied provided an insightful commentary for television viewers. Colleges from California to Massachusetts paid tribute to the departed educator. Milton Eisenhower sent a message of sympathy from the general membership of the Association of Land-Grant Colleges and Universities. The Baptist Church eulogized the lay leader from the pulpit and through the printed page. With the possible exception of Will Rogers, the death of Henry Bennett received more attention than anyone in the state's history. All of the tributes paid the deceased man were noteworthy. But perhaps the lines delivered by Senator Robert Kerr on January 10, 1952, were the most moving. He tied the educator to the state that had given him fame by whispering that his "vision was an unlimited as an Oklahoma sky. His courage as boundless as her horizons; his loyalty as steadfast as the roots of her forests, and his devotion as constant as the fertility of her soil."[59]

In death, Henry Garland Bennett received the honor that should have been given him during his life. Memorials now enshrine his name and work. The citizens of Oklahoma and of Iran marked the spot where he died with a circular monument made from the stone of the hillside where the ill-fated plane had crashed.

Oliver Willham, R. T. Stuart, Fred Drummond, and J. R. Vandegrift supervised the collection of nearly one million dollars to construct a memorial chapel on the campus site where the Bennett family had lived. The three hundred delegates from thirty-five nations gathered in Washington, D. C. for a conference sponsored by the International Economic and Social Development Agency in 1952 pledged money to establish the Bennett Memorial Scholarship Fund. In the future, one thousand foreign students from underdeveloped areas of the world would be able to study agriculture and engineering each year in the United States without personal cost.[60] This gesture seems more than appropriate to commemorate the name of a man who once said that Point Four would provide impoverished countries with a

window into the 20th century through which they can see the evidences of progress long denied to them and through which they can hear those great ideas of self government, economic progress and social justice that we have been championing. They are looking for a door and we are helping them find one.[61]

Point Four permitted the American land-grant college to lengthen its shadow. Some ideas and institutions cannot be confined to one time or place.

XVII   "WE ARE PRIVILEGED TO REAP WHERE
        OTHERS HAVE SOWN"

The Board of Regents elected Oliver Siralvo Willham as president
of the Oklahoma A. and M. College on January 17, 1952. Names
from outside the state were introduced into the discussions which
preceded the formal appointment. The trustees, however, believed
that someone familiar with the former administrator's policies and
programs should be selected. In part, this decision stemmed from
the fact that the Board wanted to pay a further tribute to Henry
Bennett. But it also recognized the need to nominate an experienced
person who could cope with a bonded indebtedness which fluctuated
between fifteen and twenty million dollars. The most difficult problem the regents faced in making a choice related to the advanced
age of the institution's executive officers. After all, the "Durant
Gang" had been in office for almost a quarter of a century. Of the
vice-presidents, both Philip Donnell and Randall Klemme were
ruled out. The former neared retirement and the latter was deeply
involved in an overseas project funded by the Ford Foundation.

His resignation had been rumored for many months. Oliver Willham, by the process of elimination, seemed the only logical choice for the presidential position.[1]

Willham had much in his background to commend him for the position. He had graduated from the institution and had learned much about Oklahoma during his tenure at the Panhandle A. and M. College from 1923 to 1934, a place where he rose to the second in command. The executive returned to Stillwater in 1935 as an assistant professor of animal husbandry. The following year he was placed in charge of reproduction research for the Oklahoma division of the Regional Swine Breeding Laboratory that had been created under the Bankhead-Jones Act. This move brought the educator a promotion in rank. Less than twenty-four months later he became vice-dean of agriculture. The vice-presidency tendered in 1950 had been earned but it also had been extended because of personal loyalty to Bennett. If the regents had any doubts about whom to designate, the manner in which the vice-president handled the crisis immediately following the death of Bennett dispelled them. Willham, with the aid of Earle Albright and Welden Barnes, set up quarters in Whitehurst Hall to deal with the situation. Their performance was nearly perfect.[2]

Oliver Willham received a unanimous vote from the Board of Regents. His salary of $16,000 indicated that Oklahoma A. and M. had achieved a degree of parity with the University of Oklahoma, for the amount paid coincided with that allotted George L. Cross. The vote and salary figure reflect as well a high degree of public confidence. Willham knew most of the state's political leaders and he proved more than capable of maintaining good relations with three Democratic governors, Johnston Murray, Raymond Gary, and J. Howard Edmonson, and one Republican, Henry Bellmon, in the future. None of these men were unfriendly toward higher education but each were tight-fisted in the area of school expenditures. The new president had been a student of politics since his undergraduate years and he came from the right geographic section of the state. In addition, Willham and Bennett worked well together in what the former man called the "lap-over," the period between the Point Four appointment and the plane crash in Iran. In fact, the younger man had helped his former employer to become a respected agriculturalist. The two had talked about farming when Bennett came to Goodwell for tours of Panhandle A. and M. Last, Willham possessed most of the qualities that every day citizens expected of the educational leaders. He was a devoted husband to Susan and a kind father to his son Richard. All of the family embraced the Presbyterian faith. Many people, too, applauded Willham's pledge when he assumed office to provide an educational opportunity for all the young in the state.[3]

Even though the incoming executive had the confidence and goodwill of almost everyone in Oklahoma, no president in the history of the institution had a more difficult tenure than Oliver Willham from 1952 to 1957, the initial five of his fifteen years as chief executive. First, his presidency was a transitional one, both in terms of the office itself and because the institution was ready for conversion to a university. Second, there were numerous complex problems which had to be dealt with. The building program in process had to be completed and the institution's coffers contained no money. Also, Oklahoma A. and M. had a contract with the Technical Cooperation Administration to modernize the educational system in Ethiopia. Then, too, the organization had to reckon with accreditation difficulties, a McCarthy purge, and the social and civil rights revolution aborning in the country. Personal tragedy struck at the same time. Susan contracted an extended illness and Oliver's father died shortly after major executive responsibilities had been assumed. The weight of the office became apparent when papers for an emergency loan had to be signed while Willham stared into the open cemetery grave prepared for his deceased parent. Yet, throughout the first half-decade of his presidency, the senior colleague of the faculty never lost his composure, sense of humor, or his ability to inspire confidence in others.

Though Oliver Willham differed from Henry Bennett in his conception of the institutional presidency, he did share with his predecessor a love of state and country. In general, Willham made the chief executive's office more open. He invited the public to inspect the financial affairs of the organization at any time. Graduates were even encouraged to examine in advance the budgets prepared for submission to the Oklahoma State Regents for Higher Education. The money that did become available was allocated directly to departments and schools instead of being retained by the central accounting office. Moreover, few items concerning Oklahoma in newspapers were not thoroughly digested. Hundreds of letters were mailed to friends of the institution on special occasions. Neither were events on the campus and in the community neglected. In fact, a day seldom passed without a luncheon or dinner speech being given. Willham, as vice-president and president, urged people to vote and he visited military installations in Stillwater and elsewhere. The great personal popularity and the broad social contacts led some to speculate that the official might run for national office upon retirement.[4]

In spite of narrow academic training, Oliver Willham exemplified an understanding of the new scientific and technological age dawning in the United States. What he did not know himself, he learned from others. The man had an uncanny ability to learn from listening. Two developments during the early years indicate that henceforth A. and M. was to be a leader, not a follower. First, Dean M. R. Lohman of the Oklahoma Institute of Technology attempted to counteract the failure of the German diesel laboratory by requesting funds from the Atomic Energy Commission to bring the first nuclear reactor in the Southwest to Stillwater. Washington's W. Kenneth Davis approved a grant to purchase equipment manufactured by the Aerojet-General Corporation. Installation began in

1955. Professor John B. West offered two courses in this field: "Introduction to Nuclear Engineering" and "Introduction to Nuclear Technology." Second, L. Wayne Johnson, a professor in the mathematics department, paved the way for the institution to develop the first college-wide computer system in the Southwest. An educational discount permitted the hardware to be used for instruction and research as well as for accounting purposes. The administration placed the reactor in the Chemical Engineering Building and the IBM 650 in the new Home Economics Building.[5]

From 1952 to 1957, many important personnel and organizational changes were made. These decisions stemmed from a tight financial situation, and an effort to decentralize the decision-making process, and the retirement of several influential members of the Bennett team. In the former year, the Board of Regents decided to move their office from Oklahoma City to Stillwater, locating in the space provided by the completion of the Student Union. The trustees, too, created a new position, that of administrative assistant to the Board. Governor Johnston Murray, upon the recommendation of the regents and the college president, appointed Forrest McIntire to fill the post. His principal function was to execute policy and to bring a closer coordination among the eight colleges governed by the A. and M. regents. Simultaneously, Willham received approval to take a step which should have been instituted many years before. He elevated the position of manager of the Student Union to one called director of auxiliary enterprises. This job involved putting the student services of the organization on a paying basis. Edward Morrison assumed this function, replacing C. A. Tibbetts. The Alumni Association opened an office in the Student Union, too. Murl Rogers, Hugo's "Citizen of the Year" in 1954, succeeded A. O. Martin. The growth of the institution, the heavy demands placed upon the placement services, and the increased number of alumni made division of the placement services and the responsibility for the alumni program of activities desirable. Kenneth Ricker, former assistant to the head of the English department, became personal secretary to the president. His family had been associated with the institution since its founding days. The men who received the above appointments were all graduates of the Oklahoma A. and M. College.[6]

These same years also witnessed widespread changes in the academic structure of the campus. Randall Klemme resigned effective January 1, 1953, in order to take a permanent position with the Ford Foundation in Pakistan. W. L. Blizzard retired about the same time, making it possible for A. E. Darlow to become director of the Oklahoma Experiment Station, dean of agriculture, and vice-president of agriculture. Darlow, with the exception of seven years before World War II, had been a member of the faculty since 1919. He held a Ph. D. in animal husbandry from the University of Wisconsin and had made the Stillwater department of the same name one of the largest and best in the United States. Harry Orr, who joined the faculty the same year as Darlow, succeeded Clarence

McElroy as dean of veterinary medicine in 1953. He had been one of the instructors who had taught Willham while he was a student. Born in Mystic, Iowa, in 1895, and a graduate of his state's land-grant college, Orr was an outstanding teacher and had held rank as a full professor since 1928. He died only three years after his promotion. Glenn C. Holm, his successor, came to Oklahoma from the North Dakota State College in Fargo. Though a young man, he had achieved a national reputation as a result of his numerous publications in plant pathology.[7]

Other significant leadership substitutions took place in the school of business and the graduate college. Raymond Thomas, who had pioneered a name change from commerce and marketing to business in 1956, retired the following year. Eugene L. Swearingen filled the vacancy. The thirty-six year old economist possessed two degrees from A. and M. and a doctorate from Stanford. He specialized in petroleum economics. Daniel McIntosh decided to turn his position as graduate dean over to a younger man three years before Thomas left office. The importance of his pioneering work is reflected in the fact that he had personally awarded 3,500 of the 4,300 graduate degrees awarded by A. and M. His replacement, Robert MacVicar, was one of Willham's best appointments. He had earned degrees from the University of Wyoming and the University of Wisconsin, holding several prestigious fellowships in the process. In spite of his youth, he had published extensively in animal metabolism and nutrition and belonged to many professional organizations. He became the first executive director of the Oklahoma Frontiers of Science Foundation and assumed a vice-presidential post at A. and M. in 1957. Both Swearingen and MacVicar were intense and dedicated men. Many people felt that one of them would replace Willham when he retired.[8]

While Willham nominated men to office who had proven records of success in their chosen fields, he did not consult the faculty on administrative appointments. His position was a personal one but it also mirrored official policy. The members of the Board of Regents were entrepreneurs, individuals not accustomed to following democratic processes in their own business operations. Opposition developed in 1954. After making several changes in the office of dean of students, the president appointed Walter W. Hansen as vice-dean of the college of arts and sciences. Hansen, head of botany and plant physiology, had been a respected member of the faculty, so protest did not occur. The appointment of Homer Knight by Schiller Scroggs to replace Tom Reynolds of the history department in 1954, however, did signal trouble. Knight, a graduate of the University of Missouri and currently dean at Westminster College had gotten acquainted with Scroggs during the summer conference of academic deans held on the A. and M. campus. The row which followed was not personal. But some faculty let it be known that they felt the instructional staff should be consulted at least in regard to the hiring of the administrators with whom they had daily contact. Some of the bitterness that evolved challenged the authoritarian manner in which Scroggs ran the school under his supervision.[9] A spokesman for a faculty committee which looked into the situation stated: "The explanation sometimes given, as in the history department case, that secrecy in making appointments is necessary, we regard as untenable."[10] The instructional staff received more consideration in the future. Power continued to emanate from the presidential office in Whitehurst Hall, however.

The instructional staff took steps to create a modern faculty organization in 1953. In October, H. I. Featherly met with the faculty in the Classroom Building to discuss its future role on the campus. Those assembled voted favorably upon a constitutional document which had been prepared the previous summer. The purpose of the Faculty Council, as the assemblage would be known, was to

promote effectiveness of the organization in discharge of its responsibilities to the people of Oklahoma, to effect closer coordination among the various divisions of the college and to provide a means by which the special competencies of the members of the faculty may be used more fully in the formulation and execution of the academic program of the college.[11]

Election of officers followed shortly thereafter. The positions to be chosen by ballot were vice-chairman, secretary, one representative from each of the six undergraduate schools, and three representatives from the five subject matter divisions of the institution. Willham served as chairman by virtue of his office as president. There was only a light turn out. But when the counting had been completed Featherly received confirmation as vice-chairman and Helmer E. Sorenson as secretary. The absence of a large vote had significance. It reflected low faculty morale and resentment that Willham served in an official instead of an *ex officio* capacity. Under the leadership of Randall Jones, the faculty formed a dining club the same month as the election of the Faculty Council.

The major reason for poor morale on the part of the faculty stemmed from the substandard salaries paid them. Willham, even as early as his vice-presidency, recognized the problem and attempted to secure more money for the staff. The improvement of the physical plant made by Bennett and him had made for good working conditions and improved teaching and research facilities. Yet it was not enough to compensate for the $1,500 difference between A. and M. and other land-grant college salaries. Other state college and university presidents, such as E. T. Dunlap, George Cross, Max Chambers, and Bruce Carter, joined Willham in a quest for additional revenues. Carter explained on one occasion that students who worked at a local Goodrich Rubber Plant made as much as $3,000 more than instructors with doctorates. Federal grants and the presence of the Research Foundation helped a little, because some faculty were able to publish their way out of the institution. In general, however, the heavy inbreeding and the presence of large numbers without terminal degrees prevented extreme reaction.[12]

Another factor contributing to a reserved response pertains to public charges of disloyalty on the part of higher educational personnel in the state. In 1949, approximately one year before Joseph McCarthy issued his famous statement that he had a list of fifty-seven names of Communists in the State Department, Representative Walter Bailey of Vinita requested that the Oklahoma Legislature enact a bill which would require teachers and professors to take a Loyalty Oath. The House of Representatives passed such a measure in less than a month. Opposition developed, because some people felt that legislation was not stringent enough. Representative Bob Reynolds, Jr., Oklahoma City, believed that all adults should be required to attest to such a document before voting. D. C. Cantrell, Stigler, wanted a general investigation of higher education. His proposal was directed at the University of Oklahoma, an organization which still suffered from similar charges made by William Murray during the Great Depression. Another legislator felt that George Cross was un-American because he opposed the measure. Finally, a former OU student, who now represented his hometown of Medford, stated that he knew there were Communists at Norman. If they were prosecuted, he felt that other subversives would not move to the state.[13]

On March 1, 1949, Henry Bennett, a vigorous opponent of Communism himself, wrote to Edwin Langley, the chairman of a special investigating committee of the House of Representatives. He told Langley that he wished to cooperate and then said:

I wish to further acknowledge your request for a written statement, made under oath, from myself regarding communistic activities, if any, on the part of deans and heads of departments at Oklahoma A. and M. College; for similar statements from each of the heads at our institution regarding members of the faculty assigned to their respective departments; and, an additional statement from myself concerning communistic activities, if any, among our students.[14]

Ten days later department heads gathered with their respective deans to discuss the situation further. In the college of arts and sciences, Dean Scroggs made clear that the investigation was no laughing matter. He, in fact, charged that the teaching of history at the institution was suspect. When asked to clarify his position, he retorted: "There is no objection to teaching the facts of history in an unbiased manner, but each person should know whether an instructor is teaching the facts or is instilling beliefs in students."[15] Thus, he implied that instruction should only be concerned with the cognitive, not the affective, domain of learning. Unless, of course, the latter coincided with the right wing element of the state and nation.

On April 9, 1951, Governor Johnston Murray signed a bill which made it mandatory for certain public employees, including faculty and students, to sign a Loyalty Oath. Murray placed his signature on the roll reluctantly, becaused he believed certain aspects of it would not hold up in courts. The bill's well-intentioned author, William S. Shibley of Bristow, was a wholesale grocer who had come to the United States from Lebanon. His proposal required all city, county, and state employees to swear that they had not belonged to the Communist Party in the last five years and that they would bear arms for the defense of the country if requested to do so. Those who did not affix their names to the Loyalty Oath by May 9 would be dropped from the state payroll. Many individuals and organizations, such as the Westminster Foundation, believed the law to be unconstitutional. It left it up to the attorney-general to decide which groups were subversive and there were no provisions made to excuse conscientious objectors from bearing arms. Furthermore, the provision which based suitability for employment on past, instead of present and future, loyalty smacked of being a bill of attainder.[16]

Henry Bennett visited the campus in April but did not take a public stand on the bill. This left Willham to handle the situation. To his credit, he did not issue any inflammatory statements, either for or against the measure. One newspaper quoted him to the effect that he planned to let those who did not sign leave the campus without fanfare or publicity.[17] On another occasion, he stated simply: "It is just another law and as such we must honor it."[18] It became obvious, however, as the May deadline approached that the situation was more serious than initially thought. Foreign students and visiting professors were advised by their American embassies not to sign. Then, too, if the institution lost many of its better faculty, then some federal contracts might be endangered. Malcolm Correll, a professor of physics, branded the Loyalty Oath as a witch-hunt and William Newton, English, requested that people who opposed the measure write to their legislators and ask for repeal. Collectively, a group in the state hired the Oklahoma City law firm of Emery and Emery to try to get the bill declared unconstitutional. Colonel R. T. Stuart attempted to prevent A. and M. faculty from participating in this movement by stating that any professor who did not sign, regardless of whether the law was declared invalid, would not be rehired when his or her contract expired.[19]

It was apparent on May 10 that a major crisis in the history of the college was at hand. Some faculty had signed the oath, some refused, and others crossed out objectionable portions before affixing their names to the bottom of the statement. Three students, Judy Anderson, Paul Palmer, and Alan Thompson, were fired from their part time jobs in the library. Neither Willham nor Edmon Low would make a statement. William Coffman, head of the arts and science testing bureau, chaired a meeting which consisted of some 150 participants on May 11. In it, Paul Foreman, sociology, called for a strengthening of the local chapter of the American Association of University Professors. He further suggested that the instructional staff needed to form a faculty senate. The executive committee of the AAUP met six days afterwards and joined its sister chapter in Norman in asking that certain provisions of the oath be changed. O. C. Dermer, T. L. Agnew, and Lloyd Young issued the statement. On the same day, eight members of the faculty and staff were notified of their suspension. These included: Warner Baum, Luella Neitz, Allen D. and Nancy Siebur, S. H. Lee, Robert Wieman, Lillian Schmoer, and Malcolm Correll.[20] One observer wrote to a friend that the "oath has lost us some of our brainiest faculty members."[21] She also pointed out that the Legislature had severely cut the budget for higher education in Oklahoma.

The Board of Regents met in Oklahoma City on May 20. Chairman Stuart had called a special meeting so that Attorney-General Mac Q. Williamson could discuss a recent decision of Oklahoma County District Judge W. A. Carlile. His case number 125,417, entitled "Updegraff v. Board of Regents of the Oklahoma Agricultural and Mechanical Colleges, et al" had been brought by a Norman resident to have salaries stopped for those people who did not sign the state's Loyalty Oath. Carlile ruled on this matter but went further so as to clarify some vague points. The Board expressed an interest in the decision as it was fearful of stopping salary payments without being on firm legal ground for such action could be interpreted as a breach of contract. Insofar as the Oklahoma A. and M. College was concerned, the decision had some important connotations, because seven people did not sign and thirty-two had modified the Loyalty Oath. Williamson told the regents that, according to the way he interpreted it, none of the thiry-nine people should be permitted to man their classrooms the following Monday morning. The Board requested Williamson to seek additional information from the Supreme Court and then ordered salaries stopped for the non-signers.[22]

On May 21, 1951 most of the non-signers were discharged. Oklahoma Supreme Court Justice Ben Arnold upheld Carlile's decision, stating that public officials could prescribe loyalty procedures in order to preserve peace and the public welfare. The United States Supreme Court agreed to hear the case the following spring. The outcome was uncertain for this body had recently upheld non-Communist oaths for school teachers in Los Angeles and political candidates in Maryland. The crucial issue centered upon whether or not a state could terminate an employee's contract for belonging to a subversive organization, regardless of whether one had committed an unloyal act. In late 1952, the Supreme Court declared the Loyalty Oath unconstitutional by a vote of 8 to 0. Tom C. Clark wrote the decision. He stated that membership alone is not cause for discharging an employee. A person must, he said, know that an organization was subversive. Three months later the Oklahoma Supreme Court ratified the decision. The Board of Regents moved to pay the $7,000 owed in back salaries to those who had been discharged. Both Oliver Willham and J. L. Sanderson refused to release the files related to the situation, so that a public taint permanently surrounded those who had been forced to leave the institution. [Privately, however, some administrators did offer some assistance in helping the non-signers to attain other positions.] The winners acted more generously than the losers. They did not request return of their jobs nor did they seek damages in connection with relocation expenses.[23]

To the credit of the people of Oklahoma, they did not lose faith in the educational system of the state. The classroom provided a practical method of preparing the young men and women of rural communities with a means of making the transition to city life. Strangely enough, however, the public became more incensed over the spring "Pantie Raids" that gripped the state's campuses from 1952 to 1955 than the Loyalty Oath controversy. But while irate citizens complained to Willham that A. and M. had become a playground, underwear manufacturers applauded the incidents as being good for business. James Lowry, vice-president of Lingerie, Incorporated, suggested that the raids become progressive in the future. He thought that freshman should take the panties, sophomores the bras, juniors the slips, and seniors the nighties. Other higher educational institutions in the Southwest, including the University of Oklahoma, had similar occurrences. Norman girls in 1953 even added a new twist. They initiated a "Shorts Raid" on Jefferson Hall, the home of the football squad. In 1955, some 3,000 Stillwater students participated in a riot that caused considerable damage to state property. The suspension of twenty-four students brought more responsible behavior in the future. The Aggies then became caught up in the "bop" music and the "I Go Pogo" craze.[24]

Underneath the frivolous facade, it is clear that some of these activities masked Cold War anxieties and increased social tensions at home. The students invited more and more politicians to the campus to discuss political issues, leading the Board of Regents to adopt an official policy on guest lecturers. Moreover, the student government waged war from 1951 to 1954 against Theta Nu Epsilon, the secret political fraternity which had existed in Stillwater for so many years. The student body itself seemed to be divided on the merits of the organization. Some letters to the editor of the *O'Collegian* branded TNE as undemocratic, while others maintained it was needed to combat general apathy. Race, however, was the most important social issue of the day. Both blacks and whites joined together to force improvements in civil rights.[25]

Oklahoma had many problems in the area of racial relations, but it was segregation of the educational system that came to the forefront first. A. and M., as compared to other southern institutions, had a reasonably good record in this regard. The organization, as early as 1931, had loaned faculty, both male and female, to serve as consultants for the Rosenwald Foundation. During the Great Depression, the college employed blacks in the extension division to implement New Deal programs. In the next decade, Henry Bennett, aided by "Ned" Conger, worked with President G. L. Harrison to develop a plan of action for upgrading Langston University and for bringing this institution under the jurisdiction of the Board of Regents for the Oklahoma A. and M. Colleges. The trustees obtained the funds and personnel to get the organization accredited by North Central. Insofar as can be determined, all of these improvements came without pressure from either the national government or the black masses.[26]

Accreditation, however, did not resolve the growing racial educational crisis in Oklahoma. In theory, the state had provided equal undergraduate opportunities but no provisions had been made for graduate work. Langston did not have the faculty nor the physical facilities and equipment to offer advanced instruction. The problem became compounded in 1941 when the Legislature made it unlawful for blacks and whites to attend the same college. In addition, it forbade white instructors from teaching, even part time, at a black school. Other states, during the same period, started to form separate graduate institutions for Negroes. In Oklahoma this procedure seemed unfeasible financially, for the black population numbered only seven per cent of the total population as compared, for example, with Mississippi's forty-nine per cent. In 1948, Ada Lois Sipuel, a twenty-three year old girl from Chickasha, challenged the state's segregation policy. She applied for admission to the law school of the University of Oklahoma. Denied entrance, she appealed to the United States Supreme Court. This body ruled that she must be enrolled if Oklahoma did not have a black law school. Governor Roy Turner, who believed that the people still wanted segregation in their schools, provided leadership in developing law classes for blacks which were held in the State Capitol Building. About the same time, G. W. McLaurin, a retired professor, did gain admittance to the OU college of education. But under orders from the state, he received instruction in a classroom which was separated from whites by a specially-constructed partition. The Oklahoma Regents for Higher Education sought and obtained some modification of state law so that the Oklahoma A. and M. College and the University of Oklahoma could offer integrated summer workshops.[27]

In January, 1949 events began to unfold in Stillwater which would lead to the eventual admittance of Negroes. It was students, however, not the administration, who provided the impetus for change. During this month, eighty people, from Langston and A. and M., gathered on the latter campus in an open forum to discuss the economic, moral, and international aspects of Jim Crow laws. Professor Darrel Troxel served as moderator. James Ray Johnson and Vernel Fuller of Langston and Orville Sandlin and Neil Hendricks of Stillwater led the discussion. The Aggies, as a result of this meeting, formed a new organization on the campus and elected the latter two individuals as officers of the American Committee for Equality. Troxel, along with R. R. Oglesby and O. K. Campbell, served as faculty sponsors. In consultation with Roscoe Dunjee of the Oklahoma chapter of the American Association for the Advancement of Colored People, this organization sought admittance of Henry W. Floyd, Eufaula, and Jane Ellison, Oklahoma City, to A. and M. in February. These two blacks wanted to transfer from Langston to Stillwater to study political science and textiles, respectively. Concurrently, Thomas A. Brown and William Scofield, both

291

A. and M. students, attempted to enroll at nearby Langston. The applications of the black students were denied because their present institution had programs in existence in the area of their interest. On the other hand, the reasoned atmosphere which prevailed indicated that desegregation at the Oklahoma A. and M. College could come without a rash of lawsuits.[28]

The relative racial calm in Stillwater was broken in an explosive manner. In 1950, the Cowboy football team played Drake University to a 14 to 14 stalemate. The tie pleased Aggie fans, because the Iowa team contained a black player named Johnny Bright who would end the season as the nation's rushing and scoring leader. There had been some concern about a Negro playing in the Missouri Valley Conference. But no incidents resulted. After the game, Frank M. Gardner of Drake publicly commended the A. and M. coaching staff and football players for the lack of attention to the bi-racial nature of the contest. The next year, the Drake University eleven appeared in Stillwater with a 5-0 record. Led by All-American Bright, the team hoped to beat the Cowboys, even though sports forecasters had made Stillwater the slight favorite. Coach J. B. Whitworth predicted that the game would be the toughest of the season.[29]

In the opening seconds of the game, Bright was grounded hard. Later, a film revealed that Wilbank Smith had blocked him with his arms in an illegal position. Three Aggies, moments after the first play, tackled Bright as he plunged past the line of scrimmage. One of the men grazed the Drake player with his helmet. The ball carrier stayed in the game long enough to pass for a touchdown but Coach Warren Gaer removed him so that he could receive medical attention. The A. and M. infirmary found that Bright's jawbone had been broken. Testimony of the participants disagree. There is evidence, however, that neither Bright or Gaer immediately felt that a wrong had been intentionally committed. The October 21st edition of the *Des Moines Register* reported the story in sensational fashion and published photographs and comment that created a national incident of major proportions. *Time* and *Life* magazines carried the story to the rest of the nation in print and Paramount News distributed film to movie theaters throughout the country. Subsequently, hate mail poured over Willham's desk in unbelievable quantities.[30]

Henry Bennett, then in national office, refused to attach much significance to the incident or its aftermath. Again, Willham was left to cope with a problem which generated attention as far away as Latin America and Europe. The Missouri Valley Intercollegiate Athletic Conference investigated the affair and Willham personally invited Norman Burns of the North Central Association to come to Stillwater in order to let a third party review the situation. The Oklahoma A. and M. College offered to pay for any expenses incurred. Nothing, however, seemed to do any good. The nation's sports fans lost the pleasure of viewing an exciting football player and Drake University withdrew from the conference. And, before the controversy fully subsided, the United States Supreme Court issued its famous *Brown v. the Topeka Board of Education* decision. The Johnny Bright incident itself closed with everyone concerned having lost something important.[31]

In spite of unfavorable publicity, Oklahoma A. and M. continued to move toward desegregating. In 1953, three black undergraduates enrolled; two in electrical engineering and one in veterinary medicine. A new law passed in 1949 provided for admission to previously lily-white schools if Langston did not have a course of study in a particular area. The black students were, however, required to stay in segregated facilities. Governor Raymond Gary and M. A. Nash, Chancellor of the Oklahoma State Regents for Higher Education, provided excellent political and educational leadership. Gary believed the *Brown v. the Topeka Board of Education* decision of 1954 a "fair one" and he felt that the people of the state were ready for a change. In 1955, the Oklahoma Education Association opened its doors to the 1,600 black teachers who had belonged to the Oklahoma Association of Negro Teachers. The black teachers were happy to join but one-third of them lost their jobs in the next five years. No public outcry accompanied the organizational desegregation. The extreme intolerance of the past had vanished but perhaps the Johnny Bright case tempered racial attitudes in the state even more.[32]

Having been baptised by fire as vice-president and president, Oliver Willham decided to delay his formal inauguration as chief executive officer of the Oklahoma A. and M. College until May 9, 1953. He was the first to have such a ceremony since dignitaries had gathered to welcome the scholarly James B. Eskridge at the end of World War I. The decision to postpone the event was wise in many ways. Willham's handling of several difficult problems had delivered him from the living under the shadow of Henry Bennett. He now was an executive in his own right. The specific time chosen coincided with the dedication of the new library. The building was important in and of itself but it symbolized as well the virtual completion of the "Twenty-Five Year Plan." It provided an impressive square of Georgian architecture in the center of the campus. Whitehurst Hall, the Classroom Building, the Student Union, and the Library stood facing the same landscaped common. The impressive physical plant and the fact that Willham was the first president in the history of the organization to take office without a political squabble suggested that a new era was about to dawn.

Philip Wilber presented the Library to Colonel Robert Stuart on May 8. The latter man accepted it with a moving speech entitled "A Dream Realized." With Edmon Low presiding, Robert Bingham Downs, President of the American Library Association, and Guy R. Lyle dedicated and launched the building. Oliver Willham and Agnes Berrigan spoke on behalf of the faculty while the Very Reverend Eric Beevers provided the invocation. Arthur Lynds Bigelow, bellmaster at Princeton University and Louvain, Belgium, was featured in a carillon concert which contained many of the favorite hymns of Henry and Vera Bennett. The next day delegates from over one hundred colleges and universities gathered to honor Willham. His remarks were preceded by Reuben G. Gustavson, who spoke on "The Place of the Land-Grant College in the Culture of Today."[33] Then Oliver Willham arose to give his inaugural address. He discussed the importance of higher education and then paid tribute to the men and women who had preceded the present generation of Aggies. In words that resemble Bradford Knapp's idea that institutions have souls, he said: "We are privileged to reap where others have sown, a privilege which can appropriately be exercised only with a sense of profound obligation."[34]

Unknown to many people in the audience, the double ceremony on May 8 and 9 marked the end of still another crisis in the history of the college. In December, 1952, President Willham reminded the Board of Regents that the North Central Association would soon be on the campus to renew the institution's accreditation. The visit was a routine one and it did not cause any specific fears, except that it was known that faculty salaries were low and that Oklahoma A. and M. would be the first organization inspected under Criterion "F," a new policy in regard to intercollegiate athletics. Point shaving scandals and charges of paying athletes had dictated the need for closer supervision in this area. Both Bud Wilkinson and Henry Iba, the athletic directors of the University of Oklahoma and Oklahoma A. and M., expressed shock at the severity of the code but each man promised the public that he would follow it in conduct of his job. Willham had served on the North Central Committee which met at the Palmer House in Chicago to draft the document. The completed statement, however, did not seem realistic and he advised A. and M.'s Andrew Holley to cast a ballot against it when the final draft came up for a vote.[35]

On February 7, 1953, the inspection team delivered a preliminary report to the Board of Regents. Verbal comments offered by M. G. Neale of the University of Minnesota and B. L. Stradley of Ohio State indicated a few problems existed, especially in the area of faculty salaries. Conversely, the visitors praised the physical facilities of the institution. The essence of Neale's and Stradley's report was received in written form the next month. The regents expressed a desire to correct as many of the deficiencies as quickly as possible. But toward the end of the month, a bombshell exploded. North Central officials announced that Oklahoma A. and M. would be dropped from the list of members as of July 1. President Henry G. Harmon of Drake University, who chaired the committee on athletics, made the motion. The most serious charge against the Stillwater institution was that the administration, not the faculty, had charge of athletics. Low salaries and a substandard number of doctorates also received attention. Bradley University, also a perennial basketball power, came under fire at the same time as a result of another visitation.[36]

The North Central announcement initiated dozens of newspaper editorials and crash meetings throughout the state. Fortunately, Johnston Murray, M. A. Nash, Oliver Willham, and the members of the Board of Regents for the A. and M. Colleges, agreed that immediate steps should be taken to preserve accreditation. Willham received much public criticism from the press because he refused to release the full text of the Chicago report. But he and Governor Murray did meet with reporters to give them a summary of the document in laymen's words. Later, Milo Bali, Charles Boardman, Manning Patrillo, and Norman Burns, all executives of North Central, responded favorably to a plea from Willham for an extension of time so that the institution could correct the alleged deficiencies. Thirty days were granted. Murray and Willham requested an additional $824,066 in legislative appropriations to make salary adjustments, hire more instructors, and provide more support for the school of veterinary medicine. Meanwhile, a faculty committee consisting of Guy Donnell, James Webster, Jack Byrom, Fred Jewett, U. Christopherson, Roger Flanders, and D. R. Peterson drew up a document which placed the faculty in charge of the intercollegiate athletic program. On May 8, 1953, the day before his inauguration President Willham placed proof in the hands of the Board of Regents that the college had met all of the requirements laid down by the North Central Association. Charles Boardman wired the next month that the organization was again in good standing and that its membership would be continued. Locally, it was announced, too, that A. and M. would seek admission into the Big Seven Athletic Conference.[37]

From 1954 to 1957, the college began moving ahead. The institution retired the bonds on Willard and Cordell Halls ahead of time and then started to plan for new construction. Private funds were found for an engineering research laboratory. Multi-million dollar plans were formulated to provide better facilities for agriculture, chemistry, and veterinary medicine. The national government expanded the size of the campus by giving title to the lake west of the city to the college. It was named in honor of Carl Blackwell. Two million in funds were sought from the Education Facilities Division of the Federal House and Home Financial Agency in order to get new projects underway. Furthermore, the institution attempted, but failed, to secure nineteen million dollars from the Department of Agriculture for an animal disease laboratory. Additional physical facilities were needed to keep pace with student growth. Enrollments had recently increased by some thirty-six per cent.[38]

Whether intentional or not, President Willham made one serious error of judgment during this period. It caused a momentary loss of popularity with certain older members of the institution's alumni. In 1955, he wrote an article for the *Oklahoma A. and M. Magazine* entitled "Looking To the Future." In it, he hinted that some of the buildings constructed in the territorial period had outlived their usefulness. In particular, he referred to Old Central, Williams Hall, the Old Library Building, and the Student Publications Building. He said:

These buildings will continue to be used by A. and M. College as long as it is possible for us to economically keep them in repairs. It is said that 50 years is the life of such a building. If so, most of our older buildings are past retirement age.[39]

Some former students and members of the faculty took these remarks to mean that Old Central had already been marked for destruction. Jessie Thatcher Bost, president of the Half Century Club, appointed Thomas J. Hartman chairman of the group called the Committee to Save Old Central. Hartman vigorously promoted the protest. One member of the faculty, who had labored for years to preserve the reminiscences of the first students, subsequently published a book about the incident wherein he called Willham a farmer-president. Assurances that the building would not be torn down brought the crisis to a quick end. But the matter was not completely forgotten. The affair created strong sentiment for restoring the structure and making it a state and federal historical landmark.[40]

While the Oklahoma A. and M. College was modernizing at home, it undertook commitments to pioneer in land-grant education abroad. President Bennett, just before he died, met with the Board of Regents in regard to developing an overseas educational program for the Ford Foundation. Randall T. Klemme was selected to help the young nation of Pakistan increase agricultural production and better utilize mineral resources. From Karachi, Klemme, aided by several Oklahoma A. and M. graduates, devised a plan for improvement which closely resembled the idea behind the agricultural and mechanical colleges of America. Klemme became so engrossed in the project that he presented Oliver Willham with his resignation in 1952.[41] Two years later, the Ford Foundation hired E. R. Stapley, Henry P. Adams, and Paul S. Wheeler to make an extended survey to "explore three levels of technical education in Pakistan, professional engineering, technician and trade school training."[42] Immediately afterwards, officials announced that Pakistani young men would come to Stillwater and Okmulgee to study the philosophy, principles, methods, and techniques of American education. They, upon graduation, were to return to their home land to set up an engineering school in Karachi and a polytechnic institute in East Bengal. The initial agreement called for a three year program with a one-half million dollar budget. During the same period, C. G. Bauman served as a technical advisor for the government of Burma.[43]

The most impressive foreign undertaking assumed by the college occurred in Ethiopia. This nation, which had 15,000,000 people who occupied a geographic area the size of Oklahoma and Texas, was rich in natural resources. This country, however, had not been developed. On June 16, 1951, the State Department drew up an agreement between the United States and Ethiopia called "The Point Four General Agreement for Technical Cooperation Between the United States of America and the Ethiopian Empire." Three months later, Ed Morrison and Elmo W. Baumann went to Addis

Ababa for six weeks under a grant from the Foreign Development Corporation to see if the Oklahoma A. and M. College could assist Haile Selassie's country to revamp its educational system. Their visit led to a second contract between the two countries, "The Agreement for a Cooperative Agricultural Educational Program Between the Imperial Ethiopian Government and The Government of the United States." On May 16, 1952, the Stillwater land-grant college signed an "Agreement Between the Technical Cooperation Administration and Oklahoma Agricultural and Mechanical College." This document implemented certain provisions of the second treaty signed by Ethiopia and the United States. Specifically, A. and M. agreed to:

1. Give assistance to the Government of Ethiopia in the establishment and operation of a college of agriculture.
2. Give assistance to the Government of Ethiopia in the establishment and operation of a country-wide system of agricultural extension services to the people of rural areas.
3. Give assistance to the Government of Ethiopia in the establishment and operation of agricultural research and experiment stations.
4. Administer such other specific projects and operations, and give such other assistance to the Government of Ethiopia in related fields pertaining to the economic development of Ethiopia, as the TCA may request and the College may accept.[44]

Randall Klemme and Luther Brannon worked out the details for the technical assistance to be supplied by the college. The initial contract called for an expenditure of $620,000. The latter man was selected to serve as president of the College of Agriculture to be constructed in Ethiopia. Brannon, at present, served as vice-director of the extension division. He had joined the experiment station staff as an agronomist in 1940 and had become an administrator three years later. He held two degrees from A. and M. and a Ph. D. from Harvard University. Prior to the Ethiopian assignment, the United States government had used him as an advisor for the Marshall Plan. Other staff members who participated in the early stages included C. L. Angerer. H. W. Staten, Everett Little. D. B. Jeffrey, and A. E. Darlow. Eventually, almost 200 faculty served in Ethiopia before the program was terminated in 1968.[45] The venture proved so successful that Harold Stassen decided that the Foreign Operations Administration should "utilize on an expanded basis the services of colleges, universities, and other institutions through the United States under contractual arrangements similar to those . . . with Oklahoma."[46] Thus, after almost one hundred years, the land-grant idea was ready for export to the underdeveloped countries of the world.

The people of Oklahoma approved of the involvement of their land-grant college with the nation of Ethiopia. The Sooner State, a part of the American Bible Belt, felt sympathy for a country that legend connected with the early days of Christianity. Then, too, it had been a former Oklahoma school teacher, Henry M. Stanley, who had put Africa on the modern world map. The initial ventures in Ethiopia fell into three major categories. First, a variety of tasks were performed for the Imperial Government. Statisticians, such as Carl Marshall, formed a census bureau and gathered basic agricultural data. Insect eradication, soil surveys, and improvement of utility systems were other projects that received attention. Second, a high school was constructed at Jimma. The Italians had formed a school there during World War II but the surrounding area had gone back to its natural state and the buildings were left in poor state of repair. From a high school, the Jimma Agricultural Technical School gradually became the equivalent of an American community college. Third, the technical advisors assisted in the establishment of the Imperial Ethiopian College of Agriculture and Mechanical Arts. It was located in the eastern province of Harar, near the village of Alemaya on the shores of Lake Ikake. In general, the educators of the two nations worked in harmony, both being dedicated to increasing the quality of life in Ethiopia.[47]

The Jimma Agricultural Technical School started under an agreement signed on June 24, 1952. The village of Jimma, located southwest of Addis Ababa, served as the capital of Kaffa Province. The only dependable contact with it was by air. The school began with a faculty of seven and a student body of eighty. Evert Little served as principal. He was assisted by Hugh Rouk (agronomy), John McCrary (farm shop), Jack Herron (animal husbandry), Robert Loomis (biological sciences), Willie D. Mitchell (science); and James W. Murray (social science). Nineteen students graduated in the spring of 1953. One study of the eighty who were admitted the first year reported:

Fifty, after graduating from Jimma, completed the requirements for a B.S. degree at Alemaya. Of this number, 26 have received M.S. degrees from U.S. institutions, and 16 have completed or are in the process of completing doctoral programs.[48]

Besides offering instruction, the school served as an agricultural research center for the immediate locality. Coffee, cattle, and egg production received attention as well as grain storage and soil testing. The teachers and community got along without problems until 1956. In that year, a substitute had to be hired for a professor who failed to return to his assignment. The school nurse assumed the function of teaching a general science class. A misunderstanding resulted in the expulsion of all students enrolled in the course. Politicians from Ethiopia and the United States then became involved. At this point, more local control was given to the Jimma School.[49]

The Imperial College was situated near Addis on 1,100 acres. Six A. and M. staff members spent four months in a four-wheel drive vehicle and traveled approximately 5,000 miles to find an appropriate site for the campus. The delegation felt that the institution should be established in Addis, instead of Gondar, Asmara,

Lechemti, Gambella, Jimma, Soddu, Harar, or Asba Tafara, because that city served as the hub of the nation. In addition, it was located in the central geographic section of the nation. On March 11, and 27, the committee met with Haile Selassie. He convinced them to locate the college in Harar instead. The reaching of an agreement made it necessary to evacuate the natives of this region and permitted the Oklahoma A. and M. architectual staff to draft plans for buildings. The lack of local contractors and good building materials posed several difficult problems, all of which were solved without incident. Except for a controversy as to whether bathrooms should be located in or outside the buildings, the construction project moved ahead, though not always at a rapid pace. The first class graduated in 1957, five years after the experiment began. Their course of study consisted of work in one or more of the following areas: plant science (including soils and forestry) ; agricultural business and economics; animal science; and agricultural engineering technology. In 1966, the Americans assumed purely an advisory role, thereby permitting graduates of the institution to accept direct responsibility for operation of the organization.[50]

In June, 1954, Haile Selassie visited Stillwater to thank Oliver Willham and the Oklahoma A. and M. College staff for their assistance in the educational modernization of his nation. A crowd of some 1,000 people, including national, state, and local dignitaries, greeted His Imperial Majesty as he stepped from the plane at Searcy Field. Lidj Endalkatchew Makkonnen, Selassie's translator, expressed gratitude for the warm reception that had been provided. The college sponsored a formal dinner for 300 and a reception for nearly three times as many. President Willham presented the Emperor with a bronze plaque which the latter man ordered mounted in the entrance of the administration building of the Imperial Ethiopian College. In turn, Johnston Murray, A. E. Darlow, and Willham received service citations. The next year, Willham returned the visit. He arrived in Ethiopia in time to attend the closing events of the Silver Jubilee Fair, an event which marked the twenty-fifth anniversary of the Lion of Judah.[51] When the president arrived back in Stillwater, he wrote: "I sincerely feel that when the history of our time is written, Point Four will be listed as one of the programs that made a major contribution toward a more enlightened world . . . ."[52] If this is true, Oliver Willham deserves much personal credit. He spent long hours supervising the work overseas and he was the catalyst who made the project successful.

On September 12, 1956, the Oklahoma A. and M. College began a new academic year. The worst of the financial crisis was over and some 3,000 new students started classes amidst the din of new construction noises. The next month, Governor Gary, having exhausted man's efforts to end a drought as severe as the "Year of the Turnip" in 1890, asked the residents of the state to pray for rain. On the same day, heliocopters flew over the nation of Ethiopia for the first time to begin mapping that country in detail. In March, ex-president Harry Truman visited the campus to deliver a speech and to inquire about the Point Four projects which had been inaugurated during his administration. About the same time, James Goodrich, a student, reported in the *O'Collegian* that certain people in the state believed the name of the college should be changed. The institution now seemed to resemble a university more than a college. Among others, Goodrich suggested that legislators consider titles such as, Stillwater University, Great Plains University, North American University, Midcontinental University, International University, Atomic University, and Bennett University.[53]

Appropriately, the Oklahoma State University of Agriculture and Applied Science was born during the fiftieth anniversary celebration of statehood. It also had been five decades since the family of Oliver Willham moved from Kansas to Oklahoma. James Arrington and H. L. Sparks of the House of Representatives and Everett S. Collins of the Senate introduced the necessary legislation for a change of status. Raymond Gary signed the bill into law on May 15, 1957. He did not file it until the next day, however, so that sponsors could appear in his office for a short ceremony. Shortly afterward, the Big Seven Athletic Conference announced that Oklahoma State University had been admitted into membership. The University of Oklahoma assisted in both of these efforts, making a move which promised closer cooperation between the two organizations in the near future. Oklahoma and her university in Stillwater had matured together. The political institution had made the transition from a rural to an urban society while the educational establishment had grown from a bare plot in the middle of a prairie to a multi-campus university with a physical plant valued in excess of one hundred million dollars. Increased excellence accompanied program development and Stillwater now served as an international center for the creation and dissemination of knowledge. But, even with new life, the institution vowed to keep its democratic mission. It was to remain a college of and for the people.[54]

CHAPTER NOTES

I

[1]Historians have tended to romanticize the Oklahoma territorial period, particularly overemphasizing the isolated, but colorful, activities of the first generation of immigrants. Individuals did, on occasion, contribute to the modernization of the state, but corporations and organizations, because of their large aggregates of capital and experienced leadership, were in a better position to lobby for change. The presence of the Populist Party in Oklahoma, and the fact that the national government appointed Republicans to office at a time when most of the people were registered as Democrats, rendered political institutions less effective than usual. Later, after statehood, the Democrats so dominated elections that there was little competition for governmental offices. Consequently, social and economic institutions had to assume the responsibility of keeping politicians "honest" and offering alternative solutions to the state's problems. For an excellent analysis of the early political situation, see James Scales, "A History of the Democratic Party in Oklahoma," (unpublished Doctoral dissertation, University of Oklahoma, 1949). The impact of corporations and national political carpetbagging in other western territories is discussed in William Lyon, "The Corporate Frontier in Arizona," *The Journal of Arizona History,* IX, No. 1 (1968), pp. 1-17 and Earl Pomeroy, "Carpet-Baggers in the Territories, 1861-1890," *The Historian,* II, No. 2 (1939), pp. 53-64.

[2]Altogether, thirteen states were created from the Louisiana Purchase. These included Arkansas, Colorado, Iowa, Kansas, Louisiana, Minnesota,

Missouri, Montana, Nebraska, North Dakota, Oklahoma, South Dakota, and Wyoming. A brief comparative journalistic analysis of these entities' struggles for statehood may be read in *The* (Stillwater, Oklahoma) *People's Press,* November 14, 1907. Howard Lamar's *The Far Southwest, 1846-1912* (New Haven, 1966) deals with other late nineteenth century territories.

[3]Seven counties were formed after the initial territorial run. Their names and population figures are as follows: Beaver (2,674); Canadian (7,158); Cleveland (6,605); Kingfisher (8,332); Logan (12,770); Oklahoma (11,742); and Payne (7,225). Greer, which was first claimed by the state of Texas, had 5,338 inhabitants. U. S. Department of the Interior, Census Division, *Abstract of the Eleventh Census: 1890* (Washington, 1896), pp. 27, 96.

[4]James D. Richardson, *Messages and Papers of the Presidents,* 1889-1898, VII (New York, 1912), p. 5453; Robert Cunningham, *Stillwater; Where Oklahoma Began* (Stillwater, 1969), pp. 4-8.

[5]*Portrait and Biographical Record of Oklahoma* (Chicago, 1901), p. 1.

[6]Seth Humphrey, *Following the Prairie Frontier* (Minneapolis, 1934), pp. 229-265; "Memories of Oklahoma," (Payne County Historical Society), p. 9; Dan Peery, "The First Two Years," *The Chronicles of Oklahoma,* VII, No. 2 (1929), p. 294; Edward E. Dale, "Teaching on the Prairie Plains, 1890-1900," *The Mississippi Valley Historical Review,* XXXIII, No. 2 (1946), p. 293; Frederick Jackson Turner, *The Frontier in American History* (New York, 1920), p. 1; Theodore H. White, "Action Intellectuals: Scholarly Impact on the Nation's Past," *Life,* 62, No. 24 (1967), p. 56; Henry Nash Smith, *Virgin Land: The American West as Symbol and Myth* (New York, 1950), pp. 291-305.

[7]"Selections from the Record Book of Oklahoma Agricultural and Mechanical College, 1891-1941," (Oklahoma State University), p. 69. All citations from this document will be from copy two. Second citations for documentary collections, manuscript collections, and secondary sources will be abbreviated. Initial references to newspapers will carry name and state.

[8]Dale, "Teaching on the Prairie Plains, 1890-1900," p. 293.

[9]Fulmer Mood (ed.), "Frederick Jackson Turner's Address on Education in a United States Without Free Lands," *Agricultural History,* XXIII, No. 4 (1949), pp. 254-259. Also, see Wilbur Jacobs (ed.), *Frederick Jackson Turner's Legacy* (San Marino, 1965), pp. 193-207 and the Turner essay entitled "Pioneer Ideals and the State University" in *The Frontier in American History.*

[10]Richard Hofstadter, *Anti-Intellectualism in American Life* (New York, 1963), pp. 299-322; Donald F. Tingley, "Anti-Intellectualism on the Illinois Frontier," in *Essays in Illinois History* (Carbondale, 1968), pp. 3-17.

[11]Ray Billington, *America's Frontier Heritage* (New York, 1966), p. 80.

[12]Eldon Clemence, "A History of the Democratic Party in Oklahoma Territory," (unpublished Master's thesis, Oklahoma State University, 1966), pp. 15-16; James Albert Barnett, "A History of the Empire of Greer," (unpublished Master's thesis, Oklahoma Agricultural and Mechanical College, 1938), pp. 116-121; *Portrait and Biographical Record of Oklahoma,* pp. 758-759; 844-847; 868, 889, 1053, 1210-1211; *The Stillwater* (Oklahoma) *Daily Press,* June 15, 1939.

[13]*The Stillwater* (Oklahoma) *Gazette,* January 22, 1892. Myers and Davis were both Presbyterian ministers. Brief references to their educational activities may be found in James K. Hastings, "First Presbyterian Church, Stillwater, Oklahoma," (Stillwater Public Library), p. 2; "Stillwater's First School Board Minutes," (Payne County Historical Society), p. 72.

Apparently Oklahoma clergymen differed somewhat in their support for public education. Since the territory for eighteen months had only subscription public schools, one minister believed a "few thousand dollars at this critical time would erect a school building which would be a great factor in promoting the Church in this field." *The* (Guthrie) *Oklahoma Churchman,* February, 1892. Contrasted to this is a resolution of the Episcopal Church convention of 1899 urging an "intelligent and earnest interest in the schools and colleges of Oklahoma and Indian Territories." Quoted from Alvin Hock, "Religious and Cultural Efforts of the Protestant Episcopal Church in Early Oklahoma," (unpublished Master's thesis, Oklahoma Agricultural and Mechanical College, 1926), p. 51.

[14]This concentration of elite seems not to be entirely peculiar to the city of Stillwater. For instance, see the lists of professional people compiled by William Murray in his *Memoirs of Governor Murray and True History of Oklahoma,* III (Boston, 1945), pp. 260-266.

[15]Other counties had similar ideas. See, Gerald Forbes, *Guthrie Oklahoma's First Capitol* (Norman, 1938), p. 11.

[16]James K. Hastings, "Oklahoma Agricultural and Mechanical College and Old Central," *The Chronicles of Oklahoma,* XXVIII, No. 1, (1950), p. 81.

[17]"Historical Pageant—Oklahoma Agricultural and Mechanical College," (Oklahoma State University), p. 20; Gene Aldrich, "Pioneers and Pioneer Life in Payne County," (unpublished Master's thesis, Oklahoma Agricultural and Mechanical College, 1938), p. 15; Bee Guthrey, "Early Days in Payne County," *The Chronicles of Oklahoma,* III, No. 1 (1925), p. 76; Houston Overby, "The Story of Aggieland The Nineteenth Century," *Oklahoma Agricultural and Mechanical College Yesterday and Today* (Guthrie, 1938), n.p.

[18]Wikoff later wrote that all "the other county seats had announced their intentions to go after the various prospective state institutions . . . . None had mentioned the A. and M. college . . . . Lowry had lived in Ames, Iowa, and knew what such a college was; I had attended the state university of Illinois at Champaign and Urbana . . . . I knew it had the Morrill and Hatch fund, and we all knew there was a section of . . . land close to Stillwater . . ." "Selections from the Record Book," p. 98.

[19]Gaston Litton, *History of Oklahoma at the Golden Anniversary of Statehood,* I (New York, 1957), p. 460.

[20]Quoted from *The* (Stillwater) *Oklahoma A. and M. College Mirror,* May 15, 1895.

[21]*Journal of the First Session of the Oklahoma Legislative Assembly,* (1890), p. 19.

[22]*Ibid.,* p. 127.

[23]It has often been alleged that this limiting amendment was included in the Second Morrill Act of 1890 at the request of the National Grange and the Farmers' Alliance. A somewhat typical statement reads: "Due to the pressure of the Grange and the Farmers' Alliance who were not satisfied that enough emphasis had been given to instruction in agriculture and mechanic arts," the bill was amended in the House, "so that the funds were to apply 'only to instruction in agriculture, the mechanic arts, the English Language and the various branches of mathematics, physical, natural, and economic science, with special reference to their applications in the industries of life.' " Richard Axt, *The Federal Government and Financing Higher Education* (New York, 1952), p. 56.

Henry Elijah Alvord, who became the second president of the Oklahoma A. and M. College, asserted in his presidential address to the Association of American Agricultural Colleges and Experiment Stations that such credit was erroneous. He said: "I have the original draft of that amendment in my possession; it was first written by one college president who cared more for object than for form; was carefully trimmed and punctuated by another college president, and cordially adopted by the others on the committee, none of these being grangers although entirely friendly to that order and its general work. The Association committee did not believe the amendment necessary, but willingly proposed it and supported it until adopted . . . . Therefore, instead of this limiting amendment being of Grange origin . . . the plain facts are that it originated with college men and had their honest support from the first to the last . . . ." United States Department of Agriculture, Office of Experiment Stations, Miscellaneous Bulletin Number 30, *Proceedings of the Ninth Annual Convention of the Association of American Agricultural Colleges and Experiment Stations* (Washington, 1896), pp. 24-25.

[24]*Journal of the First Session of the Oklahoma Legislative Assembly,* pp. 133, 151-152.

[25]*Ibid.,* pp. 127-128.

[26]Otis Wile, "Sixth Founder's Day Celebration is Best Yet," *The Oklahoma A. and M. College Magazine,* V, No. 6 (1934), p. 3.

[27]Overby, n. p.

[28]Freeman E. Miller, *The Founding of the Oklahoma Agricultural and Mechanical College* (Stillwater, 1928), p. 2.

[29]John H. Florer, "Major Issues in the Congressional Debate of the Morrill Act of 1862," *The History of Education Quarterly,* VIII, No. 4 (1968), p. 460.

[30]*Journal of the First Session of the Oklahoma Legislative Assembly,* pp. 118, 124, 130, 169-171, 221-222.

[31]*Ibid.,* p. 301. For the actual provisions of the Second Morrill Act, see *United States Statutes at Large,* XXVI, (1890), pp. 417-419.

[32]*Journal of the First Session of the Oklahoma Legislative Assembly,* pp. 380, 590-593, 663, 411-412, 564-565, 850, 920-921, 1000-1001, 1084, 1087, 1093, 1104, 1112-1113.

[33]*Ibid.,* pp. 992-995, 1013-1015.

[34]*Ibid.,* p. 1015.

[35]*The College Mirror,* May 15, 1895.

[36]*The Statutes of Oklahoma,* (1890), p. 2.

[37]*Ibid.,* pp. 81-82.

[38]John Alley, *City Beginnings in Oklahoma Territory* (Norman, 1939), p. 94; *Annual Catalog,* Session of 1894-1895, pp. 8-9; *Portrait and Biographical Record of Oklahoma,* pp. 202, 890, 1197; Berlin Chapman, "The Men Who Selected Stillwater as the Site for the College," *The Oklahoma A. and M. College Magazine,* II, No. 4 (1930), p. 108.

[39]Amos Ewing, "The First Board of Regents," *The Oklahoma A. and M. College Magazine,* 1, No. 4 (1929), p. 4; *Annual Catalog,* Session of 1894-1895, pp. 8-9.

[40]Miller, *The Founding of the Oklahoma A. and M. College,* pp. 8-9; "Record of the Minutes of the Board of Trustees of the Town of Stillwater," (Stillwater Municipal Building, Office of the City Clerk), p. 33.

[41]Miller, *The Founding of the Oklahoma A. and M. College,* p. 18.

[42]Berlin Chapman, *The Founding of Stillwater* (Oklahoma City, 1948), p. 145.

[43]A. E. Jarrell to B. B. Chapman, June 25, 1956, "The Jarrell Collection," (Oklahoma State University); A. E. Jarrell, "I Remember When . . . ," *Oklahoma State University Magazine,* II, No. 11, (1958), p. 7.

[44]"Selections from the Record Book," pp. 319-320. For a farmer's appraisal of the value of land-grant institutions, see James Hastings, "Log Cabin Days in Oklahoma," *The Chronicles of Oklahoma,* XXVII, No. 2 (1950), p. 153.

[45]Chapman, *The Founding of Stillwater,* pp. 146, 183; Overby, n. p.

[46]*The Stillwater Daily Press,* December 14, 1938; "Register of the Stillwater City Hotel," (Payne County Historical Society), n.p.

[47]*The Stillwater Daily Press,* December 14, 1938.

[48]Quoted from Oklahoma Agricultural Experiment Station, *Bulletin Number 1* (Stillwater, 1891), p. 7.

[49]Chapman, *The Founding of Stillwater,* p. 147.

[50]*The Stillwater Gazette,* January 22, 1892.

[51]"Minutes of the Stillwater Board of Trustees," p. 64.

[52]*The Stillwater Daily Press,* January 1, 1939.

[53]This legislation may be read in its entirety in *Supplement to the Revised Statutes of the United States,* 1874-1891, I (1891), p. 504. Known as Harrison's Law, the bill most likely became enacted because of certain financial problems in Arizona Territory. One account of its origin may be surveyed in *The* (Globe) *Arizona Silver Bell,* September 4, 1886.

[54]*The Stillwater Gazette,* July 29, 1892; Miller, *The Founding of the Oklahoma A. and M. College,* p. 18.

[55]*The Stillwater Daily Press,* December 26, 1939; *The Stillwater Gazette,* August 26, 1892; "Minutes of the Stillwater Board of Trustees," pp. 83-89.

[56]*The Stillwater Gazette,* September 23, 1893; Hays Cross, "Memories to be Revived," *The Oklahoma A. and M. College Magazine,* XI, No. 4

(1939), p. 4; "We Get the College," *The Oklahoma A. and M. College Magazine,* I, No. 4 (1929), p. 31; *The Stillwater Daily Press,* December 14, 1938; "Minutes of the Stillwater Board of Trustees," p. 89.

⁵⁷"Minutes of the Stillwater Board of Trustees," p. 98; "We Get the College," p. 31.

⁵⁸*The* (Stillwater) *Oklahoma Hawk,* April 27, 1893.

⁵⁹*The Stillwater Daily Press,* January 1, 1939; *The Stillwater Gazette,* March 28, 1913.

⁶⁰*The Stillwater Gazette,* January 22, 1892; Miller, *The Founding of the Oklahoma A. and M. College,* pp. 20-21; *The Stillwater Daily Press,* January 1, 1939; "Minutes of the Stillwater Board of Trustees," pp. 206, 252, 314.

⁶¹Frank Wikoff to Tom Hartman, November 30, 1940, "The Hartman Collection," (Oklahoma State University).

⁶²*The Oklahoma Hawk,* April 27, 1893.

⁶³*Ibid.*

⁶⁴*Annual Catalog,* Session of 1894-1895, pp. 13-14.

⁶⁵Miller, *The Founding of the Oklahoma A. and M. College,* pp. 23-24.

⁶⁶American communities often sought colleges for economic rather than for intellectual reasons. See, Thomas Cochran, *The American Business System* (New York, 1957), p. 172. The most penetrating critique of the influence of businessmen on colleges and universities is Thorstein Veblen, *The Higher Learning in the United States* (New York, 1918).

⁶⁷Emma Dent to B. B. Chapman, November 14, 1965, "Early Student Letter Collection," (Oklahoma State University).

⁶⁸For a summary of the status of higher education at the close of the territorial period, consult Oscar William Davidson, "Education at Statehood," *The Chronicles of Oklahoma,* XXVIII, No. 1 (1950), p. 79. Much valuable information is also available in Elijah T. Dunlap, "The History of Legal Controls of Public Higher Education in Oklahoma," (unpublished Doctoral dissertation, Oklahoma State University, 1956), *passim.*

⁶⁹Litton, I, p. 458. Even the early students had second thoughts about the advisability of so many educational institutions. A newspaper reporter wrote: "It will always be a question, however, whether a few strong, well-equipped colleges will not do greater good than will a larger number each with poorer facilities." Quoted from *The College Mirror,* January, 1898.

II

¹The regents were not only unfamiliar with higher education, but some of them during the "itinerant years" were not terribly interested in devoting their time to a venture which did not have profit as a motive. This situation also occurred at other land-grant institutions. For example, see Louis Geiger, *University of the Northern Plains: A History of the University of North Dakota,* (Grand Forks, 1958), p. 28.

²In contrast to the poverty of some land-grant institutions in the late nineteenth and early twentieth century, the new privately endowed graduate colleges, such as Johns Hopkins University, the University of Chicago, and Stanford University, had abundant resources. In fact, one historian, Laurence R. Veysey, suggests that the modern university could not have developed without the aid of philanthropists. *The Emergence of the American University* (Chicago, 1965), p. 3. Yet, this richness may have been a mixed blessing, for Upton Sinclair, after a two year tour of the American educational system, declared in his book *The Goose-Step* (Pasadena, 1922) that it often was difficult for these private organizations to carry on research that countered traditional values, especially in the area of economics. (p. 198)

³There are few specialized studies which deal with the history of the American college student. Some comparative data, however, may be found in Morris Bishop, *Early Cornell, 1865-1900* (Ithaca, 1962), pp. 121-152.

⁴It should be remembered here that land-grant colleges were both regional and national institutions. Agencies and associations, such as The Society

for the Promotion of Agricultural Science, the American Society of Civil Engineers, the Association of American Agricultural Colleges and Experiment Stations, and the National Cattlemen's Association, helped to establish general guidelines for Morrill institutions, but individual colleges still had to adapt to local conditions. Philip Rulon and Ronald Butchart, "Henry Elijah Alvord, 1844-1904: Soldier, Scientist, and Scholar," *The Chronicles of Oklahoma,* LII, No. 1 (1974), p. 61-81.

5As with the case of college students, university trustees have not been the object of intensive historical research. A contemporary study which includes valuable bibliographic information is Rodney T. Hartnett, *College and University Trustees: Their Backgrounds, Roles, and Educational Attitudes* (Princeton, 1969), pp. 1-71.

6*The Statutes of Oklahoma,* (1890), p. 83.

7Alexander Magruder to S. M. Tracy, July 29, 1892, "Manuscript Letter Collection," I (Oklahoma State University), p. 66.

8A revision of the 1890 statute somewhat clarified this situation. In addition, the name of the educational organization was changed from the Agricultural and Mechanical College of the Territory of Oklahoma to the Agricultural and Mechanical College of Oklahoma. For the complete text, see *The Statutes of Oklahoma,* (1893), pp. 79-83.

9Gilmore, F. R., "A Historical Study of the Oklahoma Agricultural Experiment Station," (unpublished Doctoral dissertation, Oklahoma State University, 1967), p. 35.

10*Journal of the First Session of the Oklahoma Legislative Assembly,* (1890), p. 1094; *Portrait and Biographical Record of Oklahoma,* p. 173, 535; Miller, *The Founding of the Oklahoma A. and M. College,* p. 11; *Council Journal* (1895), pp. 668-783. Regents were required to repeat the following oath: "I, John Doe, do solemnly swear I will support the Constitution of the United States, and the Organic Act of Oklahoma Territory; and faithfully discharge the duties as member of the Board of Regents of the Oklahoma Agricultural and Mechanical College, so help me God." "Manuscript Letters," IV, p. 80.

11Ewing, p. 4.

12*House Journal* (1893), pp. 347-348. It should be noted at this point that the regents' minutes for the "itinerant years" are not available. Frequent changes of administration, fires, and the fact that early officials were not conscientious about keeping records, have reduced the number of primary sources.

13OAES, *Bulletin No. 1,* (1891), pp. 8, 12; Miller, *The Founding of the Oklahoma A. and M. College,* pp. 11-12.

14"We Get the College," p. 31. The expenditure of federal funds under the Second Morrill Act was in theory carefully regulated; however, in practice the "illegal" use of such monies was sanctioned under certain conditions. During these years William Torrey Harris, the United States Commissioner of Education, worked with the executive committee of the Association of American Land-Grant Colleges to ascertain what expenditures were just, and the nature of the reports that land-grant colleges should submit to the Secretary of the Interior. Harris expressed his personal views on this matter to Professor E. F. Ladd. He wrote: "Under this interpretation of the law the following are a few of the items which are held as not properly chargeable to the funds granted by the act of August 30, 1890: Salaries of president, treasurer, secretary, librarian, bookkeepers, accountants, janitors, watchmen; salaries of professors of ancient and modern languages, of pedagogics, of mental and moral philosophy, of music; also furniture, cases, shelving, musical instruments, fuel for heating purposes, lighting, tableware, and cooking utensils . . . ." North Dakota Agricultural and Mechanical College, *Third Biennial Report of the Board of Trustees of the North Dakota Agricultural College,* Session of 1895-1896 (Bismarck, 1896), p. 14.

15Horace J. Harper, "Margruder Field," *The Oklahoma A. and M. College Magazine,* XIII, No. 9 (1942), p. 6; *House Journal,* (1893), pp. 347-348.

16Alfred Edwin Jarrell, "The Founding of Oklahoma A. and M. College: A Memoir," *The Chronicles of Oklahoma,* XXXIV, No. 3 (1956), pp. 323-324. The officials of the college hoped in the near future to be eligible for a military officer to be detailed from West Point to assume the position of Commandant and Tactician. Thus Darnell's appointment was only temporary. Major Henry Alvord, who was the first regular military officer detailed by the academy to train students enrolled in Morrill institutions, and C. W. Dabney, Tennessee University, carried the fight in the association of land-grant colleges for continuance of such activities. Some of the older organizations, such as the Massachusetts Institute of Technology, maintained similar relationships with the Naval Academy at Annapolis. For details, consult, USDA, OES, Miscellaneous Bulletin No. 3, *Proceedings of the A. A. A. C. E. S.* (Washington, 1890), pp. 68-69; (Washington, 1899), pp. 64-65; (Washington, 1894), p. 25; Massachusetts Institute of Technology, *Annual Report of the President and Treasurer,* Session of 1898 (Boston, 1899), p. 16.

[17]Miller, *The Founding of the Oklahoma A. and M. College,* pp. 12-13; Gale Wallin, "I Remember When—," *The Oklahoma A. and M. College Magazine,* No. 5, I (1930), p. 5.

[18]*The Stillwater Gazette,* January 15, 1892; July 1, 1892; Miller, *The Founding of the Oklahoma A. and M. College,* p. 15.

[19]The dates of the presidential administrations of these men are: Barker, June 21, 1891—June 15, 1894; Alvord, June 16, 1894—January 17, 1895; Murdaugh, January 18, 1895—June 30, 1895; Morrow, July 1, 1895—June 30, 1899; and Scott, July 1, 1899—June 30, 1908. J. C. Neal served as acting president for an unknown period. Robert Cunningham, *Oklahoma Agricultural and Mechanical College: A Book of Photographs* (Stillwater, 1955), n.p.

[20]*Portrait and Biographical Record of Oklahoma,* p. 535; Personal interview by author with Angie Debo, August 3, 1967, in Marshall, Oklahoma.

[21]H. E. Thompson to B. B. Chapman, June 3, 1954, "The Thompson Collection," (Oklahoma State University).

[22]Ewing, p. 4; Harry E. Thompson, "The Territorial Presidents of Oklahoma A. and M. College," *The Chronicles of Oklahoma,* XXXII, No. 4 (1954), pp. 364-365.

[23]"Selections from the Record Book," p. 80.

[24]*Ibid.,* p. 313.

[25]Robert Barker to John Noble, March 8, 1892, "The OSU Collection," (Oklahoma State University).

[26]"Selections from the Record Book," p. 57; *Annual Catalog,* Session of 1891-1892, n.p.

[27]Sherman B. Barnes, "The Entry of Science and History in the College Curriculum, 1865-1914," *The History of Education Quarterly,* IV, No. 1 (1964), p. 46.

[28][Willa Adams, "Scrapbook," n.p.] in "The Dusch Collection," (Oklahoma State University).

[29][Berlin Chapman, "President Robert Barker," n.p.] in "The Angie Debo College Collection," (Author's Library); H. E. Thompson to Angie Debo, March 14, 1957, "The Debo Collection."

[30]*House Journal,* (1893), p. 351.

[31]Julius T. Willard, *A History of the Kansas State College of Agriculture and Applied Science* (Manhattan, 1940), p. 351.

[32]"Minutes of the First Faculty," (Oklahoma State University), pp. 113-114.

[33]*Ibid.,* p. 116.

[34]*Ibid.,* p. 119.

[35]*Ibid.,* pp. 127-140.

[36]*House Journal,* (1893), p. 249; H. E. Thompson to B. B. Chapman, June 3, 1954, "The Thompson Collection"; *The Stillwater Daily Press,* December 9, 1937; December 14, 1937.

[37]Emma Dent to B. B. Chapman, November 14, 1965, "Early Student Letter Collection."

[38]The standard history of such institutions is USDA, OES Bulletin No. 80, A. C. True and V. A. Clark, *The Agricultural Experiment Stations in the United States* (Washington, 1900).

[39]*United States Statutes at Large,* XXIV (1887), p. 440.

[40]Allan Nevins, *The State Universities and Democracy* (Urbana, 1962), p. 102.

41USDA, OES, Miscellaneous Bulletin No. 2, *Proceedings of the A. A. A. C. E. S.* (Washington, 1891), pp. 86-87.

42Gilmore, pp. 74-78.

43D. C. McIntosh, Don M. Orr, and C. White, "The Story of Agriculture of Less than College Grade in the Oklahoma Agricultural and Mechanical College from December 25, 1890 to June 1, 1940," (Oklahoma State University), p. 3; *The College Mirror,* January 16, 1896.

44James Neal to Jennie Neal, November 22, 1894, "The Neal Collection," (Oklahoma State University).

45Aime Neal Jamison to E. A. Jarrell, n.d., "The Neal Collection"; "Selections from the Record Book," pp. 80.

46"Minutes of the First Faculty," p. 229.

47*The Tulsa* (Oklahoma) *World,* November 28, 1965.

48James Neal to Jennie Neal, January 28, 1864, "The Neal Collection."

49Nancy B. Kremkus to B. B. Chapman, September 29, 1965, "The Neal Collection"; [Willa Adams, "Scrapbook," n.p.] in "The Dusch Collection."

50OAES, *Bulletin No. 1,* pp. 8-11.

51For example, see USDA, OES, Miscellaneous Bulletin No. 3, *Proceedings of the A. A. A. C. E. S.* (Washington, 1892), p. 55.

52[John Fields, "Stock Raising in Oklahoma," p. 21] in "Manuscript Letters," VII; Gilmore, p. 31.

53Hastings, "Oklahoma Agricultural and Mechanical College and Old Central," p. 83.

54"Selections from the Record Book," p. 39.

55Amie Neal Jamison to B. B. Chapman, May 31, 1962, "The Neal Collection"; *The Stillwater Gazette,* July 4, 1895.

56Quoted from *The* (Stillwater, Oklahoma) *Payne County Populist,* August 22, 1895.

57*Ibid.,* September 26, 1895.

58"Minutes of the First Faculty," p. 230.

59In 1909, John Dewey made the following observation concerning the impact of Charles Darwin's *The Origin of Species.* "No wonder, then, that the publication of Darwin's book, a half century ago, precipitated a crisis. The true nature of the controversy is easily concealed from us, however, by the theological clamor that attended it. The vivid and popular features of the anti-Darwinian row tended to leave the impression that the issue was between science on one side and theology on the other. Such was not the case—the issue lay primarily with science itself, as Darwin clearly recognized." John Dewey, "The Influence of Darwin on Philosophy," in Bert James Loewenberg (ed.), *Darwinism: Reaction or Reform?* (New York, 1966), p. 52.

By 1900, the conflict in the sciences was nearing resolution. The idea of taking factual data and formulating all-encompassing natural laws seemed to be passing from vogue. Instead, modern scientists were looking for causal relationships, being content to work with small pieces of the evolutionary cycle. Furthermore, land-grant college professors broadened the area in which they did experiments, especially in relation to man and his environment. In other words, they believed the farmer "had other problems besides insects, hail, frost, and the sterility of his prize boar." White, p. 56.

60Hastings, "Oklahoma Agricultural College and Old Central," p. 83; Edward Danforth Eddy, *Colleges for Our Land and Time: The Land-Grant Idea in American Education* (New York, 1956), p. 9.

61Jarrell, "The Founding of the Oklahoma A. and M. College: A Memoir," p. 324.

62Frank Northup to B. B. Chapman, December 22, 1962, "The Northup Collection," (Oklahoma State University); *The Peoples Press,* August 11, 1910.

63For glimpses of the elder Magruder's career, see John K. Bettersworth, *People's College: A History of Mississippi State* (Birmingham, 1953), pp. 80-83, 157, 166, 219, 333, 397.

64Medals were presented to Katie Neal, George Bowers, and Arthur Adams. Magruder got the idea of giving an award to the best declaimer in the freshman class from his father. A. C. Magruder to John Fields, May 22, 1893, "Manuscript Letters," I, p. 389. Also, see Berlin Chapman, "Medal Collection

Complete," *The Oklahoma A. and M. College Magazine,* XV, No. 3 (1943), p. 7; *The Stillwater News-Press,* August 26, 1956.

Portions of the winning speeches may be read in *The Stillwater Gazette,* June 23, 1893; June 13, 1895; *The* (Stillwater, Oklahoma) *Eagle-Gazette,* June 21, 1894.

[65]Besides requesting advice from the most prominent American land-grant colleges and experiment stations, Magruder and Holter sought information from stations in Guelph, Canada, Königsberg, Germany, Rothamshed, England, and Halle, Germany.

[66][Alexander Magruder, "Report to the Board of Regents," p. 124] in "Manuscript Letters," I.

[67]H. G. Magruder to H. Thompson, August 31, 1892, "Manuscript Letters," II, p. 101.

[68]Harper, p. 6; "Selections from the Record Book," p. 630.

[69]Miller, *The Founding of the Oklahoma A. and M. College,* p. 15.

[70]Quoted from *The College Mirror,* February, 1898.

[71]*Ibid.*

[72]The article "Ideals of Horticultural Instruction" was published after Frank Waugh left the Oklahoma A. and M. College campus. Many of the students' essays, however, that were written while Waugh taught in Stillwater evidence this point of view. For instance, see the oration entitled "Landscape Gardening" given by J. H. Adams in June, 1895, at the annual closing exercises. It may be read in part by consulting *The Stillwater Gazette,* June 13, 1895.

While such changes in agricultural courses have been widely publicized, it should not be forgotten that the same was also true in the engineering area. Speaking on this subject, President Francis A. Walker of M. I. T. said: "Our shops are not factories, but laboratories. It is not the thing made, but the training, the discipline, the practice, which the students obtains in the making, which forms the object in view." Massachusetts Institute of Technology, *Annual Report of the President and Treasurer,* Session of 1896 (Cambridge, 1897), p. 39.

[73]Frank Northup to B. B. Chapman, December 22, 1962, "The Northup Collection"; [Willa Adams, "Scrapbook," n.p.] in "The Dusch Collection."

[74]A. E. Jarrell to B. B. Chapman, September 22, 1957, "The Jarrell Collection."

[75]Jarrell, "The Founding of the Oklahoma A. and M. College: A Memoir," pp. 316-317.

[76]"Stillwater's First School Board Minutes," p. 81; *The Stillwater Daily Press,* September 18, 1934; Jarrell, "The Founding of the Oklahoma A. and M. College: A Memoir," pp. 316-317.

[77]Quoted from *The College Mirror,* June 15, 1895.

[78] B. B. Chapman, "First Faculty Set Standards," *The Oklahoma A. and M. College Magazine,* XV, No. 4 (1943), p. 3; B. B. Chapman, "I Remember the University When," *The Oklahoma State Alumnus,* II, No. 10 (1961), p. 13; "Last of the A. and M. Faculty," *The Oklahoma A. and M. College Magazine,* XXI, No. 4 (1949), p. 13.

[79]["Biographical Sketch of Harry Thompson," n.p.] in "The Hartman Collection."

[80]*Ibid.*

III

[1]*The Stillwater Gazette,* December 26, 1930. Also, see Roy Gittinger, *The Formation of the State of Oklahoma* (Norman, 1939), p. 189 and *The Stillwater Press,* June 15, 1939.

[2]Peery, p. 289.

[3]Lawrence Cremin, *The Genius of American Educators* (New York, 1965), pp. 113-114; Everett Dick, *The Dixie Frontier* (New York, 1948), pp. 170-180.

[4]Cunningham, *Stillwater: Where Oklahoma Began,* pp. 55-68.

[5]"Stillwater's First School Board Minutes," p. 88.

6Stillwater High School Journalism Class of 1935-1936, "Stillwater Public Schools, 1889-1938," (Stillwater Public Library).

7*Annual Announcement*, Session of 1897-1898, p. 6.

8*The Stillwater News-Press*, September 3, 1963.

9Frederick Rudolph, *The American College and University: A History* (New York, 1965), p. 281.

10*Annual Announcement*, Session of 1896-1897, p. 6; *Annual Catalog, Session of 1893-1894*, p. 34; Thompson, "The Territorial Presidents of the Oklahoma A. and M. College," p. 364. Harry Thompson taught the pedagogical courses during the summer months. Perhaps the first person to receive a certificate as a result of these classes was Miss Gertie Diem. *The Stillwater Gazette*, August 26, 1892.

11*The Statutes of Oklahoma*, (1890), p. 85.

12*Ibid.*, (1893), p. 83.

13*The College Mirror*, October 15, 1895; May, 1898; *Annual Catalog, Session of 1894-1895*, pp. 33-34; [Alexander Magruder, "Report to the Board of Regents," p. 126], in "Manuscript Letters," I.

14Berlin Chapman to Edward Morrison, June 28, 1951, "The Debo College Collection."

15William E. Bittle and Gilbert L. Geis, "Racial Self-Fulfillment and the Rise of an All-Negro Community in Oklahoma," in August Meier and Elliot Rudwick (eds.), *The Making of Black America*, II (New York, 1969), p. 108.

16Henry Allen Bullock, *A History of Negro Education in the South* (New York, 1967), p. 172; A. C. Scott to Amy Gordon Bruce, September 5, 1905, "Manuscript Letters," XXXVII, p. 379. Negro literacy statistics published in Oklahoma newspapers differ substantially with those complied by the United States Bureau of Census. For example, compare the figures cited by Professor Bullock with those in *The* (Stillwater, Oklahoma) *New Education,* June 1, 1912.

17Gerald Gutek, "An Analysis of Formal Education in Edward Bellamy's *Looking Backward,*" *The History of Education Quarterly,* IV, No. 4 (1964), p. 253. The Turner paper is reprinted in Theodore Rawson Crane, *The Colleges and the Public,* 1787-1862 (New York, 1963), pp. 172-189.

18[Untitled Address, June 15, 1894], in "The Chapman Clipping and Letter Collection," (Oklahoma State University).

19*Ibid.*

20*Report of Oklahoma Educational Institutions* (Guthrie, 1902), p. 28; Harry Thompson, "1892—A. and M. College—1930," *The Oklahoma A. and M. College Magazine,* I, No. 8 (1930), p. 4; J. H. Adams, "In Retrospect and Prospect," *The Oklahoma A. and M. College Magazine,* XIII, No. 5 (1942), p. 8; *Church Directory of the First Methodist Church* (Stillwater, n.d.), n.p.

21"Selections from the Record Book," p. 40.

22George Holter, "When the School Was Young," *The Oklahoma A. and M. College Magazine,* I, No. 4 (1929), p. 31.

23Jarrell, "The Founding of the Oklahoma A. and M. College: A Memoir," p. 318.

24Hastings, "Oklahoma Agricultural College and Old Central," p. 83.

25Jarrell, "The Founding of the Oklahoma Agricultural and Mechanical College: A Memoir," p. 316; "Selections from the Record Book," pp. 29, 81.

26"Selections from the Record Book," p. 59.

27USDA, OES, Miscellaneous Bulletin No. 65, *Proceedings of the A. A.-A. C. E. S.* (Washington, 1899), p. 65.

28Kansas State Agricultural College, *Sixteenth Biennial Report of the Board of Regents and Faculty,* Session of 1907-1908 (Topeka, 1908), p. 82.

29*Annual Catalog,* Session of 1893-1894, p. 42.

30*Ibid.*

31"Selections from the Record Book," p. 310.

32Jarrell, "I Remember When . . . ," p. 24.

33"Selections from the Record Book," p. 310.

34*Ibid.*

35George Bowers, "Early Military Training," *The Oklahoma A. and M.*

College Magazine, I, No. 7 (1930), p. 4; A. C. Magruder to W. C. Renfrow, March 17, 1895, "Manuscript Letters," II, p. 11; *The Eagle-Gazette,* December 13, 1894.

36Holter, p. 12.

37"Minutes of the First Faculty," pp. 179-180.

38*Ibid.,* p. 102.

39*Ibid.,* p. 120.

40"Selections from the Record Book," p. 26.

41For example, see "Minutes of the First Faculty," pp. 269-275.

42*Ibid.,* p. 217.

43*Ibid.,* p. 235.

44*Annual Catalog,* Session of 1891-1892, n.p.

45Jarrell, "The Founding of the Oklahoma Agricultural and Mechanical College: A Memoir," p. 317; A. C. Magruder to R. J. Barker, July 23, 1892, "Manuscript Letters," I, p. 55; A. C. Magruder to Richard Krey, June 14, 1892, "Manuscript Letters," I, p. 7; *Annual Catalog,* Session of 1894-1895, p. 99.

46*Ibid.,* pp. 99-100. For an analysis of nineteenth century textbooks, see Ruth Miller Elson, *Guardians of Tradition* (Lincoln, 1964).

47*The College Paper,* October, 1902; October 15, 1903.

48*The College Mirror,* May 15, 1895. Enrollment statistics for the territorial period are available in Ruth Howard, "The Development of the Oklahoma Agricultural and Mechanical College," (unpublished Master's thesis, Oklahoma A. and M. College, 1926), p. 40.

49North Dakota Agricultural College, *Sixth Biennial Report of the Board of Trustees,* Session of 1901-1902, p. 65.

50Mary Jean Bowman, "The Land-Grant Colleges and Universities in Human-Resource Development," *Journal of Economic History,* XXII, No. 4 (1962), p. 530.

51*The Stillwater Gazette,* August 4, 1893.

52A. E. Jarrell to Berlin Chapman, n.d., "The Jarrell Collection."

53Miller, *The Founding of the Oklahoma A. and M. College,* p. 14; *Council Journal,* (1895), pp. 74-75; "Selections from the Record Book," p. 53; *The Stillwater Gazette,* March 31, 1893.

54*The Stillwater Gazette,* August 18, 1893.

55*Ibid.*

56*Ibid.*

57*Ibid.*

58*Ibid.,* December 1, 1893.

59*The Eagle-Gazette,* January 26, 1894.

60"Minutes of the First Faculty," p. 151.

61*The* (Stillwater) *Oklahoma State Sentinel,* February 1, 1894; *The Eagle-Gazette,* February 9, 1894; March 30, 1894; *Council Journal,* (1895), p. 713; Berlin Chapman, *Old Central in the Crisis of 1955* (Oklahoma City, 1965), p. 79.

62*The Oklahoma State Sentinel,* May 10, 1894.

63*The College Paper,* November 28, 1902.

64Nevins, p. 66.

65For the development of the high school during this period, see Edward Krug, *The Shaping of the American High School* (Madison, 1969).

IV

1Miller, *The Founding of the Oklahoma A. and M. College,* p. 16; "Selections from the Record Book," p. 80.

2*The Eagle-Gazette,* June 28, 1894.

3*Ibid.,* May 4, 1894; *The Oklahoma State Sentinel,* May 10, 1894.

4The earliest activities of this agency are detailed in Earle D. Ross, "The United States Department of Agriculture During the Commissionership: A Study in Politics, Administration, and Technology, 1862-1889," *Agricultural History,* XX, No. 3 (1946), pp. 129-143.

5Vernon Carstensen, "A Century of the Land-Grant Colleges," *The Journal of Higher Education,* XXXIII, No. 1 (1963), p. 34: H. E. Thompson to B. B. Chapman, June 3, 1954, "The Thompson Collection," (Oklahoma

State University); George H. Calcott, *A History of the University of Maryland* (Baltimore, 1966), p. 192.

⁶Samuel Morgan Alvord, *Genealogy of the Descendants of Alexander Alvord* (New York, 1908), pp. 365-366, 570-573. Also, see his *History of the Connecticut Valley in Massachusetts*, II (Philadelphia, 1879), pp. 980-981.

⁷Liberty Hyde Bailey, *Cyclopedia of American Agriculture*, IV (New York, 1909), p. 551.

⁸Alfred C. True, "Henry Elijah Alvord," in *Dictionary of American Biography*, I, ed. Allen Johnson (New York, 1928), p. 238; U. S. Government, USDA, *Twenty-First Annual Report of the Bureau of Animal Husbandry* (Washington, 1904), pp. 41-43; William Arba Ellis (ed. and comp.), *Norwich University, 1819-1911: Her History, Her Graduates, Her Roll of Honor*, II (Montpelier, 1911), p. 668; Gould P. Colman, "Pioneering in Agricultural Education: Cornell University, 1867-1890," *Agricultural History*, XXXVI, No. 4 (1962), p. 206.

⁹Rulon and Butchart, pp. 61-81.

¹⁰Eddy, p. 10; William Belmont Parker, *The Life and Public Services of Justin Smith Morrill* (Boston, 1924), p. 261; Ellis, I, pp. 124, 138, 485-486; III, pp. 650, 667-668; Henry Alvord, "Early's Attack on Washington, July, 1864," in *Military Order of the Loyal Legion* (Washington, 1897), pp. 1-32; Caroline B. Sherman, "A New England Boy in the Civil War," *The New England Quarterly*, XXII, No. 5 (1932), pp. 310-344.

¹¹U. S. Government, General Services Administration, "Service and Pension Records of Henry Alvord," Claim Papers No. 2429833 (National Archives and Record Service); Caroline B. Sherman, " A Young Army Officer's Experience in Indian Territory," *The Chronicles of Oklahoma*, XII, No. 2 (1935), pp. 146-153; *The Eagle-Gazette*, December 20, 1894; William B. Hazen, "Some Correction of 'Life on the Plains'," reprint in *The Chronicles of Oklahoma*, III, No. 4 (1925), pp. 296-318; F. Stanley, *Satanta and the Kiowas* (Borger, 1968), pp. 185-193.

¹²U. S. Government, Secretary of the Interior, *Report of the Commissioner of Indian Affairs for 1869* (Washington, 1869), p. 42.

¹³U. S. Government, Department of the Interior, *Annual Report of the Commissioner of Indian Affairs for 1880* (Washington, 1880), pp. 178-181.

¹⁴Harold Whiting Cary, *The University of Massachusetts: A History of One Hundred Years* (New York, 1962), p. 43; U. S. Government, Department of the Interior, *Annual Report of the Commissioner of Indian Affairs for 1872* (Washington, 1872), pp. 128-148; James Mooney, "Calendar History of the Kiowa Indian," in *Seventeenth Annual Report of the Bureau of Ethnology to the Secretary of the Smithsonian Institution 1895-1896*, I, ed. John W. Powell, (Washington, 1898), pp. 193-195; Rupert Norval Richardson, *The Commanche Barrier to South Plains Settlement* (Glendale, 1933), pp. 143-359; Flora Warren Seymour, *Indian Agents of the Old Frontier* (New York, 1941), pp. 83-105; Grant Foreman, "Historical Background of the Kiowa-Comanche Reservation," *The Chronicles of Oklahoma*, XIX, No. 2 (1941), pp. 129-140; Aubrey L. Steele, "The Beginning of Quaker Administration of Indian Affairs in Oklahoma," *The Chronicles of Oklahoma*, XVII, No. 4 (1939), pp. 364-392; Berlin Basil Chapman, "Establishment of the Wichita Reservation," *The Chronicles of Oklahoma*, XI, No. 4 (1933), pp. 1044-1055; Carolyn Thomas Foreman, "Black Beaver," *The Chronicles of Oklahoma*, XXIV, No. 3 (1946), pp. 269-292; True, "Henry Elijah Elvord," p. 238; J. P. Sheldon, *Dairy Farming; Being the Theory, Practice, and Methods of Dairying* (London, 1881), pp. 369-496; Henry Alvord, " The American Cattle Trade," *The Journal of the Royal Agricultural Society of England*, XIII, No. 2 (1887), pp. 356-374.

¹⁵Earle D. Ross, *Democracy's College; The Land-Grant Movement in the Formative Stage* (Ames, 1942), p. 139; USDA, OES, Miscellaneous Bulletin No. 1, *Proceedings of the A. A. A. C. E. S.* (Washington, 1889), p. 23-25, 68-71; Kansas State Agricultural College, *Eighth Biennial Report of the Board of Regents and Faculty*, Session of 1891-1892 (Topeka, 1893), p. 55.

¹⁶Thompson, "The Territorial Presidents of Oklahoma A. and M. College," p. 365.

[17]James Neal to Robert Lowry, January 16, 1895, "The Cunningham Manuscript Collection," (Oklahoma State University).

[18]*Council Journal,* (1895), p. 76; USDA, OES, Miscellaneous Bulletin No. 16, *Proceedings of the A. A. A. C. E. S.* (Washington, 1893), p. 15; (Washington, 1894), p. 14.

[19]*Council Journal,* (1895), p. 78.

[20]*Ibid.,* p. 80.

[21]*Ibid.,* p. 81.

[22]"Minutes of the First Faculty," pp. 175-176.

[23]*Ibid.,* pp. 178-183.

[24]See, *The Eagle-Gazette,* October 11, 1894 and December 20, 1894 for examples of speeches delivered in the Territory.

[25]*Prospectus of the A .and M. College,* Session of 1894-1895, pp. 2-3.

[26]*Ibid.,* pp. 3-8.

[27]*Council Journal,* (1895), p. 692.

[28]A. C. True to Henry Alvord, November 9, 1894, "The Cunningham Manuscript Collection."

[29]*The Eagle-Gazette,* November 22, 1894; USDA, OES, Miscellaneous Bulletin No. 24, *Proceedings of the A. A. A. C. E. S.* (Washington, 1895), p. 62.

[30]Freeman Miller, "Founding the College Library," *The Oklahoma A. and M. College Magazine,* I, No. 4 (1929), p. 19.

[31]*The Eagle-Gazette,* January 17, 1895.

[32]*Ibid.*

[33]*Ibid.*

[34]*Ibid.*

[35]*The Stillwater* (Oklahoma) *Messenger,* January 11, 1895.

[36]*Ibid.*

[37]*Ibid.*

[38]J. C. Neal to Robert Lowry, January 12, 1895, "The Cunningham Manuscript Collection." Neal assessed the situation correctly. In 1925, the wife of Representative Ben Tanersley reported that her husband had been offered $10,000 and a section of land near Oklahoma City to vote for removal of the college to El Reno. *The* (Stillwater, Oklahoma) *O'Collegian,* October 23, 1925.

[39]Hays Hamilton to Robert Lowry, January 16, 1896, "The Cunningham Manuscript Collection."

[40]J. C. Neal to Robert Lowry, January 16, 1895, "The Cunningham Manuscript Collection."

[41]*The Oklahoma State Sentinel,* January 17, 1895; Hays Hamilton to Robert Lowry, January 17, 1895, "The Cunningham Manuscript Collection."

[42]*Council Journal,* (1895), p. 318.

[43]*The Statutes of Oklahoma,* (1895), p. 271.

[44]*Ibid.*

[45]J. C. Neal to Robert Lowry, January 16, 1895; J. A. Stephenson to Robert Lowry, January 31, 1895; C. D. Shaffer to Robert Lowry, January 31, 1895, "The Cunningham Manuscript Collection."

[46]*Report of the President,* December 31, 1894, pp. 1-20. Local newspaper editorial comment may be read concerning the report in *The Oklahoma Sentinel,* January 17, 1895 and *The Eagle-Gazette,* January 17, 1895.

[47]*Council Journal,* (1895), p. 669.

[48]*Ibid.,* pp. 670-679.

[49]*Ibid.,* p. 682.

[50]*The Stillwater News-Press,* April 1, 1963.

[51]*Council Journal,* (1895), p. 669.

[52]*Ibid.,* p. 697.

[53]*The College Mirror,* May 15, 1895; *Council Journal,* (1895), pp. 700-711.

[54]*Council Journal,* (1895), pp. 717-739.

[55]*Ibid.,* p. 755.

[56]*Ibid.,* pp. 755-785.

[57]*Ibid.,* pp. 788-791.

[58]*House Journal,* (1895), p. 721.
[59]*Ibid.,* pp. 722-724.
[60]*Ibid.,* p. 725.
[61]J. C. Neal to Robert Lowry, February 11, 1895, "The Cunningham Manuscript Collection."
[62]*The Eagle-Gazette,* February 14, 1895.
[63]*The Daily Democrat,* August 27, 1904.
[64]*The Oklahoma State Sentinel,* February 14, 1895.
[65]Charles McGraw to Robert Lowry, February 24, 1895, "The Cunningham Manuscript Collection."
[66]F. C. Hunt to Robert Lowry, March 6, 1895, "The Cunningham Manuscript Collection."
[67]*The Stillwater News-Press,* March 18, 1963.

V

[1]*The Oklahoma State Sentinel,* December 5, 1894; *The Eagle-Gazette,* January 31, 1895; St. Louis, Missouri, Department of Health, *Certified Copy of Death,* No. 8167. The most extensive published bibliography of Alvord's writing is *The National Union Catalog Pre-1956 Imprints,* II (Chicago, 1969), pp. 120-122.
[2]Frank Wikoff to Tom Hartman, November 30, 1940, "The Hartman Collection."
[3]H. E. Thompson to B. B. Chapman, June 3, 1954, "The Thompson Collection"; George O. Ferguson to James D. Morrison, July 10, 1947, "Author's Library"; Charles P. McCurdy, Jr. to James D. Morrison, October 24, 1947, "Author's Library"; Merle Bateman to James D. Morrison, December 17, 1947, "Author's Library"; Francis Coram Oakes, "Edmond Dandridge Murdaugh, 1895-1901," (Oklahoma State University) p. 27.
[4]Oakes, p. 25.
[5]*The Stillwater News-Press,* April 15, 1963.
[6]*The Stillwater Gazette,* February 28, 1895.
[7]*The College Mirror,* May 15, 1895.
[8]"Minutes of the First Faculty," pp. 201-208.
[9]*The Stillwater Gazette,* July 4, 1895.
[10]*The Payne County Populist,* August 1, 1895; July 18, 1895; July 4, 1895; *The Stillwater Gazette,* July 4, 1895.
[11]H. E. Thompson to Freeman Miller, July 2, 1895, "The Cunningham Manuscript Collection."
[12]C. E. Regnier to Freeman Miller, July 7, 1895, "The Cunningham Manuscript Collection."
[13]*The Guthrie* (Oklahoma) *Leader,* June 30, 1895; July 2, 1895.
[14]*The Stillwater Gazette,* July 18, 1895.
[15]Frank Wikoff to Tom Hartman, November 30, 1940, "The Cunningham Manuscript Collection."
[16]*The Oklahoma State Sentinel,* May 9, 1895.
[17]*The Stillwater Gazette,* July 18, 1895.
[18]Richard Hofstadter and Walter Metzger, *The Development of Academic Freedom in the United States* (New York, 1955), p. 424.
[19]Thompson, "The Territorial Presidents of Oklahoma A. and M. College," pp. 365-366; Oakes, pp. 25-26. For highlights of Murdaugh's career at the Frostburg Normal School, see *The Frostburg* (Maryland) *Mining Journal,* August 23, 1902-June 26, 1909.
[20]S. H. Kelsey to George E. Morrow, June 29, 1895, "Manuscript Letters," IV, p. 150.
[21]H. E. Thompson to B. B. Chapman, June 3, 1954, "The Thompson Collection."
[22]Nevins, p. 64; Bailey, IV, p. 598.
[23]Quoted from Earle Dudley Ross, *A History of the Iowa State College of Agriculture and Mechanic Arts* (Ames, 1942), p. 123.
[24]Bailey, IV, p. 598.

25Roger Ebert, *An Illini Century* (Urbana, 1967), pp. 17-18.

26Winton Solberg, "The University of Illinois Struggles for Recognition," *Journal of the Illinois State Historical Society,* LIX, No. 2 (1966), pp. 21-24.

27H. E. Thompson to B. B. Chapman, June 3, 1954, "The Thompson Collection."

28Richard Hatch (comp.), *Some Founding Papers of the University of Illinois* (Urbana, 1967), p. 98.

29Quoted from *The College Paper,* October 1, 1900.

30USDA, OES, Miscellaneous Bulletin No. 24, *Proceedings of the A. A.- A. C. E. S.* (Washington, 1895), pp. 26-31.

31*The College Mirror,* September 16, 1895.

32USDA, OES, Miscellaneous Bulletin No. 1, *Proceedings of the A. A.- A. C. E. S.* (Washington, 1889), p. 44.

33USDA, OES, Miscellaneous Bulletin No. 7, *Proceedings of the A. A.- A. C. E. S.* (Washington, 1892), p. 68.

34*The College Mirror,* September 16, 1895.

35H. E. Thompson to B. B. Chapman, June 3, 1954, "The Thompson Collection."

36*The Stillwater Gazette,* August 22, 1895; September 26, 1895; *The College Mirror,* September 16, 1895.

37*The Stillwater Gazette,* October 17, 1895.

38*Ibid.,* December 12, 1895.

39*Ibid.,* July 17, 1897.

40*Ibid.,* October 24, 1896.

41*Ibid.,* November 24, 1898.

42Frank Wikoff to Tom Hartman, November 30, 1940, "The Hartman Collection."

43*Ibid.; The College Mirror,* March 16, 1896; June 15, 1896; *The Stillwater Democrat,* September 2, 1898; *The College Paper,* October 1, 1899; *The Stillwater Gazette,* June 8, 1898. For illustrations of faculty delegation of power to the president, see "Minutes of the First Faculty," pp. 216-217; 305-337; 352-353.

44*Report of the Governor of Oklahoma to the Secretary of the Interior* (Washington, 1896), p. 9.

4554th Congress, 2nd Session, U. S. House of Representatives, Document Number 5. *Report of the Secretary of the Interior,* III (Washington, 1896), p. 429; *Biennial Report of the Secretary of the Board of Leasing School Lands to the Governor of the Oklahoma Territory* (Guthrie, 1898), p. 3; *Third Annual Report of the Territorial Treasurer to the Governor of Oklahoma* (Guthrie, 1897), p. 9; *Biennial Reports of the Board of Regents, Clerk, and Treasurer of the Territorial Agricultural and Mechanical College.* Session of 1897-1898 (Guthrie, 1898), p. 50.

46*Biennial Reports of the Board of Regents, Clerk, and Treasurer of the Territorial Agricultural and Mechanical College,* Session of 1897-1898 (Guthrie, 1898), p. 39.

47*The College Mirror,* May 15, 1895.

48The Langston University founding law can be read in *Session Laws of Oklahoma,* (1897), pp. 37-41.

49*The Stillwater Gazette,* April 1, 1897.

50*The College Mirror,* January, 1898.

51*Ibid.,* April, 1898.

52USDA, OES, Bulletin No. 51, *Statistics of the Land-Grant Colleges and Agricultural Experiment Stations in the United States* (Washington, 1898), pp. 10-27; Pennsylvania State College, *Annual Report,* Session of 1897 (Harrisburg, 1898), pp. 8-11.

53*The College Mirror,* September 15, 1897; April, 1898; *The Stillwater Gazette,* March 24, 1898.

54*Council Journal,* (1899), p. 31; *The College Paper,* May 15, 1899.

55"Selections from the Record Book," p. 26; *The Payne County Populist,* September 19, 1896.

56*First Commencement Program* (Stillwater, 1896), n.p.

57Quoted from *The Stillwater Gazette,* May 28, 1896.

58Quoted from Nevins, p. 104.

[59]*The College Paper,* June 15, 1899; April 1, 1900.
[60]Quoted from *The College Paper,* April 1, 1900.

VI

[1]US Congress, House of Representatives, Annual Report of the Department of the Interior, *Report of the Commissioner of Education,* I, Document Number 5, 55th Congress, 2nd Session (Washington, 1898), p. 427; Eddy, p. 103; Ross, *Democracy's College,* pp. 173-174; Nevins, p. 53; Earle D. Ross, "The Great Triumvirate of Land-Grant Educators," *The Journal of Higher Education,* XXXII, No. 9 (1961), pp. 480-481. Wellford Addis, the statistician for the Department of Agriculture, estimated in 1896 that land-grant colleges were receiving $620,000 annually from the federal government. US Congress, House of Representatives, *Report of the Secretary of Interior,* Document Number 5, 54th Congress, 2nd Session (Washington, 1897), pp. 1243-1244.
[2]Quoted from Chapman, *Old Central in the Crises of 1955,* p. 100.
[3]*Ibid.*
[4]Cornell University, *Annual Report of the President,* Session of 1903-1904 (New York, 1904), p. liv, appendix.
[5]*The Statutes of Oklahoma* (1890), p. 84.
[6]*Annual Catalog,* Session of 1906-1907, pp. 75-76.
[7]*Ibid.,* p. 31.
[8]"Minutes of the First Faculty," pp. 218-220.
[9]*Annual Catalog,* Session of 1906-1907, pp. 75-76.
[10]*Ibid.,* Session of 1894-1895, pp. 37-40.
[11]*The College Mirror,* April, 1898; *The Stillwater Gazette,* June 23, 1898; Barnes, p. 44; Solon Justus Buck, *The Granger Movement: A Study of Agricultural Organization and Its Political, Economic and Social Manifestations, 1870-1880* (Lincoln, 1913), pp. 290-292. Also, see J. P. Powell, "Some Nineteenth Century Views on the University Curriculum," *The History of Education Quarterly,* V, No. 1 (1955), pp. 97-107.
[12]*The College Paper,* November 16, 1903; February, 1905; October 1, 1899; May 1, 1900; March, 1903; December 20, 1902; March, 1904; November 28, 1902; January 1, 1900; December 2, 1901; November 1, 1900; May, 1902; *The College Mirror,* April, 1898; March, 1898; November 15, 1895; January 16, 1896; *The Stillwater Gazette,* December 19, 1895.
[13]Finley Peter Dunne, *Mr. Dooley at His Best* (New York, 1938), p. 218.
[14]*The College Mirror,* May, 1898.
[15]The first collegiate curriculum is listed in the *Annual Catalog,* Session of 1891-1892, n.p.
[16]*The Sunday* (Oklahoma City) *Oklahoman,* October 17, 1965; "Minutes of the First Faculty," pp. 142, 170.
[17]*Annual Catalog,* Session of 1893-1894, p. 35.
[18]*Ibid.,* pp. 36-38.
[19]*Ibid.,* pp. 43-45.
[20]*Ibid.,* pp. 46-47. The Gray textbooks are analysed in Charles Ford, "Botany Texts: A Survey of Their Development in Higher Education, 1643-1906," *The History of Education Quarterly,* IV, No. 1 (1964), pp. 62-65.
[21]*Annual Catalog,* Session of 1893-1894, p. 35.
[22]*Ibid.,* pp. 39-40.
[23]*Ibid.,* pp. 40-42.
[24]*Ibid.,* pp. 41-42.
[25]*Annual Announcement of the College,* Session of 1896-1897, p. 8.
[26]A complete list of alumni for this period is contained in *The College Paper,* February 1, 1901. See also, W. L. English to B. B. Chapman, October 16, 1964, "Miscellaneous Student Letter Collection"; George Stiles, "Reminiscenses of the Class of 1900," *The Oklahoma A. and M. College Magazine,* XVII, No. 9 (1945), pp. 3-4, 6; *The College Paper,* May 1, 1900; March 1, 1900; *The College Mirror,* October 15, 1897; January, 1898.
[27]A. C. Scott to Charles Sheldon, April 28, 1905, "Manuscript Letters," XXIV, p. 308.

316

[28]Eddy, p. 10; Ellis, I, pp. 346-368. For the further development of engineering at West Point Academy, see Stephen Ambrose, *Duty, Honor, and Country: A History of West Point* (Baltimore, 1966).

[29]"Manuscript Letters," XVI, p. 396; "Selections from the Record Book," p. 34. Engineering placement statistics are available in *The New Education,* July 1, 1911.

[30]A. C. Scott to Walter E. Rowe, July 18, 1905, "Manuscript Letters," XXVII, p. 134; *The New Education,* May 1, 1914.

[31]*The New Education,* July 1, 1912.

[32]John Fields to Martin Dodge, August 29, 1901, "Manuscript Letters," X, p. 381; A. C. Scott to J. Barnes, April 23, 1903, "Manuscript Letters," XVI, p. 201; *The New Education,* February 15, 1912; A. C. Scott to R. Morton House, June 15, 1903, "Manuscript Letters," XVI, p. 262.

[33]A. C. Scott to T. B. Ferguson, July 27, 1904, "Manuscript Letters," XX, pp. 588-600; A. C. Scott to Albert Moore, June 27, 1905, "Manuscript Letters," XXIV, p. 485.

[34]Minutes of the First Faculty," p. 148.

[35]*The College Mirror,* April 15, 1896.

[36]"Minutes of the First Faculty," p. 248-250.

[37]*Ibid.,* p. 254.

[38]*The College Mirror,* October 15, 1897; "Minutes of the First Faculty," p. 321.

[39]*The College Paper,* April 1, 1900.

[40]Miller, "Founding the College Library," p. 18; *The Eagle-Gazette,* December 13, 1894; *The College Mirror,* May 15, 1895; *The Stillwater Gazette,* August, 19, 1897.

[41]*Annual Catalog,* Session of 1906-1907, p. 13.

[42]Hastings, "Oklahoma Agricultural and Mechanical College and Old Central," pp. 83-84.

[43]*The College Paper,* February 1, 1900.

[44]Willa Adams Dusch, *The Sigma Literary Society, 1893-1897: A Chapter in the History of Oklahoma A. and M. College* (Stillwater, 1951), pp. 14-18; "Minutes of the Sigma Literary Society," (Oklahoma State University), n.p.

[45]*The Eagle-Gazette,* December 13, 1894; *The College Paper,* May 1, 1900; *The College Mirror,* May 15, 1895.

[46]Alvord, *Report of the President,* p. 9.

VII

[1]The same statement may be made in regard to the universities themselves. In 1947, Samuel Eliot Morison and Henry Steele Commager wrote: "Practically every college and university has its 'history' but most of them are concerned largely with finances and athletics, and the character of university histories as of church histories is a major scandal in American scholarship." *The Growth of the American Republic,* II (New York, 1947), p. 622.

[2]White, pp. 45-56. The American conception of *in loco parentis* is closely associated with the decline of the family, the church, and the apprenticeship institutions on the frontier. See, Bernard Bailyn, *Education in the Forming of American Society* (Chapel Hill, 1960), pp. 3-52. Also, see Herman E. Harms, "In Loco Parentis in Higher Education," *Phi Kappa Phi Journal,* LI, No. 3 (1971), pp. 24-34.

[3]Hofstadter and Metzger, *The Development of Academic Freedom in the United States,* p. 283.

[4]Ewing, p. 30. The chronological age of the students increased later in the territorial period. In 1898, the college newspaper reported: "The average age of students at time of entrance to the college and preparatory classes during the last three years has been 17 3/5; thirty-three per cent being below and forty-three per cent above seventeen years of age." *The College Mirror,* May, 1898.

[5]A. E. Jarrell to B. B. Chapman, September 22, 1957, "The Jarrell Collection"; Tom Hartman, "1898 Class History," *The Oklahoma A. and M. College Magazine,* XIV, No. 9 (1943), pp. 3-8.

[6]"Selections from the Record Book," p. 41.

[7]*The* (Stillwater, Oklahoma) *Farmers Fact and Fancy,* January 4, 1904.

[8]"Selections from the Record Book," p. 47.

[9]Fern Hurley, "That Which They Built," *The Oklahoma A. and M. College Magazine,* I, No. 5 (1930), p. 27; *The College Paper,* October 1, 1899.

[10]*The Payne County Populist,* September 26, 1895.

[11]John Slack to Freeman Miller, August 10, 1897, "The Cunningham Manuscript Collection."

[12]*The Eagle-Gazette,* November 8, 1894; November 15, 1895; Hastings, "Oklahoma Agricultural College and Old Central," p. 83.

[13]*The College Mirror,* January 15, 1896.

[14]*The Eagle-Gazette,* November 15, 1896; December 3, 1895; January 3, 1895; *The College Mirror,* May 15, 1895; *The Stillwater Gazette,* October 31, 1895.

[15]*The Stillwater News-Press,* October 19, 1964.

[16]*The College Paper,* February 1, 1900; *The College Mirror,* February, 1898.

[17][Willa Adams, "Autograph Book," n.p.] in "The Dusch Collection."

[18]Edward Everett Dale, "The Frontier Literary Society," *Nebraska History,* XXXI, No. 2 (1950), p. 168.

[19]Dale, "Teaching on the Prairie Plains, 1890-1900," p. 303.

[20]*The Stillwater Gazette,* January 22, 1892; J. H. Adams, "When the College Was Young," *The Oklahoma A. and M. College Magazine,* I, No. 4 (1929), p. 9.

[21]*The Stillwater Gazette,* January 22, 1892; April 15, 1892.

[22]*The College Paper,* December-January, 1905-1906; [Willa Adams, "Scrapbook," n.p.] in "The Dusch Collection"; *Annual Catalog,* Session of 1894-1895, pp. 114-115; *The College Mirror,* June 15, 1895; *The Payne County Populist,* January 18, 1900; *The Stillwater Gazette,* September 26, 1895.

[23]"Minutes of the Webster Literary Society," October 16, 1893 (Oklahoma State University); October 20, 1893; *Constitution of the Webster Debating Society* (Stillwater, 1896), p. 1; "Minutes of the First Faculty," p. 150; A. E. Jarrell to B. B. Chapman, September 1, 1958, "The Jarrell Collection."

[24]*Constitution of the Webster Debating Society,* p. 1, 10; "Minutes of the First Faculty," p. 161.

[25]Compiled from the "Minutes of the Webster Literary Society," October 28, 1893 to October 3, 1896.

[26]Dusch, *The Sigma Literary Society,* p. 17.

[27]*The College Paper,* November, 1902.

[28]Dusch, *The Sigma Literary Society,* p. 3.

[29]*The College Mirror,* May 15, 1895; "Minutes of the First Faculty," pp. 150-152; *Constitution of the Sigma Literary Society* (Stillwater, n.d.), p. 1.

[30]James Whitcomb Riley, "At the Literary," *The Complete Works of James Whitcomb Riley* (New York, 1916), pp. 1292-1295; Dusch, *The Sigma Literary Society,* p. 17; "Minutes of the Sigma Literary Society," February 8, 1895, to November 28, 1896.

[31]"Selections from the Record Book," p. 30.

[32]"Minutes of the Webster Literary Society," December 9, 1893.

[33]"Minutes of the Sigma Literary Society," pp. 37-38; "Minutes of the Webster Literary Society," October 26, 1895; Dusch, *The Sigma Literary Society,* p. 23; "Minutes of the First Faculty," p. 267.

[34]Dusch, *The Sigma Literary Society,* p. 25.

[35]*The Eagle-Gazette,* January 17, 1895.

[36]*The College Mirror,* January 15, 1896.

[37]"Minutes of the First Faculty," pp. 270-276; "Treasurer's Book of the Sigma Literary Society," (Oklahoma State University), p. 21.

[38]"Minutes of the First Faculty," p. 300.

[39]*The College Mirror,* December 15, 1897; *The College Paper,* January, 1905; April 1, 1900; April, 1905; March 1, 1902; October, 1902; February, 1906; February, 1904.

[40]Compiled from *The Stillwater Gazette* and *The Payne County Populist,* January 1, 1892, to January 1, 1895.

[41]["The Riverside Review," n.p.] in "The Dusch Collection."

42"Minutes of the Sigma Literary Society," p. 7.

43*The Stillwater Gazette,* May 9, 1895.

44*The College Mirror,* May 15, 1895.

45*The College Paper,* April, 1902; February 1, 1902. For reprints of reviews, see *The College Mirror,* June 15, 1895.

46*The College Mirror,* September 16, 1895.

47*Ibid.,* June 15, 1895, to June 15, 1896.

48*Ibid.,* June 15, 1896.

49*Ibid.,* September 15, 1897; "Minutes of the First Faculty," p. 318.

50*The College Paper,* May 15, 1899. President Scott had had experience with student newspapers before coming to Stillwater. He and two of his 1876-1877 classmates at the University of Kansas printed the first student newspaper at that institution. In addition, he and a brother owned a newspaper in Oklahoma City. *The College Paper,* October, 1906.

51Gilmore, p. 63.

52"Selections from the Record Book," p. 29.

53*The College Mirror,* September 15, 1895.

54*Ibid.,* May, 1895.

55*The College Paper,* November 1 ,1901.

56*Ibid.,* October 1, 1899.

57*Ibid.,* April 1, 1900; January 1, 1900; *The Tulsa World,* April 3, 1966; *The Payne County Populist,* January 18, 1900; *The Stillwater Gazette,* May 10, 1900.

58*The College Paper,* February, 1904; "Minutes of the First Faculty," p. 330.

59This enthusiasm corresponded with an increased national interest in the sport. See, Rudolph, pp. 371-393.

60*The College Paper,* October 1, 1899.

61[Mrs. A. C. Scott, "Biographical Notebook of Angelo Scott," p. 9.] in "The Scott Collection," (Oklahoma State University).

62A. E. Jarrell to B. B. Chapman, September 1, 1958, "The Jarrell Collection"; Sam Barnes, "Early Day Football Reviewed," *The Oklahoma A. and M. College Magazine,* VI, No. 4 (1934), p. 6; *The Stillwater Gazette,* April 26, 1900; *The College Paper,* January 1, 1900; *The* (Phoenix) *Arizona Republic,* October 21, 1970.

63*The College Paper,* July, 1902.

64*Ibid.,* November 28, 1902.

65*Ibid.,* January 28. 1903.

66Angelo Scott, "The A. and M. College Song" in *Songs of the Western Colleges,* (New York, 1902), p. 151.

VIII

1Angelo C. Scott, *The Story of an Administration* (Stillwater, 1929), p. 3; Fayette Copeland to Mrs. A. C. Scott, March 31, 1949, "The Scott Collection."

2Quoted from *The College Mirror,* January, 1899.

3Undated newsclipping, Kansas University, *Graduate Magazine,* "The Scott Collection"; *The College Paper,* June 15, 1899. Midwestern institutions of higher education frequently were called the "Yales" or "Harvards" of their region. Russell B. Nye, *Midwestern Progressive Politics* (East Lansing, 1959), p. 7.

4For a concise statement of the beliefs of such men, see John Brubacher and Willis Rudy, *Higher Education in Transition* (New York, 1958), pp. 155-156.

5Gilmore, p. 10; Nevins, p. 102.

6Earle D. Ross, "On Writing the History of Land-Grant Colleges and Universities," *Journal of Higher Education,* XXIV, No. 8 (1953), p. 412; USDA, OES, Miscellaneous Bulletin Number 115, *Proceedings of the A. A. A.-C. E. S.* (Washington, 1900), p. 66.

7Quoted from Howard, p. 3.

319

8For a good summary of Scott's analysis of the attitude of Oklahoma farmers toward agricultural education, see *Second Biennial Report of the Oklahoma Territorial Board of Agriculture* (Guthrie, 1906), pp. 261-276. An overview of the national situation in this regard is Rudolph, pp. 241-263, 513.

9W. J. Jamison to Edith Copeland, April 29, 1949, "The Scott Collection"; Blanche Little, "The Oklahoma A. and M. College," *The School Journal,* LXXIV, No. 2 (1907), p. 664.

10[Angelo Scott, "The Mission of Books," n.p.] in "The Scott Collection."

11[Angelo Scott, "Which Way Education? At the Crossroads," p. 2] in "The Scott Collection."

12*Biennial Reports of the Territorial A. and M. College and Experiment Station of the Territory of Oklahoma* (Guthrie, 1900), p. 15.

13[Angelo Scott, "The Place of the College of Agriculture and Mechanic Arts in the School System of the State," pp. 10-11] in "The Scott Collection."

14*The College Paper,* October, 1902.

15*Report of Oklahoma Educational Institutions* (Guthrie, 1902), p. 21.

16Undated newspaper clipping in "The Wikoff Collection."

17*The College Paper,* October 15, 1903. Other land-grant institutions were also carrying on advertising campaigns. Generally speaking, these activities were designed to solicit students for Morrill institutions and to persuade legislators to appropriate larger sums of money. For more detailed information, see Solberg, "The University of Illinois Struggles for Public Recognition, 1867-1894," pp. 5-29. The same ground is covered in his *The University of Illinois, 1867 to 1894* (Urbana, 1968).

18The rural background of progressive ideals and leadership may be read in Wayne Fuller, "The Rural Roots of the Progressive Leaders," *Agricultural History,* XLII, No. 1 (1968), pp. 1-13. It is disappointing to note in this otherwise fine article that Professor Fuller does not show the relationship of the land-grant movement to progressivism. But on the other hand, he does, commendably, briefly discuss the influence of country and small town schools in shaping the reform values of the period, thereby alleviating some important criticisms of progressive historiography in Lawrence Cremin, *The Transformation of the School: Progressivism in American Education* (New York, 1961), pp. 355-356.

19[Mrs. A. C. Scott, "Biographical Notebook of Angelo C. Scott, pp. 14-15] in "The Scott Collection."

20Quoted from *The College Paper,* October, 1902.

21*Report of the Superintendent of the Territorial Board of Health for Oklahoma* (Guthrie, 1902), p. 50; [Angelo Scott, "Temperance Address," p. 36] in "The Scott Collection." The extent of the alcohol problem is evidenced in this local newspaper item. "Some of the farmers who occasionally get full of booze when in town have the idea that the city authorities take peculiar pains to run them in on the least provocation and at the same time permit residents of the town go unmolested no matter how drunk they get. This notion should be dismissed now since the city marshal has been hauled up before 'his honor' and treated as any other plain drunk." *The Stillwater Gazette,* March 25, 1897.

22[Angelo Scott, "Opening of College Year 1901-1902," pp. 14-15] in "The Scott Collection."

23*The College Paper,* April, 1901.

24*Ibid.,* June 1, 1901.

25[Angelo Scott, "Honor," p. 10] in "The Scott Collection."

26B. B. Chapman, "Author Discovered by A. C. Scott," *The Oklahoma A. and M. College Magazine,* VII, No. 7 (1945), p. 3; [Vingie Roe, "Scrapbook," p. 10] in "The Roe Collection" (Oklahoma State University).

27Vingie E. Roe to Berlin Chapman, September 19, 1929, "The Roe Collection."

28"Selections from the Record Book," p. 48.

29*The Farmers Fact and Fancy,* December 7, 1904.

30For further information about midwestern agrarian business attitudes, see Louis Galambos, "The Agrarian Image of the Large Corporation, 1879-1920: A Study in Social Accommodations," *The Journal of Economic History,*

XXVIII, No. 3 (1968), pp. 341-362.

31This type of administrative practice had already passed from business organizations to other agencies. Examine, for instance, the activities of certain governmental department heads detailed in Samuel P. Hays, *Conservation and the Gospel of Efficiency: The Progressive Conservation Movement, 1890-1920* (Cambridge, 1959).

32"Advice at Presidential Level," *The Oklahoma A. and M. College Magazine*, XXV, No. 9 (1954), pp. 20-21; *The Daily Oklahoman*, December 30, 1937; John Fields to William Scott, March 1, 1901, "Manuscript Letters," VII, p.113. In spite of ill health, John Scott held a number of positions in Kansas and Oklahoma. In the former state he served in both the territorial and state Legislatures, including selection as speaker of the House of Representatives and president *pro tem* of the Senate. Moreover, he was a farmer, a representative for the Leavenworth, Lawrence, and Galveston Railroad, a druggist, a regent for the University of Kansas, and a member of the federal government livestock inspection board in Kansas City. In Oklahoma, then a retired physician, he was appointed Indian Agent for the Ponca, Pawnee, and Otoe tribes and a member of the Oklahoma Legislature. He died in 1899, becoming the first lawmaker in the territory to expire in office. *Portrait and Biographical Record of Oklahoma*, pp. 817-818; *The National Cyclopedia of American Biography*, XXXVII (New York, 1951), p. 337; *House Journal* (1899), pp. 347-355.

33*The* (Lawrence) *Kansas University Weekly*, September 17, 1898; *The Iola* (Kansas) *Register*, June 6, 1910; [Charles Scott, "Boyhood Journal," n.p.] in "The Scott Collection." Little has been written about the career of Charles Scott, but David Donald hints that he may not have been as progressive as his educator brother. See, David Donald, *Lincoln Reconsidered* (New York, 1956), pp. 12-13.

34*Portrait and Biographical Record of Oklahoma*, p. 818; *The National Cyclopedia of American Biography*, p. 338; The Kansas University *Graduate Magazine*, March, 1949; Berlin Chapman, "Oklahoma City, From Public Land to Private Property," *The Chronicles of Oklahoma*, XXXVII, Nos. 2, 3, 4 (1959), pp. 211-237, 330-353, 440-479.

35*The* (no city) *Southwestern State Banker*, December, 1902.

36Scott, p. 10.

37*The College Paper*, July 25, 1900; November 1, 1901; October 15, 1903.

38Quoted from *The College Paper*, November 16, 1903.

39*Ibid.*, March 1, 1901; *The Daily Democrat*, August 27, 1904; John Fields to A. C. True, February 27, 1901, "Manuscript Letters," VII, p. 99.

40*The Stillwater Democrat*, January 16, 1903.

41*The Stillwater Gazette*, January 17, 1903; A. C. Scott to W. F. Hendricks, January 24, 1907, "The Scott Collection." In this same letter, the president said: "I have never attended or participated in a partisan political convention since I have been president. I have had many invitations from individuals to deliver political addresses, but I have always declined giving as my reason that I considered it inappropriate for me, in my position, to take part in any partisan politics."

42Scott, pp. 13-16; *The College Paper*, January, 1905; John Fields to E. A. Bryan, October 24, 1901, "Manuscript Letters," XII, p. 109; John Fields to the Oklahoma A. and M. Regents, September 5, 1903, "Manuscript Letters," XIX, p. 208; A. C. Scott to Chester Long, February 8, 1904, "Manuscript Letters," XXIV, pp. 136-140.

43*The College Paper*, February, 1905; John Fields to J. B. Thoburn, May 6, 1904, "Manuscript Letters," XXII, p. 188.

44"Minutes of the State Board of Agriculture," (Oklahoma State Board of Agriculture, Archives), pp. 24-25.

45*The Stillwater Gazette*, February 21, 1905.

46*The College Paper*, April, 1905.

47John Fields to L. H. Bailey, March 9, 1905, "Manuscript Letters," XXXI, p. 50.

48*Session Laws* (1905), pp. 49-51; *The College Paper*, April, 1905.

[49]John Fields to George L. Bishop, May 15, 1906, "Manuscript Letters," XXXI, p. 50.

[50][Frank Wikoff, "Scrapbook," n.p.] in "The Wikoff Collection"; *The Daily Democrat*, October 18, 1906; November, 1905; *The College Paper*, November, 1906; *The Peoples Press*, September 26, 1907; *The Advance Democrat*, September 28, 1905.

[51]*The Advance Democrat*, November 16, 1905.

[52]Reprinted in *The Advance Democrat*, November 16, 1905.

[53]Scott, p. 18. Details of this law are in Everett Dick, *The Lure of the Lands* (Lincoln, 1970), pp. 213-214.

[54]Scott, p. 18.

[55]"Minutes of the Board of Agriculture," I. pp. 125-151.

[56]*The Breeder's Gazette*, March 17, 1909; Keith Bryant, Jr., *Alfalfa Bill Murray* (Norman, 1968), pp. 45-72.

[57]Scott, p. 19.

[58]*The Stillwater Gazette*, June 8, 1908; *The Peoples Press*, June 4, 1908; *The Farmers Fact and Fancy*, February 22, 1905.

[59][Angelo Scott, "Farewell Address," pp. 6-7] in "The Scott Collection."

[60]A Memorandum dated June 30, 1908, "Manuscript Letters," XXIV, p. 323.

[61]A. C. Scott to J. H. Connell, February 17, 1908, "Manuscript Letters," XXXIX, p. 61; *The Peoples Press*, June 11, 1908.

[67]Undated newsclipping, Kansas University *Graduate Magazine*, "The Scott Collection."

IX

[1]The relationship between the educational and political progressive movements has been neglected by historians. For an overview of the former, see Cremin, *The Transformation of the School*. A survey of the latter is contained in Benjamin Parke De Witt, *The Progressive Movement* (New York, 1915). Recent scholarship may be reviewed in Eric Goldman, *Rendezvous with Destiny* (New York, 1952); Richard Hofstadter, *The Age of Reform* (New York, 1955); and Henry May, *The End of American Innocence* (New York, 1959).

[2]*The Peoples Press*, November 14, 1907.

[3]This point of view is best expressed in the Sequoyah Constitution which served as a model for the Oklahoma Constitution. See, Joseph B. Thoburn and Muriel Wright, *Oklahoma: A History of the State and Its People*, II (New York, 1929), p. 629. Conner's statement may be read in its entirety in *First Biennial Report of the Oklahoma State Board of Agriculture to the Legislature of the State*, Part II (Guthrie, 1908), pp. 1-8.

[4]Gordon Hines, *Alfalfa Bill* (Oklahoma City, 1932), p. 63; Bryant, p. 79; Murray, *Memoirs of Governor Murray and True History of Oklahoma*, II, pp. 125-126; *First Biennial Report of the Oklahoma State Board of Agriculture*, Part I, pp. 7-8.

[5]Murray, *Memoirs of Governor Murray*, II, p. 127.

[6]*Ibid.*, p. 115; Bryant, p. 79; Davidson, p. 80; "Selections from the Record Book," pp. 310-312.

[7]*The Peoples Press*, January 23, 1908.

[8]For a survey of educational changes in Oklahoma as a result of the new constitution, see Paul Monroe, *A Cyclopedia of Education*, I (New York, 1914), pp. 540-545.

[9]*The Peoples Press*, February 13, 1908.

[10]*The New Education*, November 15, 1912.

[11]*Ibid.*, March 1, 1913.

[12]A. P. Posey to author, August 31, 1970, "Author's Collection"; "Selections from the Record Book," p. 44; John F. Hopkins, *The University of Kentucky* (Lexington, 1951), p. 219; Texas A. and M. College, Bulletin No. 8, Clarence Ousley, *History of the Agricultural and Mechanical College of Texas* (College Station, 1913), p. 27.

[13]*The Advance Democrat*, February 27, 1908; March 26, 1908; *The Peoples Press*, April 23, 1908; January 23, 1908; USDA, OES, Miscellaneous

Bulletin No. 30, *Proceedings of the A. A. A. C. E. S.* (Washington, 1896), pp. 32-35.

[14]For example, see "Opening Address to Farmers' Short Course" in *The Peoples Press,* January 28, 1909 and "Agricultural and Industrial Education in Oklahoma" in *First Biennial Report of the Oklahoma State Board of Agriculture* (Guthrie, 1908), pp. 1-23.

[15] Quoted from the reprint in *The New Education,* October 15, 1911.

[16]*The Peoples Press,* September 17, 1908; September 24, 1908; October 22, 1908; November 12, 1908; *The New Education,* December 1, 1912.

[17]*The Stillwater News-Press,* August 24, 1952.

[18]Personal interview by Angie Debo with H. G. Seldomridge, May 22, 1952, "Debo College Collection."

[19]*The Orange and Black,* September, 1909. For further information in regard to the faculty see the various editions of *The Redskin,* the college yearbook. Connell authorized the publication of this document in 1910.

[20]*The Peoples Press,* September 23, 1909; September 15, 1911; September 1, 1913; February 15, 1913.

[21]*Ibid.,* October 15, 1911.

[22]*The New Education,* September 1, 1911; September 21, 1911; *The O'Collegian,* January 12, 1949; *Annual Catalog,* Session of 1909-1910, p. 139.

[23]*The New Education,* September 1, 1911; *The Orange and Black,* April, 1909; *The Redskin,* 1911, pp. 146-147, 150-151.

[24]*The Orange and Black,* November 8, 1908; December 18, 1909; November 9, 1910; February 9, 1910; March 9, 1910; *The Redskin,* 1910, pp. 196-198.

[25]*The Peoples Press,* October 29, 1908; October 1, 1911; September 15, 1911; October 15, 1911, January 15, 1912.

[26]*Ibid.,* March 30, 1911.

[27]Quoted from *The New Education,* December 1, 1913.

[28]*The O'Collegian,* January 13, 1949; November 9, 1941; November 25, 1941; *Annual Catalog,* Session of 1909-1910, pp. 10-11, 21, 54, 139.

[29]*The Peoples Press,* December 31, 1908; September 1, 1912; September 15, 1912; August 15, 1911; October 15, 1913; August 7, 1914.

[30]*The O'Collegian,* April 14, 1942; "Selections from the Record Book," p. 96.

[31]*The Peoples Press,* July 30, 1908; July 1, 1911; September 2, 1909; September 1, 1912; November 15, 1912; October 15, 1911.

[32]Quoted from Philip Dorf, *Liberty Hyde Bailey,* (Ithaca, 1956), p. 150.

[33]*Annual Catalog,* Session of 1910-1911, pp. 60-61.

[34]*The Redskin,* 1912, p. 266; *The Peoples Press,* April 13, 1911.

[35]*The Peoples Press,* April 13, 1911.

[36]*The Redskin,* 1914, pp. 111-120; *The New Education,* December 1, 1912; January 15, 1912.

[37]*The New Education,* July 1, 1911.

[38]*Ibid.,* July 1, 1913.

[39]*Ibid.,* January 1, 1912.

[40]*The Peoples Press,* June 20, 1906.

[41]*The New Education,* August 15, 1913.

[42]*The Orange and Black,* October 26, 1910; November 2, 1910; *The New Education,* October 15, 1911.

[43]Quoted from Gilmore, p. 118, citing OES, *Annual Report,* 1913, p. 72.

[44]*The Stillwater Gazette,* June 10, 1910.

[45]*Ibid.,* April 23, 1909. Also, see April 30, 1909.

[46]*Ibid.,* June 4, 1909.

[47]*Ibid.,* April 8, 1910; May 20, 1910; August 26, 1910.

[48]*Ibid.,* April 29, 1910.

[49]Quoted from *The Peoples Press,* August 11, 1910.

[50]Quoted from *The Stillwater Gazette,* April 29, 1910.

[51]*Ibid.*

[52]*Ibid.,* May 6, 1910; June 16, 1910.

[53]"Selections from the Record Book," p. 86.

[54]Charles Scott to W. A. Tucker, July 4, 1911, "The Tucker Collection,"

(Oklahoma State Board of Agriculture).

[55]G. N. Kneeland to Charles Lamb, July 18, 1911, "The Tucker Collection."

[56]*The Peoples Press*, August 10, 1911.

[57]For details of the meeting, see *The Peoples Press*, August 10, 1911; September 7, 1911, September 21, 1911.

[58]*The Stillwater Gazette*, September 8, 1911.

[59]*Ibid.*, November 3, 1911.

[60]Quoted from *The Peoples Press*, October 5, 1911.

[61]*Ibid.*, December 14, 1912.

[62]*The Stillwater Gazette*, December 15, 1911.

[63]*Ibid.*, September 6, 1912; September 13, 1912; October 11, 1912.

[64]*The New Education*, November 1, 1912; *The Stillwater Gazette*, February 7, 1913; February 21, 1913; April 18, 1913; July 4, 1913; July 25, 1913; January 2, 1914; June 12, 1914.

[65]*The Stillwater Gazette*, December 15, 1911.

[66]Quoted from *The Stillwater Gazette*, November 28, 1913.

[67]*Ibid.*, June 12, 1914; June 19, 1914; June 26, 1914; July 24, 1914; November 20, 1914.

[68]*Ibid.*, July 24, 1914; *Annual Catalog*, Session of 1913-1914, pp. 176-183.

[69]*Biennial Report of the Oklahoma State Board of Agriculture, 1914-1915* (Oklahoma City, 1915), p. 4.

X

[1]E. E. Dale and M. Wardell, *History of Oklahoma* (New York, 1940), pp. 328-329.

[2]Edwin C. McReynolds, *Oklahoma: A History of the Sooner State* (Norman, 1954), pp. 326-327; *The Stillwater Gazette*, April 3, 1914.

[3]*The Stillwater Gazette*, May 8, 1914; November 13, 1914; McReynolds, p. 326.

[4]Thoburn and Wright, II, p. 733.

[5]Insofar as using educational institutions for patronage purposes, the Oklahoma Board of Education operated in a manner similar to the Oklahoma Board of Agriculture. See, Melvin Frank Fiegel, "A History of Southwestern State College, 1903-1953," (unpublished Doctoral dissertation, Oklahoma State University, 1968), *passim*.

[6]*Men of Affairs and Representative Institutions of Oklahoma* (Tulsa, 1916), n.p.

[7]*The Oklahoma Farm Journal*, August 1, 1914.

[8]*Ibid.*, May 15, 1914; "Minutes of the Board of Agriculture," I, p. 488; Personal interview by author with Oliver Willham, July 10, 1971.

[9]"Minutes of the Board of Agriculture," I, pp. 477, 570; *Annual Catalog*, Session of 1913-1914, p. 29; Session of 1914-1915, pp. 116-121, 68-97; *The Stillwater News-Press*, February 9, 1964; Richard Phillips to Author, December 24, 1971; October 26, 1971; February 1, 1972 (Author's Collection).

[10]"Minutes of the Board of Agriculture," I, pp. 473, 481, 485.

[11]*The Orange and Black*, September 28, 1922.

[12]*Annual Catalog*, Session of 1914-1915, p. v; *The Stillwater Gazette*, July 2, 1915; July 10, 1914; "Minutes of the Board of Agriculture," I, p. 481.

[13]*The Redskin*, 1910, pp. 9-10; *The Orange and Black*, October 10, 1914; *The Stillwater Gazette*, September 29, 1922; *The O'Collegian*, October 2, 1927.

[14]*The Stillwater Gazette*, July 24, 1914.

[15]*The Redskin*, 1915, p. 41.

[16]*The Orange and Black*, October 17, 1914; *The Stillwater Gazette*, August 14, 1914; Oklahoma Extension Bulletin, I, No. 5 *Report of the Boys and Girls Clubs in Oklahoma for 1915* (Stillwater 1915), p. 3.

[17]*The Redskin*, 1915, p. 144.

[18]*Ibid.*, p. 150; *The Stillwater Gazette*, October 23, 1914; November 13, 1914; February 5, 1915.

19"Minutes of the Board of Agriculture," II, p. 49, 120-121; *The Orange and Black,* January 9, 1915.

20"Minutes of the Board of Agriculture," II, p. 490; *The Stillwater Gazette,* November 26, 1914; August 6, 1928.

21"Minutes of the Board of Agriculture," I, pp. 582-583; *U. S. Statutes at Large,* XXXVIII, pp. 372-375 (1913-1915). Also, see Edd Roberts, "The History of the Extension Service in Oklahoma," "The OSU Collection."

22*The Stillwater Gazette,* October 30, 1914.

23*Ibid.,* April 16, 1915; *The Orange and Black,* April 16, 1917.

24*The Redskin,* 1914, n.p.

25*The O'Collegian,* September 10, 1925.

26"Minutes of the Board of Agriculture," II, p. 156.

27*Ibid.,* III, p. 305.

28*Ibid.,* II, p. 56.

29*Proceedings of the A. A. A. C. E. S.* (Montpelier, Vt., 1915), p. 14; (Burlington, Vt., 1917), p. 15; (Burlington, Vt., 1916), p. 15. After 1910, the Association of American Agricultural Colleges and Experiment Stations began publishing their own bulletins instead of issuing them through the Office of Experiment Stations. Also, from 1920 to 1954, the organization changed its name several times, finally deciding upon the title American Association of Land-Grant Colleges and State Universities. Subsequent citations will reflect these name changes.

30*The Orange and Black,* June 26, 1915.

31"Minutes of the Board of Agriculture," II, p. 199.

32*Ibid.,* III, pp. 221, 253; *The Stillwater Gazette,* August 6, 1915; October 29, 1916.

33Quoted from *The Stillwater Gazette,* December 7, 1917.

34*Ibid.,* February 1, 1918; *The Orange and Black,* July 12, 1920; March 4, 1916.

35Barbara Schott, "Introducing Carl P. Thompson," *The Oklahoma A. and M. College Magazine,* XIX, No. 4 (1948), p. 11; *The Orange and Black,* May 14, 1917; June 18, 1920; *The Stillwater Gazette,* November 27, 1936.

36H. M. Trimble, "Fifty Years of Chemistry at Oklahoma A. and M. College," (Stillwater, 1942), *passim; The Stillwater Gazette,* August 6, 1920; *The Orange and Black,* February 2, 1922: January 19, 1922.

37*The O'Collegian,* May 20, 1917.

38J. W. Cantwell, "Report of the President," in *Annual Report of the State Board of Agriculture for 1915* (Oklahoma City, 1916), p. 84.

39*The Orange and Black,* September 20, 1915.

40*Ibid.,* September 4, 1915; September 27, 1915; *The Stillwater Gazette,* July 30, 1915; "Minutes of the Board of Agriculture," III, pp. 12-13.

41"Minutes of the Board of Agriculture," III, pp. 78-79.

42*The Stillwater Gazette,* December 31, 1915.

43*Ibid.,* January 14, 1916.

44"Minutes of the Board of Agriculture," III, pp. 85-88, 141, 222-224, 307; *The Stillwater Gazette,* May 19, 1916.

45*The Orange and Black,* May 13, 1916.

46*The Stillwater Gazette,* June 9, 1916.

47Quoted from *The Stillwater Gazette,* May 26, 1916. Also, see Gilmore, pp. 122-133.

48J. W. Cantwell, "Report of the President," in *Annual Report of the Oklahoma State Board of Agriculture* (Oklahoma City, 1917), pp. 44-47. Good background comments on the transition of normal schools to teachers colleges are available in Helen Marshall, *Grandest of Enterprises* (Normal, Illinois, 1956), pp. 247-278 and H. C. Johnson and E. V. Johanningmeier, *Teachers for the Prairie: The University of Illinois and the Schools 1865-1956* (Urbana, 1972).

49"Minutes of the Board of Agriculture," IV, pp. 184-187; *The Orange and Black,* March 24, 1917; *Proceedings of the A. A. A. C. E. S.* (Burlington, 1917), pp. 27, 54; *U. S. Statutes at Large,* XXXVIII, pp. 373-374 (1914).

50Arthur Walworth, *Woodrow Wilson* (Baltimore, 1969), pp. 101-122.

51Henry Steele Commager, *Documents in American History* (New York, 1963), p. 132.

[52]*Proceedings of the A. A. A. C. E. S.* (Burlington, Vt., 1918), p. 34.

[53]Dale and Wardell, pp. 331-332; *The Stillwater Gazette*, January 26, 1918; June 28, 1918; January 11, 1918; January 21, 1918; *The Orange and Black*, October 13, 1917; April 6, 1918; October 27, 1917; April 12, 1918; "Minutes of the Board of Agriculture," IV, pp. 26-28. Also, see Fiegel, pp. 73-94; O. A. Hilton, "The Oklahoma Council of Defense and the First World War," *The Chronicles of Oklahoma*, XX, No. 1 (1942), pp. 18-42; "Public Opinion and Civil Liberties in Wartime, 1917-1919," *The Southwestern Social Science Quarterly*, XXVIII, No. 3 (1947), pp. 201-224.

[54]"Minutes of the Board of Agriculture," IV, pp. 272-273.

[55]J. W. Cantwell, "Report of the President," in *Annual Report of the Oklahoma State Board of Agriculture for 1917* (Oklahoma City, 1918), p. 48.

[56]"Minutes of the Board of Agriculture," IV. pp. 282-283.

[57]*The Stillwater Gazette*, January 10, 1919.

[58]*Ibid.*, November 20, 1925; November 2, 1923; January 4, 1918; "Minutes of the Board of Agriculture," V, pp. 155-156, 26-27, 72-73.

[59]*The Redskin*, 1915, p. 143; *The Stillwater Gazette*, March 1, 1918; *The Orange and Black*, September 8, 1916; "Minutes of the Board of Agriculture," IV, pp. 59-60.

[60]*The Stillwater Gazette*, April 27, 1917; May 4, 1917; May 18, 1917; August 17, 1917.

[61]"Minutes of the Board of Agriculture," V, pp. 214-215, 277-278; VI, pp. 64-66; *The Stillwater Gazette*, September 7, 1918.

[62]Eddy, p. 164.

[63]"Minutes of the Board of Agriculture," VI, pp. 106-107, 183-184, 145-146; *The Stillwater Gazette*, October 4, 1918; *The Orange and Black*, March 11, 1920; *Proceedings of the A. A. A. C. E. S.* (Burlington, Vt., 1920), pp. 30-34.

[64]*The Stillwater Gazette*, September 12, 1919.

[65]"Minutes of the Board of Agriculture," V, pp. 42-43; VII, pp. 198-199; VIII, pp. 156-157; *The Stillwater Gazette*, September 27, 1918; May 7, 1926.

[66]*Proceedings of the A. A. A. C. E. S.* (Burlington, Vt., 1919), pp. 74-79; "Minutes of the Board of Agriculture," VII, p. 267; *The Orange and Black*, September 17, 1919; November, 1921; *The Stillwater Gazette*, December 12, 1919.

[67]*The Stillwater Gazette*, February 25, 1921.

[68]McReynolds, pp. 334-339; *The Stillwater Gazette*, July 9, 1920.

[69]"Minutes of the Board of Agriculture," VII, pp. 183-184.

[70]"In Memoriam: John Whitehurst," *The Oklahoma A. and M. College Magazine*, I, No. 8 (1930), p. 6; *The Orange and Black*, April 12, 1919; George Whitehurst to Henry S. Johnston, July 2, 1918, "The Johnston Collection," (Oklahoma State University).

[71]"Minutes of the Board of Agriculture," V, pp. 298-299, 300-302; VI, pp. 201-203, 268-269; *The Stillwater Gazette*, January 31, 1919.

[72]*The Stillwater Gazette*, April 4, 1919.

[73]*Ibid.*, June 20, 1919.

[74]*Ibid.*, July 9, 1920; "Minutes of the Board of Agriculture," IX, 97-98; VIII, pp. 296-299; VII, p. 27-28, 62-63.

[75]*The Stillwater Gazette*, May 28, 1920.

[76]*The Orange and Black*, July 2, 1920.

[77]"Minutes of the Board of Agriculture," IX, pp. 137-141.

[78]*Oklahoma Session Laws*, (1921), p. 236; *The Stillwater Gazette*, April 8, 1921; December 21, 1928; "Minutes of the Board of Agriculture," IX, pp. 265-266; 313-314.

[79]"Minutes of the Board of Agriculture," X, pp. 7-9; *The Orange and Black*, September 22, 1921; *The Stillwater Gazette*, January 13, 1922; March 9, 1923; April 3, 1931.

[80]*The Stillwater Gazette*, April 10, 1931.

XI

[1]Hilton, "The Oklahoma Council of Defense and the First World War," pp. 18-42.

[2]Sheldon Neuringer, "Governor Walton's War on the Ku Klux Klan: An Episode in Oklahoma History," *The Chronicles of Oklahoma,* XLV, No. 2 (1967), p. 154.

[3]McReynolds, p. 343; Thoburn and Wright, II, p. 697.

[4]Angie Debo, *From Creek Town to Oil Capitol* (Norman, 1943), p. 101.

[5]*Proceedings of the Association of Land-Grant Colleges* (Burlington, Vermont, 1922), pp. 19-20.

[6]*Ibid.,* 1923, p. 35. Hereafter, this citation will read *Proceedings of the A. L. G. C.*

[7]*The Stillwater Gazette,* April 22, 1921; *The Redskin,* 1923; "Ninth A. and M. President is Dead," *The Oklahoma A. and M. College Magazine,* XXIII, No. 9 (1952), p. 17; *Who's Who in America,* XIX, p. 826.

[8]*The Oklahoman,* May 16, 1921; April 26, 1921; Fiegel, p. 109; *The Stillwater Gazette,* April 22, 1921; "Ninth President is Dead," p. 17.

[9]See, for example, J. B. Eskridge to Henry S. Johnston, May 21, 1917, "The Johnston Collection"; Fiegel, pp. 80-84.

[10]Fiegel, p. 104.

[11]*The Orange and Black,* December 15, 1921; *The O'Collegian,* February 6, 1942; "Minutes of the Board of Agriculture," X, pp. 166-168; Personal interview by author with Oliver Willham, July 10, 1971.

[12]*The Stillwater Gazette,* June 10, 1921; July 22, 1921; *The Oklahoman,* September 2, 1921.

[13]*The Tulsa World,* October 2, 1921.

[14]"Minutes of the Board of Agriculture," X, pp. 57-60, 118, 200-206; *The Orange and Black,* September 22, 1921; *The Stillwater Gazette,* October 20, 1922.

[15]*The Orange and Black,* September 15, 1921.

[16]*Ibid.,* October 20, 1921; November 3, 1921; October 27, 1921; *The Stillwater Gazette,* October 28, 1921.

[17]*The Stillwater Gazette,* November 4, 1921.

[18]*Ibid.* The complete text of the speech is not available.

[19]*Proceedings of the A. L. G. C.* (Burlington, Vermont, 1922), p. 12.

[20]*Annual Catalog.* Session of 1920-1921, p. 111; "Minutes of the Board of Agriculture," X, p. 236; *The Orange and Black,* November 3, 1921; *The Stillwater Gazette,* February 3, 1922; September 9, 1922; June 28, 1935; December 17, 1927; "A. and M. Is His Life," *The Oklahoma A. and M. College Magazine,* XXIV, No. 4 (1952), pp. 17-19.

[21]*The Stillwater Gazette,* June 14, 1918; May 3, 1918; *The Orange and Black,* July 9, 1918; February 10, 1917; July 2, 1917; November 2, 1918; *The Redskin,* 1919, pp. 38-39. Also, see *Extension Division Circulars,* 17, 18, 20, 21, 22, 23, 24, 25, 26, 27, 29, 31 (Stillwater, 1916).

[22]*The Orange and Black,* September 15, 1921; November 10, 1921.

[23]*Ibid.,* December 22, 1921.

[24]*Ibid.,* October 6, 1921; February 2, 1922; September 21, 1922.

[25]*Ibid.,* November 16, 1922; November 24, 1922.

[26]H. N. MacCracken, "Religio Magistri," *Atlantic Monthly,* CXXVII, No. 1 (1921), pp. 76-84.

[27]"The Oklahoma Educational Survey Commission," *School and Society,* XIV, No. 366 (1921), p. 637.

[28]*Ibid.*

[29]*The Orange and Black,* March 4, 1916; July 12, 1920; December 8, 1921; *The Agricultural News Service,* December 3, 1928; *The Stillwater Gazette,* July 28, 1922; "Minutes of the Board of Agriculture," IV, pp. 308-309.

[30]H. Patterson, "Can College Teaching Be Improved?" *Educational Review,* 64, No. 1 (1922), pp. 68-73; "An Experiment in Supervising College Teaching," *School and Society,* XXI, No. 527 (1925), pp. 146-147; "An Experiment in Automatic Spelling," *School and Society,* XVII, No. 444 (1923), pp. 719-720; "Teaching Ethics Through Manual Training," *School*

and *Society,* XVI, No. 415 (1922), pp. 650-653; "A New Approach to the 'Formal Discipline' Controversy," *School and Society,* XII, No. 307 (1920), pp. 471-473; "Common Sense and Teachers' Contracts," *School and Society,* X, No. 254 (1919), pp. 553-556.

[31]*The Orange and Black,* April 23, 1922; "Minutes of the Board of Agriculture," XI, pp. 24-25, 54-56, 161; The *Stillwater Gazette,* February 17, 1922.

[32]"Minutes of the Board of Agriculture," XI, p. 177; *The Stillwater Gazette,* January 19, 1923; January 26, 1923; September 8, 1922; November 17, 1922.

[33]Neuringer, pp. 153-158.

[34]Gilbert Fite, "The Non Partisan League in Oklahoma," *The Chronicles of Oklahoma,* XXIV, No. 2 (1946), pp. 146-157; *The Stillwater Gazette,* June 16, 1922; August 11, 1922; October 20, 1922; April 27, 1923; January 12, 1923.

[35]Dale and Wardell, p. 337; *The Stillwater Gazette,* January 19, 1923; March 30, 1923; February 2, 1923; February 9, 1923; March 2, 1923; March 23, 1923.

[36]*The Stillwater Gazette,* April 20, 1923.

[37]McReynolds, pp. 343-344; "Minutes of the Board of Agriculture," I, p. 390; V, p. 158; *The O'Collegian,* February 1, 1925.

[38]*The Stillwater Gazette,* May 11, 1923.

[39]"Minutes of the Board of Agriculture," XIII, pp. 1-2.

[40]*The Stillwater Gazette,* May 25, 1923.

[41]*The Orange and Black,* May 10, 1923; *The Stillwater Gazette,* May 18, 1923.

[42]*The Stillwater Gazette,* May 25, 1923.

[43]*Ibid.,* June 1, 1923; May 25, 1923.

[44]*The Oklahoma Farmer,* June 10, 1923.

[45]*The Stillwater Gazette,* May 11, 1923.

[46]*Ibid.,* May 11, 1923.

[47]*The O'Collegian,* February 1, 1925; *The Stillwater Gazette,* May 25, 1923; June 8, 1923.

[48]*The Stillwater Gazette,* June 8, 1923.

[49]Personal interview by author with Oliver Willham, July 10, 1971.

[50]See reprints in *The Stillwater Gazette,* June 8, 1923; May 25, 1923.

[51]*The Wichita Daily Eagle,* June 5, 1923.

[52]*Ibid.,* June 6, 1923.

[53]*The Stillwater Gazette,* June 8, 1923; "Minutes of the Board of Agriculture," I. p. 608.

[54]*The Stillwater Gazette,* June 8, 1923.

[55]*Ibid.,* May 25, 1923.

[56]"Minutes of the Board of Agriculture," XIII, p. 64.

[57]*The Stillwater Gazette,* June 8, 1923.

[58]"Minutes of the Board of Agriculture," XIII, pp. 83-89, 90-91; *The Stillwater Gazette,* July 20, 1923.

[59]*The New York Times,* July 25, 1923; July 26, 1923; July 28, 1923; *The Stillwater Gazette,* July 27, 1923; August 3, 1923; *The O'Collegian,* March 27, 1942.

[60]*The O'Collegian,* April 1, 1942.

[61]*The Stillwater Gazette,* August 17, 1923; August 24, 1923; "Minutes of the Board of Agriculture," XIII, pp. 72-75.

[62]"Minutes of the Board of Agriculture," I, p. 164; III, p. 274; V, p. 113; *The Stillwater Gazette,* September 28, 1922.

[63]"Minutes of the Board of Agriculture," XI, p. 288.

[64]*The Stillwater Gazette,* June 1, 1923; June 8, 1923; "Minutes of the Board of Agriculture," XIII, pp. 72-75.

[65]*The Stillwater Gazette,* January 4, 1924.

[66]*Ibid.,* January 18, 1924.

[67]*The Stillwater Gazette,* February 22, 1924; May 16, 1924; May 23, 1924; February 13, 1925; March 6, 1925; June 27, 1928; November 3, 1933.

[68]Neuringer, pp. 170-175; Extraordinary Session of the Senate, Ninth

Oklahoma Legislature, *Transcript of Impeachment Proceedings,* October-November, 1923 (Oklahoma City, 1924), pp. 19-55.

[69]*The Stillwater Gazette,* November 2, 1923; April 11, 1924; *The O'Collegian,* February 1, 1925.

XII

[1]Joseph Bailey, *Seaman A. Knapp: Schoolmaster to American Agriculture* (New York, 1945), p. 79; C. R. Barnett, "Seaman Knapp" in *Dictionary of American Biography,* X, Dumas Malone, ed. (New York, 1933), pp. 452-453; Lincoln D. Kelsey, *Cooperative Extension Work* (Ithaca, 1955), p. 17; M .C. Barritt, *The County Agent and the Farm Bureau* (New York, 1922), pp. 33, 153, 172, 176; Ronald J. Slay, *The Development of the Teaching of Agriculture in Mississippi* (New York, 1928), pp. 73-76; R. K. Bliss (ed.), *The Spirit and Philosophy of Extension Work* (Washington, 1952), pp. 185-195; *The O'Collegian,* February 1, 1925; *Proceedings of the A. L. G. S.* (Burlington, 1925), p. 56.

[2]Earle D. Ross, *The Land-Grant Idea at Iowa State College* (Ames, 1958), pp. 71, 77, 169, 186-188; *Who's Who in America,* XIV, p. 1127; *National Cyclopedia of American Biography,* XXXIV, pp. 285-286; *The Stillwater Gazette,* April 23, 1926; June 8, 1928; October 1, 1926; *The O'Collegian,* September 19, 1927.

[3]Bailey, p. 86.

[4]*The O'Collegian,* December 5, 1924; June 25, 1925; December 19, 1925; *Annual Catalog,* Session of 1922-1923, p. 5.

[5]*The O'Collegian,* October 17, 1925.

[6]*Ibid.,* September 28, 1926.

[7]*The Orange and Black,* January 16, 1915; *The Stillwater Gazette,* September 14, 1925.

[8]*Proceedings of the A. A. A. C. E. S.* (Montpelier, 1915), pp. 203-213; *Ibid.,* (Burlington, 1917) pp. 305-311; *Ibid.,* (Burlington, 1920), pp. 266-271; *Library of Congress Printed Cards,* Number 81 (Paterson, 1963), p. 300; *Who's Who in American Education,* II (New York, 1930), p. 414; *National Cyclopdedia of American Biography,* XXXIV, pp. 285-286; *The Stillwater Gazette,* July 31, 1925.

[9]*The Stillwater Gazette,* September 14, 1923; "Minutes of the Board of Agriculture," XIII, p. 125; XIX, pp. 48-49.

[10]Quoted from *The Stillwater Gazette,* September 14, 1923.

[11]*The O'Collegian,* March 18, 1928; October 26, 1926; *The Stillwater Gazette,* September 14, 1923.

[12]Helen Freudenberge, "Records and Reminiscences," *The Oklahoma A. and M. College Magazine,* VIII, No. 4 (1937), p. 13. Also, see *The O'Collegian,* December 14, 1936.

[13]*The Stillwater Gazette,* October 10, 1924; July 24, 1924; July 25, 1924; October 12, 1923; October 16, 1923; *The Oklahoma City Farmer,* September 25, 1923; *The O'Collegian,* January 29, 1925.

[14]*The Stillwater Gazette,* October 19, 1923; January 25, 1924; February 27, 1925; November 16, 1923; *The O'Collegian,* March 16, 1924.

[15]*The O'Collegian,* April 29, 1925.

[16]*Ibid.,* December 15, 1927.

[17]Personal interview by author with Oliver S. Willham, July 8, 1971; "Minutes of the Board of Agriculture," XVII, pp. 243-244; XIX, pp. 48-49; XV, pp. 40, 90.

[18]"Minutes of the Board of Agriculture," XX, pp. 315.

[19]*The Stillwater Gazette,* January 8, 1926; "Minutes of the Board of Agriculture," XIII, pp. 26-27; XVIII, pp. 32-34; XIV, pp. 193-194, 70-72, 267-269.

[20]*The Stillwater Gazette,* June 4, 1926; November 5, 1926; May 7, 1926; *The O'Collegian,* February 1, 1928.

[21]*The Stillwater Gazette,* September 21, 1923.

[22]*The O'Collegian,* October 22, 1925; *The Stillwater Gazette,* December

28, 1923; January 4, 1924; November 9, 1924; June 3, 1927; "Minutes of the Board of Agriculture," XIX, p. 247.

23The O'Collegian, September 17, 1925; April 19, 1925; October 23, 1927; October 27, 1923; October 30, 1927; The Oklahoma City Times, April 17, 1925.

24The O'Collegian, November 10, 1927.

25Ibid., April 19, 1925.

26The Stillwater Gazette, March 14, 1924; July 24, 1924; April 22, 1927; July 18, 1924; The O'Collegian, September 17, 1927.

27"Minutes of the Board of Agriculture," XVI, pp. 50-51.

28Ibid., XV, pp. 191-192.

29Quoted from The Stillwater Gazette, December 11, 1925.

30Ibid., July 11, 1924; "Minutes of the Board of Agriculture," XVII. pp. 139-142.

31"Minutes of the Board of Agriculture," XX, pp. 214-215.

32The O'Collegian, September 25, 1924; November 9, 1924; March 18, 1925; The Stillwater Gazette, January 23, 1925; "Minutes of the Board of Agriculture," XIII, pp. 167-168.

33The O'Collegian, October 6, 1926; September 22, 1925.

34"Minutes of the Board of Agriculture," XVII, pp. 322-323; The O'Collegian, September 17, 1926; October 29, 1927.

35The O'Collegian, January 8, 1927; February 7, 1928; September 30, 1927; December 9, 1927; The Agricultural News Service, August 22, 1927.

36Jerome L. Rodnitzky, "Getting the Ear of the State: A Pioneer University Radio Station in the 1920's," The History of Education Quarterly, VIII, No. 4 (1968), pp. 505-509.

37The O'Collegian, January 13, 1925; March 21, 1925.

38The Stillwater Gazette, October 23, 1925.

39The Agricultural News Service, September 5, 1927; The O'Collegian, April 7, 1925; April 18, 1925; October 5, 1926; The Stillwater Gazette, April 17, 1925; June 11, 1926; October 8, 1926.

40The O'Collegian, January 24, 1925.

41The Agricultural News Service, May 31, 1926; The O'Collegian, February 25, 1925; January 20, 1928; The Stillwater Gazette, March 12, 1926; August 22, 1924; "Minutes of the Board of Agriculture," XIX, pp. 109-112; Berlin Chapman, "Old Central of Oklahoma State University," The Chronicles of Oklahoma, XLII, No. 3 (1964), pp. 273-290.

42The O'Collegian, February 8, 1925; The Stillwater Gazette, February 13, 1925.

43The Stillwater Gazette, July 16, 1926.

44"Minutes of the Board of Agriculture," XVI, p. 287.

45Ibid., p. 197.

46The O'Collegian, July 19, 1925.

47George F. Herod, "The Administration, Impeachment, and Removal of Governor Henry S. Johnston," (unpublished MA thesis, Tulsa University, 1962), pp. 1-4; The Stillwater Gazette, April 22, 1927.

48McReynolds, p. 357; Dale and Wardell, p. 349; Herod, p. 39.

49The Stillwater Gazette, June 10, 1927.

50Ibid., January 14, 1937; November 13, 1931; "Minutes of the Board of Agriculture," XVIII, p. 87; Personal interview by author with Oliver S. Willham, July 8, 1971.

51"Minutes of the Board of Agriculture," XVIII, p. 178.

52The O'Collegian, September 13, 1927; September 14, 1927; October 8, 1926; The Stillwater Gazette, October 15, 1926.

53"Minutes of the Board of Agriculture," XX, pp. 71-76; The Stillwater Gazette, April 7, 1927.

54The Stillwater Gazette, October 15, 1926; The O'Collegian, June 11, 1925; October 14, 1925; October 29, 1925; February 8, 1927; February 9, 1927; December 20, 1927; April 1, 1927.

55The O'Collegian, October 14, 1925; February 16, 1927; December 19, 1924; January 26, 1927; April 3, 1927.

56Ibid., January 14, 1927.

57*Ibid.*, January 19, 1927.
58*Ibid.*, February 18, 1927.
59*Ibid.*, May 4, 1927.
60*Ibid.*, May 29, 1927.
61"Minutes of the Board of Agriculture," XIX, p. 203; *The O'Collegian*, May 4, 1927.
62Bradford Knapp, "Policies on Finances and Appointments to the State Board of Agriculture," in "Minutes of the Board of Agriculture," XVIII, p. 150.
63*Ibid.*, p. 48.
64*The Stillwater Gazette*, June 17, 1927.
65Fiegel, p. 130; *The Stillwater Gazette*, July 15, 1927; *The O'Collegian*, September 28, 1927; October 14, 1927; December 13, 1927.
66Dale and Wardell, p. 349; Herod, p. 118; "Minutes of the Board of Agriculture," XXI, p. 104; *The O'Collegian*, February 26, 1928; *The Stillwater Gazette*, March 23, 1928.
67*The O'Collegian*, March 1, 1928.
68*The Stillwater Gazette*, March 23, 1928; March 15, 1928; *The O'Collegian*, March 18, 1928; March 20, 1928; March 2, 1928; April 27, 1928; "Minutes of the Board of Agriculture," XXI.
69"Minutes of the Board of Agriculture," XXI, pp. 51-52.
70*The Stillwater Gazette*, March 30, 1928; April 13, 1928.
71*The Stillwater Gazette*, May 18, 1928; June 1, 1928; *The O'Collegian*, May 24, 1928; Berlin Chapman, "Dr. Henry G. Bennett As I Knew Him" *The Chronicles of Oklahoma*, XXXIII, No. 2 (1955), p. 159.
72*The Stillwater Gazette*, June 8, 1928; July 22, 1932; "Dr. Bradford Knapp," *The Oklahoma A. and M. College Magazine*, I, No. 9 (1938), p. 12.
73Ruth Horn Andrews, *The First Thirty Years: A History of Texas Technological College*, 1925-1955 (Lubbock, 1956), p. 49.

XIII

1Rush Welter, *Popular Education and Democratic Thought in America* (New York, 1962), p. 303.
2Quoted from Andrew Turnbull (ed.), *The Letters of F. Scott Fitzgerald* (New York, 1963), p. 74.
3B. H. Lehman, *Wild Marriage* (New York, 1925), pp. 1-324; *The O'Collegian*, January 27, 1925.
4Max Heirich and Sam Kaplan, "Yesterday's Discord," in *The Berkeley Student Revolt*, S. M. Lipset and Sheldon Wolin, eds. (Garden City, 1965), p. 10.
5Calvin B. T. Lee, *The Campus Scene, 1900-1970* (New York, 1970), p. 11.
6Lehman, p. 324.
7"Theta Pond Gets A Facial," *The Oklahoma A. and M. College Magazine*, XV, No. 6 (1944), p. 8; *The O'Collegian*, June 12, 1953.
8*The Orange and Black*, September 26, 1914; *The O'Collegian*, October 27, 1925; *The Stillwater Gazette*, February 9, 1923; April 8, 1921.
9*The Redskin*, 1929, pp. 296-299; *The Orange and Black*, March 11, 1920.
10*The Stillwater Gazette*, February 23, 1923.
11*The O'Collegian*, March 5, 1953.
12*The Redskin*, 1919, pp. 81, 89, 101, 137, 249; 1920, pp. 258, 260; *The Orange and Black*, November 12, 1919; November 26, 1919; September 24, 1919; October 22, 1919.
13*The Redskin*, 1920, pp. 79, 284, 277; *The Orange and Black*, March 24, 1920; *The O'Collegian*, March 5, 1953.
14See Glenn Shirley, *Pawnee Bill: A Biography of Major Gordon W. Lillie* (Albuquerque, 1958).
15Frank Martin, "Dick Tracy's Creator," *The Oklahoma A. and M. College Magazine*, IX, No. 5 (1938), p. 6.

[16]*Ibid.,* For a brief analysis of the Dick Tracy comic strip, see William H. Young, Jr., "The Serious Funnies: Adventure Comics During the Depression, 1929-1938" in *Things in the Driver's Seat: Readings in Popular Culture,* H. R. Huebel, ed. (Chicago, 1972), pp. 85-87.

[17]*The O'Collegian,* May 9, 1953; Personal interview by author with Oliver Willham, July 8, 1971.

[18]Oliver Willham, "Early Days at the Oklahoma A. and M. College," (Oklahoma State University), p. 3.

[19]*Ibid.,* pp. 7, 8; Personal interview by author with Oliver Willham, July 8, 1971; Oliver Willham, "Twentieth Anniversary Report," *The Oklahoma A. and M. College Magazine,* XIV, No. 9 (1943), p. 4.

[20]Personal interview by author with Oliver Willham, July 8, 1971; "A. and M's New President," *The Oklahoma A. and M. College Magazine,* XXIII, No. 8 (April, 1952), pp. 8-10.

[21]"Graduate School Offerings at A. and M.," *The Oklahoma A. and M. College Magazine,* XXIV, No. 7 (1953), p. 12.

[22]*Annual Catalog,* Session of 1911-1912, p. 14.

[23]Wendall Hagood, "The Graduate School Grows," *The Oklahoma A. and M. College Magazine,* I, No. 7 (1930), pp. 11, 27, 29.

[24]For background on the development of graduate education in the United States, see Richard Storr, *The Beginnings of Graduate Education* (Chicago, 1953) and Jurgen Herbst, *The German Historical School in American Scholarship* (Ithaca, 1965).

[25]*Annual Catalog,* Session of 1914-1915, pp. 10-11; *The Stillwater Gazette,* August 24, 1920.

[26]"Stillwater and A. and M. College Booster," *The Oklahoma A. and M. College Magazine,* VI, No. 1 (1934), p. 16.

[27]"Minutes of the Board of Agriculture," XVIII, pp. 35-40; *The O'Collegian,* September 10, 1925; February 18, 1925; October 2, 1927; October 9, 1925; December 17, 1927.

[28]Hagood, pp. 11, 27, 29; *The O'Collegian,* October 9, 1926; November 13, 1927; June 9, 1953; January 4, 1953.

[29]"Minutes of the Board of Agriculture," XII, p. 213: *The Orange and Black,* April 27, 1922; *The Stillwater Gazette,* July 2, 1926; May 24, 1920; June 15, 1923.

[30]*The Stillwater Gazette,* August 9, 1929; Lawrence Thompson, "Poor Boys Get a Break," *The Oklahoma A. and M. College Magazine,* I, No. 1 (1929), p. 19.

[31]*The Stillwater Gazette,* January 17, 1930; June 20, 1930; January 24, 1930; May 9, 1930; June 27, 1930.

[32]*Ibid.,* August 23, 1929; February 7, 1930; March 7, 1930.

[33]*The Orange and Black,* April 10, 1915; May 8, 1915; September 20, 1915.

[34]Quoted from *The Orange and Black,* September 13, 1915.

[35]*The O'Collegian,* April 3, 1925; April 17, 1925; October 16, 1925.

[36]"Minutes of the Board of Agriculture," XV, p. 90; *The O'Collegian,* September 4, 1924.

[37]*The O'Collegian,* September 14, 1924.

[38]*The Stillwater Gazette,* January 3, 1930; July 8, 1932.

[39]*The Stillwater Gazette,* April 25, 1914.

[40]*The Redskin,* 1910, p. 16.

[41]*The Orange and Black,* September 22, 1921.

[42]*Ibid.,* October 6, 1921; September 22, 1921.

[43]*Ibid.,* September 4, 1915; February 23, 1918; October 13, 1921; *The Stillwater Gazette,* October 24, 1919; *The O'Collegian,* September 5, 1925.

[44]*The O'Collegian,* October 4, 1925.

[45]*Ibid.,* September 11, 1925; September 30, 1925; December 16, 1925; December 13, 1925; April 11, 1929; November 1, 1925; January 1, 1926; October 13, 1926; *The Agricultural News Service,* July 19, 1926.

[46]Undated newsclipping in "YMCA Scrapbook," (Oklahoma State University), n.p.; *The O'Collegian,* September 21, 1929.

47*The O'Collegian,* February 28, 1953.

48*Ibid.,* October 3, 1925; January 7, 1925; *The Stillwater Gazette,* October 2, 1931; October 19, 1923; May 18, 1923; December 16, 1932; *The Orange and Black,* March 4, 1920.

49*The Orange and Black,* November 6, 1916; September 22, 1917; March 24, 1920; May 20, 1920; September 10, 1919; *The Stillwater Gazette,* September 12, 1919; *The Redskin,* 1929, pp. 313-330.

50*The Orange and Black,* October 9, 1916; March 4, 1916; February 4, 1920.

51*The Redskin,* 1929, pp. 364-381.

52*The Stillwater Gazette,* October 30, 1936; February 25, 1921; *The Orange and Black,* February 2, 1922. Geneva Holcomb, "Makovsky: The Man and the Musician," *The Oklahoma A. and M. College Magazine,* II, No. 1 (1930), pp. 8-9, 19.

53*The Orange and Black,* April 29, 1920.

54For example, see *The O'Collegian,* March 31, 1925 and April 4, 1925.

55*The Orange and Black,* September 4, 1915; *The Stillwater Gazette,* September 10, 1915; *The O'Collegian,* October 16, 1954; B. B. Chapman, "Living Cowboy Emblem," *The Oklahoma A. and M. College Magazine,* XXVI, No. 5 (1955), p. 1. Also, see Frank Eaton, *Pistol Pete: Veteran of the Old West* (Boston, 1952).

56*The Orange and Black,* December 2, 1914; October 6, 1921; *The Stillwater Gazette,* December 11, 1914; December 2, 1922; *The O'Collegian,* December 7, 1924; September 30, 1927. For a detailed history of sports, see Otis Wile, "The Chronological Story of Sports at Oklahoma State University from the Beginning in the 1890's Through the 1960's" (Oklahoma State University).

57*The Stillwater Gazette,* October 31, 1919; July 18, 1924; *The Orange and Black,* October 9, 1916; November 5, 1919.

58"Minutes of the Board of Agriculture," I, p. 282; *The Orange and Black,* October 3, 1914; June 12, 1915; *The Redskin,* 1918, pp. 169-171.

59*The Orange and Black,* December 6, 1915; November 25, 1916; September 20, 1915.

60*The Redskin,* 1916, p. 132.

61*The Orange and Black,* September 8, 1917.

62*The Redskin,* 1918, p. 46; 1920, p. 188; 1921, p. 193; *The Orange and Black,* December 1, 1917.

63*The Stillwater Gazette,* May 24, 1919; December 3, 1926; *The O'Collegian,* January 22, 1927; *The Redskin,* 1925, pp. 202-216; 1927, p. 244; 1928, pp. 247-253; 1923, p. 99; 1929, p. 249.

64*The Redskin,* 1929, Preface.

65*The Stillwater Gazette,* May 24, 1929; *The O'Collegian,* May 9, 1920; October 15, 1926; *The Redskin,* 1930, p. 211; "Minutes of the Board of Agriculture," XIX, pp. 309-314; "Waldorf Takes Place with Kansas Aggies," *The Oklahoma A. and M. College Magazine,* V, No. 7 (1934), p. 7.

66*The Redskin,* 1915, p. 184; 1917, p. 128.

67*Ibid.,* 1920, p. 210; 1921, p. 206; 1922, p. 76.

68*Ibid.,* 1923, p. 120; 1924, p. 125; 1925, pp. 214-215; 1926, pp. 200-204; 1927, pp. 256-260; 1928, pp. 256-257; 1929, pp. 264-266; 1930, pp. 224-226; 1931, p. 358.

69*The Daily Oklahoman,* December 25, 1951; *The Redskin,* 1935, p. 190.

70*The Redskin,* 1915, pp. 197-206; 1919, p. 136; 1922, pp. 66-70; 1927, p. 241; 1929, pp. 284-286; 1931, p. 363.

71Melvin Sidney Anderson, "History of Wrestling at Oklahoma Agricultural and Mechanical College: Brief Biography of Edward Clark Gallagher" (unpublished M. A. thesis, Oklahoma Agricultural and Mechanical College, 1935), pp. 15, 45-46. Also, see E. C. Gallagher, *Amateur Wrestling* (Guthrie, 1925), pp. 1-35 and *Wrestling* (New York, 1939), p. 1-91.

72Anderson, pp. 7-14.

73*Ibid.,* p. 15.

74*Ibid.,* p. 16.

[75]Bennie L. DeWitt, "Oklahomans' Attitude Toward John Steinbeck Since 1937," *Proceedings of the Oklahoma Academy of Science,* XLVII (1968), pp. 303-307.

XIV

[1]"Minutes of the Board of Agriculture," XIX, p. 263; *The O'Collegian,* March 20, 1928; March 25, 1928; *The Stillwater Gazette,* March 23, 1928; *Harlow's Weekly,* May 19, 1928.

[2]"Minutes of the Board of Agriculture," XIX, p. 264.

[3]Dial Currin, *Beyond the Gold Fields* (Stillwater, 1951), p. 1.

[4]*The Stillwater Gazette,* June 8, 1928.

[5]*The New York* (New York) *Herald Tribune,* January 1, 1940. Also, see William G. Ariett, "Double Birthday," *The Oklahoma A. and M. College Magazine,* XXI, No. 7 (1950), pp. 5, 8-9; *The Stillwater Gazette,* December 13, 1934.

[6]Thoburn and Wright, IV, p. 806; Frank Taylor to Author, February 22, 1972 (Author's Library); "Lifetime Land-Grant Missionary," *The Oklahoma A. and M. College Magazine,* XXIII, No. 6 (1952), p. 5; *The O'Collegian,* June 5, 1928; *The Stillwater Gazette,* September 21, 1928; October 5, 1928; *The Stillwater News-Press,* December 24, 1951.

[7]*The Oklahoman,* December 25, 1951; "Lifetime Land-Grant Missionary," pp. 5-6.

[8]*The O'Collegian,* December 14, 1927; "Lifetime Land-Grant Missionary," pp. 28-29; *The Stillwater Gazette,* July 6, 1928; *The Stillwater News-Press,* December 24, 1951.

[9]"Lifetime Land-Grant Missionary," p. 6; *The O'Collegian,* June 5, 1928; June 30, 1928; *Harlow's Weekly,* November 10, 1928, pp. 6-8.

[10](Henry Bennett, "What Makes a College Great," p. 2) in Box 1 "The Henry Bennett Speech Collection," (Oklahoma State University).

[11] H. G. Bennett, *The Coordination of the State Institutions for Higher Education in Oklahoma* (Durant, 1926); (Thomas Briggs to Henry Bennett, February 3, 1931) File Folder "Dr. Thomas Briggs," "The OSU Collection"; (Henry Bennett, "Aspirations and Achievements of Oklahoma Public Education, pp. 3-4) in Box 1 "The Bennett Speech Collection;" *The O'Collegian,* February 1, 1933; *The Stillwater Gazette,* July 6, 1928.
Strayer, in collaboration with N. L. Englehardt [and others] wrote dozens of books on educational administration. About two dozen of the most important titles are in the Oklahoma State University Library and bear accession numbers which date them as being purchased during the Bennett administration. Strayer's educational philosophy is contained in G. D. Strayer and Edward S. Evenden, *Syllabus of a Course in the Principles of Educational Administration* (New York, 1912).

[12]Schoolmen from southeastern Oklahoma came to dominate both public and higher education in Oklahoma. Ferman Phillips, G. T. Stubbs, Farris E. Willingham, Clark White, A. L. Bondurant, Bill Gillham, A. L. Crable, and Russell Conway are examples of men from this section who were instrumental in shaping the influential Oklahoma Education Association. Their backgrounds and accomplishments are detailed in Joe Hubbell, "A History of the Oklahoma Education Association, 1945-1965," (unpublished Doctoral dissertation, Oklahoma State University, 1970), *passim.* Henry Bennett, Schiller Scroggs, Dial Currin, M. A. Nash, Napoleon Conger, Elijah Dunlap, and Forrest McIntire are representative of the Little Dixie element who headed colleges or served in important positions for the Oklahoma State Regents for Higher Education. Ferman Phillips, long time executive of the Oklahoma Education Association, was offered a state college presidency, provided he was "cleared" by Henry Bennett. He believed that no one was appointed to these jobs unless they had Bennett's personal approval. Joe Hubbell to Author, August 29, 1972 (Author's Collection).

[13](A. O. Martin, "The Ancient and Beneficient Order of the Red Red Rose," p. 9) in "The Red Red Rose Collection" (Oklahoma State University). Also, see A. DeWitt Hanry to Roy R. Tompkins, February 14, 1953; Hilton

Ira Jones to Roy R. Tompkins, February 24, 1953 in "The Red Red Rose Collection."

[14](E. C. Foster, "Order of the Red Red Rose," p. 53) in "The Red Red Rose Collection."

[15]"Minutes of the Board of Agriculture," XXI, June 1, 1928, p. 269; *The O'Collegian,* June 8, 1928.

[16]*The O'Collegian,* June 30, 1928.

[17]*Ibid.,* June 5, 1928; June 12, 1928; June 30, 1928.

[18]"Minutes of the Board of Agriculture," XXII. p. 28. Bennett promised the residents of Stillwater that he would introduce such a statement. *The Stillwater Gazette,* July 6, 1928.

[19]Randle Perdue, "That Man Bennett," *The Oklahoma A. and M. College Magazine,* I, No. 1 (1929), p. 8, 29; "Minutes of the Board of Agriculture," XXI, pp. 286-287; *The Stillwater Gazette,* August 10, 1928; September 21, 1928; August 8, 1930; January 9, 1931. An example of a speech written for Governor Holloway is (Henry Bennett, "The Oklahoma University Library") in Box 6 "The Bennett Speech Collection." It also is obvious that the section of Holloway's address to the Twelfth Oklahoma Legislature which deals with higher education coordination was written by Bennett. The speech may be read in *Harlow's Weekly,* May 18, 1929.

[20]*The Stillwater Gazette,* September 30, 1932; December 5, 1930; January 17, 1930.

[21]Personal interview by author with Oliver Willham, July 10, 1971.

[22]"Lifetime Land-Grant Missionary," p. 7; "Minutes of the Board of Agriculture," XXXI, pp. 174, 250; XXXIV, p. 97;*The O'Collegian,* January 6, 1933; September 17, 1936; *The Stillwater Gazette,* January 24, 1930; June 7, 1935; (Henry Bennett, "I Had a Friend," p. 1) in Box 6 "The Bennett Speech Collection."

[23]"Minutes of the Board of Agriculture," XXI, p. 5; XLIII, p. 158; *The Stillwater Gazette,* June 16, 1933; Otis Wile, "Brick, Stone, Dreams, and Travail," *The Oklahoma State Alumnus,* VI, No. 1 (1956), p. 6.

[24]*The Stillwater Gazette,* July 20, 1928; December 7 ,1928; February 10, 1933; August 9, 1935; March 5, 1937; January 13, 1939; "Sojourning in Chile," *The Oklahoma A. and M. College Magazine,* I, No. 2 (1937) pp. 5, 16; Hilton Briggs, "The New Dean of Agriculture," *The Oklahoma A. and M. College Magazine,* X, No. 5 (1939), pp. 4, 14; "Minutes of the Board of Agriculture," XXI, p. 183; XXXV, p. 31.

[25]"World Power Conference," *The Oklahoma A. and M. College Magazine,* II, No. 4 (1930), pp. 106, 122; "Donnell . . . A Sketch," *The Oklahoma A. and M. College Magazine,* I, No. 7 (1929), pp. 7, 29; "Minutes of the Board of Agriculture," XI, p. 103; XLIV, p. 244; *The Stillwater Gazette,* September 14, 1928; August 29, 1930; April 11, 1930; February 28, 1936.

[26]*The O'Collegian,* December 3, 1940.

[27]*The Redskin,* (1940), p. iii.

[28]*The Stillwater Gazette,* June 28, 1935; June 27, 1930; August 29, 1941; *The O'Collegian,* October 8, 1954; "Staff and Faculty Changes," *The Oklahoma A. and M. College Magazine,* VII, No. 1 (1936), p. 3; *The Redskin,* 1936, p. 114; "Minutes of the Board of Agriculture," XXXI, p. 174. For the dean's views on educational administration, see Schiller Scroggs, "Science and Literature Makes Changes," *The Oklahoma A. and M. College Magazine,* VIII, No. 6 (1937), pp. 3, 4, 16; "General Administrative Organization of the College," *The Oklahoma A. and M. College Magazine,* II, No. 4 (1930), pp. 112-113; Schiller Scroggs and Henry Bennett, "Sabbatical Leave," *The Journal of Higher Education,* III, No. 4 (1932), pp. 196-199.

[29]Napoleon Conger, *Professional Adjustment Service Rendered by Teacher Training Institutions* (Durant, 1930), pp. i, 191; *The Stillwater Gazette,* August 20, 1937.

[30]*The Stillwater Gazette,* September 21, 1928; April 24, 1928; March 21, 1930; "Looking Ahead with the School of Commerce," *The Oklahoma A. and M. College Magazine,* II, No. 7 (1931), p. 196; "School of Commerce Gets Results from Six Objectives," The Oklahoma A. and M. College Magazine, II, No. 7 (1931), pp. 197, 222; "Fifteen Years of Growth by School of Commerce,"*The Oklahoma A. and M. College Magazine,* II, No. 7 (1931), p.

199.

[31]Raymond D. Thomas, "The Land-Grant College in the Changing Times," *The Oklahoma A. and M. College Magazine,* IV, No. 4 (1933), p. 3.

[32]"Alumni and Faculty Recognized," *The Oklahoma A. and M. College Magazine,* VI, No. 5 (1935), p. 3.

[33]Henry Bennett (ed.), *Annual Report of the President for 1928* (Stillwater, 1928), pp. i-xxiii.

[34]Henry Bennett (ed.), *Report of the President for 1930* (Stillwater, 1930), pp. 1-230; Henry Bennett (ed.), *Report of the President for 1931* (Stillwater, 1931), pp. xix.

[35]*The O'Collegian,* October 4, 1931; "Minutes of the Board of Agriculture," XXXIV, p. 53.

[36](Henry Bennett, "Greetings from the Oklahoma A .and M. College," pp. 1-2) in Box 5 "The Bennett Speech Collection."

[37](Henry Bennett, "Annual Address to the Faculty—September 11, 1939," p. 8) in Box 5, "The Bennett Speech Collection."

[38](Henry Bennett, "Institutional Greatness," p. 10) in Box 1 "The Bennett Speech Collection."

[39]"Minutes of the Board of Agriculture," XXI, p. 183.

[40]John W. Hamilton, "Saga of a Little Red Schoolhouse," *The Oklahoma A. and M. College Magazine,* XIX, No. 3 (1947), p. 2; Genevieve Braley, "Classes Resumed in Old Central," *The Oklahoma A. and M. College Magazine,* I, No. 8 (1930), p. 5.

[41]"Minutes of the Board of Agriculture," XXIII, p. 119; XXI, p. 286; XXXII, p. 5; *The Stillwater Gazette,* May 16, 1930; October 10, 1930; "Future College Being Planned for 25 Years," *The Oklahoma A. and M. College Magazine,* I, No. 1 (1929), p. 26; "Oklahoma A. and M. of the Future," *The Oklahoma A. and M. College Magazine,* II, No. 3 (1930), pp. 80-81; Bennett, *Report of the President for 1931,* pp. xix-xxvii; Vick Lindley, "The Aggie Campus Reminds Me," *The Oklahoma A. and M. College Magazine, XXII,* No. 3 (1950), pp. 8-11; Wile, "Brick, Stone, Dreams, and Travail," pp. 6-7.

[42]*The Stillwater Gazette,* August 10, 1928.

[43]*Ibid.,* December 12, 1930.

[44]*Ibid.,* December 19, 1930; January 9, 1931; January 23, 1931; January 30, 1931; February 13, 1931; October 2, 1931; May 19, 1933.

[45]*Ibid.,* August 28, 1931; November 28, 1930; March 6, 1931; June 5, 1931; June 19, 1931; August 12, 1932; November 4, 1932; January 13, 1933; March 3, 1933; December 15, 1933.

[46]*Ibid.,* July 17, 1931; November 18, 1932; November 20, 1936; *The O'Collegian,* November 15, 1932; November 14, 1936; "Minutes of the Board of Agriculture," XXXV, p. 82; XLI, p. 19.

[47]"Minutes of the Board of Agriculture," XX, p. 36; *The Stillwater News-Press,* February 26, 1954; *The Stillwater Gazette,* April 17, 1931; September 29, 1933.

[48]*Harlow's Weekly,* April 25, 1931; "On the Campus," *The Oklahoma A. and M. College Magazine,* X, No. 4 (1934), p. 7; "New Dormitory Under Construction," *The Oklahoma A. and M. College Magazine,* V, No. 6 (1934), pp. 5, 15; *The Stillwater Gazette,* March 30, 1934; "Minutes of the Board of Agriculture," XXXII, p. 295.

[49]*Bulletin of the American Association of University Professors,* XVIII, No. 5 (1932), p. 352. The tenure statement may be read in Louis Joughin (ed.), *Academic Freedom and Tenure* (Madison, 1969), pp. 155-176.

[50]*The Stillwater Gazette,* January 24, 1930. For Bennett's position on public school tenure, see (Henry Bennett, "A Civil Service for Teachers," n.p.) in Box 3 "The Bennett Speech Collection."

[51]*The O'Collegian,* January 25, 1933.

[52]Henry Bennett, "Ten Years of Progress," *The Oklahoma A. and M. College Magazine,* IX, No. 1 (1937), p. 3.

[53]*The Stillwater Gazette,* April 10, 1931; May 27, 1928.

[54]*The O'Collegian,* September 11, 1931; January 10, 1932; "Minutes of the Board of Agriculture," XXI, p. 348.

[55]Bennett, "Ten Years of Progress," p. 4.

[56]*The Stillwater Gazette,* April 15, 1932; October 11, 1935; January 29, 1937; May 10, 1940; *The O'Collegian,* February 7, 1956; "Minutes of the Board of Agriculture," XXXI, pp. 129-131; XVI, p. 169; XVII, p. 5. Also, see (Henry Bennett, "Proposed Salary Schedule Oklahoma A. and M. College," n.p.) File Folder "Salary List for 1932-1933," in "The OSU Collection."

[57]*The Stillwater Gazette,* September 19, 1930; *The O'Collegian,* October 19, 1934; September 26, 1933; September 13, 1931.

[58]*Harlow's Weekly,* September 21, 1929.

[59]*The Stillwater Gazette,* June 13, 1930; September 12, 1930; October 3, 1930; April 10, 1931; September 22, 1933; September 14, 1934; October 11, 1935; August 21, 1936; September 25, 1936; May 13, 1938; September 23, 1938; Warren E. Shull, "The Next Governor of Oklahoma," *The Oklahoma State Alumnus,* III, No. 11 (1962), pp. 5-8.

[60]*Annual Catalog,* Session of 1939-1940, pp. 38-41; *The O'Collegian,* October 24, 1939; February 21, 1936; "Minutes of the Board of Agriculture," XXVIII, pp. 316-321.

[61]*The O'Collegian,* November 5, 1931.

[62]"Minutes of the Former Students Association," November 1, 1931 (Oklahoma State University), p. 1; October 29, 1932, pp. 9-10; December 14, 1938, p. 2; "Minutes of the Board of Agriculture," XXI, pp. 163-164; (Harry Cordell to Henry Johnston, June 11, 1930) in Box C "The Johnston Collection;" Henry Bennett, "A Message from the President," *The Oklahoma A. and M. College Magazine,* I, No. 1 (1929), p. 4; Harry Cordell, "Broadcasting Loyalty," *The Oklahoma A. and M. College Magazine,* I, No. 3 (1929), p. 5.

[63]"Minutes of the Board of Agriculture," XXI, p. 184; *The Stillwater Gazette,* December 13, 1929; December 18, 1931.

[64]*The Oklahoma A. and M. College Magazine,* I, No. 1 (1929), p. 4.

[65]"Minutes of the Former Students Association," October 16, 1931, p. 2.

[66]*The Orange and Black,* December 7, 1922; *The Stillwater Gazette,* July 25, 1924; *The O'Collegian,* July 26, 1927; "Minutes of the Board of Agriculture," XX, p. 61; XIX, p. 297; W. H. Moulton, "A and M's New Stadium" *The Oklahoma A. and M. College Magazine,* I, No. 5 (1929), pp. 7, 29.

[67]Randle Perdue, "The Goal is $500,000," *The Oklahoma A. and M. College Magazine,* I, No. 6 (1929), pp. 6, 29; Randle Perdue, "The Stadium Campaign Unfolds," *The Oklahoma A. and M. College Magazine,* I, No. 7 (1929), p. 6; *The Stillwater Gazette,* February 7, 1930; February 21, 1930; March 7, 1930; March 21, 1930; April 11, 1930; May 30, 1930; October 28, 1932; "Minutes of the Board of Agriculture," XXV, p. 42; (Philip Wilber to H. G. Bennett, January 7, 1933) File Folder "Stadium Corporation and Other Matters," in "The OSU Collection."

[68]*The Stillwater Gazette,* November 4, 1932; June 22, 1922; June 14, 1928; August 14, 1928; December 28, 1928.

[69]Orville M. Savage, "What About This Separate Board of Regents?" *The Oklahoma A. and M. College Magazine,* I, No. 2 (1929), p. 18.

[70]*The Stillwater Gazette,* February 28, 1930; May 30, 1930; October 10, 1930; October 24, 1930; November 7, 1930; November 8, 1930; November 28, 1930; January 20, 1933; May 18, 1934; March 15, 1935; March 22, 1935; May 3, 1935; March 13, 1936; August 7, 1936; August 28, 1936; September 25, 1936; October 9, 1936; August 28, 1936; September 25, 1936; September 17, 1937; October 29, 1936; *The O'Collegian,* March 7, 1936; November 4, 1936; September 15, 1937; "Minutes of the Board of Agriculture," XXIV, p. 21; "Minutes of the Former Students Association," May 4, 1934, p. 1; May 16, 1937, p. 1; November 15, 1937, p. 1; "Legislature Backs Separate Board Plan," *The Oklahoma A. and M. College Magazine,* II, No. 1 (1930), pp. 6-7.

[71]Perdue, "That Man Bennett," p. 8.

XV

[1]*The Stillwater Gazette,* April 17, 1931; September 11, 1931; March 27, 1931; August 14, 1931; *The O'Collegian,* June 6, 1933.

[2]*Ibid.,* August 21, 1931.

[3]Bryant, pp. 151-172; *Harlow's Weekly,* June 21, 1930, August 16, 1930.

[4]"Minutes of the Board of Agriculture," XXIV, p. 2; *The Stillwater Gazette,* January 24, 1930; Bryant, pp. 173-189.

[5]Hubbell, p. 13.

[6]*Harlow's Weekly,* January 17, 1931.

[7]*Ibid.,* August 8, 1931.

[8]*The Stillwater Gazette,* January 16, 1931.

[9]*Harlow's Weekly,* July 11, 1931; *The Stillwater Gazette,* January 30, 1931; February 6, 1931; July 10, 1931; July 24, 1931; September 4, 1931; September 11, 1931; May 1, 1931.

[10]*Harlow's Weekly,* September 12, 1931.

[11](Henry Bennett, "Introduction of Governor Murray," pp. 1-5) in Box 6 "The Bennett Speech Collection;" *Harlow's Weekly,* November 21, 1931; *The Stillwater Gazette,* October 23, 1931; *The O'Collegian,* October 13, 1931; October 20, 1931; October 17, 1931; October 27, 1931; October 22, 1931; November 12, 1931.

[12]Bennett's "friendship" with Murray saved a number of faculty from being dismissed. He could not, however, dissuade the Murray men from releasing Mrs. Elsie Hand, *The O'Collegian,* June 6, 1933; June 16, 1933.

[13]*The Oklahoma State System of Higher Education* (Oklahoma City, 1971), pp. 8-9; *A System of Higher Education for Oklahoma* (Oklahoma City, 1942), pp. 100-103.

[14]*A System of Higher Education for Oklahoma,* p. 102.

[15](Henry Bennett, "Problems Confronting Oklahoma University and Oklahoma A. and M. College," p. 5) in Box 5 "The Bennett Speech Collection;" *Harlow's Weekly,* April 15, 1933; "Minutes of the Board of Agriculture," XXVIII, p. 9; *The O'Collegian,* March 16, 1933; *The Stillwater Gazette,* March 17, 1933; September 8, 1933. For an in depth look at Murray's educational views, see Murray, II, pp. 545-553; III, pp. 362-384, 611-621.

[16]*The Tulsa World,* May 24, 1933; *The O'Collegian,* December 20, 1933; May 26, 1933; June 23, 1933; *The Stillwater Gazette,* June 23, 1933; September 1, 1933; "On the Campus," *The Oklahoma A. and M. College Magazine,* V, No. 4 (1934), p. 7.

[17]The Institute for Government Research of the Brookings Institution, *Organization and Administration of Oklahoma* (Washington, 1935), *passim; The Stillwater Gazette,* March 15, 1935.

[18]William H. Murray, *The Negro's Place in the Call of Race* (Tishomingo, 1948); *The Stillwater Gazette,* August 10, 1934; June 24, 1938; September 2, 1938. For newspaper comment in regard to Bennett's candidacy for governor, see *The Stillwater Gazette,* December 22, 1933; January 29, 1937; March 26, 1937; October 22, 1937.

[19]*Harlow's Weekly,* December 16, 1933; "Minutes of the Board of Agriculture," XXIX, p. 37; *The Stillwater Gazette,* January 17, 1930; *The O'Collegian,* December 9, 1933.

[20]*Annual Catalog,* Session of 1934-1935, p. 13; *The O'Collegian,* September 29, 1935; *The Stillwater Gazette,* June 1, 1934.

[21]Wile, "Brick, Stone, Dreams and Travail," p. 8.

[22]McReynolds, pp. 361-377; *The Stillwater Gazette,* March 23, 1934; April 20, 1934; May 12, 1933.

[23]*The Stillwater Gazette,* August 11, 1933; August 25, 1933; October 6, 1933; October 27, 1933; *The Redskin,* 1938, p. 20; *The O'Collegian,* September 26, 1934; September 30, 1933; "Minutes of the Board of Agriculture," XXIX, p. 1.

[24]*The O'Collegian,* January 15, 1935; *The Stillwater Gazette,* January 25, 1935; November 5, 1937.

[25]*The Stillwater Gazette,* June 4, 1937.

[26]"Minutes of the Board of Agriculture," XXX, pp. 69-70; XXXI, pp.

171, 228; *The Stillwater Gazette,* March 22, 1935; February 22, 1935; August 23, 1935; November 22, 1935.

[27]*The Stillwater Gazette,* May 21, 1937; June 4, 1937.

[28]"Minutes of the Board of Agriculture," XXXIV, pp. 54-56; XXXI, p. 124; *The O'Collegian,* June 4, 1937; *The Stillwater Gazette,* November 23, 1934; January 11, 1935; September 4, 1936; February 7, 1936; January 7, 1938; June 11, 1937.

[29]*The Stillwater Gazette,* January 11, 1935; January 15, 1937; January 22, 1937; February 19, 1937.

[30]*The O'Collegian,* January 12, 1937.

[31]"Joe C. Scott Heads Aggie Board," *The Oklahoma A. and M. College Magazine,* VIII, No. 6 (1937), p. 4; *The Stillwater Gazette,* February 26, 1937; June 18, 1937; April 15, 1938; July 7, 1939.

[32]*The Stillwater Gazette,* August 18, 1933; *The O'Collegian,* March 3, 1934; December 9, 1933; Clement Trout, "A. and M. College Does It's Part," *The Oklahoma A. and M. College Magazine,* V, No. 1(1933), pp. 5, 15-16; "Federal Government Continues to Call on A. and M.," *The Oklahoma A. and M. College Magazine,* V, No. 5 (1934), p. 5, 13; "Minutes of the Board of Agriculture," XXXII, p. 30; XXXIV, p. 90.

For a complete roster of the men and women who held government positions in the New Deal period, see (Henry Bennett, "The Land-Grant College: A Federal College in a State Setting," pp. 5-8) in Box 3 "The Bennett Speech Collection."

[33]*The Stillwater Gazette,* January 5, 1934.

[34]*Ibid.,* September 18, 1936; March 19, 1937; March 26, 1937; April 9, 1937.

[35](Henry Bennett, "Dedicatory Remarks 4-H Club and Student Activity Building," p. 2) in Box 3 "The Bennett Speech Collection;" "Minutes of the Board of Agriculture," XXXII, p. 297; *The Stillwater Gazette,* August 19, 1938; August 21, 1936; October 6, 1933; January 4, 1935; February 25, 1938; April 16, 1937; July 2, 1937; May 28, 1937.

[36]"Minutes of the Former Students Association," May 27, 1939, p. 1; "Minutes of the Board of Agriculture," XLI, pp. 17-18; XLII, *passim; The Stillwater Gazette,* February 14, 1936; March 12, 1937 April 8, 1938; June 3, 1938; July 29, 1938.

[37]*The Stillwater Gazette,* October 3, 1937; October 8, 1937; November 3, 1939; *The O'Collegian,* September 28, 1937; March 23. 1950; *Annual Catalog,* Session of 1941-1942, p. 14; "Minutes of the Board of Agriculture," XXXVII, p. 317; *Proceedings of the A. L. G. C. U.* (Washington, 1948), p. 48.

[38]*Harlow's Weekly,* October 14, 1933; "Minutes of the Board of Agriculture," XXXIII, p. 22; XXXIV, p. 53; *The Stillwater Gazette,* October 6, 1933; May 25, 1934; October 30, 1936; *The O'Collegian,* October 3, 1933.

[39]*The Stillwater Gazette,* November 5, 1937; September 2, 1938; *The O'Collegian,* November 2, 1937; October 30, 1936; "Minutes of the Board of Agriculture," XXXIV, p. 6; XXXIV, p. 97.

[40]G. A. Hale, "Parking Meter Aggie Designed," *The Oklahoma A. and M. College Magazine,* XXII, No. 4 (1950), pp. 5-8; LeRoy H. Fischer and Robert E. Smith, "Oklahoma and the Parking Meter," *The Chronicles of Oklahoma,* XLVII, No. 2 (1969), pp. 168-208; *The O'Collegian,* January 23, 1933.

[41]Additional information on the parking meter is in H. G. Thuesen (with annotation and bibliography by LeRoy Fischer), "The Reminiscences of the Development of the Parking Meter," *The Chronicles of Oklahoma,* XLV, No. 2 (1967), pp. 1-31.

[42]*The Stillwater Gazette,* December 30, 1938; September 22, 1939; Mc-Reynolds, pp. 377-382; "Minutes of the Board of Agriculture," XXXIV, p. 295; IXV, pp. 53-54.

[43]McReynolds, pp. 377-382; *The Redskin,* 1939, p. 171.

[44]*The Stillwater Gazette,* January 13, 1939.

[45]*The Daily O'Collegian,* March 30, 1940; *The Stillwater Gazette,* February 2, 1940.

[46]*The Stillwater Gazette,* March 17, 1939; August 4, 1939; October 6, 1939; January 12, 1940; March 22, 1940; March 15, 1940; January 3, 1941; September 1, 1941.

47The committee published its report. See, *A System of Higher Education,* pp. 1-131. In addition, consult *Oklahoma State System of Higher Education,* p. 9; "Minutes of the Oklahoma State Regents for Higher Education," I, (Office of the Chancellor, Oklahoma State Regents for Higher Education), pp. 1-5.

48*The Stillwater Gazette,* September 11, 1942.

49"Flying Course Progress," *The Oklahoma A. and M. College Magazine,* XI, No. 6 (1940), pp. 4, 16; "Minutes of the Board of Agriculture," XLII, p. 154; *The Stillwater Gazette,* January 8, 1943; August 18, 1939; September 29, 1939; June 7, 1940.

50Richard Caldwell, "A. and M.'s Fighting Dean Returns," *The Oklahoma A. and M. College Magazine,* XVIII, No. 4 (1946), pp. 3, 13;; "Lifetime Land-Grant Missionary," pp. 8-13; *The Stillwater Gazette,* September 6, 1940; December 13, 1940; April 25, 1941; January 12, 1940; November 23, 1945; September 7, 1951.

51*The O'Collegian,* May 19, 1940.

52*Ibid.,* September 27, 1940.

53*The Stillwater Gazette,* September 27, 1940.

54*The O'Collegian,* February 4, 1941.

55"Minutes of the Former Students Association," February 16, 1939, p. 1; "Minutes of the Board of Agriculture," XLV, p. 220; *The Stillwater Gazette,* January 31, 1941.

Oklahomans were not the only ones who did not differentiate between Communism and Fascism. See, Les K. Adler and Thomas G. Paterson, "Red Fascism: The Merger of Nazi Germany and Soviet Russia in the American Image of Totalitarianism, 1930's-1950's," *The American Historical Review,* LXXV, No. 4 (1970), pp. 1046-1064.

56*The Stillwater Gazette,* August 11, 1939; April 19, 1940; February 7, 1941; February 11, 1941; May 30, 1941; October 10, 1941; October 31, 1941.

57*Ibid.,* October 31, 1941; November 7, 1941; November 18, 1941; December 4, 1941; January 9, 1942; July 17, 1942; November 13, 1942; March 6, 1942; May 8, 1942; *The O'Collegian,* December 5, 1942.

58*Harlow's Weekly,* December 9, 1933;*The Stillwater Gazette,* November 7, 1941; *The Daily Oklahoman,* December 24, 1941; *The Redskin,* 1943, n.p.; McReynolds, pp. 383-389.

59"Minutes of the Board of Agriculture," XXVI, p. 26.

60*The O'Collegian,* January 8, 1937.

61*The Stillwater Gazette,* October 28, 1938.

62*Ibid.,* December 11, 1942.

63*Ibid.,* November 19, 1943; July 19, 1946. Gilmer promised to fire Ned Conger, Schiller Scroggs, and H. G. Bennett, if elected.

64*Ibid.,* November 26, 1943; December 3, 1943; January 7, 1944; February 11, 1944.

65*Ibid.,* February 11, 1944.

66*Ibid.*

67*Fiftieth Anniversary Celebration* (Stillwater, 1941), n.p.; "Fiftieth Anniversary Observed," *The Oklahoma A. and M. College Magazine,* XIII, No. 4 (1942), pp. 2-3, 15; *The Stillwater Gazette,* December 4, 1941; October 24, 1941.

68*The O'Collegian,* December 9, 1941.

69*Ibid.,* December 16, 1941.

XVI

1Henry Bennett, *A Report on Public Works Plannings* (Oklahoma City, 1938), p. 4.

2Personal interview by author with Forrest McIntire, June 5, 1972; *The Stillwater Gazette,* July 3, 1942; September 27, 1946; November 8, 1946; January 5, 1951; June 2, 1950; "Oklahoma's Legislators' Wives Make 1947 Trek to Aggie Campus," *The Oklahoma A. and M. College Magazine,* XVIII, No. 7 (1947), pp. 8-10; McReynolds, pp. 298-390, 392-393.

³*The Stillwater Gazette,* April 30, 1943; July 23, 1943; August 2, 1946; *The O'Collegian,* May 10, 1949.

⁴*The O'Collegian,* September 17, 1948; September 21, 1950; September 23, 1950; October 21, 1950; *The Stillwater Gazette,* April 16, 1951; September 1, 1948.

⁵Personal interview by author with Oliver Willham, July 8, 1971; *The Stillwater Gazette,* April 17, 1942; August 28, 1942; October 6, 1944; *The O'Collegian,* December 1, 1949; "Minutes of the Board of Regents for the Oklahoma A. and M. Colleges," March 7, 1950 (Oklahoma State University), p. 52.

⁶("Report of the Committee to Appraise the Work of the Committee on Appraising and Improving College Education," pp. 1-7); (Faculty Committee on Appraising and Improving Education," January 8, 1935, pp. 1-18); ("Report on the Committee for Student Advisement," April 17, 1936, pp. 1-19); ("American Association of University Professors College and University Government Survey," 1939, pp. 1-4); ("Resolutions Adopted by the Association of American Colleges," 1942, pp. 1-2); ("Minutes of the School of Arts and Sciences," May 16, 1940, n.p.) in "The OSU Collection."

⁷*The O'Collegian,* June 12, 1942.

⁸*The Stillwater Gazette,* January 23, 1942; January 16, 1942; January 23, 1942; May 22, 1942; July 24, 1942; September 18, 1942; October 2, 1942; October 16, 1942; November 6, 1942; November 27, 1942; October 19, 1945.

⁹*Ibid.,* December 12, 1941; July 24, 1942; May 14, 1948; April 15, 1948; *The O'Collegian,* January 27, 1942; January 17, 1945; January 28, 1949; January 23, 1951.

¹⁰(Henry Bennett, "Contributions of the Oklahoma A. and M. College to the State and Nation in World War II," pp. 1-6) in "The OSU Collection"; Howard Floyd, "Campus Fire Station in War Time," *The Oklahoma A. and M. College Magazine,* XVI, No. 7 (1944), p. 8; "Minutes of the Oklahoma State Regents for Higher Education," June 15, 1945, pp. 312-314; *The O'Collegian,* June 11, 1943; *The Stillwater Gazette,* June 29, 1945; September 21, 1945; July 20, 1945.

¹¹*The O'Collegian,* February 10, 1942; February 20, 1942; May 7, 1942; May 20, 1942; May 21, 1942; *The Stillwater Gazette,* April 17, 1942; June 26, 1942; January 23, 1942; March 21, 1943; March 27, 1942; April 6, 1945; July 27, 1945; "Minutes of the Oklahoma State Regents for Higher Education," June 18, 1942, p. 74.

¹²*The Stillwater Gazette,* November 6, 1942; March 17, 1944; *The O'Collegian,* November 20, 1942; November 28, 1942; January 6, 1943; January 13, 1943; February 10, 1944; "Minutes of the Board of Agriculture." XLVII, p. 182.

¹³Howard M. Yost, "Military Training Expands at Oklahoma A. and M." *The Oklahoma A. and M. College Magazine,* XV, No. 3 (1943), pp. 8-10, 14; *The O'Collegian,* September 24, 1946.

¹⁴Richard Caldwell, "Rhapsody of the Waves," *The Oklahoma A. and M. College Magazine,* XVII, No. 3 (1944), p. 5; *The Stillwater Gazette,* February 19, 1943; April 9, 1943; April 23, 1943; May 14, 1943; July 9, 1943; August 6, 1943; April 20, 1945; *The O'Collegian,* October 16, 1942; January 16, 1943; May 11, 1943; January 31, 1945.

¹⁵Personal interview by author with Robert B. Kamm, June 10, 1972; *The O'Collegian,* April 11, 1945; June 21, 1946; *The Stillwater Gazette,* May 4, 1945; May 18, 1945; June 8, 1945; June 22, 1945; "Minutes of the Board of Regents for the Oklahoma A. and M. Colleges," August 3, 1945.

At least one other person associated with the Oklahoma A. and M. College wrote a famous World War II novel. Thomas Heggen published *Mr. Roberts* with Houghton Mifflin Company in 1946. Heggen served in the navy for four years.

¹⁶"Contributions of the Oklahoma A. and M. College to the State and Nation in World War II," pp. 1-6; *The Stillwater Gazette,* August 18, 1944; September 14, 1945; "Minutes of the Board of Regents for the Oklahoma A. and M. Colleges," July 6, 1946, n.p.

[17]*The O'Collegian,* March 12, 1943.

[18]"Minutes of the Former Students Association," May 28, 1944, p. 1.

[19]*Ibid.,* June 15, 1944, p. 1; "New Board of Regents," *The Oklahoma A. and M. College Magazine,* XVII, No. 1 (1944), pp. 3-4; *The Stillwater Gazette,* August 11, 1944; June 9, 1944; "State Question No. 310," *The Oklahoma A. and M. College Magazine,* XVI, No. 10 (1944), p. 3.

[20]"Colonel Robert Terry Stuart," *The Oklahoma A. and M. College Magazine,* XXII, No. 4 (1950), pp. 18-19; "Minutes of the Board of Regents for the Oklahoma A. and M. Colleges," April 16, 1946, p. 34. Colonel Stuart became chairman in 1946.

[21]Henry G. Bennett, *This Is Colonel Stuart: A Gentleman from Texas* (n.p., 1945); "Minutes of the Board of Regents for the Oklahoma A. and M. Colleges," August 7, 1944, pp. 1-7; May 5, 1945, p. 38.

[22]"Minutes of the Board of Regents for the Oklahoma A. and M. Colleges," May 3, 1951, n.p.; October 28, 1944, pp. 1-26; August 7, 1944, pp. 1-7; May 5, 1945, n.p.

[23]*Ibid.,* September 2, 1944, pp. 5, 7.

[24]*Ibid.,* August 1, 1947, p. 25; *The Stillwater Gazette,* November 24, 1950; *The O'Collegian,* November 18, 1950; "A. and M's Vice President," *The Oklahoma A. and M. College Magazine,* XIX, No. 1 (1947), p. 3.

[25]"Minutes of the Board of Regents for the Oklahoma A. and M. Colleges," January 6, 1945, n.p.; May 3, 1947, p. 20; "Minutes of the Oklahoma State Regents for Higher Education," May 24, 1948, p. 556 .

[26]"Tribute is Given to Dr. O. M. Smith," *The Oklahoma A. and M. College Magazine,* XXVII, No. 2 (1955), p. 15; *The Stillwater Gazette,* July 22, 1946; "Minutes of the Board of Regents for the Oklahoma A. and M. Colleges," December 2, 1944, pp. 18-19.

[27]*Annual Catalog,* Session of 1939-1940, p. 225; *Ibid.,* 1946-1947, p. 206; *The O'Collegian,* November 9, 1954; "Graduate School Offerings at A. and M.," *The Oklahoma A. and M. College Magazine,* XXIV, No. 7 (1953), p. 12. For the historical roots of the Doctor of Education and Doctor of Philosophy degrees, see Walter Crosby Eells, *Degrees in Higher Education* (Washington, 1963), pp. 20-37.

[28]*The Stillwater Gazette,* April 25, 1947; March 2, 1951; April 16, 1951; *The O'Collegian,* October 20, 1949; *Annual Catalog,* Session of 1947-1948, pp. 217-219; "Graduate School Offerings at A. and M.," p. 12; "Minutes of the Oklahoma State Regents for Higher Education," October 23, 1950, p. 733; April 26, 1952, pp. 851-852.

[29]("Provisional Qualifications and Selection of Graduate Faculty," October 4, 1948, pp. 1-3); ("Members of the Graduate Faculty," June 16, 1949, pp. 1-2); ("Organization of the Graduate School and Graduate Faculty," n.d., pp. 1-5); ("The Graduate School," June 22, 1948, pp. 1-2); ("Summary of the Minutes of the Graduate Faculty Meeting," March 24, 1949, pp. 1-2); (Otto M. Smith, "Third Annual Report on Fellowships and Scholarships Committee," pp. 1-8); ("Handbook of the Graduate School," pp. 1-25) in "The OSU Collection."

[30]"Minutes of the Board of Regents for the Oklahoma A. and M. Colleges," January 24, 1949, n.p.; March 13, 1948, p. 23; Richard Caldwell, "German Diesel Lab Here!" *The Oklahoma A. and M. College Magazine,* XIX, No. 8 (1948), pp. 16-17; Richard Caldwell, "Engine Research at A. and M.," *The Oklahoma A. and M. College Magazine,* XXI, No. 1 (1949), pp. 34-35.

[31](Philip Donnell to Henry Bennett, February 4, 1949) File Folder "Memorandums to President Bennett," in "The OSU Collection."

[32](Philip Donnell to Henry Bennett, July 1, 1947) File Folder "Veterans" in "The OSU Collection"; "Minutes of the Board of Regents for the Oklahoma A. and M. Colleges," December 8, 1945, pp. 19-20; October 6, 1945, p. 230.

[33]*The Stillwater Gazette,* September 22, 1944; April 27, 1945; November 23, 1945; January 4, 1946; January 5, 1946; February 15, 1946; March 15, 1946; November 1, 1946.

[34]"Veterans Village Comes of Age," *The Oklahoma A. and M. College Magazine,* XX, No. 1 (1948), pp. 4-5; *The Stillwater Gazette,* March 8, 1946; March 22, 1946; *The O'Collegian,* January 9, 1946; March 29, 1946.

35The (Stillwater, Oklahoma) *Village Times,* September 10, 1946 to July 22, 1949; *The O'Collegian,* January 17, 1949; January 13, 1949; February 24, 1949; March 8, 1949; January 10, 1950; February 10, 1947; March 11, 1950; February 17, 1949; *The Stillwater Gazette,* June 4, 1948; *The Stillwater News-Press,* January 23, 1949.

36"Minutes of the Board of Regents for the Oklahoma A. and M. Colleges," March 9, 1946, p. 23; June 8, 1948, p. 27; June 22, 1949, p. 39; February 8, 1947, p. 24; May 3, 1951, p. 35; July 5, 1951, p. 67; "Minutes of the Oklahoma State Regents for Higher Education," October 28, 1946, pp. 416-417; January 27, 1947, pp. 438-439; June 27, 1949, p. 629; *The Oklahoman,* September 15, 1950; *The Stillwater News-Press,* March 18, 1955; *The O'Collegian,* May 7, 1946; January 25, 1949; *The Stillwater Gazette,* June 4, 1948; March 2, 1951.

37Wile, "The Chronological Story of Sports at Oklahoma State University from the Beginning in the 1890's Through the 1960's," pp. 334-485; *The Redskin,* 1946, pp. 143-149, "Cowboys Play Difficult Schedule," *The Oklahoma A. and M. College Magazine,* XVII, No. 4 (1945), pp. 8-9; "Oklahoma Aggies Sugar Bowl Bound," *The Oklahoma A. and M. College Magazine,* XVIII, No. 3 (1945), p. 3; *The O'Collegian,* January 9, 1946; November 30, 1949; *The Stillwater Gazette,* December 2, 1938; December 1, 1944; December 21, 1945; February 9, 1945; November 30, 1945; January 18, 1946; February 1, 1946; March 29, 1946; January 27, 1950.

38"Minutes of the Oklahoma State Regents for Higher Education," August 20, 1942, p. 86; April 19, 1943, pp. 133-135; "Minutes of the Board of Regents for the Oklahoma A. and M. Colleges," September 7, 1945, p. 23; *The Stillwater Gazette,* February 23, 1945; July 27, 1945.

39*The New York* (New York) *Herald Tribune,* January 1, 1950.

40*The Stillwater Gazette,* November 5, 1945; December 20, 1946; March 28, 1947; April 18, 1947; June 27, 1947; July 4, 1947; September 19, 1947; April 30, 1948; May 20, 1949; March 3, 1950; *The O'Collegian* April 15, 1947; February 10, 1950; "Toward a Greater A. and M.," *The Oklahoma A. and M. College Magazine,* XX, No. 1 (1948), pp. 14-18; "Minutes of the Board of Regents for the Oklahoma A. and M. Colleges," March 11, 1947, p. 21; January 24, 1948, n.p.; May 6-7, 1948, appendix; February 9, 1949, p. 22; October 27, 1950, appendix; May 23, 1951, n.p.

41*The O'Collegian,* February 15, 1949; December 17, 1949; January 19, 1951; September 9, 1952; *The Stillwater Gazette,* February 2, 1951; "Minutes of the Board of Regents for the Oklahoma A. and M. Colleges," March 4, 1949, p. 25; *The Oklahoma A. and M. College Magazine,* XXIV, No. 3 (1952), p. 23.

42*The Henry G. Bennett Birthday Party Program* (Stillwater, 1949), p. 2.

43*The Oklahoman,* October 1, 1950; *The Stillwater Gazette,* August 13, 1938; May 20, 1950; May 26, 1950; September 14, 1950.

44("Supreme Court of Oklahoma, Case No. 34352," pp. 1-50) File Folder "Washington Street Closing" in "The OSU Collection"; "Minutes of the Board of Regents for the Oklahoma A. and M. Colleges," December 14, 1948, p. 38; Edmon Low, "Knowledge Storehouse," *The Oklahoma A. and M. College Magazine,* XXIV, No. 8 (1953), pp. 20-21; *The O'Collegian,* May 12, 1950; June 6, 1950; January 29, 1953; February 27, 1953; April 30, 1954, *The Oklahoman,* May 9, 1953; *The Stillwater News-Press,* May 28, 1950; *The Stillwater Gazette,* July 29, 1949; June 2, 1950.

45*The O'Collegian,* January 11, 1950; October 26, 1954; October 22, 1954; *The Stillwater Gazette,* February 9, 1951; March 23, 1951; June 22, 1951; June 29, 1951; August 3, 1951.

46Henry Bennett to Harry Truman, May 24, 1944, Official File 192, "The Truman Papers" (Harry S. Truman Library, Independence, Missouri); "Minutes of the Board of Regents for the Oklahoma A. and M. Colleges," October 6, 1945, p. 24; *The O'Collegian,* March 8, 1949; *The Stillwater Gazette,* March 11, 1949.

47*The Stillwater News-Press,* March 3, 1949.

48*The O'Collegian,* July 6, 1949; September 30, 1949; September 24, 1949; March 30, 1950; *The Stillwater Gazette,* March 31, 1950; "Minutes of the Board of Regents for the Oklahoma A. and M. Colleges," June 22, 1949, p. 40; "President Returns from Abroad," *The Oklahoma A. and M. College Magazine,* XXI, No. 3 (1949), pp. 4-5; (Henry Bennett to Philip Donnell, Summer, 1949) File Folder "Memorandums to President Bennett" in "The OSU Collection"; Elmer Thomas to Harry Truman, June 6, 1950, OF 192-E and Harry Truman to Robert Kerr, July 13, 1950, OF 192-E in "The Truman Papers."

[49]Quoted from Commager, II, p. 554.

[50]"Statement by the President of September 8, 1950," OF 192-A and Harry Truman to D. W. Brooks, December 31, 1951, President's Personal File, 5929, "The Truman Papers"; Jonathan Bingham, *Shirt-Sleeve Diplomacy; Point Four in Action* (New York, 1953), pp. 1-15.

[51]*The O'Collegian,* November 10, 1950.

[52]*Ibid.,* November 15, 1950; November 17, 1950; *The Stillwater Gazette,* November 24, 1950; Nelson Rockefeller to Harry Truman, November 27, 1950, OF 192-A Technology, "The Truman Papers"; "Minutes of the Board of Regents for the Oklahoma A. and M. Colleges," November 17, 1950, pp. 2-3; Personal interview by author with Oliver Willham, July 10, 1972.

[53]*The Washington* (District of Columbia) *Daily News,* August 14, 1951; " 'Big Brother' to a Free World," *The Oklahoma A. and M. College Magazine,* XXIII, No. 1 (1951), pp. 4-8; *The Stillwater Gazette* ,December 15, 1950; January 12, 1951; "Minutes of the Board of Regents for the Oklahoma A. and M. Colleges," February 8, 1951, p. 39; December 13, 1950, pp. 6-7.

[54]"Funeral Message for Henry Bennett," PPF 5929, "The Truman Papers."

[55]*The Kansas City* (Missouri) *Star,* December 26, 1951; *The Stillwater News-Press,* January 2, 1952; *The Stillwater Gazette,* July 20, 1951; *The O'Collegian,* February 3, 1951; February 7, 1951; September 12, 1951.

[56]Henry Bennett, *The Great Basic Hope for Peace* (Stillwater 1951), p. 2.

[57]Henry Bennett, "The Human Side of Point Four," in *Proceedings of A. L. G. C. and U.* (Houston, 1951), p. 69.

[58]"A. and M. Mourns Loss of President, Wife," *The Oklahoma A. and M. College Magazine,* XXIII, No. 5 (1952), p. 7; *The Oklahoman,* December 24, 1951; *The Stillwater News-Press,* December 24, 1951.

[59]*The O'Collegian,* January 11, 1952. Many of the letters, telegrams, and newspaper editorials were published in *The Oklahoma A. and M. College Magazine* for February, 1952. Unpublished items are in a file folder marked "Henry Bennett" and are available in the main office of the Board of Regents for the Oklahoma A. and M. College in Stillwater, Oklahoma.

[60]For background on the three memorials, see: (Teheran) *The Oklahoman,* November 18, 1955; December 25, 1956; *The Stillwater News-Press,* December 24, 1956; (The Bennett Memorial Chapel) *The Stillwater News-Press,* May 4, 1955; *The O'Collegian,* January 16, 1952; February 15, 1952; December 17, 1952; October 8, 1954; (The Bennett Memorial Scholarship Foundation Fund) *The Stillwater News-Press,* May 14, 1954; September 21, 1954; *The O'Collegian,* April 16, 1952; April 30, 1952; April 23, 1952; March 16, 1954.

[61]*The O'Collegian,* April 4, 1952.

XVII

[1]"Minutes of the Board of Regents for the Oklahoma A. and M. Colleges," January 17, 1952, p. 23.

[2]*The Oklahoman,* December 24, 1951; Hilton Briggs, "The New Dean of Agriculture," *The Oklahoma A. and M. College Magazine,* X, No. 5 (1939), pp. 4, 14.

[3]*The O'Collegian,* January 19, 1952; *The Stillwater Gazette,* January 18, 1952; Personal interview by author with Oliver Willham, July 8 and 10, 1971; "Minutes of the Board of Regents for the Oklahoma A. and M. Colleges," January 17, 1952, p. 23.

4Oliver Willham, "A Report on College Needs," *The Oklahoma A. and M. College Magazine,* XXIV, No. 6 (1953), pp. 8-9; Oliver Willham, "The Challenge Facing A. and M.," *The Oklahoma A. and M. College Magazine,* XXV, No. 2 (1953), pp. 5-7; *The O'Collegian,* September 19, 1951; January 17, 1951; January 19, 1952; *The Stillwater Gazette,* April 4, 1952; Hubbell, pp. 270-177; *The Redskin,* 1956, p. 43.

5*The Stillwater News-Press,* September 21, 1955; May 10, 1957; "The 'Electronic Brain,' " *The Oklahoma A. and M. College Magazine,* XXVIII, No. 5 (1957), pp. 5-8; "Scientific Tools for Nuclear Technology," *The Oklahoma A. and M. College Magazine,* XXVIII, No. 7 (1957), p. 5.

6*The O'Collegian,* November 22, 1952; July 10, 1953; March 2, 1954; March 27, 1954; *The Stillwater Gazette,* December 19, 1952; December 18, 1953; "Rogers is Named Alumni Secretary," *The Oklahoma A. and M. College Magazine,* XXVI, No. 7 (1955), p. 17; *The Faculty News,* February 25, 1955, n.p.; "Auxiliary Enterprises at Oklahoma A. and M.," *The Oklahoma A. and M. College Magazine,* XXV, No. 2 (1953), pp. 8-10; "Biography of William Forrest McIntire," pp. 1-2.

7"Minutes of the Board of Regents for the Oklahoma A. and M. Colleges," December 6, 1951, p. 6; January 8, 1953, p. 23; "Darlow Takes Over; Dean Blizzard Retires," *The Oklahoma A. and M. College Magazine,* XXIV, No. 6 (1953), p. 41; "Named Dean of Veterinary Medicine," *The Oklahoma A. and M. College Magazine,* XXVIII, No. 2 (1956), p. 11; *The Stillwater News-Press,* August 17, 1956; January 20, 1956; *The Stillwater Gazette,* November 7, 1952; *The O'Collegian* November 7, 1952; January 9, 1953, April 15, 1953; July 7, 1954; October 12, 1954; September 11, 1956.

8*The O'Collegian,* June 9, 1953; October 6, 1953; *The Stillwater News-Press,* May 25, 1956; January 27, 1957; *The Oklahoman,* March 10, 1957; "Minutes of the Board of Regents for the Oklahoma A. and M. Colleges," November 4, 1955, p. 17; "Dr. Swearingen is Appointed Dean," *The Oklahoma A. and M. College Magazine,* XXVIII, No. 8 (1957), p. 31; "Dr. MacVicar Named Vice-President," *The Oklahoma A. and M. College Magazine,* XXVIII, No. 7 (1957), p. 30.

9*The Stillwater Gazette,* February 12, 1954; *The O'Collegian,* April 1, 1954; April 9, 1954; September 15, 1954.

10*The O'Collegian,* May 20, 1954.

11*Ibid.,* October 2, 1953.

12*Ibid.,* October 6, 1953; October 9, 1953 October 22, 1953; October 27, 1953; October 29, 1953; October 30, 1953; November 5, 1953.

13"Minutes of the Board of Regents for the Oklahoma A. and M. Colleges," June 2, 1951, n.p.; Oliver Willham, "Measuring the Values of Higher Education," *The Oklahoma A. and M. College Magazine,* XXVIII, No. 6 (1957), pp. 8-9; *The O'Collegian,* May 5, 1955; January 12, 1949; February 16, 1949. Other colleges and universities experienced similar problems at the same time. See, Verne A. Stadtman, *The University of California, 1868-1968* (New York, 1970), pp. 319-339.

14Henry Bennett to Edwin Langley, March 1, 1949, "The OSU Collection."

15"Minutes of the School of Arts and Sciences," May 10, 1949, p. 1.

16*The O'Collegian,* March 29, 1951; *The Stillwater Gazette,* March 30, 1951; April 13, 1951; April 20, 1951; April 27, 1951.

17*The O'Collegian,* April 29, 1951.

18*Ibid.,* April 26, 1951.

19Governor Murray asked the attorney-general's office to advise him on the Constitution. See, Fred Hansen to Johnston Murray, April 30, 1951, File Folder "Loyalty Oaths" in "The OSU Collection." Also, read *The O'Collegian,* May 5, 1951; May 9, 1951.

20*The O'Collegian,* May 10, 1951; May 11, 1951; May 19, 1951.

21Ruth Hammond to Angie Debo, June 6, 1951, "The Debo College Collection."

22"Minutes of the Board of Regents for the Oklahoma A. and M. Colleges," May 20, 1951, pp. 1-8.

23*The Stillwater Gazette,* July 13, 1951; March 7, 1952; December 19,

1952; December 26, 1952; *The O'Collegian,* October 19, 1951; February 21, 1952; December 11, 1952; December 16, 1952; "Minutes of the Board of Regents for the Oklahoma A. and M. Colleges," April 9, 1953, p. 25; *United States Supreme Court Records,* 97 (Rochester, 1953), pp. 218-230.

24John H. Dunkin to Oliver Willham, May 27, 1952 and Oliver Willham to John Dunkin, June 2, 1952, File Folder "General File" in "The OSU Collection;" *The Stillwater Gazette,* October 17, 1952; May 23, 1953; *The O'Collegian,* September 23, 1954; September 25, 1954; May 18, 1955.

25"Minutes of the Board of Regents for the Oklahoma A. and M. Colleges," April 18, 1954, pp. 33-35; *The O'Collegian,* April 17, 1951; May 18, 1951; October 29, 1952; March 13, 1953; March 21, 1954; April 30, 1954; May 5, 1954; May 6, 1954; May 13, 1954.

26"Minutes of the Board of Agriculture," XLVIII, pp. 135, 253; *Annual Catalog,* Session of 1932-1933, p. 91; "Minutes of the Oklahoma State Regents for Higher Education," May 13, 1946, p. 392.

27*Higher Education for Negroes* (Oklahoma City, 1949), pp. 1-21; Edgar Knight, *Higher Education in the South* (Chapel Hill, 1947), p. 101; "Minutes of the Oklahoma State Regents for Higher Education," May 27, 1947, pp. 473-474; "Minutes of the Board of Regents for the Oklahoma A. and M. Colleges," January 24, 1948, pp. 1-3; *The Stillwater Gazette,* May 2, 1947; August 6, 1948; September 12, 1948; October 15, 1948; *The O'Collegian,* January 13, 1948.

28*The O'Collegian,* January 15, 1949; January 21, 1949; February 5, 1949; February 10, 1949; February 23, 1949; February 25, 1949; March 1, 1949; March 4, 1949; March 5, 1949; April 1, 1949; "Minutes of the Board of Regents for the Oklahoma A. and M. Colleges," April 8, 1949, pp. 23-26; May 6, 1949, p. 11; Neil Hendricks to Henry Bennett, April 14, 1949, File Folder "Applications of Negro Students" in "The OSU Collection."

29*The O'Collegian,* October 7, 1950; November 17, 1950; October 20, 1951.

30*The Stillwater Gazette,* October 26, 1951; *The O'Collegian,* October 23, 1951; November 28, 1951; *The Des Moines* (Iowa) *Register,* October 4, 1951; October 21, 1951.

31Personal interview by author with Oliver Willham, July 8, 1971; Norman Burns to Oliver Willham, December 12, 1951 and Oliver Willham to Norman Burns, December 22, 1951, File Folder "The Johnny Bright Case" in "The OSU Collection"; *The O'Collegian,* January 18, 1952.

32*The Stillwater News-Press,* September 17, 1954; June 3, 1955; *The O'Collegian,* September 15, 1954; Hubbell, pp. 109, 112; "Minutes of the Board of Regents for the Oklahoma A. and M. Colleges," June 9, 1955, p. 23.

33*The O'Collegian,* May 8, 1953; May 9, 1953; *Inauguration of Oliver Siralvo Willham* (Stillwater, 1953), n.p.

34*The Oklahoman,* May 10, 1953.

35*The O'Collegian,* November 12, 1949; February 16, 1952; December 10, 1952; December 11, 1952; "Minutes of the Board of Regents for the Oklahoma A. and M. Colleges," December 13, 1952, p. 21.

36*The Oklahoma City Times,* March 26, 1953; *The Oklahoman,* March 26, 1953; *The O'Collegian,* March 26, 1953; "Minutes of the Board of Regents for the Oklahoma A. and M. Colleges," March 12, 1953, p. 27; March 12, 1953, p. 35; Personal interview by author with Oliver Willham, July 8, 1971.

37"Minutes of the Board of Regents for the Oklahoma A. and M. Colleges," April 2, 1953, n.p.; April 9, 1953, pp. 26-43; May 8, 1953, pp. 31-34; "The North Central Report," *The Oklahoma A. and M. College Magazine,* XXIV, No. 9 (1953), pp. 8-11; Oliver Willham to Don Boydston, August 17, 1953, File Folder "National Collegiate Athletic Association" in " The OSU Collection"; *The O'Collegian,* March 26, 1953; April 7, 1953; April 21. 1953; April 25, 1953; May 16, 1953; May 30, 1953; July 21, 1953; July 24, 1953; *The Stillwater Gazette,* April 24, 1953; May 1, 1953.

North Central, when it visited the Oklahoma A. and M. College again in 1966, commended President Willham for his leadership. See, *The North Central Association Report* (Stillwater, 1966), pp. 1-19.

[38]"Minutes of the Board of Regents for the Oklahoma A. and M. Colleges," September 4, 1952, p. 48; June 7, 1956, p. 24; *The Stillwater Gazette,* January 9, 1952; *The Stillwater News-Press,* May 14, 1954; December 24, 1954; June 17, 1955; September 30, 1955; November 11, 1955; April 6, 1956; June 29, 1956; February 11, 1957; *The Oklahoman,* November 17, 1956; *The O'Collegian,* May 16, 1953; September 15, 1953; March 18, 1955; July 22, 1955; July 19, 1955; September 4, 1955; June 22, 1956; November 20, 1956; "Lake Blackwell Deeded to the College," *The Oklahoma A. and M. College Magazine,* XXVI, No. 6 (1955), pp. 24-25.

[39]Oliver Willham, "Looking Ahead to the Future," *The Oklahoma A. and M. College Magazine,* XXVI, No. 6 (1955), p. 7.

[40]Chapman, *Old Central in the Crisis of 1955, passim.*

[41]*The Stillwater Gazette,* December 14, 1951; "Minutes of the Board of Regents for the Oklahoma A. and M. Colleges," May 26, 1952, p. 4; November 6, 1952, p. 20.

[42]*The O'Collegian,* April 1, 1954.

[43]*Ibid.,* April 8, 1954; "Minutes of the Board of Regents for the Oklahoma A. and M. Colleges," April 18, 1954, p. 32; December 8, 1954, p. 31; May 9, 1952, p. 33.

[44]*Oklahoma State University in Ethiopia* (Stillwater, 1969), 6. Also, see *The Stillwater Gazette,* December 21, 1951; July 18, 1952.

[45]"Minutes of the Board of Regents for the Oklahoma A. and M. Colleges," April 3, 1952, pp. 22-27; July 10, 1952, pp. 27-28; September 4, 1952, p. 49.

[46]Marcus J. Gordon to Oliver S. Willham, September 28, 1953, File Folder "Ethiopian College, 1950-1965" in "The OSU Collection,"

[47]*The O'Collegian,* January 1, 1953; "The A. and M. Counterpart in Ethiopia," *The Oklahoma A. and M. College Magazine,* XXV, No. 3 (1953), pp. 12-14; *Oklahoma A. and M. in Ethiopia* (Stillwater, 1955), pp. 1-2; Oliver Willham to Acting Administrator, TCA Administration, September 9, 1953, File Folder "Ethiopian College, 1950-1965" in "The OSU Collection." The impact of the Italians on Ethiopian education is discussed in Richard Parnhurst. "Education in Ethiopia During the Italian Fascist Occupation (1936-1941)," *The International Journal of African Historical Studies,* X, No. 3 (1972), pp. 361-396.

[48]*Oklahoma State University in Ethiopia,* 1952-1968, p. 10.

[49]Hugh Rouk to E. R. Eichholzer, January 9, 1956, File Folder "Ethiopian College, 1950-1965" in "The OSU Collection."

[50]*Oklahoma A. and M. in Ethiopia,* pp. 1-12; *Oklahoma State University in Ethiopia, 1952-1968,* pp. 18-48; Philip Wilber to Oliver Willham, June 22, 1953; L. H. Brannon to C. Bills, May 21, 1953; I. Eknor to Luther Brannon, May 6, 1953, File Folder "Ethiopian College, 1950-1965" in "The OSU Collection."

[51]*The Stillwater Gazette,* June 25, 1954; May 21, 1954; *The O'Collegian,* October 7, 1955; January 24, 1956; "Minutes of the Board of Regents for the Oklahoma A. and M. Colleges," July 9, 1954, pp. 47-48.

[52]Oliver Willham to Luther Brannon, February 1, 1956, File Folder "Ethiopian College, 1950-1965" in "The OSU Collection."

[53]*The O'Collegian,* September 12, 1956; October 24, 1956; March 2, 1957; March 1, 1957.

[54]*The Stillwater News-Press,* May 16, 1957; May 17, 1957; March 12, 1957; March 13, 1957; March 22, 1957; *Session Laws of Oklahoma* (1957), pp. 507-509; "Minutes of the Oklahoma State Regents for Higher Education," May 29, 1957, p. 2,022; "Minutes of the Board of Regents for the Oklahoma A. and M. Colleges," June 6, 1957, p. 26.

BIBLIOGRAPHY

BIBLIOGRAPHY
COLLECTIONS, MANUSCRIPTS, AND MANUSCRIPT RECORDS
Aldrich, Gene. "Pioneers and Pioneer Life in Payne County." (Unpublished Master's Thesis, Oklahoma Agricultural and Mechanical College, 1938).
Anderson, Melvin Sidney. "History of Wrestling at Oklahoma Agricultural and Mechanical College: Brief Biography of Edward Clark Gallagher." (Unpublished Master's Thesis, Oklahoma Agricultural and Mechanical College, 1935).
"The Henry E. Alvord Collection." Social and Economics Records Division, National Archives, Washington, D.C.
Barnett, James Albert. "A History of the Empire of Greer." (Unpublished Master's Thesis, Oklahoma Agricultural and Mechanical College, 1938).
Chapman, Berlin B. "Clipping and Letter Collection." Oklahoma State University Library, Archives.
———. "Early History of Stillwater and Vicinity: A Document Collection." Payne County Historical Society, Stillwater Public Library.
———. "Early Student Correspondence Collection." Oklahoma State University Library, Office of the Reference Librarian.
———. "Oklahoma State University Materials Concerning Its History." Microfilm reels numbered M 378.766 and C 4650, State Library of Oklahoma, Microfilm Division, Oklahoma City, Oklahoma.

Chapman, Berlin and Thompson, Catherine M. "Inventory to the Angelo C. Scott Collection." Oklahoma State University Library, Archives.

Chapman, Berlin (with assistance of OSU students in Oklahoma History 162). "Memorandum for the Meeting of the Lincoln County Historical Society Meeting of May 8, 1954." Oklahoma State University Library, Archives.

Clemence, Eldon L. "A History of the Democratic Party in Oklahoma Territory." (Unpublished Master's Thesis, Oklahoma State University, 1966).

Duncan, Otis Durant. "Economic Changes in American Rural Life." Oklahoma State University Library, Archives.

Dunlap, Elijah T. "The History of Legal Controls of Public Higher Education in Oklahoma." (Unpublished Doctoral Dissertation, Oklahoma State University, 1956).

Dusch, Willa Adams and Adams, A. W. "Oklahoma and "Little Gusta'." Microfilm Reels Numbered M 378.766 and C 4650. State Library of Oklahoma, Microfilm Division, Oklahoma City, Oklahoma.

Fiegel, Melvin Frank. "A History of Southwestern State College, 1903-1953." (Unpublished Doctoral Dissertation, Oklahoma State University, 1968).

Hartman, Thomas J. "Miscellaneous Notes on Professor Harry Thompson." Oklahoma State University Library, Archives.

Hastings, James K. "The Presbyterian Church of Stillwater, Oklahoma." Oklahoma State University Library, Archives.

Helms, Rosalind. "The Beginnings of Education in Stillwater." Stillwater Public Library Historical Collection, Stillwater Public Library.

Herod, George F. "The Administration, Impeachment, and Removal of Governor Henry S. Johnston." (Unpublished Master's Thesis, Tulsa University, 1952).

Hock, Alvin. "Religious and Cultural Efforts of the Protestant Episcopal Church in Early Oklahoma." (Unpublished Master's Thesis, Oklahoma Agricultural and Mechanical College, 1926).

Howard, Ruth. "The Development of the Oklahoma Agricultural and Mechanical College." (Unpublished Master's Thesis, Oklahoma Agricultural and Mechanical College, 1926).

Hubbell, Joe. "A History of the Oklahoma Education Association, 1945-1965." (Unpublished Doctoral Dissertation, Oklahoma State University, 1970).

"The Henry S. Johnston Collection." Oklahoma State University Library Archives.

McIntosh, D. C., Orr, Don, and White, C. "The Story of Agriculture of Less than College Grade in the Oklahoma Agricultural and Mechanical College from December 25, 1890 to June 1, 1940." Oklahoma State University Library, Archives.

"Minutes of the Former Students Association (1931-1944)." Oklahoma State University, Office of the Alumni Association, Student Union.

"Minutes of the Oklahoma State Regents for Higher Education (1944-1957)." State Capitol Building, Oklahoma City.

"Minutes of the Board of Regents for the Oklahoma A. and M. Colleges (1944-1957)." Oklahoma State University, Office of the Board of Regents, Student Union.

Oakes, Francis Coram. "Edmond Dandridge Murdaugh, 1895-1901." Oklahoma State University Library, Archives.

Oklahoma Agricultural and Mechanical College and Oklahoma State University. "Charging Book of the A. and M. Library, 1895." Oklahoma State University Library, Archives.

———. "The Henry G. Bennett Speech Collection." Oklahoma State University Library, Archives.

———. "The Cunningham Manuscript Collection." Oklahoma State University Library, Archives.

———. "The Cunningham Photographic Collection." Oklahoma State University Library, Archives.

———. "The Willa Adams Dusch Collection." Oklahoma State University Library, Archives.

———. "The Thomas J. Hartman Collection." Oklahoma State University Library, Archives.

———. "Historical Pageant—Oklahoma Agricultural and Mechanical College." Oklahoma State University Library, Archives.

———. "The Amos E. Lovett Collection." Oklahoma State University Library, Archives.

———. "The Manuscript Letter Collection (1892-1908)." Oklahoma State University Library, Archives.

———. "Memories of Oklahoma." A bound series of essays written by the Oklahoma History class of A. and M. College, Second Semester, 1942-1943. Payne County Historical Society, Stillwater Public Library.

———. "Minutes of the First Faculty (1892-1899)." Oklahoma State University Library, Archives.

———. "Minute Book of the Sigma Literary Society (1893-1896)." Oklahoma State University Library, Archives.

———. "Minute Book of the Webster Literary Society (1893-1896)." Oklahoma State University Library, Archives.

———. "Collection of James Clinton Neal and Family." Oklahoma State University Library, Archives.

———. "Oklahoma State University Buildings and Building Program: A Clipping Collection." Oklahoma State University Library, Office of the Reference Librarian.

———. "The OSU Collection (1891-1957)." Oklahoma State University Library, Archives.

———. "The Vingie Roe Collection." Oklahoma State University Library, Archives.

———. "The Frank J. Wikoff Collection." Oklahoma State University Library, Archives.

———. "The Red Red Rose Collection." Oklahoma State University Library, Archives.

———. "The Angelo C. Scott Collection." Oklahoma State University Library, Archives.

———. "Selections from the Record Book of the Oklahoma Agricultural and Mechanical College (1891-1941)." Oklahoma State University Library, Archives.

———. "The Harry E. Thompson Collection." Oklahoma State University Library, Archives.

———. "Treasurer's Book of the Sigma Literary Society (1894-1897)." Oklahoma State University Library, Archives.

Territory of Oklahoma. "Minutes of the State Board of Agriculture (1901-1944)." Oklahoma Board of Agriculture, State Capitol Building, Office of the President.

———. "Minutes of the Territorial Board of Education (1891-1907)." Office of the State Board of Education, State Capitol Building.

———. "The W. A. Tucker Collection." Oklahoma Board of Agriculture, State Capitol Building, Office of the President.

Santee, Mary C. "A History of the School of Agriculture of the Oklahoma Agricultural and Mechanical College." (Unpublished Master's Thesis, Oklahoma A. and M. College, 1956).

Scales, James. "A History of the Democratic Party in Oklahoma." (Unpublished Doctoral Dissertation, University of Oklahoma, 1949).

Scott, William Lester, "An Economic Survey of Stillwater." (Unpublished Master's Thesis, Oklahoma Agricultural and Mechanical College, 1931).

Stillwater, Oklahoma. "The Browning Club Minute Book (1903-1912)." Stillwater Public Library Historical Collection, Stillwater Public Library.

———. "Early Business and Industries: Stories of Stillwater's Earliest Industries and Businesses." Compiled by the Journalism Class of 1938. Stillwater Public Library Historical Collection, Stillwater Public Library.

———. "The Freeman Miller Collection." Payne County Historical Society, Stillwater Public Library.

———. "Records of Minutes of the Board of Trustees of the Town of Stillwater (1891-1901)." Stillwater Municipal Building, Office of the City Clerk.

———. "Records of the Christian Church of Stillwater." Stillwater Public Library Historical Collection, Stillwater Public Library.

————. "Records of the Payne County Sunday School Association." Stillwater Public Library Historical Collection, Stillwater Public Library.
————. "Register of the Stillwater Hotel." Payne County Historical Society, Stillwater Public Library.
————. "Stillwater's First School Board Minutes." Payne County Historical Society, Stillwater Public Library.
————. "Stillwater Public Schools, 1889-1938." Compiled by the Journalism Class of 1935-1936." Stillwater Public Library Historical Collection, Stillwater Public Library.
Trimble, H. M. "Fifty Years of Chemistry at Oklahoma A. and M. College." Oklahoma State University Library, Archives.
"The Harry S. Truman Collection." Harry S. Truman Presidential Library, Independence, Missouri.
United States Department of the Interior. Office of the Commissioner of Education. "Correspondence and Memoranda, 1890-1907." National Archives, Washington, D.C.
Wile, Otis. "The Chronological Story of Sports at Oklahoma State University from the Beginning in the 1890's through the 1960's." Oklahoma State University, Gallagher Hall.

U. S. GOVERNMENT DOCUMENTS

U. S. Department of Agriculture. *Annual Reports of the Bureau of Animal Industry.* Washington: Government Printing Office, 1900-1904.
————. *Organizational Lists of the Agricultural Colleges and Experiment Stations in the United States with a List of Agricultural Experiment Stations in Foreign Countries.* Washington: Government Printing Office, 1892-1903.
————. *Proceedings of the Annual Conventions of the Association of American Agricultural Colleges and Experiment Stations.* Washington: Government Printing Office, 1887-1909. (The Association began publishing its own reports in 1910. These documents were used through 1957.)
————. *Statistics of the Land-Grant Colleges and Agricultural Experiment Stations in the United States.* Washington: Government Printing Office, 1898-1903.
U. S. Department of the Interior. Census Division. *Abstract of the Eleventh Census: 1890.* Washington: Government Printing Office, 1896.
————. *Reports of the Commissioner of Education.* Washington: Government Printing Office, 1869-1880.
————. *Reports of the Commissioner of Indian Affairs.* Washington: Government Printing Office, 1869-1880.
————. *Report of the Secretary of the Interior.* Washington: Government Printing Office, 1869-1897.
U. S. Statutes at Large Pertaining to the Land-Grant Colleges:

Morrill Act of 1862	12, 503-505	(1862)
Hatch Act	24, 440-442	(1887)
Second Morrill Act of 1890	26, 417-419	(1890)
Adams Act	34, 63- 64	(1906)
Nelson Amendment	34,1281-1282	(1907)
Smith-Lever Act	38, 372-375	(1914)
Purnell Act	43, 970-972	(1925)
Capper-Ketcham Act	45, 711-712	(1928)
Bankhead-Jones Act	49, 436-439	(1935)
Research and Marketing Act of 1946	60,1082	(1946)

True, Alfred Charles. *A History of Agricultural Education in the United States.* Washington: Government Printing Office, 1929.
————. *A History of Agricultural Experimentation and Research In the United States, 1607-1925.* Washington: Government Printing Office, 1937.
————. *A History of Agricultural Extension Work in the United States, 1785-1923.* Government Printing Office, 1928.

LAND-GRANT COLLEGE AND UNIVERSITY DOCUMENTS

Annual Reports of the President of Cornell University. Ithaca, New York: Cornell University Press, 1886-1904.

Annual Reports of the President and Treasurer of the Massachusetts Institute of Technology. Boston: Rockwell and Churchill Press, 1897-1904.

Annual Reports of the Pennsylvania State College. Harrisburg: Pennsylvania State Printer, 1890-1909.

Annual Reports of the Regents and Faculty of the Kansas State Agricultural College. Topeka: Kansas Publishing House, 1890-1908.

Biennial Reports of the Board of Directors of the North Dakota Agricultural College. Grand Forks: North Dakota State Printer, 1900-1903.

STATE OF OKLAHOMA AND OKLAHOMA TERRITORY DOCUMENTS

A System of Higher Education for Oklahoma. Oklahoma City: Oklahoma State Regents for Higher Education, 1942.

Annual Reports of the Governor of Oklahoma to the Secretary of the Interior. Washington: Government Printing Office, 1895-1901

Annual Reports of the Oklahoma Board of Agriculture. Guthrie and Oklahoma City: State Capital Printing Company, 1893-1904.

Biennial Reports of the Territorial Superintendent of Public Instruction in Oklahoma. Guthrie: Leader Printing Company, 1898-1900.

Journals of the Oklahoma Council and Senate. Guthrie and Oklahoma City: State Capital Printing Company, 1890-1957.

Journals of the Oklahoma House of Representatives. Guthrie and Oklahoma City: State Capital Printing Company, 1890-1957.

Laws for the Regulation and Support of the Common Schools. Oklahoma City: Norman Transcript Steam Printing Company, 1893-1904.

Report of Education Institutions. Guthrie: State Capital Printing Company, 1902.

Report of the Secretary of the Board for Leasing School Lands to the Governor of Oklahoma Territory. Guthrie: State Capital Printing Company, 1898.

Report of the Superintendent of the Territorial Board of Health for Oklahoma. Guthrie: State Capital Printing Company, 1892.

The Session Laws and Statutes of Oklahoma. Guthrie and Oklahoma City: State Capital Printing Company, 1890-1957.

The Oklahoma State System of Higher Education. Oklahoma City: Oklahoma State Regents for Higher Education, 1971 (revised edition).

OKLAHOMA STATE UNIVERSITY DOCUMENTS

Annual Catalogs. Stillwater and Oklahoma City: various publishers, 1891-1957.

Bennett, Henry, *Reports of the College Presidents for 1929, 1930, and 1931.* Stillwater: College Printing Department, 1929-1931.

Biennial Reports of the Board of Regents, Clerk and Treasurer of the Territorial Agricultural and Mechanical College for 1897-1898. Guthrie: State Capital Printing Company, 1898.

Biennial Reports of the Territorial Agricultural and Mechanical College and Experiment Station of the Territory of Oklahoma for 1899-1900. Guthrie: State Capital Printing Company, 1900.

Biennial Reports of the Territorial Board of Regents of the A. and M. College and Experiment Station of the Territory of Oklahoma for 1900. Guthrie: State Capital Printing Company, 1900.

Constitution of the Sigma Literary Society. Stillwater: n.p., n.d., 1896.

Constitution of the Webster Debating Society. Stillwater: n.p., 1896.

Experiment Station Bulletins. Guthrie and Stillwater: various publishers, 1892-1957.

Extension Division Circulars. Stillwater: College Printing Department, 1916.

Oklahoma Agricultural and Mechanical College First Commencement Program. Stillwater: n.p., 1892.

Program of the Fiftieth Anniversary of the Oklahoma Agricultural and Mechanical College. Stillwater: The College Press, 1941.

The North Central Association Report. Stillwater: n.p., 1966.

The Redskin Yearbook. Stillwater: various publishers, 1910-1957.

Report of the Agricultural and Mechanical College Exhibit "E" of the Governor's Message to the Third Legislative Assembly of Oklahoma. Guthrie: State Capital Printing Company, 1895.

Report of the Financial Transactions of the Board of Regents of the Oklahoma Agricultural and Mechanical College and Experiment Station. Guthrie: State Capital Printing Company, 1902.

NEWSPAPERS*

The (Stillwater, Oklahoma) *Advance Democrat,* 1904-1906.
The (Oklahoma A. and M. College) *Agricultural News Service,* 1926-1927.
The (Phoenix) *Arizona Republic,* 1970.
The (Globe) *Arizona Silver Bell,* 1886.
The (Oklahoma A. and M. College) *College Paper,* 1899-1907.
The (Oklahoma A. and M. College) *College Mirror,* 1895-1898.
The (Stillwater, Oklahoma) *Daily Democrat,* 1904-1906.
The (Oklahoma A. and M. College) *Daily O'Collegian,* 1923-1957.
The (Oklahoma City) *Daily Oklahoman,* 1937-1956.
The (Stillwater) *Daily Oklahoma State,* 1898.
The Des Moines (Iowa) *Register,* 1951.
The (Stillwater, Oklahoma) *Eagle-Gazette,* 1895-1900.
The (Stillwater, Oklahoma) *Farmers Fact and Fancy,* 1904-1905.
The Frostburg (Maryland) *Mining Journal,* 1903-1909.
Harlow's (Oklahoma City) *Weekly,* 1928-1933.
The Iola (Kansas) *Register,* 1910.
The Kansas City (Missouri) *Star,* 1895.
The (Lawrence) *Kansas University Weekly,* 1898.
The (Oklahoma A. and M. College) *New Education,* 1911-1914.
The New York (New York) *Herald Tribune,* 1950.
The New York (New York) *Times,* 1923.
The (Guthrie) *Oklahoma Churchman,* 1892.
The Oklahoma City (Oklahoma) *Times,* 1939-1958.
The (Oklahoma City) *Oklahoma Eagle,* 1893.
The (Oklahoma City) *Oklahoma Farmer,* 1923.
The (Oklahoma City) *Farm Journal,* 1914.
The (Stillwater) *Oklahoma Hawk,* 1893.
The (Stillwater) *Oklahoma State,* 1898.
The (Guthrie) *Oklahoma State Capital,* 1897.
The (Stillwater) *Oklahoma State Sentinel,* 1893-1897.
The (Oklahoma A. and M. College) *Orange and Black,* 1908-1923.
The (Stillwater) *Payne County Journal,* 1894.
The (Stillwater, Oklahoma) *Payne County Populist,* 1893-1902.
The (Stillwater, Oklahoma) *Peoples Press,* 1907-1912.
The Perkins (Oklahoma) *Courier,* 1908.
The Perkins (Oklahoma) *Excelsior,* 1894.
The Perkins (Oklahoma) *Journal,* 1892-1893.
The (Oklahoma City, Oklahoma) *Pythian Times,* 1903.
The (no city, no state) *Southwestern Banker,* 1902.
The Stillwater (Oklahoma) *Daily Press,* 1914-1941.
The Stillwater (Oklahoma) *Democrat,* 1898-1903.
The Stillwater (Oklahoma) *Gazette,* 1891-1956.

The Stillwater (Oklahoma) *Daily News-Press,* 1941-1957.
The Tulsa (Oklahoma) *World,* 1921-1966.
The (Oklahoma A. and M. College) *Village Times,* 1946-1949.
The Washington (District of Columbia) *Daily News,* 1951.

*Oklahoma newspapers, especially in the territorial period, frequently changed hands and titles. This resulted in numerous name changes. The guide used in this study was Foreman, Carolyn Thomas, *Oklahoma Imprints, 1835-1907: A History of Printing in Oklahoma Before Statehood.* Norman, 1936.

ARTICLES

Adams, J. H. "In Retrospect and Prospect." *The Oklahoma A. and M. College Magazine,* XIII, No. 5 (1942)

Adler, Les K. and Paterson, Thomas G. "Red Fascism: The Merger of Nazi Germany and Soviet Russia in the American Image of Totalitarianism, 1930's-1950's." *The American Historical Review,* LXXV, No. 4 (1970).

"Advice at Presidential Level." *The Oklahoma A. and M. College Magazine,* XXV, No. 9 (1954).

"The A. and M. Counterpart in Ethiopia." *The Oklahoma A. and M. College Magazine,* XXV, No. 3 (1953).

"A. and M. is His Life." *The Oklahoma A. and M. College Magazine,* XXIV, No. 4 (1952).

"A. and M. Mourns Loss of President, Wife." *The Oklahoma A. and M. College Magazine,* XXIII, No. 5 (1952).

"A. and M.'s New President." *The Oklahoma A. and M. College Magazine,* XXIII, No. 8 (1952).

"A. and M.'s Vice President." *The Oklahoma A. and M. College Magazine,* XIX, No. 1 (1947).

"Alumni and Faculty Recognized." *The Oklahoma A. and M. College Magazine,* VI, No. 5 (1935).

Alvord, Henry. "The American Cattle Trade." *The Journal of the Royal Agricultural Society of England,* XIII, No. 2 (1887).

Ariett, William G. "Double Birthday." *The Oklahoma A. and M. College Magazine,* XXI, No. 7 (1950).

"Auxiliary Enterprises at Oklahoma A. and M." *The Oklahoma A. and M. College Magazine,* XXV, No. 2 (1953).

Barnes, Sherman B. "The Entry of Science and History in the College Curriculum, 1865-1914." *The History of Education Quarterly,* IV, No. 2 (1964).

Bennett, Henry. "Ten Years of Progress." *The Oklahoma A. and M. College Magazine,* IX, No. 1 (1937).

" 'Big Brother' to a Free World." *The Oklahoma A. and M. College Magazine,* XXIII, No. 1 (1951).

Bowman, Mary Jean. "The Land-Grant Colleges and Universities in Human-Resource Development." *Journal of Economic History,* XXII, No. 4 (1962).

Bowers, George. "Early Military Training." *The Oklahoma A. and M. College Magazine,* I, No. 7 (1930).

Braley, Genevieve. "Classes Resumed in Old Central." *The Oklahoma A. and M. College Magazine,* I, No. 8 (1930).

Briggs, Hilton. "The New Dean of Agriculture." *The Oklahoma A. and M. College Magazine,* X, No. 5 (1930).

Bulletin of the American Association of University Professors, XVIII, No. 5 (1932).

Caldwell, Richard. "A. and M.'s Fighting Dean Returns." *The Oklahoma A. and M. College Magazine,* XVIII, No. 4 (1946).

———. "Engine Research at A. and M." *The Oklahoma A. and M. College Magazine,* XXI, No. 1 (1949).

———. "German Diesel Lab Here!" *The Oklahoma A. and M. College Magazine,* XIX, No. 8 (1948).

———. "Rhapsody of the Waves." *The Oklahoma A. and M. College Magazine,* XVII, No. 3 (1944).

Carstensen, Vernon. "A Century of the Land-Grant Colleges." *The Journal of Higher Education*, XXXIII, No. 1 (1963).

Chapman, B. B. "Author Discovered by A. C. Scott." *The Oklahoma A. and M. College Magazine*, VII, No. 7 (1945).

――――. "Dr. Henry G. Bennett As I Knew Him." *The Chronicles of Oklahoma*, XXXII, No. 2 (1955).

――――. "Establishment of the Wichita Reservation." *The Chronicles of Oklahoma*, XXIV, No. 3 (1946).

――――. "First Faculty Set Standards." *The Oklahoma A. and M. College Magazine*, XV, No. 4 (1943).

――――. "I Remember the University When." *The Oklahoma State Alumnus*, II, No. 10 (1961).

――――. "Living Cowboy Emblem." *The Oklahoma A. and M. College Magazine*, XXVI, No. 5 (1955).

――――. "Medal Collection Complete." *The Oklahoma A. and M. College Magazine*, XV, No. 3 (1943).

――――. "The Men Who Selected Stillwater as the Site for the College." *The Oklahoma A. and M. College Magazine*, II, No. 4 (1930)

――――. "Oklahoma City from Public Land to Private Property." *The Chronicles of Oklahoma*, XXXVII, Nos. 2, 3, 4 (1959).

――――. "Old Central of Oklahoma State University." *The Chronicles of Oklahoma*, XLII, No. 3 (1964).

Colman, Gould P. "Pioneering in Agricultural Education: Cornell University, 1867-1890." *Agricultural History*, XXXVI, No. 4 (1962).

"Colonel Robert Terry Stuart." *The Oklahoma A. and M. College Magazine*, XXII, No. 4 (1950).

Cordell, Harry. "Broadcasting Loyalty." *The Oklahoma A. and M. College Magazine*, I, No. 3 (1929).

"Cowboys Play Difficult Schedule." *The Oklahoma A. and M. College Magazine*, XVII, No. 4 (1945).

Cross, Hays. "Memories to be Revived. " *The Oklahoma A. and M. College Magazine*, XI, No. 4 (1939).

Dale, Edward E. "The Frontier Literary Society." *Nebraska History*, XXXI, No. 2 (1950).

――――. "Teaching on the Prairie Plains, 1890-1900." *The Mississippi Valley Historical Review*, XXXIII, No. 2 (1946).

"Darlow Takes Over; Dean Blizzard Retires. " *The Oklahoma A and M. College Magazine*, XXIV, No. 6 (1953)

Davidson, Oscar William. "Education at Statehood." *The Chronicles of Oklahoma*, XXVIII, No. 1 (1950).

DeWitt, Bennie L. "Oklahomans' Attitude Toward John Steinbeck Since 1937." *Proceedings of the Oklahoma Academy of Science*, XLVII (1968).

"Dr. MacVicar Named Vice-President." *The Oklahoma A. and M. College Magazine*, XXVIII, No. 7 (1957).

"Dr. Swearingen is Appointed Dean." *"The Oklahoma A. and M. College Magazine*, XXVIII, No. 8 (1957).

"Donnell . . . A Sketch." *The Oklahoma A. and M. College Magazine*, I, No. 7 (1929).

"The 'Electronic Brain'," *The Oklahoma A. and M. College Magazine*, XXVIII, No. 5 (1957).

Ewing, Amos. "The First Board of Regents." *The Oklahoma A. and M. College Magazine*, I, No. 4 (1929).

"Federal Government Continues to Call on A. and M." *The Oklahoma A. and M. College Magazine*, V, No. 5 (1934).

"Fifteen Years of Growth by the School of Commerce." *The Oklahoma A. and M. College Magazine*, II, No. 7 (1931).

"Fiftieth Anniversary Observed." *The Oklahoma A. and M. College Magazine*, XIII, No. 4 (1942).

Fischer, LeRoy H. and Smith, Robert E. "Oklahoma and the Parking Meter." *The Chronicles of Oklahoma*, XLVII, No. 2 (1969).

Fite, Gilbert. "The NonPartisan League in Oklahoma." *The Chronicles of Oklahoma*, XXIV, No. 2 (1946).

Florer, John H. "Major Issues in the Congressional Debate of the Morrill Act of 1862." *The History of Education Quarterly,* VIII, No. 4 (1968).

Floyd, Howard. "Campus Fire Station in Wartime." *The Oklahoma A. and M. College Magazine,* XVI, No. 7 (1944).

"Flying Course Progress," *The Oklahoma A. and M. College Magazine,* XI, No. 6 (1940).

Ford, Charles. "Botany Texts: A Survey of Their Development in Higher Education, 1643-1906." *The History of Education Quarterly,* IV, No. 1 (1964).

Foreman, Carolyn Thomas. "Black Beaver." *The Chronicles of Oklahoma,* XXIV, No. 3 (1946).

Foreman, Grant. "Historical Background of the Kiowa-Comanche Reservation." *The Chronicles of Oklahoma,* XIV, No. 2 (1941).

Freudenberge, Helen. "Records and Reminiscences." *The Oklahoma A. and M. College Magazine,* VIII, No. 4 (1937).

Fuller, Wayne. "The Rural Roots of the Progressive Leaders." *Agricultural History,* XLII, No. 1 (1968).

"Future College Being Planned for 25 Years." *The Oklahoma A. and M. College Magazine,* I, No. 1 (1929).

Galambos, Louis. "The Agrarian Image of the Large Corporation, 1879-1920: A Study of Social Accommodation. *The Journal of Economic History,* XXVIII, No. 3 (1968).

"Graduate School Offerings at A. and M." *The Oklahoma A. and M. College Magazine,* XXIV, No. 7 (1953).

Gutek, Gerald. "An Analysis of Formal Education in Edward Bellamy's Looking Backward." *The History of Education Quarterly,* IV, No. 4 (1964).

Guthrey, Bee. "Early Days in Payne County." *The Chronicles of Oklahoma,* III, No. 1 (1925).

Hagood, Wendall. "The Graduate School Grows." *The Oklahoma A. and M. College Magazine,* I, No. 7 (1930).

Hale, G. A. "Parking Meter Aggie Designed." *The Oklahoma A. and M. College Magazine,* XXII, No. 4 (1950).

Hamilton, John W. "Saga of a Little Red Schoolhouse." *The Oklahoma A. and M. College Magazine,* XIX, No. 3 (1947).

Harms, Herman E. "*In Loco Parentis* in Higher Education." *Phi Kappa Phi Journal,* LI, No. 3 (1971).

Hartman, Tom. "1898 Class History," *The Oklahoma A. and M. College Magazine,* XIV, No. 9 (1943).

Harper, Horace J. "Magruder Field." *The Oklahoma A. and M. College Magazine,* XIII, No. 9 (1942).

Hastings, James. "Log Cabin Days in Oklahoma." *The Chronicles of Oklahoma,* XXVII, No. 2 (1950).

————. "Oklahoma Agricultural and Mechanical College and Old Central." *The Chronicles of Oklahoma,* XXVIII, No. 1 (1950).

Hazen, William B. "Some Correction of 'Life on the Plains'," *The Chronicles of Oklahoma,* III, No. 4 (1925).

Hilton, O. A. "The Oklahoma Council of Defense and the First World War." *The Chronicles of Oklahoma,* XX, No. 1 (1942).

————. "Public Opinion and Civil Liberties in Wartime, 1917-1919." *The Southwestern Social Science Quarterly,* XXVIII, No. 3 (1947).

Holcomb, Geneva. "Makovsky: The Man and the Musician." *The Oklahoma A. and M. College Magazine,* II, No. 1 (1930).

Holter, George. "When the School was Young." *The Oklahoma A. and M. College Magazine,* I, No. 4 (1929).

Hurley, Fern. "That Which They Built." *The Oklahoma A. and M. College Magazine,* I, No. 5 (1930).

"In Memoriam: John Whitehurst." *The Oklahoma A. and M. College Magazine,* I, No. 8 (1930).

Jarrell, Alfred E. "The Founding of Oklahoma A. and M. College: A Memoir." *The Chronicles of Oklahoma,* XXXIV, No. 3 (1956).

————. "I Remember When . . . ." *Oklahoma State University Magazine,* I, No. 11 (1958).

"Joe C. Scott Heads Aggie Board." *The Oklahoma A. and M. College Magazine*, VIII, No. 6 (1937).

"Lake Blackwell Deeded to the College." *The Oklahoma A. and M. College Magazine*, XXVI, No. 6 (1955).

"Last of the A. and M. Faculty." *The Oklahoma A. and M. College Magazine*, XXI, No. 4 (1949).

"Legislature Backs Separate Board Plan." *The Oklahoma A. and M. College Magazine*, II, No. 1 (1930).

"Lifetime Land-Grant Missionary." *The Oklahoma A. and M. College Magazine*, XXIII, No. 6 (1952).

Lindley, Vick. "The Aggie Campus Reminds Me." *The Oklahoma A. and M. College Magazine*, XXII, No. 3 (1950).

Little, Blanche. "The Oklahoma A. and M. College." *The School Journal*, LXXIV, No. 2 (1907).

"Looking Ahead with the School of Commerce." *The Oklahoma A. and M. College Magazine*, II, No. 7 (1931).

Low, Edmon. "Knowledge Storehouse." *The Oklahoma A. and M. College Magazine*, XXIV, No. 8 (1953).

Lyon, William. "The Corporate Frontier in Arizona." *The Journal of Arizona History*, IX, No. 1 (1968).

MacCracken, H. N. "Religio Magistri." *Atlantic Monthly*, CXXVII (January, 1921).

Martin, Frank "Dick Tracy's Creator." *The Oklahoma A. and M. College Magazine*, IX, No. 5 (1938).

Miller, Freeman, "Founding the College Library." *The Oklahoma A. and M. College Magazine*, I, No. 4 (1929).

Mood, Fulmer (ed.). "Frederick Jackson Turner's Address on Education in a United States without Free Lands." *Agricultural History*, XXIII, No. 4 (1949).

Moulton, W. H. "A and M.'s New Stadium." *The Oklahoma A. and M. College Magazine*, I, No. 5 (1929).

"Named Dean of Veterinary Medicine." *The Oklahoma A. and M. College Magazine*, XXVIII, No. 2 (1956).

Neuringer, Sheldon. "Governor Walton's War on the Ku Klux Klan: An Episode in Oklahoma History." *The Chronicles of Oklahoma*, XLV, No. 2 (1967).

"New Board of Regents." *The Oklahoma A. and M. College Magazine*, XVII, No. 1 (1944).

"New Dormitory Under Construction." *The Oklahoma A. and M. College Magazine*, V, No. 6 (1934).

"Ninth A. and M. President is Dead." *The Oklahoma A. and M. College Magazine*, XXIII, No. 9 (1952).

"The North Central Report." *The Oklahoma A. and M. College Magazine*, XXIV, No. 9 (1953).

"Oklahoma Aggies Sugar Bowl Bound." *The Oklahoma A. and M. College Magazine*, XVIII, No. 3 (1945).

"Oklahoma A. and M. of the Future." *The Oklahoma A. and M. College Magazine*, II, No. 3 (1930).

"The Oklahoma Educational Survey Commission." *School and Society*, XIV, No. 366 (1921).

"Oklahoma Legislators' Wives Make 1947 Trek to Aggie Campus." *The Oklahoma A. and M. College Magazine*, XVIII, No. 7 (1947).

"On the Campus." *The Oklahoma A. and M. College Magazine*, X, No. 4 (1934).

Pankhurst, Richard. "Education in Ethiopia During the Italian Fascist Occupation (1936-1941)." *The International Journal of African Historical Studies*, X, No. 3 (1972).

Patterson, Herbert. "A New Approach to the 'Formal Discipline' Controversy." *School and Society*, XII, No. 307 (1920).

———. "An Experiment in Automatic Spelling." *School and Society*, XVII, No. 444 (1923).

———. "An Experiment in Supervising College Teaching." *School and Society*, XXI, No. 527 (1925).

————. "Can College Teaching Be Improved?" *Educational Review*, 64, No. 1 (1922).

————. "Common Sense and Teacher's Contracts." *School and Society*, X, No. 254 (1919).

————. "Teaching Ethics Through Manual Training." *School and Society*, XVI, No. 415 (1922).

Peery, Dan. "The First Two Years." *The Chronicles of Oklahoma*, VII, No. 2 (1929).

Perdue, Randle. "The Goal is $500,000." *The Oklahoma A. and M. College Magazine*, I, No. 6 (1929).

————. "The Stadium Campaign Unfolds." *The Oklahoma A. and M. College Magazine*, I, No. 7 (1929).

————. "That Man Bennett." *The Oklahoma A. and M. College Magazine*, I, No. 1 (1929).

Pomeroy, Earl. "Carpet-Baggers in the Territories, 1861-1890." *The Historian*, II, No. 2 (1939).

Powell, J. P. "Some Nineteenth Century Views on the University Curriculum." *The History of Education Quarterly*, V, No. 1 (1955).

"President Returns from Abroad." *The Oklahoma A. and M. College Magazine*, XXI, No. 3 (1949).

Rodnitzky, Jerome L. "Getting the Ear of the State: A Pioneer University Radio Station in the 1920's." *The History of Education Quarterly*, VIII, No. 4 (1968).

"Rogers is Named Alumni Secretary." *The Oklahoma A. and M. College Magazine*, XXVI, No. 7 (1955).

Ross, Earle D. "The Great Triumvirate of Land-Grant Educators." *The Journal of Higher Education*, XXXII, No. 9 (1961).

————. "On Writing the History of Land-Grant College and Universities." *Journal of Higher Education*, XXIV, No. 8 (1953).

————. "The United States Department of Agriculture During the Commissionership: A Study in Politics, Administration, and Technology, 1862-1889." *Agricultural History*, XX, No. 3 (1946).

Rulon, Philip and Butchart, Ronald. "Henry Elijah Alvord, 1844-1904: Soldier, Scientist, and Scholar." *The Chronicles of Oklahoma*, LII, No. 1 (1974).

Savage, Orville M. "What About this Separate Board of Regents?" *The Oklahoma A. and M. College Magazine*, I, No. 2 (1929).

"School of Commerce Gets Results from Six Objectives." *The Oklahoma A. and M. College Magazine*, II, No. 7 (1931).

Schott, Barbara "Introducing Carl P. Thompson." *The Oklahoma A. and M. College Magazine*, XIX, No. 4 (1948).

"Scientific Tools for Nuclear Technology." *The Oklahoma A. and M. College Magazine*, XXVIII, No. 7 (1957).

Scroggs, Schiller, "General Administrative Organization of the College." *The Oklahoma A. and M. College Magazine*, II, No. 4 (1930).

————. "Science and Literature Makes Changes." *The Oklahoma A. and M. College Magazine*, VIII, No. 6 (1937).

Scroggs, Schiller and Bennett, Henry. "Sabbatical Leave." *The Journal of Higher Education*, III, No. 4 (1932).

Sherman, Caroline. "A New England Boy in the Civil War." *The New England Quarterly*, XXII, No. 4 (1932).

————. "A Young Army Officer's Experience in Indian Territory." *The Chronicles of Oklahoma*, XII, No. 2 (1935).

Shull, Warren. "The Next Governor of Oklahoma." *The Oklahoma State Alumnus*, III, No. 2 (1962).

"Sojourning in Chile." *The Oklahoma A. and M. College Magazine*, I, No. 2 (1937).

Solberg, Winton. "The University of Illinois Struggles for Recognition." *Journal of the Illinois State Historical Society*, LIX, No. 2 (1966).

"Staff and Faculty Changes." *The Oklahoma A. and M. College Magazine*, VII, No. 1 (1936).

"State Question No. 310." *The Oklahoma A. and M. College Magazine*, XVI, No. 10 (1944).

Steele, Aubrey L. "The Beginning of Quaker Administration of Indian Affairs, in Oklahoma." *The Chronicles of Oklahoma*, XVII, No. 4 (1939).

Stiles, George. "Reminiscences of the Class of 1900." *The Oklahoma A. and M. College Magazine*, XVII, No. 9 (1945).

"Stillwater and A. and M. College Boosters." *The Oklahoma A. and M. College Magazine*, VI, No. 1 (1934).

"Theta Pond Gets a Facial." *The Oklahoma A. and M. College Magazine*, XV, No. 6 (1944).

Thomas, Raymond D. "The Land-Grant College in the Changing Times." *The Oklahoma A. and M. College Magazine*, IV, No. 4 (1933).

Thompson, Harry. "1892—A. and M. College—1930." *The Oklahoma A. and M. College Magazine*, I, No. 8 (1930).

———. "The Territorial Presidents of Oklahoma A. and M. College." *The Chronicles of Oklahoma*, XXXII, No. 4 (1954).

Thompson, Lawrence. "Poor Boys Get a Break." *The Oklahoma A. and M. College Magazine*, I, No. 1 (1929).

Thuesen, H. G. and Fischer, LeRoy. "The Reminiscenses of the Development of the Parking Meter." *The Chronicles of Oklahoma*, XLV, No. 2 (1967).

"Toward a Greater A. and M." *The Oklahoma A. and M. College Magazine*, XX, No. 1 (1948).

"Tribute is Given to Dr. O. M. Smith." *The Oklahoma A. and M. College Magazine*, XXVII, No. 2 (1955).

Trout, Clement. "A. and M. College Does Its Part." *The Oklahoma A. and M. College Magazine*, V, No. 1 (1933).

"Veterans Village Comes of Age." *The Oklahoma A. and M. College Magazine*, XX, No. 1 (1948).

"Waldorf Takes Place with Kansas Aggies." *The Oklahoma A. and M. College Magazine*, V, No. 7 (1934).

Wallin, Gale. "I Remember When - - ." *The Oklahoma A. and M. College Magazine*, I, No. 5 (1930).

"We Get the College." *The Oklahoma A. and M. College Magazine*, I, No. 4 (1929).

White, Theodore H. "Action Intellectuals: Scholarly Impact on the Nation's Past." *Life*, 62, No. 24 (1967).

Wile, Otis. "Bricks, Stone, Dreams, and Travail." *The Oklahoma State Alumnus*, VI, No. 1 (1965).

———. "Sixth Founders' Day Celebration is Best Yet." *The Oklahoma A. and M. College Magazine*, V, No. 6 (1934).

Willham, Oliver S. "A Report on College Needs." *The Oklahoma A. and M. College Magazine*, XXIV, No. 6 (1953).

———. "The Challenge Facing A. and M." *The Oklahoma A. and M. College Magazine*, XXV, No. 2 (1953).

———. "Looking Ahead to the Future." *The Oklahoma A. and M. College Magazine*, XXVI, No. 6 (1955).

———. "Measuring the Values of Higher Education." *The Oklahoma A. and M. College Magazine*, XXVIII, No. 6 (1957).

———. "Twentieth Anniversary Report." *The Oklahoma A. and M. College Magazine*, XIV, No. 9 (1943).

"World Power Conference." *The Oklahoma A. and M. College Magazine*, II, No. 4 (1930).

Yost, Howard M. "Military Training Expands at Oklahoma A. and M." *The Oklahoma A. and M. College Magazine*, XV, No. 3 (1943).

BOOKS

Alley, John. *City Beginnings in Oklahoma Territory*. Norman, 1939.

Alvord, Henry. "Dairying at Home and Abroad," in *Yearbook of the United States Department of Agriculture*. Washington, 1903.

———. "Dairy Development in the United States," in *Yearbook of the United States Department of Agriculture*. Washington, 1906.

————. "The Dairy Herd: Its Formation and Management," in *Yearbook of the United States Department of Agriculture*. Washington, 1894.

Alvord, Samuel Morgan. *Genealogy of the Descendants of Alexander Alvord*. New York, 1908.

————. *History of the Connecticut Valley in Massachusetts*, I. II. Philadelphia, 1879.

Ambrose, Stephen, *Duty, Honor, and Country: A History of West Point*. Baltimore, 1966.

Andrews, Ruth Horn. *The First Thirty Years: A History of Texas Technological College, 1925-1955*. Lubbock, 1956.

Axt, Richard. *The Federal Government and Financing Higher Education*. New York, 1952.

Bailey, Joseph. *Seaman A. Knapp: Schoolmaster to American Agriculture*. New York, 1945.

Bailey, Liberty Hyde. *Cyclopedia of American Agriculture*, IV. New York, 1909.

Bailyn, Bernard. *Education and the Forming of American Society*. Chapel Hill, 1960.

Barritt, M. C. *The County Agent and the Farm Bureau*. New York, 1922.

Bennett, Henry Garland. *A Report on Public Works Plannings*. Oklahoma City, 1938.

————. *The Coordination of the State Institutions for Higher Education in Oklahoma*. Durant, 1926.

————. *The Great Basic Hope for Peace*. Stillwater, 1951.

————. *This is Colonel Stuart: A Gentleman from Texas*. Stillwater, 1945.

Bettersworth, John. *People's College: A History of Mississippi State*. Birmingham, 1953.

Billington, Ray. *America's Frontier Heritage*. New York, 1966.

Bingham, Jonathan. *Shirt-Sleeve Diplomacy: Point Four in Action*. New York, 1953.

Bishop, Morris. *Early Cornell, 1865-1900*. Ithaca, 1962.

Bliss, R. K. (ed.). *The Spirit and Philosophy of Extension Work*. Washington, 1952.

Brubacher, John and Rudy, Willis. *Higher Education in Transition*. New York, 1958.

Buck, Justus Solon. *The Granger Movement: A Study of Agricultural Organization and Its Political, Economic, and Social Manifestations, 1870-1880*. Lincoln, 1913.

Bullock, Henry A. *A History of Negro Education in the South*. New York, 1967.

Bryant, Keith, *Alfalfa Bill Murray*. Norman, 1968.

Calcott, George. *A History of the University of Maryland*. Baltimore, 1966.

Cary, Harold Whiting. *The University of Massachusetts*. Amherst, 1962.

Chapman, Berlin, *Early History of Oklahoma Agricultural and Mechanical College*. Stillwater, 1929.

————. *The Founding of Stillwater: A Case Study in Oklahoma History*. Oklahoma City, 1948.

————. *Old Central in the Crisis of 1955*. Oklahoma City, 1965.

Cochran, Thomas. *The American Business System*. New York, 1957.

Commager, Henry Steele. *Documents in American History*. New York, 1963.

Crane, Theodore R. *The Colleges and the Public, 1787-1862*. New York, 1963.

Cremin, Lawrence. *The Genius of American Education*. New York, 1965.

————. *The Transformation of the School: Progressivism in American Education*. New York, 1961.

Cunningham, Robert. *Oklahoma Agricultural and Mechanical College: A Book of Photographs*. Stillwater, 1955.

————. *Stillwater: Where Oklahoma Began*. Stillwater, 1969.

Conger, Napoleon. *Professional Adjustment Service Rendered by Teacher Training Institutions*. Durant, 1930.

Currin, Dial. *Beyond the Gold Fields*. Stillwater, 1951.

Dale, E. E. and Wardell, M. *History of Oklahoma*. New York, 1940.

Debo, Angie. *From Creek Town to Oil Capital*. Norman, 1943.

DeWitt, Benjamin Parke. *The Progressive Movement*. New York, 1915.

Dick, Everett. *The Dixie Frontier*. New York, 1948.
———. *The Lure of the Land*. Lincoln, 1970.
Donald, David. *Lincoln Reconsidered*. New York, 1956.
Dusch, Willa. *The Sigma Literary Society, 1893-1897*. Stillwater, 1951.
Eaton, Frank. *Pistol Pete: Veteran of the Old West*. Boston, 1952.
Ebert, Roger. *An Illini Century*. Urbana, 1967.
Eells, Walter Crosby. *Degrees in Higher Education*. Washington, 1963.
Ellis, William Arba (ed. and comp.). *Norwich University, 1819-1911: Her History, Her Graduates, Her Roll of Ronor*, I, II, III, IV. Montpelier, 1911.
Elson, Ruth M. *Guardians of Tradition*. Lincoln, 1964.
Gallagher, E. C. *Amateur Wrestling*. Guthrie, 1925.
———. *Wrestling*. New York, 1939.
Geiger, Louis. *University of the Northern Plains: A History of the University of North Dakota, 1883-1958*. Grand Forks, 1958.
Gittinger, Roy. *The Formation of the State of Oklahoma*. Norman, 1939.
Goldman, Eric. *Rendevous with Destiny*. New York, 1952.
Hartnett, Rodney T. *College and University Trustees: Their Backgrounds, Roles and Educational Attitudes*. Princeton, 1969.
Hatch, Richard (ed.). *Some Founding Papers of the University of Illinois*. Urbana, 1967.
Hays, Samuel P. *Conservation and the Gospel of Efficiency: The Progressive Conservation Movement, 1890-1920*. Cambridge, 1959.
Higher Education for Negroes. Oklahoma City, 1949.
Herbst, Jurgan. *The German Historical School in American Scholarship*, Ithaca, 1965.
Hines, Gordon, *Alfalfa Bill*. Oklahoma City, 1932.
Hofstadter, Richard. *The Age of Reform*. New York, 1955.
———. *Anti-Intellectualism in American Life*. New York, 1963.
Hofstadter, Richard and Metzger, Walter. *The Development of Academic Freedom in the United States*. New York, 1955.
Hopkins, John F. *The University of Kentucky*. Lexington, 1951.
Humphrey, Seth. *Following the Prairie Frontier*. Minneapolis, 1934.
Institute for Government Research of the Brookings Institution. *Organization and Administration of Oklahoma*. Washington, 1935.
Jacobs, Wilbur (ed.). *Frederick Jackson's Turner's Legacy*. San Marino, 1965.
Johnson, H. C. and Johanningmeier, Johanningmeier, E. W. *Teachers for the Prairie: The University of Illinois and the Schools, 1865-1956*. Urbana, 1972.
Joughin, Louis (ed.). *Academic Freedom and Tenure*. Madison, 1969.
Kelsey, Lincoln D. *Cooperative Extension Work*. Ithaca, 1955.
Knight, Edgar. *Higher Education in the South*. Chapel Hill, 1947.
Krug, Edward. *The Shaping of the American High School*. Madison, 1969.
Lamar, Howard, *The Far Southwest, 1846-1912*. New Haven, 1966.
Land-Grant Colleges and Universities: What are They and the Relations of the Federal Government to Them. Washington, 1951.
Lehman, B. H. *Wild Marriage*. New York, 1925.
Leuchtenburg, William E. *Franklin D. Roosevelt and the New Deal*. New York, 1963.
Lipset, S. M. and Wolin, Sheldon (eds.). *The Berkeley Student Revolt*. Garden City, 1965.
Lee, Calvin B. T. *The Campus Scene, 1900-1970*. New York, 1970.
Litton, Gaston. *History of Oklahoma at the Golden Anniversary of Statehood*, I. New York, 1957.
Loewenberg, Bert James (ed.). *Darwinism: Reaction or Reform?* New York, 1966.
Marshall, Helen. *Grandest of Enterprises*. Normal, 1956.
May, Henry. *The End of American Innocence*. New York, 1959.
McCormick, Richard. *Rutgers: A Bicentennial History*. New Brunswick, 1966.
McReynolds, Edwin C. *Oklahoma: A History of the Sooner State*. Norman, 1954.
Meier, August and Rudwick, Elliot (eds.). *The Making of Black America*, II. New York, 1969.

Men of Affairs and Representative Institutions of Oklahoma. Tulsa, 1916.

Military Order of the Loyal Legion. Washington, 1897.

Miller, Freeman E. *The Founding of Oklahoma Agricultural and Mechanical College.* Stillwater, 1928.

————. *The Latin Inflections: Together with their Elementary Principles.* Stillwater, 1928.

Morison, Samuel E. and Commager, Henry S. *The Growth of the American Republic,* II. New York, 1947.

Murray, William. *Memoirs of Governor Murray and True History of Oklahoma,* I, II, III. Boston, 1945.

————. *The Negroes Place in the Call of Race.* Tishomingo, 1948.

Nevins, Allan. *The Origins of the Land-Grant Colleges and State Universities: A Brief Account of the Morrill Act of 1862 and its Results.* Washington, 1962.

————. *The State Universities and Democracy.* Urbana, 1946.

Nye, Russel B. *Midwestern Progressive Politics.* East Lansing, 1959.

Oklahoma A. and M. in Ethiopia. Stillwater, 1969.

Oklahoma State University in Ethiopia. Stillwater, 1969.

Ousley, Clarence. *A History of the Agricultural and Mechanical College of Texas.* College Station, 1913.

Overby, Houston. "The Story of Aggieland in the Nineteenth Century" in *Oklahoma Agricultural College Yesterday and Today.* Guthrie, 1938.

Parker, William Belmont. *The Life and Public Services of Justin Smith Morrill.* Boston, 1924.

Richardson, James D. *Messages and Papers of Presidents, 1889-1898,* VII. New York, 1912.

Richardson, Rupert Norval. *The Comanche Barrier to South Plains Settlement.* Glendale, 1933.

Riley, James Whitcomb. *The Complete Works of James Whitcomb Riley.* New York, 1916.

Ross, Earle D. *Democracy's College: The Land-Grant Movement in the Formative Stage.* Ames, 1942.

————. *A History of the Iowa State College of Agricultural and Mechanical Arts.* Ames, 1942.

————. *The Land-Grant Idea at Iowa State College.* Ames, 1958.

Rudolph, Frederick. *The American College and University,* New York, 1965.

Scott, Angelo. *The Case for Homo Sapiens.* Oklahoma City, 1940.

————. *The Story of an Administration of the Oklahoma Agricultural and Mechanical College.* Oklahoma City, n.d.

————. *The Story of Oklahoma City.* Oklahoma City, 1939.

Seventy-Fifth Anniversary Committee. *History of New Hampshire, 1866-1941.* Durham, 1941.

Seymour, Flora Warren. *Indian Agents of the Old Frontier.* New York, 1941.

Sheldon, J. P. *Dairy Farming: Being the Theory, Practice and Methods of Dairying.* London, 1881.

Shirley, Glenn. *Pawnee Bill: A Biography of Major Gordon W. Lillie.* Albuquerque, 1958.

Sinclair, Upton. *The Goose-Step.* Pasadena, 1922.

Slay, Ronald J. *The Development of the Teaching of Agriculture in Mississippi.* New York, 1928.

Smith, Henry Nash. *Virgin Land: The American West as Symbol and Myth.* New York, 1950.

Solberg, Winton. *The University of Illinois, 1867-1894.* Urbana, 1968.

Songs of the Western Colleges. New York, 1902.

Stadtman, Verne A. *The University of California, 1868-1968.* New York, 1970.

Stanley, F. *Satanta and the Kiowas.* Borger, 1968.

Storr, Richard. *The Beginnings of Graduate Education.* Chicago, 1953.

Strayer, G. D. and Evenden, Edward S. *Syllabus of a Course in the Principles of Educational Administration.* New York, 1912.

Thoburn, Joseph B. and Wright, Muriel. *Oklahoma: A History of the State and Its People,* I, II. New York, 1929.

Tingley, Donald (ed.). *Essays in Illinois History.* Carbondale, 1968.

Turnball, Andrew (ed.). *The Letters of F. Scott Fitzgerald.* New York, 1963.

Turner, Frederick Jackson. *The Frontier in American History.* New York, 1920.

Veblen, Thorstein. *The Higher Learning in the United States.* New York, 1918.

Veysey, Laurence R. *The Emergence of the American University.* Chicago, 1965.

Walworth, Arthur. *Woodrow Wilson.* Baltimore, 1969.

Welter, Rush. *Popular Education and Democratic Thought in America.* New York, 1962.

White, Andrew D. *Autobiography of Andrew Dickson White.* New York, 1905.

Willard, Julius T. *A History of the Kansas State College of Agriculture and Applied Science.* Manhattan, 1940.

INDEX

365

Bahntage, Mrs. Harry, 159
Bailey, Liberty Hyde, 29-30, 50, 72, 75, 83, 122, 134
Bailey, Walter, 287
Baird, Marie, 168-169
Baird, R. O., 133, 204
Barker, J. W., 232
Baker University, 213
Bali, Milo, 295
Balfour, G. P., 179
Bankhead-Jones Act, 282
Barker, Robert J., first president, 11, 19-20; early life and education, 21; educational philosophy, 22; administrative problems, 23; end of administration, 24; death, 24, 30, 32, 35, 36, 44, 46, 49; testimony before Legislature, 61-62, 73, 86, 88, 97, 100, 103, 105
Bauman, C. G., 296
Barnes, Cassius, 64, 76
Barry, John, 179
Barton, L. J., 137
Bascomb, E. E., 137
Baseball, 107
Basketball, 107; modern basketball, 215-216, 249, 274-275, 323
Battenberg, J. P., 196, 222
Baum, Warner, 289
Bauman, Elmo W., 296
Baxter, L. W., 122
Baylor University, 159, 213
Beatty, Cornelius, 137
Beaver County, Oklahoma, 302
Beanblossom, Floyd, 217
Beeson, M. A., 177-178, 205-206
Beevers, Eric, 293
Beeker, Charles, 11, 44-45
Bell Telephone Company, 227
Bellatti, C. R., 263, 266, 276
Bellamy, Edward, 37
Bellis, William, 206
Bellmon, George D., 235, 282
Bellmon, Henry, student days, 234-235
Beloit College, 189
Bennett Hall, 275
Bennett, Henry, 124; background, assumes presidency, 219-283, 288, 292, 294, 296, 334
Bennett, Henry, Jr., 221, 260
Bennett, Liberty, 221, 260
Bennett, Mary, 221, 260
Bennett, Mary Elizabeth (Bright), 221
Bennett Memorial Scholarship Fund, 280
Bennett, Philip, 221, 260
Bennett, Tom, 221, 260
Bennett, Thomas Jefferson, 221
Bennett, Vera Pearl (Connell), 221, 226, 260, 279, 294
Benson, Walter, 180
Bentley, William, 149, 184

Berea College, 206
Berrigan, Agnes, 293
Beveridge, Albert J., 120, 145
Bessey, C. E., 88
Bible Belt, 2, 37, 298
Big Eight Conference, 183
Big Seven Conference, 274, 295, 300
Big Six Conference, 213
Biology, 25, 27, 114; Old Biology Building, 249
Biology Club, 85
Bivert, Raymond, 193, 208, 261
Bizzell, W. B., 196-197, 241, 253, 268
Black, Ora Ardell, 168
Blackburn, Louis, 236
Blackwell, Carl Petty, 226-227, 247-249, 294
Blake, Harry, 177
Blizzard, William L., hired, 149, 155-156, 187; influence on Oliver Willham, 203, 284
Block and Bridle, 203-204
Blue Blue Violets, 223
Bass, Edgar, 174
Board of Home Missions, 30
Board of Regents for the Oklahoma A. and M. College (1944 to present), replaces Board of Agriculture, 266; organization, 267, 270; leave for Henry Bennett, 278; Willham made president, 281-282; loyalty oaths, 289-291, 294-295; university status, 300
Boardman, Charles, 295
Bogue, E. E., 76, 107
Bolsheviks, 162, 164
Bondurant, A. L., 334
Bone, J. F., 76
Bookkeeping, 79, 84
Booth, N. O., 204
Boswell, Oklahoma, 221
Boulton, Herbert, 189
Botany, 25, 55, 76, 88, 92, 114, 187
Bowers, John, 132, 151, 170, 204
Bowline Abraham Lincoln, 175
Bowling Green State College, 226
Boyd, Alfred, 138
Boyd, David, 123
Boyd, Edward P., 188
Bradley, M. J., 231
Bradley, R. O., 250
Bradshaw, Claude, 263
Brannon, Luther, 297
Brattin, Monte, 233
Breeder's Gazette, 137
Brewer, Ed, 165, 175, 195-196, 233
Brewer, O. H., 139-140
Briggs, Eugene, 253
Briggs, Thomas H., 222
Brigham, John W., 186

Cordell, Harry, 145, 192, 196-197, 220, 226, 232, 237, 242; death, 247-248; 250, 295
Cordell, William J., 238
Covey, Jacob, 9
Cornell University, 29, 32, 50, 76, 90, 152, 168, 187, 227, 250
Correll, Malcolm, 288-289
Correspondence School, 135, 166, 184
Cosmopolitan Club, 210
Cotton Bowl, 273
Covelle, L. K., 272
Coward, Stella A., 194
Cox, Ted, 273
Coyne, Pete, 173, 175, 177
Craig, John, 130, 134, 137
Creek County, Oklahoma, 129
Creel Committee, 155, 162
Creighton University, 273
Crescent City, Oklahoma, 22-23, 49, 53
Crilley, A. Cyril, 278-279
Cross, George, 268, 282, 286, 287
Cruce, Lee, 132, 135, 139, 141, 144, 149
Crutchfield Hall, 131, 133
Crutchfield, W. W., 171
Cumberland River, 164
Cumberland University, 163, 228
Cunningham, J. Rex, 261
Curhuff, H. M., 255
Currin, Dial, 220, 275, 334
Curtain, Gerald, 235
Custer County, Oklahoma, 139
Custer, George, 51

D

Daane, Adrian, 197
Dabney, C. W., 39
Dairying, 128, 135
Dale, Edward Everett, 99-100
Daley, Charles, 175
Daniels, Arthur, 6, 19
Darby, J. F., 141
Darlow, A. E., 263, 284-285, 297, 299
Darnell, Captain L. J., first military commandant, 20, 39-40
Darnell, W. M., 240
Dartmouth College, 80
Darwin, Charles, 106; theory, 183, 308
Darwinism, 2, 27, 85
Davis, Arthur J., 156-157
Davis, Chester, 248

Davis, Edward T., 266
Davis, Kenneth W., 283-284
Davis, Paul J., 214
Davis, William, 3
Dean, Clifford T., 216
Decade Club, 233
Delta Sigma Alpha, 210
Delta Bowl, 273
Delta Sigma, first campus fraternity, 132; 210
Democratic Party, 5, 14, 19, 44-45, 48, 59, 68, 70-71, 120, 122, 127-128 133, 135, 138; attempt to control Board of Agriculture, 139, 144-145, 150, 158, 164-180, 183, 191, 220; Depression and New Deal politics, 239-258, 282
Dennis, S. D., 123
Dent, Emma, 36, 60
Dent, Harry L., 220
Dent, Oklahoma, 212
DePauw University, 49
Dermer, O. C., 288
Dewey, John, 308
Dial, Hardy, 140
Dickinson College, 214
Dickinson, H. C., 269
Diehl, D., 123
Diem, Gertie, 310
Dille, John, 64
Disney, W. E., 180
Dobie, J. Frank, 188, 221-222
Doctor of Arts, 268
Doctor of Education, 268
Doctor of Philosophy, 268-269
Doctor of Veterinary Medicine, 268
Donart, Charles, 11-12
Donart, Elmer, 263
Donnell, Guy, 271, 295
Dooley, Mister, 86
Dowell, C. T., 197
Donnell, Philip, 247-248; 252-254; made vice-president, 267, 269-270, 272, 278, 281
Dowell, Foster, 271
Downs, Robert Bingham, 293
Douglas Cup, 109
Doyle, David Cushman, 258
Drake University, 292-293
Drummond, Fred G., 266, 280
Duck, Frank, 4, 9-10, 13, 79
Duck, Simon, 171
Dudley, M. L., 266
Duff, J. A., 169
Duncan, Bessie, 29
Dungee, Roscoe, 291
Dunlap, Elijah T., 286
Dunlavy, D. W., 189
Dunlavy, Henry C., 158
Dunn _____, early Stillwater school teacher, 35
Dunne, Peter F., 86

Durant, Oklahoma, 140, 144-145; work of Henry Bennett at, 220-221; townspeople view of Bennett, 224; selection of friends for positions at OAMC, 225-226, 229, 248, 279

Dykstra, Clarence A., 258

E

Early, Jubal, 50
Earthquake, 208
East Side Academy, 163
Eastern Oklahoma Agricultural and Mechanical College, 266
Eaton, Frank, 213
Eckel, Edward Henry, 156
Ecole Militaire, 90
Economics, 127, 229, 285
Eddie, B. D., 266-267
Edmison, Marvin T., 268
Edmond, Oklahoma, 140
Edmonson, J. Howard, 282
Eggleston, Edward, 43
Eisenhower, Milton, 279
El Reno, 63, 75, 203, 271
Elective System, 86, 91-92
Ellison, Jane, 291
Elliot, Edward, 243
Elliott, J. C., 123
Ellis, Lippert S., 247, 248
Emmons, Lille, 100
Emmons, Wendell, 206
Emory College, 82
Engineering Building, 78-79, 90-91, 150
Engineering Club, 85, 132
Engineering and early industrial acts, 50, 54, 71, 76, 84-85, 90, 92, 114, 132; designation as school, 133 (see also College of Engineering)
Englehardt, N. L., 334
English and History Building, 249
English (and literature), 36, 42-43, 49, 84, 87, 89, 101, 107, 112-114, 151, 160, 168, 188, 288
Enid, Oklahoma, 182, 184
Entomology, 25, 55, 76, 84, 88, 205
Enyart, William, 254
Epworth University, 253
Eskridge, Catherine Castleman, 163
Eskridge, James Burnett, 163-173, 179, 185, 193, 293
Eskridge, John Harper, 163

F

Etheridge, Ray, 174, 178
Ethics, 87
Ethiopia, 278, 283, 296
Eufaula, Oklahoma, 291
Evans, Charles, 130, 165
Evenden, E. S., 228
Ewing, Amos, 19-20, 45-46, 60
Exendine, A. A., 215
Faculty Senate, beginning of Board of Faculty Representatives, 261, Faculty Council, 286, 288
Fannema, Pete, 217
Farm Credit Association, elects Henry Bennett to head office, 277
Farm and Ranch Magazine, 128
Farm-Labor Reconstruction League, 171-173, 175, 177, 179
Farmers' Alliance, 117, 363
Farmers' Cooperative Demonstration work, 181-182
Farmers' Union, 185
Farnsworth, Darius, 7
Featherly, H. I., 286
Federal Bureau of Investigation, 256
Federal House and Home Financial Agency, 295
Federal Works Agency, 268
Fenimore, Bob, 273
Ferguson, A. H., 175
Ferguson, Tom, 91, 122, 138
Fickel, Jacob E., 263
Fields, J. W., 76
Fields, John, 119-120, 122, 127, 144, 172
Finlayson, John D., 243
Finley, Iva M., 252
Fisher, Earl C., 236
Fisher, Frederick Vining, 237
Fitzgerald, F. Scott, 199
Flanders, Roger, 295
Flesher, Earl, 240
Florida A. and M. College, 26
Floyd, H. C., 206
Floyd, Henry W., 291
Flynn, Dennis, 120, 122
Football, 107, 110, 131, 152, 182, 201, 208; modern football, 213-215, 236, 273; Bright case, 292-293
Foraker, Joseph, 123
Foreign Development Corporation, 297
Foreign languages, 28, 76, 79, 97, 114, 174
Foreign Operations Administration, 297
Foreman, Paul, 288
Forest City, Oklahoma, 8
Forestry, 87, 299

Ford Foundation, work in Pakistan, 284, 296
Fort Arbuckle, Oklahoma 51
Fort Cobb, Oklahoma, 51
Fort Gibson, Oklahoma, 51
Fort Sill, Oklahoma, 178
Foster, R. B., gives dedication address for Old Central, 37, 93
Founder's Day Celebration, 236, 257-258
Four-H, 151, 249
Frances Willard Hall, 250
Francis, C. K., 204
Frederick, Oklahoma, 248
Freedmen's Bureau, 51
Freeling, S. P., 153
Freeman, Blanche, 177, 197
French, M. G., 206
Fresenius, C. Remigius, 87
Frostburg Normal School, 71
Fulbright, J. William, 278
Fuller, Vernel, 291
Fulton, Robert, 106

G

Gaer, Warren, 292
Galbraith, C. A., 46
Gallagher Hall, 217, 249, 274, 279
Gallagher, Alfred, 217
Gallagher, Edward, 155; athletic director and wrestling coach, 203, 218, 237, 249, 273
Gallagher, Susan, 217
Gallion, Milton R., 178
Gardenhire, George, 4; role in formulating organic legislation for college, 5-7, 9-11, 20
Gardiner Hall, construction, 131, 133; fire, 148; naming, 230
Gardiner, Maude, 230
Gardner, Frank M., 292
Gary, Raymond, governor, 282; 293, 299, 300
Gault, Frank, 141, 145, 148, 150, 153, 155, 158, 179
Geary, Oklahoma, 145
General Organization Company, 237
Geography, 25, 36, 42-43
Geology, 55-56, 88, 268
George Washington University, 166, 182
George Peabody College, 151, 166, 182, 189
Georgia Institute of Technology, 227

Georgia State College of Agriculture, 220
G. I. Bill of Rights, 270-272, 276
Gilbert, Norris, 99, 104, 105
Gillham, Bill, 334
Gilmer, Dixie, 257
Glasgow, Clarence, 251
Glazier, Henry, 27, 44, 62
Glennan General Hospital, 272-273
Graduate College, graduate work, 84, first degrees, 123; Lewis Research Club, 150; modern graduate work, 204-206; Daniel McIntosh, 205; formation as college, 225, 235; expansion of programs, 267-269; new dean, 285
Graduate Council, authorized, 269
Grady County, Oklahoma, 255
Grange Society, 50, 85, 117; Granger Amendment, 119, 238
Grant County, Oklahoma, 140
Grant, U. S., 50-51
Gray, Asa, 106
Gray, J. T., 141
Gray, Ruth, 140
Great Depression, 199, 206, 218, 225; student enrollment, 234-235, 237; college role in New Deal programs, 239-258, 270, 287, 290
"Green Corn Rebellion," 145
Green, Frank, 64
Gregory, John Milton, 73
Griener, Frank, 90
Griffith, John George, 214
Griggs, Edward Howard, 258
Goessman, Charles, 51
Goldsmith, Clarence, 250
Golf, 201
Goodrich, Gary, 300
Goodwell, Oklahoma, 127
Gore, Thomas P., 135, 156
Gould, Chester, student and cartoonist, 201-204, 208
Guberlet, John E., 177
Gunderson, Carl, 130, naming of Gunderson Hall, 133, 204
Gustavson, Reuven G., 294
Gustavus Adolphus, 151
Guthrie, Oklahoma, 12-15, 18-19, 22, 34, 45-46, 58, 60-61, 64, 75, 77, 91, 108-109, 119-120, 123
Gymnastics, 201

H

Haile Sellassie University, 297-299

Hale, Gerald A., 251
Hale Normal College, 21
Half Century Club, 296
Hall, Clyde, 216
Hall, Frank, 241
Hall, John D., 271
Halle University, 226
Hamilton, Alexander, 90
Hamilton, D. A., 226; assistance with 25 year plan, 229, 230-232
Hamilton, Hays, 6, 11, 13, 57-58
Hammonds, Mrs. O. O., 192
Hancock, G. D., 43
Hand, Elsie, 226
Hanner Hall, 249
Hanner, Carter G., 191, 263
Hansen, Walter W., 285
Harding, Warren G., 166
Hardy, Ben, 278-279
Harmon, Henry G., 294
Harper, Horace, 247
Harreld, J. E., 240
Harrill, P. F., 266
Harris, James, 240
Harris, William Torrey, 306
Harrison, Benjamin, signs proclamation opening Oklahoma, 2, 4
Harrison, Bill, 262
Harrison, G. L., 266, 290
Harrison, H. P., 152
Harrison, Jack, 262
Hartman, Tom, 31, 38, 296
Harvard University, 119, 189, 199-200, 227, 268, 276, 298
Harvey, T. W., 89
Haskell, Charles, 123, 144
Hasselle, J. L., 141
Hastings, James, 38, 98
Hatch Act of 1887, 4-5, 14-25; importance of experiment stations, 25, 50, 52, 59, 73, 77, 117; misuse of funds, 137
Hawthorne, Nathaniel, 106
Hays, George P., 265
Hearst, William Randolph, 168
Heide, B. H., 187
Helena, Oklahoma, 127
Henderson, Loy, 279
Hendricks, Neil, 291
Henshaw, O. S., 243
Hennessey, Oklahoma, 75
Hesley, Carl, 250
Herron, Jack, 298
Herner, J. T., 177
Hershowitz, Abe, 175
Hiatt, Albert S., 189, 233
Hickman, John, 145
Hilgard, Eugene, 72
Hill, Adams Sherman, 89
Hill, Boyd, 214
Hilton, O. A., 229, 261
Hinds, George H., 141

History, 3, 31, 36, 42-43, 49, 83, 87, 89, 92, 101-102, 134, 153, 159, 188, 229, 287
Hilter, Adolph, 254-255
Hockey, 201
Hodges, Mable, 98
Hodges, W. J., 98
Hoel, Henry W., 275
Hoke, Roy, 263
Holley, Andrew, 294
Holm, Glenn C., 285
Holloway, William J., 192, 220, 225, 237, 256
Holt, Fred, 145
Holt, Georgina, 147
Holter, George Latimer, hired as chemistry professor, 20-21, 23-24; background and academic views, 26-27, 32, 37-38; fired, 69, 87, 92, 98, 101-104, 108, 119, 130, 132, 137
Holzclaw, H. F., 177
Homestead Act of 1862, 2
Hoover, Herbert, 244
Hoover, Sam, 242
Hopkins, Harry, 245
Horticulture, 27, summary of views at turn of century, 29, 42, 84, 87, 92, 114
Houghton Farm, 52
House, R. Morton, 91
Houston, D. F., 154-155
Hunt, DeWitt, 206, 210
Howard, E. B., 240
Howard, J. W., 44
Howard, Oliver Otis, 51
Hueston, T. J., 9
Hughes, Roy, 240
Hugo, Oklahoma, 221, 226
Humphrey, Manly, 242
Hunt, F. C., 14, 64
Hurley, Patrick, 265
Huston, A. H., 141
Hutto, Frank, 3, 11, 48-49, 171
Hutto, Maggie, 103
Hutto, W. W., 48-49, 89
Huxley, Thomas H., 106

I

Iba, Henry, 216-217, 249, 273-275, 294
Iben, Icko, 226
Ickes, Harold L., 251
Idaho Experiment Station, 142
In loco parentis, 42, 95

Indian Territory, 50, 144
Indians, 2; Carlisle Indian Barracks, 51; Satanta, 51; 90, 102, 167, 216, 221, 272
Ingalls, Oklahoma, 8
Institutes, 128-129; cotton, 134; farmers', 134-135; summer encampment schools, 135; problems over selection of Farmers' Institute delegates, 138-143; summer, 187-188
International Economic and Social Development Agency, 280
International Relations Club, 212
International Stock Show, ribbons and trophies, 188
International Workers of the World, 162
Iowa Agricultural College, 72, 76, 137, 154, 181-182, 187, 190, 204
Isaac, J. P., 233
Irving, Washington, 106

J

Jackson, T. J., 266
James Russell Demonstration School, 228
Jarrell, Alfred Newton, 9, 38, 79, 96, 275
Jefferson, Thomas, 90
Jeffords, T. M., 136
Jeffrey, D. B., 297
Jelks, Tommy, 255
Jennings, Al, 144
Jessee, Walter, 237
Jewett, Fred, 295
Jimma Agricultural Technical School, 298
John Slack Boarding Club, 98
Johns Hopkins University, 43, 90, 119, 260
Johnson, Hiram, 145
Johnson, Hugh, 246
Johnson, James Ray, 291
Johnson, Jerry, 207
Johnson, Wayne L., 284
Johnston, Henry, 145, 164, 192; impeachment charges, 196; 219, 225, 240
Johnston, William Walter, first dean A & S, 146
Jones, Harry, 172, 174
Jones, Hilton Ira, the chemistry Wizard, 151-152, 166, 202-203
Jones, Lewis Webster, 250

Jones, Randall, 286
Jones, T. S., 20
Jordan, David Starr, 119
Julia Stout Hall, 274

K

Kamm, Robert B., succeeds Oliver Willham as president, 265
Kane, John, 253
Kansas Agricultural College, 23, 39, 71, 210, 212-213, 216
Kansas University, 90
Kappa Alpha, 210
Kappa Alpha Theta, 201, 210
Kappa Delta Pi, 211
Kappa Kappa Psi, 211-212
Kappa Phi, 211
Kappa Sigma, 210
Kappa Tau Pi, 211
Kappa Theta, 200
Katz, Jake, 185, 206
Keaton, J. R., 20
Kelley, Francis, 242, 253
Kelly, John, 271
Kelly T. W., 244
Kelsey, S. H., 59, 62, 65
Kenny, Roy W., 217
Kent, H. L., 178
Kerr, R. H., 109-110, 221, 253, 256-260, 265-267, 275, 279
Key, W. S., 252
King, Ferne (Mrs. Frank), 177, 220
King, J. Berry, 232
King, Sterling, 3
Kingfisher, Oklahoma, 22, 60
Kingfisher College, 108-109, 227
Kingfisher County, Oklahoma, 19, 48, 135
Kiowa County, Oklahoma, 135, 192
Klemme, Randall, 267, 276, 278, 281-282, 284, 296
Klockner-Humboldt-Deutz Laboratory, 269-270
Knapp, Arthur, 182
Knapp, Bradford, background and administration, 181-197; 205, 207, 210, 213-215, 219, 223, 237, 294
Knapp, Bradford, Jr., 182
Knapp, Marian, 182
Knapp, Maria Hotchkiss, 182
Knapp, Seaman, 149, 181-182
Kneeland, G. N., 139
Knight, Henry G., 258
Knight, Homer, 285

Knights of Liberty, 162
Knipe, William, 3, 11, 63
Knoblock, Charles, 9, 12, 14
Knapp, Stella, 197
Knox, Henry, 90
Kolshorn, Henrietta, 134
Korean War, 78, 257, 276
Kositzky, J. C., 190
Ku Klux Klan, 162, 171, 178, 180, 192, 202-203, 210
Kurland, Bob, 273, 275
Kvey, Richard, 43

L

Lahoma (Campus Club), 132
Lake Carl Blackwell, 249-250, 295
Lamb, Charles, 139
Lambda Chi Alpha, 210
Lane, J. P., 19-20, 59, 62
Langley, Edwin, 287
Langston, Oklahoma, 123, 266
Latin and Mathematics Boys' Training School, 163
Lawrence Scientific School of Harvard, 36, 90
Lawrence, J. F., 137
Lawrence, William, 130
Lawton, Oklahoma college, 127
Lawter, Z. H., 247
Layton, S. A., 122
League of Young Democrats, 242
LeConte, J., 88
Lee, Robert E., 50
Lee, S. H., 289
Legislation (other than appropriations), founding of college, 5-9; name of college established, 18; provisions of founding act, 18-19, 36; investigation of college, 58, 84, 86, 89, 106, 114, 116; new board of regents, 123-124, 127, 139, 140-141; attempts to change regential control, 237-238; proposals of William Murray during Great Depression, 240-245; early efforts to coordinate higher education, 242-244, 253; change in structure of regents, 265-266; loyalty oaths, 287-290; integration, 293; university status, 300
Lehman, B. H., 199-200
Lester, T. J., 9
Lever Act, 154-155
Lernfreiheit, 95

Lewis, Ervin Gibson, 79
Lewis, Jaleh, 146
Lewis, L. L., 76, 115; dean veterinary medicine, background, and acting president, 146-150, 153, 156, 160; dean of the faculty, 167-168, 183, 200, 205, 212-213, 217
Lewis, Ruth, 147
Lewis, Samuel, 147
Lewis, S. J., 146
Lewis Stadium, 150, 186-187, 249, 274
Library, 56, 79, 89, 92-94, 137, 160, 190, 193, 231, 249, 275-276, 293-294; old library building, 295
Lilienthal, David, 285
Lillie, Gordon, 202
Lincoln County, Oklahoma, 98
Lindsay, R. W., 123
Linklater, W. A., 151
Linscheid, A., 253
Little, Arlington P., 130
Little, Blanche, 113
Little, Everett, 297-298
Little, M. T., 19, 59
Litton, Gaston, 15
Livestock Pavilion, 157
Logan County, Oklahoma, 19
Logan, Dave, 238
Lomanitz, Sebastian, 152
Lohman, M. R., 283
Lomanitz, Sebastian, 152
Long, Chester, 123
Lookabaugh, Guy, 214
Lookabaugh, Jim, 273
Loomis, Robert, 278
Loring, George, 50
Louisiana Purchase, 2
Low, Edmon, 226, 275-276, 293
Lowe, T. G., 20
Lowell, James Russell, 106
Lowry, Chester H., 159, 179-180
Lowry, Fern, 207
Lowry, James, 290
Lowry, Robert, 3-4, 11, 57-58, 63-64, 76, 79, 80, 153
Loyalty Oaths, 255, 283, 287-290
Luther, Martin, 129
Lyell, Charles, 106
Lyle, Guy R., 293
Lynn, S. K., 251
Lytten, Dale, 177, 196

M

McAlpine, James A., 264
McCabe, E. S., 177

375

McCafferty, Earl, 235
McCarthy, Joseph, 283; loyalty oath controversy, 287-290
McConkey, L. E., 263
McCosh, James, 82
McCrary, John, 298
McCrary, Culley and Carhart Compan,y, architectural consultants, 230-231
McDonald, A. H., 172
McDonald, Michael, 157, 203
McDowell, A. V., 20, 48, 59
McElroy, Clarence, 166, 177, 185, 189; acting president, 197, 205, 223, 233, 237; retires as dean of men, 261, 285
McElroy, George, 236
McGraw, Charles, 3, 4, 12, 14, 64
McInnis, Louis L., 25
McIntire, Forrest, 260, 284
McIntosh, Daniel Cobb, pioneer in graduate studies, 205; 269, 285
McIntyre, Robert, 93
McKeever, Horace, 158
McLaurin, G. W., 291
McNeal, Joseph W., 9, 13, 60
McNeil, N. E., 180
McNutt, Hal, 263

MacKenzie, A. St. Clair, 142
MacVicar, Robert, 285
Magee, Carl, 251
Magruder, Alexander Covington, hired to teach agriculture, 20, 22-24, 27, background and educational philosophy, 28-29; 32, 39, 43, 46, 53-54, 62, 69, 87, 128
Magruder Medal, 28
Mahomet, 121
Mainsville Academy, 72
Makkonnen, Lidj Endalkatchew, 299
Makovsky, Bohumil, 212
Markham, B. H., 175
Marland, Ernest Whitworth, administration as governor, 245-252
Marshall, Carl, 298
Marshal Plan, 297
Martin, A. O., 265-266, 284
Martin, Frank, 201-202
Martin, Robert, 9, 11-12
Martin, Van, 3, 12
Maryland Agricultural College, 52
Maryland State Board of Education, 67
Mason-Dixon Line, 35
Massachusetts Agricultural College, 30, 52, 71, 90, 113
Massachusetts Institute of Technology, 90, 178
Mathematics, 25, 31, 42-43, 55, 84, 87, 89, 91, 101, 189, 284
Matriculation Pledge, 38-39, 40-41

Matthews, James, role in founding college, 4-6, 7, 9, 119
Maulbetsch, John Frederick, 215-216
Maxwell, Marshall, 251
Medford, Oklahoma, 287
Mellet, J. M., 174
Melton, W. A., president Former Student Association, 219, 223, 226, 235, 237
Mercer, Ford, 250
Mershon, William, 26
Merton, W., 8, 10
Meteorology, 25, 88
Merite Agricole, 50
Miami University (Ohio), 72
Michaels, Ruth, first dean of home economics, 151, 165, 168
Michigan State University, 32, 134, 211 250,
Miller, Ella Nova, 168
Miller, Floyd, 176
Miller, Freeman, 12, 14-15, 40; becomes member of faculty, 49; 54, 56, 68, 76, 86, 92-93, 97, 119, 135, 141-142, 151, 153, 180, 188
Miller, H. P., 137
Miller, Hugh, 28
Miller, James E., 242
Miller, Lewis, 90, 96-97
Miller, Paul, 193
Mills College, 258
Miltimore, Cora, 90
Milton, John, 129
Mississippi Agricultural College, 20, 28, 128
Missouri Valley Conference, 213-216, 292-293
Missouri Weslayan College, 215
Mitchell, James T., 279
Mitchell, L. A., 197
Mitchell, Willie D., 298
Montgomery, T. T., 222, 253
Mooney Recreation Hall, 271
Moore, Brown, 175
Moore, Tommie, 242
Mooring, D. C., 183
Moorhouse, L. A., 137
Morehouse, W. H., 189
Morningside Orphanage, 169
Moroney, Beissner and Company, 274
Morrill Act of 1862, 5-6, 21, 39-40, 72, 77, 90, 112-113, 123, 137, 157
Morrill Act of 1890, Granger Amendment, 5; 46, 54, 59, 77, 117, 119
Morrill Hall, construction, 122-123; destruction by fire, 147; 150
Morrill, John H., 264
Morrill, Justin Smith, 50, 112
Morris, Oscar Matison, 79, 90, 137
Morrison, Edward, 284, 296
Morrow, George Espy, 20; background, 71-73; plans for expansion

O

O'Brien, Richard, 276
O'Collegian, 105, 186, 194-195, 201, 207-208, 234-235, 254, 264, 290, 300
Oglesby, R. R., 291
O'Heggen, Tom, 341
Ohio State University, 76, 211, 294
Ohio University (Athens), 228
Oklahoma, from statehood, 125; hopes for the future, 126; educational politics, 133; educational power struggle, 137-143; political changes after WWI, social characteristics of the '20s, 162; poor ranking of public schools, 169-170; political scene, 192; relationship of politics to education, 225-226; Great Depression, 231; New Deal, 239-258; changes in governor's office, 260; industrialization, 269; attitude toward education, 282; 50th anniversary, 300
Oklahoma Academy of Science, 204-205
Oklahoma Agricultural and Mechanical College, land, 10-11, 13; redemption of bonds, 14; initial planning, 17-20; securing students, 30; beginning of preparatory school, 35-47; Old Central, 44-46; reorganization, 48-65; Murdaugh hired, 67; faculty discontent, 68-69; Morrow years, 71-81; Angelo Scott, 111-125; administration of James Connell, 126-143; Eskridge term, 162-173; George Wilson era, 173-178; Knapp tenure, 181-197; Bennett regime, 219-280; Oliver Willham, 300
Oklahoma Agricultural and Mechanical College Extension, 75; William Murray on extension, 127; formation and purpose of youth groups in the community, 134-135; political problems as result of administrative chaos, 137-143; use of films, 142; extension used for political patronage, 148; Bentley hired, 149; Lever Act importance, 155; extension program in New Deal era, 250
Oklahoma A. and M. College Magazine, 236, 295
Oklahoma Association of Negro Teachers, 293
Oklahoma Baptist University, 216
Oklahoma Board of Agriculture (1908-1944), 18, 121; assumes supervision of OAMC, 123-128, 131-132; youth extension, 134-135;

rural spoils system, 145-146, 149; hires Cantwell, 150, war policies, 155-158, 161; post-WWI leadership changes, 158-160; employes Eskridge, 164; Wilson, 177; Knapp, 181-197; Cordell replaces Whitehurst, 193; students and athletics, 199-219; Bennett administration, 219-280; 25 year plan, 229, 230-231; faculty policies, 233-234; Coffey becomes head, 248; Scott, 248, 260; new regent structure, 265-266 (see also Board of Regents for the Oklahoma A. and M. College)
Oklahoma Board of Education, 164-165, 173, 196
Oklahoma Childrens' Home, 168
Oklahoma City, 15, 75, 112, 144, 152, 175, 184, 196, 212-213, 251, 260, 284
Oklahoma City University, 125
Oklahoma City, Oklahoma, 15, 140, 174, 242, 287-289
Oklahoma College Association, 242
Oklahoma Constitutional Convention, 124-125, 192
Oklahoma Council for Defense, 155, 162
Oklahoma County, Oklahoma 179
Oklahoma Education Association, 293
Oklahoma Experiment Station, 19; director appointed, 19; first staff, 20; early philosophy, 25-26; student curriculum, 40-43; controversy, 48-65; attempt to relocate, 57; comment on soil at station, 63; loss of experienced personnel, 69, 74, 96; publication of bulletins, 107; general impact of experiment stations on higher education, 112, 118; popular bulletins, 128, 130, 134; investigation, 136-137; former director runs for governor, 144; Lewis reorganization, 149, 155, 172; purchase of Snowden Farm, 196; role in Depression self-help industries, 206; problems with Washington, 225; appointment of Blackwell, 227; new director, 284
Oklahoma Flying Farmers Association, 254
Oklahoma Frontiers of Science Foundation, 285
Oklahoma Home, 208
Oklahoma Institute of Technology, 269-270, 283
Oklahoma Intercollegiate Athletic Conference, 108-109
Oklahoma Land Rushes, 2, 26, 118, 189
Oklahoma Medical College, 163
Oklahoma National Guard, 254

Oklahoma Planning and Resources Board, 257
Oklahoma Power and Propulsion Laboratory, 269-270
Oklahoma Press Association, 149, 176
Oklahoma Shorthorn Breeders, 177
Oklahoma State Corporation Commission, 136
Oklahoma State Planning Board, 247
Oklahoma State Regents for Higher Education, beginnings of coordinating board, 242-244; 253, 267, 273-274, 283; moves offices to Stillwater, 284, 291; university status, 300
Oklahoma State Soil Conservation Committee, 247
Oklahoma State University, 152, 300
Oklahoma Supreme Court, 141-142, 145, 232, 238, 289
Oklahoma Tax Commission, 248
Oklahoma Teachers Association, 221, 238
Oklahoma Territory, early characteristics, 1; land rush of 1889, 2; 3-4, 9-10, 13, 21, 34, 48-65, 71, 79, 87, 102, 112-113; politics, 120-125
Oklahoma Territorial Superintendent of Instruction, 29
Oklahoma Women's College, 163
Okmulgee, Oklahoma, 192, 238, 245, 272-273
Okmulgee Tech, 272-273
Old Central, 1, 14, 31, 44, 47, 52-54, 79, 93, 97, 112, 147, 158, 160, 190, 193, 201, 208, 229-230, 276, 295-296
Old Music and Art Institute, 212
Old Northwest Ordinance, 34
Old Settlers Association, 185
Oldham Family, 41
Olds, Commander H. W., 263
Omega Society, 105, 131
Omicron Nu, honor society in home economics, 168, 211
"Operation Bootstrap," 276
Orange and Black, 105, 131-133, 138, 173, 201
Orlando, 13, 29-30
Orr, Harry 203, 212, 284
Otey, M. J., 137, 153, 175; court case, 178-180
Otjen, W. J., 257
O'Toole, Lela, 260
Quachita College, 192, 221; grants honorary doctorate to Bennett, 240
Ousley, Clarence, 156
Owen, Thomas, 171
Owens, R. L., 206

P

Packard, Alpheus Spring, 88
Paden, _____, 194
Page, Irving, 240-241
Pakistan Project, 296
Palmer, Paul, 288
Panhandle A. and M. College, 266, 282
Panhandle, Oklahoma, 77
Panhellenic Council, 211
Parker, Elsie, 103
Parking meter, invention of, 251
Parrish, Edward, 50
Parry, E. E., 214
Parrington, Vernon Louis, 125
Partridge, Alden, 50, 90
Pasteur, Louis, 86
Pate, J. B., 174
Patrillo, Manning, 295
Patterson, Herbert, 151, 170, 177, 228
Pauls Valley, Oklahoma, 135
Payne Center, Oklahoma, 8
Payne County, Oklahoma, 2-4, 6-9, 18, 36, 57, 63, 96, 119, 179; Great Depression, 213-263
Payne, Loyal F., 143
Pearl Harbor, 237, 258-259
Pearson, R. A., 163
Pennsylvania State University, 25, 27, 76, 78, 90, 119, 152
Peoples Power League, 140-141
Perdue, Randle, 238, 242
Perkins, Oklahoma, 3, 8, 10-11, 63, 75, 206, 213
Perkinson, Fred, 153
Perky, J. B., 247
Permanent Court of Military Justice, 207
Perry, Oklahoma, 75, 192
Persinger, J. H., 141
Petroleum, 188
Peterson, D. R., 295
Phi Kappa Phi, 204, 212-213
Phillips, J. B., 140
Phillips, Leon C., gubernatorial administration, 252-257
Phillips, Milt, 255
Phillips University, 214
Philomathian Society, 105, 131; at Ouachita College, 221
Philosophy, 87-88, 101-102
Physical Education, 39, 86; for women, 201, 203
Physics, 55, 76, 87, 288
Physiology, 25, 43, 52, 167
Pi Beta Phi, 201
Pi Delta Kappa, 211-212
Pi Epsilon Alpha, 211
Pi Zeta Kappa, 211

Pierson, Leonard, 119
Pier, Stanhope Reid, 209
Pine, W. B., 245
Pinchot, Gifford, 96
Pittuck, B. C., 130
Pistol Pete (mascot), replaces tiger emblem, 213
Pittman, Leander, 7, 153
Pixlee, James E., 215-216
Placement Bureau, 236
Plant pathology, 187, 263-264, 299
Poe, Allan, 106
Political Science, 42, 84, 101-102, 160, 271
Polo, 182
Ponca City, Oklahoma 206
Pontius, C. I., 253
Populist Party, 5, 19, 71, 93, 127, 135-136
Posey, Vance, 270
Potter, Andrew, 266
Potts, H. Clay, 261
Potts, R. C., 136
Pond Creek, Oklahoma, 75
Pratt Institute, 168
Pratt, Richard Henry, 51
Princeton University, 31, 108, 112, 199, 293
Printing and Publishing Department, 107, 116, 132-133, 208
Pritchard, E. A., 214
Progressive Agriculturalist, 105, 134
Progressive Movement, 112, 125-127; use of reform techniques to keep Populism alive, 138-139
Progressive Party (Bull Moose Republicans), 145
Prohibition, 234
Prosser, Ethel, 271
Pruett, Haskell, 226
Psychology, 71, 87-88, 166
Publicity Department, established, 68
Purdue University, 220, 243
Purdy, Daisy, 250
PWA, 252

Q

Quien, J. E., 61

R

Radar, 263-264
Radio, 100, 190
Raiford, Charles, 151
Railroads, 2, 102, 109, 120, 122, 126 132, 188
Raley, John W., 253
Ramsey, G. A., 141
Ramsey, W. F., 9
Randlett, Oklahoma, 149, 203
Ray, Joseph, 43, 89
Reconstruction Finance Corporation, 271
Red Cross, 167
Red River Dam, 253
Redpath Lyceum Bureau, 151-152
Redskin, 202; founded, 208; 211, 215, 227, 235
Reece, J. W., 179
Reed, Eli, 12-13
Reed, S. L., 151, 276
Reed, W. H., 185
Regional Council for Education, 268
Reinhardt, Aurelia H., 258
Religious Emphasis Week, 210
Renfro, I. C., 141
Renfrow, William, 29, 44, 46, 48, 61-62, 29-70
Republican Party, 14, 19, 21, 46, 48, 63, 70, 120, 122, 138; fight for control of Board of Agriculture, 139-143; 158, 183; Henry Bellmon, 235; Great Depression politics, 239-258, 282
Research Foundation, 268, 286
Reserve Officers Training Corps, 156
Reynolds, Bob, Jr., 287
Reynolds, Thomas, 189, 205, 242, 248, 285
Rice University, 213
Richardson, Thomas, 3
Ricker, Kenneth, 284
Riggs, Walter Merritt, 181
"Riverside Review," 105
Rizley, Ross, 252
PKO Pathe News, 168
Roach, J. N., 160
Robb, D. N., 123
Robert A. Peery Building, 206
Roberts, Anita, 272
Robertson, J. B. A., 144, 158-160, 165, 171
Robinson, Joe, 207
Robinson, Wayne, 251
Rockefeller, Nelson, 277
Rody, George, 216
Roe, Vingie, 46, 116, 117
Roetzel, J., 123
Rogers, Harry M., 197
Rogers, John, 253
Rogers, Murl, 284
Rogers, Will, 151, 218, 237, 279
Rolf, F. M., 151, 187

Roosevelt, Franklin D., 242, 251, 254, 261, 264, 277
Roosevelt, Theodore, 122, 134, 145
Rose, L. B., 130
Rosen, Rudolph, 137
Rosenberg, Anna, 276
Royal Agricultural Society, 50
Royal American Stock Show, OAMC ribbons, 156
Royal Economic Society of England, 183
Royce, J. E., 173, 175, 177
Rowe, Walter E., 91
Rupe, Victor L., 251
Rural Resettlement Administration, 248-249
Russell, Campbell, 137, 141
Ryan, H., 14

S

Saint Joseph Loan and Trust Company, 12-14
Saint Mary's College, 273
Sallisaw, Oklahoma, 201, 271
Sanborn, C. E., 156; organization of graduate college, 203-204, 233
Sanders, J. T., 247
Sanderson, J. L., 267, 289
Sandlin, Orville, 291
"Sanhedrin," 4, 8
Santee, L. A., 235
Sapulpa, Oklahoma, 182, 216
Sater, J. E., 9
Satanta, 51
Sauerhering, Richard, 137
Savage, Orville, 235, 237-238, 247
Scabbard and Blade, 211
Schmoer, Lillian, 289
Scholl, E. E., 247
Schull, R. J., 226
School of Firemanship, 250, 263
School Journal, 113
School of Restaurant and Hotel Management, 250
Schreiber, W. E., athletic director, 141, 213
Schurman, J. G., 83
Science Hall, 159
Scofield, William, 291
Scott, Angelo Cyrus, 20, 58, 76, 90-91, 93, 107-108, 110; administration, 111-124; ends term in office, 125; 130, 153, 176, 179, 188, 208, 246
Scott, Charles, 118, 139-140
Scott, Joe, 248, 260, 266
Scott, John, 118
Scott, William, 118
Scroggs, J. W., 227
Scroggs, Schiller, 206-207, 227-229, 244, 285, 287
Seamon A. Knapp School of Country Life, George Peabody College, 182
Searcy Field, 263, 299
Seay, A. J., 19, 62
Selassie, Haille, 277-278, 297-299
Severied, Eric, 279
Sexton, Tom, 267
Shaffer, C. D., 58
Shaffer, J. J., 14
Shallabargar, F. L., 108
Shaw, Oras A., 257
Shaw, Walter, 119
Shawnee, Oklahoma, 75, 141, 212
Shearer, Phede, 100
Shedler, Leah, 232
Sheerar, L. F., 206
Sheffield Scientific School, 90
Shelbyville Training School, 163
Sheldon, J. P., 52
Sheridan, Philip H., 50
Sherman and Kruger construction firm, 122
Shibley, William S., 288
Short courses, 128, 132, 155-156, 165-166
Short, Robert, 235
Sicks, Vivian, 251
Siebur, Allen D., 289
Siebur, Nancy, 289
Sigma Literary Society, 31, 93, 99, 105
Sigma Tau, 211
Silk, W. W. (Mrs.), 160
Simpson, C. H., 164
Sipuel, Ada Lois, 291
Skinner, Ray 201
Smallpox, 96, 98, 115
Smith, Al, 196
Smith, Annie, 168
Smith, Edith, 168
Smith, O. M., 268
Smith, Wilbank, 292
Smith-Hughes Act, 154
Smith-Lever Act, 146, 149, 181; speeches of Bradford Knapp on demonstration, 183-184
Smithsonian Institution, 26
Smoot, V. G., 253
Snapp ,Cora, 137
Snell, Vernon, 216
Snelling, Charles M., 194
Snow, Francis Huntington, 111
Soccer, 201
Social Club, 105
Socialist Party, 120, 145, 155, 158, 172, 176, 255 (see also Communism)
Social science, 27, 84, 186, 205

Society for the Promotion of
Agricultural Science, 50
Sociology, 288
Sorenson, Helmer E., 286
Soule, Andrew M., 220
Sousa, John Philip, 212
Southeastern State College, 220; development under Bennett, 222, 227, 248
Southern Association of Teaching Training Institutions, 170
Southern Cotton Growers Association, 129
Southern Methodist University, 216
Southard, George, 169
Southwest Conference, 216
Southwestern Academy, 150
Southwestern State College, 71, 163-164, 166
Southwestern University of Arkansas, 213
Spanish-American War, 156
Sparks, H. L., co-author of bill to provide university status, 300
Spaulding, H. G., 176
Stanford Univresity, 119, 130, 285
Stanley, Henry M., 298
Stapley, Edward R., 260, 296
Star-Crescent Literary Society, 100, 103
Stassen, Harold ,297
Staten, H. W., 297
Steele, George, 4, 8, 11, 15, 19, 61
Steele, Joel Dorman, 43, 88
Steinbeck, John, 218
Stenography, 79
Stephenson, J. A., 58
Stevens Institute of Technology, 76
Stigler, Oklahoma, 139, 287
Stiles, George, 90
Stillwater, township status and location, 2-5; incorporation, 9; real estate speculation, 10; community aspirations, 11-12; sale of college bonds, 13; redemption of bonds, 14, 17; early public school students, 35; use of local buildings by college students, 37; building funds, 44-45; Old Central, 46, 91, 98-99, 108-110, 114; temperance, 115-116; 119, 121, 123-130; 133, 139-140, 147, 150-152, 155, 157-160, 164-165. 167-169, 172, 174, 182, 184, 189, 195-196; college students, 199-219, 227-228; Great Depression, 231, 233, 237, 242-246; Lake Carl Blackwell, 249-250, 253; Searcy Field, 254, 260; WWII, 263-280; 282-284; 290-291
Stillwater Chamber of Commerce, 141, 149, 155, 185, 190; WWII spending, 253, 276

Stillwater Council of Churches, relief during Great Depression, 231
Stillwell, H. M., 173, 175, 177
Stimmons, Walter, 156
Stone, Sam, 226, 242
Stone, Walker, 207
Stone, William, 6
Stout, Julia, 226
Stovall, J. M., 8, 10
Stradley, B. L., 294
Strang, J. C., 122
Strayer, George D., 222
Stringtown prison, 247
Strode, Ruth, 185
Strong, Clinton R., 226, 243
Stuart, R. T., 266, 275-276, 280, 288, 293
Stubblefield, Max, 98
Student Athletic Association, 214
Student Constitution, 206
Student Union Building, 274-275, 284, 293
Student Volunteer Movement, 209
Students, early conduct, 23, comments on politics surrounding college, 30; behavior, 31; demerit system, 40-42; democratic nature of preparatory school, 47; conditions fourth academic year, 52; attendance, 53; reception accorded President Murdaugh, 68, 74; first graduation, 79. 80; first woman graduate, 83; teaching and learning, 84-85; honor system and requirements for graduation, 85; preparatory school, 86, instruction, 87-93; social life, 95-110; entrance requirements and enrollment, 114; behavioral views of President Scott, 115, 129, 131-133; protest 138, 142; support for Lewis as president, 146; Harvest Carnival, 147-148, 150-151; admonitions for conduct, 152, 155-158, 164-168; enrollments, 170, 184, 186; enrollment and fees, 193; newspaper censorship, 194-195; and '20s and '30s, 199-218; students injured, 232; Bennett's policies, 234-235; problems under Bennett, 235, 240; "Murray for President Club," 242; Great Depression, 246-247, 253-254; World War II, 258; military programs WWI, 262-265; veterans, 270-272; plans for Student Union, 274, 276; foreign scholarships, 280, 288, 293, 295
Students' Army Training Corps, 157
Sugar Bowl, 273
Summer Conference of Academic Deans, 228
Supply, Oklahoma, 237
Surveying, 89

Swearingen, Eugene L., 285
Sweat, Helen, 264
Swift, Edith 194
Swiler, William, 4, 13, 35
Swimming, 201
Swinton, William, 89
Swope, J. H., 9
Syracuse University, 168

T

Tabor, George, 208
Taft, William Howard, 159
Talbot, Nora, 151, 234, 260
Talbot, D. W., 7
Tarr, William A., receives honorary
  degree, 187
Taylor, J. E., 256
Taylor, Ross U., 98
Taylor, Stella, 217
Teachers Club, 132
Teapot Dome Scandal, 251
Technical Cooperation Administra-
  tion, 277-280, 282-283, 296-300
Television, 100
Temperance movement, 70, 115-116,
  149
Tennessee Valley Authority 248
Tennis, 201
Terrill, Ira, 6-7
Texas A. and M. College, 25, 61, 128,
  146, 204-205, 213
Texas Christian University, 163, 273
Texas Juvenile Training School, 161
Texas State Farmers Congress, 129
Texas State Teachers Association, 150
Texas Technological College, 160,
  182, 197
Thatcher Dormitory, 191, 265
Thatcher, Jessie, first woman graduate,
  83, 94, 106; Thatcher Hall con-
  struction, 191; 249, 263, 296
Theiss, George 13
Theta Nn Epsilon, 197, 210, 190
Theta Pond, history and development,
  200-201
Theusen, H. G., 251, 261-262
Thomas, Oklahoma 260
Thomas, Elmer, 264, 277
Thomas, Raymond, 228-229, 247-248,
  285
Thompson, Alan, 288
Thompson, Bryan, 200
Thompson, Carl, 151-152, 155-156
  187; recruits Oliver Willham, 203

Thompson, Grady, 207
Thompson, Harry, 20; background and
  early work at college, 30-33; 43, 52
  69, 71, 75, 100, 108, 236
Thompson, R. B., 197
Thompson, Henry L., 156
Tibbetts, C. A., 275, 284
Tiger, school nickname, 108
Tishomingo, Oklahoma, college, 127,
  240
Tolson, J. A., 174
Tomkins, Roy R., 272
Track, 109, 182
Tracy, Dick, 202-203
Trapp, M. E., 180, 184-185, 191-192,
  240
Trent, Dover, 246, 248, 250
Trout, C. E., 193
Troxel, Darrel, 291
True, Alfred, 55, 73, 76, 80, 93, 136-
  137, 151
Truman, Harry S., 260, 276-279, 300
Tuberculosis, 119
Tucker, Robert, 76
Tucker, Robert Henry, 117
Tucker, W. A., 139
Tugwell, Rexford, 248
Tulane University, 29
Tulsa, Oklahoma, 169, 174, 178, 191,
  223, 242, 257, 272, 275
Turner, Frederick Jackson, 189
Turner, J. W., 196
Turner, Jonathan Baldwin, 37, 73
Turner, M. L., 14, 45
Turner, Roy, gubernatorial adminis-
  tration, 260, 276
Tuskeegee, 266
"Twenty-Five Year Plan," 229; pre-
  liminary planning, 230-231; begin-
  ning work, 232-233, 238-239, 245,
  267, 274-276, 293
Tyler, Richard Gaines, acting pres-
  ident, 178-180, 188
Typewriting, 79, 92, 114
Typhoid, 96, 98

U

Uhl, George, 4
United National Food and Agricul-
  ture Conference, 276
United States Civilian Agricultural
  Department and Cultural Relations
  Agency, 276-277
United States Coast Guard and
  Geodetic Survey, 227

and educational philosophy, 29-30, 40, 54; released, 69, 87, 101, 103
Ware, Veta, 226
Waynick, Capus M., 277
Weatherby, L. S., 137
Weatherford, Oklahoma, 163, 179, 196
Weaver, E. R., 255
Webber, W. P., 130
Webster Debating Club, 94, 101-104
Webster, James, 295
Waddy, V., 89
Weissinger, Harold, 215
Wells, E. H., 212
Wentworth, E., 89
Wentworth Military Academy, 192
Wentz Foundation, 206
Wentz, L. H., 206, 240
West, Clyde, 272
West, John B., 284
West, Leonard, 271
West Point Academy, 40, 51, 53, 55, 90, 156
West Virginia Experiment Station, 28
Westbrook, E. J., head of printing and publishing 133; admission to Decade Club, 233
Westminister Club (Missouri), 285
Westminister Foundation, 288
Westmoreland, Ada, 150
Wheeler, Paul S., 296
White, E., 123, 127, 129, 139, 141-142
White, L. A., 182
White, Stella, 182
Whitehurst, George, 158-161, 165-166, 171-173, 175, 177, 180, 184, 191; replaced on Board of Agriculture, 192
Whitehurst, John 145
Whitehurst Hall, construction, 191, 226; damaged by fire, 232; 282, 286, 293
Whitledge, Fred E., 262
Whiteside, George, 254, 260, 263
Whittier, John Greenleaf, 106
Whitworth, A. T., 177
Whitworth, J. B., 273, 292
Wieman, Robert, 289
Wikoff, Frank, 3-4, 10, 13-14, 70, 76-77, 118-119, 123
Wilkinson, Bud, 294
Wilkinson, John W., 134
Wilber, Philip, 226; role in developing 25-year plan, 229-232; 245, 247, 250, 263, 267, 275, 293
Wilcox, Edwin Mean, 119
Wilcox and Swank, 232
Wilcox, W. H., 185
Wile, Otis, 164
Wiley, Harvey K., 90
Willard, Frances, 250

Willard Hall, 264, 295
Willets, Edwin, 25
Willham, Oliver S., 175; student days, 201-204, 267; made vice-president, 278-280; Willham presidency, 281
Willham, Richard, 282
Willham, Susan (Hurt), 282-283
Willham, Time, 203
William and Mary College, 67
William H. Murray Educational Foundation, 242, 257
William Jewell College, 43
Williams College, 118
Williams, A. Richard, 261
Williams, Jonathan, 90
Williams, Robert L., 127, 144, 153, 158
Williams, V., 102-103
Williamson, A. G., 253
Williamson, Mac Q., 275, 289
Willison Seminary, 51
Wilson, George, 148, 173, 175, 179-180, 184, 188, 259
Wilson, James, 136; fired, 137; 141, 172
Wilson, R. F., 123, 169
Wilson, Woodrow, 128, 146, 154
Wimberly, John, 19-20, 59, 61
Windom, Oklahoma, 8
Winters, Ralph, 235
Women Appointed for Voluntary Emergency Service, 264
Women's Athletic Association, 201
Woodward, Oklahoma, 212
Woodward public schools, 71
Woolrich Academy, 90
Works Progress Administration, 200, 248-249
Workman, Jerome, 3
World Power Conference, 227
World War I, 109, 145, 154-159, 164, 169, 171, 193, 200, 204-205, 209, 237, 252, 272, 293
World War II, 218, 227, 237, 253-255, 260-267, 284
Wrestling, national spotlight during Gallagher era, 217-218, 273
Wright, Frank Lloyd, 275
Wright, Houston, 251
Wright, J. K., 180
Wright, W. R., 137

Y

Yale University, 36, 90, 96, 150-151, 153, 228

Z